Seventh Edition

Exceptional Lives

Special Education in Today's Schools

Ann Turnbull
University of Kansas

Rud Turnbull
University of Kansas

Michael L. Wehmeyer
University of Kansas

Karrie A. Shogren
University of Illinois

PEARSON

Boston   Columbus   Indianapolis   New York   San Francisco   Upper Saddle River
Amsterdam   Cape Town   Dubai   London   Madrid   Milan   Munich   Paris   Montréal   Toronto
Delhi   Mexico City   São Paulo   Sydney   Hong Kong   Seoul   Singapore   Taipei   Tokyo

Vice President and Editorial Director: Jeffery W. Johnston
Executive Editor: Ann Castel Davis
Editorial Assistant: Penny Burleson
Senior Development Editor: Alicia Reilly
Vice President, Director of Marketing: Margaret Waples
Marketing Manager: Joanna Sabella
Senior Managing Editor: Pamela D. Bennett
Senior Production Editor: Sheryl Glicker Langner
Senior Operations Supervisor: Matthew Ottenweller
Senior Art Director: Diane C. Lorenzo

Cover and Text Designer: Wanda Espana
Photo Coordinator: Lori Whitley
Permissions Administrator: Rebecca Savage
Media Producer: Autumn Benson
Media Project Manager: Rebecca Norsic
Full-Service Project Management: Diane Kohnen, S4Carlisle Publishing Services
Composition: S4Carlisle Publishing Services
Printer/Binder: Quebecor World Color
Cover Printer: Lehigh/Phoenix Color
Text Font: ITC Garamond Std Light 10/12

Credits and acknowledgments for materials borrowed from other sources and reproduced, with permission, in this textbook appear on appropriate page within text.

Every effort has been made to provide accurate and current Internet information in this book. However, the Internet and information posted on it are constantly changing, so it is inevitable that some of the Internet addresses listed in this textbook will change.

Photo Credits: photo credits are on page xxvii.

Library of Congress Cataloging-in-Publication Data

Turnbull, Ann P.
  Exceptional lives : special education in today's schools / Ann Turnbull, Rud Turnbull, Michael L. Wehmeyer, Karrie A. Shogren.—7th ed.
    p. cm.
  Includes bibliographical references and index.
  ISBN-13: 978-0-13-282177-3
  ISBN-10: 0-13-282177-X
  1. Children with disabilities—Education—United States—Case studies. 2. Special education—United States—Case studies.
3. Inclusive education—United States—Case studies. I. Turnbull, H. Rutherford. II. Wehmeyer, Michael L. III. Title.
  LC4031.E87 2013
  371.90973—dc23
                                                                                          2011039372

10 9 8 7 6 5 4 3 2 1

PEARSON

ISBN 10:   0-13-282177-X
ISBN 13: 978-0-13-282177-3

Courtesy of Diane Guthrie. The photograph was taken in 2008.

Rud and Ann dedicate this book to their son, Jay Turnbull (1967–2009), who was their best professor.

Michael dedicates this book to J. T., who taught him to celebrate each day, and also to his family—Kathy, Geoff, and Graham—who make each day worth celebrating.

Karrie dedicates this book to J. T., who taught her the importance of lunch and singing with friends; Dave, who reintroduced her to the importance of laughter, love, and support; and to her Aunt J., who taught her about the importance of community.

Preface

It has been said of the city of Paris, "plus ca change, plus c'est la meme chose"—the more she changes, the more she remains the same. That is almost true of this seventh edition of *Exceptional Lives*.

What remains the same are the authors. Each is a professor of special education at the University of Kansas except for Karrie Shogren, who earned her doctorate at the University of Kansas but is on the faculty at the University of Illinois at Urbana-Champaign.

What also remains the same is our emphasis on inclusion of students with disabilities in general education. We also gave the first edition that emphasis; and at the time, some thought we were too pro-inclusion. But the capacity of special educators, general educators, related service professionals, and families to collaborate with each other for inclusion has demonstrated that inclusion is not only possible but desirable, even more so than when we wrote and published the first edition of this book.

New to This Edition

Paris changes even as she remains the same, and so does our book. Following is a list of some of the overall content changes we've made since the sixth edition, followed by a chapter-by-chapter list of topics that have been added or significantly updated.

- Chapters 1, 4, 6, 7, 8, 12, 14, 15, and 16 begin with new vignettes.
- A new feature called "Universal Design for Progress" has been added to every chapter.
- All chapters include references to the latest version of the CEC's "Knowledge and Skill Base for All Beginning Special Education Teachers of Students in Individualized General Curriculums."
- Data on the educational placement of students have been updated for every category of exceptionality.

  Chapter 1: Overview of Today's Special Education
  - The relationship between the Elementary and Secondary Education Act, formally known as the No Child Left Behind Act
  - 2009 data on reading and math assessment scores for students with disabilities
  - New information about the indicators of successful outcomes for young adults with disabilities
  - The eight guiding principles of the CEC's Code of Ethics, with a particular emphasis on the first: "Special education professionals are committed to developing the highest educational and quality of life potential of individuals with exceptionalities"

  Chapter 2: Ensuring Progress in the General Education Curriculum: Universal Design for Learning and Inclusion
  - Accommodations in assessments, including options provided by ESEA with regard to alternate assessments that should be linked with the general education curriculum
  - Accountability standards for all students
  - How students with disabilities fit into the reform movement in education
  - Student outcomes associated with inclusion
  - How inclusion facilitates progress
  - Response to intervention (RTI)

Chapter 3: Today's Multicultural, Bilingual, and Diverse Schools
- Guiding questions for implementing RTI for students who are learning English
- Updated information about students who live in poverty and students from homeless families

Chapter 4: Today's Families and Their Partnerships with Professionals
- Updated information on the domains and indicators of family quality of life
- Enhanced coverage about forming partnerships with families
- Supporting diverse parents to be active decision makers
- Improving family participation in IEP conferences
- Partnership principles and relevant key indicators

Chapter 5: Understanding Students with Learning Disabilities
- Challenges faced by students with reading disorders
- Social and emotional characteristics of children with learning disabilities
- Concerns related to use of the discrepancy model to identify students with learning disabilities
- New viewpoints on the use of RTI as a model for identifying students with learning disabilities
- The psychological processing model for identifying students with learning disabilities
- Self-directed IEPs

Chapter 6: Understanding Students with Communication Disorders
- Active listening as an important life skill

Chapter 7: Understanding Students with Emotional or Behavioral Disorders
- Bullying as a factor in teen depression and suicide and as a form of externalizing behavior
- Basic components of classwide peer tutoring (CWPT)
- The social skills improvement system (SSIS) for rating students' acquisition of social skills
- The KidTools support system for teaching self-regulation and problem solving using universally designed instruction

Chapter 8: Understanding Students with Attention-Deficit/Hyperactivity Disorder
- Computer-assisted instruction (CAI) and video self-modeling (VSM) as instructional strategies for secondary and transition students

Chapter 9: Understanding Students with Intellectual Disability
- Four main risk factors that can lead to intellectual disability (biomedical, social, behavioral, and educational)
- Community-based instruction for secondary and transition students
- Computer-based reading supports

Chapter 10: Understanding Students with Multiple Disabilities
- Assistive and educational technology

Chapter 11: Understanding Students with Autism
- Updated information on the biomedical causes of autism
- New information about the environmental factors related to autism

Chapter 12: Understanding Students with Physical Disabilities and Other Health Impairments
- Seizure types and subtypes
- Supporting students and families of students who use powered or electric wheelchairs
- Assistive technology (high- and low-tech) for students with physical disabilities

Chapter 13: Understanding Students with Traumatic Brain Injury
- Cognitive and academic changes experienced by students with TBI

Chapter 14: Understanding Students with Hearing Loss
- Using an educational interpreter in the classroom

Chapter 15: Understanding Students with Visual Impairments
- How general education teachers can work with a teacher of students with visual impairments (TVI)

Chapter 16: Understanding Students Who Are Gifted and Talented
- Origins of giftedness
- The schoolwide enrichment model

Inclusion

REAL STUDENTS, REAL ISSUES

Every chapter begins with the story of a student and his or her teachers, family, and friends. Telling these stories serves a powerful didactic purpose: it allows these people to demonstrate, in their own words and through these snapshots of their lives, how special education benefits every one of them. These students, educators, family members, and friends show you how exceptional lives can be made all the more exceptional when you approach them on the basis of principles and state-of-the-art teaching techniques.

Chapter Vignettes. These opening narratives tell the stories of students and their families, friends, teachers, and other educators and service providers. These people represent a wide range of cultural and linguistic groups, and they live in a wide variety of geographic locations across the United States. We refer to these vignettes throughout each chapter to exemplify our key points and content. We augment the vignettes and our summaries of research-based, state-of-the-art techniques by highlighting many strategies and tips for educators throughout the chapter.

2

Ensuring Progress *in the* General Education Curriculum: Universal Design *for* Learning *and* Inclusion

Who Is Dani Gonzalez?

When Arthur Laurents, Leonard Bernstein, and Stephen Sondheim collaborated to create the modern version of Shakespeare's *Romeo and Juliet,* first produced in 1958 as *West Side Story,* they could not have known how well the character Tony's expectant song "Something's Coming" would suit Dani Gonzalez, a fifth-grade student. Tony declares, "I've got a feeling there's a miracle due. . . . Something great is coming. . . . It's only just out of reach" (Laurents & Sondheim, 1979). For Dani, that something great just out of reach was sufficient self-confidence in her ability to speak out among her peers, enough to overcome her speech impairment and fully participate in her class.

But someone other than Laurents and Sondheim *is* writing down Dani's story. Meet Lauren Priest, a special education resource-room teacher, and Erin Lane, a general education fifth-grade teacher. Here's what Erin wrote to Lauren:

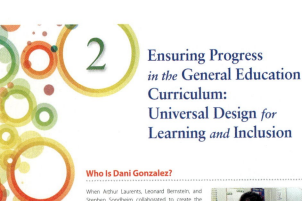

I ran down to see you. . . . I just had to tell you about Dani and the class meeting today. Normally she is always the last one to give her compliment and I really have to help her and you KNOW how quietly she can speak. Well, today was TOTALLY different! She had her [compliment] ready, said it the first time and was as loud as could be! The kids [fifteen fifth graders in general education] were all so excited for her, they gave her a big applause and all gave her a compliment for that! Then, she had ANOTHER one! It was so awesome to see her interact with her peers that way! Was so proud! Just goes to show what you [Lauren] are doing is working and that she is really benefiting from being with her peers!

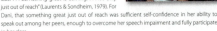

On the same day, Lauren continued Dani's story by writing to Luz Gonzalez, Dani's mother:

Some pretty incredible things went on today. . . . We are having our fifth-grade literature circles [and] . . . she is reading "Stone Fox." . . . We then have a discussion with about 15 fifth graders from all classes. Today, Dani raised her hand to participate 4 times on her own!! Her answers were also correct and appropriate and she didn't need any prompting from me at all. This is huge, considering that I have never seen her raise her hand on her own! . . . She is making such huge growths in her confidence; you have no idea how proud I am of her.

Sometimes, indeed, "something great" is just around the corner. Dani had pointed herself toward that corner, but she could not have turned it on her own. She was diagnosed as having speech-language delays (severe apraxia) when she was three years and nine months old, and she has received speech-language intervention since she was four years old (in early childhood special education and in elementary school). The intervention focuses on her ability to speak intelligibly: She has a lisp; and because her parents, Luz (from Colombia) and Carlos (from Spain), speak Spanish at home, she speaks English with a Spanish accent.

Dani is included with her nondisabled peers to learn reading, science, and social studies. To teach reading, Lauren uses an evidence-based reading program (*Horizons*), modifies the curriculum by using graphic organizers, and provides specially designed instruction in the form of direct (one-on-one) instruction to teach spelling. To teach math, Lauren uses another research-based program (*Number Worlds*). Her immediate goal is to have Dani increase her reading and math skills by another 25 percent to 30 percent; her long-term goal is to have Dani perform grade-level work without direct support. That's why direct instruction through evidence-based reading and math programs is necessary now.

With accommodations in science and social studies, Dani's grades average 90 percent or better. Lauren asks Dani to focus on the big picture and allows her to respond in different ways, but essentially the content material matches the general education program. She is making progress in the general education

Inclusion Tips. The information in the feature provides helpful advice and strategies for including students in the general curriculum. We address student behaviors, social interactions, educational performance, and classroom attitudes in relation to what teachers may see in the classroom, what they may be tempted to do, other responses, and best practices for including the student's peers in the process. Because IDEA commands that students be educated, to the maximum extent appropriate, in the general curriculum, we describe how the strategies

BOX 3.2	INCLUSION TIPS			
	What You Might See	**What You Might Be Tempted to Do**	**Alternate Responses**	**Ways to Include Peers in the Process**
Behavior	A Latino student who is an English-language learner and has learning disabilities puts her head on her desk when she does not understand written instructions. She rarely completes assignments.	Tell her that she should go to bed at a reasonable hour so that she can stay awake and complete her classwork.	List steps of the instructions in sequence on the board. Use pictures whenever possible. Ask her parents how help is requested and provided in their culture.	Model the skill of asking for help for all students and let them role-play. Provide reinforcement when they use the skill and encourage their classmates to use it.
Social interactions	She rarely initiates a greeting but usually responds to one appropriately.	Do not push her to initiate because you believe this skill will develop as her English improves.	Have students share greetings from the different languages represented in the classroom.	Have this student and others teach the different greetings and reinforce the use of them in and outside the classroom.
Educational performance	The student has strong math skills but performs poorly on word problems when she has to read them.	Request that she have more time outside of the general education classroom for intensive English instruction.	Provide word problems in her native language and English.	Establish a peer tutoring system within the class. She can tutor students who have problems with computation. Students who share the same primary language can help her read the word problems.
Classroom attitudes	She complains of a head- or a stomachache and asks to go to the clinic when assigned to read a children's novel and answer comprehension questions in written form.	Allow her to go to the clinic, hoping that she will grow out of this behavior as her English improves.	Try to obtain a copy of the book in her native language.	Have students work in cooperative groups to read and answer questions together.

lead to students' inclusion in the general curriculum. We supplement each highlighted "Inclusion Tips" with information about universally designed learning and self-determination.

Addressing the Professional Standards. Each chapter concludes with a list of relevant knowledge and skill statements from the Council for Exceptional Children's (CEC) "Knowledge and Skill Base for All Beginning Special Education Teachers of Students in Individualized General Curriculums." This will help you see how the book's content relates to your future professional educational behaviors and dispositions. A full listing of these standards is provided in an Appendix at the end of the text.

ADDRESSING THE PROFESSIONAL STANDARDS

The following Council for Exceptional Children (CEC) Common Core Knowledge and Skills are addressed in this chapter through the content and concepts we discuss. See the Appendix for a full listing of these Knowledge and Skill statements:

ICC1K2, ICC1K4, ICC1K5, ICCIK6, ICC1K7, ICC5S2, ICC5S3, ICC5S4, ICC5S6, ICC7S1, ICC7S2, ICC7S3, ICC7S6, ICC7S7, ICC7S9, ICC8K2, ICC8K3, ICC8K5, ICC8S2, ICC8S6

Universal Design for Progress

REAL STUDENTS, REAL SOLUTIONS

The majority of students with disabilities can progress in the general education curriculum if educators will apply the techniques we have described and use the strategies and tips we highlight in Chapter 2 and then throughout the rest of the text.

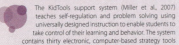

BOX 7.4   UNIVERSAL DESIGN FOR PROGRESS

The KidTools Support System

The KidTools support system (Miller et al., 2007) teaches self-regulation and problem solving using universally designed instruction to enable students to take control of their learning and behavior. The system contains thirty electronic, computer-based strategy tools that can be used in classrooms and by the student and his or her family at home (Miller et al., 2007). The software is designed and validated for use with elementary and middle school students. It provides cognitive, behavioral, and academic supports and includes templates to create the following:

- *Contracts* that students develop with their teacher to agree upon what the student will do and consequences that accrue when the contract is or is not completed
- *Checking contracts* that allow students to compare their contract-based performance with a teacher's evaluation
- *STAR plan forms*, which support students to Stop, Think, Act, and get Results" (e.g., STAR) when confronting a problem and to make a plan to address that problem
- *"Am I working?" card templates* to help students self-monitor their attention and on-task behavior in classrooms

- *Monitoring card templates* to support students to check their performance as part of a self-monitoring plan
- *Class, period, or picture point cards* that give students a way to track what they need to do in class

The middle school version of KidTools includes the above tools and adds the following:

- *Goal contract form* that gives students a way to set a behavioral goal and check their progress toward that goal
- *Homework contract form* to enable students to establish expected performances on homework completion and submission
- *Costs/payoffs card template* to support students to think about positive and negative consequences of actions before choosing how to act
- *Thinking/feeling/doing plan template* to assist students to evaluate how their actions in the past worked and to consider what might happen the next time the situation occurs

KidTools is a server-based application, so it runs from a school computer; and it incorporates features of both UDL and computer-based instruction (CBI).

NEW Universal Design for Progress. In every chapter, this feature highlights a technology that teachers can use in the classroom (or one that supports classroom instruction) to help meet the educational needs of students with disabilities. The technology featured can be anything from a software program to an assistive or adaptive technology or even specific educational websites.

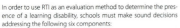

BOX 5.3   INTO PRACTICE

Responsiveness to Intervention As a Method for Determining the Presence of a Learning Disability

In order to use RTI as an evaluation method to determine the presence of a learning disability, schools must make sound decisions addressing the following six components:

1. Specify the number of prevention tiers.
   - Three key tiers in RTI programs include primary prevention, secondary prevention, and tertiary prevention.
   - Primary prevention is generally considered to be the general education program with the core curriculum and instruction associated with grade-level norms.
   - Secondary prevention consists of small-group tutoring in core academic subjects, especially reading and math.
   - Tertiary prevention consists of an individualized program characterized by systematic instruction and ongoing progress monitoring.
2. Identify students for prevention.
   - Provide quality instruction in the general curriculum (Tier 1).
   - Conduct universal screening of all students in the school at the beginning of the school year in order to identify students who are not successful with core instruction.
3. Provide intervention.
   - Implement two intervention models including problem solving and standard protocols (Tier 2).
   - ✓ Problem solving involves defining the problem related to learning, analyzing the factors contributing to the problem, developing and implementing a plan to address the problem, and evaluating the effectiveness of systematic instruction.
   - ✓ Standard protocols involve implementing instructional programs whose effectiveness has been verified through experimental research.
   - Implement intervention for a period of time, approximately 3–4 times per week for 10–20 weeks.

4. Classify response.
   - Identify criteria for determining when a student's response is adequate and when the student needs to receive more systematic instruction.
   - Consider the student's rate of improvement and actual achievement as it compares to classmates whose learning is progressing at the Tier 1 level.
5. Conduct multidisciplinary evaluation.
   - For students unable to respond adequately to Tier 2 prevention, design a multidisciplinary evaluation to address the questions and issues that are problematic for the student (Tier 3).
   - Implement the multidisciplinary evaluation in order to pinpoint learning challenges around which Tier 3 intervention should be designed.
   - Rule out the presence of other disabilities, especially an intellectual disability.
6. Provide special education.
   - Implement intervention characterized by instruction that is highly explicit, intensive, and supportive (Tier 3).
   - Ensure lower student-teacher ratios and extended instructional time.

myeducationlab

Go to the Building Teaching Skills and Dispositions section in Chapter 5 of MyEducationlab and complete the activities. As you interact with the simulations and answer the accompanying questions, think about how the RTI model is different from the traditional discrepancy model in successfully determining eligibility for special education services.

Source: Based on infomation from Fuchs, G., & Fuchs L. (2007). A model for implementing responsiveness to intervention, *Teaching Exceptional Children, 38*(5), 14–20.

Into Practice. In every chapter, this feature describes practical, step-by-step examples of how to use universal design, secure inclusion, respond to the multicultural nature of American schools, and practice collaboration and partnerships. Every categorical chapter presents strategies across grade levels to give all prospective teachers real-life examples. These strategies represent the best of the best from teachers and programs across the country.

Partnerships

REAL EDUCATORS, REAL FAMILIES

Partnership Tips. To reflect the focus on families and partnerships that guides the book, this feature provides practical, workable ways to develop and maintain effective partnerships between professionals (both in and out of school), families, and educators. This critical collaboration process makes the difference between effective learning and progress toward goals and unsuccessful attempts.

IEP Tips. For students who have disabilities, the IEP and the IEP process is the guiding force to their inclusion and progress in the general education curriculum. Throughout the chapters, we include margin notes that help link content with this practical focus. These margin notes supplement the narrative that describes how professionals can be partners with other professionals, parents, and students to provide an appropriate education in the general curriculum. All of these additional references help inform teachers of their role in the IEP and the IEP process and integrate this content into meaningful, professional contexts.

My Voice. This feature continues our focus on connecting in personal ways to the content of the book. "My Voice" is a reflection about living with exceptionalities and how education affects the person's life; it further connects you to real people and helps you understand the impact you and others can make.

BOX 9.3 **PARTNERSHIP TIPS**

Improving Interagency Collaboration

Sometimes it can feel beyond the scope of your responsibility as a teacher to contribute to interagency collaboration; however, each and every teacher can make a difference in the success of such collaborations. First, you should know best practices and encourage your team members to use them. Second, you should use these practices yourself.

Researchers identified twenty-nine high-performing school districts to determine what strategies they used to develop interagency collaborations (Noonan et al., 2010). Eleven key strategies were identified, but a major theme was that schools should have a transition coordinator whose job it is to build interagency collaborations. The strategies are as follows:

- Develop personal relationships with staff in community organizations who have responsibilities related to transition.
- Invite members of community agencies to come to IEP and other transition planning meetings; consider their scheduling preferences in arranging the time for the meetings.
- Ensure that school staff network within community settings.
- Anticipate that students and families will need support after graduation and share information with them about workshops, websites, and parent-to-parent connections.

- Recognize that administrative support is critical to flexible scheduling, compensation time, substitute teachers, and paid summer training.
- Recognize that interagency collaboration involves shared funding from multiple agencies, including government benefits for employment and housing.
- Seek technical assistance and continuing education from the state education agency, universities and colleges, and other professional development sources; encourage staff from community agencies to take advantage of continuing education opportunities.
- Partner with school, community, and state transition personnel in providing practical information and educational opportunities for students and families relating to all the key aspects of adult life planning.
- Find out about the availability of any interagency groups such as a community-wide transition council; learn who from your district is attending those meetings, and ask if that person will keep you informed about the decisions that are made.

Source: Information from Noonan, P. M., Morningstar, M. E., & Erikson, A. G. (2008). Improving interagency collaboration: Effective strategies used by high performing local districts and communities. *Career Development for Exceptional Individuals, 31*(3), 132–143.

IEP TIP

When there is an obvious connection—or even a suspicion of a connection—between the student's intellectual and adaptive functioning, such as inadequate nutrition, health care, and rest, you and related service providers such as a school social worker should develop an IEP that addresses these factors to the maximum extent you can in the general curriculum, and you should connect the student's family to appropriate school and community resources.

BOX 9.1 **MY VOICE**

Margaret's Guide to Down Syndrome

Today I'd like to tell you about Down syndrome. My purpose for talking about this is to be able to say, "Yes, I have Down syndrome. Sometimes I have to work harder to learn things, but in many ways I am just like everyone else." I would like to tell people that having Down syndrome does not keep me from doing the things I need to do or want to do. I just have to work harder.

Down syndrome is a condition and not a disease. You cannot catch Down syndrome like you can catch a cold or virus. It is something you are just born with—like blond hair and blue eyes. If you have Down syndrome when you are born, you will have it your whole life.

People without Down syndrome have 46 chromosomes, which carry all the genetic information about a person, in each of their cells. People with Down syndrome have one extra chromosome. So a person with Down syndrome has a total of 47 chromosomes in each cell. Doctors and experts are not really sure what causes it, but they say it occurs in about 1 of every 700 babies. This happens randomly, like flipping a coin or winning the lottery.

Everyone with Down syndrome is a totally unique person. The extra chromosome makes it harder for me to learn. Sometimes I need someone to say, "Settle down and get busy!" Also, it's really easy for me to be stubborn, so I don't mind if you say, "Hey, Margaret, please stop."

Even though I have one extra chromosome, the rest of my chromosomes carry information from generation to generation just like yours. Chromosomes control certain genetic characteristics, like eye color, skin color, height, and some abilities like music, art, or math.

For example, I get my blue eyes from my father, my fair skin and freckles from my mother, my blond hair from my grandmother, my long, thin feet from both my mom and my dad, and my need to wear glasses from both my grandparents and my parents. I like to concentrate on the ways that I am like everyone else.

I am very lucky to be alive today rather than 50 years or even 20 years ago because back then the doctors and experts believed that people with Down syndrome were not capable of learning. But now we know that people with Down syndrome are capable of doing many different things.

I personally am doing things that some people didn't think I could do. When I was born, somebody told my mom that it was too bad that I was named "Margaret" because I would never even be able to say my name. That person might never have expected that I could win four medals in Special Olympics swimming, be a green belt in karate, cook a pizza, read a novel, run half a mile, or get up in front of the class and give a speech! With a lot of hard work and encouragement, I have been able to do all these things.

I am not sad about the fact that I have Down syndrome. It is just part of me. I have a great brother (most of the time) and parents who love me a lot. I have wonderful friends who enjoy hanging out and having fun with me. I have teachers who help me keep on learning new things. I am glad to be a student at Lincoln Middle School because it is a great school and almost everyone is really nice. Down syndrome has not stopped me from having a worthwhile life.

—*Margaret Muller*
Cape Cod, Massachusetts

Source: By Margaret Muller, from www.patriciaebauer.com <http://www.patriciaebauer.com/>. Originally printed in the *Washington Post*, September 14, 1999.

MyEducationLab

THE POWER OF CLASSROOM PRACTICE

In *Preparing Teachers for a Changing World,* Linda Darling-Hammond and her colleagues point out that grounding teacher education in real classrooms—among real teachers and students and among actual examples of students' and teachers' work—is an important, perhaps even an essential, part of training teachers for the complexities of teaching in today's classrooms. MyEducationLab (www.myeducationlab.com) is an online learning solution that provides contextualized interactive exercises, simulations, and other resources designed to help you develop the knowledge and skills that teachers need. All of the activities and exercises in MyEducationLab are built around essential learning outcomes for teachers and are mapped to professional teaching standards. Using classroom video, authentic student and teacher artifacts, case studies, and other resources and assessments, the scaffolded learning experiences in MyEducationLab offer you a unique and valuable education tool.

On the MyEducationLab for this course you will find the following features and resources.

A Study Plan Specific to Your Text. A MyEducationLab study plan consists of a chapter quiz. Students have the opportunity to take a self-assessment after reading each chapter of the text. Each self-assessment question is tied to a chapter objective, so the students are assessed on their knowledge and comprehension of all the concepts presented in each chapter. The quiz results automatically identify areas of the chapter that still need some additional study time. In this study plan, students are presented with review, practice, and enrichment exercises to help ensure learning and to deepen understanding of chapter concepts when just rereading and studying chapter content is not enough. The study plan is designed to help each student perform well on exams and to promote deep understanding of chapter content.

Connection to National Standards. Now it is easier than ever to see how coursework is connected to national standards. Each topic, activity, and exercise on MyEducationLab lists intended learning outcomes connected to the appropriate national standards.

Assignments and Activities. Designed to enhance your understanding of concepts covered in class, these assignable exercises show concepts in action (through videos, cases, and/or student and teacher artifacts). They help you deepen content knowledge and synthesize and apply concepts and strategies you read about in the book. (Correct answers for these assignments are available to the instructor only.)

Building Teaching Skills and Dispositions. These unique learning units help users practice and strengthen skills that are essential to effective teaching. After presenting the steps involved in a core teaching process, you are given an opportunity to practice applying this skill via videos, student and teacher artifacts, and/or case studies of authentic classrooms. Providing multiple opportunities to practice a single teaching concept, each activity encourages a deeper understanding and application of concepts as well as the use of critical thinking skills. Feedback for the final quizzes is available to the instructor only.

IRIS Center Resources. The IRIS Center at Vanderbilt University (http://iris.peabody.vanderbilt .edu), funded by the U.S. Department of Education's Office of Special Education Programs (OSEP), develops training enhancement materials for preservice and practicing teachers. The center works with experts from across the country to create challenge-based interactive modules, case study units, and podcasts that provide research-validated information about working with students in inclusive settings. In your MyEducationLab course we have integrated this content where appropriate.

Simulations in Classroom Management. One of the most difficult challenges facing teachers today is how to balance classroom instruction with classroom management. These interactive cases focus on the classroom management issues teachers most frequently encounter on a daily basis. Each simulation presents a challenge scenario at the beginning and then offers a series of choices to solve each challenge. Along the way students receive mentor feedback on their choices and have the opportunity to make better choices if necessary. Upon exiting each simulation, you will have a clear understanding of how to address these common classroom management issues and will be better equipped to handle them in the classroom.

Teacher Talk. This feature emphasizes the power of teaching through videos of master teachers, who all tell compelling stories of why they teach. These videos help you see the bigger picture and consider why the concepts and principles you are learning are important to your career as a teacher. Each of these featured teachers has been awarded the Council of Chief State School Officers Teachers of the Year award, the oldest and most prestigious award for teachers.

Course Resources. This section of MyEducationLab is designed to help you put together an effective lesson plan, prepare for and begin your career, navigate your first year of teaching, and understand key educational standards, policies, and laws. It includes the following:

- The *Lesson Plan Builder* is an effective and easy-to-use tool that you can use to create, update, and share quality lesson plans. The software also makes it easy to integrate state content standards into any lesson plan.

- The *Preparing a Portfolio* module provides guidelines for creating a high-quality teaching portfolio.

- *Beginning Your Career* offers tips, advice, and other valuable information on

     Resume writing and interviewing

     Your first year of teaching

     Law and public policies

Certification and Licensure. This section is designed to help you pass your licensure exam by giving you access to state test requirements, overviews of what tests cover, and sample test items. It includes the following:

- *State certification test requirements*. Here, you can click on a state and will then be taken to a list of state certification tests.

- *Information about licensure exams*. You can learn basic information about each test, read descriptions of what is covered on each test, and find sample test questions with explanations of correct answers.

- *Pearson's National Evaluation Series®*. Here, students can see the tests in the series, learn what is covered on each exam, and access sample test items with descriptions and rationales of correct answers. You can also purchase interactive online tutorials developed by Pearson Evaluation Systems and the Pearson Teacher Education and Development Group.

- *ETS Online Praxis Tutorials*. Here you can purchase interactive online tutorials developed by the Educational Testing Service and the Pearson Teacher Education and Development Group. Tutorials are available for the Praxis I exams and for select Praxis II exams.

Supplements

This seventh edition of *Exceptional Lives: Special Education in Today's Schools* is accompanied by a comprehensive and integrated collection of supplements to assist students and professors alike in maximizing learning and instruction. The supplements also embrace universal design by using multiple ways of presenting material, multiple ways of engaging the students, and multiple ways of allowing students to respond.

For the Professor

All of the instructor supplements are available at the Instructor Resource Center. To access the manual, the PowerPoint lecture presentation, and the test bank and MyTest (see below), go to the Instructor Resource Center (www.pearsonhighered.com) and click on the Educators link. Here you will be able to log in or complete a one-time registration for a user name and password.

Online Instructor's Manual with Test Items. The instructor's manual helps to synthesize all of the resources available for each chapter but also helps to sift through the materials to match the delivery method (e.g., semester, quarter) and areas of emphasis for the course. These materials can be used for traditional courses as well as online or online-supported courses.

Pearson MyTest. This is a powerful assessment generation program that helps instructors easily create and print quizzes and exams. Questions and tests are authored online, allowing ultimate flexibility and the ability to efficiently create and print assessments anytime, anywhere. Instructors can access Pearson MyTest and their test bank files by going to www.pearsonmytest.com to log in, register, or request access. Features of Pearson MyTest include the following:

Premium assessment content
- Draw from a rich library of assessments that complement your Pearson textbook and your course's learning objectives.
- Edit questions or tests to fit your specific teaching needs.

Instructor-friendly resources
- Easily create and store your own questions, including images, diagrams, and charts using simple drag-and-drop and Word-like controls.
- Use additional information provided by Pearson, such as the question's difficulty level or learning objective, to help you quickly build your test.

Time-saving enhancements
- Add headers or footers and easily scramble questions and answer choices, all from one simple toolbar.
- Quickly create multiple versions of your test or answer key and, when ready, simply save to MSWord or PDF format and print.
- Export your exams for import to Blackboard 6.0, CE (WebCT), or Vista (WebCT).

Online PowerPoint Slides. These visual aids display, summarize, and help explain core information presented in each chapter. They can be downloaded from our Instructor's Resource Center. All PowerPoint slides have been updated for consistency and to reflect current content in this new edition.

ACKNOWLEDGMENTS

Many people have contributed to this book. From the Turnbulls' perspective, their son, Jay, has been their best professor, teaching them time and again how and why to respond to his very self-determined ways, his great expectations, and his insistence on living as a full citizen. Amy Turnbull Khare and Kate Turnbull, the Turnbulls' two daughters; Rahul Khare, their son-in-law; Dylan Kumar Khare, Cameron Turnbull Khare, and Maya Annika Khare, their grandchildren; and Chip Brookes, Kate's partner, have taught us to preserve the enthusiasm of youth as we write the seventh edition of this book and to bear in mind that every child is special.

Michael Wehmeyer would like to acknowledge the ongoing support of his wife Kathy and sons Geoff and Graham in all his professional activities as well as that of his colleagues in the University of Kansas's Department of Special Education, at the Beach Center on Disability, and in the Kansas University Center on Developmental Disabilities.

Karrie Shogren would like to acknowledge the support of Dave and her close network of friends in all of her professional endeavors. She would also like to acknowledge the ongoing support she receives from the faculty in the Department of Special Education at the University of Illinois at Urbana-Champaign.

Of course, the families, students, and teachers featured in the vignettes are indispensable to this book. If they had not opened their lives to us, we could not have written about them. In every way, they are your professors and ours, too. Our gratitude to them is unbounded.

This book is the product of collaboration among many different talented professionals. At the Beach Center on Disability at the University of Kansas, we have had the immeasurable benefit of Lois Weldon's many skills. She never flinched when presented with yet another draft of a chapter, with still another request to create figures and boxes, or with unexpected deadlines. We could not do what we do daily without her calm, cool, and composed work ethic.

Jane Wegner of the Schiefelbusch speech-language-hearing clinic at the University of Kansas and Evette Edmister, a speech-language pathologist in Des Moines, Iowa, and professor at the University of Northern Iowa (who trained with Jane at the University of Kansas), once again contributed a superb chapter on communication impairment. Sally Roberts, associate professor in the Department of Special Education and associate dean at the School of Education at the University of Kansas, did likewise with respect to the chapter on hearing impairment. Sandy Lewis at Florida State University once again wrote the chapter on visual impairment and helped us all understand how to educate students with that disability.

Alicia Reilly, our development editor, contributed her impressive organizational skills to our collaborations and added immensely to the content of each chapter by adding the special Pearson (publisher) teacher-education content. Ann Davis, the executive editor of our publisher's special education texts, has been a key member of our planning team and reminded us how important it was to humanize our book by emphasizing values and reiterating the voices of the students, teachers, and family members.

Sheryl Langner reprised her role as our production editor; no authors could have a more cheerful and eagle-eyed colleague than Sheryl has been. She and the copyeditor, Dawn Potter, caught our mistakes; if there are any left, they are attributable to us, not the publisher.

Diane Kohnen at S4Carlisle Publishing Services was immensely helpful and always cheerful in approving the last version of the text.

Our colleague at the University of Kansas, Sean Smith, had a hand in the fourth edition, and there are traces of his good work in this edition. We are grateful for his collegiality.

We also gratefully acknowledge the input and insight of several reviewers who helped us keep our book current and in step with their classrooms and students: Penny Cantley, University of Oklahoma; Allison P. Dickey, Ashland University; Lynn Gagle, Asbury College; Lorna Idol, University of Northern Colorado; Judith Presley, Tennessee State University; and Iris Roudeau, Western Carolina University.

Brief Contents

Contents

Chapter 3 • TODAY'S MULTICULTURAL, BILINGUAL, AND DIVERSE SCHOOLS 52

Chapter 8 • UNDERSTANDING STUDENTS WITH ATTENTION-DEFICIT/ HYPERACTIVITY DISORDER 172

Chapter 9 • UNDERSTANDING STUDENTS WITH INTELLECTUAL DISABILITY 194

Chapter 10 • UNDERSTANDING STUDENTS WITH MULTIPLE DISABILITIES 218

Chapter 11 • UNDERSTANDING STUDENTS WITH AUTISM 240

Chapter 12 • UNDERSTANDING STUDENTS WITH PHYSICAL DISABILITIES AND OTHER HEALTH IMPAIRMENTS 264

Chapter 13 • UNDERSTANDING STUDENTS WITH TRAUMATIC BRAIN INJURY 290

Chapter 14 • UNDERSTANDING STUDENTS WITH HEARING LOSS 312

Chapter 15 • UNDERSTANDING STUDENTS WITH VISUAL IMPAIRMENTS 342

Chapter 16 • UNDERSTANDING STUDENTS WHO ARE GIFTED AND TALENTED 370

Special Features

PARTNERSHIP TIPS

NONDISCRIMINATORY EVALUATION PROCESS

Photo Credits

Chapter 1

Courtesy of the Schwind family, pp. 2, 3; Comstock Royalty Free Division, p. 8; Courtesy of the Ellenson family, p. 9; © Robin Nelson/Photo Edit, p. 16; © Trevor Smith/Alamy, p. 19.

Chapter 2

Courtesy of the Gonzalez family, pp. 28, 29; Katelyn Metzger/Merrill, p. 31; Laima Druskis/PH College, p. 32; Courtesy of Fiskars Brands, Inc., p. 35; Lori Whitley/ Merrill, p. 39; Anthony Magnacca/Merrill, p. 40; George Dodson/PH College, p. 43.

Chapter 3

Courtesy of the McGee family, pp. 52, 53; © Bettman/Corbis, p. 57; Tom Watson/ Merrill, p. 60; Laima Druskis/PH College, p. 70; © Monkey Business Images, p. 76.

Chapter 4

Courtesy of the Stuckey family, pp. 80, 81; © Jonathan Nourok/PhotoEdit, p. 82; © Jose Carrillo/PhotoEdit, p. 84; © Michael Newman/PhotoEdit, pp. 91, 94; © Unlisted Images, Inc. All Rights Reserved, p. 97; © Image Source/ SuperStock, p. 100.

Chapter 5

Jupiterimages/Thinkstock, pp. 104, 105; Masterfile Royalty Free Division, p. 107; Digital Vision/Thinkstock, p. 108; Jupiterimages, Creatas Images/ Thinkstock, p. 117.

Chapter 6

Courtesy of the Elser family, pp 126, 127; PH College, p. 129; © Monkey Business Images/Shutterstock, p. 131; Lori Whitley/Merrill, p. 134; Courtesy of Rud and Ann Turnbull, p. 138; © Belinda Images/SuperStock, p. 139; Anthony Magnacca/Merrill, p. 143.

Chapter 7

Courtesy of the Jewitt family, pp. 150, 151; © Getty Images/Jupiter Images/ Thinkstock, p. 153; Richard Hutchings/ Photo Researchers, Inc., p. 155; Barbara Schwartz/Merrill, p. 158; © Tony Freeman/PhotoEdit, p. 166.

Chapter 8

Courtesy of the Sims family, pp. 172, 173; © Bill Aron/PhotoEdit, p. 176; Courtesy of Chris Fraser, p. 179; Aaron Haupt/ Photo Researchers, Inc., p. 186.

Chapter 9

Courtesy of the Sabia family, pp. 194, 195; Katelyn Metzger/Merrill, p. 198; © Fotosearch/SuperStock, p. 204; Images reproduced with permission of AbleLink Technologies © 2005. All rights reserved, p. 206; © Robin Nelson/PhotoEdit, p. 210.

Chapter 10

Purestock/Fotosearch, pp. 218, 219; Scott Cunningham/Merrill, p. 221; © Michael Newman/PhotoEdit, p. 227; Images reproduced with permission of AbleLink Technologies © 2005. All Rights Reserved, p. 229; © 1985–2011 AbleNet, Inc. All Rights Reserved. Used with Permission, p. 230.

Chapter 11

Courtesy of the Conroy family, pp. 240, 241, 251, 256; © Stock Connection Blue/ Alamy, p. 244; Courtesty of Western Psychological Services, p. 247; Lori Whitley/Merrill, p. 254.

Chapter 12

Courtesy of the Ellenson family, p. 264; Courtesy of the Shaffer family, pp. 265, 266; © Brian Mitchell/Alamy, p. 267; © Levent Konuk/Shutterstock, p. 276; © 1985–2011 AbleNet, Inc. All Rights Reserved. Used with Permission, p. 278; Courtesy of the Lorenzo family, p. 279; Susan Glaser, p. 282.

Chapter 13

Courtesy of the Outlaw family, pp. 290, 291; © Image Source/SuperStock, p. 294; © Glasshouse Images/SuperStock, p. 300.

Chapter 14

Courtesy of the Symanski family, pp. 312, 313; © David Young-Wolfe/PhotoEdit, p. 319; © Sally and Richard Greenhill/ Alamy, p. 320; CC Studio/Photo Researchers, Inc., p. 326; © Michael Newman/PhotoEdit, pp. 328, 338; Teacher using a Front Row Pro Digital Classroom Amplification System. Photo courtesy of Front Row™ © 2011, p. 331; Courtesy of Barbara Leutke, p. 336.

Chapter 15

Courtesy of the Thornberry family, pp. 342–343; Lori Whitley/Merrill, p. 345; Todd Yarrington/Merrill, p. 346; Scott Cunningham, pp. 347, 362, 364; Katelyn Metzger, p. 361; Bob Rowan/Corbis/ Bettman, p. 366.

Chapter 16

Courtesy of the Tabb family, pp. 370, 371; Getty Images, Inc. – Photodisc, p. 373; Courtesy of the Wehmeyer family, p. 382; Keith Weller/USDA Natural Resources Conservation Services, p. 384; © Will Hart/PhotoEdit, p. 387.

1 Overview *of* Today's Special Education

Who Is Dylan Schwind?

Let's start at the beginning. He's the 8½-year-old adopted son of Darlene and Lieutenant Colonel Matthew Schwind. He was born in China and adopted when he was two years old. He has lived in China and in four different places in the United States, moving as his father was reassigned from one duty post to another. He has one sister and no brothers. His mother does not work outside the home. Those are the beginning facts you need to know about him.

Now what about his education? Here, the answers are far less clear-cut. Professionals identified him as needing supports and services and

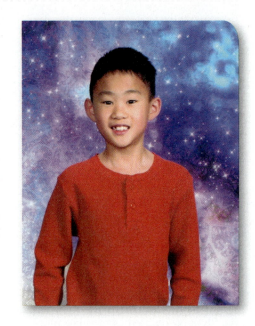

have provided them since he was a toddler. Soon after adopting him, Darlene noticed he had delays in some areas: He isolated himself from other children, he did not want to be touched, and he was content with entertaining himself for hours on end. During the next three years, Darlene talked to several pediatricians; each assured her that Dylan would catch up. Upon arriving in Washington, D.C., she finally convinced a physician to have Dylan tested for motor delays. At the age of five, he had the motor skills of a 2½- to 3-year-old. His occupational therapist suggested he be evaluated for autism or attention-deficit/

hyperactivity disorder (AD/HD). (You will learn about these disabilities in Chapters 11 and 8, respectively.) He then referred Dylan to a developmental pediatrician who abandoned the unjustified conclusion that "he's just developing slowly" and confirmed that Dylan had autism and AD/HD.

Dylan has a strong advocate in his mother, Darlene. Special educators either quickly become partners with her—or fail to, at their peril. Dylan can prosper when special educators provide the services he needs, according to the evaluations he has had, in the settings that allow him to prosper, and in collaboration with his mother and other professionals.

But Dylan is also a child whom some special educators seem to want to overlook; and if not for Darlene, they might get away with overlooking him. That's not a comfortable judgment to reach, but it's defensible. Even though he was diagnosed by a pediatrician, schools in two different districts, each in a different state, stonewalled on giving him early education services even though he was eligible for them.

Finally, but not insignificantly, he is also a "military brat"—the son of a career army officer. That is significant because he and his family move every two to three years, not just from one school district to another in the same state but from one state to another. These moves or deployments are involuntary: Family members comply with orders, uprooting themselves and, at times, jeopardizing Dylan's development in service to their country. Given the huge numbers of servicemen and -women who are being activated from the reserve and the National Guard or who belong to the regular armed forces, special educators can expect to serve more and more of their families.

Military families are not the only ones who are mobile. In-state and interstate immigration occurs within the civilian population. The challenge to special

OBJECTIVES

- You will learn about six values that should guide you as you teach.

- You will learn about students such as Dylan, who are in special education, and about the professionals who work with them.

- You will learn about the federal special education law, its six principles, and how the law benefits infants and toddlers (birth through age three), young children (ages three through six), and school-aged students (ages six through twenty-one).

- You will learn about the federal general education law, its six principles, and how the special education and general education laws are aligned with each other.

- You will learn about other federal laws that benefit students with disabilities.

- You will learn about the outcomes that these laws have helped achieve for students, and you will discover that much more remains to be achieved.

educators is to provide continuity in appropriate services, which ensure that a student makes progress toward academic, developmental, functional, and emotional-behavioral goals and that he or she is educated with peers without disabilities to the maximum extent appropriate for that student. So Dylan represents a significant portion of the population whom special and general educators will teach.

Has he received an appropriate education from them? You be the judge. He was in three different states before he began to have stability and receive an appropriate education; that means he was 5½ years old before he began to benefit from special education because his disabilities were not formally diagnosed until he started kindergarten. Even with that diagnosis, the school resisted a special education evaluation well into that school year.

Darlene believes the school districts he had previously attended tried to pacify her by offering some services, based only on a rudimentary screening, with the hope that she and her family would soon be transferred out of the district and thus allow it to avoid the cost of providing Dylan with special education services. These districts screened Dylan for his academic skills, which were good. But they paid little heed to his behavioral needs or his fine-motor deficits. In a word, they refused to collaborate with other professionals. Not surprisingly, his behaviors got worse: He withdrew socially and melted down when challenged by a difficult task that educators did not adapt for him, throwing objects, sweeping items off his desk, and screaming and crying.

Although Dylan was included in classrooms with students who did not have disabilities, he seemed not to benefit from inclusion; indeed, he was being bullied by some students because of his disabilities, not because of his Chinese heritage. (Schools on military bases or in communities impacted by a heavy military presence are unusually diverse in their populations.) And to Darlene's frustration, many of his teachers ignored her, thinking they knew more than she did about Dylan and resenting that she had found reliable allies among military families whose children had disabilities and who knew how to navigate their ways through obstacles in the local schools.

Finally, however, Dylan began receiving an appropriate education. Then came the next move: New testing determined that he needed no social, educational, or behavioral assistance. He is now in the second grade, receiving only occupational therapy and physical therapy, but he is regressing. His mother, with help from other professionals, is trying to implement the social, behavioral, and academic interventions he needs. She continues to fight for Dylan's needed services before he loses any more time.

What lessons can we take away from this story? Darlene thinks there are three. First, educators must serve children first and foremost, not themselves or the systems that employ them. Their primary job is to benefit the students. Second, educators must be true partners with other professionals and parents: Collaboration invariably leads to good outcomes. Third, educators must plan carefully so that students such as Dylan, who move frequently, will have a consistent education, which is another foundation for good outcomes.

Let's reframe Darlene's three lessons so that they fit more precisely into the topic of this chapter. Students' progress depends on their right to an education, which Dylan had from the moment he was diagnosed as having disabilities. Their progress also depends on educators' practices. Those lessons hold true not just for this chapter but for all the chapters in this book. They can turn a none-too-encouraging story into a wholly upbeat one. To appreciate how, read on.

PEARSON
myeducationlab

Visit the MyEducationLab (www.myeducationlab.com) for *Exceptional Lives* to enhance your understanding of chapter concepts with a personalized Study Plan. You'll also have the opportunity to hone your teaching skills through video- and case-based assignments and activities, IRIS Center Resources, and Building Teaching Skills and Disposition lessons.

Profile of Special Education Students and Personnel in Today's Schools

Perhaps you have heard these lines. Although they apply to all of us today, they were written in 1624 by poet John Donne: "Never send to know for whom the bell tolls; It tolls for thee" (Donne, 1986).

Disability affects 8.8 percent of the U.S. school-aged population (U.S. Department of Education, 2011); it eventually affects most of us as we age. For you, then, the disability bell could toll at least twice: once as you teach, and once as you age. For some of you,

FIGURE 1.1 *Values to guide you in your career*

Envisioning great expectations. Students have many capabilities that have not been tapped. We can develop new visions of what is possible. These visions can become realities. We need new perspectives of what life can be as well as support for fulfilling these dreams.

Enhancing positive contributions. Students contribute positively to their families, schools, friends, and communities. We need to develop greater opportunities for these contributions.

Building on strengths. Students and families have many natural capacities. They need opportunities for educational programs to identify, highlight, and build upon their strengths.

Becoming self-determined. Students and families can direct their own lives. Enabling them to act on their own preferences promotes their self-determination.

Expanding relationships. Connections are crucial to quality of life. Students and families need to connect with each other, educators, and friends in the community.

Ensuring full citizenship. Less able does not mean less worthy. All students, including those with exceptionalities, and their families are entitled to full participation in American life.

the bell peals more frequently because you have a family member or a close friend with a disability or because you yourself have special needs.

When the bell tolls, it tolls not only for people with a disability but also for their families, friends, teachers, school administrators, and communities. That is why, in this book, we offer stories about real families, real children and youth, and real educators at the beginning of each chapter. But stories alone are not enough to introduce you to the field of special education, so we also review the most recent research data, combining the real-life personal face of exceptionality with evidence-based practices in special education, public policy, and overarching values that we encourage you to adopt. In particular, we discuss three themes: inclusion, universal design for learning, and partnerships.

Remember Dylan? He is included in the general curriculum, and he benefits from teachers who adapt their teaching for him and others. (These teachers are applying *universal design* to their instruction, a strategy we will discuss throughout this book.) They also use assistive technology for him. (We define assistive technology in Figure 1.3.)

Exemplary special education occurs when values guide practices. And when values-guided practices are as state-of-the-art as the ones you will read about in this book, no student, family, school, or teaching challenge will be too daunting. Figure 1.1 identifies these values.

WHO ARE THE STUDENTS?

To answer this question, we describe the total number of students with disabilities, the gender of those students, the provision of gifted education, the categories of disabilities, and issues of labels and language. First, however, let's define *special education*. It is specially designed instruction, at no cost to a child's parents, that meets a child's unique needs in school. It consists of related services (Figure 1.3) and supplementary aids and services (which we describe in Chapter 2 and then in Chapters 5 through 16).

Total Number of Students Served

In the 2007–2008 school year, 321,894 infants and toddlers (ages birth through two), or 2.7 percent of U.S. infants and toddlers, received early intervention services; and 709,004 preschool children (ages three through five), or 5.7 percent of the preschool-aged population, received early childhood services (U.S. Department of Education, 2011). Approximately 6 million (5,889,849, to be exact) students ages six through twenty-one received some form of special education. Also, 346,258 students from ages eighteen to twenty-one years of age received special education services. This brings the total number of children, youth, and young adults served by special education to 7,267,005.

Gender of Students

In the general education school population, males and females are enrolled in equal proportion, but in special education approximately two thirds (67 percent) of the students are male and one third (33 percent) are female (U.S. Department of Education, 2011).

Gifted Students

Special education also serves students who have unusual gifts and talents (see Chapter 16). The percentage of students identified as gifted ranges from a low of 1.8 percent to a high of 18 percent in different states (National Association for Gifted Children, 2007). In the 2006 school year, 3,236,990 students were identified as gifted and talented in elementary and secondary schools, representing 6.7 percent of the school population (U.S. Department of Education, 2009). Females slightly outnumber males.

Disability Categories

The U.S. Department of Education collects data from states according to students' type or category of disability. Figure 1.2 sets out the percentages of students associated with the highest frequency categories (U.S. Department of Education, 2011). Nearly two thirds of students with disabilities are classified into two categories: specific learning disabilities (42.9 percent) and speech or language impairments (19 percent). These two categories, when combined with the categories of intellectual disability (8.1 percent) and emotional or behavioral disorders (7.1 percent), account for 77 percent of all students with disabilities. In each chapter, you will meet students who have disabilities, just as you have been introduced to Dylan. You will read about their characteristics, their families, and the education they receive. But before you read about educational characteristics, a word of caution is in order.

FIGURE 1.2   *Disability distribution for students ages six through twenty-one receiving special education and related services under IDEA: School year 2008–2009*

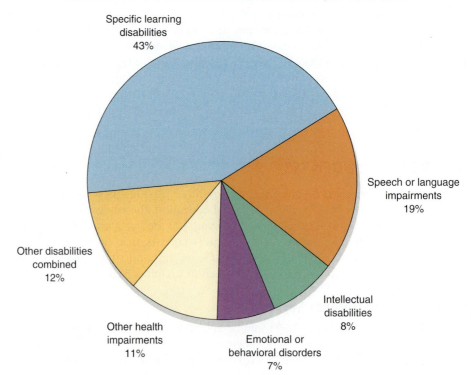

Source: U.S. Department of Education. (2011). *Data Accountability Center: Individuals with Disabilities Education Act (IDEA) data.* Retrieved on February 12, 2011, from https://www.ideadata.org.

Note: Percentages have been rounded and collapsed across categories.

Labels and Language

How would you feel if you were Dylan and if other students or even teachers referred to you as "the autistic kid"? Now imagine being called "the crippled kid" or "the handicapped student." How would you feel if you were known only by your disability and not according to your abilities? Devalued? Probably. Indeed, that is precisely how many families and special educators respond when a child with disabilities is labeled, first and foremost, as a disabled person.

There is controversy about labeling and its consequences, which include classification into special education. Some students may benefit if a label qualifies them to receive services because the benefit of those services can outweigh the stigma that accompanies some labels. Indeed, certain people, including those with hearing and visual impairments (see Chapters 14 and 15), accept and celebrate the labels because they create cultural solidarity.

On the other hand, labeling can lead educators to make biased decisions about a student's strengths and needs. In one study, researchers gave preservice teacher educators videos of students and asked them to identify students' behavior as on task or off task (Allday, Duhon, Blackburn-Ellis, & Van Dycke, 2011). They told some of the preservice teacher educators that students had oppositional defiant disorder (a type of emotional or behavioral disorder), others that students had attention-deficit/hyperactivity disorder (AD/HD), and still others that students were gifted and talented. The students' labels made a difference: Teachers were less likely to rate the behavior of students who were gifted and talented as off task.

So we ask you to be cautious about using labels. While they may not be objectionable to a minority of people with disabilities, they are to most and to their families and friends. Our best advice is this: Let Dylan be Dylan, not a youngster with a label. Refer to him by his name, not his label. And if you or other educators must use labels for legal or other valid reasons, such as to secure services for the student, avoid those that demean and stigmatize, for they always separate and devalue people, both inside and outside school (Goffman, 1963; Smith, 1999), and they impair students' self-esteem (Lapadat, 1998).

Three changes in terminology have occurred over the past three decades. They are important to understand because they reflect values that you should adopt in your practice. The first change abandons the term *handicap* and favors the term *disability*. To be handicapped is to have your cap in your hand, begging for a service such as education. Dylan does not have to beg; he is not handicapped but does have a disability.

The second change abandons stigmatizing words altogether. For example, the terms *retarded* and *mentally retarded* have been replaced by the term *intellectual disability*. Indeed, the word *retard* is highly offensive and should never be used in professional or casual conversations. The "R word" is tantamount to racial and ethnic slurs that have long been off limits. In other words, calling Dylan a "retard" would be not only inaccurate but also pejorative and debasing. Similar changes in wording apply to other students: For instance, *crippled* has been replaced by *physically challenged*.

The third change, called *people-first language,* puts the person before the disability. For example, instead of using phrases such as "physically disabled children," teachers say "students with physical disabilities." Even better, they and you might consider not labeling at all. Why not just say "students"? Best of all, just say "Dylan."

In Chapter 2 you will learn about a current approach in special education: *responsiveness to intervention (RTI)*. It directs teachers to intensify their instruction for students who experience learning challenges before referring them for special education testing and ultimately for a formal label. This approach—respond and intensify—can help teachers avoid labeling because RTI applies to all students.

WHO ARE SPECIAL EDUCATION PERSONNEL?

According to the U.S. Department of Education (2011), 426,001 special education teachers were employed in 2007 to teach students ages three through twenty-one. If you are considering a career in special education, your job prospects are good. To understand your opportunities completely, you should know that a study of supply and demand for sixty-two

The profession of special education offers you many career paths.

education fields identified fourteen as having a considerable shortage, nine of which were in areas related to special education (American Association for Employment in Education, 2008). The four areas with the most critical shortages were teachers trained to support students with emotional or behavioral disorders, visual impairments, and severe disabilities as well as those who specialize in early childhood. The regions of the country that had the most severe shortages were the northwest and the southeast.

Not all special education professionals are teachers. Other educational personnel include school social workers, occupational therapists, physical therapists, recreation and therapeutic specialists, medical/nursing staff, orientation and mobility specialists, physical education teachers, psychologists, audiologists, counselors, rehabilitation counselors, interpreters, and speech pathologists. The number of nonteaching personnel who provided special education services for students ages three through twenty-one totaled 214,040 during 2007. Additionally, 389,824 paraprofessionals served special education students during autumn 2005 (U.S. Department of Education, 2011).

You now know that there is a broad range of roles in the special education field. What you may not know is how rewarding it can be to be a special educator or how federal law provides a structure for that rewarding career. Let's consider those matters.

Overview of the Law and Special Education

For more than thirty years now, the education of students with disabilities has been governed by a law that Congress enacted in 1975 called the Individuals with Disabilities Education Act (IDEA). Whatever role you play in American schools, you almost certainly will have to know about this law, the rights it gives to students, and the duties it imposes on schools. Let's begin with a bit of its history.

TWO TYPES OF DISCRIMINATION

During the early and middle decades of the 20th century, schools discriminated against students with disabilities in two significant ways (Turnbull, Stowe, & Huerta, 2007). First, they often completely excluded many students with disabilities. If such students were admitted, they were not provided with an effective or appropriate education. Second, schools often classified students as having disabilities who in fact did not have disabilities. This practice is known as misclassification. Frequently, these students were members of culturally or linguistically diverse groups.

Beginning in the early 1970s, advocates for students with disabilities—primarily their families, parent advocacy organizations, and civil rights lawyers—began to sue state and local school officials, claiming that exclusion and misclassification violated students' rights to an equal education opportunity under the U.S. Constitution (Turnbull, Shogren, & Turnbull, 2011). Relying on the Supreme Court's decision in the school race-desegregation case *Brown v. Board of Education* (1954), they argued that because the Court held that schools may not segregate by race, schools also may not segregate or otherwise discriminate by ability and disability. Students are students, regardless of their race or disability. You will learn more about *Brown*'s impact in Chapter 3, when we describe the deplorable history of discrimination against students from culturally diverse backgrounds, especially in special education.

JUDICIAL DECISIONS AND LEGISLATION

Advocates for students with disabilities were successful. In 1972, federal courts ordered the Commonwealth of Pennsylvania and the District of Columbia to (1) provide a free appropriate public education to all students with disabilities, (2) educate students with disabilities in the same schools and basically the same programs as students without disabilities, and (3) put into place certain procedural safeguards so that parents of students with disabilities could challenge schools that did not live up to the courts' orders (*Mills v. Washington, DC, Board of Education*, 1972; *Pennsylvania Association for Retarded Citizens [PARC] v. Commonwealth of Pennsylvania*, 1972).

These two cases prompted Congress to act. In 1975, it enacted IDEA (then called the Education of All Handicapped Students Act, or Public Law [P.L.] 94–142). At that time Congress intended to open up the schools to all students with disabilities and make sure that those students had the chance to benefit from education.

Nowadays the challenge is to provide access and ensure that students really do benefit. Special education is explicitly outcome-driven. There are four outcomes: equality of opportunity, full participation, independent living, and economic self-sufficiency. Later in this chapter you will read about these outcomes, but first you need to know about IDEA's basic components.

When Congress reauthorized IDEA in 2004, it enacted the Individuals with Disabilities Education Improvement Act. Sometimes you will hear people refer to the law by that name or its abbreviation, IDEIA. But Congress recognized that people are familiar with the law's former name (before the 2004 reauthorization), so it provided that the short title of the reauthorized law is Individuals with Disabilities Education Act (abbreviated as IDEA). Therefore, in every place in which we refer to the 2004 law, we call it Individuals with Disabilities Education Act or IDEA.

The Span of Special Education: Birth Through Age Twenty-One

Having enacted IDEA in 1975 to benefit students ages six to eighteen, Congress has expanded the group of students who have a right to special education. The law now applies to infants and toddlers from birth through age two, young children (ages three through five), and older students (through age twenty-one). IDEA recognizes that infants and toddlers have needs unlike those of older children (ages three through twenty-one). Accordingly, it consists of two parts, each of which is age-specific: Part B and Part C. (Part A sets out Congress's intent and national policy to provide a free appropriate public education to all students with disabilities, from birth to age twenty-one.)

Part B

Part B benefits students (such as Dylan Schwind) who are ages three through twenty-one. To define eligible students, IDEA combines a categorical approach (that is, it describes the categories of disabilities; Dylan's is autism) with a functional approach (that is, it provides that the student must be unable to function successfully in the general curriculum without special education). The IDEA categories for students ages three through twenty-one, in order from the most frequent to the least frequent, are specific learning disabilities, speech or language impairments, intellectual disability (IDEA uses the term *mental retardation* although Congress enacted a law in 2010 that replaces that term with *intellectual disability* in all federal laws, including IDEA), emotional disorders, multiple disabilities, hearing impairments, other health impairments, autism, visual impairments, and traumatic brain injury. In this book we provide a chapter about each

The purpose of IDEA is to ensure that all students with disabilities have a free appropriate public education in the least restrictive setting.

disability (including physical disabilities). We also cover attention deficit/hyperactivity disorder (AD/HD), which is a component of other health impairments, as well as students who are gifted.

These same categories apply to children ages three to six (those in early childhood special education), but each state may also provide special education to children who do not yet have a disability label but meet the functional criteria for special education services, which include the following:

- Are experiencing developmental delays in one or more of the following areas— physical development, cognitive development, communication development, social or emotional development, or adaptive behavior and development—and
- Because of these delays, need special education and related services

IDEA gives the states discretion about whether they will choose to serve children ages three through five (early education). As of early 2010, all states do so.

Part C

IDEA also gives the states discretion about whether they will choose to serve infants and toddlers (ages birth through two, also known as zero to three). As of early 2010, all states do. **Part C** benefits any child under age three who (1) needs early intervention services because of developmental delays in one or more of the areas of cognitive development, physical development, communication development, social or emotional development, and adaptive development or (2) has a diagnosed physical or mental condition that has a high probability of resulting in a developmental delay.

Part C does more than benefit the children who have identified delays. It also gives each state the option of serving at-risk infants and toddlers (children under age three). These are children who would be at risk of experiencing a substantial developmental delay if they did not receive early intervention services. Note the difference: A child with a diagnosed condition that has a "high probability" of resulting in a developmental delay is not the same as a child who is "at risk" of having a delay.

SPECIAL EDUCATION AND STUDENTS' ELIGIBILITY

Eligibility Based on Need

As you have already read, IDEA (Part B, ages three through five optional, ages six through twenty-one not optional) defines special education as specially designed instruction, at no cost to the child's parents, that meets the unique needs of a student with a disability. A student with a disability is one who has the disabilities identified previously in this chapter (the categorical definition) and who, because of the disability, needs special education and related services (the functional definition). Thus, special education is reserved for students who need it because of their disabilities and because their needs cannot be met in general education without special education services and supports. Dylan is one of the beneficiaries of IDEA: He has a disability that requires special education services and supports.

Where Special Education Is Provided

Special education occurs in classrooms (where Dylan receives his), students' homes, hospitals and institutions, and other settings. Under IDEA, special education must be available wherever there are students who qualify for its benefits.

COMPONENTS OF SPECIAL EDUCATION

Special education is individualized to the student; that is the meaning of "to meet the unique needs" of a student. To meet a student's needs, it is usually necessary to provide more than individualized instruction. Educators and other professionals in special education do this by supplementing their instruction with what are known as *related services*. These are services that are necessary to assist the student in benefiting from special education. Figure 1.3 identifies and defines related services. Note that speech therapy, which Dylan receives, is a related service.

FIGURE 1.3 *Definitions of related services in IDEA*

The related services apply to Part B and students ages three through twenty-one unless we note that they belong to Part C only and thus only to children ages birth through two.

- *Assistive technology and services:* acquiring and using devices and services to restore lost capacities or improve impaired capacities (Part C, but also a "special consideration" for Part B students' IEPs).

- *Audiology:* determining the range, nature, and degree of hearing loss and operating programs for treatment and prevention of hearing loss.

- *Counseling services:* counseling by social workers, psychologists, guidance counselors, or other qualified professionals.

- *Early identification:* identifying a disability as early as possible in a child's life.

- *Interpreting services:* various means for communicating with children who have hearing impairments or who are deaf-blind.

- *Family training, counseling, and home visits:* assisting families to enhance their child's development (Part C only).

- *Health services:* enabling a child to benefit from other early intervention services (Part C only).

- *Medical services:* determining a child's medically related disability that results in the child's need for special education and related services.

- *Occupational therapy:* improving, developing, or restoring functions impaired or lost through illness, injury, or deprivation.

- *Orientation and mobility services:* assisting a visually impaired or blind student to get around within various environments.

- *Parent counseling and training:* providing parents with information about child development.

- *Physical therapy:* services by a physical therapist.

- *Psychological services:* administering and interpreting psychological and educational tests and other assessment procedures and managing a program of psychological services, including psychological counseling for children and parents.

- *Recreation and therapeutic recreation:* assessing leisure function, recreation programs in schools and community agencies, and leisure education.

- *Rehabilitative counseling services:* planning for career development, employment preparation, achieving independence, and integration in the workplace and community.

- *School health services:* attending to educationally related health needs through services provided by a school nurse or other qualified professional.

- *Service coordination services:* assistance and services by a service coordinator to a child and family (Part C only).

- *Social work services in schools:* preparing a social or developmental history on a child, counseling groups and individuals, and mobilizing school and community resources.

- *Speech pathology and speech-language pathology:* diagnosing specific speech or language impairments and giving guidance regarding those impairments.

- *Transportation and related costs:* providing travel to and from services and schools, travel in and around school buildings, and specialized equipment (e.g., special or adapted buses, lifts, and ramps).

- *Vision services:* assessing vision in an infant/toddler (Part C only).

IDEA: Six Principles

It is not enough for IDEA simply to identify the eligible students and to specify the services they have a right to receive. Because of schools' past discrimination through exclusion and misclassification, IDEA also establishes six principles that govern students' education (Turnbull et al., 2007). Figure 1.4 describes those six principles. Because IDEA is complex and contains general rules, exceptions to the general rules, and even exceptions to the exceptions, we will describe the general rules and, sometimes, the exceptions.

ZERO REJECT

The **zero-reject** principle prohibits schools from excluding any student with a disability (as defined by IDEA) from a free appropriate public education. The purpose of the zero-reject principle is to ensure that all children and youth (ages three through twenty-one), no matter how severe their disabilities, will receive an appropriate education provided at public expense. To carry out this purpose, the zero-reject rule applies to the state and all of its school districts and private schools (if the public system places a student into a private school), state-operated programs such as schools for students with visual or hearing impairments, psychiatric hospitals, and institutions for people with other disabilities.

Educability

To carry out the zero-reject rule, courts have ordered state and local education agencies to provide services to children who traditionally (but unjustly) have been regarded as not able to learn because of the profound extent of their disabilities. The courts say that "all" means "all": Congress was very clear that it intends IDEA to benefit *all* children with disabilities, no matter how severe their disability.

Discipline

To assure that all students with a disability receive an appropriate education and that the schools are safe places for teaching and learning, IDEA regulates how schools may discipline students who qualify for IDEA's protection. The principles of the IDEA discipline amendments are simple, but their details are complex. The general principles are as follows:

- *Equal treatment*. The school may discipline a student with a disability in the same way and to the same extent as it may discipline a student without a disability, for the same offense, subject to the nine exceptions that we now describe.
- *No cessation*. No matter what the student does to violate a school code, the school may not expel or suspend the student for more than ten school days in any one school year.
- *Unique circumstances*. The school may take into account any unique circumstances related to the student and the student's behavior in violating a school code of behavior when the school is deciding whether to change the student's placement in order to discipline the student.
- *Short-term removals*. The school may suspend the student for not more than ten school days in any one school year. It has no duty to offer any services to the suspended student during those ten days.
- *Manifestation determinations*. When the school proposes to change the student's placement for more than ten days, it must determine whether the student's behavior

is a manifestation of the student's disability. A manifestation exists when the student's behavior was caused by the disability or had a direct and substantial relationship to the disability or when the student's conduct was the direct failure of the school to implement the student's IEP.

- *Response to no manifestation.* If the school determines that the student's behavior is not a manifestation of the disability, it may discipline the student in the same way as it disciplines students without disabilities except that it may not terminate the student's education (the "no cessation" rule). It may, however, place the student in an interim alternative educational setting.

- *Response to manifestation.* When a school determines that the student's behavior is a manifestation of the disability, the school must take immediate steps to remedy any deficiencies contributing to the school's failure to implement the student's IEP. The school also must conduct a functional behavioral assessment and develop a behavioral intervention plan to address the student's behavior (whether or not the manifestation is IEP-deficiency based). Unless the school and parents agree to place the student in an interim alternative setting, the student then returns to the student's previous school placement.

- *Services in interim alternative educational settings.* When it places a student in such a setting, the school must still offer an education that assures that the student will make progress according to the student's IEP.

- *Weapons, drugs, and injury.* When a student has weapons or knowingly has or uses illegal drugs in school or when a student seriously injures another person at school, the school may place the student in an interim alternative educational setting, without first making any manifestation determination, for up to forty-five days.

NONDISCRIMINATORY EVALUATION

The effect of the zero-reject rule is to guarantee all students with a disability access to an appropriate education. To assure such an education, IDEA requires educators to conduct a **nondiscriminatory evaluation** of the student.

Two Purposes

The nondiscriminatory evaluation has two purposes. The first is to determine whether a student has a disability. If the student does not have a disability, then she has no right to receive special education under IDEA or any further evaluation related to special education under IDEA.

If the evaluation reveals that the student has a disability, the evaluation process must then accomplish its second purpose: to identify special education and related services the student will receive. As you just learned, this information is necessary to plan an appropriate education for the student and determine where the student will be educated—the "what" and "where" of individualized education. In Dylan's case, the "what" is the specific educational program he receives, and the "where" is the general and special education setting in which he receives it.

Nondiscriminatory Evaluation Requirements

Because evaluation has such a significant impact on students and their families, IDEA surrounds the evaluation process with procedural safeguards. Figure 1.5 highlights IDEA's procedural safeguards and its additional provisions for notice to students' parents and the rights of parents to consent or not to what their child's educators propose.

Once the evaluation team has determined that a student has a disability (or, in some states, is gifted) and has identified the special education and related services the student needs, then educators must provide the student with that kind of education and those services, describing them in the student's individualized education program (IEP). In short, the nondiscriminatory evaluation leads to, and is the very foundation of, the student's appropriate education.

IDEA does not specify who the members of the evaluation team must be. It simply says that a local educational agency must ensure that qualified personnel and the student's parents are part of the evaluation team. But because one of the members of the student's IEP team must be a person qualified to interpret the evaluation results, usually at least one member of the evaluation team will be a member of the IEP team. To the greatest extent possible, it is helpful to have overlap between the members of the multidisciplinary evaluation team and the members of the IEP team. Regardless of the precise team membership, however, the result is the same: The evaluation leads to IEP decisions about program (appropriate education) and placement (least restrictive environment).

APPROPRIATE EDUCATION

By enrolling students (zero reject) and evaluating their strengths and needs (nondiscriminatory evaluation), schools still do not ensure that students' education will be appropriate and beneficial. That is why Congress has given each student in special education the right to an **appropriate education** and related services.

As we have already noted, the key to an appropriate special education is *individualization:* for example, tailoring Dylan's education to build on his strengths and meet his learning needs. Educators individualize by developing an **individualized education program (IEP)** for each student ages three through twenty-one. Children from birth through age two and their families receive an **individualized family services plan (IFSP)**. To guide you through IDEA's appropriate education requirements, we will discuss (1) the basic contents of IEPs/IFSPs; (2) age-specific provisions, including early intervention and transitions to adulthood; (3) the participants who develop the IEP/IFSP; and (4) timelines. You will learn more about the IEP in Chapter 2.

FIGURE 1.5 *Nondiscriminatory evaluation safeguards*

Assessment Procedures

- They use a variety of assessment tools and strategies to gather relevant functional, developmental, and academic information, including information provided by the student's parent that may enable the team to determine if the student has a disability and the nature of specially designed instruction needed.
- They should include more than one assessment because no single procedure may be used as the sole basis of evaluation.
- They may be requested by a parent, the state education agency, another state agency, or the local education agency (initial evaluations).
- They are selected and administered so as to not be discriminatory on a racial or cultural basis.
- They are administered in the language and form most likely to produce accurate information about the student's current levels of academic, development, and functional performance.
- They must be used for the purposes for which the assessments are valid and reliable.
- They are administered by trained and knowledgeable personnel and in conformance with instructions by the producer of the tests or material.

Parental Notice and Consent

- Inform the parents fully and secure their written consent before the initial evaluation and each reevaluation.
- If the parents do not consent to the initial evaluation, the school may use dispute resolution (due process) procedures to secure approval to proceed with the evaluation or reevaluation.
- Obtain parents' consent before any reevaluation unless the school can demonstrate that it has taken reasonable measures to obtain their consent and parents have failed to respond.
- Provide to the parents a full explanation of all due process rights, a description of what the school proposes or refuses to do, a description of each evaluation procedure that was used, a statement of how the parents may obtain a copy of their procedural safeguards and sources that they can contact to obtain assistance in understanding the provisions of the notice, a description of any other options considered, and an explanation of any other factors that influenced the educators' decisions.
- Do not treat the parents' consent for evaluation as their consent for placement into or withdrawal from a special education program; secure separate parental consent for these changes.
- If the parents do not consent to placement, the school has no duty to provide special education and is not liable to the parents or child if it does not use dispute resolution (due process) to get authority to provide services.

As you've just read, each student's IEP/IFSP is based on the student's evaluation and is outcome-oriented. Taken as a whole, the IEP/IFSP is the foundation for the student's appropriate education; it is the assurance that Dylan and other students covered by IDEA will benefit from special education and have real access to equality of opportunity, full participation, independent living, and economic self-sufficiency.

The IFSP describes the services that both the infant (or toddler) and the family will receive. Like the IEP, the IFSP is based on the child's development and needs; it specifies outcomes for the child. Unlike the IEP, however, the IFSP also provides the option for families to identify their resources, priorities, and concerns related to enhancing their child's development. Furthermore, the IFSP must include outcomes and services for the child's family if the family wants to achieve specific outcomes related to the child's development.

Participants Who Develop the IEP/IFSP

At the beginning of our discussion about appropriate education, we wrote that the non-discriminatory evaluation lays the foundation for the student's individualized plan (IEP or IFSP). We also wrote that the IEP team therefore must include at least one person who can link the evaluation to the IEP. But the team must include others as well:

- The student's parents (In Dylan's case, Darlene or Matthew, or both)
- At least one general education teacher with expertise related to the student's educational level
- At least one special education teacher
- A representative of the school system who is qualified to provide or supervise special education and is also knowledgeable about the general education curriculum and the availability of school resources
- An individual who can interpret the evaluation results
- At the discretion of the parent or agency, other individuals with expertise regarding the student's educational needs, including related-service personnel
- The student, when appropriate

Other people may be included in the IEP or IFSP conference. For example, a parent might wish to bring another family member or a friend who knows about the special education process. We discuss parent rights later in this chapter and in Chapter 4 (about partnerships).

Timelines

IDEA requires an IEP to be in effect at the beginning of each school year. Educators and parents may make changes in the IEP either through a team meeting or by developing a written document that amends or changes the current IEP. Also, the team must review and, if appropriate, revise the student's IEP at least once a year.

IDEA requires an IFSP to be developed within "a reasonable time" after the child has been assessed for early intervention services. The IFSP must be evaluated at least annually, and families have the right to at least a semi-annual review based on the needs of the family, infant, and/or toddler.

IEP/IFSP Conferences

IDEA does not have detailed requirements about the process that must be followed at IEP/IFSP conferences. Ideally, however, those conferences reflect partnerships among educators and parents. Sadly, research on the IEP/IFSP has generally reported that the traditional process tends to involve legal compliance—a paperwork process—rather than problem-solving, dynamic teamwork (Turnbull, Turnbull, Erwin, Soodak, & Shogren, 2011). That fact is regrettable because the U.S. Supreme Court, in interpreting IDEA, has said that the "core" of the law is the "cooperative process" that occurs among the IEP team members, especially the student's parents (*Schaffer v. Weast*, 2005).

To ensure that the conference is indeed a meeting of partners, including the parents, IEP conferences should incorporate ten activities (Turnbull et al., 2011):

1. Prepare in advance
2. Connect and start
3. Review formal evaluation and current levels of performance
4. Share thoughts about resources, priorities, and concerns
5. Share visions and great expectations
6. Consider interaction of proposed student goals, placement, and services
7. Translate priorities into written goals or outcomes
8. Determine nature of services
9. Determine modifications in assessments and special factors
10. Conclude the conference

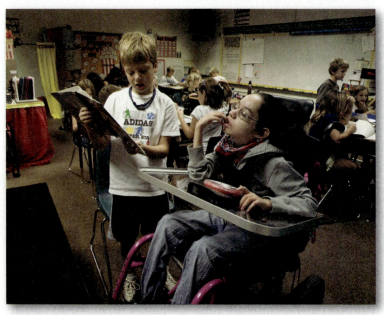

IDEA seeks the full inclusion of persons with disabilities and presumes they will be in general education programs while in school. Here, a student with a disability and a student without a disability learn their lessons together. Togetherness is an essential element of full inclusion.

The purpose of the required IEP/IFSP review is to determine whether the student is making progress toward achieving annual goals (IEP) or outcomes (IFSP). Accordingly, IDEA requires the IEP team to review the student's IEP and revise it as appropriate to secure that kind of progress. A review may cause a reevaluation and even a change of placement. Throughout this book, you will find IEP tips, which are suggestions for how you can participate effectively in the IEP conference and in the development of students' IEP documents.

LEAST RESTRICTIVE ENVIRONMENT

Once the schools have enrolled a student (the zero-reject principle), fairly evaluated the student (the nondiscriminatory evaluation principle), and provided an IEP/IFSP (the appropriate education principle), they must contribute one more element to the student's education—namely, education alongside students who do not have disabilities. This is the principle of the **least restrictive environment (LRE)**, formerly known as the mainstreaming or integration rule and now known as the inclusion principle. Dylan benefits from the LRE presumption, as you learned by reading about him and the "where" of his education earlier in this chapter.

In early intervention (ages zero through two), IDEA favors education in the student's "natural environment," which could be home or an out-of-home child care or education center. In all other education (ages three through twenty-one), IDEA favors placement in general education. The term *general education* has three dimensions: the academic curriculum, extracurricular activities, and other nonacademic activities (for example, recess, transportation, mealtimes, dances, and sports).

The Rule: A Presumption in Favor of Inclusion

IDEA creates a presumption in favor of educating students with disabilities alongside those who do not have disabilities. It does this by requiring that (1) a school must educate a student with a disability with students who do not have disabilities to the maximum extent appropriate for the student and (2) a school may not remove the student from the regular education environment unless, because of the nature or severity of the student's disability, he or she cannot be educated there successfully (appropriately, in the sense that the student will benefit), even after the school provides supplementary aids and support services for the student.

Access to General Education Curriculum

IDEA specifically states that the education of children with disabilities can be made more effective by having "high expectations" for them and ensuring their maximum access to the general education curriculum in the regular classroom in order to meet both their developmental goals and, to the greatest extent possible, the challenging academic expectations established for all children.

Setting Aside the Presumption

The school may set aside this presumption of inclusion only if the student cannot benefit from being educated with students who do not have disabilities and only after the school has provided the student with supplementary aids and services in general education settings. In that event, the school may place the student in a less typical, more specialized, less inclusive program.

The Continuum of Services

Schools must offer a continuum, or range, of services from more to less typical and inclusive—that is, from less to more restrictive or separate. The most typical and inclusive setting is general education, followed by resource rooms, special classes, special schools, homebound services, and hospitals and institutions (also called residential or long-term-care facilities). You will learn more about these different settings in Chapter 2.

Extracurricular and Nonacademic Inclusion

Schools also have to ensure that students with disabilities may participate in extracurricular and other nonacademic activities and services such as meals, recess periods, counseling, athletics, transportation, health services, recreational activities, special interest groups or clubs, and referrals to agencies that assist in employment and other aspects of life outside school. In short, when providing academic, extracurricular, and other nonacademic activities and services to students who do not have disabilities, schools must include students with disabilities (such as Dylan) in all those activities and services to the maximum extent appropriate for each child with a disability. That is because, as Congress said in 1997 and repeated in 2004, special education is a service for children rather than a place to which they are sent.

PROCEDURAL DUE PROCESS

Schools do not always carry out IDEA's first four principles: zero reject, nondiscriminatory evaluation, appropriate education, and least restrictive environment. What's a parent to do? Or what if a school believes that one type of special education is appropriate but a parent disagrees and believes that the proposed placement will not benefit the student? The answer lies in the **procedural due process** principle, which basically seeks to make schools and parents accountable to each other for carrying out the student's IDEA rights.

When parents and educators disagree, IDEA provides each with three different ways to resolve their disagreements. First, they may meet face to face in a resolution session. Second, they may resort to mediation. IDEA does not require mediation, and it may not be used to deny or delay the right to a due process hearing. But IDEA strongly encourages mediation. Third, if the parties still cannot resolve their disagreements, each has a right to a due process hearing (a mini-trial) before an impartial hearing officer. The due process hearing is similar to a regular courtroom trial. At the hearing, the parents and schools are entitled to be represented by lawyers, present evidence, and cross-examine each other's witnesses. If the local education agency or the parent is dissatisfied with the decision of the hearing officer, either may appeal to state or federal courts. Dylan's parents have not yet exercised any of their due process rights. Perhaps they never will, but they may have to if they want Dylan to benefit fully from his IDEA rights.

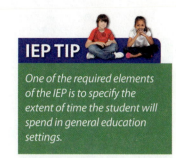

IEP TIP

One of the required elements of the IEP is to specify the extent of time the student will spend in general education settings.

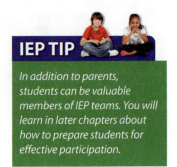

IEP TIP

In addition to parents, students can be valuable members of IEP teams. You will learn in later chapters about how to prepare students for effective participation.

PARENT AND STUDENT PARTICIPATION

Although due process hearings and other procedural safeguards provide a system of checks and balances for schools and parents, IDEA also offers another, less adversarial accountability technique: the parent-student participation principle. You have already read that parents have many rights. They have the right to be members of the IEP team, to receive notice before the school does anything about the student's right to a free appropriate public education, and to use three dispute-resolution techniques (procedural due process).

In addition, parents have the right to have access to school records concerning their child and to control who has access to those records. Further, the state education agency must include parents on state and local special education advisory committees, thereby ensuring that their perspectives are incorporated into policy and program decisions.

Finally, one year before a student reaches the age of majority (usually age eighteen), the school must advise him or her that all of the IDEA rights that belonged to the parent will transfer to the student when he or she attains the age of majority. The only exception to this transfer-of-rights rule is that the parents' rights will not transfer to the student if the student has been determined, under state law, to be incompetent. In that event, the rights transfer to the student's legally appointed guardian.

BRINGING THE SIX PRINCIPLES TOGETHER

How do the six principles ensure an appropriate education for students with disabilities? Figure 1.6 highlights the fact that the first four principles—zero reject, nondiscriminatory evaluation, appropriate education, and least restrictive environment—are the *inputs* into a student's education. The other two principles—procedural due process and parent-student participation—are *accountability techniques*, ways to make sure that the other four principles are implemented correctly. The figure identifies the principles and their purposes and shows their relationships.

FIGURE 1.6 *The relationships among the six principles of IDEA*

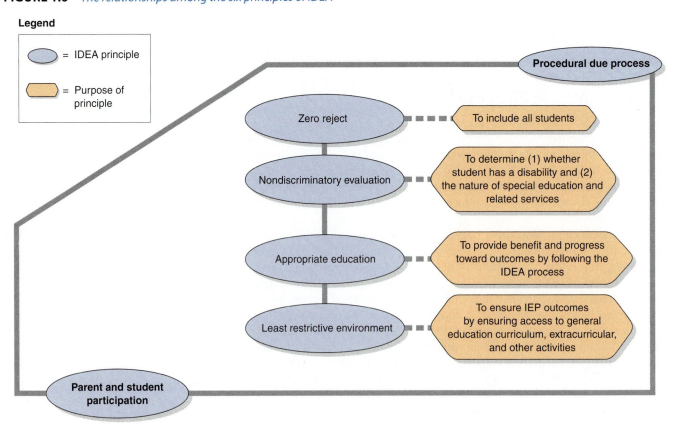

How, you may ask, should I and my colleagues in schools carry out these laws? That's a good question, and we answer it by (1) describing the principles of nondiscriminatory evaluation, appropriate education, least restrictive environment, and parent participation in Chapters 5 through 16 and (2) giving you evidence-based strategies to apply as you implement these principles.

ESEA and Other Federal Laws

Other federal laws affect special education and students in those programs. There are two types of laws: Some authorize services for students; others prohibit students from discrimination based on their disabilities.

ELEMENTARY AND SECONDARY EDUCATION ACT AS AMENDED BY NO CHILD LEFT BEHIND ACT

The principal federal law affecting general education is the Elementary and Secondary Education Act (ESEA). It authorizes services for all children, including those with disabilities. Congress amended it in 2001 by enacting the No Child Left Behind Act (NCLB). Consistent with current practice, we will refer to the federal law as ESEA, but you may hear people speak about NCLB. Remember, however, that ESEA is the proper name of the federal law.

ESEA seeks to improve educational outcomes for all students—those with and those without disabilities. Figure 1.7 identifies its six principles and highlights two requirements associated with each. IDEA is aligned with ESEA because each seeks improved outcomes for students with disabilities (Turnbull et al., 2007).

REHABILITATION ACT

Like ESEA, the Rehabilitation Act authorizes services for people with disabilities. If a person has a severe disability but, with rehabilitation, is able to work despite the disability, the person is entitled to two types of vocational rehabilitation services. First, when the person is sixteen years old, he may receive work evaluations, financial aid to pursue job training, and job locator services, all from the state rehabilitation agency.

Second, a person with severe disabilities, including a student, may enroll in a supported employment program. There, the student will work with the assistance of a job coach whose duties are to teach the person how to do a job and then help her to do it independently. The supported worker must be paid at least the minimum wage, work at least twenty hours a week in a typical work setting, and be able, after eighteen months of supported employment, to do the job alone without support.

TECH ACT

The Technology-Related Assistance to Individuals with Disabilities Act of 1988 (as amended), often called the Tech Act, grants federal funds to the states so that they can help create statewide systems for delivering assistive technology devices and services to people with disabilities, including students with disabilities. In Chapters 5 through 16, we describe how technology benefits students.

ANTIDISCRIMINATION LAWS

IDEA and the Rehabilitation Act create personal entitlements; they provide direct services to eligible people. By contrast, the Tech Act creates a

Assistive technology helps all students learn. Just think of the many devices teachers use and of the widespread use of computers in classrooms. Students with disabilities also benefit from technology to master their lessons, although their technology may be somewhat different and perhaps more sophisticated than the technology their peers without disabiltiies use.

FIGURE 1.7 *Principles and implementing activities of the ESEA*

1. *Accountability for results.* Schools should sufficiently educate all students so that they demonstrate proficiency in certain core academic subjects (English, mathematics, and others). School districts that achieve student outcomes will be rewarded, and those that do not will be reformed.

   • By the 2005–2006 school year, each state must test students annually in grades 3 through 8 in reading and math and students in grades 10–12 at least once in reading and math.

   • Every student will be assessed accordng to each state's standard for proficiency in reading/language arts, math, and science by the end of the 2013–2014 school year.

2. *School safety.* Because all students need a safe environment in which to learn and achieve outcomes, schools are required to establish a plan for keeping schools safe and drug-free.

   • States must establish a uniform procedure for reporting data to parents and other citizens regarding school safety and drug-free schools.

   • When a state identifies a school as being persistently dangerous, the state must notify parents of every student and offer them opportunities to transfer to a safe school.

3. *Parental choice.* Parents of all students should have the opportunity to stay informed, in a full and accurate manner about achievement and safety so that they will be in a position to be full partners in their child's education.

   • Parents must receive a report about the overall achievement of students and the particular school their child attends, the qualifications of their child's teacher, and school safety.

   • Parents must be notified if their child is eligible to move to another school or district when their child's school is not making adequate progress in student outcomes, the school is considered to be "persistently dangerous," or the student has been a victim of a violent crime while on school grounds.

4. *Teacher quality.* Teachers should be proficient to teach and thus must meet certain federal and states' standards before they are certified to teach. States' receipt of federal funds will depend on their record in hiring "highly qualified" teachers.

   • Each state must have developed a plan to ensure that all teachers of core academic subjects will be highly qualified by the end of the 2005–2006 school year. ("Highly qualified" means that each teacher has full certification and a bachelor's degree and has passed a state-administered test on core academic subject knowledge.)

   • Paraprofessionals hired after January 2002 must have an associate's degree or higher, or they must have completed two years of postsecondary study at an institution of higher education.

5. *Scientifically based methods of teaching.* Highly qualified teachers must use research-based curricula and instructional methods in order to ensure students' academic success.

   • Each state is responsible for establishing a Reading Leadership Team to ensure that schools that need to improve their reading achievement scores are using scientifically based instructional methods.

   • Schools that fail to meet adequate student achievement goals are required to use scientifically based instructional methods in order to remain open.

6. *Local flexibility.* State and local educational agencies have some discretion in using federal and state matching funds in order to respond to local problems in particularly local ways.

   • Education funding programs are consolidated so they will be easier to administer at the local level.

   • Money may be transferred from many federal programs to another federal program in order to address local needs (but no transfers of IDEA money are allowed).

statewide capacity to serve people with disabilities. Instead of directly benefiting the people themselves, it helps the states meet the people's needs.

Education and rehabilitation are, of course, necessary to address the need for support created by a student's disability. But they are not sufficient by themselves. IDEA, for example, does not prohibit public or private agencies from discriminating against the student on the basis of the student's disability. Yes, a student such as Dylan may receive special education, but that service might not create opportunities for the student to use the skills in college or the workplace that he or she has acquired through special education. Prejudice against people with disabilities may still limit opportunities for students to show that, although they have a disability, they are nonetheless still able.

How can society attack the prejudice? One answer is to use antidiscrimination laws such as those that prohibit discrimination based on race or gender. The first such law, enacted in 1975 as an amendment to the Rehabilitation Act, is known as Section 504 (29 U.S.C. Section 794). The second, enacted in 1990, is the Americans with Disabilities Act (ADA) (42 U.S.C. Sections 12101–12213). These are similar laws. They provide that no otherwise qualified individual with a disability shall, solely by reason of the disability, be discriminated against in certain realms of American life. Figure 1.8 sets out the meaning of "person with a disability" under Section 504 and ADA.

Section 504 applies to any program or activity receiving federal financial assistance. Because state and local education agencies receive federal funds, they may not discriminate against students or other persons with disabilities on account of their disabilities. As you will learn in Chapters 8 and 13, not all students with disabilities are entitled to IDEA benefits. But they are entitled to be free from disability discrimination. That's the effect of Section 504.

Clearly, Section 504 is limited in scope. What if a student attends a private school that receives absolutely no federal funds? What if an individual seeks employment from a company that does not receive any federal funds, wants to participate in state and local government programs that are not federally aided, or wants to have access to telecommunications systems such as closed captioning for people with hearing impairments? In none of those cases will the person receive any protection from Section 504. Here, ADA comes to the person's rescue.

ADA extends civil rights/nondiscrimination protection to people with disabilities in the following sectors of American life: private-sector employment, transportation, state and local government activities and programs, privately operated businesses that are open to the public ("public accommodations"), and telecommunications.

Basically, IDEA and the Rehabilitation Act authorize federal, state, and local educational agencies to undertake programs in education and employment, respectively. Both laws provide funds for the state and local agencies to pay for those programs. By contrast, Section 504 and ADA prohibit discrimination solely on the basis of disability in education, employment, and other sectors of American life. But these two laws do not provide federal aid.

Together, these four laws support students' transition from school to post-school activities, including work. That is why the transition components of a student's IEP anticipate outcomes that are largely consistent with those that any student, with or without a disability, typically will want: work, education, and opportunities to participate in the community. Those results cannot be achieved so long as discrimination exists.

IEP TIP

Some students who do not qualify for coverage under IDEA do qualify under Section 504. You may be involved in developing a 504 plan for these students as opposed to an IEP.

Special Education Goals and Results

After the schools started to implement IDEA in 1977, the federal criteria for evaluating special education results were primarily numerical. The questions were "How many more students are being served annually and in what types of placements are they being served?" Numbers, however, do not tell the full story. That is why Congress amended IDEA in 1997 to require state and local education agencies to report outcomes. State and local education agencies still count and report to the U.S. Department of Education the number of students being served and tally their placements. But they now must also report data that show that students are making progress toward their individual goals and toward other goals, too.

The reasoning behind this outcome-based accountability is that IDEA declares that improving education results for students with disabilities is an "essential element" of the nation's policy of ensuring equal opportunity, full participation, independent living, and economic self-sufficiency. Those are the nation's goals. Without documented results, it is difficult to know how well schools support students to attain these goals. So results count. They count for Congress. They count for your students. They count for Dylan. They certainly count for Stelios Gragoudas, who has cerebral palsy. Read about Stel in Box 1.1 and consider his outcome.

The same outcome-related task exists for general education under ESEA: to improve educational results for all students. Each state and each of its school districts must set goals for improving the academic scores of all students, whether in general or special education, on standardized tests. If students do not meet these goals by obtaining higher scores, ESEA provides several ways of improving the schools.

Like IDEA, ESEA emphasizes that outcomes—measured by academic achievement—count for all students. For that reason, each student with a disability must take the state and district assessments, the tests of student achievement. As evidenced by the 2009 data reported in Figure 1.9, scores for students with disabilities on national assessments indicate that there are still miles to go in increasing the results for students with disabilities (National Center for Educational Statistics, 2011). The other good news is that there has been a steady increase in math scores since they were first measured in 1996. There has been, however, only slight improvement in reading, with unevenness across the years (increases in some years, drops in subsequent years).

What does IDEA stipulate in terms of results? Is the focus on academic achievement alone or on longer-term results? Congress went beyond academic subjects alone in emphasizing equality of opportunity, full participation, independent living, and economic self-sufficiency as national goals and thus the appropriate outcomes for students with disabilities. Here are the four terms and general definitions for each:

- *Equality of opportunity.* People with disabilities will have the same chances and opportunities in life as people without disabilities. Without equal opportunity, they cannot achieve the other three outcomes. Dylan has a right to equal opportunity to benefit from education. He has always had this right, even though some of the schools he attended failed to give him equal opportunities to benefit from education.

IEP TIP

As you participate in IEP conferences and collaboratively develop goals and objectives, you should always consider how the goals and objectives that you recommend will advance equality of opportunity, full participation, independent living, and economic self-sufficiency.

FIGURE 1.9

Data on reading and math national assessment scores for students with disabilities: 2009

	Below Basic	**At or Above Basic**	**At or Above Proficient**	**At Advanced**
Reading	62	30	8	0
Math	64	26	9	1

Source: National Center for Education Statistics. (2011). *Grade 8 national results.* Retrieved July 24, 2011, from http://nationsreportcard.gov/math_2009 and http://nationsreportcard.gov/reading_2009/.

BOX 1.1   **MY VOICE**

Stel Achieves His Great Expectations

Education has always been an important part of my life. My parents always stressed the importance of having the best education you possibly could obtain. It wasn't only learning that excited me; it was also being with other students, playing kickball, and making friends that enriched my educational experience.

I began my school career at the same time that P.L. 94–142 (better known today as IDEA) was passed. Therefore, educating students with disabilities was a new experience for my school district. The faculty did not know how to include students with disabilities into a program for students without disabilities. My teachers did the best they could by including me in all the instances they thought were appropriate. For the subjects that I needed extra help in, I went to a resource room where I could receive the extra assistance I needed. Thinking back, I liked that system. Even though I was out of my homeroom for a couple of hours a week, I still felt as if that room was my base. It was where all my friends were and where I could do exactly what all the other students were doing.

All that changed when I went to middle school and high school. It was as if my education took a 360-degree turn. When a student moves up to middle school, academics are the focal point of the educational experience. Therefore, my educational team had to answer a very important question: Could I keep up with the academic program that was offered at the middle school? My teachers were not too optimistic. They believed that even though I had fared well in elementary school, middle school was going to be too challenging for me. My parents, however, insisted that I be included in the general curriculum as much as possible. So my IEP called for me to be placed in the general curriculum for some of my subjects and in a resource room for the others.

This program was similar to my elementary school experience, with one great distinction. In middle school, my base was not the place where I felt included. It was the place where I felt excluded. That base was my resource room, where I was excluded from most of the students who were in my academic classes. This did not allow me to form the kinds of friendships that I did in elementary school. I do not have many fond memories of that period of my educational career.

High school was a similar situation. Even though I had good grades in all of my academic classes, my teachers still recommended that academics should not be the focal point of my education and that I should focus on vocational goals. My parents did not agree with this plan. They always believed that I should be pushed to my limit.

The school agreed with hesitation and opted to place me in a collaborative program within the high school. I would be able to participate in the high school classes, and the collaborative program would provide me with a tutor and other supports that I needed to succeed in high school. As I look back, the program was not all that bad. It provided me with additional services that I needed to succeed in my high school, such as speech therapy and adapted gym.

However, the same thing that had happened in middle school was happening all over again. Instead of feeling like a student at my high school, I felt like a guest. Even though I had my classes with students in the high school, when class was over, they would go in one direction and I would go back to the collaborative program. Even though I was free to eat lunch with them, I chose not to because I felt like an outsider who was only a guest in the high school and I felt at home eating lunch with my fellow classmates in the collaborative program.

I always knew that I wanted to go to college. It was what everyone else in my class was thinking about, so I caught the bug as well. Once again, however, I met opposition from my special education teachers. The teachers from my high school classes were more supportive because they knew the work I had done in their classes and felt that I was ready for college-level academics.

The process of applying to school was very exciting. The experience of going to visit schools, meeting students with disabilities who were already in college, writing essays, and finding out how colleges supported people with disabilities was extremely informative.

It also provided me with a new idea of what it meant to be independent. To that point, independence to me meant going to the mall by myself or going on a trip with my friend instead of my family. In college, independence meant making sure I had all of the supports that I needed to live independently or talking with professors about accommodations that I needed in class. College gave me two things. It gave me the academic background that I needed to begin the career that I am still in today. Equally important, it gave me the skills I needed to live independently and to direct my own future.

I have earned my Ph.D. and am working in higher education in Massachusetts. Sometimes I think it would be amusing to go back to my high school and show some of my old teachers what I have accomplished since I started postsecondary education, but then I think it would be a better idea to focus my attention on improving special education and education as a whole so that every student with a disability can receive the most appropriate education alongside classmates without disabilities.

—*Stelios Gragoudas*

- *Full participation*. People with disabilities will have opportunities to be included in all aspects of their community and will be protected from any attempts to segregate them solely on the basis of their disability. Dylan is not segregated in schools at Fort Campbell, and that fact assures that he can fully participate in school and then in his community.

- *Independent living*. People with disabilities will have the opportunity to fully participate in decision making and to experience autonomy in making choices about their lives. In school, training in self-determination advances this goal. If Dylan's schools deal appropriately with his behaviors, they will advance his ability to make choices.

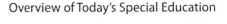

(We will describe in Chapters 5 through 16 how schools can apply self-determination and positive support to change Dylan's behaviors.)

- *Economic self-sufficiency.* People with disabilities will be provided with opportunities to engage fully in income-producing or unpaid work that contributes to a household or a community. Given an appropriate education, Dylan should be able to get, keep, and advance in a job of his choice.

What is the evidence related to these results? Unfortunately, research on results for students with disabilities does not provide definitive answers. However, data on several indicators suggest that substantial work is needed to improve student outcomes.

The first indicator is the extent to which students with disabilities are receiving a high school diploma. The national rate of students receiving a high school diploma is 90 percent (Chapman, Laird, & KewalRamani, 2010); whereas the rate for students with disabilities is 34 percent (U.S. Department of Education, 2011). Receiving a diploma or a general educational development (GED) certificate has been linked to a number of positive outcomes, including substantially higher income, employment, increased health, and decreased likelihood of being in prison (U.S. Department of Education, 2010).

The second indicator relates to the area of postsecondary education or employment. Clearly, adults who receive postsecondary education and/or are employed increase their chances for full participation, independent living, and especially economic self-sufficiency. The good news is that, during the past two decades, young adults with disabilities have substantially improved their likelihood of attending postsecondary school or being employed—a 65 percent likelihood in 1990 compared with an 80 percent likelihood in 2005 (Newman, Wagner, Cameto, Knokey, & Shaver, 2010).

The third indicator relates to household circumstances and social/community involvement for young adults with disabilities within four years of leaving high school. Figure 1.10 highlights comparisons between 1990 and 2005 on a number of indicators that are tied to equality of opportunity, full participation, and independent living.

The fourth and final indicator focuses on overall satisfaction with life. Approximately two thirds of individuals without disabilities report that they are very satisfied with life in general; by contrast, approximately one third of individuals with disabilities report the same satisfaction. The following trends contribute to general life satisfaction (National Organization on Disability, 2010):

- Adults with disabilities are almost three times less likely to be employed full or part time as compared to people without disabilities (21 percent versus 59 percent).

- Slightly more than half of adults with disabilities report that they are struggling financially (living paycheck to paycheck, going into debt) as compared to one third of people without disabilities (58 percent versus 34 percent).

FIGURE 1.10

Indicators of postschool results related to household circumstances and social/community involvement for young adults with disabilities: 1990 and 2005

	1990	2005
Having a savings account	56%	44%
Having a checking account	47%	25%
Participating in volunteer or community service	13%	25%
Being registered to vote	53%	67%
Having been arrested	16%	27%

Source: Newman, L., Wagner, M., Cameto, R., Knokey, A. M., & Shaver, D. (2010). *Comparisons across time of the outcomes of youth with disabilities up to 4 years after high school. A report of findings from the National Longitudinal Transition Study (NLTS) and the National Longitudinal Transition Study-2 (NLTS2)* (NCSER 2010-3008). Menlo Park, CA: SRI International.

- Approximately one fifth of adults with disabilities report going without needed health care as compared to one tenth of people without disabilities (19 percent versus 10 percent).
- Adults with disabilities are approximately twice as likely to have inadequate transportation as compared to people without disabilities (34 percent versus 16 percent).
- Slightly more than half of adults with disabilities report accessing the Internet as contrasted to the vast majority of adults without disabilities (54 percent versus 85 percent).

Here's the question you have to answer for yourself: Given that there is a great deal of room for improvement in achieving results for students with disabilities, what role will you play in helping students with disabilities make progress in the general curriculum so that their long-term results are as positive as possible? We call your attention to Figure 1.11. It includes the eight guiding principles of the Council for Exceptional Children's code of ethics. We particularly draw your attention to the first principle: "Special education professionals are committed to developing the highest educational and quality of life potential of individuals with exceptionalities" (CEC, 2008, p. 389). We hope our book helps you achieve this and many other vital goals.

FIGURE 1.11 *Guiding principles of the Council for Exceptional Children's Code of Ethics and Standards for Professional Practice*

A. Special education professionals are committed to developing the highest educational and quality of life potential of individuals with exceptionalities.

B. Special education professionals promote and maintain a high level of competence and integrity in practicing their profession.

C. Special education professionals engage in professional activities which benefit individuals with exceptionalities, their families, other colleagues, students, or research subjects.

D. Special education professionals exercise objective professional judgment in the practice of their profession.

E. Special education professionals strive to advance their knowledge and skills regarding the education of individuals with exceptionalities.

F. Special education professionals work within the standards and policies of their profession.

G. Special education professionals seek to uphold and improve where necessary the laws, regulations, and policies governing the delivery of special education and related services and the practice of their profession.

H. Special education professionals do not condone or participate in unethical or illegal acts, nor violate professional standards adopted by the Delegate Assembly of CEC. (CEC, 2008, p. 389).

Source: CEC. (2008). CEC code of ethics and standards for professional practice for special educators. *Exceptional Children, 74*(3), 389–393.

ADDRESSING THE PROFESSIONAL STANDARDS

The following Council for Exceptional Children (CEC) Common Core Knowledge and Skills are addressed in this chapter through the content and concepts we discuss. See the Appendix for a full list of these Knowledge and Skill statements:

ICC1K1, ICC1K2, ICC1K3, ICC1K4, ICC1K5, ICC1K6, ICC1K7, ICC1S1, ICC5S2, ICC5S3, ICC5S4, ICC5S6, ICC7S1, ICC7S2, ICC7S3

Summary

PROFILE OF SPECIAL EDUCATION STUDENTS AND PERSONNEL IN TODAY'S SCHOOLS

- The six key values that permeate this book include envisioning great expectations, enhancing positive contributions, building on strengths, becoming self-determined, expanding relationships, and ensuring full citizenship.
- More than 7 million children, youth, and young adults, ages birth through twenty-one, have disabilities and receive special education services.
- Approximately two thirds of special education students are male.
- Students who are gifted and talented represent 6.7 percent of the schools' enrolled students.
- Slightly more than three fourths of all students with disabilities are classified into the categories of specific learning disabilities, speech or language impairments, intellectual disabilities, and emotional or behavioral disorders.
- Language sensitivity is important. Along with nearly all professionals, we recommend the use of *disability* rather than *handicapped, intellectual disability* rather than *mentally retarded* (never *retard*), and people-first language ("students with intellectual disability" rather than "intellectually disabled students").
- Of the fourteen fields of teacher education with the greatest shortages, nine are in areas of special education.

OVERVIEW OF THE LAW AND SPECIAL EDUCATION

- The preludes to today's federal special education law were the school desegregation case (*Brown*) and two cases requiring schools to educate students with disabilities.
- The federal law, enacted in 1975 and reauthorized in 2004, is the Individuals with Disabilities Education Act.
- There are twelve categories of disabilities for children ages six through twenty-one.
- The law benefits infants and toddlers (Part C) and students ages six through twenty-one (Part B).

IDEA: SIX PRINCIPLES

- IDEA has six principles:
  - Zero reject, a rule against exclusion
  - Nondiscriminatory evaluation, a rule of fair assessments
  - Appropriate education, a rule of individualized benefit
  - Least restrictive placement, a rule of presuming placement in general education programs
  - Procedural due process, a rule of fair dealing and accountability
  - Parent and student participation, a rule of shared decision making
- The first four principles are inputs into a student's education. The last two are accountability techniques.
- Federal funding of special education supplements state and local funding.

ELEMENTARY AND SECONDARY EDUCATION ACT AND OTHER FEDERAL LAWS

- ESEA has six principles:
  - Accountability for results, a rule for enhanced student academic outcomes
  - Teacher quality, a rule to improve teacher credentials
  - Scientifically based methods of teaching, a rule to increase the delivery of research-based instruction
  - School safety, a rule to keep schools safe and drug-free
  - Local flexibility, a rule to increase local decision making
  - Parental choice, a rule to provide options for parents to transfer their child
- The Rehabilitation Act provides for work training, especially supported employment.
- The Tech Act makes assistive technology available in each state.
- The Americans with Disabilities Act and Section 504 of the Rehabilitation Act prohibit discrimination solely on the basis of disability in a wide range of services, both inside and outside of school.

SPECIAL EDUCATION GOALS AND RESULTS

- Approximately two thirds of students with disabilities scored below basic levels in reading and math in grade 8.
- Congress stipulated IDEA's four major results as equality of opportunity, full participation, independent living, and economic self-sufficiency.
- Students with disabilities are three times less likely to complete high school than are students without disabilities.

- Over the past two decades, young adults with disabilities have improved their likelihood of attending postsecondary school or being employed from 65 percent in 1990 to 80 percent in 2005.
- On indicators related to social/community involvement, young adults with disabilities have had some improvements and some setbacks, according to comparative data from 1990 to 2005.
- Approximately two thirds of individuals without disabilities report that they are very satisfied with life in general, as contrasted to approximately one third of individuals with disabilities.

MyEducationLab

Go to Topic #1: Special Education Law in the MyEducationLab (www.myeducationlab.com) for *Exceptional Lives*, where you can do the following:

- Find learning outcomes for Special Education Law along with the national standards that connect to these outcomes.
- Complete assignments and activities that will help you more deeply understand the chapter content.
- Apply and practice your understanding of the core teaching skills identified in the chapter with the Building Teaching Skills and Dispositions learning units.
- Examine challenging situations and cases presented in the IRIS Center Resources.
- Access video clips of CCSSO National Teachers of the Year award winners responding to the question, "Why Do I Teach?" in the Teacher Talk section.
- Check your comprehension on the content covered in the chapter with the Study Plan. Here you will be able to take a chapter quiz, receive feedback on your answers, and then access review, practice, and enrichment activities to enhance your understanding of chapter content.
- Use the Online Lesson Plan Builder to practice lesson planning and integrating national and state standards into your planning.

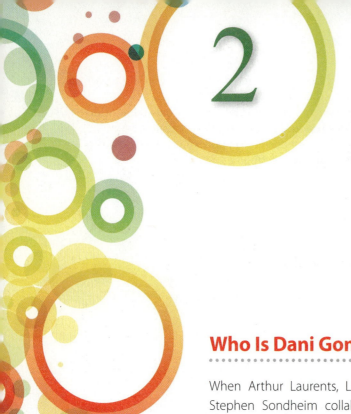

2

Ensuring Progress *in the* General Education Curriculum: Universal Design *for* Learning *and* Inclusion

Who Is Dani Gonzalez?

When Arthur Laurents, Leonard Bernstein, and Stephen Sondheim collaborated to create the modern version of Shakespeare's *Romeo and Juliet,* first produced in 1958 as *West Side Story,* they could not have known how well the character Tony's expectant song "Something's Coming" would suit Dani Gonzalez, a fifth-grade student. Tony declares, "I've got a feeling there's a miracle due. . . . Something great is coming. . . . It's only just out of reach" (Laurents & Sondheim, 1979). For

Dani, that something great just out of reach was sufficient self-confidence in her ability to speak out among her peers, enough to overcome her speech impairment and fully participate in her class.

But someone other than Laurents and Sondheim *is* writing down Dani's story. Meet Lauren Priest, a special education resource-room teacher, and Erin Lane, a general education fifth-grade teacher. Here's what Erin wrote to Lauren:

> I ran down to see you. . . . I just had to tell you about Dani and the class meeting today. Normally she is always the last one to give her compliment and I really have to help her and you KNOW how quietly she can speak. Well, today was TOTALLY different! She had her

> [compliment] ready, said it the first time and was as loud as could be! The kids [fifteen fifth graders in general education] were all so excited for her, they gave her a big applause and all gave her a compliment for that! Then, she had ANOTHER one! It was so awesome to see her interact with her peers that way! Was so proud! Just goes to show what you [Lauren] are doing is working and that she is really benefiting from being with her peers!

On the same day, Lauren continued Dani's story by writing to Luz Gonzalez, Dani's mother:

Some pretty incredible things went on today. . . . We are having our fifth-grade literature circles [and] . . . she is reading "Stone Fox." . . . . We then have a discussion with about 15 fifth graders from all classes. Today, Dani raised her hand to participate 4 times on her own!! Her answers were also correct and appropriate and she didn't need any prompting from me at all. This is huge, considering that I have never seen her raise her hand on her own! . . . She is making such huge growths in her confidence; you have no idea how proud I am of her.

Sometimes, indeed, "something great" is just around the corner. Dani had pointed herself toward that corner, but she could not have turned it on her own. She was diagnosed as having speech-language delays (severe apraxia) when she was three years and nine months old, and she has received speech-language intervention since she was four years old (in early childhood special education and in elementary school). The intervention focuses on her ability to speak intelligibly: She has a lisp; and because her parents, Luz (from Colombia) and Carlos (from Spain), speak Spanish at home, she speaks English with a Spanish accent.

Dani is included with her nondisabled peers to learn writing, science, and social studies. To teach reading, Lauren uses an evidence-based reading program (*Horizons*), modifies the curriculum by using graphic organizers, and provides specially designed instruction in the form of direct (one-on-one) instruction to teach spelling. To teach math, Lauren uses another research-based program (*Number Worlds*). Her immediate goal is to have Dani increase her reading and math skills by another 25 percent to 30 percent; her long-term goal is to have Dani perform grade-level work without direct support. That's why direct instruction through evidence-based reading and math programs is necessary now.

With accommodations in science and social studies, Dani's grades average 90 percent or better. Lauren asks Dani to focus on the big picture and allows her to respond in different ways, but essentially the content material matches the general education program. She is making progress in the general education

OBJECTIVES

As you read in Chapter 1, three major themes of this book are progress through inclusion, universal design, and family-professional partnerships. In this chapter, you will learn about inclusion and universal design.

- You will learn about inclusion, or, as IDEA terms it, how Dani participates and makes progress in the general curriculum.

- You will learn the definitions of supplementary aids and services and universal design for learning and how they benefit Dani and other students.

- You will learn the meaning of inclusion and how it and a student's IEP make it possible for students such as Dani to participate and make progress in the general curriculum.

- Finally, you will learn what you and your colleagues in general and special education can teach students so they will make the progress that IDEA wants and that Dani, her teachers, and her parents want for her as well.

curriculum, which is the goal for all children and the intent of federal laws such as IDEA and ESEA.

Dani's speech challenges, with their resulting impact on her self-confidence and her ability to read, are not her only challenges. She has been diagnosed with diabetes and receives insulin through a pump that she and the school nurse both monitor. And she still needs instruction in some functional academic skills (stating and writing completely her name, birthday, address, and important telephone numbers) and self-help skills (knowing how many carbohydrates she is ingesting and then giving herself appropriate amounts of insulin).

Her teachers describe Dani as "extremely happy . . . social . . . gets along wonderfully with her peers and adults . . . very responsible, always completing her homework and able to independently follow a schedule and make changes/judgments as needed . . . extremely hard worker who is eager to learn . . . always puts forth her best effort . . . beginning to demonstrate more self-confidence than in past years." So how did Dani find "something great" just around the corner? What led to her self-confidence among her peers? Was it her well-trained teachers? Their use of evidence-based practices? The support she receives at home from Luz, Carlos, and her brother Juan? The fact that she has been included in the general education classroom during her fifth-grade year (in contrast to her fourth-grade year)? Her personality? Will her social self-confidence become academic self-confidence, too? There is no single, right answer. Instead, the answer to all of these questions is "yes."

Still, just around the corner lie two challenges. First, Dani's teachers and other supporters must sustain her progress in all aspects of fifth grade. Second, they must continue planning her transition from the substantially separate curriculum that comprised her work in fourth grade into the general education curriculum, extracurricular, and other school activities she is part of in fifth grade. A multidisciplinary team of general and special educators from Dani's current school and the middle school started planning in August of her last year in elementary school. The planning will continue throughout the school year, with Luz and Carlos fully participating in it.

Is it unrealistic for Dani's teacher-parent team to expect something great just around the school-year corner? No. Indeed, it would violate IDEA's theme of high expectations achieved through qualified teachers who are using evidence-based interventions for them to expect anything less.

PEARSON
myeducationlab

Visit the MyEducationLab (www .myeducationlab.com) for *Exceptional Lives* to enhance your understanding of chapter concepts with a personalized Study Plan. You'll also have the opportunity to hone your teaching skills through video- and case-based assignments and activities, IRIS Center Resources, and Building Teaching Skills and Disposition lessons.

IEP TIP

The IEP team must design an IEP that ensures that the student will be involved in and make progress in the general education curriculum, and it must do so by addressing the student's education and education-related needs.

What Is "Progress in the General Education Curriculum"?

In this chapter, we address universal design and inclusion as foundations for progress in the general education curriculum. In Chapter 3 we discuss multiculturalism, and in Chapter 4 we discuss partnerships. Universal design and inclusion are means to an end: The goal is that students such as Dani will receive an appropriate education by participating in and making progress in the general education curriculum. And that end is a means to still four other ends: equal opportunity, independent living, full participation, and economic self-sufficiency. When you read Chapter 1, you learned about those four national goals. So universal design and inclusion are means to an appropriate education and progress in the general curriculum, which, in turn, are a means to those four overarching goals. Before we talk about the means, then, we should think more about the end. What does "progress in the general education curriculum" mean?

First, progress is what federal law promotes and requires. As you learned from reading Chapter 1, IDEA requires each student's IEP to state how the student will be involved with and progress in the general education curriculum, how the student's progress will be assessed, and how state- and district-wide assessments will be modified (as appropriate) for the student. As you learned in Chapter 1, one of the six principles of the federal Elementary and Secondary Education Act (ESEA) is accountability. Accordingly, ESEA requires assessment of students' proficiency and exempts no students from assessment. ESEA covers students with disabilities but, like IDEA, it allows for appropriate individualized modifications as set out in a student's IEP.

Second, progress in the general education curriculum is achieved by **standards-based reform**. This process identifies the academic content (reading, mathematics, science, etc.) that students must master, the standards for students' achievement of content proficiency, a **general education curriculum** aligned with these standards, assessment of student progress in meeting the standards, and information from the assessments to improve instruction and to demonstrate that the schools are indeed accountable to students, their families, and the public.

Third, ESEA requires states to establish challenging academic content and student achievement standards that apply to all students, including students with disabilities. **Academic content standards** define the knowledge, skills, and understanding that students should attain in academic subjects. **Student achievement standards** define the levels of achievement that students must meet to demonstrate their proficiency in the subjects. States may establish **alternate achievement standards** for students with the most significant cognitive disabilities; but even so, those alternate standards must align with the same academic content standards for all students so that these students will be able to make progress in the general education curriculum (U.S. Department of Education, 2005a).

Finally, a student's IEP team must consider what accommodations in the assessment process the student might need to ensure that his or her achievement is fairly evaluated. Accommodations do not change the content of the assessment; rather, they change teachers' ways of presenting information (for example, changing the order of taking subtests), students' ways of responding (for example, using a computer or dictating answers), assessment timing (for example, having extended time or frequent breaks), and assessment settings (for example, taking the test in a quiet room or a small group away from the larger class) (Perie, 2010).

Standards-based assessment applies to all students, including students with disabilities.

HOW DOES THE GENERAL EDUCATION CURRICULUM BENEFIT STUDENTS WITH DISABILITIES?

Connecting the Curriculum to Standards

As we just pointed out, the general education curriculum for students without disabilities is aligned with academic content and student achievement standards set by each state education agency for students at various grade levels. Alignment, however, does not mean that educators should overlook the individual needs of each student with a disability. Indeed, they should not. If they were to overlook Dani's needs, they would be unable to provide her with an appropriate education, one that occurs in general education. IDEA requires them to provide an appropriate education based on each student's strengths and needs and to do so by including the student (to the maximum extent appropriate) in the general academic curriculum. Further, IDEA requires educators to assess the student's progress toward stated goals. Educators often do this by determining how well a student with a disability performs on the state- or district-wide assessments of all students, with and without disabilities.

Typically, states use three approaches to assessments. First, they define *standards*. These are general statements of what a student should know and be able to do in any given academic subject. Then they define *benchmarks*, specific statements of what the student should know and be able to do in that subject. Finally, they define *indicators*. These are statements of knowledge or skills that a student must demonstrate in order to meet a benchmark. Some students with disabilities will be expected to meet the same

IEP TIP

You and your colleagues on an IEP team must determine what constitutes the "maximum extent" to which the student will be involved with the general education curriculum. You and they must presume, as IDEA does, that they should maximize, not minimize, the student's involvement and set high expectations for student performance.

standards and benchmarks as students without disabilities; they will be assessed by the same indicators as students without disabilities. Other students with disabilities will have different standards, benchmarks, and indicators, depending on the extent of their disability. They benefit from these accommodations because, although their curriculum is aligned with that of students without disabilities, they are receiving individualized education specially tailored to them. It is reasonable to assess their progress according to their individualized education even while that education aligns with that of students without disabilities.

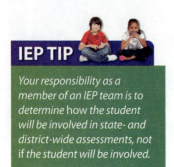

Making Accommodations in Assessments

Many students with disabilities will require modifications in the methods of assessment to provide evidence of their knowledge. States that administer state-level assessments have written policies or guidelines concerning accommodations in assessments (Lazarus, Thurlow, Lail, & Christensen, 2009). Studies of frequent test accommodations, such as dictated responses, extended time, large print, read-aloud, and computer-based assessment, have produced mixed results about their effectiveness (Cormier, Altman, Shyvan, & Thurlow, 2010).

Under IDEA, a student who (according to the IEP team) cannot learn the same content as same-age peers who do not have disabilities and who cannot take the state assessment even if modified may provide evidence of progress through an **alternate assessment**. ESEA provides a number of options, but any such assessment must be linked or aligned with the general education curriculum. **Alternate assessments based on grade-level achievement standards** (AA-GLAS) enable students to demonstrate skills and knowledge on grade-level assessments, but the assessments are modified versions of the general assessment. **Alternate assessments based on alternate academic achievement standards** (AA-AAS) refer to assessment for use with students with the most significant cognitive disabilities that involve multiple accommodations and links to alternate achievement standards. Finally, **alternate assessments based on modified achievement standards** (AA-MAS) are used for students across disability categories (other than primarily students with the most significant cognitive disabilities) who need both accommodations and some modifications to the grade-level standards (National Center on Educational Outcomes, n.d.). The traditional alternate assessment was the AA-AAS version. The AA-GLAS version is the least frequently offered, while the AA-MAS is the newest option and is gaining in use (Thurlow, 2008).

As you will learn in Chapter 4, students from diverse racial and ethnic backgrounds disproportionately receive special education services, and there have been disproportionate results for many students from diverse backgrounds in terms of educational outcomes. Further, many students from diverse backgrounds are disadvantaged in the processes of referral and eligibility for special education and for test taking.

On a global basis, the question has to be "do assessments disadvantage students from racially and ethnically diverse backgrounds?" Data from the U.S. Department of Education's National Assessment of Educational Progress (NAEP) testing seem to suggest so. For example, data from the NAEP have shown that children with more highly educated parents earned higher average reading and math scores on the NAEP than did children with less well educated parents. Given that the NAEP shows that in 2008 African American mothers and fathers and Hispanic mothers and fathers had the lowest levels of educational attainment among all groups, one can surmise that children from certain ethnic groups are disadvantaged in large-scale assessments.

Of course, lower educational levels result in lower income. The NAEP also showed that in 2009 74 percent of African American fourth graders, 77 percent of Hispanic fourth graders,

High-stake assessment can be a barrier to some students graduating from high school, but can also help students who do graduate to be better prepared for adult life in college or at work.

and 68 percent of American Indian/Alaska Native fourth graders were eligible for free or reduced-price lunch, compared to just 29 percent of white fourth graders (Aud, Fox, & KewalRamani, 2010). There is little question that issues such as poverty, education, and race and ethnicity impact test scores.

WHY IS PROGRESS IN THE GENERAL EDUCATION CURRICULUM VALUED?

Dani's parents, Luz and Carlos, are adamant that Dani will participate in the general education curriculum. They accept no arguments to the contrary; both are well-educated professionals, and both have high expectations for Dani and believe that her inclusion in the general education curriculum and classroom is the route to achieving those expectations. Dani herself wants to be with her age-similar peers in general education, and indeed her inclusion has boosted her self-confidence and her ability to read. Still, there is the global question: Is it good to hold students with disabilities accountable for progress in the general education curriculum? Is it fair to determine those students' accountability for progress toward the same standards? There are two reasons to answer "yes" to each question (Wehmeyer, 2011):

- Holding schools accountable for the progress of all students when compared on identical standards may result in higher expectations and higher achievement for students with disabilities.
- By being part of the standard process for assessment, students with disabilities will be part of the reform movement of education.

Of course, there are legitimate concerns that an identical-standards approach will conflict with the individualized needs of students as set out in their IEPs, limiting needed instruction in important areas such as vocational education and basic life skills, or that students may be frustrated, discouraged, and drop out. Yet despite the difficulties of involving students with disabilities in standards-based reform, evidence shows that it is important to hold them to high expectations and provide them with access to a challenging curriculum while being vigilant to ensure that negative impact on other instructional areas or student motivation are minimized. Underlying high expectations is the value of full citizenship: To deny students the opportunity to benefit from the general education curriculum may actually limit their education and postschool opportunities. That certainly reflects the Gonzalez family's perspectives. Research backs up their beliefs and shows that even students with the most significant cognitive disabilities can benefit from instruction in core content areas (Wehmeyer, 2011).

How do you provide standards-based education for all students? We will answer that question throughout all chapters in this book. We begin by describing how you can design curriculum, instruction, and assessment to enable students with exceptionalities to progress in the general education curriculum.

How Do Supplementary Aids and Services and Universal Design for Learning Support Progress?

As you learned in Chapter 1, a student has a right to special education, necessary related services, and supplementary aids and services.

WHAT ARE SUPPLEMENTARY AIDS AND SERVICES?

IDEA defines **supplementary aids and services** as "aids, services, and other supports that are provided in regular education classes, other education-related settings, and in extracurricular and nonacademic settings, to enable children with disabilities to be educated

IEP TIP

As a member of the IEP team, you and your colleagues must identify and itemize the supplementary aids and services the student needs to participate in the general curriculum to the maximum extent appropriate and to make progress in that curriculum.

FIGURE 2.1

Supplementary aids and services

Domain	Definition	Examples
Universal design for learning	Modifications to how curriculum is presented or represented or to the ways in which students respond to the curriculum	Digital Talking Book formats, advance organizers, video or audio input/output
Access	Modifications to the community, campus building, or classroom to ensure physical and cognitive access	Curb cuts, wide doors, clear aisles, nonprint signs
Classroom ecology	Modifications to and arrangements of features of the classroom environment that impact learning	Seating arrangement, types of seating, acoustics, lighting
Educational and assistive technology	Technology that reduces the impact of a person's impairment on his or her capacity	Calculator, augmentative communication device, computer
Assessment and task modifications	Modifications to time or task requirements (but not content or material) to assist in participation in assessment or educational task	Extended time, scribe, note taker, oral presentation
Teacher, paraprofessional, or peer support	Support from another person to participate in instructional activities	Peer buddy, paraeducator, teacher

with nondisabled children to the maximum extent appropriate." These services and aids supplement the student's specially designed instruction and related services and, like that instruction and those related services, ensure that a student receives an appropriate education, especially to ensure participation and progress in the general education curriculum.

Supplementary aids and services are noninstructional modifications and supports. As Figure 2.1 shows, they include modifications to ensure physical and cognitive access to the environment, classroom ecological variables such as seating arrangements and classroom acoustics, educational and assistive technology, assessment and task modifications, and support from other persons. Dani has a nurse-care plan and assistance from the school nurse so she can administer the proper dosage of insulin, through her implanted Cosmo pump, to treat her diabetes. Although all of these aids and services are important, we will focus on the role of universal design in promoting progress in the general education curriculum.

WHAT IS UNIVERSAL DESIGN?

Universal design (UD) refers to the design of buildings, environments, and products with features that ensure that all people can access the building or environment or use the product (Erlandson, 2008). This is an important point: UD features ensure accessibility for *all* people, not just people with disabilities. For example, the designs of most scissors limit people who have fine-motor difficulties from using them easily. Did you know, however, that most such scissors are also designed for people who are right-handed? People who are left-handed must purchase specially designed scissors. However, scissors such as those shown in the photo here can be used by people with limited hand strength or fine-motor difficulties as well as by people who are left-handed or right-handed. They are universally designed.

So what does universal design have to do with special education services? As schools began to implement standards-based reforms, it became obvious that instructional materials impeded many students' progress in the general education curriculum. Students who could not read because of their visual impairments did not have access to the information they needed to learn content. Likewise, students who spoke a language other than English experienced barriers. In fact, traditional ways of representing content (written formats such as textbooks), presenting information (whole-class lectures), and having students demonstrate their knowledge and skills (through written papers and examinations) were barriers for a lot of children, not only students with disabilities.

Universally designed scissors.

That's where IDEA and **universal design for learning (UDL)** come in. UDL refers to the design of instructional materials and activities to make the content information accessible to all children (Rose & Meyer, 2006). You'll learn more about the work of CAST, a research and development center that has pioneered the concept of UDL, in Chapter 9. Basically, though, UDL ensures that students with disabilities can access the general education curriculum via curriculum modifications achieved through technology and instruction (that is, pedagogy).

HOW DOES UNIVERSAL DESIGN FOR LEARNING FACILITATE PROGRESS?

Universal design for learning contributes to progress in the general education curriculum by ensuring that all students can access academic content information and provide evidence of their learning through more than one means. Notice the words "all students."

There are three elements of universal design for learning. The first, *multiple means of representation*, relates to the materials that teachers use to represent the content they are asking their students to learn. The second, *multiple means of action and expression*, concerns how the materials provide alternative ways for students to demonstrate knowledge. The third, *multiple means of engagement*, deals with how the materials take advantage of student interests and motivations to engage them in learning (Rose & Meyer, 2006).

Teachers achieve universal design in representing content when they use multiple formats, such as text, graphics or pictures, digital and other media formats (audio or video), and performance formats (plays, skits) and when they use different means to deliver content information, including lectures, computerized visual presentations such as PowerPoint, role playing, and computer-mediated instruction. Similarly, students can provide evidence of their learning through reports, exams, portfolios, drawings, performances, oral reports, videotaped reports, and other alternative means.

It is also important that instructional materials be universally designed. In fact, the National Instructional Materials Accessibility Standard (NIMAS), which was included in IDEA 2004 (U.S. Department of Education, n.d.), requires that publishers provide electronic formats of all instructional materials to ensure that students who have print-related disabilities can access written content.

In the "Planning for Universal Design for Learning" sections in Chapters 5 through 16, you will learn how UDL principles apply to students with disabilities and how technology and pedagogy enable them to participate and make progress in the general education curriculum, from digital talking books and e-readers, to the use of pedagogical means of achieving access, such as advance organizers and concept maps. The bottom line is simply this: Universal design for learning tailors instruction to the needs of each student. It focuses on a student's strengths, takes the student's learning capacities into account, and offers each student a full opportunity to benefit from the general education curriculum.

How Does Inclusion Support Progress?

You already know that progress in the general education curriculum is one of IDEA's goals, and you know why it is important for students. You have just started to learn about one way to advance that goal: universal design for learning. There is a second important way. It is called inclusion. You learned, while reading Chapter 1, that IDEA has a principle called the *least restrictive environment*. This principle underlies inclusion: Students with disabilities should participate in the school's academic, extracurricular, and other activities with students without disabilities. We introduce you to this essential concept here and then elaborate on it in Chapters 5 through 16.

WHAT ARE STUDENT PLACEMENT TRENDS?

First, it is important to understand issues pertaining to student placement. The U.S. Department of Education reports annually on students with disabilities who receive special education and related services in different educational settings. Figure 2.2 lists the department's categories of educational placement (also called *environment*) and defines each one.

Figure 2.3 shows the percentage of students with disabilities who are educated in each placement category, according to the most recent U.S. Department of Education report. If you were to graph changes in these percentages over time, you would observe that more students with disabilities are being served in regular classrooms for most of their school day, that fewer students with disabilities are being served outside the general education classroom, and that the amount of time they spend outside the general education classroom has decreased. In addition, the number of students in self-contained and separate facilities has gradually decreased. The number of students in residential facilities and in homebound or hospital placements has remained at a low level over this entire time period.

Not surprisingly, the percentage of students with disabilities in the different placement categories varies according to the age of students and their type of disability. More elementary students than secondary students are served in typical schools with peers who do not have disabilities. Students with less intensive support needs (for example, speech or language impairments and learning disabilities) are more likely to be in general education classrooms for the largest percentage of time compared with students with more intensive support needs (for example, students with intellectual disability or multiple disabilities). In Chapters 5 through 16 you will learn what percentage of students, by disability category, are in general education. In Chapter 3, you will learn that placement category also varies based on students' racial or ethnic background.

FIGURE 2.2 *Placement categories designated by U.S. Department of Education and the percentage of all students with disabilities, ages six through twenty-one, placed in those categories: School year 2008–2009*

Time spent inside regular class

80 to 100 percent of a student's time: 58 percent of all students with disabilities

40 to 79 percent of a student's time: 21 percent of all students with disabilities

Less than 39 percent of a student's time: 15 percent of all students with disabilities

Time spent in separate settings

Settings include separate school, residential facility, parental placement in private school, correctional facility, and home or hospital. Although each is a separate placement category, Figure 2.3's "separate setting" includes all of them: 5 percent of all students with disabilities

FIGURE 2.3 *Percentage of students (rounded upward) ages six through twenty-one in different education environments: School year 2008–2009*

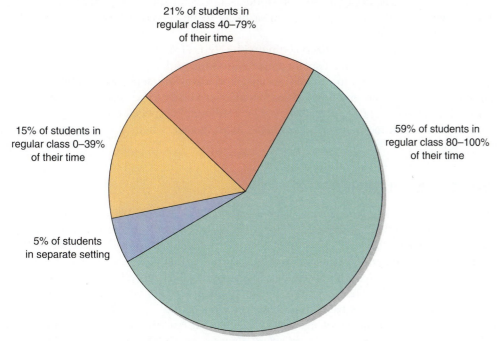

21% of students in regular class 40–79% of their time

15% of students in regular class 0–39% of their time

5% of students in separate setting

59% of students in regular class 80–100% of their time

Source: U.S. Department of Education. (2011). *Data accountability center: Individuals with Disabilities Education Act (IDEA) data.* Retrieved on February 12, 2011, from https://www.ideadata.org
Note: Percentages have been rounded and collapsed across categories.

Issues in Residential, Home, and Hospital Placements

Settings that have a residential component—special boarding schools, hospitals, and students' homes—are generally regarded as the most restrictive placements. Students who attend residential schools sometimes do so because their local schools have not developed the capacity to provide special education services for them. Sometimes, however, they attend special schools to acquire capacity to learn in more typical settings, as, for example, when they are relearning after a traumatic brain injury (Chapter 13). Thus, it is important to distinguish situations in which a student needs a more restrictive environment from those in which schools need to expand their capacity to serve all students.

As compared with other students with disabilities, students with hearing impairments, visual impairments, and deaf-blindness are most likely to attend residential schools (U.S. Department of Education, 2011). Similarly, students with multiple disabilities, physical disabilities, and traumatic brain injury are most likely to be educated in a hospital or their home (U.S. Department of Education, 2011). As illustrated in Figure 2.3, however, a low percentage of students are in these settings, and this percentage has remained relatively stable over time.

Issues in Special-School Placements

Separate schools typically congregate students from a specific disability category and provide services specifically related to the characteristics of that disability. As compared with other students with disabilities, students with multiple disabilities are those most likely to be educated in special schools; the next most likely are students with deaf-blindness and emotional and behavioral disorders (U.S. Department of Education, 2011). Students, particularly those with emotional disorders, are frequently placed in special schools because of problem behavior that many teachers do not know how to address.

Issues in Specialized-Settings Placements Within Typical Schools

Specialized settings in many schools include resource rooms and self-contained classes. Students who are in regular classes for 40 to 79 percent of their education are often served

IEP TIP

The IEP team is responsible for making placement decisions. While IDEA allows placement across several settings, it presumes, as you must, that students will be educated in the general education classroom and will participate in extracurricular and other school activities with their nondisabled peers.

in resource rooms. Resource rooms are staffed by special education teachers who work with students with disabilities for as little as one period or as many as several periods during the school day, depending upon students' needs for specially designed instruction. Students with learning disabilities are most likely to be served in resource rooms (U.S. Department of Education, 2011).

The second type of specialized setting within typical schools is the special education classroom. Special classrooms usually are provided for students with more intense needs than those students served in resource rooms. Students with intellectual disability, autism, multiple disabilities, and emotional disorders are most likely to be served in special classrooms (U.S. Department of Education, 2011). Traditionally, special education classrooms serve students with more severe disabilities; there, teachers help students acquire functional skills.

WHAT IS INCLUSION?

In the previous section, you learned that students in particular disability categories may be more likely to be served outside of the general education classroom. It is important, though, that you understand that a disability label is not destiny when it comes to placement. There are examples of successful inclusion across age and disability categories; and it is IDEA's presumption that students with disabilities, independent of category, be educated with their nondisabled peers. So what exactly is meant by inclusion? As we said at the beginning of this section, inclusion is based on IDEA's principle of the least restrictive environment. IDEA's presumption in favor of inclusion declares that "each state must establish procedures to assure that, to the *maximum extent appropriate, children with disabilities . . . are educated with children who are not disabled*, and special classes, separate schooling, or other removal of children with disabilities from the regular educational environment occurs *only when the nature or severity of the disability of a child is such that education in regular education with the use of supplementary aids and services cannot be achieved satisfactorily.*"

Inclusion, then, refers to the participation of students with disabilities alongside their nondisabled peers in academic, extracurricular, and other school activities. Inclusive practices have a long history in the field of special education. Figure 2.4 summarizes that history.

The provision of supplementary aids and services is important to IDEA's emphasis. **Supplementary aids and services** are defined as "aids, services, and other supports that are provided in general education classes, other education-related settings, and in extracurricular and nonacademic settings, *to enable children with disabilities to be educated with nondisabled children to the maximum extent appropriate.*" These aids and

---

FIGURE 2.4

Four consecutive phases of inclusion

1. *Mainstreaming:* an educational arrangement of returning students from special education classrooms to general education classrooms, typically for nonacademic portions of the school day, such as art, music, and physical education (Grosenick & Reynolds, 1978; Turnbull & Schulz, 1979)

2. *Regular Education Initiative:* an attempt to reform general and special education by creating a unified system capable of meeting individual needs in general education classrooms (Gartner & Lipsky, 1987; Reynolds, Wang, & Walberg, 1987; Will, 1986)

3. *Inclusion through accommodations (instructional adaptations):* an additive approach to inclusion that assumes the only viable approach to including students with disabilities in general education classrooms is to add instructional adaptions to the predefined general education teaching and learning approaches (Pugach, 1995)

4. *Inclusion through restructuring:* a design to inclusion that re-creates general and special education by merging resources to develop more flexible learning environments for all students and educators (McGregor & Vogelsberg, 1998; Pugach & Johnson, 2002; Sailor, 2002; Thousand, Villa, & Nevin, 2002)

services facilitate placement in and compliance with the regulations for the least restrictive environment: *"To the maximum extent appropriate, children with disabilities . . . are educated with children who are nondisabled."* IDEA allows placements other than the general education classroom, but it presumes that the setting of choice for students is the general education classroom and that students will not be removed from that setting unless inclusion in the general education classroom cannot be achieved satisfactorily with the use of supplementary aids and services and specially designed instruction. Consistent with IDEA and with Luz and Carlos Gonzalez's expectations for their daughter, Dani has a placement (the general education classroom with support for writing, science, and social studies, plus the resource room for highly individualized reading instruction) and supplementary aids and services (the school nurse's assistance with her diabetes pump) that exemplify the inclusion principle.

Characteristics of Inclusion

Inclusion has four key characteristics: home-school placement, the principle of natural proportions, restructuring teaching and learning, and age- and grade-appropriate placements.

Home-School Placement. Within an inclusive model, students attend the same school they would have attended if they did not have a disability. This is the same school other children in the student's neighborhood attend. Dani attends her neighborhood school and contributes to a sense of a learning community (Munk & Dempsey, 2010).

Principle of Natural Proportions. The principle of natural proportions holds that students with exceptionalities should be placed in schools and classrooms in natural proportion to the occurrence of exceptionality within the general population (Brown et al., 1991). If, for example, 10 percent of students in a school district receive special education services, the principle of natural proportions holds that, if a classroom has thirty students, not more than three should have a disability.

Restructuring Teaching and Learning. Inclusion through restructuring requires general and special educators to work in partnership with related service providers, families, and students to provide supplementary aids and services and special education and related services. You will recall from "Who Is Dani Gonzalez?" how closely her special educator and general educator work together. Tremendous variability exists in how teachers provide special education services within general education classrooms. Just consider the descriptions in Figure 2.4 of inclusion through add-on services and inclusion through restructured services. State-of-the-art schools such as Dani's, which implements inclusion through restructuring, pool the strengths and talents of educators who have different types of training and capacities to provide individualized instruction within the general education classroom.

Age- and Grade-Appropriate Placements. Finally, inclusion favors educating all students in age- and grade-appropriate placements. Therefore, Dani spends most of her time at school with other fifth graders.

Two major issues are at the heart of the inclusion debate: (1) eliminating the continuum of placements and (2) increasing the amount of time students spend in the general education classroom.

Eliminating the Continuum of Placements. The concept of a continuum of services has been part of special education ever since Congress enacted IDEA in 1975. The continuum refers to services that range from the most typical and most inclusive settings to the most atypical and most segregated settings.

There was a time when accommodating students with disabilities in general education classrooms through supplementary aids and services

The four characteristics of inclusion guide general and special educators.

was not considered an option. That limited perspective caused Taylor (1988) to observe that students with disabilities were caught in the continuum of services. Unfortunately, once students were placed in more restrictive settings, few ever left them for general education classrooms.

The inclusion movement has tried to limit the need for more restrictive settings by creating a new partnership between special and general educators. This partnership seeks to provide individualized instruction to students in general education classrooms through a universally designed general education curriculum (Jackson, Ryndak, & Wehmeyer, 2010). The priority for inclusion in the general education classroom is now predicated on the premise that it is not often appropriate or even necessary to remove some students from the general education classroom and place them in a more specialized and restrictive setting to provide individualized and appropriate education; that in order to gain access to the general education curriculum, students must be in the general education classroom (Wehmeyer, 2011); and that there is now sufficient evidence to support inclusion as a research-based practice (Jackson et al., 2010).

Increasing the Amount of Time in General Education Classrooms. Research confirms that students with disabilities can be successfully educated in the general education classroom, given adequate support and instruction (Bruns & Mogherraban, 2007); and IDEA expresses a preference for inclusion. So how can teachers increase the amount of time students with disabilities are served in the general education classroom? In Chapters 5 through 16, you will learn about strategies to promote universal design for progress, supplementary aids and services to promote inclusion and progress, and ways to support students with disabilities in inclusive settings. In the next section, you will learn why it's important to increase student inclusion.

WHAT STUDENT OUTCOMES ARE ASSOCIATED WITH INCLUSION?

By now, most stakeholders in the education of students with disabilities have accepted the importance of including students. For many parents of younger children with disabilities, inclusion is an expectation (Turnbull, Turnbull, Erwin, Soodak, & Shogren, 2011). So what benefits accrue when students are included?

First, there is almost universal agreement that students with disabilities gain social and communication benefits from their involvement in inclusive settings (Jackson, Ryndak, & Wehmeyer, 2009). Dani's increased self-confidence and ability to read underscore this finding. Second, and particularly important in light of current trends in standards-based reform, research shows that students with disabilities can and do benefit academically from involvement in the general education classroom (Snell, 2009). Cole, Waldron, and Majd (2004) found that students without disabilities educated in inclusive classrooms made significantly greater academic progress in mathematics and reading than did students without disabilities who did not have students with disabilities in their classroom. Cole and colleagues offer an explanation: The additional supports provided in the general education classroom that are intended to support the students with disabilities benefit all students. Now that's universal design for learning!

In particular, research shows that students with disabilities receiving their education in the general education classroom are significantly more likely to have access to the general education curriculum. Students being educated in the general education curriculum are more likely to be working on activities linked to grade-level standards in the general education classroom (Wehmeyer, 2011). Clearly, inclusion with

Students who are included benefit socially and make more friends.

BOX 2.1

INCLUSION TIPS

	What You Might See	What You Might Be Tempted to Do	Alternate Responses	Ways to Include Peers in the Process
Behavior	The student shows an apparently poor attitude toward other students and does not easily cooperate with them during instructional activities.	Discipline him for his poor behavior and separate him from the rest of the class.	Identify his strengths and work together on a list of positive things he can say when responding to other students during instructional activities.	Ask him to identify peers he would like to work with. Then work with this small group to practice verbal responses that would be helpful.
Social interactions	He has few friends and doesn't appear to want any.	Encourage him to take the initiative toward others but also allow him to be by himself whenever he chooses.	Collaborate with the school counselor to paln ways to teach him specific social skills.	Work with identified peers to practice the specific social skills with him in and out of the classroom.
Educational performance	His work is acceptable, but he needs constant supervision.	Assign an aide to work with him and allow him to complete unfinished work at home.	Collaborate with the special education teacher to create step-by-step assignments that he can do on his own. Set up a reward system for each step sucessfully completed without supervision.	Encourage him to work with his peers to monitor the assignments. Ask peers to work with him to construct a tracking system for class assignments.
Classroom attitudes	He never volunteers answers and is reluctant to participate in class activities.	Carefully choose activities that allow him to work alone.	Together with the special education teacher, work with him ahead of time on content to be covered and plan specific things for him to contribute.	Plan with peers positive contributions that each can make to upcoming class activities.

support (through individually designed instruction, related services, supplementary aids and services, and universal design in learning) is feasible and important. Box 2.1 illustrates some effective practices to promote inclusion. The Inclusion Tips boxes in Chapters 5 through 16 will provide similar information for students covered in each of those chapters.

HOW DOES INCLUSION FACILITATE PROGRESS?

Until now, the inclusion movement has consisted of two generations of different practices. The first generation focused on moving students with disabilities from segregated settings into the general education classroom. The second focused on developing and evaluating practices to support the presence of students with disabilities in the general classroom. Both phases focused primarily on the place in which students were educated.

Now, however, ESEA's standards-based reforms and IDEA's command for access to the general education curriculum have created conditions for a third generation of inclusive practices. Today, the focus is no longer exclusively on where a student is taught. It also includes (1) "what"—curriculum mastery, or what a student is taught and learns; and (2) "how"—the methods and pedagogy that teachers use. Nothing about the first two generations of inclusive practices is obsolete or unimportant. In fact, as we describe in Chapters 5 through 16, efforts to achieve outcomes associated with first- and second-generation inclusive practices (inclusion in the general education classroom and implementation of high-quality instructional strategies to support students in the general education classroom) continue but with new emphasis on "what" and "how."

How Does a Student's IEP Support Progress?

You have learned about two initiatives, universal design for learning and inclusion, that promote students' progress in the general education curriculum. We discuss other practices in future chapters. To lay the foundation for those chapters, however, we turn your attention to other important practices, beginning with students' Individualized Education Programs (IEPs). We discussed the IEP in Chapter 1, but we add to that discussion here.

In developing a student's IEP, you should remember two basic propositions of special education practices. First, individualization is a hallmark of these practices (Turnbull, Turnbull, Wehmeyer, & Park, 2003), and nothing about standards-based reform changes that basic fact. Second, IDEA requires a student's IEP to ensure involvement with and progress in the general education curriculum and also to address his or her unique learning needs.

WHO DESIGNS AN IEP AND WHAT ARE THEIR DUTIES?

In Chapter 1, you learned that the Individualized Education Program (IEP) is the plan for an education program for each student ages three through twenty-one. For children from birth through age two, that plan is called the Individualized Family Services Plan (IFSP). You also learned who participates in an IEP meeting and how the IEP process aligns with the priorities of the six principles of IDEA. To refresh your memory, we'll restate who must be involved in writing an IEP: the student's parents, a general educator, a special educator, a school representative who supervises or provides special education and knows about general education and school resources, a person who interprets the results of the student's nondiscriminatory evaluation, any other person with expertise about the student's educational needs (at the parents' discretion), and, when appropriate, the student.

The members of Dani's IEP team were Luz Gonzalez (her mother), two general education teachers, a school psychologist, a speech-language pathologist, her special education teacher, a paraprofessional, and the school nurse. Because a special educator and two general educators were on the team, Dani's special education under IDEA is aligned with ESEA. As you learned in Chapter 1, IDEA and ESEA align with each other; so does Dani's IEP.

You should also know that Dani participated in and signed off on her IEP. There is an expression in the disability world: "nothing about me without me." It means that the person with a disability is the focus of the action and has the right and should be supported to participate in decisions about him or herself. Dani's participation reflects that saying.

Now let's consider these participants' duties when writing the IEP. They must do all of the following:

- Ensure that all of the individuals identified by IDEA as mandatory members of the team participate.
- Follow IDEA's process for developing an IEP by considering the student's strengths; the parents' concerns about how to enhance their child's education; the results of the nondiscriminatory evaluations; the student's academic, developmental, and functional needs; and five "special factors." (We describe those later in this chapter under "Components of the IEP.") In Chapters 5 through 16, you'll learn how to conduct a nondiscriminatory evaluation for a student with a particular disability label and how to assess the student's progress in the general education curriculum and other educational needs.
- Include all of the required components of an IEP. (We describe them later in this chapter under "Components of the IEP.")
- Specify the student's educational placement, consistent with the principle of the least restrictive environment (which you read about in Chapter 1 and have learned more about in this chapter).

WHAT ARE THE COMPONENTS OF THE IEP?

IDEA requires the IEP to include eight components, which are shown in Figure 2.5. To comply with IDEA and ensure that the student will benefit from special education, a student's IEP team *must* include every component in each IEP.

FIGURE 2.5 *Required components of every IEP*

The IEP is a written statement for each student ages three through twenty-one. Whenever it is developed or revised, it must contain the following statements:

1. The student's present levels of academic achievement and functional performance, including
   - How the student's disability affects the student's involvement and progress in the general curriculum (for students ages six through twenty-one)
   - How a preschooler's disability affects the child's participation in appropriate activities (for children ages three through five)
   - A description of the benchmarks or short-term objectives for students who take alternate assessments that are aligned to alternate achievement standards

2. Measurable annual goals, including academic and functional goals, designed to
   - Meet each of the student's needs resulting from the disability in order to enable the student to be involved in and make progress in the general curriculum
   - Meet each of the student's other educational needs that result from the disability

3. How the student's progress toward annual goals will be measured and when periodic reports on the student's progress and meeting annual goals will be provided

4. The special education and related services and supplementary aids and services, based on peer-reviewed research to the extent practicable that will be provided to the student or on the student's behalf and the program modifications or supports for school personnel that will be provided for the student to
   - Advance appropriately toward attaining the annual goals
   - Be involved in and make progress in the general curriculum and participate in extracurricular and other nonacademic activities
   - Be educated and participate in those three types of activities with other students with disabilities and with students who do not have disabilities

5. An explanation of the extent, if any, to which the student will not participate with students who do not have disabilities in the regular classroom and in extracurricular and other nonacademic activities

6. Any individual appropriate accommodations that are necessary to measure the student's academic and functional performance on state- and district-wide assessments; if the IEP team determines that the student will not participate in a regular state- or district-wide assessment or any part of an assessment, an explanation of why the student cannot participate and the particular alternate assessment that the team selects as appropriate for the student

7. The projected date for beginning the special education, related services, supplemental aids and services, and modifications, as well as the anticipated frequency, location, and duration of each

8. Beginning no later than the first IEP that will be in effect after the student turns sixteen, and then updated annually, a transition plan that must include
   - Measurable postsecondary goals based on transition assessments related to training, education, employment, and, where appropriate, independent living skills
   - A statement of transition services, including courses of study, needed to assist the student to reach those postsecondary goals
   - Beginning no later than one year before the student reaches the age of majority under state law (usually age eighteen), a statement that the student has been informed of those rights under IDEA that will transfer to the student from the parents when the student comes of age

In addition to addressing each of these eight required components, the IEP team must also carefully consider five special factors when developing a student's IEP. If any factors apply to the student, the team must address them through the IEP as part of that student's special education, related services, or supplementary aids and services:

- If the child's behavior impedes his or other students' learning, the IEP team must consider whether to use positive behavioral interventions and supports or other strategies

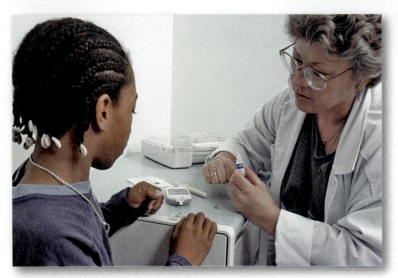
School nurses are members of some IEP teams.

to address the child's behavior. This consideration does not apply to Dani; she does not have any behavior support needs.

- If the child has limited English proficiency, the IEP team must consider her language needs in the IEP. This does not apply to Dani.

- If the child is blind or visually impaired, the IEP team must provide (not merely consider providing) instruction in braille and the use of braille. The team may determine that such instruction is not appropriate for the child but only after it evaluates the child's reading and writing skills, needs, and appropriate reading and writing media, including an evaluation of his future needs for instruction in braille or the use of braille. Dani is not visually impaired, so this consideration does not apply to her.

- For every child, the IEP must consider the child's communication needs. If the child is deaf or hard of hearing, the team must consider language and communication needs, opportunities for direct communication with peers and professional personnel in her language and communication mode, academic level, and full range of needs, including opportunities for direct instruction in language and communication mode. It is important that Dani's IEP team consider her communication needs, although, because she does not have a hearing impairment, these specific considerations do not apply to her.

- Also for every child, the IEP team must consider whether he needs assistive technology devices and services. Dani does use a device (a pump) that administers insulin, but her device is implanted. That makes a difference because IDEA does not regard an implanted device as a related service. Still, IDEA does require the school to support Dani in monitoring the pump and assisting her to use it.

You learned in Chapter 1 that IDEA defines special education as specially designed instruction, and you have just learned about the required eight components of an IEP and the five special factors the IEP must consider. Now let's consider the IDEA definition of special education and the component requirements as they apply to Dani.

Dani's IEP has a "long-range vision" section ("expressing and communicating her thoughts and opinions with confidence in herself"); a statement of her academic and functional achievement; and a specification of the types of education she will have in reading, math, life skills, writing, science, and social studies. It also identifies her speech-language challenges but does not provide the related service of speech-language therapy. If those were the only issues Dani's IEP team were to consider and the only ones her teachers were to address, Dani might be shortchanged. That is because IDEA requires each IEP team not only to address the eight components and consider the five factors but also to consider the following:

- The child's strengths
- The child's parents' concerns for enhancing their child's education
- The results of initial or subsequent nondiscriminatory evaluations
- The child's academic, developmental, and functional needs

Dani, her parents, and her teachers have taken into account her strengths (determination to learn), the concerns that Luz and Carlos have (integrated education that leads to a life more like that of people who do not have disabilities), Dani's evaluations, and Dani's various needs. It is especially important for the IEP team to consider a student's strengths, as Dani's team has done, because it is too easy for educators to focus primarily on a student's needs. A student's present strengths, especially as educators build on them to address the student's needs, often shape the expectations that educators, parents, and even the students have. In Box 2.2, My Voice, you will read about a student who knew her strengths and had great expectations for herself and her future.

Knowlton (2007) recommends that well-written annual goals should be clear and concise; expressed in terms of observable behavior and the conditions under which it will occur; logically derived from one or more present levels of educational performance; related to relevant academic, social, vocational, and or community-referenced skills appropriate to the age of and expectations for the student; and readily accomplished in one year's time. Heinich, Molenda, Russel, and Smaldino (1999) recommend that well-written goals address the ABCDs of goal writing:

(A)udience. Who is the target of the goal?

(B)ehavior. What do you expect the target for the goal to be able to do? This should be an overt, observable behavior, even if the actual behavior is covert or mental in nature. Otherwise, it is not measurable.

(C)ondition. Under what conditions or circumstances do you expect the student to perform the behavior?

(D)egree of proficiency. What criteria will you use to determine if the student has met the goal?

ADDRESSING PROGRESS THROUGH THE IEP

It is worthwhile to repeat that one of IDEA's purposes is to ensure that the student has equal opportunities in education and that those opportunities will lead to economic self-sufficiency, independent living, and full participation. To secure these outcomes, educators must address the student's progress in school. Because the IEP is the linchpin to the student's education and progress, they have to take into account the supplementary aids and services the student will need and how special education, related services, and supplementary aids and services shape annual goals and progress toward those goals.

BOX 2.2 | **MY VOICE**

The Power of Great Expectations and Visions

I had a learning disability throughout grades K–12, but in May 2002 I graduated with my first bachelor of science degree (in geography) from Western Kentucky University in Bowling Green. I have gone for two more degrees at WKU. One is the bachelor of fine arts in graphic design and the other a bachelor of arts in broadcasting. I received both degrees in May 2004. I never imagined so much success as I am now having in my life.

My teachers in high school believed it was impossible for me to attend a major university and graduate due to my severe learning disability. I was determined to succeed in life, though, and get a good college education despite what the test scores said, the Board of Education said to me, and my teachers said to me. It took a while for them to accept my goals in life and to support me. My high school teachers wanted me to just graduate with an associate's degree and never attend a university. I just wish they had pushed me more to my full potential in high school and had me reach for my dreams.

One of my goals had been to work for the Weather Channel as an on-camera meterologist. I have had to abandon that goal because the math and physics required to be a meterologist are just too hard for me and too challenging. But I am looking in to attending the University of Hawaii—Manoa to get a bachelor of science degree in global environmental science and to take other courses in geography and oceanography.

I am getting a lot of support from my professors, but accomplishing these degrees at Western Kentucky University was extremely challenging. Still, I got through them all right with hard work and persistence. My learning disability was in math, which is a weak subject for me; so you can understand why being a meterologist was beyound my reach, even with all the work I put in and all the support I received. But I can pursue other work in the area of the natural sciences, and that is what I will do at the University of Hawaii.

I also got support from the president of my university, the dean, the professors, and the advisors and alumni association. However, they don't know the entire story and all that I had to go through to get to this point in my life. I really can't believe my dreams of working in the natural sciences are coming true. That is why I would also like to help out in some way with kids who have learning disabilities.

—*Chandra Beyerck,*
Western Kentucky University, Bowling Green

Determining Supplementary Aids and Services

Relying on the student's nondiscriminatory evaluation and IEP, the IEP team should ask what supplementary aids and services the student needs to be educated with his non-disabled peers and to progress in the general education curriculum. There is a connection between supplementary aids and services and the five special considerations that a student's IEP team must take into account. To repeat, those five considerations are (1) strategies to address a student's behavior that impedes his or other students' learning; (2) language needs of students with limited English proficiency; (3) instruction in braille for students who are blind; (4) communication needs, especially when the student is deaf or hard of hearing; and (5) use of assistive technology devices and services.

Each factor can guide the IEP team as it considers what supplementary aids and services a student needs. Does she need to be seated near the teacher to see or hear the lesson? Does she work best when seated individually or with other students around a table? What is the role of the paraprofessional in providing supports? What assistive technologies might promote access? Does the student need certain assessment or task modifications to succeed? These are all part of determining needed supplementary aids and supports.

Determining Annual Goals

As you know, the IEP must state the student's annual goals and how educators will measure his progress toward those goals, especially as the student participates in the general curriculum. The goals must relate to both the student's educational goals and his other educational needs.

With regard to goals addressing the student's other educational needs, students with severe disabilities need functional or life-skills content that other students acquire outside of school or at a younger age and that may not be part of the general education curriculum, particularly for older students. Most students, whether receiving special education services or not, need instruction related to making the transition from school to the adult world, including instruction in employment and community living; yet this is often lacking in general curriculum standards. Further, some students with disabilities (especially those who have visual impairments) need specialized instruction in areas such as orientation and mobility—namely, how to get from place to place—that other students do not need.

The IEP team should take into account the content of the general education curriculum and how it will fail to provide the student with the skills and knowledge she needs to be a productive, independent adult. Then the team should develop goals and objectives to address those areas. Historically, the IEPs of students with disabilities began with these alternative or functional curricular content areas. That practice, however, limited students to instruction in only those areas that the IEP team believed were important or possible. In the end, those IEPs failed to hold students to the high expectations of the general education curriculum.

Remember that IDEA does not limit a student's educational program to content in the general education curriculum. IDEA allows educators to address students' other educational needs, but it requires them to begin by considering how a student can participate and make progress in the general education curriculum. Thus, the team will consider the other educational needs of a student with disabilities (such as how Dani can learn to calculate the proper dosages of her insulin), but it will start by asking how the student can participate and make progress in the general education curriculum.

Determining Specially Designed Instruction

Having considered supplementary aids and services and written goals, the IEP team should identify the **specially designed instruction** the student needs to ensure participation and progress in the general education curriculum. Ordinarily, the IEP team does not have to identify all possible instructional techniques and strategies a student might need; that is the role of the student's teachers for each course. Dani's IEP specifies the reading program she will have (*Horizons*), her math program (*Number Worlds*), and her life-skills program (which teaches her to use a calculator; read nutritional labels; write her name, address, and telephone number; and so on). Consistent with IDEA's requirement that the IEP must identify a student's strengths, Dani's IEP begins by acknowledging that she is "an extremely happy and social child . . . gets along wonderfully with her peers and adults . . . is very responsible . . . is an extremely hard worker . . . is proud of herself when she succeeds and is beginning to demonstrate more self-confidence than in past years." In Chapters 5 through 16, you will learn about an array of specially designed instruction across all age and grade levels and about how students' IEPs, like Dani's, can reflect their strengths as well as their educational needs.

Specifying Related Services

Next, the IEP team should consider related services (identified in Chapter 1) that are necessary to enable a student to benefit from special education and to participate and make progress in the general education curriculum.

Determining Test Accommodations or Alterations

Finally, the IEP team should consider whether the student can take the state or district assessments without modification, needs a modified test or other accommodations, or needs to take an alternate assessment. The IEP team cannot completely exempt the student from assessments. That is not an option.

What Should Educators Do to Support Progress?

Promoting access begins with inclusive practices, UDL, and effective planning, but the heavy lifting occurs day in and day out in the classroom. Three campus- and classroom-level actions promote student progress in the general education curriculum: creating learning communities, designing unit and lesson plans, and implementing schoolwide quality instruction.

CREATING LEARNING COMMUNITIES

Effective instruction begins when educators intentionally create learning environments in which students learn to respect and value each other and everyone's individual differences, understand their roles and responsibilities, work in a self-directed manner, and participate in setting classroom rules. You can create an effective learning community by discovering the abilities of all your students; developing systematic ways to collect information on student progress for use in planning future lessons; and using collaborative teaching, grouping, and differentiated instructional strategies to individualize student educational experiences. In Chapters 3 and 4 you will learn more about the community, about respecting and valuing diversity, and about creating partnerships with families.

DESIGNING UNITS AND LESSONS

Think of units of study as the maps teachers create to organize and plan content and to support student learning and achievement in the general education curriculum. Units of study identify end-of-school-year goals, standards for determining whether the goals are met, and knowledge that students will acquire. Once you as a teacher understand the big picture for the school year, you must map backward to determine what your students will need to know and do at the middle of the school year and then plan for manageable instructional units. When you have an overall idea of what you need to accomplish by the end of the school year and have chunked the content, skills, and knowledge into midyear and quarterly components, you are ready to plan specific units of instruction.

Having identified the learning targets, you can plan day-to-day activities to support students in achieving the outcomes of each unit of instruction. Generally, lesson plans identify the theme of a lesson, the purpose of the lesson, how the lesson will be conducted, what students are expected to accomplish, and how those accomplishments will be measured. Dani's teachers use evidence-based reading and math curricula that are highly specific about what to teach (curriculum), how to teach (methodology), and how to measure progress.

At both the unit- and lesson-planning level, you should identify the skills, processes, or knowledge that *all* students, including students with disabilities, should master and how the teacher and other educators will support all students in doing so. Spooner, Baker, Harris, Ahlgrim-Delzell, and Browder (2007) found that as little as one hour of training on UDL enabled teachers to implement lesson plans that were accessible for all students, so it is important for school administrators to ensure that teachers have those opportunities to learn about how to write lesson plans and units that incorporate UDL features. You will learn about more of these practices in Chapters 5 through 16.

One such strategy is to identify the big ideas that all students should learn from the lesson or unit. Once you know what you want all students to know, you can develop lesson objectives that allow students to demonstrate, through different means, that they grasp the big ideas (Grossen et al., 2002). Dani's IEP calls for her to "focus on the basic concepts being taught."

One way to create those objectives is to use **cognitive taxonomies**. Cognitive taxonomies classify the cognitive demands of learning targets. Perhaps the most familiar cognitive taxonomy is the one developed by Bloom and associates. Bloom's taxonomy is a means of categorizing the cognitive skills students use when achieving learning targets. As one ascends Bloom's taxonomy, the cognitive demands on students are more complex. By developing lesson objectives that range from less to more complex cognitive demands, you can ensure that all of your students acquire knowledge about the content and have flexible options for providing evidence of that knowledge.

IMPLEMENTING SCHOOLWIDE INSTRUCTIONAL STRATEGIES

In subsequent chapters you will learn more about high-quality, schoolwide instructional strategies that promote students' progress in the general education curriculum. Pay careful attention to the word *schoolwide*. These strategies are effective not in just one classroom but in all school environments. Indeed, their payoff comes in every classroom. Further, like UDL, these strategies benefit all students, not just those who have qualified for special education under IDEA or reasonable accommodations under Section 504. They include learning communities, differentiated instruction, positive behavior support, cooperative learning, collaborative teaming, peer-mediated learning, and many more. You will learn about them in future chapters. Two innovative schoolwide procedures, *response to intervention* and *positive behavior supports,* are critical to student progress through schoolwide implementation strategies. We briefly referred to these procedures in Chapter 1 in reference to Dylan Schwind. Now, let's move from "briefly" to "more deeply."

Response to Intervention

Response to intervention (RTI) is a means to determine whether any student, regardless of type of disability, needs more intensive instruction. RTI is "a multilayered system for struggling learners that provides increasingly intense levels of academic interventions and assessment" (Byrd, 2011, p. 33).

Implementing RTI. Hoover and Love (2011) identified a number of steps in the successful implementation of RTI models. First, most of these models involve three tiers of instruction, increasing in duration and intensity at each level:

- *Tier 1:* implementation of a high-quality, universally designed general education curriculum for all students, with necessary supplementary aids and services and supports.
- *Tier 2:* implementation of supplemental instruction to address specific student needs that arise in the course of Tier 1 instruction.
- *Tier 3:* implementation of highly specialized instruction to meet intensive needs for a small group of students.

Next, RTI involves the use of data to make decisions about instructional needs. Data are gathered through multiple, frequent assessments. You will learn strategies to monitor progress in the general education curriculum in Chapters 5 to 16. RTI emphasizes the implementation of high-quality educational interventions called *evidence-based practices.* The U.S. Department of Education provides information on evidence-based practices via the

What Works Clearinghouse (http://ies.ed.gov/wwc/). The evidence for a particular practice is evaluated using an evidence rating, ranging from *positive effects, potentially positive effects,* and *mixed effects* to *no discernable effects, potentially negative effects,* and *negative effects.*

RTI is a component of the third generation of inclusive practices because it emphasizes universal practices. That is, RTI does not focus on singling out students who are different because they have certain characteristics. Instead, it asks teachers to implement high-quality, research-based interventions for all students. Having done so and having used systematic and ongoing measurement of student progress and universal screening procedures, teachers then can determine which students are not responding to an intervention—that is, which students are not learning. Only at that point should teachers implement increasingly intense, individualized, and specialized instruction until, quite simply, the student receives the instruction he or she needs to succeed. The National Association of State Directors of Special Education (2005) has emphasized the problem-solving nature of RTI, as shown in Figure 2.6.

Positive Behavior Support

In Chapter 11, you will learn more about **positive behavior support** (PBS). At this point, however, you need to know only that positive behavior support is a systems-level, problem-solving-oriented, data-based approach to reducing problem behavior; improving appropriate behavior; and achieving important academic, social, and communication outcomes for a particular student and for all students throughout the school building (Bambera & Kern, 2005). Teachers instruct students to replace their problem behavior with appropriate behavior, enabling them to benefit much more effectively from the general curriculum.

In addition, PBS seeks to rearrange school environments and change school systems to eliminate the value for students of engaging in problem behaviors in the first place. Because a student's problem behavior often results from someone else's failure to provide individualized and comprehensive support (Janney & Snell, 2008), positive behavior support involves tailoring students' environments to their preferences, strengths, and needs.

School reform models have adopted RTI and PBS, with some researchers applying RTI to students' social domains as well as academic domains (Fairbanks, Sugai, Guardino, & Lathrop, 2007). But there's more to practices such as RTI, PBS, and UDL than their useful application in different domains and populations: The principles underlying these practices are requiring educators to rethink inclusion and to generate new models for school reform.

For example, Sailor, Stowe, Turnbull, and Kleinhammer-Tramill (2007) have argued that schoolwide PBS is especially desirable today, when standards-based reforms (under the Elementary and Secondary Education Act, as amended by No Child Left Behind Act) are so important. They regard schoolwide PBS as an inclusive and preventive approach and contend it is fundamentally different from previous educational models. Earlier models, even when directed at students with and without disabilities, were still reactive: They responded to a student's failure, did not seek to prevent the failure, and did not increase the intensity of interventions to head off potential failure experiences.

FIGURE 2.6   *Response to intervention as a problem-solving approach*

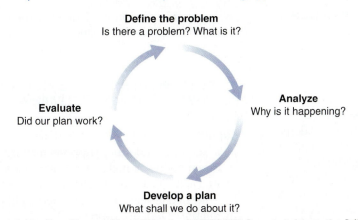

Define the problem
Is there a problem? What is it?

Analyze
Why is it happening?

Develop a plan
What shall we do about it?

Evaluate
Did our plan work?

Source: National Association of State Directors of Special Education (NASDSE). 2005. Response to Intervention: Policy Considerations and Implementation. Available at www.nasdse.org.

Sailor (2009) suggests that the new conceptualization of inclusion should take into account the entire school, not merely the classrooms where students with disabilities learn. Sailor advocates using RTI, PBS, and UDL together and on a schoolwide basis and has developed the Schooldwide Applications Model (SAM), incorporating six guiding principles (pp. 506–508):

1. General education guides all student learning.
2. All school resources are configured to benefit all students.
3. Schools address social development and citizenship forthrightly.
4. Schools are democratically organized, data-driven, problem-solving systems.
5. Schools have open boundaries in relation to their families and communities.
6. Schools enjoy district support for undertaking an extensive systems-change effort.

Approaches such as SAM incorporate aspects of RTI, PBS, and UDL. In doing so, they create new and universal approaches to education: They benefit all students, not just those with disabilities. That is why they are particularly important to members of a student's IEP team. If the team calls for and the student's teachers use RTI, PBS, and UDL, the student has a greater chance of being included alongside students who do not have disabilities, just as the legal principle of least restrictive environment wants and just as the theory of inclusion envisions.

ADDRESSING THE PROFESSIONAL STANDARDS

The following Council for Exceptional Children (CEC) Common Core Knowledge and Skills are addressed in this chapter through the content and concepts we discuss. See the Appendix for a full listing of these Knowledge and Skill Statements:

ICC1K2, ICC1K4, ICC1K5, ICCIK6, ICC1K7, ICC5S2, ICC5S3, ICC5S4, ICC5S6, ICC7S1, ICC7S2, ICC7S3, ICC7S6, ICC7S7, ICC7S9, ICC8K2, ICC8K3, ICC8K5, ICC8S2, ICC8S6

Summary

WHAT IS "PROGRESS IN THE GENERAL EDUCATION CURRICULUM"?

- IDEA requires each student's IEP to state how the student will be involved and progress in the general education curriculum, how the student's progress will be assessed, and how state- and district-wide assessments will be modified (as appropriate) for the student.
- ESEA requires states to establish challenging academic content and student achievement standards that apply to all students, including those with disabilities.
- The general education curriculum refers to the same curriculum taught to nondisabled students, and IDEA requires that students with disabilities be involved in the general education curriculum to the maximum extent appropriate (i.e., beneficial) for the particular student.

HOW DO SUPPLEMENTARY AIDS AND SERVICES AND UNIVERSAL DESIGN FOR LEARNING SUPPORT PROGRESS?

- Supplementary aids and services are noninstructional aids, services, and other supports that are provided in general education classes or other education-related settings to enable children with disabilities to be educated alongside nondisabled children to the maximum extent appropriate.

- Supplementary aids and services include modifications to ensure physical and cognitive access to the environment, classroom ecological variables such as seating arrangements or classroom acoustics, educational or assistive technology, assessment or task modifications, and support from other persons.
- Universal design for learning refers to the design of instructional materials and activities to make the content information accessible to all children.
- The three elements of UDL are multiple means of representing the curriculum, multiple means of using materials, and multiple means of engaging students in learning.

HOW DOES INCLUSION SUPPORT PROGRESS?

- Inclusion refers to students with disabilities learning in general education classes and having a sense of belonging in these classes. There has been a steady increase in the number of students with disabilities who are placed in general education.
- Inclusion has four key characteristics: home-school placement, the principle of natural proportions, restructuring teaching and learning, and age- and grade-appropriate placements.
- When supplementary aids and services are readily available within general education classrooms and universal design for learning has been fully implemented, students with disabilities will be more likely to perceive themselves as valued classroom members and will not need to leave the classroom as often to receive an appropriate education.

- The general education classroom is the place in which the general education curriculum is most likely to be taught to students with disabilities, and inclusion ensures that students will have access to the general education curriculum.

HOW DOES A STUDENT'S IEP SUPPORT PROGRESS?

- A student's IEP must be based on both the general education curriculum and the student's unique learning needs.
- There are required members of the IEP team.
- The team must develop the IEP based on the student's strengths, the parents' concerns, the nondiscriminatory evaluation, the student's needs, and five special factors.
- There are eight required components of an IEP; the team must address each component.

WHAT SHOULD EDUCATORS DO TO SUPPORT PROGRESS?

- Educators should create learning communities that enable students with disabilities to become integrated into their classrooms.
- Educators should create unit and lesson plans that incorporate universal design features and include goals and objectives that vary in complexity, thereby ensuring that all students can show progress.
- Educators should use schoolwide strategies such as response to intervention and positive behavior support because these approaches promote students' progress in the general education curriculum.

MyEducationLab

Go to Topic #2: IEPs in the MyEducationLab (www.myeducationlab.com) for *Exceptional Lives*, where you can do the following:

- Find learning outcomes for IEPs along with the national standards that connect to these outcomes.
- Complete assignments and activities that will help you more deeply understand the chapter content.
- Apply and practice your understanding of the core teaching skills identified in the chapter with the Building Teaching Skills and Dispositions learning units.
- Examine challenging situations and cases presented in the IRIS Center Resources.
- Access video clips of CCSSO National Teachers of the Year award winners responding to the question, "Why Do I Teach?" in the Teacher Talk section.
- Check your comprehension on the content covered in the chapter with the Study Plan. Here you will be able to take a chapter quiz, receive feedback on your answers, and then access review, practice, and enrichment activities to enhance your understanding of chapter content.
- Use the Online Lesson Plan Builder to practice lesson planning and integrating national and state standards into your planning.

3 Today's Multicultural, Bilingual, *and* Diverse Schools

Who Is De'ja McGee?

You are about to meet De'ja and Sharilyn McGee. De'ja is in the sixth grade and has been classified as having a specific learning disability. That fact alone does not mean much, for it does not tell you much about her. All it really says is that she has a certain type of disability. It does not tell you any of the other information that you need to know: De'ja has scored in the 97th percentile on her standardized reading test; she struggles with mathematics; she receives special services for both reading and math, including support in the general education classroom; and she participates in after-school tutoring. A person is far more than her label or test scores.

Let's look at De'ja's photograph. Here, too, you can find some clues about her. Perhaps you can see what her teachers and friends see in her: a cheerfulness that might seem difficult to maintain if you knew more about her life. Even though she is only eleven years old, De'ja lives the life of a young woman, not a girl. This is because she is indispensable to her mother, Sharilyn.

Sharilyn is divorced from De'ja's father, and she and De'ja are the only members of their household. What's more, as a consequence of various work-related injuries, Sharilyn has significant disabilities and is unable to work. De'ja is responsible for changing her mother's surgical dressings, injecting pain-killing medicines, and assisting her with simple but essential matters of daily living, such as getting dressed. Sharilyn has another child, a son who lives about forty miles away; but he is an adult and has his own family responsibilities. So for De'ja and Sharilyn, *family* means the two of them and no one else. As a result, De'ja has a maturity—born of necessity and experience—beyond her years.

Together, De'ja and Sharilyn exemplify certain aspects of the culture of American families. They are a single-parent family; they deal with disability within the family (in this case, both

De'ja's and Sharilyn's); and because De'ja's father rarely provides child support and Sharilyn is unable to work, they live on the economic edge. This is typical: For many families, disability and single-parent status go hand in hand with financial hardship

These traits sometimes coincide with another aspect of De'ja's and Sharilyn's life: intra-district migrancy. De'ja and Sharilyn move from apartment to apartment, nearly once every year. One reason is that De'ja's father does not provide child support and Sharilyn cannot work, so the family's income depends on public support and private charity. Another is that some landlords do not want to rent to people who receive public support for housing (assistance in paying their rent). Yet another is that rents increase faster than public support does. So to find acceptable housing, the family has to move often. This means that De'ja is likely to attend several different schools during her middle-school years. It also means that consistency in teaching and the development of crucial parent-teacher/student-teacher relationships will be hard to achieve.

Sharilyn herself was a student in special education, and she, too, was classified as having a specific learning disability. She dropped out of high school to give birth to her son, but she later earned her GED. From time to time, her own experiences as a student shape her relationships with De'ja's teachers; skepticism about their commitment to De'ja creeps into her attitudes about her daughter's school experiences.

Another fact to note is that De'ja and Sharilyn are African American. This should not lead you to make any assumptions about them. Parents from all ethnic, cultural, and linguistic backgrounds have children with disabilities, including specific learning disabilities. Similarly, parents from all backgrounds have disabilities, are or will become poor, and are or will become skeptical about schools and teachers. What race does mean, for De'ja and Sharilyn, is this: It is one, and only one, aspect of their culture.

People are like puzzles, and no puzzle is complete without all of its parts. Teachers who work for De'ja understand that. Seeing De'ja as a student with a label tells you something but not everything; it is just one piece of the puzzle. It is far more accurate

OBJECTIVES

- You will learn that there are challenges in providing effective special education to students from different cultural, ethnic, and linguistic backgrounds. You also will learn how to respond to the challenges.

- You will learn about the history of discrimination in education and the beliefs that supported discrimination against students from various cultural, ethnic, and linguistic backgrounds.

- You will learn that schools still disproportionately place into special education students who are not European American, do not speak English as their first language, and come from families who meet the federal definition of *poor*.

- You will learn that family structure and parents' education also correlate with placement into special education.

- You will learn how to become a culturally responsive educator by being introspective about yourself. Then you will learn how to take into account your students' cultures, broaden your education about people who do not share your culture, and teach in culturally responsive ways.

- You will be challenged to be not just a teacher but also an advocate for your students from diverse backgrounds.

to regard her and Sharilyn as people who have disabilities, face economic uncertainty, are intra-district migrants, have had their own experiences with teachers and peers, are optimistic about their future, and are determined to benefit from school. By understanding each of them as a whole person and both of them as a whole family—a completed puzzle—you will begin to understand that, when educators use the term *culturally diverse* to refer to students, families, and schools, you can interpret it as we present it in this chapter.

Culture refers to customary beliefs, forms of a person's life, and material traits. You have your own culture. We all do. Seeing De'ja and Sharilyn—indeed, seeing yourself—in only one way is deceptive. Worse, it impedes your ability to be an effective teacher.

It is natural for some people to think that "my way" is "the right way"—that how we ourselves teach, learn, and live is how others should, too. Of course, that's not true in America. There is no single "right" way, no culture that is more "right" or less "right" than any other. Diversity is a fact in American life. It always has been, and it is increasingly a fact of life in all schools. An effective teacher will see through De'ja's classification and understand and respond nonjudgmentally to the beliefs, forms, and material traits that characterize De'ja's and Sharilyn's lives.

PEARSON
myeducationlab

Visit the MyEducationLab (www .myeducationlab.com) for *Exceptional Lives* to enhance your understanding of chapter concepts with a personalized Study Plan. You'll also have the opportunity to hone your teaching skills through video- and case-based assignments and activities, IRIS Center Resources, and Building Teaching Skills and Disposition lessons.

Defining Culture and Its Implications for Special Education

Culture refers to the "customary beliefs, social forms, and material traits of a racial, religious, or social group; also, the characteristic features of everyday existence (as diversions or a way of life) shared by people in a place and time" (*Merriam-Webster's Collegiate Dictionary,* 2003, p. 304). Culture reflects the basic values of a particular group of people. When the members of a particular group perceive themselves, others, and their communities and nation in a particular way, they are reflecting their culture. It is likely that you are acutely conscious of your own culture—how you interpret yourself and your community and how you act on those interpretations. But do you have sufficient knowledge of how to understand and show respect for the cultures of your future students, their families, and other educators as well as your school, your community, and society at large? By asking that question, we are not suggesting that you do not understand and respect diverse cultures. We mean only that the question is worth asking and answering, as we do, in part, in this chapter.

There is no single culture in the United States or in its schools. Indeed, our country and schools consist of many microcultures. Americans who are Scottish or Irish in origin have certain traditions and cultures; their own native language (Gaelic, Celtic, or English); common music; common religions (Protestant or Roman Catholic); and common geographic origins (England, Scotland, Ireland, and Wales). Common race/ethnicity, religion, language, and geographic origin apply to other Americans as well, whether they are from parts of Scandinavia, Europe, Southeast Asia, Central and South America, Africa, or the Middle East. Groups from each area within these larger places have distinct traditions and cultures; each is a *micro,* or "smaller," group within the *macro,* or "larger," group known as Americans.

Figure 3.1 identifies the principal microcultures that you will encounter in your schools, according to race/ethnicity, language, income, religion, disability, gender, sexual orientation, age, and geography. Throughout this chapter we use the term *diverse backgrounds,* or terms similar to it, to refer to students or others who are traditionally regarded as being from nonmajority ethnic, cultural, or linguistic backgrounds. We base our terminology on IDEA's, which refers to individuals who are from "minority" backgrounds,

FIGURE 3.1 *Cultural and microcultural identity*

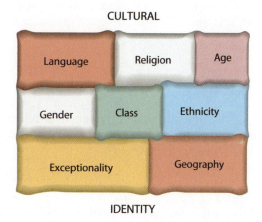

meaning that they, as a group, do not constitute the majority of people in the United States. Indeed, IDEA specifically refers to students who are not proficient in English and to African American students when it describes its intent to help schools respond to "the growing needs of an increasingly diverse society."

Reflect on Figure 3.1. What microcultures comprise your own culture? With whom do you experience a sense of "we-ness"—a sense of identity with others' behaviors, communication styles, interests, and traditions? At her school, De'ja's team of educators consists entirely of European American individuals. Their culture differs from De'ja's and Sharilyn's in significant ways: by race, income, and education. (Remember, Sharilyn was in special education; she earned her GED after leaving school to deliver her son.) Let's consider what these facts mean as we begin to explore the IDEA language about a diverse society and its rapidly changing ethnic profile, and let's do so by returning to the term *culture*.

Banks and Banks (2001) emphasize the "everyday existence" feature of culture: "Culture is in us and all around us, just as is the air we breathe. It is personal, familial, communal, institutional, societal, and global in its scope and distribution" (p. 31). Janet Vohs, the mother of a daughter who has cerebral palsy as well as special artistic talents, is a professional in the field of disabilities. She describes culture by means of a metaphor. She notes that in medieval times, small rooms used for baking became so full of the remains of yeast from years and years of baking that it was unnecessary to add yeast to bread dough. The yeast culture "simply lived in the air." Like our own assumptions and presuppositions, yeast is invisible but powerful. Like bread, we "inherit" our "invisible" assumptions and presuppositions—namely, our culture and its premise: those "sentences, metaphors, and stories about life that we have learned to call true." Sometimes they change, but they "usually linger" long after they are no longer useful or correct (Vohs, 1993, pp. 56–57).

In this chapter, we will lay a foundation for you to become a culturally responsive educator. As you read this chapter, note that *cultural responsiveness* in education involves instruction and assessment of student learning that takes into account the each student's "cognitive, linguistic, and social assets": that is, the student's "epistemologies, world views, and learning, teaching, and communication styles" (Klingner & Solano-Flores, 2007, p. 231). These derive from the student's culture and affect how the student learns and interprets what happens. Given the way in which culture is deeply embedded within each student, educators should build on the student's culture and not denigrate it (Klingner & Solano-Flores, 2007). With the goal of helping you become more culturally responsive, we start with a history lesson.

The Social Context of Special Education

You cannot fully understand the social and cultural context of special education (or, for that matter, general education) without knowing something about the history of special education in U.S. schools. That history is problematic. Educators who worked diligently to create effective and equal educational opportunities for *all* students often met resistance. Does resistance still exist today, and, if so, how does it affect the school systems, teachers and other professionals, and students and their families? Those are questions we try to answer in this chapter.

HISTORY JUSTIFYING IDEA

The history underlying IDEA's statements about diversity is reflected in theories about diversity, school systems' responses to those theories, and court cases related to nondiscriminatory evaluation.

Theories About Diversity

Three main theories of diversity exist: genetic deficit, cultural deficit, and cultural difference. Beginning in the 1700s, pseudo-scientists developed **genetic deficit theories**. These theories held that white people were genetically superior to nonwhite people. For instance, craniologists—professionals who measured people's head size and classified their head shape—disagreed on whether whites and nonwhites evolved from the same species. For the most part, however, they agreed that the supposedly larger brains of whites rendered them superior to nonwhites. Their theories contributed to justifying a two-track system of education, one for the "superior" whites and another for other people (McCray, Webb-Johnson, & Neal, 2003).

Other professionals have resorted to a **cultural deficit theory**. It blames the academic failure of students from diverse backgrounds on the inherent disadvantages that exist within the students' cultures. These professionals argue that the students' cultural deprivation (for example, a lack of books in their schools or homes or parents' lack of attendance at teacher-parent conferences) explains why there are significantly disparate academic and behavioral outcomes between students from racially/ethnically diverse backgrounds or poverty backgrounds and their middle-class European American counterparts (Blanchett, 2009).

Genetic and cultural deficit theories reemerged in the early 1990s with the publication of *The Bell Curve* (Herrstein & Murray, 1994). In that book, the authors discussed the role that IQ (genetic deficit theory) plays in the social and economic differences among racial groups (cultural deficit theory). The book spurred intense controversy because it asserted that African Americans and other people of color are biologically less intelligent than European Americans. In an effort to bring evidence into the debates, the American Psychological Association (1996) issued a report stating that research does not support a genetic interpretation of IQ test-score differences between African Americans and European Americans. Nor does it support segregation or racial **eugenics**—procedures that claim to improve the human race by encouraging the birth of children with allegedly "good" hereditary qualities and discouraging or preventing the birth of those with allegedly "undesirable" hereditary qualities.

Still other professionals have advanced a theory of **cultural difference**. That theory is not identical with the cultural deficit theory, which we have just discussed, because cultural difference adherents argue that the academic failures of students from diverse backgrounds cannot be attributed to perceived disadvantages existing within a culture. Instead, school failure results principally because there is a mismatch (difference) between students' cultures and the cultures of the schools themselves (Blanchett, 2009; Artiles, Kozleski, Trent, Osher, & Ortiz, 2010).

Within the broad cultural difference theory there is a subtheory called the **cultural reproduction theory** (Bowles & Gintas, 1976; Skiba et al., 2008). It holds that inequity is created and reproduced continually through individual and organizational decisions that create privilege for some groups at the expense of curtailing privilege for others.

How might these theories be educationally useful for De'ja's teachers? Certainly the genetic deficit theories are unhelpful. What about the cultural deficit theory? Undoubtedly, Sharilyn has lived on the economic edge; poverty is a fact of her everyday existence.

But her ambition for De'ja—"De'ja, you have to go to school and work hard every day. A young black girl has to get her education or else end up like me"—belies any surrender to that harsh reality and in fact uses it as a motivator for her daughter.

What about the cultural difference theory? Although De'ja's teachers do not use the theory of cultural difference to explain how they relate to De'ja and Sharilyn, it might serve them well to do so. Consider what you learned about Sharilyn in the vignette that opened this chapter, and then remember that all of De'ja's teachers and school administrators are fully certified, highly qualified professionals. We will return to the cultural difference theory throughout this chapter because it has so many implications for what you do and how you do it when working with students and families from diverse backgrounds.

School Systems' Responses to Theories

The theories about genetic deficit, cultural deficit, and cultural difference have played important roles in American education. During the early to mid-19th century, for example, advocates of the common school focused on developing educational programs that would provide all children with equal educational opportunities in integrated settings. They believed that an education that focused on basic skills, morality, and citizenship would put students from immigrant backgrounds (those from culturally or linguistically diverse backgrounds) on par with even the most privileged European American students born in the United States.

Nonetheless, students whose families immigrated to America still experienced school failure in large numbers and were often blamed for those failures, as though the fault were inherent in them and not in a school system that did not take their cultural differences into account but remained rigidly Eurocentric. Interestingly, at the same time, some states were enacting antiliteracy laws that prohibited educators from teaching free or enslaved African Americans how to read (Span, 2003).

During the last half of the 19th century, educators commonly retained in grade second- and third-generation students from immigrant backgrounds as well as African American students. These retention rates were alarmingly high, yet only rarely did these same educators entertain the notion that students' poor performance might be linked to a combination of factors such as inappropriate instruction and racial discrimination (Deschenes, Cuban, & Tyack, 2001).

Inequities in education have existed for centuries in the United States.

The progressive movement of the first half of the 20th century produced educational reforms designed to promote educational equity for all students through differentiated instruction. Many educators believed that the new technology of standardized testing, when combined with differentiated instruction, would result in school placements that were more aligned with students' abilities and that differentiated placements—tracking—would provide the differently placed students with the skills they needed to be successful in life (Safford & Safford, 1998).

However well intentioned, the consequence of differentiated instruction and standardized testing (administered in English) was that many children from immigrant backgrounds were retained in grade or assigned to schools' remedial and vocational tracks. In turn, many students from racially/ethnically diverse backgrounds were segregated from their more "typical" European American peers largely because of their race, socioeconomic status, immigrant status, and language (Safford & Safford, 1998). School segregation mirrored segregation in nearly every other facet of public life (Mickelson, 2003).

In the middle of the 20th century, civil rights activists and their allies frontally attacked segregation itself, in all of its forms. These reformers focused on the most American of American institutions: schools and school racial segregation. They argued that the 14th Amendment to the U.S. Constitution, which prohibits a state from denying equal protection of the laws to anyone in its jurisdiction, required the schools to desegregate by race. In what many regard as one of its most far-reaching decisions, the U.S. Supreme Court, in *Brown v. Board of Education* (1954), agreed and ordered the defendants in the case (school boards in Topeka, Kansas, and state education agencies in Delaware, South Carolina, and Virginia) to desegregate by race with all due deliberate speed (Blanchett, 2009; Skiba et al., 2008).

One early consequence of school racial desegregation was that, as enrollment of culturally and linguistically diverse children in previously all-white schools increased, so did their enrollment in self-contained programs for students who allegedly were "mildly mentally retarded" (Blanchett, 2009; Dunn, 1968; Mercer, 1973; National Research Council, 2002). History was repeating itself. Educators were tracking both African American and Latino students into programs for students with intellectual disability (at that time, the term was *mental retardation*) and justifying their decisions with students' scores on standardized tests, which were usually administered in English and not in students' native languages (Mercer, 1973).

Inarguably, *Brown* and other school-classification/segregation cases were the legal foundation that made it possible for advocates for students with disabilities to challenge classification procedures and seek the remedy of a free appropriate public education in the least restrictive environment (Turnbull, Stowe, & Huerta, 2007; Turnbull, Shogren, & Turnbull, 2011). As you learned in Chapter 1, these advocates were successful: Congress enacted P.L. 94–142, the Education for All Handicapped Children Act, in 1975. That law remains in effect today, renamed Individuals with Education Disabilities Act, or IDEA, and amended to account for research on teaching and learning and to reflect modern understandings about the lives of students with disabilities and the nation's four goals: equal opportunity, independent living, full participation, and economic self-sufficiency (which you learned about in Chapter 1).

Just as African American students used the theory of equal opportunity and the facts of racial segregation to defeat school segregation, advocates for both Latino and African American students subsequently used the same theory and the same kinds of data—the demographics of segregated placement—to successfully attack special education classification based on standardized tests administered in English to students who were not English-speaking (*Diana v. State Board of Education,* 1970; *Larry P. v. Riles,* 1972/1974/1979/1984).

The basis for IDEA's nondiscriminatory evaluation principle was a lawsuit brought by advocates for students with disabilities against the state of California (Turnbull et al., 2007). In that suit, the advocates alleged that the state and its schools classified students by relying on tests that were inherently biased against students from racially and linguistically diverse backgrounds. They even sought to prevent the state's school system from using standardized tests for evaluating students and classifying them into special education. They were resoundingly successful. In *Larry P. v. Riles* (1972/1974/1979/1984), a federal court held that the tests were inherently discriminatory and ordered the state and its schools to abandon the tests, use tests that were not discriminatory, and use other means for evaluating students for school placement. Each of those three remedies found its way into IDEA's principle of nondiscriminatory evaluation (Chapter 1). You will find them in the evaluation processes we describe in Chapters 5 through 16.

Disproportionate Representation

Because you know something about the history of special education and its relationship to segregation, you may be wondering about segregation in special education nowadays. The fact is that students from so-called diverse backgrounds are disproportionately segregated. There are three data sources related to disproportionality: (1) the proportion of students served in special education by disability and race/ethnicity, (2) the percentage of students in special education in different educational environments by race/ethnicity, and (3) the percentage of students in racial/ethnic groups participating in education for students who are classified as gifted.

As you read in Chapter 1, terminology is important, so a note about our use of terms is appropriate. Throughout all chapters, when we refer to racial/ethnic groups, we primarily use the terms *African American, Asian, European American, Latino,* and *Native American/Alaska Native.* In this section, when we include figures with data from the U.S. Department of Education, we use the terms that are cited in the figures, which usually results in replacing *black* for *African American* and *white* for *European American.* As you learned in Chapter 1, the term *intellectual disability* now has replaced the term *mental retardation.* We use *mental retardation* only when we are referring to government charts that still use this outdated term.

RISK RATIOS

Risk ratio is the first aspect of disproportionality. Figure 3.2 identifies the **risk ratios** for students ages six through twenty-one receiving special education and related services by race/ethnicity and disability category (U.S. Department of Education, 2010). Risk ratios compare the proportion of a specific racial/ethnic group receiving special education services to the proportion among the combined total of other racial/ethnic groups receiving special education.

FIGURE 3.2

Risk ratios for students ages six through twenty-one receiving special education and related services for a given primary disability category under IDEA, Part B, by race/ethnicity: Autumn 2005*

Disability**	American Indian/ Alaska Native	Asian/Pacific Islander	Black (not Hispanic)	Hispanic	White (not Hispanic)
Specific learning disabilities	1.80	0.40	1.43	1.17	0.78
Speech or language impairments	1.37	0.73	1.03	0.93	1.06
Mental retardation	1.29	0.48	2.86	0.69	0.61
Emotional disturbance	1.57	0.27	2.28	0.55	0.84
Multiple disabilities	1.36	0.63	1.50	0.68	1.01
Hearing impairments	1.34	1.20	1.10	1.28	0.77
Orthopedic impairments	0.97	0.83	1.01	1.15	0.94
Other health impairments	1.23	0.35	1.16	0.47	1.50
Visual impairments	1.45	0.97	1.21	0.94	0.92
Autism	0.73	1.28	0.98	0.57	1.33
Deaf-blindness	1.67	1.09	0.84	1.09	0.99
Traumatic brain injury	1.48	0.59	1.16	0.67	1.21
All disabilities above	1.54	0.51	1.47	0.92	0.89

Source: U.S. Bureau of the Census. (2005). Population data. Retrieved August 2006, from http://www.census.gov/popest/states/asrh/files/sc_est2004_alldata6.csv.

U.S. Department of Education, Office of Special Education Programs, Data Analysis System. (2004). Children with disabilities receiving special education under Part B of the Individuals with Disabilities Education Act. (OMB #1820-0043), Vol. 2, Tables 1-16, 1-16a–1-16m, B-7. These data are for the fifty states, the District of Columbia, and Bureau of Indian Affairs schools and were updated on July 17, 2006.

U.S. Department of Education. (2010). 29th annual report to Congress on the implementation of the Individuals with Disabilities Education Act, 2007 (Vo1. 1). Washington, DC: Author.

*This and the following notes refer to text within the U.S. Department of Education's 29th Annual Report explaining how the department calculated risk ratios. The document's Tables 1-12 and 1-13, mentioned in the notes to our figure, accompany its explanation of the risk ratios. Risk ratios were calculated by dividing the risk index for the racial/ethnic group by the risk index for all other racial/ethnic groups combined and rounding the result to two decimal places. See Table 1-12.

**States' use of the developmental delay category, which is optional for children between ages six and nine and not applicable to children older than nine years of age, is not listed in Table 1-13. For more information on the category and states with differences in developmental delay reporting practices, see Appendix B, Table B-3.

The risk ratio of 1.0 represents expected representation. Risk ratios higher than 1.0 reflect overrepresentation for a particular racial/ethnic group as compared to the combination of all other groups; likewise, a risk ratio below 1.0 indicates underrepresentation of a particular group as compared to the combination of others. For example, in the column for black students, you can see that their risk ratio for specific learning disabilities is 1.43, meaning that they are 1.43 times more likely to receive special education for learning disabilities than are their chronological age peers from all other racial/ethnic groups combined. As you review and analyze Figure 3.2, you will note the following trends:

- Across all disability categories, American Indian/Alaska Native and black students are 1.54 and 1.47, respectively, as likely to receive special education and related services as are Asian/Pacific Islander, Hispanic, and white students.

- The largest risk ratio for students who are American Indian/Alaska Native is learning disabilities (1.80), and the largest for students who are black is intellectual disability (2.86).

- Asian/Pacific Islander (.51), Hispanic (.92), and white (.89) students are underrepresented in special education.

These are national figures for students ages six through twenty-one. An analysis of preschool trends in five states reveals that Native American/Alaska Native and African American students were each overrepresented in one state out of five (Morrier & Gallagher, 2010). Results from this state study of preschool disproportionality underscore the importance of examining state rather than national data. For example, Native American students range from a low risk ratio of .29 in one state to a high risk ratio of 2.25 in another state. This variability underscores the importance of analyzing data by state as well as considering national trends. Variations also exist at local levels, as you will learn later in this chapter.

PERCENTAGE OF STUDENTS IN SPECIAL EDUCATION IN DIFFERENT ENVIRONMENTS BY RACE/ETHNICITY

The second aspect of disproportionality is the extent to which students are included in general education classrooms rather than more restrictive settings. Figure 3.3 highlights the percentage of students ages six through twenty-one who receive special education and related services in different educational environments, according to race/ethnicity (U.S. Department of Education, 2010).

Overrepresentation of culturally and linguistically diverse students in special education placements remains a problem today.

Black students with disabilities are least likely to spend the greatest amount of time in the general education classroom and are most likely to spend the greatest time in special settings. Alternatively, white students with disabilities are most likely to experience inclusiveness rather than restrictiveness. De'ja, however, participates in the general education courses in reading, writing, science, math, and social studies with support in reading, math, and study hall from a special educator.

GIFTED EDUCATION PLACEMENT

What about the representation of students across racial/ethnic groups in programs for students regarded as gifted? The answer comes from data about the percentage of gifted and talented students in public elementary and secondary schools by race/ethnicity (U.S. Department of Education, 2009). In the following list, each

FIGURE 3.3 *Percentage of students ages six through twenty-one with disabilities receiving special education and related services under IDEA, Part B, in each educational environment, by race/ethnicity: Autumn 2005*

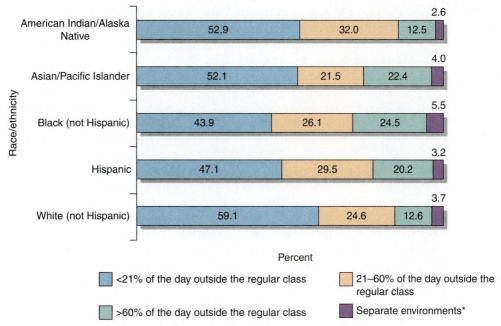

Source: U.S. Department of Education, Office of Special Education Programs, Data Analysis System. (2005). *Part B, Individuals with Disabilities Education Act, implementation of FAPE requirements* (OMB # 1820-0517), Vol. 2, Tables 2-7a–2-7e. These data are for the fifty states, the District of Columbia, Bureau of Indian Affairs schools, Puerto Rico, Guam, American Samoa, the Northern Marianas, and the Virgin Islands and were updated on July 17, 2006.

*The category of separate environments includes public and private residential facilities, public and private separate schools, and homebound/hospital environments.

percentage reported is the percentage of the total population of each racial/ethnic group within the gifted and talented public school programs.

- American Indian/Alaska Native: 5.2 percent
- Asian/Pacific Islander: 13.1 percent
- African American: 3.6 percent
- Latino: 4.2 percent
- European American: 8.8 percent
- Average total: 6.8 percent

Clearly, Asian/Pacific Islander and European American students are overrepresented in gifted programs, and American Indian/Alaska Native, African American, and Latino students are underrepresented.

Factors Associated with Disproportionate Representation and Educational Equality

You will better understand the data on disproportionality when you understand more about three key microcultures: race/ethnicity, language, and income level. It is difficult to separate these microcultures because they often overlap. To distinguish them, it helps to take two steps: First, understand the factors associated with each microculture; second, understand how these factors, individually and collectively, affect the educational success of many students from diverse backgrounds. It cannot be said that De'ja is not making progress in school; the data her teachers have accumulated show that she *is* progressing, although she is gaining faster in some courses than in others. Yet race and poverty may well have influenced her educational experiences and progress, as you will discover in the next section.

RACIAL/ETHNIC CONSIDERATIONS

The national data on placement in special education programs make it clear that African American and American Indian/Alaska Native students are at special risk of being identified as having a disability. They are also at risk for not being identified as eligible for gifted education. Most research and commentary on racial disproportionality have focused on African American students.

There are three special education categories in which educators have the greatest leeway for exercising their judgments about students' abilities and needs: learning disabilities, intellectual disabilities, and emotional and behavioral disorders (Artiles, Kozleski, Trent, Osher, & Ortiz, 2010). Often called "high-judgment categories," they include students with milder disabilities who are usually identified after starting school; and they rely on educational and psychological assessments that entail professional judgment. Review Figure 3.2 and note the risk ratios for American Indian/Alaskan Native and African American students in the areas of specific learning disabilities, intellectual disabilities, and emotional disturbance. What do you detect about the risk ratios for those three categories? Now compare those to the so-called "nonjudgment categories," such as orthopedic impairments and other health impairments, which tend to use assessments that rely more heavily on objective criteria. Do you see the discrepancies? Do you understand how high-judgment categories may reflect bias based on culture?

Figure 3.4 provides a composite of numerous factors that contribute to disproportionate opportunities for educational equality broken down by racial/ethnic groups. Note trends in terms of factors that are likely to facilitate and impede educational progress, especially the first factor (b.1).

Disproportionality exists because African American students are suspended approximately three times more than European American and Asian students and are expelled thirteen times more than European American students. Yet discipline can negatively influence opportunities to learn and achieve academically (Skiba, Eckes, & Brown, 2009/2010; Wallace, Goodkind, Wallace, & Bachman, 2008).

Figure 3.4 and its data on the percentage of students suspended or expelled by race/ethnicity do not reveal how many instructional hours these students lost, but the lost learning opportunities were certainly substantial and damaging. Culturally responsive discipline—discipline that is fair, caring, and committed to the student—is especially important as an effective way to reduce suspensions and expulsions and increase opportunities to learn (Cartledge & Kourea, 2008; Skiba, Eckes, & Brown, 2009).

IEP TIP

At the IEP conference, you should develop a discipline plan for a student who needs one, and you should make the plan culturally appropriate.

To use culturally responsive discipline, you should know about each student's culture and the intersection of your own cultural values with the student's. You should also set high academic and behavioral expectations for all students, use proactive strategies such as teaching social skills, and provide culturally relevant instruction (Cartledge, Singh, & Gibson, 2008). Equally important, you should employ positive behavior support strategies to reduce suspensions/expulsions and provide students from diverse backgrounds with greater opportunities to learn (Skiba & Sprague, 2008). You will learn about these strategies in Chapters 7, 10, and 11.

Discipline is not a problem for the educators who work with De'ja. They note in her IEP that she sometimes is "easily upset and pulled off task by others" and can become "very frustrated with the other students" because she "has some difficulty distinguishing between a person doing something by accident and a person doing something on purpose." But they also speak about her personality as a "plus" for her, and they praise her resiliency in dealing with the challenges she faces.

When a male classmate began to bully her verbally (with sexual and racial innuendos constituting the majority of his taunts), De'ja responded by not going to school. Her truancy impeded her progress; her IEP addressed that issue and her academic scores. Nothing that Sharilyn did—no degree of complaining to the school staff—seemed to blunt the bullying . . . until Sharilyn told one of De'ja's teachers that, the year before, she had been so angry that she had thought about giving De'ja a gun to bring to school. Upon hearing that comment, the teacher immediately contacted the school security officer, who was duty-bound to investigate. He went to Sharilyn's home, confronted her, determined she had no intention to give a gun or other weapon to De'ja, and then filed a report with the local police department.

FIGURE 3.4

Factors differentially associated with students from diverse racial/ethnic backgrounds
(rounded to the nearest percentage point)

Indicator	Total	White	Black	Hispanic	Asian	American Indian/ Alaska Native
A. Student/family						
a.1 Percentage distribution of family households, by female householder, no husband present	25	17	56	28	11	38
a.2 Percentage of children ages 6–18 whose mother had not completed high school	13	5	13	39	15	19
a.3 Percentage distribution of elementary and secondary students who speak a language other than English at home	21	6	6	69	64	16
a.4 Percentage of fourth graders eligible for free or reduced-priced lunch	48	29	74	77	34	68
a.5 Percentage of children ages 12–17 who used alcohol during past month	16	18	10	15	8	*
a.6 Number of live births per 1,000 females ages 15–19	43	27	64	82	17	59
a.7 Percentage of people ages 18–24 enrolled in colleges and universities	40	44	32	26	58	22
B. School factors						
b.1 Percentage of public school students in grades 6–12 who had ever been suspended	22	16	43	22	11	14
b.2 Percentage of public school students in grades K–12 who had ever been expelled	3	1	13	3	*	*
b.3 Percentage of public school students in grades K–12 who had ever repeated a grade	12	9	21	12	4	13
b.4 Percentage of people ages 16–24 who were high school dropouts in 2003	9	5	8	21	6	19
b.5 Percentage distribution of students below basic reading achievement levels in grade 8	26	16	43	42	20	44
b.6 Percentage distribution of students below basic math achievement levels in grade 8	27	17	50	43	15	44
b.7 Percentage of high school students who reported that they had engaged in a physical fight on school property	12	10	18	16	15	10

Source: From Aud, S., Fox, M. A., & KewalRamani, A. (2010). *Status and trends in the education of racial and ethnic minorities.* Washington, DC: U.S. Department of Education.

*Reporting standards not met.

Incensed that the school staff would cause a police officer to investigate a conversation that related to the previous year, Sharilyn cut off almost all contact with De'ja's teachers. Now the school social worker communicates with one of Sharilyn's friends, who in turn communicates with Sharilyn. The school began closely monitoring the bully and has developed a plan to shape the boy's behavior. The plan is working: De'ja is back in school.

Box 3.1 adds a valuable perspective about mediating cultural differences. Its author, Michael Lamb, graduated from an elite private school in Chicago and from an equally selective university. Turning his back on law school and an unquestionably bright financial future, he chose to return to Chicago and teach in the general education program in its public schools. His story is worth your careful attention. Notice how he converts the traditional "three Rs" (reading, writing, and arithmetic) into the "four Rs": respect, relationships, rigor, and resilience. Just consider how supported De'ja and Sharilyn would feel if they had the benefits of the four-R approach.

BOX 3.1 **MY VOICE**

The Four-R Approach

"Mr. Lamb, why do I gotta raise my hand?"

"I ain't no little kid!"

"You not my daddy!"

As a first-year reading teacher on Chicago's South Side, I often heard these comments. On good days, I faced skepticism; on bad, defiance.

To my students, I had no depth. Why, I asked myself, can't they detect my good intentions? Why don't they give me the benefit of the doubt? How can I reach and convince them?

I was shocked when my assistant principal told me in my second month at the school, "I think you've lost them for the year. You'll just have to try to find some way to make the best of it." Was this how my teaching career would go: Was I a white liberal with good intentions who would ultimately fail? I intended to make the opposite result happen.

Critical self-reflection forced me to realize that I had no context to my students. Half of the staff left the school each year, and students had no idea why I would stay, let alone genuinely care about them. I had been operating on assumptions about myself and my students, but to communicate with them, I had to ask myself: Why am I here? Is it about me or about them? Who am I and where did I come from? What do I bring to them? What strengths do they bring to the table? I found that the most important tools were concepts any teacher can use.

I needed to make my respect for my students, their families, and their lives clear. No matter who I was, what decisions I had made in my own life, or what my values were, I had to show them that I respected their essential humanity, their innate goodness.

Nor could I let their misbehavior cause me to think that they were flawed. Equally, I could not judge them by their test scores alone. I had to affirm that each could become a better reader, regardless of his or her scores.

Now I started to connect with my students. However, it was not until I brought my mother to school for Thanksgiving that relationships began to form. I knew about the importance of relationships, but I was not sure exactly how to build them.

I had determined that my students' parents were essential for both me and their children's education. I called all of them the first day of school, seeking their trust. At the first parent-teacher conference, I said I was all about power and opportunity for our students. From then on, they were major resources for me. I do not remember one interaction that ended negatively that year. But I couldn't get my students to buy in.

I thought about relationships and differences and realized I needed to find roots with my students. Could they and I transcend the power-over relationship in which I was dominant and they were acquiescent? I believed so; now, my duty would be to reach out and learn about my students.

To reach out meant giving them the benefit of the doubt and teaching them to give the same to me. We had to find ways to create relationships. With a relationship, we could understand; with understanding, we could give each the benefit of any doubts. We could begin to trust, to solve our problems together.

When I brought my mother to class before Thanksgiving, my students saw me as not just their teacher but as a man with a visible origin and palpable values.

They asked her, "What was he like as a kid?"

They asked me, "What was your most embarrassing moment?" We began to see each other as people; the common humanity became manifest. Now my students saw me as a more whole person; they also could get some dirt on me. My mother was now "Grandma," making me "School Daddy." They were still skeptical, but less so; still angry, but less so.

Late in the fall term, I asked my assistant principal for guidance. She turned the question back on me, asking what I had learned at my high school and what I thought my students deserved to know. That was a turning point: thereafter, I built rigor into my curriculum. We would become critical thinkers together, whether reading Shakespeare's *Much Ado About Nothing* or Bradbury's *Fahrenheit 451*.

I knew I could not control whether my students liked me or thought I was cool. But I could control my academic expectations of them. I knew hard work in school gave me power to make my own decisions about the opportunities that came to me because of that work.

I was determined to give my students this same sense of control over their own futures by insisting on hard work and academic rigor. At the start of the school year, only 12 percent of my eighth-grade students met standards on the Illinois Test of Basic Skills (ITBS) reading test; at the end, 71 percent met national standards on the state test. The next year I began a two-year loop with my new homeroom. After the seventh- and eighth-grade years, these students had the same success: from only 12 percent achieving standards, 67 percent did. Three of them who had started below the thirty-sixth percentile ended up scoring in the ninety-fourth during their eighth-grade year.

Expecting hard work also caused the students to feel more respected. When low expectations exist, students feel unchallenged; they believe their teachers are condescending.

When challenges arise, resilience is essential. My students usually would get into trouble or fail academically because they let little issues spiral out of control; they were uncertain of forgiveness and lacked strategies to resolve routine problems. When called to account for minor matters, they would escalate their reactions; they did not expect understanding and forgiveness.

Challenged by test questions or difficult reading passages, they would make the problem appear to be a question of their behavior instead of their intelligence.

But I talked about overcoming obstacles. And they began to open themselves up to conflict- and problem-resolution strategies, whether they were interacting with other students or reading a difficult passage. Simply shifting their mindset to one that left them open to solutions and resolution was a major accomplishment for them.

For us as teachers, the question is this: What respect, relationships, rigor, and resilience have we helped put into place to provide our students with opportunities to respond with better versions of themselves? Arguments about each other's mommas and their struggles to comprehend Shakespeare or Bradbury will happen. But who will students become as a result of these challenges?

—*Michael Lamb*
Chicago, Illinois

LANGUAGE CONSIDERATIONS

It is difficult to teach you about language as an element of culture unless we lay a foundation that consists of several points. The first point has to do with terminology. Formerly, teachers described students who need special language instruction because of their cultural background as being limited English proficient (LEP). More often nowadays, they refer to them as English language learners. They may even use the abbreviation ELLs. In the spirit of using person-first language, as we recommend in Chapter 1, we use the phrase "students who are learning English." That phrase, rather than LEP or ELL, is consistent with Barrera's (2006) recommendation to use a "more respectful manner of reference to these students" (p. 142).

The second point relates to students' English proficiency. Quite naturally, students vary in their English proficiency. That proficiency can be represented by a continuum of five stages (Hoover, Klingner, Baca, & Patton, 2008):

- *Stage 1: Silence/receptive or preproduction stage.* Students understand approximately 500 English words but cannot use them. For one to six months, students tend to rely on gestures, body language, or yes/no responses.
- *Stage 2: Early production stage.* Students expand their receptive vocabulary to about 1,000 words and begin to use short phrases to respond to simple questions. This stage lasts for about six months.
- *Stage 3: Speech emergence stage.* Students' receptive vocabulary expands to about 3,000 words. They begin to use simple sentences. This stage often lasts for one year.
- *Stage 4: Intermediate language proficiency stage.* For another year or so, students expand their understanding and use about 6,000 words. They move from simple to complex statements, provide opinions, and are able to write essays.
- *Stage 5: Advanced language proficiency stage.* During the final stage, students have a vocabulary and grammar comparable to same-age native speakers. They can participate in content discussions at grade level and can succeed in complicated writing tasks. Reaching Stage 5 may take five to seven years.

Obviously, it takes a student who does not use English a long time to master it for school purposes. While the student is learning English, she also must master the content of a curriculum offered in English. The lack of useful English undoubtedly impedes that mastery and may suggest to some teachers that the student has a disability. But be cautious of reaching that conclusion: The student may simply need to learn the majority language.

Demographics about students who are learning English are astonishing (Skinner, Wight, Aratani, Cooper, & Thampi, 2010):

- Among children ages five through seventeen, 21 percent speak a language other than English at home. Over the past thirty years, this rate has grown four times faster than the rate of the nation's population growth.
- The states with the largest number of children and families with limited English proficiency include California, Florida, Illinois, New Jersey, New York, and Texas. Only 19 percent of students learning English scored above the state norm on reading comprehension assessments given in English. Students who receive bilingual education perform better than students who are in all-English classrooms.

Of the students who are receiving English instruction, 454,332 between the ages of six and twenty-one are also served in special education, as are 47,746 between the ages of three and five (U.S. Department of Education, 2008). Remarkably, students who are learning English speak more than 400 different languages, with Spanish by far the most prevalent (U.S. Department of Education, 2001). Look again at the data in Figure 3.4, especially "a.3 Percentage distribution of elementary and secondary students who speak a language other than English at home." Clearly, the fact that approximately two thirds of Latino and Asian students do not speak English at home provides evidence of a link between language proficiency and race/ethnicity.

IEP TIP

At the IEP conference, you must comply with IDEA by communicating with students' parents in their preferred language, which may be their native language.

There is a positive relationship between participating in programs for students who are learning English and being identified as having a learning disability. Nationally, an analysis of patterns from 750 schools documented the likelihood that students who are learning English have a greater chance of being identified as having a learning disability than are students who are proficient in English (Shifrer, Muller, & Callahan, 2010). An analysis of placement trends of students learning English (with more than 90 percent being of Latino heritage) found that in California the proportion of students receiving special education services across the state was proportional; however, within this overall statewide proportionality, there were pockets of disproportionality (Artiles, Rueda, & Salazar, 2005):

- In the three largest urban districts, students learning English were disproportionately identified as having a disability.

- Elementary-level placement patterns were proportional; however, at the end of elementary school and throughout high school, placement patterns were disproportional.

- Students with limitations in both their native language and in English had the highest rate of being identified as having a disability.

- Students learning English who were also from low-income backgrounds had larger representation in special education programs than did their counterparts with middle and higher incomes

Similarly, an analysis of district placement trends in a school district comprised of 12.1 percent students who were learning English indicated that these students were more likely to be identified as having learning disabilities and to be placed in more segregated educational settings than were students with English proficiency (de Valenzuela, Copeland, Qi, & Park, 2006).

Consistent with IDEA and best practices, assessments used in the nondiscriminatory evaluation process to identify students for possible special education placement must not penalize students who are learning English (Hoover & Méndez Barletta, 2008). Yet there is evidence of the extensive misuse of assessment instruments (Klingner, deSchonewise, Onis, & Méndez Barletta, 2008; Rodriguez, 2009). Under IDEA, students must be tested in their primary language so that educators can make careful distinctions between disabilities and language proficiency. Additionally, good practice is that students must be provided with instruction that enables them to advance their conceptual and academic development through their primary language while learning English in a way that is contextualized, relevant, and understandable (Klingner, Hoover, & Baca, 2008; Rodriguez, 2009). The inclusion tips provided in Box 3.2 will help you consider how to be culturally responsive to students who are learning English.

An overlooked issue is language diversity as it relates to Native American students. Native American students and families have experienced *language loss*. More than 300 Native American languages were used in the United States in the 19th century, but approximately half of those still exist today (Aguilera & LeCompte, 2007). As of about ten years ago, only about fifty of these languages were being taught to children, and only about twenty were used widely by children.

When a student loses his or her native language, the student also loses the "soul" of his or her culture, the "wisdom of ancestors," the "gods" deserving of prayers, the "land" lived on, and his or her own "government and sovereignty" (Kameyeleihiwa, cited in Aguilera & LeCompte, 2007, p. 11). Fortunately, language programs have been developed to promote the maintenance of the language of Native American students and to teach them English (Hermes, 2007; Holgate, 2009; Yazzie-Mintz, 2007).

POVERTY CONSIDERATIONS

Although children represent approximately one fourth of the U.S. population, 36 percent of all people living in poverty in the United States are children (Chau, Thampi, & Wight, 2010). Although *poverty* is officially defined as having an income of $22,050 a year for a family of four, families need approximately twice this income level to meet their expenses

BOX 3.2 **INCLUSION TIPS**

	What You Might See	**What You Might Be Tempted to Do**	**Alternate Responses**	**Ways to Include Peers in the Process**
Behavior	A Latino student who is an English-language learner and has learning disabilities puts her head on her desk when she does not understand written instructions. She rarely completes assignments.	Tell her that she should go to bed at a reasonable hour so that she can stay awake and complete her classwork.	List steps of the instructions in sequence on the board. Use pictures whenever possible. Ask her parents how help is requested and provided in their culture.	Model the skill of asking for help for all students and let them role-play. Provide reinforcement when they use the skill and encourage their classmates to use it.
Social interactions	She rarely initiates a greeting but usually responds to one appropriately.	Do not push her to initiate because you believe this skill will develop as her English improves.	Have students share greetings from the different languages represented in the classroom.	Have this student and others teach the different greetings and reinforce the use of them in and outside the classroom.
Educational performance	The student has strong math skills but performs poorly on word problems when she has to read them.	Request that she have more time outside of the general education classroom for intensive English instruction.	Provide word problems in her native language and English.	Establish a peer tutoring system within the class. She can tutor students who have problems with computation. Students who share the same primary language can help her read the word problems.
Classroom attitudes	She complains of a head- or a stomachache and asks to go to the clinic when assigned to read a children's novel and answer comprehension questions in written form.	Allow her to go to the clinic, hoping that she will grow out of this behavior as her English improves.	Try to obtain a copy of the book in her native language.	Have students work in cooperative groups to read and answer questions together.

(Wight, Chau, & Aratani, 2010). Some of the implications of poverty are as follows (Chau et al., 2010; Wight et al., 2010):

- 69 percent live with a single parent.
- 17 percent do not have health insurance.
- 21 percent do not have adequate food.

Race/ethnicity and disability status are both highly related to poverty levels. Children who are African American, American Indian/Pacific Islander, and Latino are approximately three times more likely to experience poverty as compared to European American students and twice as likely as compared to Asian students (Wight et al., 2010). Further, slightly more than one third of students with disabilities live in households with incomes of $25,000 or less as compared to approximately one fourth of students in the general population (Wagner, Marder, Blackorby, & Cardoso, 2002).

Homelessness is also highly associated with poverty. The McKinney-Vento Homeless Assistance Improvements Act of 2001 authorizes services to assist schools to educate students who are homeless. When Congress reauthorized IDEA in 2004, it required state and local education agencies to make special efforts to serve homeless students with disabilities (Jozefowicz-Simbeni & Israel, 2006). A child who is homeless is defined as one who does not have a stable and consistent nighttime residence (U.S. Department of Education, 2002). In part because Sharilyn cannot always pay rent, she and De'ja have lived in different places, sometimes several different ones each school year, in their hometown. They are not exactly homeless. But their residence is not particularly stable. Because she moves from one place to another, De'ja misses school more often than many other students do, and her academic progress suffers.

Approximately 1.5 million children live in families that are homeless (Aratani, 2009). Children who are African American and American Indian/Alaska Native have higher rates of homelessness as compared to children from other racial/ethnic groups (National Center for Family Homelessness, 2009).

A number of trends contribute to the problem of homelessness (Aratani, 2009):

- The availability of affordable housing units has declined over the past decade.

- The rate of unemployment has increased, especially for adults who have jobs not requiring professional education.

- More than 80 percent of families who are homeless are female-headed.

- Slightly more than 80 percent of mothers who are homeless have experienced domestic violence.

- Among youth in foster care, 49 percent report a history of running away; and among American Indian/Alaska Native youth, the rate of running away is twice that of European American youth.

As an effective teacher, you can use several strategies to make a positive difference for students who experience poverty (Turnbull, Turnbull, Summers, & Poston, 2008):

- "Standing in the shoes" of students who experience poverty and seeking to understand the increased difficulties of concentrating on academic work given challenges associated with hunger, health care, cleanliness, and stress that result from environmental factors such as unsafe neighborhoods

- Partnering with the school social worker and/or school counselor to provide information to families on government benefits that are designed to assist families who experience poverty and have children with disabilities, such as Supplemental Security Income and Medicaid

- Partnering with other educators in referring families to community agencies that provide economic resources related to food banks, job training, and affordable housing

- Connecting students with organizations interested in providing direct support to students who have economic needs, such as Big Sister/Big Brother programs, community service programs, and religious programs

- Providing clear and understandable information to parents who have low levels of education to ensure that they are comfortable in developing a trusting partnership with you to support their child's educational success

RELATIONSHIPS AMONG RACE/ETHNICITY, LANGUAGE, AND POVERTY

As the evidence indicates, race/ethnicity, language, and income intersect to affect the classification of students into a disability category or into programs for students who have unusual gifts and talents. Figure 3.5 depicts the many factors that ultimately influence classification and student outcomes. It consists of six levels, starting from the macro (largest) perspective of values and then reflecting increasingly smaller (macro to micro) factors (Bronfenbrenner, 1979).

Figure 3.5 shows you the big picture, the multiple influences that affect children, families, and schools and how those influences align with race, language, and poverty. It suggests that it is wrong to conclude that all of the problems you may face in educating

IEP TIP

When school social workers and school counselors are members of the IEP team, you can partner with them to identify how schools can reduce the educational challenges facing students from poverty backgrounds.

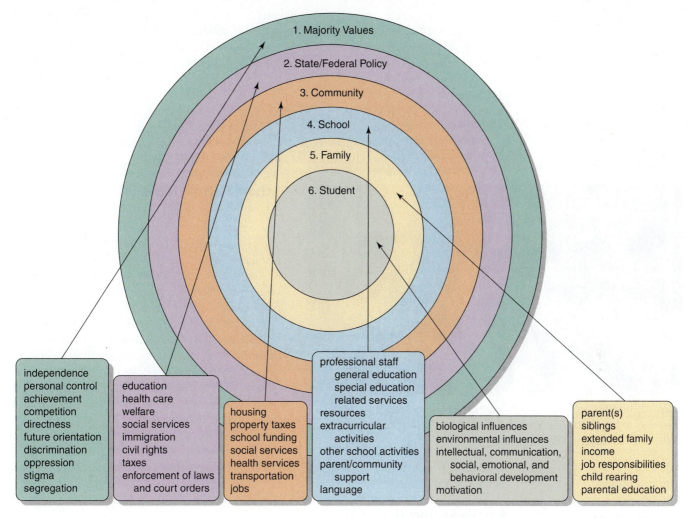

students reside in and originate from the students and their families (Blanchett, 2009; Skirtic & McCall, 2010). Let's examine Figure 3.5 in depth.

Majority Values (Layer 1)

As a rule, Americans value independence, personal control, achievement, competition, directness, future orientation, and so on (Hanson, 2004). These values are culturally rooted in our nation's history, but that does not mean they are the only acceptable ones.

Some American families have different cultural values. They believe in interdependence rather than independence, elder control rather than personal control, contentment rather than achievement, cooperation rather than competition, indirectness rather than directness, and present orientation rather than future orientation (Lynch & Hanson, 2004). Nevertheless, the standard expectation is that students will adhere to majority values and use English at school (Artiles et al., 2010; Blanchett, Klingner, & Harry, 2009; Monzo & Rueda, 2009).

State/Federal Policy Factors (Layer 2)

The second ecological layer, state/federal policy, includes legislation and court decisions, especially those dealing with education, health care, welfare, immigration, and civil rights. But tax policy is also important: Without funds, schools are impoverished. Thus, if communities (Layer 3) and schools (Layer 4) are going to be able to make improvements, state and federal policy, including tax policy, must be taken into account (Skrtic & McCall, 2010).

Community Factors (Layer 3)

The interaction of race, language, and poverty is especially acute in urban communities and their schools (Blanchett et al., 2009; Gregory, Skiba, & Noguera, 2010; Skiba et al., 2008). The 100 largest school districts in the United States provide education to approximately 68 percent of students of color (Ayers, Ladson-Billings, Michie, & Noguera, 2008; National Center for Educational Statistics, 2001). These urban communities, as well as communities around the country that are not in urban settings, must deal with issues of housing, property taxes, school funding, social services, health services, transportation, and jobs in order to provide a community context that advances the education of students from diverse backgrounds. Schools (Layer 4), families (Layer 5), and students (Layer 6) are rarely able to improve unless their communities do too (Blanchett, Mumford, & Beachum, 2005).

Rarely do highly qualified teachers (such as the one pictures here) find their way to the classrooms where students from diverse background constitute the majority of all students.

School Factors (Layer 4)

School factors include the professional staff's qualifications, cultural responsiveness, and ongoing professional development. They also include resources in general education, special education, related services, and other supports. Other factors come into play, too: parental support of schools, community support of schools, extra curricular opportunities, and transportation. Unfortunately, schools that have the highest number of students from diverse backgrounds tend both to be in low-poverty districts and to have the greatest number of noncertified teachers, the highest teacher turnover, the most inadequate resources for providing differentiated instruction, the lowest overall funding, the highest class sizes, the least support from the principal and colleagues, the most distrusting relationships with families, and the greatest deficit of support from the community (Blanchett, 2010; Fall & Billingsley, 2011).

Family Factors (Layer 5)

You have already learned about a number of family factors that are associated with different racial/ethnic, language, and poverty trends: number of parents in the home, parental education, and family income (see Figure 3.4). According to Delgado and Scott (2006), the low education of mothers has a positive correlation with various risks for disability. For example the risk for mild intellectual disability is 9.9 times higher, for an emotional or behavioral disorder 5.3 times higher, and for a specific learning disability 2.1 times higher. Unfortunately, some educators blame parents for their children's problems when these educators should recognize that many parents from diverse backgrounds have been marginalized or oppressed. All too often, parents of the students are themselves victims of unequal opportunities and are so encased within the ecological layers of Figure 3.5 that they are not as free to change as some people who have not experienced oppression might believe. That is not to say that they do not have strengths related to their survival skills, religious faith, access to extended family support, diligence in spite of adversity, and strong desire for their children to have opportunities that they did not have as a child (Harry, 2008; Turnbull, Turnbull, Erwin, Soodak, & Shogren, 2011).

How does Sharilyn prevail? She and De'ja both receive Social Security benefits—Sharilyn because she has a disability and De'ja because she, too, has a disability and is in a family that the federal government classifies as poor. Sharilyn is active in a small church; some of its members have created a circle of support for her, substituting for her mother who lives an hour's drive away and is raising some of her other grandchildren. As you have already read, Sharilyn is adamant that De'ja should go to school, telling her that an education is the key to achieving De'ja's goal of being a chef. De'ja herself is resilient; she still attends school, is making progress there, and has endeared herself to her teachers.

Student Factors (Layer 6)

At last, we come to the students. It may be easy for some educators to criticize the students who do not achieve academically, whose behavior leads to classroom disruption, or who have excessive absenteeism. Using the ecological framework shown in Figure 3.5, however, they might easily understand that biological and environmental factors shape students' achievement, behavior, school attendance, and other characteristics.

What's the take-away message? It is that disproportionality in special education placement needs to be understood within the context of disproportionality in society across all six ecological layers of Figure 3.5 (Kozleski & Smith, 2009). To ensure equal opportunities for students from culturally diverse backgrounds, it is necessary to provide not only culturally responsive instruction of students but also culturally responsive support of families, culturally responsive support of schools, culturally responsive community living, culturally responsive state/federal policy, and culturally diverse societal values. Being a culturally responsive educator means being not only an effective teacher of students but also being an advocate at all six ecological layers.

Becoming a Culturally Responsive Teacher and Advocate

In this section, we offer four strategies that will assist you to be a culturally responsive teacher: enhancing your self-awareness, increasing your knowledge and experiences concerning other cultures, implementing culturally responsive instruction, and advocating for systems change across layers.

ENHANCING YOUR SELF-AWARENESS

To become more self-aware culturally, we all should examine our own cultural values; realize that they are cultural values rather than the ultimate truth about what is right and wrong; and become aware of our stereotypes, biases, and prejudices. Change may follow awareness; certainly change requires awareness (Cartledge & Kourea, 2008; Harry, 2008).

To examine your own culture, study Figure 3.6. You will see that it incorporates the picture of microcultures from Figure 3.1 and adds questions for you to consider in light of each one. As you use Figure 3.6 to reflect on your culture, keep a journal of your reflections, have conversations with friends and acquaintances within your own culture and across cultures, be perceptive to the social and political media, examine your own values, and ask whether your culture is really the one and only right way or just another way to follow.

INCREASING YOUR KNOWLEDGE AND EXPERIENCES OF OTHER CULTURES

It is fascinating to learn about other cultures. As students, you can join community and campus organizations with a diversity focus, have extended conversations with people from diverse backgrounds, and develop friendships with people from diverse backgrounds. In time, you may be invited to partake in their cultural traditions, holiday celebrations, and routines. You can follow international and national news stories about people from other cultures, read books about them, go to movies produced in other countries, take courses in cultural sociology or anthropology, and, if time and money permit, travel to other countries and try, while there, to get into spiritual community with the places you visit. Your studies of different cultures should identify the similarities and dissimilarities of that culture and your own. Consider the issues of independence and interdependence; determine which values the two cultures have in common and which they do not.

As you learn about other cultures, you will begin to understand how cultural values influence the ways in which families interpret the instruction that feels right to them. It

1. As you reflect on Figure 3.1 in terms of your own overall cultural identity and the microcultures that shape your cultural identity, which microcultures are most influential in how you characterize your culture and which are least influential?

2. In light of your overall cultural identity and the contributing factors associated with each microculture, what do you consider to be your core cultural values?

3. In light of your own experiences and cultural values, what are your preferences and biases regarding the microcultures that are different from your own? (Go through each microculture and think carefully about what it is that draws you to other people and what it is that makes you uncomfortable or tends to make you feel judgmental about other people.)

4. How might your cultural values influence your preferences to work with students with particular characteristics and your biases against working with students with other characteristics?

5. How do your cultural values influence your views of standards and expectations associated with
   - Academic achievement
   - Classroom behavior
   - Participation in extracurricular activities
   - Developing trusting partnerships with families
   - Likelihood of becoming a culturally responsive teacher
   - Likelihood of becoming a culturally responsive systems advocate

6. How do your own microcultures influence your reaction to the information in this chapter? Were there any times in reading this chapter that you felt uncomfortable or impatient? If so, how does your own cultural identity contribute to those reactions? If not, why not?

can be easy for European American educators not to realize how many educational approaches rely on European American values (Kalyanpur & Harry, 1999). For example, researchers describe the implementation of positive behavior support (you will learn about this approach in Chapter 10) with Chinese American families (Wang, McCart, & Turnbull, 2007). They provide a case study showing how educators who wanted to offer positive behavior support for Meng, a fourteen-year-old middle school student identified as having AD/HD and problem behavior, needed to take into account the fact that Meng's grandmother was the family's decision maker. Meng's father and mother were not, and certainly Meng was not.

The researchers had to acknowledge that it was consistent with the family's culture for Meng's parents to give her a cold face (a stern, reprimanding look) and not allow her to eat dinner if she had not finished her homework; these were punishing, not positive, responses. They had to understand that Meng's grandmother believed that Meng's problem behaviors resulted from something she, the grandmother, had done wrong in her previous life and were influenced by bad spirits. In short, they had to understand Meng's culture and then develop a culturally responsive intervention to suit her and her family.

IMPLEMENTING CULTURALLY RESPONSIVE INSTRUCTION

You can use the following four strategies to implement culturally appropriate instruction.

Use the Adapted Posture of Cultural Reciprocity

Let's return to Meng. Having expanded your knowledge and experience about different cultures theoretically, you should be able to enter into a partnership with Meng's family and then use an educational practice that is acceptable to them. That's easier said than done. Under this approach, you and Meng's family share your respective views about how to teach Meng; and you listen carefully (Harry, 2008; Kalyanpur & Harry, 1999). Box 3.3

BOX 3.3

PARTNERSHIP TIPS

Implementing Adapted Posture of Cultural Reciprocity

Steps in Adapted Posture of Cultural Reciprocity

1. Learn about the family's strengths, needs, preferences, and priorities by having informal conversations with them and by welcoming them and their child into your classroom. Identify their priorities and preferences for their child's educational program: IEP, placement, related services, extracurricular activities, and other school activities. Try to understand and honor their cultural values and priorities in order to establish a trusting partnership with them.

2. Invite the family to describe their cultural values and how they relate to their strengths, needs, preferences, and priorities. Ask why they have those values.

3. Identify any disagreements or alternative perspectives that you or other professionals have about providing educational supports and services to the student and/or family. Identify the cultural values embedded in *your* interpretation or in that of the other professionals. Identify how the family's views differ from your own.

4. Acknowledge and explicitly show respect for any cultural differences. Fully explain the cultural basis of your and your colleagues' professional assumptions or the assumptions of the student and family.

5. Through discussion and collaboration, determine the most effective way of adapting your and your colleagues' professional interpretations to the family's value system.

Decisions Made for Meng's Positive Behavior Support Plan

1. The behavior support team decided to use informal contacts (phone calls and home visits) rather than formal planning meetings at the beginning.

2. After Meng's family became more comfortable with her teachers, the behavior team asked a Chinese American teacher in her school to facilitate the behavior team.

3. The team recognized that Meng's family did not feel comfortable about being an equal partner and accommodated to their choice.

4. The team respected Meng's family priority about addressing learning issues before behavior issues.

5. The team demonstrated respect for Meng's grandmother and listened to and accepted her suggestions about herbal treatments.

6. The team did not criticize Meng's family or make judgments about their practices.

7. The team had many conversations about punishment and did not ask the family to give up their current discipline practices but did share information with them about alternative strategies.

8. The team supported the family's goal for Meng's academic expectations and encouraged her family to recognize the importance to Meng of having some after-school time without stress.

Readers interested in a much more detailed description of the partnership between the behavior team and Meng's family can read about it in Wang, M., McCart, A., & Turnbull, A. (2007). Implementing positive behavior support with Chinese American families: Enhancing cultural competence. *Journal of Positive Behavior Interventions, 9*(1), 38–51.

describes the adapted posture of cultural reciprocity and decisions that were made by Meng's positive behavior support team based on team members' responsiveness to the Chinese American values of Meng's family. Kalyanpur and Harry (1999) describe the purpose of the strategy of *posture of cultural reciprocity* as follows:

> Awareness of cultural differences provides merely the scaffolding for building collaborative relationships. Knowledge of the underlying belief and value that brings about the difference in perspective provides the reinforcing strength to the relationship. . . . We suggest that professionals . . . engage in explicit discussions with families regarding different cultural values and practices, bringing to the interactions an openness of mind, the ability to be reflective in their practice, and the ability to listen to the other perspectives. Furthermore, they must respect the new body of knowledge that emerges from these discussions and make allowances for differences in perspectives when responding to the family's need. (p. 118)

IEP TIP

During the IEP conference, you should use the adapted posture of cultural reciprocity to learn from culturally diverse parents their priorities and how those relate to their child's education.

Incorporate Five Components for Delivering Culturally Responsive Instruction

Having reached agreements with your students' families about their culturally driven priorities, you will need to instruct in ways that honor those understandings and the student's culture. Your instruction should "take into consideration the cognitive, linguistic, and social assets of an individual . . . that are culturally determined and shape the ways in which individuals learn and make sense of [their] experiences" (Klingner & Solano-Flores, 2007, p. 231). Box 3.4 depicts a useful framework for tailoring your instruction to the five components of culturally responsive instruction: (1) Integrate content into your curriculum, (2) help students understand cultural assumptions and biases, (3) create a curriculum that facilitates the academic growth of students from diverse backgrounds, (4) use your curriculum and teaching methods to modify your students' unacceptable racial attitudes, and (5) include your students in various decisions about their education (van Garderen & Whittaker, 2006).

Capitalize upon Instructional Consultation Teams

The good news is that you are not alone in your efforts to seek cultural responsiveness. A standard practice in schools is to have a referral process for special education. It is at the point of referral to special education that many problems associated with disproportionate placement begin. Thus, it has become increasingly prevalent for schools to develop a broad range of prereferral supports for students and for teachers in order to prevent inappropriate special education referrals.

Different methods for implementing prereferral strategies are often described by different names: for instance, instructional consultation teams (Gravois & Rosenfield, 2006; McDonough, 2009), child study teams (Klingner & Harry, 2006), intervention assistance teams (Ortiz, Wilkinson, Robertson-Courtney, & Kushner, 2006), and teacher assistance teams (Papalia-Beradi & Hall, 2007). The teams usually consist of general and special educators, bilingual specialists, school psychologists, and other specialists. Together, these professionals observe the student, brainstorm about the challenges and solutions, and create action plans to address the student's learning and behavioral challenges and ensure participation and progress in the general education curriculum.

These teams have been able to influence the disproportionate referral and placement of students from diverse backgrounds into special education. According to a study by Gravois and Rosenfield (2006), there were major differences between thirteen schools that used instructional consultation teams and nine schools that did not. After using such teams for two years, schools had lower rates of students from diverse backgrounds being placed in special education when compared to schools that did not use the teams. The consultation-team schools offered training, online coaching, and follow-up support related to collaborative and reflective communication skills, problem-solving skills, curriculum-based assessment, and collection and analysis of classroom data.

Comparable research confirmed that (1) instructional consultation teams lower the risk for special education placement for each racial/ethnic group (McDonough, 2009) and (2) parent involvement in prereferral processes decreases the likelihood that students are referred for special education evaluation (Chen & Gregory, 2010). Teachers' perspectives on satisfaction range from highly positive to neutral/slightly dissatisfied, probably linked to the quality of the support that they receive to improve the decisions they make about instruction (Kaiser, Rosenfield, & Gravois, 2010; Papalia-Berardi & Hall, 2007). The take-away lesson is this: Wherever you work in schools, inquire from the outset whether prereferral assistance is available and especially whether it is culturally responsive. If it is, take advantage of it.

Implement Response to Intervention

In Chapter 2 you learned about response to intervention (RTI). Just as RTI is effective for students with disabilities, so it seems to be effective at blunting diversity-based discrimination and unjustified placement into special education but only if it is comprehensively implemented through evidence-based practices (Kashi, 2008; Klingner, Méndez Barletta, & Hoover, 2008; Xu & Drame, 2008). Using RTI, educators explore how the students' social/cultural context influences their readiness and opportunities to learn and the extent to which evidence-based instruction is being delivered. Using a social/cultural perspective, you and other educators do not presume that a student's educational needs arise from cultural differences, disabilities, or other factors associated with that student (Haager, Klingner, & Vaughn, 2007). Instead, you and they inquire into issues surrounding the student's language and the cultural roots of his or her behavior, doing so before

BOX 3.4   **INTO PRACTICE**

Components and Action Steps for Culturally Responsive Instruction

Offering a culturally responsive curriculum can involve five different components. This box identifies each component, defines it, and describes the relevant action steps.

Components	Definition	Action Steps
Content Integration	Content integration involves teachers using examples and content from a variety of cultures and groups to illustrate key concepts, principles, generalizations, and theories in their subject area or discipline.	• Reading biographies of women and people of color who are scientists and mathematicians • Learning about demographics of diverse groups • Using primary documents about the history of non–Anglo-European peoples • Reading multicultural literature • Including images of many kinds of families in the curriculum
The Knowledge Construction Process	The knowledge construction process includes teachers helping students to understand, investigate, and determine how the implicit cultural assumptions, frames of references, perspectives, and biases within a discipline influence the ways in which knowledge is constructed within it.	• Examining the degree to which authors in the curriculum are female and/or people of color • Including the perspectives of both the dominant and non-dominant cultures in any description of historical conflict • Examining labels applied to people with disabilities from the perspective of the person • Validating the importance of languages other than English • Discussing the difference between Western and non-Western views on science • Interviewing community elders about their immigration experiences
An Equity Pedagogy	An equity pedagogy exists when teachers modify their teaching to facilitate the academic achievement of students from diverse racial, cultural, and social-class groups. This includes using a variety of teaching styles consistent with the wide range of learning styles within various cultural and ethnic groups.	• Knowing the cultural background of students and incorporating them into classroom instruction and procedures • Using cooperative learning or group experiences with students who learn best collaboratively • Placing students in pairs to encourage question-and-answer exchanges
Prejudice Reduction	This dimension focuses on the characteristics of students' racial attitudes and how they can be modified by teaching methods and materials.	• Making cooperative learning groups heterogeneous by gender, race, and language • Developing racial identity (e.g., through a family tree) • Teaching the concept of race as a social, not biological, construct • Studying various religions in the context of a winter holiday season or historical event
An Empowering School Culture and Social Structure	Grouping and labeling practices, sports participation, disproportionality in achievement, and the interaction of staff and students across ethnic and racial lines are components of the school culture that empowers students from diverse racial, ethnic, and cultural groups.	• Including students in determining classroom rules or allowing them choices of assignments • Including students with disabilities or all students who try out for a performance • Actively recruiting and hiring teachers of color • Reducing the numbers of African Americans and Latinos who are inappropriately placed in special education programs • Working with community groups to provide mentoring and tutoring programs • Involving families in school decision-making bodies

Source: Information from James A. Banks, *Cultural Diversity and Education*, 2006, p. 5. Upper Saddle River, NJ: Allyn & Bacon/Pearson Education.

Response to intervention is effective in all classrooms, especially in those with a mix of students from different backgrounds.

referring the student for special education evaluation or placement (Rinaldi & Samson, 2008).

We have already said that RTI is related to issues of diversity. Let's explore that statement. Box 3.5 identifies questions that you and other educators should address at each of RTI's three tiers to gather sufficient information about universal design for students who are learning English. Answers to these questions will enable you to consider and identify different means of representation, action/expression, and engagement to support students' progress in the general curriculum.

Encouragingly, an RTI program in kindergarten helped students who were learning English perform significantly better than their counterparts who were not part of the RTI program; further, the RTI program was just as effective for students who were learning English as it was for those

---

BOX 3.5

UNIVERSAL DESIGN FOR PROGRESS

Guiding Questions for Implementing RTI for Students Who Are Learning English

Tier 1
- Is scientifically-based instruction in place for the target student and consideration given to his/her cultural, linguistic, socioeconomic, and experiential background?
- Is instruction targeted to the student's level of English proficiency?
- Is the concern examined within the context (i.e., language of instruction, acculturation)?
- Have the parents been contacted and their input documented?
- Have accurate baseline data been collected on what the student can do as well as what he/she must still learn?
- Are L1 and L2 language proficiency monitored regularly?
- Have the *ecology* of the classroom and school been assessed?
- What were the child's preschool literacy experiences, if any?
- Have hearing and vision been screened?
- What tasks *can* the student perform and in what settings?
- Have specific Tier 1 RTI interventions that are culturally, linguistically, and experientially appropriate been developed?

Tier 2
- Will instruction in a small group setting lead to success?
- Has the student's progress been compared to him or herself using data collected over time and across settings?
- Does the child's learning rate appear to be lower than that of an average learning "true peer"?

- Is the child responding to intervention?
- Will an alternate curriculum help the student succeed?
- Is scientifically-based instruction in place for the target student and consideration given to his/her cultural, linguistic, socioeconomic, and experiential background?

Tier 3
- How many rounds of Tier 2 instruction has the student had?
- Is there evidence of progress from previous interventions?
- Is the student successful with different curriculum, teaching approaches and an individualized setting?
- Does the student differ from the "true peers" in the following ways:
  - Level of performance?
  - Learning slope?
- What are the child's functional, developmental, academic, linguistic, and cultural needs?
- If additional assessments are used, are the instruments technically sound, valid, and used appropriately for the ELL student?
- Are test results interpreted in a manner that considers student's language proficiency in L1 and L2 and their level of acculturation?
- Do assessments include information in the student's home language and English?
- Has the student received continuous instruction (i.e., absences do not make up a good portion of the student's profile)?

Source: From Brown, J. E., & Doolittle, J. (2008). A cultural, linguistic, and ecological framework for response to intervention with English Language Learners. *Teaching Exceptional Children, 40*(5), 66–72.

already proficient in English (McMaster, Kung, Han, & Cao, 2008). This program involved providing twenty to thirty minutes of reading instruction per session for each of four days per week. Students who were learning English were more responsive to this program than they were to traditional instruction. Because language is only one aspect of culture, it may be that, for students who already speak English but whose behavior reflects their cultural background rather than their school's, RTI is effective at preventing them from being unjustifiably referred for special education evaluation and placement. A caveat is that when RTI is implemented without sufficient knowledge of evidence-based practices within a negative school culture, it can be insufficient to promote the appropriate learning of students from diverse backgrounds, including those who are learning English (Orosco & Klingner, 2010).

ADVOCATING FOR SYSTEMS CHANGE

Providing culturally responsive quality instruction is a big enough challenge in and of itself, but it is not your only challenge. As you know from Figure 3.5 (depicting the six ecological levels that contribute to cultural barriers), culturally responsive schools depend on culturally responsive societies. As a teacher and a citizen, you will want to ask yourself, What can I do to contribute to a culturally responsive society? You can begin by reflecting on the barriers associated with each of the six layers. What can you do within each? For starters, we suggest in Box 3.6 two actions that you might take at each of the six levels.

BOX 3.6 **INTO PRACTICE**

Taking Action to Create a More Culturally Responsive Society

Unlike Box 3.4, which suggested action you can take as you teach, this box suggests what you might do if you want to extend your culturally responsive teaching.

Layer 1: Majority Values
- In all of your words and actions, demonstrate and model for others respect for people whose cultural values are different from your own.
- Hold your family, friends, fellow educators, and community citizens accountable for being respectful in their comments about interactions with others from diverse backgrounds. For example, if your fellow teachers make critical comments in the teacher's lounge about the culture of students or families, let them know that their comments make you uncomfortable and highlight a cultural strength of the student or family as an example of how cultural differences might be viewed more positively.

Layer 2: Federal/State Policy
- Participate actively in elections by learning the positions of candidates, volunteering for candidates who demonstrate cultural respect, and voting for them.
- Advocate actively with state and federal policy leaders in support of legislation that will provide equal opportunities for all citizens and will improve the capacity of the educational system, as well as other human service systems, to be responsive.

Layer 3: Community Factors
- Serve as a volunteer in your community with agencies and nonprofit organizations whose mission is to respond to the needs of citizens who experience oppression.

- Vote in local elections for candidates who demonstrate cultural responsiveness and a track record of supporting policies that will make a positive difference in the lives of citizens from diverse backgrounds.

Layer 4: School Factors
- Volunteer to serve on committees for the school district that particularly focus on developing and implementing programs related to cultural responsiveness.
- Provide information to decision makers in your community about the importance of increasing educational resources that can equalize educational opportunities for students from diverse backgrounds.

Layer 5: Family Factors
- "Go the second mile" in providing information and responsive support to families who face challenges associated with ethnicity/race, language diversity, and poverty.
- Be a partner in your school in creating school policies that value family partnerships and encourage families from diverse backgrounds to share their experiences, traditions, and culturally related hobbies with the school community.

Layer 6: Student Factors
- Seek to "walk in the shoes" of students from culturally diverse backgrounds in your class and suspend your own perceptions in order to see the world from their point of view.
- Explore every opportunity to highlight the strengths and value the contributions of all students, particularly those from culturally diverse backgrounds who feel marginalized.

As you reflect on your own commitments to being a systems advocate, we encourage you to remember the Japanese proverb: "When I want to think, I sit. When I want to change, I act." Your actions at each of the six ecological layers, in combination with the actions of others, can indeed create a more just society.

ADDRESSING THE PROFESSIONAL STANDARDS

The following Council for Exceptional Children (CEC) Common Core Knowledge and Skills are addressed in this chapter through the content and concepts we discuss. See the Appendix for a full listing of these Knowledge and Skill statements:

ICC1K2, ICC1K4, ICC1K5, ICCIK6, ICC1K7, ICC5S2, ICC5S3, ICC5S4, ICC5S6, ICC7S1, ICC7S2, ICC7S3, ICC7S6, ICC7S7, ICC7S9, ICC8K2, ICC8K3, ICC8K5, ICC8S2, ICC8S6

Summary

DEFINING CULTURE AND ITS IMPLICATIONS FOR SPECIAL EDUCATION

- *Culture* is defined as the "customary beliefs, social forms, and material traits of a racial, religious, or social group; it is also the characteristic features of everyday existence (as diversions or a way of life) shared by people in a place and time" (*Merriam-Webster's Collegiate Dictionary,* 2003, p. 304).
- "Cultural responsiveness is the extent to which research and practice in instruction and assessment take into consideration the cognitive, linguistic, and social assets of an individual (such as epistemologies, world views, and learning, teaching, and communication styles) that are culturally determined and shape the ways in which that individual learns and makes sense of his or her experiences. Cultural responsiveness refers to the fact that, in order to be fair and effective, education should be compatible with those assets and build on them, rather than disparage or ignore them." (Klingner & Solano-Flores, 2007, p. 231)

THE SOCIAL CONTEXT OF SPECIAL EDUCATION

- Three theories about diversity have influenced the history that justified IDEA: genetic deficit theory, cultural deficit theory, and cultural difference theory.
- Early in the 20th century, tracking led to segregation by race and disability.
- Court cases, including *Brown v. Board of Education* (1954), *Diana v. Board of Education* (1970), and

Larry P. v. Riles (1972/1974/1979/1984), were instrumental in systematically addressing problems related to segregation.

DISPROPORTIONATE REPRESENTATION

- National data on disproportionality indicate that African American and Native American students are much more likely to receive special education for a disability. The largest risk ratio for students who are American Indian/Alaska Native involves learning disabilities, and the largest for students who are black involves intellectual disabilities.
- African American students are least likely to spend the greatest amount of time in the general education classroom and are most likely to spend the greatest amount of time in special settings.
- American Indian/Alaskan Native, black, and Latino students are underrepresented in gifted education.

FACTORS ASSOCIATED WITH DISPROPORTIONATE REPRESENTATION AND EDUCATIONAL EQUALITY

- Racial/ethnic considerations are major factors in disproportionate placement. A strong predictor of disproportionate placement is the rate of school suspensions and expulsions. Culturally responsive discipline is especially important in reducing suspensions and expulsions and increasing opportunities to learn.

- Language considerations are also a major contributor to disproportionate placement. Developing English proficiency for students who do not speak English involves five stages of development and usually takes five to seven years.
- Language loss is a major concern for many Native American families, and language immersion schools seek to ensure that Native American students learn to speak their indigenous languages.
- Poverty substantially contributes to disproportionate placement and is identified by teachers as a major factor limiting their ability to focus on academics.
- IDEA addresses the need to provide appropriate instruction to children and youth who are homeless.
- Strong relationships exist among ethnic/race, language, and poverty considerations in creating educational disadvantages for students who face these challenges.
- An ecological perspective requires educators to understand the powerful influences of factors at the following six layers: majority values, state/federal policy, community, school, family, and student. Being a culturally responsive educator carries responsibilities to address barriers at each of these levels.

BECOMING A CULTURALLY RESPONSIVE TEACHER AND ADVOCATE

- Enhancing self-awareness involves analyzing one's own cultural values as well as stereotypes, biases, and prejudices.
- It is essential to increase your knowledge and experiences concerning other cultures as a context for culturally responsive instruction.
- Four strategies for delivering culturally responsive instruction are using the adapted posture of cultural reciprocity, incorporating five areas of focus for delivering culturally responsive instruction, capitalizing upon support from instructional consultation teams, and implementing RTI in the delivery of systematic instruction.
- Advocating for systems change across ecological layers is the responsibility of all educators and of all citizens.

MyEducationLab

Go to Topic #5: Cultural and Linguistic Diversity in the MyEducationLab (www.myeducationlab.com) for *Exceptional Lives,* where you can do the following:

- Find learning outcomes for Cultural and Linguistic Diversity along with the national standards that connect to these outcomes.
- Complete assignments and activities that will help you more deeply understand the chapter content.
- Apply and practice your understanding of the core teaching skills identified in the chapter with the Building Teaching Skills and Dispositions learning units.
- Examine challenging situations and cases presented in the IRIS Center Resources.
- Access video clips of CCSSO National Teachers of the Year award winners responding to the question, "Why Do I Teach?" in the Teacher Talk section.
- Check your comprehension on the content covered in the chapter with the Study Plan. Here you will be able to take a chapter quiz, receive feedback on your answers, and then access review, practice, and enrichment activities to enhance your understanding of chapter content.
- Use the Online Lesson Plan Builder to practice lesson planning and integrating national and state standards into your planning.

4

Today's Families *and* Their Partnerships *with* Professionals

Who Is the Stuckey Family?

Let us introduce you to the Stuckey family. As you meet them, ask yourself three questions: How typical or atypical are they? What is their quality of life? What are their partnerships with the teachers and administrators in the schools their children attend?

Oldest child, Brianna, age fifteen. Born dead. Seizures. Cerebral palsy. Deaf. Blind. Spinal curvature. Muscle contractions. Placed into body casts. Wears braces. Uses prescription drugs. Has had a tracheotomy and requires suctioning almost every minute of every day. Weak immune system. Frequently hospitalized. Typical? Quality of life?

Middle child, Samuel, age fourteen. Tested into the gifted and talented program in the fourth grade. Boy Scout. Musically talented in piano and percussion. Lego maniac and mathematics whiz. Fascinated by science, especially astronomy and aerospace physics. Horrible at spelling but loves to read and write. A procrastinator who gets by on natural talent and good manners. Typical? Quality of life?

Youngest child, Merissa, age eleven. Has hearing loss and uses a hearing aid. Skipped kindergarten and admitted early to first grade. Bored in fourth grade. Developed asthma and was sick most of that year. Tested into gifted and talented program in fourth grade. Always the youngest child in her class. Plays piano, flute, and handbells. Is on student council and in Girl Scouts. Gymnast. Typical? Quality of life?

Mother, Dinell, the daughter of a teacher. "Raised poor" in Arkansas. Taught by her family to be independent and self-reliant. Musician. Won scholarships and beauty contests in college. Was a teacher and still regards herself as one. Believes she is equal to any of her children's teachers. Taught herself about assistive technology. Serves on state and regional assistive technology council. Is a key player in the state's deaf-blind technical assistance consortium. Believes in partnership but is willing to confront others when her children's educators are unwilling or unable to provide an appropriate education. Typical? Quality of life? Partnerships with professionals?

Father, Michael, an aerospace engineer. Works overtime daily. Shares Dinell's belief that Brianna's purpose in life is to teach the

world about people with disabilities. Asserts that Samuel and Merissa are more mature, compassionate, and empathetic because of Brianna. Makes the family home in the suburb of a city in which aerospace companies and the military are major employers. Typical? Quality of life?

If you answered "Typical," you would be both right and wrong about the Stuckey family. If you answered "Good, average, or poor" about their quality of life, you again would be both right and wrong about them. If you thought these family members would be exceptionally challenging to you as a teacher, you would be both correct and incorrect. And if you answered "Poor or good" to questions about their long-term prospects as individuals and as a group, you also would be both right and wrong.

Like nearly every family of the students you will teach, the Stuckeys are a confusing and complex organism. Your job as a teacher includes knowing how to learn about each family and then how to be a partner in their child's education.

OBJECTIVES

- You will learn how to think about *family* in a new way and find out more about the characteristics of today's families and their children in special education—bearing in mind that many parents, like Dinell and Michael Stuckey, are on a mission on their children's behalf.

- You will learn why parents and professionals should form partnerships with each other, just as Dinell and her children's teachers strive to be and almost always are partners.

- You will understand how children with exceptionalities shape their families' quality of life, just as Brianna and her gifted brother and sister powerfully shape their family's quality of life; and you will understand the relationship between family quality of life and student outcomes.

- You will learn strategies for becoming a partner with parents, especially those who, like Dinell, are undaunted by any challenge in their children's schools.

- You will learn that the key for partnerships is trust and that it rests on your communication, professional competence, respect for your students' family members, commitment to your students and their families, willingness to treat them as your equals when it comes to knowing their child, and willingness to advocate for them.

Understanding Today's Families

DEFINING FAMILY

Who is in your family? Before answering, try to define the word *family* as it applies to you. Does it include only your blood relatives? What about uncles, aunts, and grandparents? How nuclear or extended is your family? How much has your family changed in the past ten years? What changes in your family can you project for the next five years? How do others define *family?*

The U.S. Census Bureau (2010) defines *family* as a group of two or more people related by birth, marriage, or adoption who reside together. The Stuckeys perfectly match the standard definition. We, however, define **family** as two or more people who regard themselves to be a family and who carry out the functions that families typically perform (Poston et al., 2003). This means that people who do not reside together and who may not be related by birth, marriage, or adoption qualify as family if each person regards the others as family members and if, together, they carry out some of the various family functions.

You will find that some of your students have families whose composition is surprisingly varied. To make this point, we cite the following research, applicable to twelve African American families (Harry, Klingner, & Hart, 2005). Only one family was nuclear, with two biological parents living in the home and working full time. Three families were headed by fathers only, one by a grandmother, five by mothers, two by a mother and a stepfather, and one by an uncle. Two families had a parent with mental illness. In two families, an absent parent was living abroad.

Although this research was about one racial group, it illustrates the vast diversity of families you are likely to encounter in your work as an educator. Do not expect to communicate primarily with mothers of children with and without disabilities and to only have mothers involved in parent-teacher conferences, progress reporting, and school activities. There may well be other family members—even *many* other family members—who are willing and able to be involved in educating them. That is because of the demographics of families.

IEP TIP

As you develop a partnership, ask the family member who is most involved with the student whether there are other family members whom they want you to include as partners.

DEMOGRAPHICS OF TODAY'S FAMILIES

Demographics is defined as the statistical comparison of populations (*Merriam-Webster,* 2003). In other words, demographics are about numbers. But numbers do not tell enough about families. So before we introduce you to the demographics of today's families, let's return to the Stuckey family and consider some of their characteristics.

Families vary tremendously in the number of members and even the number of generations within the same household.

They move from place to place: from the state where Dinell and Michael were married to the state where they live now. They have had job changes: Dinell no longer is employed as a teacher, and Michael's former employer has sold the company for which he now works but he continues to do the same work for his new employer. They have faced death: Brianna was born dead, and her life has been in jeopardy many times since. They have been confronted by Brianna's numerous illnesses and disabilities and by challenges to meeting the needs of their two talented children, Stephen and Merissa. They have had financial challenges because, for some years, they lacked any public support for the services and technologies Brianna needed. Both recognize that they may never be empty-nest parents unless they can find a residential option

FIGURE 4.1

Household composition of youth with disabilities and youth in the general population

Family Characteristics	Youth with Disabilities	Youth in the General Population
Percentage of students whose family has an annual income of less than $25,000	36	24
Percentage of students whose families' head of household has less than a high school education	22	13
Percentage of household with		
No biological parents present	19	3
Biological father present	4	3
Biological mother present	35	21
Both biological parents present	42	73
Percentage living in a single-parent household	36	26
Average number of children in the household	3	2

Source: U.S. Department of Education. (2003). *To assure the free appropriate public education of all children with disabilities: Twenty-fifth annual report to Congress on the implementation of the Individuals with Disabilities Education Act.* Washington, DC: Author.

for Brianna that is not a hospital or a nursing home; after all, Brianna needs a tremendous amount of support just to breathe, much less communicate and participate in her school and, later, her community. Here's the point: As a teacher, you will have to consider families' characteristics as much as family demographics. But you should be aware of the demographics of families as you enter your profession.

As you learned in Chapter 3, families of children with disabilities, as a group, are disproportionately from culturally and linguistically diverse populations and have fewer socioeconomic resources. Figure 4.1 provides information that compares the characteristics of families with and without children with disabilities in terms of family income, educational level, and household composition. Note the differences in poverty. As compared to families of children without disabilities, families of children with disabilities have the following characteristics (Parish, Rose, Grinstein-Weiss, Richman, & Andrews, 2008):

- They are 89 percent more likely to skip meals because of lack of money.
- They are 72 percent more likely to be unable to pay rent.
- They are 61 percent more likely to postpone necessary medical care.
- They are 83 percent more likely to postpone needed dental care.

In Figure 4.1, you can note the differential percentage of families of youth with disabilities, as compared to youth in the general population, who are part of a single-parent household. After you study Figure 4.1, ask yourself, "What can I do to improve these families' quality of life by being their partner in education?"

Understanding Family Quality of Life and Your Role as an Educator

For nearly fifty years, researchers have been documenting the impact of children with disabilities on their families. What they have found is what we know about the Stuckey family: increased caregiving responsibilities and occasional or even frequent stress levels for families who have children with disabilities as contrasted to those in the general population (Meadan, Halle, & Ebata, 2010; Turnbull, Summers, Lee, & Kyzar, 2007). Indeed, a recent comprehensive analysis of many research studies related to maternal depression concluded that approximately one third of mothers of children with disabilities experienced depression; by contrast, approximately 18 percent of mothers who have children without disabilities experience depression (Singer, 2006). Alternately stated, approximately two thirds of the mothers of children with disabilities do not experience depression. It should not surprise you that, because of Brianna's life-threatening health issues, stress and depression have affected the Stuckey family.

But research has also documented positive impacts within families of children with disabilities in areas such as resilience, empowerment, social networks, and problem solving (Bayat, 2007; Hastings & Taunt, 2002; Summers, Behr, & Turnbull, 1988). Given Brianna's status at her birth and her multiple disabilities, Dinell and Michael have had to be resilient. And there is no doubt about Dinell's empowerment: She has mastered knowledge about Brianna's medical needs and opportunities for communication and participation through assistive technology, and she regularly must teach Brianna's teachers and nurses how to provide for her daughter's physical, communication, and socialization needs.

Nor are Dinell's social networks constrained because of Brianna. Dinell serves on state and regional assistive technology and deaf-blind consortia and for many years was a paid consultant on assistive technology in Brianna's schools. As for problem solving, Dinell and Michael are experts, having designed much of Brianna's assistive technology and programmed books for her to read by using homemade and specially designed technologies that keep her alive and allow her to learn. So what is there to know about the quality of life of families such as the Stuckeys who are affected by disabilities?

We and our colleagues at the Beach Center on Disability at the University of Kansas have investigated what "quality of life" means to families who have children with and without disabilities (Hoffman, Marquis, Poston, Summers, & Turnbull, 2006; Zuna, Turnbull, & Summers, 2009; Zuna, Summers, Turnbull, Hu, & Xu, 2010). Using the families' descriptions, we have concluded that **family quality of life** refers to the extent to which (1) the families' needs are met, (2) family members enjoy their life together, and (3) family members have a chance to do the things that are important to them. According to these criteria, you are on solid ground to conclude that the Stuckey family has a good quality of life. The academic and social needs of their three children are well met, though some of Brianna's teachers still need to overcome their fear of her physical needs (suctioning her trach and keeping her clean) and to take lessons from Dinell about how to use the many technologies on which Brianna depends. The Stuckeys enjoy their life together; divorce or separation has never been an issue. And they have a chance to do what they want to do: Dinell as an assistive technology expert, Michael as an engineer, Brianna as the child who joyfully rides with her brother and sister to their many after-school activities, and Stephen and Merissa as outstanding participants in school and community activities. But as you have learned, a "good" quality of life does not equal a "perfect" one. There are challenges, real ones, in every domain of their life. Let's consider those domains.

Through open-ended interviews with families as well as national surveys, we identified five **domains of family quality of life** (Hoffman et al., 2006; Summers et al., 2005): emotional well-being, parenting, family interaction, physical/material well-being, and disability-related support. Figure 4.2 briefly defines each domain and highlights some of the indicators associated with each.

When families incorporate their child into family activities, they often promote family interaction and family quality of life.

FIGURE 4.2 *Family quality of life: Domains and indicators*

Emotional well-being: the feelings or affective considerations within the family. Indicators include

- Have friends or others who provide support
- Have support needed to relieve stress
- Have some time to pursue individual interests
- Have outside help available to take care of the special needs of all family members

Parenting: those activities that adult family members do to help children grow and develop. Indicators include

- Know how to help their child learn to be independent
- Know how to help their child with schoolwork and activities
- Know how to teach their child to get along with others
- Know how to have time to take care of the individual needs of every child

Family interaction: the relationships among family members. Indicators include

- Enjoy spending time together
- Talk openly with each other
- Solve problems together
- Show they love and care for each other

Physical/material well-being: the resources available to the family to meet its members' needs. Indicators include

- Have transportation to get to the places they need to be
- Have a way to take care of expenses
- Feel safe at home, work, school, and in their neighborhood
- Get medical and dental help when needed

Exceptionality-related support: support from family members and others to benefit the child with exceptional needs. Indicators for the child with exceptional needs include

- Achieves goals at school or work
- Makes progress at home
- Makes friends

Let's apply these domains to the Stuckeys. The Stuckeys are doing well in the domain of emotional well-being; but because of Brianna's chronic life-threatening conditions and need for constant support, they are justifiably anxious about whether they can keep nurses and paraprofessionals available for Brianna throughout her life and across her life cycle. There also is no doubt that Dinell and Michael delight in and promote their children's growth. Just consider the wide range of academic, extracurricular, and out-of-school activities that Stephen and Merissa have and that recently Brianna joined a cheer-leading team for the special education basketball team.

In light of Michael's long work hours, Dinell's regular travel throughout the state to teach parents and teachers about assistive technology, and the busy schedules of each child, there could well be more time for the Stuckeys to spend time with each other. But when it comes to problem solving, they make the time to solve problems about Brianna's health and education.

Brianna's health aside—and that's a big "aside"—the Stuckeys have entirely satisfactory physical and material well-being. Their greatest uncertainty relates to exceptionality-related support. Brianna has a good deal of intelligence. But her deaf-blindness, her inability to communicate without assistive technology, her lack of mobility, and her teachers' inexperience are troublesome. Dinell wonders what more she can do to be a partner with

Brianna's teachers. She recognizes that partnership is a necessary means to an end—namely, that Brianna can have a decent chance at living in her community with support, volunteering at an agency if not actually being on an agency staff, and participating actively, not as a passive observer, in her small home town where nearly everyone knows her and her family. The question, then, is what kinds of partnerships do Brianna, Dinell, and the school staff need to advance these IDEA outcomes?

Understanding Partnerships and Why They Are Important

DEFINING PARTNERSHIPS

Partnership refers to a relationship involving joint responsibilities and close cooperation (*Merriam-Webster,* 2003). **Family-professional partnerships** are relationships in which families and professionals collaborate, capitalizing on each other's judgments and expertise in order to increase the benefits of education for students, families, and professionals (Turnbull et al., 2011). In Chapter 1, you learned that both IDEA and ESEA set out the rights and responsibilities of educators with respect to families and professionals. Taken as a whole, these reciprocal rights and responsibilities mean that families and professionals should become partners in making decisions about a student's education (Turnbull, Turnbull, Erwin, Soodak, & Shogren, 2011). That's the IDEA principle of parent participation.

There is, however, no federal law granting parents of children who are gifted the right to make decisions in partnership with teachers. In a national survey, twenty-six states (out of forty-seven reporting) indicated that there are state or local requirements related to the involvement of parents of children who are gifted in educational decision making (National Association for Gifted Children, 2010). Whether required by federal or state policy or not, it is sound educational practice to form partnerships with the families of all of your students. To that point, let's consider the Stuckey family again and their partnership with the director of special education. It is perfectly clear that the special education director regards Stephen and Merissa, in the gifted and talented classes, as beneficiaries of the same partnership he has with Dinell concerning Brianna. A candid but civil conversation he recently had with Dinell about her children dispelled his fears that she was out to "get" the district. He wrote to her, "I appreciate your framing [our school district] in a positive light." The ripple effect of partnerships based on a positive approach will be significant for the Stuckey family, just as it was for Jay Turnbull, his parents Ann and Rud, and his teacher Mary Morningstar, all of whom you will meet in Box 4.1.

IMPORTANCE OF PARTNERSHIPS

Partnerships are important for several reasons. First, schools that foster partnerships among administrators, faculty, families, and students are more likely to have high levels of trust than are schools in which partnerships are fragile or nonexistent (Hoy, 2002; Mueller, Singer, & Draper, 2008). When trust exists, morale is better; the school climate is more positive; and problems with teaching, learning, and behavior are easier to solve. Second, student achievement in the elementary grades (Goddard, Tschannen-Moran, & Hoy, 2001), middle school grades (Sweetland & Hoy, 2000), and high school grades (Hoy & Tarter, 1997) is likely to be higher in schools in which trusting partnerships exist than in schools in which partnerships and trust do not abound. At each of the following levels, trust contributes to outcomes for children who do not have disabilities:

- *Early childhood:* associated gains in child skills (language, self-help, social, motor, pre-academic skills), more positive engagement with peers and adults, higher promotion rate from kindergarten into first grade, fewer referrals to special education (Barnard, 2004; Mantizicopoulos, 2003; Reynolds & Shlafer, 2010; Webster-Stratton & Reid, 2010)

BOX 4.1 | MY VOICE

Dual Perspectives on a Trusting Partnership

Ann's Perspective

Jay was in Mary's class for his last year of high school, and it was a very positive experience for him and our entire family. The first evening we met Mary, we were impressed with her energy, state-of-art knowledge, and obvious commitment to her students. Mary quickly earned our confidence in terms of the programming that she was doing, and we were totally together in our values for integration, productivity, and independence.

Mary organized an in-service program that allowed teachers and parents to work together and to share information about disabilities with the typical students in the school to help prepare them for positive interactions. It gave us a chance to go to classes, meet students and teachers, and to feel like "part of the school." Right away, Mary got Jay established as a manager of the football team. She helped facilitate relationships between Jay and typical students (an opportunity he had never really had before) by helping him dress "cool," walk "cool," and generally fit into the school.

In terms of family contact, Mary treated us, Jay's parents, and his sisters, Amy and Kate, with respect and dignity. There had been times in the past that I have felt judged by teachers, and often, it made me defensive. To the contrary, I always felt that Mary was able to see my strengths and to value how conscientiously our family was trying to support Jay.

We exchanged a notebook back and forth, and I always looked forward to reading Mary's positive messages. It was a great source of connection and camaraderie for all of us. It was as if we had a visit each day. . . . One of the confidences that I had throughout the entire year was that Jay was in a quality program and that Mary knew exactly what she was doing. It was an incredible relief for our family to not feel that we had to advocate during every spare minute to ensure opportunities for Jay. We knew that Mary was doing a good job, and we could relax and spend time in family recreation rather than in evening advocacy meetings. What a relief from previous years!

All in all, the partnership that we established worked to the advantage of our entire family, and the happy memories of Jay's last year at Walt Whitman High School will forever be part of the legacy that we hope to pass on through our professional work to other families and educators.

Mary's Perspective

Books and articles written by Ann and Rud Turnbull were required reading at the University of Maryland where I was enrolled as a masters student. Needless to say, I was a bit nervous about having such well-known experts as parents of one of my students. But from the first time we met over ice cream sundaes at their home, I felt at ease and excited about the possibilities of working with them and their son, Jay.

The most critical part of my school program always started during that first meeting with the family. I have always preferred that my first visit take place in the family's home. This puts the family more at ease, lets me get a feel for how the family lives, and lets me meet the brothers and sisters.

As with all my families, my first visit with Ann, Rud, Jay, Kate, and Amy included completing a parent inventory and a skills preference checklist. The inventory included such items as Jay's daily schedule: What did he do each day? What did he need help with? What was important to him and to his family? It also identified his level of performance and past experiences with certain functional activities, such as grocery shopping, domestic chores, riding a public bus, and having a job. Finally, it looked at future goals: Where did Jay want to work? Where was he going to live? Who would be his friends?

From this inventory, we moved to the preference checklist. Based on Jay's activities and skill levels, we figured out what Jay should spend his time learning while in school. Once all this was done, we picked specific goals and objectives to work on for that year and plugged them into a weekly schedule. What seemed to me to be "just doing my job as a special education teacher" often had a profound effect on families. I remember Ann and Rud's being awed by this process. As parents of a young man with disabilities, they greatly valued the opportunity to work with the schools to tailor a program for their son. Their enthusiasm and excitement with Jay's program helped sustain me through some of the more trying school days.

Continued communication with the family is critical to the success of any school program. As I did for all my students, Jay carried his home-school communication notebook back and forth with him each day. This was my lifeline with the family. Any issues, problems, great ideas, changes in schedule, or good things that had happened were written down in that notebook. In fact, it was such an important chronicle of our school year that when Jay graduated, we "fought" over who would keep the notebook! Our compromise was to make a copy for me as a keepsake.

Parent-professional partnerships require give and take on both sides. What was most important to me in my relationship with the Turnbulls was their willingness to support me and follow through with Jay's program at home. Ann mentioned that Jay was the manager of the football team, but what she left out was that Rud and Kate enthusiastically attended just about every game, both home and away. They were there not only to cheer on the Whitman Vikings but also to support Jay, and through Jay, me and my program.

Knowing that Ann and Rud were there to support my efforts was the most critical component of Jay's successful year. Their involvement provided me with the sustenance to continue my efforts and to continue to improve my program. A school- and community-based program requires more than an 8-hour school day. It touches the lives of not only the student and teacher but also the family, school friends, neighbors, employers, store workers, bus drivers, and all who come in contact with that student and family. Establishing a trusting mutually beneficial family-professional partnership requires much effort and skill, but the outcomes of such a relationship far outweigh the efforts.

Source: From Turnbull, A. P., & Morningstar, M. (1993). Parent-professional interaction. In M. Snell (Ed.), *Instruction of students with severe disabilities.* Upper Saddle River, NJ: Merrill/Pearson Education.

- *Elementary school:* increased academic achievement, reduction in problem behavior, increase in social skills, reduction of gap between white and nonwhite students, increased literacy performance (Dearing, Kreider, Simpkins, & Weiss, 2006; Ginsburg-Block, Manz, & McWayne, 2010; Jeynes, 2005a; McBride, Schoppe-Sullivan, & Moon-Ho, 2005; Nokali, Bachman, & Votruba-Drzal, 2010; Nye, Turner, & Schwartz, 2006)
- *Middle/high school:* improved academic achievement, improved compliance with academic standards, successful transitions from middle to secondary school, a greater likelihood of attending a postsecondary institution (Houtenville & Conway, 2008; Jeynes, 2005b; Jeynes, 2007; Lohman & Matjasko, 2010; Stormshak, Dishion, & Falkenstein, 2010)

A national longitudinal study of family involvement in the education of secondary students with disabilities also reported a strong relationship between family-professional partnerships and student achievement (Newman, 2005). This study found the following:

- Youth whose families are more involved in their schools are less behind grade level in reading, tend to receive better grades, and have higher rates of involvement in organized groups (many of which are school-based) and more individual friendships than do youth with less family involvement at school.

- In the independence domain, youth whose families are more involved in their schools are more likely than youth from less-involved families to have had regular paid jobs in the preceding year.

In addition, positive family-professional partnerships can enhance families' quality of life (Kyzar, 2010; Summers et al., 2007). Think about that finding in these terms: You can very likely boost families' quality of life by partnering with them in educating their children. They will be grateful to you, and your quality of life as a teacher is likely to be better as a result.

Forming Partnerships with Families

How can you develop and carry out your partnerships with families? Let's start with the proposition that partnerships build on the strengths, talents, resources, and expertise of educators, families, students, and others who are committed to making a positive difference in the lives of children and youth with exceptionalities. Then let's develop that proposition by considering how to make it a reality in your work.

Figure 4.3 illustrates the seven principles of partnerships, using the structure of an arch with a keystone in its center (Turnbull et al., 2011). A keystone is the wedge-shaped piece in the arch's crown that secures the other pieces in place (*Merriam-Webster,* 2003). On each side of the arch, there are three partnership principles. Trust, the final partnership principle, is the arch's keystone, holding all of the other principles together.

Each of the seven partnership principles relies on three to five key indicators (Blue-Banning, Summers, Frankland, Nelson, & Beegle, 2004; Turnbull et al., 2011). Figure 4.4 briefly defines each partnership principle and some indicators associated with it.

A few paragraphs ago, you read how grateful the special education director was when Dinell framed the school district in a positive light. On the same day he wrote that letter to her, he also wrote another letter to a person who was not affiliated with this district but who was interested in learning about how the district and Dinell were or were not accommodating each other. In it he said, "Thank you for posing questions [to our staff] about programming [in our district]. I think that participating in this shared experience will help the [school] team bond."

What are the key words and phrases in these two letters? They are "in a positive light," "shared experience," and "bond." Why? Because they reflect the intent to be positive, the willingness of parents and teachers to confront the challenges they face together, and their commitment to be a team. These are elements of partnership. How? Because they reflect communication, commitment, competence, reliability, advocacy, equality, and trust. Let's consider each of these seven elements of partnership one by one.

FIGURE 4.3 *The arch and its seven partnership principles*

COMMUNICATING WITH FAMILIES

Figure 4.4 defined the partnership principle of communication (verbal, nonverbal, or written messages that partners exchange among themselves) and identified the following indicators: listening, being friendly, being clear, being honest, and providing and coordinating information. We particularly want to emphasize the critical importance of listening. Educators often believe that it is most important to provide information to families and that talking more rather than less when providing information is useful. It is easy to underestimate the power of listening—of taking time to hear and truly understand families' perspectives and priorities. Stephen Covey (1990), the author of a series of books on the habits of highly effective people, describes the importance of not just listening but listening with empathy: "Empathetic listening involves much more than registering, reflecting, or even understanding the words that are said. . . . In empathetic listening, you listen with your ears, but you also, and more importantly, listen with your eyes and with your heart. You listen for feeling, for meaning. You listen for behavior. You use your right brain as well as your left. You sense, you intuit, you feel" (pp. 240–241).

How does Covey's advice apply in Dinell's and Brianna's case? Here's how Dinell answers that question, speaking to her daughter's teachers:

Put yourself in my place as Brianna's mother. Consider everything we've been through. Take into account all the effort I have made to bring assistive technology and statewide consultants into her classrooms to develop her skills and your own. Remember that I scanned the regular education reading books and workbooks and designed a switch on Brianna's computer so she would have access to the curriculum. Remember that I provided the switches and switch interface for

FIGURE 4.4 *Partnership: Principles and key indicators*

Communication: the verbal, nonverbal, or written messages that partners exchange among themselves. Indicators include

- Being friendly
- Listening
- Being clear
- Being honest
- Providing and coordinating information

Professional Competence: being highly qualified for one's professional role. Indicators include

- Providing a quality education
- Continuing to learn
- Setting high expectations

Respect: relationships in which each partner regards all others with esteem and communicates that esteem through actions and words. Indicators include

- Honoring cultural diversity
- Affirming strengths
- Treating students and families with dignity

Commitment: feeling loyalty to each other. Indicators include

- Being available and accessible
- Going above and beyond
- Being sensitive to emotional needs

Equality: situations in which each partner has roughly equal opportunity and talent to influence the decisions that the partners make. Indicators include

- Sharing power
- Fostering empowerment
- Providing options

Advocacy: situations in which individuals speak out and take action to pursue a cause on a personal, organizational, or societal level. Indicators include

- Seeking win-win solutions
- Preventing problems
- Keeping your conscience primed
- Pinpointing and documenting problems
- Forming alliances

Trust: having confidence in another person's word, judgment, and action and believing that the trusted person will act in the best interest of the person who trusts him or her. Indicators include

- Being reliable
- Using sound judgment
- Maintaining confidentiality
- Trusting yourself

her computer. Remember I supplied her computer and software and then found state money so your school could get new devices for Brianna. Know how much you understand me and I understand you, and that we have made it possible for Brianna to be the first student with severe multiple disabilities to be included in any regular education classes. Consider that I bring in state consultants and work regularly with school nurses. (Stuckey, 2011, personal communication)

As they listen to Dinell, Brianna's teachers will understand not just the words she uses but also that she is equal to them in competence about Brianna, is wholly committed to Brianna, is an advocate for Brianna and the school, treats them with respect because she assumes their good faith and commitment to Brianna, and, in her words, believes that communication and respect are the essential ingredients of partnerships: "They know I am there to help them, not cause them more work. It truly does take a team approach."

Reflect on the people in your life whom you believe engage in empathetic listening with you—the ones who listen to you with not only their ears but also their eyes and hearts. Now consider people you encounter who listen to you with judgment, disapproval, unsolicited advice, and even reprimand. What difference does empathetic listening make to you? Don't you, like others, gravitate toward people who truly seek to understand you? Empathetic listening is a solid foundation for trusting partnerships.

Here are some helpful strategies for engaging in positive communication (Christenson, Palan, & Scullin, 2009; Staples & Diliberto, 2010):

- At the beginning of the school year, ask parents how they prefer to communicate with you. Then try to match your communication with their priorities.

- Communicate with families in their preferred language, using an interpreter they trust.

- For students with limited communication who are not able to describe their school day to their parents, consider daily communication by means of a dialogue notebook or email to inform parents about events they can discuss with their child.

- Consider weekly (newsletter), monthly (telephone), and quarterly (parent-teacher conferences, report cards) communication methods to keep parents informed of school progress and challenges.

- Communicate with parents to share good news, not just bad news.

- Highlight for families their child's strengths and positive contributions to others at school.

Here, a teacher works with two student. But her work is not limited to the students. Under IDEA, she is required to be competent to be a partner with the parents of her students. Parent participation and parent-professional collaboration ensure student's progress in the general curriculum and indeed in all aspects of their education.

Although these communication strategies typically are appreciated by families, each family also has its own individual resources and preferences for individualized communication. Individualizing communication requires you to consider the family's language facility in English, language facility in the native language, access to a telephone and time of day when a telephone call is possible, access to a computer and knowledge about using email, availability of transportation to attend school meetings, and work schedule that permits or does not permit communication with educators during work hours. Let's consider families whose primary language is not English. How can you respond to them and their cultures?

Cultural responsiveness begins when you understand families' communication preferences. Appropriateness varies across and also within cultures (Araujo, 2009; Ivey, Ivey, & Zalaquett, 2010; Lee, Turnbull, & Zan, 2009). You learned in Chapter 3 how you can increase your knowledge of diverse cultures through a variety of experiences and relationships.

When you are unsure about how to best approach communication because of cultural considerations, ask for assistance from a "cultural broker"—a person who has particular specialization and deep experience in specific cultural traditions and mores (Smiley, Howland, & Anderson, 2009). You can find cultural brokers within your school. They may be other educators or related service providers. Cultural brokers also may be available within the community, such as individuals who are employed by agencies whose staff members have particular expertise in reaching out to families from diverse backgrounds. Take

IEP TIP

During IEP conferences, ask your student's parents if they understand the meaning of what you are saying, and invite them to contribute their perspectives and participate actively in decision making.

another look at Box 3.3 and the cultural reciprocity approach. It provides a context within which you can learn about each family's strengths, needs, preferences, and priorities by listening to them and then having a dialogue to explore their cultural values (Sheehey, Ornelles, & Noonan, 2009).

SHARING INFORMATION WITH FAMILIES ABOUT RESOURCES

Families of children with exceptionalities frequently cannot find the services and supports they need to enhance their child's in-school success and enhance their family quality of life (Eves & Ho, 2008; Meadan et al., 2010). Four networks guide families to helpful resources: parent training and information centers, community parent resource centers, parent-to-parent programs, and family-to-family health information centers. You should know about each of them and refer families to them.

Parent Training and Information Centers

Parent training and information centers (PTIs) are funded by the U.S. Department of Education. The majority of PTI staff and board members are parents of children with disabilities. PTIs' mission is to assist families in ensuring that their children have an appropriate education. They help families (1) understand the nature of disabilities, (2) communicate with educators, (3) know their rights and responsibilities, (4) obtain appropriate educational services, and (5) link with other community resources. PTIs serve families of children with all disabilities, from birth to age twenty-six. They offer workshops, publications, websites, and one-to-one support.

Currently there are seventy-three PTIs, with at least one in each state. You can locate and learn about the PTI in your state by visiting http://www.taalliance.org and then linking to your state on the map, where you will find not only contact information but also a link to your state PTI's website. If there is more than one PTI in your state, link to the one that is the geographically closest to your home.

You help families by letting them know about the availability of the PTI in your locality, and you can also benefit by receiving newsletters and attending conferences to gain more information about developing trusting partnerships with families. Dinell has relied on the PTI in her home state to teach her the fundamentals of special education law (IDEA, Section 504, and ADA), to give her examples of how other students with severe multiple disabilities have gained access to and participated in the general curriculum, and to bolster her expectations for Brianna's life after high school. She also learned about the state's deaf-blind technical assistance consortium through PTI contacts and now is a member of its governing board and contributes ideas and strategies to Brianna's school district.

Community Parent Resource Centers

Community parent resource centers (CPRCs) operate in traditionally underserved communities to provide support to families who experience cultural and linguistic diversity. Unlike PTIs, which have a state or regional focus, CPRCs are funded at the community level and provide in-depth supports and services to families who are challenged by poverty, lower education levels, and language differences. CPRCs are similar to PTIs in their funding source (U.S. Department of Education), mission (preparing families to ensure that their children have an appropriate education), and staffing (many parents on staff and as board members). The primary difference is that CPRCs specialize in one-to-one assistance, preparation of culturally responsive materials, and mentoring of new family leaders. There are approximately thirty CPRCs. Most are located in large cities in which there is a high concentration of poverty and disability among ethnically, linguistically, and culturally diverse populations (for example, Hispanic and Latino populations in New York City and African American populations in Houston and New Orleans).

As you learned in Chapter 2, universal design for learning and progress in the general curriculum consist of multiple means of representation, action and expression, and engagement for students. The UDL principle, however, also applies to CPRC-supported families. Box 4.2, Universal Design for Progress, describes how a Korean parent was

IEP TIP

When you are developing an IEP for a student from a diverse background, you may want to suggest to the parents that they invite staff or volunteers from a CPRC to attend.

| BOX 4.2 | **UNIVERSAL DESIGN FOR PROGRESS** |

Supporting Diverse Parents to Be Active Decision Makers

Mrs. Jong Fagan is a single Korean mother who receives daily services from Yvone Link. Mrs. Fagan explains, "I know I have a harder time living without my husband. I'm treated inhumanely because I don't understand all the paperwork that comes in the mail. I believe it's my fate that I need to care for our son either with or without my husband."

Mrs. Fagan is challenged by very basic needs related to language barriers, financial resources, providing 24-hour care for her son, and participating in educational decision making with the school. She is not able to speak or read English, and she is very frustrated by having no concept of when she needs to respond to written requests from the school or to her mail. Facing these cultural and language barriers, it is understandable why Mrs. Fagan often describes that she feels "helpless and inferior."

Yvone Link, of Parent to Parent Power in Tacoma, Washington, provides daily support to Mrs. Fagan. Mrs. Fagan calls each morning and the conversation might last from fifteen minutes to an hour and a half. Mrs. Link helps Mrs. Fagan get organized for the day, making plans to care for her son and herself. During frequent face-to-face meetings, Mrs. Link reads Mrs. Fagan's mail to her, helps her write letters, including correspondence to her husband and to her son's school, teaches her English, and attends IEP meetings with her. Mrs. Link frequently received requests from the school staff to provide services for Mrs. Fagan in her native Korean language.

Through Parent to Parent Power, Mrs. Fagan is empowering herself to get the best education she can for her son and also to learn English. Mrs. Link says that she "will never say no to helping her," because she realizes how very much Mrs. Fagan needs her support.

Source: From Link, Y. (1999). [Untitled article]. *Tapestry, 3*(1), p. 23.

supported by one of the CPRCs, Parent to Parent Power in Tacoma, Washington, to communicate with her son's teacher, learn about her IDEA rights, and receive assistance so that she could participate in IEP decision making.

Parent-to-Parent Programs

The mission of parent-to-parent programs (P2P) is to provide emotional support and information to families who have children and youth with a full range of disabilities. P2P programs establish one-to-one matches between a veteran parent who has successfully resolved a challenge and a referred parent who is facing the challenge for the first time. P2P programs match veteran and referred parents typically on the basis of a similar disability, specific challenges, age proximity of children, and geographical proximity.

P2P has approximately thirty statewide programs. According to a recent survey, more than 65,000 parents are involved with P2P in approximately 600 local programs (Santelli, Turnbull, Marquis, & Lerner, 2000). To find out about programs in your state, go to http://www.p2p.org and link to the map for contact information. If you are in one of the states that has a program, encourage families to contact it.

Compared to other family-directed networks, P2P has been the most thoroughly researched in terms of its particular outcomes for families. More than 80 percent of parents find P2P to be helpful in making them feel more prepared to deal positively with their child and family situation, view their circumstances in a more positive light, and make progress on priority goals (Singer et al., 1999). A mother who was referred to her local P2P group described her "veteran" parents as "warm, optimistic, 'normal' people" who "gave us hope." A year later, this mother and her husband were trained to be support parents, although most husbands/fathers decline to be veterans. This mother, having found that support for non-English-speaking families is hard to come by, has found it satisfying to be able to serve the Spanish-speaking community (Santelli et al., 2001, p. 66).

P2P is also a resource for professionals. A school administrator said that he was certain the program would help families but "didn't realize until later that it would also be helpful to our staff. As professionals, we often feel inadequate because we cannot understand what families are going through because we haven't actually experienced what they have. Our staff was aware that the Parent to Parent program could fulfill a need for families that they could not" (Santelli et al., 2001, p. 66).

Family-to-Family Health Information Centers

Family-to-family health information centers (F2F HICs) are funded by the Maternal Child Health Bureau within the U.S. Department of Health and Human Services. Their mission is to provide assistance to parents and caregivers who have children and youth with special health care needs. Like the other family-directed networks, F2F HICs are typically staffed by parents of children with special health care needs who have learned firsthand about successful strategies for addressing health care. F2F HICs are affiliated with Family Voices, a national organization that advocates for family-centered care for children and youth with special health care needs and/or disabilities. They carry out their mission by supporting families to (1) make informed decisions, (2) advocate for improved policies, (3) establish partnerships with professionals, and (4) serve as a trusted resource related to quality health care. There currently are forty-three F2F HICs, and many are located in states that also have PTIs and/or a P2P. Given that PTIs have a primary educational mission and F2F HICs have a primary health mission, a state program that has both of these components has greater breadth for meeting the families' needs. To find out if there is a F2F HIC program in your state, use the state directory at http://www.familyvoices.org/info/ncfpp/f2fhic.php/.

ENHANCING FAMILY PARTICIPATION IN THE IEP CONFERENCE

The IEP conference can be a context for in-depth communication and decision making with families (Staples & Diliberto, 2010). We wrote "can be" because research on parent participation in IEP conferences has consistently reported that professionals tend to dominate discussion and decision making and that parents, especially those from culturally diverse backgrounds, often feel confused, intimated, and disrespected (Harry, 2008; Lo, 2008; Trainor, 2010a, 2010b). Typically, only one family member (the mother) attends as compared to the three or more professionals who attend. And in spite of the four resources we have just described, parents often have not had opportunities to learn about their IDEA-based rights and responsibilities or to understand the meaning of the terms that the educators will use. Sadly, the whole IEP process can bewilder many families. What can you do to avoid having an IEP conference that confuses parents?

First and foremost, you can help families prepare for the IEP conference by putting them in touch with the state or local parent training and information center and/or community parent resource center. Because these programs are staffed by experienced parents, they can be exceedingly helpful in supporting families to know their rights and to learn how to be active participants in the IEP conference.

No one teacher can fully satisfy the educational needs of all of her students. That is why collaboration among professionals—especially those from the "related service" disciplines—is essential. IDEA provides for that collaboration through its IEP provisions.

In some situations, these programs might even have a staff member who will accompany parents to IEP conferences and support them in expressing their perspectives about their child's strengths, needs, and preferences.

You can also advocate within your school by encouraging administrators, other educators, and related service providers to structure IEP conferences in these ten ways (Turnbull et al., 2011, p. 217):

1. Prepare in advance.
2. Connect and start.
3. Review the student's nondiscriminatory evaluation and current levels of performance.
4. Share your thoughts and take into account the parent's and student's thoughts about resources, priorities, and concerns.

5. Share each others' visions and great expectations and attainment of equal opportunity, independent living, full participation, and economic self-sufficiency.

6. Consider the interaction of the proposed and prioritized goals, services, and placement.

7. Translate priorities into written goals or outcomes.

8. Determine the nature of special education, related services, least restrictive placement, and supplementary aids and services.

9. Determine appropriate modifications in assessment and take into account the five special factors that we will describe throughout this book. Those factors are positive behavior supports, limited English proficiency, visual impairment and the use of braille, hearing impairment and the benefits of learning from and with others with hearing impairments, and assistive technology.

10. Conclude the conference.

In Box 4.3, you will find tips for partnering with families in each of those ten ways.

BOX 4.3 **PARTNERSHIP TIPS**

Tips for Collaborating with Parents in Developing Individualized Plans

Prepare in Advance

- Appoint a service coordinator to organize the conference.
- Make sure evaluation has included all relevant areas, is complete, and has clearly synthesized results.
- Ask about the family's preferences regarding the conference. Reflect on what you know according to the family systems consideration. Find out whom the family wants to invite.
- Arrange for a translator to attend the conference if needed.
- Decide who should attend the conference and include the student if appropriate. Discuss with the student his or her preferences about who should attend.
- Arrange a convenient time and location for the conference, based on family preferences.
- Help the family with logistical needs such as transportation and child care.
- Inform the family and students who are at least fourteen years of age (in jargon-free language) orally and/or in writing about the following:
  - Purpose of the conference
  - Time and location of the conference
  - Names and roles of participants
  - Option to invite people with special expertise
- Exchange information in advance by giving the family and student the information they want before the conference.
- Encourage and arrange for the student, family members, and their advocates to visit optional educational placements for the student before the conference.
- Review the student's previous IFSP/IEP and document the extent to which each goal has been met. Identify factors and barriers that contributed most to these results.
- Request an informal meeting with any teachers or related service providers who will not attend the conference. Document and report their perspectives at the conference.
- Consider whether providing snacks is appropriate and possible and make arrangements accordingly.

Connect and Start

- Greet the student, family, and their advocates.
- Share informal conversation in a comfortable and relaxed way.
- Serve snacks if available.
- Share an experience about the student that was particularly positive or one that reflects the student's best work.
- Provide a list of all participants or use name tags if there are several people who have not met before.
- Introduce each participant, briefly describing his or her role in the conference.
- State the conference's purpose, review its agenda, and ask if additional issues need to be covered.
- Ask the participants how long they can stay, discuss the conference time frame, and, if needed to complete the agenda, offer to schedule a follow-up conference.
- Ask if family members want you to clarify their legal rights, and do so if they request.

Review Formal Evaluation and Current Levels of Performance

- Give family members written copies of all evaluation results.
- Avoid educational jargon and clarify terms that puzzle the family, student, or their advocates.
- If a separate evaluation conference has not been scheduled, discuss evaluation procedures and tests and the results and implications of each.

(continued)

BOX 4.3   **PARTNERSHIP TIPS (continued)**

- Invite families and other conference participants to agree or disagree with evaluation results and to state their reasons.

- Review the student's developmental progress and current levels of performance in each subject area or domain.

- Ask families if they agree or disagree with the stated progress and performance levels.

- Strive to resolve disagreements among participants using the Skilled Dialogue or other strategy, as we will discuss in Chapter 9.

- Proceed with the IFSP/IEP only after all participants agree about the student's current levels of performance.

Sharing Thoughts about Resources, Priorities, and Concerns

- Plan how all participants can share expertise and resources to create the most comprehensive support system possible in addressing priorities and responding to concerns.

- Ask participants to share their priorities.

- Encourage all participants to express their concerns about their own roles in supporting the student, especially in areas in which they believe they will need support or assistance.

- Note the resources that all committee members can contribute.

Share Visions and Great Expectations

- If a MAPs process has been completed, share the results with everyone (see Chapter 10).

- If a MAPs process has not been completed, consider incorporating it into the conference.

- Encourage the student and family members to share their visions and great expectations for the future as well as the student's strengths, gifts, and interests.

- Identify the student's and family's visions and great expectations as well as those of the professionals (those attending and absent).

- Express excitement about the visions and great expectations and about commitment to goals and objectives (or outcomes) that will be planned at the conference.

Consider Interaction of Proposed Student Goals, Placement, and Services

- Assure the family that the decisions about the student's IFSP or IEP will be made together.

- State that interactive factors between the student's proposed goals, placement, and services will be examined carefully before final decisions are made.

Translate Priorities into Written Goals or Outcomes

- Discuss and prioritize the student's needs in light of the student's and family's visions, great expectations, strengths, interests, and preferences.

- Generate appropriate goals for all academic and functional areas that require specially designed instruction, consistent with stated great expectations, priorities, and MAPs process.

- Determine the evaluation criteria, procedures, and schedules for measuring the goals and how parents will be regularly informed.

Determine Nature of Services

- Identify placement options that reflect the least restrictive environment (e.g., regular class with necessary supports in the first option considered; close to student's home).

- Consider characteristics of placement options (e.g., building characteristics, staff and student characteristics).

- Specify supplementary aids/services and related services the student will receive to ensure appropriateness of the educational placement.

- Explain the extent to which the child will not participate in the general education program.

- Identify the supplementary aids/supports and related services the student will need to access education and achieve goals and objectives.

- Document and record the timeline for providing supplementary aids/services and related services.

- Discuss benefits and drawbacks of types, schedules, and modes of providing related services the student needs.

- Specify dates for initiating supplementary aids/services and related services, frequency, and anticipated duration.

- Share names and qualifications of all personnel who will provide instruction, supplementary aids/services, and related services.

Determine Modifications in Assessments and Special Factors

- Determine necessary modifications for the student to participate in state- or districtwide assessments of student achievement.

- If the student is not able to participate in state or district assessment, provide a rationale and specify how the student will be assessed.

- Consider the five special factors identified in IDEA (for example, positive behavioral support, limited English proficiency, use of braille, language and communication modes for people who are deaf or hard of hearing, and assistive technology), and make plans as needed for the student.

- Identify any other modifications or special factors that apply to the student, and develop appropriate plans to address those.

Conclude the Conference

- Assign follow-up responsibility for any task requiring attention.

- Summarize orally and on paper the major decisions and follow-up responsibilities of all participants.

- Set a tentative date for reviewing IFSP/IEP implementation.

- Identify preferred options for ongoing communication among all participants.

- Reach a consensus decision with parents on how they will be regularly informed of the student's progress toward the annual goals and the extent to which that progress is sufficient in achieving the goals by the end of the year.

- Express appreciation to all team members for their collaborative decision making.

- Affirm the value of partnership, and cite specific examples of how having a trusting atmosphere enhanced the quality of decision making.

When parents and educators have a history of conflict, it is especially helpful to have a facilitated IEP meeting. That meeting includes a facilitator from outside of the school who can objectively structure the meeting to ensure fairness to all parties (CADRE, 2008; Mueller, 2009) and foster partnerships through positive communication and ground rules. As an alternative to outside facilitator, related service personnel such as school social workers or school counselors might be helpful in mitigating conflict and planting the seeds for partnership (Alfred, Slovak, & Broussard, 2010; Geltner & Leibforth, 2008; Milsom, Goodnough, & Akos, 2007).

FACILITATING FRIENDSHIPS FOR CHILDREN WITH DISABILITIES

Many families of children with exceptionalities worry because their children are lonely and generally lack friends (D'Haem, 2008; Taub, 2000; Turnbull & Ruef, 1997). You can facilitate friendships among children with and without disabilities. An excellent approach is the technique called **circle of friends**, an approach that has been effective for many students with disabilities (Turnbull et al., 2011). Box 4.4 provides guidance from Leia Holley, the mother of a son, Sean, who experiences autism. Leia has worked for many years for the Kansas Parent Training and Information Center and has consulted with many educators and families about how to implement a circle of friends for other students with special needs. Circle of friends involves educators and/or parents inviting peers to form a support network for a student with a disability so that the student will have friends (Falvey, Forest, Pearpoint, & Rosenberg, 2002). Will the children always be friends? No, but elementary school students with emotional and behavior disorders who have circles of friends are more socially accepted than those who do not (Frederickson & Turner, 2003). That is the case for Sean Holley. But what about Brianna, who does not have a circle of friends?

You may be surprised to know that Brianna participates in the general education reading class and is motivated by her peers' activities; she wants to work hard and uses the assistive technology that Dinell has designed to demonstrate that she can read. But learning to read is not the only benefit of her participation in that class. Because some of her technologies make noises that can disturb her peers, she sometimes takes her reading lessons in a room adjacent to the classroom. There, she might be isolated but is not. Her peers volunteer to read with her when they have finished their reading assignments. In a sense, they are becoming her friends; in another, they are teaching their teachers and peers that Brianna has competencies that might be harder to reach but are still worth reaching.

SUPPORTING PARENTS IN PROVIDING ASSISTANCE IN THEIR CHILD'S HOMEWORK

On the whole, it can be challenging for parents and children to work together to complete a child's homework. Yet many children with disabilities rely on their parents for help with homework. Approximately 20 percent of secondary students with disabilities receive homework assistance from families five or more times a week, and students with disabilities are five times as likely as their classmates without disabilities to get frequent homework assistance. Students with disabilities receive more assistance from their families with homework than do their classmates without disabilities (Newman, 2005). For example, parents of

What more can be said than this photo says? Three students, one with a disability, two from different ethnic backgrounds, and all of them happily involved in school together. Inclusion in school programs, especially the general education programs, means being "in" and, more to the point, being "of" the school. It's one thing to "be there". It's entirely another thing to "participate" there. Friends without disabilities make the "of" happen.

BOX 4.4 | **INTO PRACTICE**

Tips for Implementing a Circle of Friends

When Sean was in first grade we knew very little about how to help peers get to know "the real Sean." His outbursts, head banging, biting, and other self-injurious behaviors reinforced the wall autism was building around him. He couldn't talk. His receptive language skills were very poor. He didn't play like or with other kids. His actions screamed, "Let me be by myself," while his eyes said, "I need you to need me."

We needed to create a circle that would include Sean and other students. But we knew the key was to build on Sean and other students' strengths and interests. It would not be "Sean's Circle." It would be and is "The Students' Circle." Here's what we did and what we recommend:

Recruit students. Send a letter to all age-appropriate peers' parents: "Participation in this group would allow your child the opportunity to model appropriate social skills such as compassion, empathy, and understanding. Our objective is to ensure that children at our school are included in social activities and feel peer acceptance." Do not address a specific child who needs help. Do emphasize the importance of social and communication skills for all students. All of the parents sent back an "agreed" permission slip.

Identify a facilitator. Select a general or special education teacher, social worker, related service provider, paraprofessional, or a peer. No one person should be solely responsible. Find some professionals or parents who can resonate with the student's likes, dislikes, interests, cultural needs, and environmental needs. The student's age and gender are important. The facilitators for Sean's circle were the school social worker and special education teacher, with great support from the general educators. The social worker was a woman; the special education teacher was a man. The circle had boys and girls in it.

Determine the size of the group based on the student's needs. It wasn't good for the entire class to be in the circle at the same time. Sean was distracted. So the students divided themselves into groups that met on rotating weeks. Sean's core group took hold when he was in elementary school and continued to provide support throughout high school. In fifth grade, students desperately wanted to be a part of the students' circle.

Decide where and when to meet. During lunch, recess, and clubs at school? Sean's friends met in the school counselor's office weekly. During these times activities focused on similarities and the gifts of each child. The key is to set up a safe environment for all members and to build on success.

Identify the activities the group will do. Will the activities be based on the general education curriculum or special interests of the group? In the beginning (first grade), Sean's group watched *Winnie the Pooh* and *The Right Thing to Do*, read and acted out "The Three Bears" story, and sang "Happy Birthday." In sixth grade, as the group transitioned into middle school, the focus turned to the needs of the group. Topics included transitioning to the new school, new teachers, new friends, and bullying.

Adjust activities and approaches as the students grow older. In middle school the group became a lunch bunch versus a circle. Students met during lunch and ate in a classroom or a meeting room. Because so many students were involved, they divided themselves into two smaller circles, sometimes going to KFC for lunch, sometimes having a pizza I bought for them, and always enjoying a special treat from the school principal. Starting in sixth grade, the group facilitated Autism Awareness Week. They made posters and pins and provided information during morning announcements. Each class had activities to do weekly, thanks to the group. Members went to other classes to answer peers' questions regarding autism. Prior to sixth grade, the subject of autism was not a primary topic. Questions about why Sean hit himself or couldn't talk were answered when asked. Books about various disabilities were read, yet the focus remained on the strengths of each student. Everything was fun and functional.

Establish three ground rules. (1) Everyone has access to all of the materials used during meetings, (2) all activities must be age appropriate, and (3) everyone participates in all activities.

Give students ownership of their circle. Once the routine and rules are established, let students determine and suggest activities. Stay away from formal learning. Circle of friends should be a fun social time for all students. Make sure there are planned activities or discussions for each meeting.

Peers have come and gone since first grade, yet by high school eight core students still remained connected. All students in the circle have benefited over the years. Through the circle, Sean's peers learned to see him as just another student who likes to have fun, even though he has unique ways of doing things. They became Sean's natural teachers and began to show the adults how to best support Sean. They instinctively knew when to push Sean and when to back off. They knew how to communicate with him and got frustrated when adults talked down to him. They looked at Sean as a peer and a friend. They became his voice when he couldn't find his, but they made him use his voice when they knew he could.

A circle of friends/lunch bunch is a safe place for all students to be themselves. Everyone in the circle is accepted and cared for and about. All students learn to grow together without worrying about cliques, peer pressure, or bullying.

—Leia Holley
Bonner Springs, Kansas

children with AD/HD report that their children often have homework difficulties related to inattention, avoidance, and anxiety and that, as a result, their children fail to complete and submit homework (Powers, Werba, Watkins, Angelucci, & Eiraldi, 2006). Furthermore, parents of children with disabilities believe that teachers need to know how to use universal design for homework (Munk et al., 2001).

Box 4.5 contains tips on how you can partner with students and parents around homework. Communication at the beginning of the school year about expectations for homework and regular communication throughout the school year are especially important to ensure mutual understanding about homework expectations, completion, and grading (Munk et al., 2001). This understanding yields benefits. Students in general education programs whose parents help them with homework usually take more responsibility for completing their work, experience more self-confidence, and have a more positive attitude about homework (Hoover-Dempsey et al., 2001). Furthermore, students

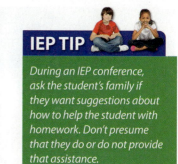

IEP TIP

During an IEP conference, ask the student's family if they want suggestions about how to help the student with homework. Don't presume that they do or do not provide that assistance.

BOX 4.5 | **INTO PRACTICE**

Tips for Partnering with Students and Parents for Homework Completion

Research has documented a number of strategies that you can implement to help ensure that students complete homework and that they become as independent as possible in doing so.

- Recognize that parents can be assets in homework completion (Sheridan, 2009).

- Set firm guidelines and teach students that they do not have a hedge factor in turning in homework (Bryan & Burstein, 2004).

- Ensure that homework is the appropriate length, especially for students who require more time for completion or who have lower levels of energy. Seek feedback from students after each assignment: For instance, have them circle a face that matches their feeling about the assignment so that you can make continual adjustments (Bryan & Burstein, 2004).

- Ask students to evaluate the time required and accuracy of their homework when they complete it while watching television, listening to the radio, or working in a quiet setting. Encourage them to reflect on the most effective setting as well as on their personal preferences (Bryan & Burstein, 2004).

- Provide reinforcement, such as extra resource time or special treats for homework completion. Reinforcement can be given to students on an individual basis or to students based on a class average. Another option is to choose a randomly selected student and provide a reward to the entire class based on that student's performance (Lynch, Theodore, Bray, & Kehle, 2009).

- Teach students to graph homework completion and then explain the graphs to their parents in parent-student-teacher conferences (Bryan & Burstein, 2004).

- Provide homework that links the classroom with real life, such as learning to tell time by developing a schedule of favorite television shows (Bryan & Burstein, 2004).

- Teach students to use homework planners and have them write down all of their homework assignments (Bryan & Burstein, 2004).

- Use cooperative homework teams in which three or four students work together to submit assignments to one team member, who is assigned to be the checker and who then grades the papers and gives them to the teacher. Students work together on corrections (Bryan & Burstein, 2004).

- Teach students self-management strategies for homework, including how to listen to and correctly write down the assignment, estimate the time it will require for completion, identify materials needed in order to take them home, recruit assistance when needed, monitor progress, and self-reward homework completion (Bryan & Burstein, 2004).

- Use a tape recorder with a beep-tape set at ten-minute intervals or less and have students log whether or not they were engaging in on-task homework behavior at the time of the beep (Axelrod, Zhe, Haugen, & Klein, 2009). Today, iPods are so commonly used that a student or the student's family might use them to record their time doing homework.

- Have a single teacher communicate with parents about homework (Harniss et al., 2001).

- Schedule after-school sessions in which students can receive assistance with homework and provide peer tutoring (Harniss et al., 2001).

You also can inform parents about how to assist with homework (Jayanthi, Sawyer, Nelson, Bursuck, & Epstein, 1995; Munk et al., 2001; Salend, Duhaney, Anderson, & Gottschalk, 2004; Turnbull et al., 2008).

- Provide them with teachers' names and preferred times and methods for being contacted with questions about homework.

- Discuss homework expectations with them during conferences and seek to identify strategies that will work best for each family.

- Use regular communication (notes, progress reports, phone calls, email messages) to communicate with them, especially when challenges exist.

- Use the Internet to provide guidance to them about homework, including directions, an exemplary model, an evaluation rubric, and the link between homework and general curriculum standards.

Homework is unavoidable, even for middle-school students. An effective teacher learns how to assist students' parents to balance the homework needs of the students with the needs of other family members.

who receive special education services and who complete homework typically show greater improvement in academic achievement (Epstein, Polloway, Foley, & Patton, 1993).

BEING AN ADVOCATE

Two national studies, one focusing on elementary/middle schools and one focusing on high schools, reported the following about parents' satisfaction with special education programs (U.S. Office of Special Education Programs, 2005):

- Approximately one in five parents of secondary students reports general dissatisfaction with his or her children's school.

- Parents of students with disabilities tend to be less satisfied with their child's education than are parents of their peers in general education.

- Across all disability categories, parents of students with emotional and behavioral disorders have the lowest levels of satisfaction.

- Parents of younger African American students with disabilities are less likely to be satisfied with their children's schools, overall education, and teachers than are parents of white or Hispanic students.

- Parents' satisfaction tends not to differ in light of household income.

Parents sometimes complain that educators are not adequately trained to deal with the challenges associated with some exceptionalities. Approximately one half of parents of children with autism, Down syndrome, and learning disabilities have reported that educators need more training in order to teach their children effectively (Starr, Foy, Cramer, & Singh, 2006). For example, many parents complain about receiving calls from educators to come pick up their children from school when behavior problems occur.

> Because [my daughter's] teacher was late or she was coming a half-day, the school is calling me to see if I could pick [up my daughter] because the "aide is nervous" . . . that's exactly what they said—"the aide is nervous," and [the teacher] wants to do a lot of work. You know, and I couldn't believe that the school was calling me. And I told them no—first of all I asked them, "Is she okay? Is she ill?" "She's not ill." "Did she hit anybody?" "She didn't hit anybody." "Well, what are you telling me?" "She wanted to do a lot of work that the aide could not do." . . . I said, "No, she needs to stay in school." (Wang, Mannan, Poston, Turnbull, & Summers, 2004, p. 150)

A different national survey of parents of children in special education found that approximately 16 percent of parents reported that they had considered legal action to secure an appropriate special education program (Johnson, Duffett, Farkas, & Wilson, 2002). Among parents of children with severe disabilities, 31 percent indicated that they had considered suing, as contrasted with 13 percent of parents of students with mild disabilities. But suing is costly, and many parents cannot afford to hire a lawyer. As one parent noted:

> You have no rights actually unless you're wealthy enough to defend yourself in court. That's what it boils down to. If you don't have the money to challenge the system, they don't care about your complaining; they don't care that you're unhappy. You can sit in the IEP meeting, fine, so what are you gonna do about it? Like, "We're not doing what you want, Ms. C, what ARE you gonna do about it? Unless you take us to court, we're finished talking to you." So, now the laws are

only in place to defend the people who are wealthy enough to hire an attorney and take them to court over that. (Beach Center, 1999)

Having financial resources to pursue legal remedies is especially important given the Supreme Court case *Schaffer v. Weast* (2005). In it, the Court held that parents must bear the burden of proof when pursing litigation against a school district. This means that parents have to demonstrate why their child's education is not appropriate. This decision has tremendous implications for families, especially for those from low-income and low-education backgrounds. As you can imagine, it is exceedingly difficult for parents, especially parents from culturally diverse backgrounds, to go up against a school district and prove why it is not providing an appropriate education (Trainor, 2010b).

The good news is that substantial numbers of parents of children with disabilities are satisfied (U.S. Office of Special Education Programs, 2005). That is often so because teachers and school administrators become their partners, as one parent observed:

The last two years have been like in a dream world. It is like I want to call them up and say, "You do not have nothing negative to say?" This educational system—this school itself has worked wonders with my son. It has taken a lot of stress off ME, so that when I go home, I do not have to get into it with him and say, "Oh, you know, the school called me today about this and that." They will call me, but they have already worked it out. Or they will call me to praise him and tell me how wonderful and how positive a role model he is now, and it's because they have worked with us. It is like I said, it has been a dream world to me. (Beach Center, 2000)

We encourage you to consider two courses of action in order to make a positive contribution to a child and, in turn, a family's quality of life. First, provide such excellent services that parents do not need to become advocates to resolve major problems related to the quality of their child's special education program. Second, be cautious about assuming that parents should be advocates for their children and should invest substantial time, energy, and resources into their children's education. Instead, regard yourself as a problem solver. Begin by identifying how to improve the quality of services to students and their families and by joining with others to be part of a solution rather than part of a problem. Remember that one of the key components of a trusting partnership is advocacy.

ADDRESSING THE PROFESSIONAL STANDARDS

The following Council for Exceptional Children (CEC) Common Core Knowledge and Skills are addressed in this chapter through the content and concepts we discuss. See the Appendix for a full listing of these Knowledge and Skill statements:

ICC1K4, ICC1K7, ICC2K3, ICC2K4, ICC5S2, ICC5S3, ICC5S6, ICC7S3, ICC7S7, ICC9S2, ICC9S3, ICC9S5, ICC10K2, ICC10K3, ICC10S3

Summary

UNDERSTANDING TODAY'S FAMILIES

- Families consist of two or more people who regard themselves to be a family and carry out the functions that families typically perform.
- As contrasted with the families of children without disabilities, a greater proportion of families of children with disabilities have a higher rate of poverty, lower educational levels, and greater likelihood of being a single-parent household.

UNDERSTANDING FAMILY QUALITY OF LIFE AND YOUR ROLE AS AN EDUCATOR

- Family quality of life refers to the extent to which (1) the families' needs are met, (2) family members enjoy their life together, and (3) family members have a chance to do the things that are important to them.
- The five domains of family quality of life are emotional well-being, parenting, family interaction, physical/material well-being, and disability-related support.

UNDERSTANDING PARTNERSHIPS AND WHY THEY ARE IMPORTANT

- Family-professional partnerships are relationships in which families and professionals collaborate with each other and capitalize on each other's judgment and expertise in order to increase benefits for students, families, and professionals alike.
- Family-professional partnerships are important because (1) schools with strong partnerships are more likely to have high levels of trust, (2) partnerships result in more positive student outcomes, and (3) positive family quality of life is more likely when families experience positive partnerships with professionals.

FORMING PARTNERSHIPS WITH FAMILIES

- The seven partnership principles are communication, professional competence, respect, commitment, equality, advocacy, and trust.
- Communication is an essential principle of trusting partnerships. It is especially important to engage in empathetic listening and to carry out strategies that are individualized according to each family's communication preferences.
- Families can gain valuable information about resources from parent training and information centers, community parent resource centers, parent-to-parent programs, and family-to-family health information centers. All of these programs are primarily staffed by families who have children with disabilities, and they offer beneficial, practical assistance to families.
- Planning for IEP conferences should take into account ten components, and there are specific strategies that you can carry out within each component that will help you serve as a trusted partner with families.
- Many families worry that their child with a disability does not have friends, and a helpful way to facilitate friendships is through the strategy known as circle of friends.
- Students with disabilities often need homework assistance, and parents can provide this assistance, especially when they are supported by educators to be effective in this role.
- Educators can be advocates for students and families by ensuring that they provide quality services and by identifying problems and taking action to resolve problems in order to improve services for students and families.

5 Understanding Students *with* Learning Disabilities

Who Is Louise Hastings?

There is a special place in this world for the peacemakers. However much we might worship the victorious warrior, we value still more the person who offers the olive branch and induces opposing parties to accept it. That is one reason why Louise Hastings is so well respected at her middle school. She's the one who, in her words, tells her classmates to "calm down, sit down, chill out, and leave it alone" when they get "really hyper" or start crying or fighting. She's the one who, in the words of one of her teachers, Myra Graham, is a candidate for the school-designated role of peer mediator.

There is a special place, too, for the problem solvers. However much we admire a person who acts passionately about issues, we look to the analyst to figure out what the problem is, why something is a problem, what the possible solutions are, and how to evaluate whether the solutions are working once they are applied. That is another reason why Louise is so important in school. She brings her analytical ability to bear as a member of a clique of white and African American girls who are the school's leaders.

Myra, too, is a problem solver. As a special educator, she teaches Louise and other students to use various strategies for learning how to calculate, learn to read, and read to learn. She also teaches other teachers how to be effective in educating students who, like Louise, have a specific learning disability in math. Her basic job is to ensure **differentiated instruction** by teaching strategies to learn, altering some students' tasks, and modifying how they perform those tasks.

As an eighth grader, Louise takes courses in math, English, science, social studies, fine arts, gym, music, and technology (using computers). If you were to visit her school, you would find her in class among students who have no disabilities and those who do. You might find her working in a small group with other students, receiving one-on-one help from Myra, or serving

as a tutor for a small group of her peers. But you would find her using the same strategies that all eighth graders use to understand her curriculum, although at times she, like other students, reads somewhat below that grade level. Differentiated instruction promotes her inclusion in the general curriculum.

If you were to explore further, you would find that Myra is a "Jill of all trades." Sometimes she collaborates with a general educator to teach math, language arts, and reading; sometimes she provides consultation for the general educators who teach science or social studies. In these roles, she focuses on differentiated instruction and collaborative teaching.

You would always find Myra among the educators who convene as a student's individualized education team; you would always find her advocating for Louise to have some extra time to take the math section of the statewide assessments of student proficiency; and you would always find her following up on what Louise is learning, how she is learning, and how her teachers are instructing her. Myra's a collaborator, a specialist, an advocate, and a monitor on behalf of Louise and the school as a whole. She's also a person who encourages Louise to advocate for herself because Myra knows that a self-determined student ultimately becomes a more effective adult.

Louise's reliable allies—not only Myra but also her parents, Harry and Elizabeth—agree that Louise brings something extra to her education and her school. That "something extra" underlies her peacemaking and her happy personality and perhaps explains both. It's a sense that Louise can do whatever she chooses to do if she puts her mind to it, learns the strategies for doing it, and

applies her problem-solving skills to make her choices come true, whether on her own or with help. Louise puts it this way: What she most likes about school is "learning new things." Elizabeth describes that sense of great expectations somewhat differently: "I tell Louise that there is nothing she can't accomplish." And Myra explains why Louise's future seems bright. It's because there are "so many positives" in Louise's life: her leadership capacities, her ability to advocate for herself and others, her willingness to work, her diligent use of the strategies she is learning for mastering her coursework, her circle of friends, and her family's support.

OBJECTIVES

- You will learn what a specific learning disability is and how to identify a student with a learning disability by using procedures and standards that apply especially to specific learning disabilities—namely, response to intervention and IDEA's inclusionary and exclusionary criteria.

- You will learn strategies for teaching students with learning disabilities in the general curriculum, such as embedded learning, self-determination, and differentiated instruction.

- You will learn how to use curriculum-based measurements to determine how well a student is progressing.

Identifying Students with Learning Disabilities

DEFINING LEARNING DISABILITIES

IDEA defines the term **specific learning disability** as a "disorder in one or more of the basic psychological processes involved in understanding or in using language, spoken or written" (Individuals with Disabilities Education Act, 2004). IDEA provides that the "disorder may manifest itself in an imperfect ability to listen, think, speak, read, write, spell, or do mathematical calculations."

IDEA also establishes criteria for determining whether a student has a specific learning disability. Under IDEA, the evaluation team may determine that a student has a specific learning disability under two circumstances (one inclusionary and one exclusionary), and both must exist. First, the student must have "a disorder in one or more of the basic psychological processes involved in understanding or using written or spoken language." The "disorder may manifest itself in an imperfect ability to listen, think, speak, read, write, spell, or do mathematical calculations." The disorder includes "perceptual disabilities, brain injury, minimal brain dysfunction, dyslexia, and developmental aphasia." This is the **inclusionary standard**; it identifies what conditions are included.

Second, a student may not be classified as having a learning disorder if the student has "a learning problem that is primarily the result of visual, hearing, or motor disabilities of intellectual disability, of emotional disturbance, or of environment, cultural, or economic disadvantage." This is the **exclusionary standard**; it says that these causal conditions are excluded.

Learning disabilities continue to be the most prevalent of all disabilities. Slightly fewer than half (42.9 percent) of all students with disabilities served under IDEA have specific learning disabilities (U.S. Department of Education, 2011). Boys are two to four times more likely than girls to be identified as having a learning disability (Coutinho & Oswald, 2005). American Indian/Alaska Native, African American, and Hispanic students are all overrepresented in the category of learning disabilities. Asian/Pacific Islander and European American students are slightly underrepresented (U.S. Department of Education, 2010).

DESCRIBING THE CHARACTERISTICS

There is no such thing as a typical student with learning disabilities. One student may exhibit strengths in math and nonverbal reasoning but weaknesses in receptive and expressive language skills. Another student may be strong in motor skills, reading, and receptive language but weak in math and expressive language. Individuals with learning disabilities commonly have average or above-average intelligence (Snowling & Hulme, 2008). Nevertheless, they almost always demonstrate low academic achievement in one or more areas and challenges in how they learn and process new information (Johnson, Humphrey, Mellard, Woods, & Swanson, 2010). Louise, for example, has powerful social skills, satisfactory language skills, and average reading skills; math, however, challenges her greatly.

Academic Achievement

Reading. One of the most significant challenges facing students with learning disabilities relates to reading (Peterson & Pennington, 2010). That fact is especially troublesome because reading is so important to performance in most academic domains and to adjustment to most school activities.

Two different terms are often used to describe reading disorders. The phrase *reading disorder* is often used in the educational literature, whereas **dyslexia** is used in the medical literature (Strauss, 2011). Sometimes the terms are used interchangeably; however, dyslexia typically indicates a more severe reading disorder that is associated with a neurological impairment. Students who experience a *reading disorder* typically experience challenges related to the following types of reading tasks (Stasi & Tall, 2010):

- *Phonemic analysis:* demonstrating sound-simple awareness that leads to being able to break down words into their basic phonemic parts.
- *Word identification:* decoding words that do not follow phonemic guidelines.
- *Reading fluency:* reading in an automatic fashion with appropriate speed and smoothness.
- *Reading comprehension:* accurately interpreting the meaning of reading passages and drawing appropriate conclusions.

Approximately 4 to 8 percent of school-age children and youth experience reading disorders. Higher rates are found in urban areas that are characterized by multiple risk factors such as poverty (Snowling & Hulme, 2008). In early elementary school, students with reading disorders often struggle with phonemic analysis, word identification, and reading fluency, whereas reading comprehension becomes a greater challenge for students with reading disorders as they progress through the school years, when reading comprehension of content subjects becomes increasingly important.

Mathematics. Students' mathematical difficulties can range from mild to severe; it is likely that Louise's are mild to moderate. Students' difficulties with math may include the following (Geary, 2005):

- *Procedural problems:* frequent errors in understanding math concepts and difficulty sequencing the steps of complex problems.
- *Semantic memory problems:* difficulty remembering math facts.
- *Visual-spatial problems:* difficulty reproducing numerals.

Researchers have reported incidence rates of math disabilities ranging from 6 to 11 percent (Snowling & Hulme, 2008). Math disability can occur in isolation or in combination with reading and written expression disorders. Approximately one half of children with math disabilities have been found to experience a reading disability as well (Barnes, Fuchs, & Ewing-Cobbs, 2010). It stands to reason that these students would have difficulty with word problems because of the language-processing requirements. A major contributor to math disability is working memory (Swanson & Jerman, 2006).

Memory

Many students with learning disabilities have difficulty with short-term, long-term, and working memory (Kibby, 2009; Swanson, Zheng, & Jerman, 2009). **Short-term memory** challenges cause difficulty in recalling information shortly after it is presented. **Long-term memory** challenges involve difficulty in storing information permanently for later recall. **Working memory** refers to how students process information in order to remember it.

Our conclusions from approximately two decades of research are that WM [working memory] deficits are fundamental problems of children and adults with LD [learning disabilities]. Further, these WM problems are related to difficulties in reading, mathematics, and perhaps writing. Students with LD in reading and/or math demonstrate WM deficits related to the phonological loop, a component of WM that specializes in the retention of speech-based information. This system is of service in complex

Computers can help students with learning disabilities write more easily.

Teachers, parents, and students should agree on strategies for improving the students's executive functions.

cognition, such as reading comprehension, problem solving, and writing. (Swanson & Sáez, 2006, p. 196)

Efficient learners take control and direct their own thinking process, but students with learning disabilities tend to lack these skills and have deficits in the following areas of executive function (Marzocchi et al., 2008; Meltzer & Krishnan, 2007):

- Acquiring, organizing, and prioritizing key informational themes without getting overloaded by details
- Checking and revising performance during learning tasks
- Initiating new strategies or tasks
- Shifting to different approaches when a given approach is not working
- Evaluating correct and incorrect solutions
- Predicting which problems they can and cannot solve correctly

Emotional and Social Characteristics

The research on the emotional and social characteristics of students with learning disabilities is useful for you to know.

- Students with learning disabilities often have high-quality friendships, including a best friend and a satisfactory number of friends; there is a higher likelihood of friendships with others who also experience a learning disability (Estell, Jones, Pearl, & Van Acker, 2009).
- Approximately three fourths of students with learning disabilities experience higher levels of anxiety than do students without learning disabilities (Nelson & Harword, 2010).
- Children with reading disorders have a higher incidence of behavioral and emotional problems. These problems are linked to problems with inattention and to increased levels of anxiety (Carroll, Maughan, Goodman, & Meltzer, 2005).
- Although there is a higher incidence of social and emotional challenges for children with learning disabilities than for students without disabilities, the majority of children with learning disabilities do not experience mental health problems (Snowling & Hulme, 2008).

IEP TIP

The IEP should address a student's social and emotional needs, not just the student's academic needs.

Given what you know about Louise, you should not be too surprised to learn that students with specific learning disabilities are held to high expectations (consistent with IDEA and ESEA) and have bright futures if they receive the proper supports in school and after they leave school. Box 5.1, My Voice, should help you understand the importance of high expectations and bright futures.

DETERMINING THE CAUSES

Neurological Mechanisms

Learning disabilities are linked to neurological problems and structural brain differences (Stasi & Tall, 2010). New neuroimaging technologies have enhanced scientists' ability to assess brain activity accurately. These technologies have enabled researchers to pinpoint specific areas of the brain associated with specific types of learning deficits. For example,

BOX 5.1   **MY VOICE**

Rachel's Story: A College Graduate

This past spring, Rachel—like thousands of other college and university students throughout the country—received her bachelor of arts degree from Mitchell College. Challenged by attention and learning issues throughout her life, Rachel succeeded through hard work, by using structured support, and by making the most of the modifications that had been put into place for her. Rachel's story is like that of many of her peers who are challenged with attention, organization, and time management skills because of a learning disability.

Rachel did well in school until the fifth grade. Attending a private school at the time, she began to notice difficulties in completing her schoolwork and staying on task. Her teachers noticed these difficulties as well and suggested that her parents have her tested.

Rachel and her parents discovered from these tests that she had attention-deficit/hyperactivity disorder as well as learning problems associated with memory and organization. The test results were a relief in that they helped to explain some of the challenges Rachel was having. She explains, "I was surrounded by all these bright friends that weren't having trouble with the assignments and the homework we had. I, on the other hand, was feeling pretty overwhelmed, and extra effort didn't seem to pay off." Finding out she had a disability didn't offer an immediate answer. Rachel's school was not prepared to meet the needs of students with disabilities, so her parents hired a tutor.

Amy became not just Rachel's tutor but also her advocate and friend. She began tutoring Rachel shortly after Rachel had been Identified with attention and learning problems. Amy began by helping Rachel set up an organized and complete notebook. "Before Amy, my notes were all over the place, and I couldn't find what I needed half the time. Amy helped with my studying but really helped empower me through organization." Amy also taught Rachel how to decide what was important to study, how to study, and how to prepare for tests and exams.

In the classroom, Rachel quickly realized her teachers were not prepared to accommodate her attention and learning needs. At times, some of her teachers were opposed to providing any accommodations for her needs. They seemed to say that if Rachel couldn't be successful on her own, that particular school wasn't the right one for her.

Fortunately, her advisor and Amy were able to advocate for her. Even with all of this support, however, Rachel continued to have problems; and by February of her junior year she was at risk of failing. It was then that her parents sent her to a private boarding school, where she repeated her junior year.

Rachel excelled in this small, supportive environment. Under the guidance of an academic advisor who advocated for her needs in the classroom while also working with her to establish these skills for her own independence, Rachel found the support she needed to remain on task and address some of her learning challenges. "I know most people hated the required study hall, but I loved it. We were all required to study, and this was so necessary for me." Rachel also received additional tutoring, which once again focused on empowering her as a learner. "We focused a lot on learning strategies and memory techniques that I could use to learn the material and, more important, remember what I learned."

Rachel's professors also accommodated themselves to Rachel's learning needs. "They all offered me various ways to do my assignments. For instance, instead of papers, I was able to do a number of oral presentations. I got so good at the oral part that I joined debate team and drama club and performed in several plays."

it is now known that, with respect to math disorders, writing dictated numbers is aligned with the left temporal lobe, whereas computation is aligned with the prefrontal and inferior parietal lobe (Stasi & Tall, 2010). Further, children and youth with reading disorders typically have less activity in left-hemisphere regions of their brain than do peers without disabilities; these differences are associated with genetic and environmental factors (Snowling & Hulme, 2008).

Genetics

Evidence continues to accumulate that specific types of learning disabilities can be linked to specific genes (Lagae, 2008). A review of research on genetics and learning disabilities points out that genetic factors account for slightly more than half of the differences that individuals with a reading disability experience (Peterson & Pennington, 2010). It appears that generalist genes may influence learning disabilities across academic areas, whereas specific genes are unique to certain specific disorders (Plomin & Kovas, 2005).

Environmental Causes

Environmental factors that enhance or impede development can affect the extent to which neurological abnormalities and genetic factors impact learning (Goldstein & Schwebach, 2009). Environmental factors that can contribute to learning disabilities include the quality and type of instruction that parents provide to their children and the quality and quantity of the home literacy environment (Paratore & Dougherty, 2011; Peterson & Pennington, 2010). In addition, the quality of schools and the reading instruction provided are also key environmental factors. Researchers have concluded that some reading disorders are caused by poor instruction (Vellutino, Scanlon, Small, & Fanuele, 2006).

Evaluating Students with Learning Disabilities

As we pointed out when we described IDEA's definition of a learning disability, a student must have a disorder that manifests itself in an imperfect ability to listen, think, speak, read, write, spell, or do mathematical calculations. The question facing state and local education agencies is how to operationalize that definition. Just how much of an impairment must a student demonstrate?

To answer that question, IDEA regulations had long authorized education agencies to apply a discrepancy standard: that is, a "severe discrepancy" between the student's intellectual ability and achievement. A severe discrepancy is one that is statistically significant. During the 1970s and 1980s, 98 percent of the states used the discrepancy standard for identifying students as having a learning disability (Frankenberger & Fronzaglio, 1991).

The current IDEA, however, adopts a different approach. First, it provides that a state or local educational agency may take into consideration whether a student has a severe discrepancy between achievement and intellectual ability in oral expression, listening comprehension, written expression, basic reading skill, reading comprehension, mathematical calculation, or mathematical reasoning. An agency *may* use the discrepancy standard; it is simply not required to do so under federal law.

Second, an agency can now use a process to determine if the student responds to scientific, research-based intervention. This is the response-to-intervention approach we first discussed in Chapter 2. We discuss it again later in this chapter.

Third, the regulations for implementing IDEA state that the identification of students as having a learning disability "may permit the use of other alternative research-based procedures for determining whether a child has a specific learning disability" (34 C.F.R., Parts 300, 301, 2006).

DETERMINING THE PRESENCE OF A LEARNING DISABILITY

Box 5.2 shows the traditional nondiscriminatory evaluation procedure for identifying learning disabilities (Gormley & McDermott, 2011; Naglieri & Goldstein, 2009). Generally, students are referred for evaluation because, even after prereferral, they seem to have more ability than is indicated by their academic performance in one or more subject areas.

Discrepancy Model

A nondiscriminatory evaluation commonly establishes a discrepancy between the student's intellectual ability, as measured by an IQ test, and the student's achievement, as measured by a standardized achievement test. Educators use *discrepancy model* as the shorthand term for the difference between a student's intellectual ability and her achievement.

In the field of learning disabilities, educators usually use an intelligence test, such as the Wechsler Intelligence Scale for Children—IV (WISC-IV) (Hale et al., 2010; O'Donnell, 2009), to measure a sample of a student's performance on tasks related to reasoning, memory, learning comprehension, and ability to learn academic skills. They infer the student's intellectual capacity based on the student's performance. IQ tests yield an intelligence quotient (IQ) that is a ratio of the student's mental age (MA) to his or her chronological age (CA): $IQ = MA \div CA \times 100$. So if a student has a mental age of twelve and a chronological age of ten, the student's IQ would compute at $12 \div 10 \times 100 = 120$.

The bell-shaped curve in Figure 5.1 shows below-average, average, and above-average ranges of intelligence on the WISC-IV. Note that 50 percent of the students at

| BOX 5.2 | NONDISCRIMINATORY EVALUATION PROCESS |

Determining the Presence of a Learning Disability

Observation

Teacher and parents observe:
Student appears frustrated with academic tasks and may have stopped trying.

Screening

Assessment measures:

Classroom work products: Work is inconsistent or generally poor. Teacher feels student is capable of doing better.

Group intelligence tests: Usually the tests indicate average or above-average intelligence. However, tests may not reveal true ability because of reading requirements.

Vision and hearing screening: Results do not explain academic difficulties.

Prereferral

Teacher implements suggestions from school-based team:
The student still experiences frustration and/or academic difficulty despite interventions. Ineffective instruction is eliminated as the cause for academic difficulty.

Referral

Multidisciplinary team submits referral.

Nondiscriminatory evaluation procedures and standards

Assessment measures:

Individualized intelligence test: Student has average or above-average intelligence, so intellectual disability is ruled out. Student may also have peaks and valleys in subtests. The multidisciplinary team makes sure that the test is culturally fair.

Individualized achievement test: A significant discrepancy (difference) exists between what the student is capable of learning (as measured by the intelligence test) and what the student has actually learned (as measured by the achievement test). The difference exists in one or more of the following areas: listening, thinking, reading, written language, mathematics. The team makes sure the test is culturally fair.

Curriculum-based assessment: The student is experiencing difficulty in one or more areas of the curriculum used by the local school district.

Behavior rating scale: The student's learning problems cannot be explained by the presence of emotional or behavioral problems.

Anecdotal records: The student's academic problems are not of short duration but have been apparent throughout time in school.

Direct observation: The student is experiencing difficulty and/or frustration in the classroom.

Ecological assessment: The student's environment does not cause the learning difficulty.

Portfolio assessment: The student's work is inconsistent and/or poor in specific subjects.

Determination

The nondiscriminatory multidisciplinary evaluation team determines that the student has a learning disability and needs special education and related services.

any particular age average an IQ below 100, and 50 percent average an IQ above 100. Most states identify students with IQs at or above 130 as gifted (Chapter 16) and students with IQs at or below 70 as having an intellectual disability if they also meet other criteria (Chapters 9 and 10).

FIGURE 5.1 *Ranges of intelligence*

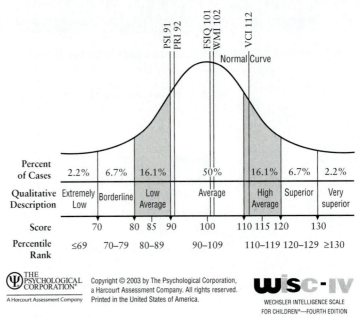

Percent of Cases	2.2%	6.7%	16.1%	50%	16.1%	6.7%	2.2%
Qualitative Description	Extremely Low	Borderline	Low Average	Average	High Average	Superior	Very superior
Score	70	80	85 90	100	110 115 120	130	
Percentile Rank	≤69	70–79	80–89	90–109	110–119 120–129	≥130	

Source: Weschler Intelligence Scale for Children, Fourth Edition (WISC-IV). Copyright © 2003 NCS Pearson, Inc. Reproduced with permission. All rights reserved.

The WISC-IV is appropriate for use with students from ages six to sixteen years, eleven months. It provides scores related to the following four indexes: verbal comprehension, perceptual reasoning, processing speed, and working memory (Prifitera, Weiss, Saklofske, & Rolfhus, 2005). Diagnosticians compare and contrast index scores in discerning patterns of relative strengths and weaknesses. Sixteen subtests measure the four index areas.

In addition to using intelligence tests, educators typically also administer a **norm-referenced** achievement test. The Wechsler Individualized Achievement Test—Second Edition (WIAT-II) is one of the tests often used (Choate, 2009). This test reveals the student's academic skills in reading, written language, and mathematics.

One benefit of using IQ and norm-referenced tests is that the same group of students (called a **norm group**) took the tests initially to develop standard scores. Both tests have a **mean** (or average) score of 100 and a **standard deviation** (a way to determine how much a particular score differs from the mean) of fifteen points. Therefore, even with two different scores, evaluators can directly compare a student's IQ and achievement scores.

Woodcock (1990) has described three types of discrepancies:

- *Aptitude-achievement (also called ability-achievement):* the discrepancy between an ability and a related area of achievement (e.g., IQ and reading score).
- *Intracognitive:* the discrepancy between different abilities (e.g., performance and verbal scores).
- *Intra-achievement:* the discrepancy between different areas of academic achievement.

When educators determine that a student has a severe discrepancy, they nearly always look at the first type: aptitude-achievement. States have different criteria for defining a severe discrepancy. Your state might use 1 standard deviation (fifteen points, as in the hypothetical case), 1.5 standard deviations (twenty-two or twenty-three points), or 2 standard deviations (thirty points). Regardless of the extent of discrepancy that a particular state specifies, the discrepancy model rests on the premise that students do not achieve at their expected level of ability. Thus, measurement compares and contrasts what a student is expected to achieve based on IQ and what a student actually achieves based on achievement test scores. Some states change the discrepancy requirement based on age, while others use complicated statistical formulas to determine discrepancy (Mercer & Pullen, 2005).

Key concerns related to the discrepancy model include identifying students from diverse backgrounds disproportionally, delaying identification and waiting for the student to experience failure, failing to have an assessment profile that can be aligned with specific instructional strategies, and failing to distinguish students whose poor reading is due or not due to IQ-achievement discrepancies (Hale et al., 2010). A national survey of school psychologists, who have a major role in the identification of students with learning disabilities, reported that the majority of respondents indicated that they do not find the discrepancy approach to learning disabilities identification to be useful (Machek & Nelson, 2010). Increasingly, the discrepancy model is in disfavor, even though it has been the predominant way to identify students with learning disabilities in the past.

Response-to-Intervention Model

As we have noted, IDEA now takes into account criticisms of the IQ-achievement discrepancy approach by specifying that schools are not required to document a severe discrepancy between intellectual functioning and achievement and that they may use alternative processes. Accordingly, it provides that a local educational agency may use a process that determines if the child responds to "scientific, research-based intervention." This process has become known within the field of special education as response to intervention (RTI) (Glover & Vaughn, 2010). In Chapter 2, you learned about RTI as a problem-solving approach that involves multiple tiers of evidence-based interventions matched to each student's needs. Each of the tiers within the RTI model (there are typically three) involves increasing degrees of intensive instruction (Harlacher, Walker, & Sanford, 2010; Wharton-McDonald, 2011). Although RTI is a model for instruction, it also is used to identify students with learning disabilities, with an emphasis on discovering optimal instruction for the child to make academic progress (Fletcher & Vaughn, 2009). Box 5.3, Into Practice, describes the steps that schools should follow in using RTI to evaluate whether a student has a learning disability.

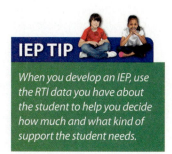

IEP TIP

When you develop an IEP, use the RTI data you have about the student to help you decide how much and what kind of support the student needs.

Proponents of the RTI approach to identification emphasize the importance of screening and monitoring all students from the earliest elementary years and then providing evidence-based instruction. The Consortium for Evidence-Based Early Intervention Practices (2010) characterizes its commitment to RTI as follows: "The interventions are powerful and decisions are data based, with a strong emphasis on individual student progress and systems accountability. Our burden shifts from finding fault with students to providing interventions that make a difference. If the interests of students with SLD [specific learning disabilities] are at the forefront, we argue that proactive and preventive practices are best" (p. 5). As students progress through the tiered system, identification of learning disabilities is based on three criteria: (1) response to instruction in terms of progress rates and performance levels, (2) assessment of low achievement using norm-referenced achievement tests, and (3) determination that the learning problems are not caused by another disability or environmental or cultural factors (exclusionary standard) (Bradley, Danielson, & Hallahan, 2002; Fletcher & Vaughn, 2009).

There are strong differences of opinion within the field of learning disabilities about the appropriateness of using an RTI approach for identification. Key concerns include the fact that there are multiple RTI approaches and no clear consensus on the most appropriate one, insufficient emphasis on determining the presence of a learning disability, no clear-cut criteria for identifying accurately the failure to respond to instruction, and a lack of emphasis on the specific psychological processing profile of students (Hale et al., 2010).

Psychological Processing Model

A third option for the identification of students with learning disabilities is a cognitive and neuropsychological assessment that can identify students' strengths and weaknesses in psychological processing (e.g., executive function, processing speed, short-term memory, working memory) (Hale et al., 2010). Proponents of the psychological processing approach strongly support a definition of learning disabilities that emphasizes that children have psychological processing strengths and weaknesses. Based on research that documents that students with disabilities have psychological processing differences as compared to students without disabilities (Aaron, Joshi, Gooden, & Bentum, 2008; Johnson et al., 2010), the proponents favor assessments focused on psychological processing.

Experts often disagree. Leaders in the field who support the RTI approach disagree with the psychological processing model because they believe it lacks scientific evidence,

| BOX 5.3 | # INTO PRACTICE |

Responsiveness to Intervention As a Method for Determining the Presence of a Learning Disability

In order to use RTI as an evaluation method to determine the presence of a learning disability, schools must make sound decisions addressing the following six components:

1. Specify the number of prevention tiers.
   - Three key tiers in RTI programs include primary prevention, secondary prevention, and tertiary prevention.
   - Primary prevention is generally considered to be the general education program with the core curriculum and instruction associated with grade-level norms.
   - Secondary prevention consists of small-group tutoring in core academic subjects, especially reading and math.
   - Tertiary prevention consists of an individualized program characterized by systematic instruction and ongoing progress monitoring.

2. Identify students for prevention.
   - Provide quality instruction in the general curriculum (Tier 1).
   - Conduct universal screening of all students in the school at the beginning of the school year in order to identify students who are not successful with core instruction.

3. Provide intervention.
   - Implement two intervention models including problem solving and standard protocols (Tier 2).
     - ✓ Problem solving involves defining the problem related to learning, analyzing the factors contributing to the problem, developing and implementing a plan to address the problem, and evaluating the effectiveness of systematic instruction.
     - ✓ Standard protocols involve implementing instructional programs whose effectiveness has been verified through experimental research.
   - Implement intervention for a period of time, approximately 3–4 times per week for 10–20 weeks.

4. Classify response.
   - Identify criteria for determining when a student's response is adequate and when the student needs to receive more systematic instruction.
   - Consider the student's rate of improvement and actual achievement as it compares to classmates whose learning is progressing at the Tier 1 level.

5. Conduct multidisciplinary evaluation.
   - For students unable to respond adequately to Tier 2 prevention, design a multidisciplinary evaluation to address the questions and issues that are problematic for the student (Tier 3).
   - Implement the multidisciplinary evaluation in order to pinpoint learning challenges around which Tier 3 intervention should be designed.
   - Rule out the presence of other disabilities, especially an intellectual disability.

6. Provide special education.
   - Implement intervention characterized by instruction that is highly explicit, intensive, and supportive (Tier 3).
   - Ensure lower student-teacher ratios and extended instructional time.

Go to the Building Teaching Skills and Dispositions section in Chapter 5 of MyEducationlab and complete the activities. As you interact with the simulations and answer the accompanying questions, think about how the RTI model is different from the traditional discrepancy model in successfully determining eligibility for special education services.

Source: Based on infomation from Fuchs, G., & Fuchs L. (2007). A model for implementing responsiveness to intervention, *Teaching Exceptional Children, 38*(5), 14–20.

it has no reliable criteria for identifying students, many students with learning disabilities do not have a unique profile of psychological processing, and the psychological processing does not focus on instructional strategies that will be effective (Consortium for Evidence-based Early Intervention Practices, 2010).

It is encouraging that efforts are under way to reconcile diverse viewpoints and build on the strengths of RTI *and* psychological processing models (Fletcher-Janzen & Reynolds, 2008). Hale and colleagues (2010) recommend using both RTI and psychological processing models: "This combination of empirically-supported best practices could reduce the need for special education referral and evaluation by providing children with learning delays early intervention services using RTI methods, but for those children who do not respond to our best attempts at intervention, additional evaluation of processing strengths and weaknesses could lead to more accurate identification of SLD [specific learning disabilities]" (Hale et al., 2010, p. 231). It is also encouraging that no single educator has the sole responsibility to implement RTI. That's the point of Box 5.4, Partnership Tips.

BOX 5.4 **PARTNERSHIP TIPS**

Implementing Tiers 1, 2, and 3 for Reading Instruction

	Tier 1	Tier 2	Tier 3
Definitions	Implement reading instruction and programs and administer benchmark assessments (3 times per year).	Use instructional intervention in small groups to supplement, enhance, and support Tier 1.	Extend individualized reading instruction in groups of 1–3 students beyond the time allocated for Tier 1.
Focus	Include all students.	Identify students with reading difficulties who have not responded to Tier 1 efforts.	Identify students with marked difficulties in reading or reading difficulties who have not responded adequately to Tier 1 and Tier 2 efforts.
Program	Provide scientifically based reading instruction and curriculum emphasizing the critical elements.	Provide specialized, scientifically based reading instruction and curriculum emphasizing the critical elements.	Provide sustained, intensive, scientifically based reading instruction and curriculum highly responsive to students' needs.
Instruction	Provide sufficient opportunities to practice throughout the school day.	Provide additional attention, focus, and support.	Provide carefully designed and implemented, explicit, systematic instruction.
Interventionist	Provide instruction through general education teacher.	Provide instruction through personnel determined by the school (e.g., classroom teacher, specialized reading teacher, other trained personnel).	Provide instruction through personnel determined by the school (e.g., specialized reading teacher, special education teacher).
Setting	Provide instruction in a general education classroom.	Provide instruction in an appropriate setting designated by the school.	Provide instruction in an appropriate setting designated by the school.
Grouping	Provide instruction through flexible grouping.	Provide instruction through homogeneous small group instruction (e.g., 1:4, 1:5).	Provide instruction through homogeneous instruction in smaller groups (e.g., 1:2, 1:3).
Time	Provide instruction for minimum of 90 minutes per day.	Provide instruction for 20–30 minutes per day in addition to Tier 1.	Provide instruction for 50-minute sessions (or longer) per day depending upon appropriateness of Tier 1
Assessment	Administer benchmark assessments at beginning, middle, and end of academic year.	Administer progress monitoring twice a month on target skill to ensure adequate progress and learning.	Administer progress monitoring at least twice a month on target skill to ensure adequate progress and learning.

Source: Adapted from Vaughn Gross Center for Reading and Language Arts at The University of Texas at Austin, (2005). *Implementing the 3-tier reading model: Reducing reading difficulties for kindergarten through third grade students,* (2nd ed), Austin, TX, in Vaughn, S. & Roberts, G. (2007). Secondary interventions in reading: Providing additional instruction for students at risk *TEACHING Exceptional Children, 39(5)*, 40–46. Reprinted with permission from The Council for Exceptional Children.

DETERMINING THE NATURE OF SPECIFICALLY DESIGNED INSTRUCTION AND SERVICES

Although the discrepancy model has largely relied on general achievement tests for evaluating a student, test scores do not provide explicit guidance for intervention and instruction. For example, a grade-equivalent score for reading does not provide sufficient guidance in developing an individualized instructional program.

An alternative, at least with respect to reading, is to zero in on fundamental skills that are necessary for reading proficiency. These include **phonological processing**, which is the capacity to use the sound system of language to process oral and written information

(Morris, 2011; Wagner & Torgesen, 2009). Using this sound system involves skills related to phonological awareness, phonological memory, rapid naming of letters, and oral vocabulary. Phonological processing at the kindergarten level predicts reading achievement through the primary grades up to eighth grade (Adlof, Catts, & Lee, 2010).

The Comprehensive Test of Phonological Processing is a standardized way to evaluate a student's current level of performance related to the first three skills: awareness, memory, and rapid naming (Wagner & Torgesen, 2009). The test identifies students whose achievement is significantly below their peers. It also identifies a student's strengths and weaknesses and is useful for monitoring a student's progress based on intervention. One version of the test is appropriate for children ages five and six, who are at the very beginning stage of reading. Another is appropriate for students ages seven through twenty-four. The test requires about thirty minutes for administration. Scores are stated according to percentiles, standard scores, and grade-equivalent scores. Separate scores also are given for each of the three major skills areas.

Designing an Appropriate IEP

PARTNERING FOR SPECIAL EDUCATION AND RELATED SERVICES

Often, students become involved in developing their IEPs when they are transitioning out of secondary school. IDEA requires them to be notified the year before they attain the age of majority (usually age eighteen) that they will become adults and have rights to make decisions for themselves when they are eighteen. But why wait until then?

Martin and colleagues had the same question, and they have pursued it by investigating the extent to which students participate in their IEP conferences during their secondary education years. Their research confirmed that special education teachers conversed during the meetings approximately one half of the time, while families conversed 15 percent of the time and students only 3 percent of the time (Martin, Van Dycke, Greene, et al., 2006). To promote greater student involvement, these researchers developed the Self-Directed IEP. This instructional program includes eleven lessons. Each one requires six to ten forty-five-minute sessions (Martin, Van Dycke, Christensen, Greene, Gardner, & Lovett, 2006), and the instructional package includes videos, a student workbook, and a teacher's manual. Figure 5.2 shows the eleven lessons.

What difference does it make when students receive instruction through the Self-Directed IEP? Martin and colleagues (Arndt, Konrad, & Test, 2006; Martin, Van Dycke, Christensen, et al., 2006) found positive outcomes, including higher student attendance at IEP meetings,

IEP TIP

Prepare your students to participate in an IEP conference. This enhances their self-determination and ensures that the IEP team takes their preferences and insights into account.

FIGURE 5.2 *Steps of the Self-Directed IEP*

1. Begin meeting by stating the purpose.
2. Introduce everyone.
3. Review past goals and performance.
4. Ask for others' feedback.
5. State your school and transition goals.
6. Ask questions if you don't understand.
7. Deal with differences in opinion.
8. State what support you'll need.
9. Summarize your goals.
10. Close meeting by thanking everyone.
11. Work on IEP goals all year.

Source: Martin, J. E., Marshall, L. H., Maxson, L. M., & Jerman, P. L. (1996). *The self-directed IEP.* Longmont, CA: Sopris West.

more active participation, more expressions of interest and skills related to transition goals, and more positive perceptions of the IEP process. Martin and colleagues have extended their work to increasing the participation of students in transition planning (Woods, Sylvester, & Martin, 2010). Recent research with students with learning disabilities focused on implementing an intervention, Student-Directed Transition Planning, to enable students to understand transition terms and concepts before an IEP meeting. Advanced preparation resulted in significant gains in student knowledge and self-efficacy in transition planning.

DETERMINING SUPPLEMENTARY AIDS AND SERVICES

In Chapter 2, you learned about the types of supplementary aids and services that enable students with disabilities to gain access to the general education curriculum and the benefit of universal design for learning. For most of these aids and services to be effective, however, it is often necessary for teachers, schools, and IEP teams to know the scope and sequence of content being delivered in the general curriculum. They can learn this information by engaging in a curriculum mapping process. While not necessarily a supplementary aid and service in and of itself, the curriculum mapping process helps educators implement these supports and ensures high-quality planning.

When members of a student's IEP team engage in curriculum mapping, they use the school calendar as an organizer because it is a statement of what must occur and when. The IEP team members then collect information about each teacher's curriculum. The information includes descriptions of the content to be taught during the year, the processes and skills emphasized, and the student assessments used. After discussing the curriculum with each of the student's teachers, they often develop a curriculum map for the school, identifying gaps or repetitions in the curriculum content. At that point, they can determine how to support students to access the curriculum framework, performance objectives, and other standards at the appropriate grade or course (Hale & Dunlap, 2010).

The curriculum mapping process helps you identify those points in the curriculum at which students with disabilities should receive instruction that is based on their unique learning needs. So, for example, Louise's teacher, Myra, may be looking for opportunities across the school day to provide Louise with additional opportunities to learn and practice math skills. If Louise's school leadership had conducted a curriculum map, she could turn to that document and explore where these additional math opportunities exist—maybe in the math-rich musical notations in band class or through history-related activities that deal with numbers. Also, if Myra were an active participant in the school curriculum mapping team, she could make sure that the type of information that will benefit the educational planning for students such as Louise is, in fact, available.

PLANNING FOR UNIVERSAL DESIGN FOR LEARNING

As you also learned in Chapter 2, you can apply principles of universal design for learning by using technology (such as digital or electronic texts, which you will learn more about in Chapter 12) and pedagogical methods.

Advance organizers are pedagogical methods that design the curriculum universally so that all students can benefit. They present information before students begin to learn it

Here, the teacher, the student, and the student's father are partners in planning for the student's transition and IEP meeting.

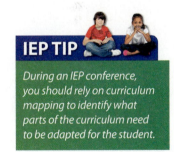

IEP TIP

During an IEP conference, you should rely on curriculum mapping to identify what parts of the curriculum need to be adapted for the student.

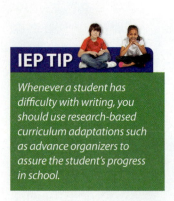
(Deshler, Robinson, & Mellard, 2009). Think of advance organizers as cognitive road maps. Maps tell us where we are and help us determine how to arrive at our destination. Similarly, advance organizers help students anticipate the relationships between their prior knowledge and the new curriculum they must master (Scheuermann et al., 2009). Advance organizers help students organize and process new material and become more active learners in traditionally passive instructional activities such as lectures and reading (Ausubel, 1963). Other ways to organize information include lesson organizers, chapter survey routines, unit organizers, and course organizers, some of which you will learn about later in this chapter.

Advance organizers are useful for students with learning disabilities across various content areas. Gajria, Jitendra, Sood, and Sacks (2007) conducted a research synthesis of interventions to improve the comprehension of expository text for students with learning disabilities and identified advance organizers as among the most effective. Bulgren, Deshler, and Lenz (2007) showed that advance organizers were effective in promoting higher-order thinking about history concepts. Schumaker and Deshler (2009) demonstrated that the advance organizers were effective in enabling students with learning disabilities to learn complex writing skills.

PLANNING FOR OTHER EDUCATIONAL NEEDS

A critical area of concern for many students with learning disabilities is their transition from high school to postsecondary education. Despite the fact that during the past decade colleges and universities have increased their support services for individuals with disabilities to assist them in their transition to and through two- or four-year institutions, many students with learning disabilities struggle in postsecondary programs.

One solution to this problem is to ensure that students with learning disabilities acquire the skills they need to advocate on their own behalf in college. They also must possess knowledge about how their disability affects their learning. A survey by researchers at Virginia Commonwealth University's Rehabilitation Research and Training Center on Workplace Supports asked college students with disabilities to identify the skills they believed were necessary for success in postsecondary education. The students identified the following skills, in priority order (Thoma & Wehmeyer, 2005):

1. Understanding their disability
2. Understanding their strengths and limitations
3. Learning to succeed despite their disability and learning what accommodations facilitate learning
4. Setting goals and learning how to access resources needed to attain those goals
5. Acquiring problem-solving skills
6. Acquiring self-management skills
7. Forming relationships with instructors, university or college disability support staff, friends, and mentors

One research-based intervention to enable students with learning disabilities to transition to postsecondary education is the Self-Advocacy Strategy (SAS) (Lancaster, Schumaker, & Deshler, 2002). The SAS includes a variety of universally designed features that support its implementation, as you will learn in Box 5.5.

Using Effective Instructional Strategies

EARLY CHILDHOOD STUDENTS: EMBEDDED LEARNING OPPORTUNITIES

There is no substitute for early intervention for children from birth to age three who have or are at risk of having a learning disability or other disabilities. Numerous early childhood special educators have recommended incorporating instruction into these

BOX 5.5 | **UNIVERSAL DESIGN FOR PROGRESS**

Using Hypermedia to Promote Self-Advocacy

The self-advocacy strategy is one of the instructional strategies developed by researchers at the University of Kansas Center for Research on Learning. You learned about several such strategies in this chapter. The intent of the self-advocacy strategy is to enable students with learning disabilities to participate more fully and meaningfully in educational planning and decision making. One important component of the strategy is the implementation of the I PLAN process. I PLAN is an acronym to assist students to remember the steps in setting goals. To set their own goals, students follow the five steps:

- **I**nventory your strengths, areas of needed improvement, and learning needs.
- **P**rovide your inventory information.
- **L**isten and respond.
- **A**sk questions.
- **N**ame your goals.

Lancaster, Schumaker, and Deshler (2002) developed an interactive hypermedia version of the self-advocacy strategy. Interactive hypermedia formats allow the use of video and audio segments, text, and graphics and provide multiple paths for students to follow in a nonlinear fashion as they interact with the material. The most common form of interactive hypermedia format is HTML (hypertext markup language), which is used to design web pages. The hypermedia version of the self-advocacy strategy allows students to navigate through the process at their own pace and with minimal teacher supervision. Students can begin and end lessons at any time. The hypermedia version includes video clips of instructors modeling each step in the strategy, including each of the I PLAN steps. At the end of the lesson, students model what they've learned to the teacher.

As with the I PLAN process itself, the goal of instruction using the hypermedia version is to assist students with learning disabilities to set academic and extracurricular goals. Using the hypermedia version of the strategy is straightforward, and students go through the process as follows:

1. The hypermedia version of the self-advocacy strategy is provided on a compact disc (CD), so students simply begin by inserting the CD into a CD-ROM player in a personal computer.

2. Students are presented content in the self-advocacy strategy in a nonlinear fashion. That is, as when they're navigating a web page, students can click between links leading to different activities and different components.

3. Once they are familiar with the CD program, students begin to work at their own pace through each of six lessons. The first screen of each lesson reviews the content in that lesson. Each lesson includes video files that students can watch. Here are the six lessons:

- *Introduction*, which provides an overview of the self-advocacy strategy
- *SHARE*, which teaches students an acronym related to how they should present themselves during an IEP meeting (*S*it up straight; *H*ave a pleasant tone of voice; *A*ctivate your thinking; *R*elax; *E*ngage in eye contact)
- *Inventory*, which lists three strengths, three areas to improve, and three learning or testing preferences
- *I PLAN*, which presents the steps of the I PLAN process discussed previously
- *Model conference*, which provides a video of an IEP using the self-advocacy strategy process.
- *Review*, which reviews the SHARE and I PLAN processes and their use in the IEP meeting

The hypermedia version of the self-advocacy strategy is available from the Center for Research on Learning (http://www.ku-crl.org/iei/index.html), but creating your own hypermedia materials is relatively simple. Authoring software packages such as Microsoft DreamWorks allow you to develop HTML-based materials, and most word processors have the capacity to save any text document as an HTML file, which then can be viewed with a web browser. Moreover, if you are using a Macintosh platform, you'll find it relatively simple to create hypermedia materials that incorporate video and audio clips, which can then be burned to a CD.

Is creating hypermedia worth the additional effort? Yes! Lancaster and colleagues (2002) found that students with learning disabilities, other health impairments, and behavioral disorders who learned the self-advocacy strategy through the hypermedia program were able to run their own IEP conferences.

Source: Based on information from Lancaster, P. E., Schumaker, J. B., & Deshler, D. D. (2002). The development and validation of an interactive hypermedia program teaching a self-advocacy strategy to students with disabilities. *Learning Disability Quarterly, 25*(4), 277–302.

children's daily activities by using a strategy called *embedded learning opportunities* (Horn & Bannerjee, 2009). The strategy calls on teachers to "identify the opportunities that are most salient to the individualized learning objectives for each child and embed short, systematic instructional interactions that support the child's goals into existing routines and activities" (Horn, Leiber, & Li, 2000, p. 210). The embedded learning opportunities strategy is often useful for teaching language skills (Horn & Bannerjee, 2009); but any skill can be taught using this approach, including reading and math skills during circle time for early childhood students (Cook, 2008). Some teachers combine

embedded learning opportunities strategies with a strategy called *constant time delay* (see Chapter 8). Constant time delay simply involves delaying the time between the teacher's instruction to a student to perform a task and the teacher's prompt that elicits the student's correct response. In constant time delay, the time delay between the instruction and the prompt remains the same. In progressive time delay, the time between instruction and prompt becomes progressively shorter.

The embedded learning approach is a promising intervention strategy because it does the following (Cook, 2008; Horn & Banerjee, 2009):

- Provides children with lots of practice within the context of their daily activities and events
- Can be used in inclusive environments
- Capitalizes on a child's interest and motivation
- Is available to parents, teachers, therapists, and peers
- Is compatible with a wide range of curricular models

ELEMENTARY AND MIDDLE SCHOOL STUDENTS: DIFFERENTIATED INSTRUCTION

Differentiated instruction is a prevalent strategy for promoting participation in and progress through the general curriculum. *To differentiate* means to make something different by altering or modifying it. Differentiated instruction modifies traditional instruction.

In differentiated instruction, a teacher uses more than one instructional methodology, such as increasing students' access to instructional materials in a variety of formats, expanding test-taking and data collection options, and varying the complexity and nature of content presented during the course of a unit of study (Tomlinson, 2003).

Differentiated instruction is a logical companion to universal design for learning. Both attempt to ensure that content or instruction reaches all students, regardless of their abilities, disabilities, language, or preparation for school. When working with Louise, Myra uses the same curriculum with her as with all students in her class, but she and Louise work in a special reading program for about thirty minutes each week so that Myra can teach Louise how to anticipate what she will read, how to review and recall what she has already read or will read in class that week, and how to implement other advance-organizer techniques. In addition, Myra, Jean Clark (an instructional coach at Louise's school), and Louise's general education mathematics teacher also break down the word-math problems for Louise because she not only has to read the problem but also has to solve it. Differentiated reading and math instruction go hand in hand.

This kind of instruction differentiates curricular content, instructional process, product requirements, and/or assessment practices to promote students' access to and success within the general curriculum (Bender, 2007). Examples of curricular content differentiation include reducing the number of math problems assigned to certain students and giving students the option of taking a weekly spelling pretest to opt out of spelling for that week. Each of the following techniques is effective for Louise when applied by Myra and Louise's general education teachers, as well as for students without disabilities (Bender, 2007):

- Providing visual or graphic organizers to accompany oral presentations
- Incorporating models, demonstrations, or role play
- Using teacher presentation cues (e.g., gestural, visual, or verbal) to emphasize key points
- Scaffolding key concepts that students must learn
- Involving students by implementing every-pupil response techniques (e.g., lecture response cards) or incorporating manipulatives for students to use

SECONDARY AND TRANSITION STUDENTS: LEARNING STRATEGIES

Don Deshler and his team of researchers at the University of Kansas's Center for Research on Learning have developed strategies for teaching students with learning disabilities (Deshler & Schumaker, 2006; Fagella-Luby & Deshler, 2008). These **learning strategies** help students with learning disabilities to learn independently and to generalize, or transfer, their skills and behaviors to new situations (Deshler & Schumaker, 2006).

Learning strategies work especially well for students who have learning disabilities in basic skill areas such as reading, language arts, writing, spelling, and math. They are effective for specialized school tasks such as taking tests, writing paragraphs, and comprehending lectures (Lancaster, Schumaker, Lancaster, & Deshler, 2009; Schumaker & Deshler, 2009). They can also help students comprehend content-oriented classes such as science and social studies.

The first step in using a learning strategy in any instructional area is to assess how well a student can perform a skill. The second step is to point out the benefit of using learning strategies so the student will ultimately discover how to learn on her own. The third step is to explain specifically what a student will be able to accomplish when she has learned the skill. Although it is not possible in this chapter to introduce you to all of the learning strategies, we can give you some examples.

Acquiring Information

As we have noted, students with learning disabilities have difficulty acquiring information; they do not have particularly strong metacognition skills. The self-questioning strategy is one of six strategies for acquiring information. It requires students to create questions, predict answers to those questions, and search for the answers while they read a passage. Self-questioning is advantageous because

- It requires students to actively interact with the material.
- It helps divide the passage into small, manageable units so students can more easily acquire the information.
- It promotes intrinsic motivation for learning by having students identify their own reasons for reading a passage.
- It requires students to verbalize the information they are learning, thereby enhancing their understanding and later recall of the information.

Storing Information and Remembering

Students with learning disabilities also have difficulty recalling what they have read or mastered. To help them, teachers instruct them to use organizational strategies. The purpose is to help students understand the direction they are taking when they are trying to learn and later recall information. Advance organizers are especially helpful (Deshler, Robinson, & Mellard, 2009).

One type of advance organizer is called a graphic organizer. Sometimes referred to as webs, maps, or concept diagrams, graphic organizers assist students to (1) identify key concepts and subconcepts, (2) compare and contrast information, and (3) relate cause to effect (Bulgren, Marquis, Lenz, Schumaker, & Deshler, 2009). The styles of graphic organizers vary depending on concepts being taught and the maturity of the students. Generally, teachers and students brainstorm together to identify one or more effective models.

Including Students with Learning Disabilities

As Figure 5.3 shows, students with learning disabilities have some of the highest rates of inclusion in the general education classroom when compared to students with other disabilities. Nevertheless, their inclusion cannot be effective unless educators use evidence-based strategies for instructing them. Box 5.6 provides tips for increasing success for students with learning disabilities in the general education classroom.

FIGURE 5.3 *Educational placement of students with specific learning disabilities: School year 2008–2009*

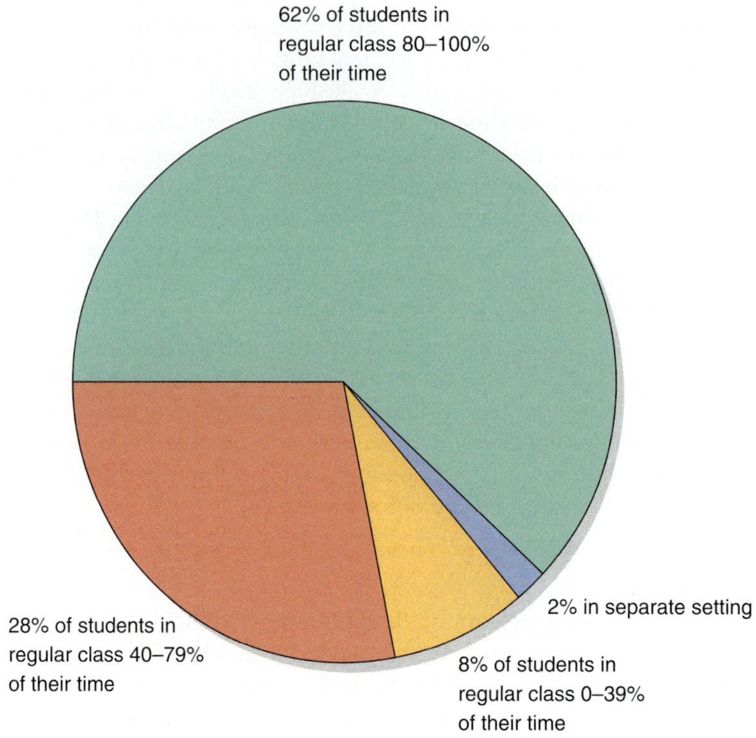

62% of students in regular class 80–100% of their time

2% in separate setting

28% of students in regular class 40–79% of their time

8% of students in regular class 0–39% of their time

Source: U.S. Department of Education. (2011). *Data accountability center: Individuals with Disabilities Education Act (IDEA) data.* Retrieved on February 12, 2011, from https://www.ideadata.org.

Note: Percentages have been rounded and collapsed across categories.

BOX 5.6 INCLUSION TIPS

	What You Might See	**What You Might Be Tempted to Do**	**Alternate Responses**	**Ways to Include Peers in the Process**
Behavior	She continually disrupts other students when she needs to be working independently on assignments.	Move her away from peers or send her to the principal's office.	Use advance organizers to guide her learning on independent assignments.	Match her with a peer tutor whom she can question when she is not sure what she is supposed to be doing.
Social interactions	She misinterprets social cues. She misinterprets facial gestures and/or verbal inflections.	Point out the misinterpretation and tell her how to do it "right."	Include her in the IEP conference to plan collaboratively a social skills curriculum.	Establish a peer partnership in which the peer can practice specific social cues with her.
Educational performance	Her work is inconsistent or generally poor.	Grade her down for poor or incomplete work.	Use differentiated instruction to ensure that her learning strengths and needs are addressed.	Use differentiated instruction with all students.
Classroom attitudes	She easily gives up in areas of weakness to get out of work.	Excuse her from some assignments or reprimand her for her unwillingness to try.	Use curriculum-based measurement to enhance her awareness about the progress she is making.	Give her opportunities to tutor others (peers or younger students) in areas of her success.

Assessing Students' Progress

MEASURING STUDENTS' PROGRESS

Progress in the General Curriculum

Curriculum-based measurement (CBM) is a useful method for tracking a student's progress in reading, writing, spelling, and math and is frequently used in the context of a response-to-intervention approach (Searle, 2010; see Chapter 2). It involves directly assessing a student's skills in the content of the curriculum that is being taught (Stecker, Fuchs, & Fuchs, 2005). Under standardized conditions, the teacher gives the student brief timed samples or probes based on the student's course content. The teacher then scores the student's performance for speed, fluency, and accuracy. Because curriculum-based measurement probes are quick to administer and simple to score, they can be given repeatedly.

CBM tracks students' progress in various content areas, including math (Montague, Penfield, Enders, & Huang, 2010; Foegen & Morrison, 2010), reading (Christ, Silberglitt, Yeo, & Cormier, 2010; Yeo, 2010), and social studies (Espin, Shin, & Busch, 2005). A review of the CBM research literature shows that teachers who adjust their instruction as a function of data generated through CBM can significantly improve student performance across content areas, that the use of CBM enables teachers to be more responsive to student needs, and that students of teachers who used classwide CBM showed more growth across content areas than did students whose teachers used other strategies (Stecker et al., 2005).

The types of probes vary according to content. Reading probes typically involve two measures: a maze task, in which a student reads a passage (aloud or silently) with words deleted and then selects words to replace the missing words; and reading aloud for a specified duration while a teacher counts the correct number of words read (oral reading fluency). CBM of spelling requires students to write words dictated to them for a specified time; the teacher counts the correct letter sequences. When CBM is applied to math, students answer computational questions for a set time period; the teacher then counts the number of correct answers (Searle, 2010).

Progress in Addressing Other Educational Needs

Although this is not the case for Louise, the biggest barrier to successful inclusion and positive postsecondary outcomes for many students with disabilities seems to be their limited social skills (Womack, Marchant, & Borders, 2011). That is why the strategies for tracking student social skills and relationships that we will discuss in Chapter 7, including using rating scales and sociometric ratings, are equally important for students with learning disabilities. There are few checklists to track progress in the types of self-advocacy skills discussed previously in this chapter, although there are standardized measures of self-determination that have been used with students with learning disabilities (Wehmeyer & Field, 2007). The Arc's Self-Determination Scale (available at http://www.beachcenter .org) is a student self-report measure of self-determination for students with cognitive disabilities, including students with learning disabilities.

MAKING ACCOMMODATIONS FOR ASSESSMENT

Perhaps in no other category of disability is the issue of test accommodations as controversial as it is in the area of specific learning disabilities. This is because many test givers (teachers, local educational agencies, and state educational agencies) are concerned that students who do not require accommodations will seek and obtain the accommodations and be placed at a competitive advantage relative to other students.

The most frequently implemented accommodation is extra time to take a test. Gregg and Nelson (2010) conducted a meta-analysis of the effectiveness of extra time as a test accommodation for students with learning disabilities. They examined score comparability between scores from students with LD who got extra time and students without disabilities who did not. They concluded that there is too little information available to be able to say much about issues of score comparability, but that, across all studies, students with LD did not out-achieve students without disabilities on tests in which accommodations were in place. It seems unlikely that providing accommodations such as extra time is unfair to students without disabilities.

The fact remains, however, that students with learning disabilities may need a wide array of accommodations to be able to perform at their highest level on standardized tests. Even if those accommodations are in place, students with learning disabilities may not demonstrate the full range of their abilities. That may be because students with learning disabilities experience higher test anxiety than do students without disabilities (Sena, Low, & Lee, 2007).

ADDRESSING THE PROFESSIONAL STANDARDS

The following Council for Exceptional Children (CEC) Common Core Knowledge and Skills are addressed in this chapter through the content and concepts we discuss. See the Appendix for a full listing of these Knowledge and Skill statements:

ICC2K1, ICC2K2, ICC2K4, ICC2K5, ICC2K6, ICC4S2, ICC4S3, ICC4S4, ICC4S5, ICC5S2, ICC5S3, ICC5S4, ICC5S9, ICC7S1, ICC7S3, ICC7S6, ICC7S9, ICC8K3, ICC8S2, ICC8S6, ICC8S8, ICC10S2, ICC10S3, ICC10S4, ICC10S5

Summary

IDENTIFYING STUDENTS WITH LEARNING DISABILITIES

- IDEA has inclusionary (disorder in one or more of the basic psychological processes involved in understanding or using written or spoken language) and exclusionary (not due to an intellectual disability or environmental/economic disadvantages) criteria for determining whether a student has a learning disability.
- Learning disabilities is the most prevalent disability category, comprising 42.9 percent of all students with disabilities.
- Students with learning disabilities typically have average or above-average intelligence.
- Students with learning disabilities are a heterogeneous population with varied academic challenges related to reading and math.
- Students with learning disabilities often have difficulty with short-term, long-term, and working memory.
- Students with learning disabilities often have deficits in their abilities to manage themselves and their school responsibilities. (The skill is known as *executive functioning*.)

- Although students with learning disabilities often experience higher levels of anxiety and more social and emotional challenges than do students without learning disabilities, as a group they do not experience more mental health problems.
- Research suggests that different neurological regions of the brain are associated with particular learning problems and that learning disabilities have genetic and environmental causes.

EVALUATING STUDENTS WITH LEARNING DISABILITIES

- The traditional nondiscriminatory evaluation practice in the field of learning disabilities has been to use standardized intelligence and achievement tests to pinpoint a severe discrepancy between aptitude and achievement.
- IDEA 2004 allows states to use RTI to identifying the presence of a learning disability as contrasted to using the severe discrepancy approach.
- A third option for identifying learning disabilities is to use assessments of psychological processing.

- A future direction in the learning disabilities field is to combine an RTI approach with assessment of psychological processing skills.

DESIGNING AN APPROPRIATE IEP

- Students with learning disabilities can be taught to successfully self-direct their IEP and transition meetings.
- Curriculum mapping involves a determination of the scope and sequence of the delivery of content in a school and can be a critical source of data for IEP teams when making decisions about a student's educational program.
- Advance organizers have been shown to be very powerful pedagogical tools that enable learners with learning disabilities to perform more effectively.
- Promoting student self-advocacy skills can enable students with learning disabilities to make the transition from high school to college.

USING EFFECTIVE INSTRUCTIONAL STRATEGIES

- Embedded learning opportunities involve instruction in key skills that are embedded in other routines or tasks. These strategies have been shown to be very useful with young children with learning disabilities.

- Differentiated instruction involves the differentiation of content and instructional strategies to ensure that all students in a classroom have the opportunity to learn. This is among the most important strategy to ensure effective inclusive practices.
- Learning strategies instruction provides the opportunity for students with learning disabilities to acquire "learning-to-learn" strategies that impact knowledge acquisition, information storage and retrieval, and other higher-order cognitive functions.

INCLUDING STUDENTS WITH LEARNING DISABILITIES

- Students with learning disabilities have a high rate of inclusion in general education classes.

ASSESSING STUDENTS' PROGRESS

- Curriculum-based measurement involves the use of multiple, frequent probes that collect samples of student progress in content areas, including math, reading, science, and social studies.
- There are a number of test accommodations, including extended time, oral presentation, computer administration, and calculator use, that may benefit students with learning disabilities.

MyEducationLab

Go to Topic #9: Learning Disabilities in the MyEducationLab (www.myeducationlab .com) for *Exceptional Lives,* where you can do the following:

- Find learning outcomes for Learning Disabilities along with the national standards that connect to these outcomes.
- Complete assignments and activities that will help you more deeply understand the chapter content.
- Apply and practice your understanding of the core teaching skills identified in the chapter with the Building Teaching Skills and Dispositions learning units.
- Examine challenging situations and cases presented in the IRIS Center Resources.
- Access video clips of CCSSO National Teachers of the Year award winners responding to the question, "Why Do I Teach?" in the Teacher Talk section.
- Check your comprehension on the content covered in the chapter with the Study Plan. Here you will be able to take a chapter quiz, receive feedback on your answers, and then access review, practice, and enrichment activities to enhance your understanding of chapter content.
- Use the Online Lesson Plan Builder to practice lesson planning and integrating national and state standards into your planning.

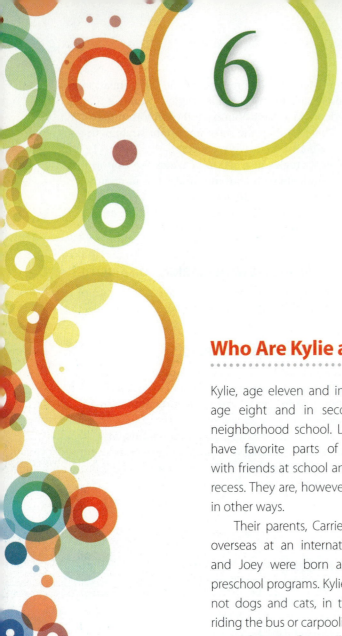

6 Understanding Students *with* Communication Disorders

Contributing authors: Jane Wegner, Ph.D., University of Kansas, and Evette Edmister, Ph.D., University of Northern Iowa

Who Are Kylie and Joey?

Kylie, age eleven and in fourth grade, and Joey, age eight and in second grade, attend their neighborhood school. Like their age-peers, they have favorite parts of the school day—being with friends at school and playing outside during recess. They are, however, quite unlike their peers in other ways.

Their parents, Carrie and Paul, were working overseas at an international school when Kylie and Joey were born and while they attended preschool programs. Kylie and Joey had elephants, not dogs and cats, in their backyard. Instead of riding the bus or carpooling to school, they logged many frequent-flyer miles traveling back to the

United States from Singapore, Saudi Arabia, and Indonesia. Compared to their same-age peers, they are apt to have a richer understanding of the world and its cultures. But unlike many of their peers, both use a variety of alternative and augmentative communication (AAC) tools to assist their communication. Yes, most of their peers use a computer and make facial expressions to communicate. But few use the AAC device that Kylie can activate with her eyes or Joey's iPod with voice output software. For Carrie and Paul, the question always has been, What should they do to satisfy Kylie's and Joey's need to communicate?

Step 1: Get Help. Carrie and Paul first observed changes in Kylie's development when she was

thirteen months old. After stressful months of observing her, visiting local physicians in Saudi Arabia, searching the Internet, and flying back to the United States, they obtained a diagnosis: Rett syndrome, "a disorder of the nervous system that leads to developmental reversals, especially in the areas of expressive language and hand use" (National Institute of Health, 2011). Joey was diagnosed by a physician in Singapore with autism spectrum disorder (ASD) at approximately two years of age. Both diagnoses strongly suggested that further communication challenges were on the horizon.

Step 2: Provide Intensive Intervention. According to Carrie, these diagnoses did not change who her children were.

They were still the same children she had always known. But what she and Paul needed now were people to fight with them to secure early intervention services, so the family moved back to their home state so that Joey could attend kindergarten. Kylie and Joey now receive therapy services in their local school, at a nearby university, and within their community. They are involved in recreational activities in the community, music camp at the university, and art camp.

Kylie has explored and used a variety of low- and high-tech communication aids. For her low-tech communication she currently uses a pragmatic organization dynamic display (PODD) communication book (Porter & Burkhart, 2010). Each page of her communication book has nine choices. She accesses her choices with the assistance of a communication partner. Her partner points to each message, and Kylie indicates, "That's the one I want," either by activating a voice output switch at her left cheek or looking to the left while the partner touches the item she wants. She also uses eye gaze (looking at what she wants from choices held up) to select from a smaller set of choices. Yet she has difficulty gaining attention to initiate communication without partner assistance. Her parents are still concerned that she is not able to initiate communication unless someone approaches her. So Kylie has a high-tech device

that reads her eye movements. Her eyes move the cursor similar to the way in which other people use a hand-controlled computer mouse to move a cursor. When she holds her gaze on a particular item for a set amount of time, she can activate the voice output or programmed command for that item.

Joey also uses low- and high-tech communication tools. He uses his speech, his gestures, and a communication book with line-drawn picture symbols and written text to assist his communication. Joey comprehends many words and phrases and reads well. He accesses his technology by touching the picture or words observed. He has explored a variety of mid- to high-tech voice output communication systems to assist his speech and gestures, and he currently uses an iPod with voice output communication software. None of these AAC tools and strategies would have been effective without parent-professional teamwork and careful observations by team members in all the settings in which the children participate.

Step 3: Assemble a Team. Carrie and Paul have chosen and lead a special group of individuals. This team includes extended family, friends, physicians, speech-language pathologists, physical therapists, college students to assist with child care for an occasional night out or work obligations, teachers, paraprofessionals, school principals, AAC consultants, and technical support personnel from AAC companies. Of course, they know that it's important to make sure that Kylie and Joey are members of their own teams as well. Consistent with the principle of self-determination, they have the ultimate say in choosing their own communication tools.

Step 4: Expect Great Results and Celebrate Them. Applaud Kylie and Joey, their parents Carrie and Paul, and the professionals who work with them when the children make progress. Make it clear to everyone, including Kylie and Joey, that they should expect and work for great results, and then celebrate the results together.

Step 5: Face the Challenges. Carrie and Paul acknowledge that they still have much to learn. Both Kylie and Joey continue to work to learn how to use their communication systems. Adults and peers are learning strategies to scaffold language and to model communication systems. Kylie is working to improve her motor skills for walking, transferring from her chair to a classroom chair, and activating switches. Both are continuing to learn literacy and math skills. At their school, professionals are determining how to increase the amount of time Kylie and Joey spend with their age-peers in the general education classroom. The school and community team members meet with Carrie and Paul every other week to discuss current progress for each child and to plan for the future.

Identifying Students with Communication Disorders

DEFINING COMMUNICATION DISORDERS

Communication entails receiving, understanding, and expressing information, feelings, and ideas. It is such a natural part of our daily lives that most of us take our ability to communicate for granted. We participate in many communicative interactions each day. For example, we talk with others face to face or on the phone; we email a colleague or a friend; we post messages on Facebook; we demonstrate social awareness by lowering our voices when we see a raised eyebrow or a frown; and we wink at friends over private jokes.

Although we usually communicate through speech, we also communicate in other ways. Some people communicate manually, using sign language and/or gestures. Others add nonlinguistic cues while speaking, such as body posture, facial and vocal expressions, gestures, eye contact, and head and body movements. Many speakers vary their voices by changing their pitch or rate of speaking. All of these skills make our communication more effective.

Communication by spoken or written language, or both, is the cornerstone of teaching and learning. Although most children come to school able to understand others and express themselves and thus are able to participate in school effectively, many children do not. A student with a communication disorder can encounter challenges with classroom activities, social interactions, instructional discourse exchanges, acquisition of knowledge and language, and the development of literacy skills. Let's consider the different types of communication disorders that students experience.

Speech and Language Disorders

Communication disorders relate to the components of the process affected: speech, language, or both (American Speech-Language-Hearing Association, 2008; Hulit, Howard, & Fahey, 2011; Justice, 2010). A **speech disorder** refers to difficulty producing sounds as well as disorders of voice quality (for example, a hoarse voice) or fluency of speech, often referred to as stuttering. A **language disorder** entails difficulty receiving, understanding, or formulating ideas and information. A **receptive language disorder** is characterized by difficulty receiving or understanding information. An **expressive language disorder** is characterized by difficulty formulating ideas and information. Both speech disorders and language disorders can adversely affect a student's educational performance.

Communication involves speaking as well as a multitude of nonverbal behaviors, such as facial expression, gestures, and head and body movements.

Speech and language disorders are often associated with other disorders. Specifically, speech disorders are sometimes associated with a **cleft palate or lip**, a condition in which a person has a split in the upper part of the oral cavity or the upper lip. Language disorders are sometimes the primary feature through which other disorders are identified. For example, a child with a hearing disorder may initially be referred for evaluation because he is not talking as well as other children his age.

Cultural Diversity in Communication

Students from different cultural backgrounds may have speech or language differences that affect their participation in the classroom. Although many individuals have a speech or language *difference,* they do not necessarily have a language or speech *disorder.* Difference does not always mean disorder (Battle, 2002).

Some students are bilingual, while others have dialectical differences or accents. An accent is a phonetic trait carried from a first language to the second (American Speech-Language-Hearing Association, 2007a). Every language contains a variety of forms, called dialects. A **dialect** is a language variation that a group of individuals uses and that reflects shared regional, social, or cultural/ethnic factors. Examples of culturally and linguistically diverse populations that may use an accent or a social dialect include African Americans, Latinos, Asian/Pacific Islanders, and Native Americans. Accents and dialects are not communication disorders; rather, they are differences (American Speech-Language-Hearing Association, 2007a).

Incidence

Approximately 19 percent (1,121,961) of all students ages six through twenty-one in special education are classified as having a speech-language disability (U.S. Department of Education, 2011). These figures do not include children who have communication disorders secondary to other conditions. Most students with communication disorders spend the majority of their day in the general education classroom.

DESCRIBING THE CHARACTERISTICS

For most children, the development of communication is uneventful and follows a typical, predictable pattern and timetable. For others, such as Kylie and Joey, it does not; these children may need assistance of a speech-language pathologist (SLP). It is helpful to

FIGURE 6.1 *Speech mechanism*

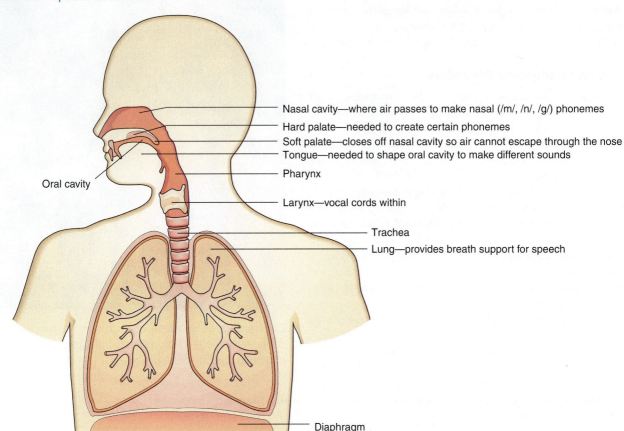

Nasal cavity—where air passes to make nasal (/m/, /n/, /g/) phonemes
Hard palate—needed to create certain phonemes
Soft palate—closes off nasal cavity so air cannot escape through the nose
Tongue—needed to shape oral cavity to make different sounds
Pharynx

Oral cavity

Larynx—vocal cords within

Trachea
Lung—provides breath support for speech

Diaphragm

understand the typical pattern of acquiring speech and language skills so you can recognize instances when communication disorders are present and then request assistance from an SLP.

Typical Development

Speech is the oral expression of language. This expression occurs when a person produces sounds and syllables. Figure 6.1 illustrates the speech mechanism that, through a coordinated effort, allows for sound production. As a person pushes air from the lungs, the muscles in the larynx move the vocal folds, producing sounds. The larynx sits on top of the trachea and contains the vocal folds (ligaments of the larynx); voice is produced here. A person forms sounds by varying the position of the lips, tongue, and lower jaw as air passes through the larynx (voice box), pharynx (a space extending from the nasal cavities to the esophagus), mouth, and nose.

Language is a structured, shared, rule-governed, symbolic system for communicating. The five components of our language system are phonology (sound system), morphology (word forms), syntax (word order and sentence structure), semantics (word and sentence meanings), and pragmatics (social use of language). Each dimension works together with the others to create a robust language system.

Phonology is the use of sounds to make meaningful syllables and words. Phonology encompasses the rules and sequencing of individual speech sounds (called **phonemes**) and how they are produced, depending on their placement in a syllable or word. For example, consonants at the beginning of syllables or words (e.g., "*t*ap") are produced slightly differently from those in the middle (e.g., "ca*tt*le") or at the end of syllables or words (e.g., "pa*t*"). Phonological use requires correct pronunciation as well as awareness of sound differences as they signal change in meaning. In English, for instance, the word *bill* is different from *pill* by only one phoneme: /b/. By changing one phoneme, a speaker can produce a totally different word. Although English spelling has twenty-six letters, English speakers use them to produce forty-five different sounds. For example, /th/, /sh/, /oy/, and /ou/ are four completely different sounds that are represented in spelling as different combinations of two of the twenty-six letters (Owens, 2012).

Morphology is the system that governs the structure of words (Owens, 2012). Phonemes or single sounds have little meaning on their own, but some can be grouped into syllables or words that have meaning. The smallest meaningful unit of speech is called a morpheme. For instance, when -s is added to *bill,* the word becomes plural. Formerly having had one **morpheme**, the word now has two: *bill* (a mouth structure on a bird, a written document) and -s (denoting plurality). Morphological rules allow speakers to add plurals, inflection, affixes, and past-tense markers to verbs. For example, correct use of morphological rules allows a child to change *swim* to *swimmed* and then, as the child matures, to *swam,* an irregular past-tense verb. An understanding of morphological rules allows us to recognize meaning just by hearing it.

Syntax provides rules for putting together a series of words to form sentences (Owens, 2012). Receptively, a child must be able to note the significance in the order of others' words. For example, "I want that cookie" means that the speaker desires a cookie, whereas "Do I want that cookie?" indicates a question in which the speaker is determining if she wants a cookie. Expressively, a child must be able to use word order to generate new sentences and to know when sentences are not grammatically correct. Just as phonology provides the rules for putting together strings of phonemes to form words, syntax provides rules for putting together a series of words to construct sentences.

The first three dimensions of language—phonology, morphology, and syntax—combine to determine the form of language, that is, what the language looks like. The next two dimensions of language—semantics and pragmatics—determine the content and social use of language (Bloom & Lahey, 1978).

Semantics refers to the meaning of what is expressed. Semantic development has both receptive and expressive components. Children first learn to understand the meaning of words and then to verbally or manually use the words and sentences meaningfully. Children start out with a small number of words that represent a large number of objects in their environments; for example, to young children, all men may be "daddy." This is called an overextension and is typical in semantic development (Owens, 2012).

Pragmatics refers to the use of communication in contexts. Pragmatics is the overall organizer for language (Owens, 2012). Caregivers and infants use the rules of pragmatics in their interactions, and children learn to use social communication very early (Kuder, 2008). After using smiles and simple verbalizations, children request objects, actions, or information; protest actions; comment on objects or actions; greet; and acknowledge comments. These skills allow them to use language socially to interact within their environments and with people in those environments more efficiently.

No one knows for sure just how the five dimensions of language come to work together so that children acquire useful language. Theories explaining how children acquire language abound (Hoff, 2009). In the 1950s, linguist Norm Chomsky (1957) proposed that children are born ready to develop language skills because of an inborn language acquisition device. Later, behaviorists proposed that the ability to learn and use language is not inborn but happens as children imitate and practice. Today, researchers investigate the effects of a child's imitation, practice, and other social interactions on language development. Their research has been compiled into social interaction theories.

Social interaction theories emphasize that communication skills are learned through social

It is important that young children learn and practice pragmatics in and outside of school.

interactions (Hoff, 2009). Parents and caregivers teach language during their interactions. These theories hold that language development is the outcome of a child's drive for attachment with his or her world; communication develops in order for the child to convey information about the environment to others and is learned through interactions with others.

The philosopher Lev Vygotsky (1978, 1987) is one of the advocates of the theory that social context and interaction within that context influence communicative choice. He argues that children develop by supplementing their independent problem-solving abilities with adult guidance or peer collaboration. Children learn by doing and from interacting with their more experienced partners. Social interactionists agree with Vygotsky's premise that children learn language by interacting either with adults, who naturally have more experiences, or with peers, who may have more or different experiences.

Children quickly learn to produce speech sounds during their early years. By the age of eight, they have learned to produce nearly all the consonants and vowels that make up the words of the family's native language. Learning these sounds usually proceeds in a fairly consistent sequence, but there may be variation among children in the time of acquisition.

Children's language development is complex. It begins early and depends on biological preparation, successful nurturance, sensorimotor experiences, and linguistic experiences (McCormick, 2003). Within the first month, babies begin to respond to human voices; and by three months, they turn, smile, and coo when spoken to (American Speech-Language-Hearing Association, 2011a). By their first birthdays, babies make sounds when spoken to, vary vocal pitch and intensity, and experiment with rhythm; they may even say their first words. Within the next year, their spoken vocabularies increase to 200 to 300 words, and the two-year-old's "no shoe" may become the three-year-old's "I don't want shoes." Three-year-old toddlers understand simple questions and prepositions such as *in, on, under,* and *up* and are able to follow two-step directions. They have a vocabulary of 900 to 1,000 words and use three- to four-word sentences. Their rapid development continues; and by age four, preschoolers ask questions using *who, what, when, where, why,* and *how* and have vocabularies of 1,500 to 1,600 words. By age six, they use irregular verbs such as *be, go, run,* and *swim* and can verbally share their feelings and thoughts with an expressive vocabulary of 2,600 words (Owens, 2012).

Although most language development takes place in the preschool years, it continues throughout the school years. This later development occurs in the areas of language structure, vocabulary, and language use. During the school years, the child learns the language skills of reading and writing (Hulit et al., 2011).

Speech Disorders

Speech disorders include disorders of articulation, voice, and fluency (rate and rhythm of speech). These disorders can occur alone, in combination, or in conjunction with other disorders. For example, students who have hearing losses (Chapter 14) or cerebral palsy (Chapter 12) often have articulation or voice disorders as well as language disorders. Similarly, a few students with intellectual disability (Chapter 9) may demonstrate slight communication delays, while others demonstrate speech delays, language delays, or both speech and language delays.

Articulation Disorders. Articulation disorders are among the most frequent communication disorders in preschool and school-aged children. **Articulation** is a speaker's production of individual or sequenced sounds. An articulation disorder occurs when the child cannot correctly produce the various sounds and sound combinations of speech.

Articulation errors may be in the form of substitutions, omissions, additions, and distortions. **Substitutions** are common, as when a child substitutes /d/ for the voiced /th/ ("doze" for "those"), or /w/ for /r/ ("wabbit" for "rabbit"). It is common for young children to make sound substitutions that disappear with maturation, but pervasive and ongoing substitutions are of concern.

Omissions occur when a child leaves a phoneme out of a word. Children often omit sounds from consonant pairs ("boo" for "blue") and from the ends of words ("ap" for "apple"). **Additions** occur when students place a vowel between two consonants, converting "tree" into "tahree."

Distortions are modifications of the production of a phoneme in a word; a listener gets the sense that the sound is being produced, but it seems distorted. Common distortions, called lisps, occur when /s/, /z/, /sh/, and /ch/ are mispronounced.

Articulation problems, like all communication disorders, vary. Children often are identified in early childhood settings through school-based speech-language screenings. Many of them have mild or moderate articulation disorders; their speech is understood by others yet contains sound-production errors. Other children have articulation disorders that have a more significant impact on their interactions, making it nearly impossible for others to understand them. When children have serious articulation disorders, they usually benefit from evaluation for an AAC device.

There are many reasons for teachers such as you to refer a student with articulation problems to a speech-language pathologist. If a student's articulation problem negatively affects his interactions in your class or his educational performance, referral is in order. Likewise, if a child's sound-production errors make her speech difficult or impossible to understand, you are justified in referring the child to an SLP. Furthermore, articulation problems resulting from neurological injuries (e.g., cerebral palsy and stroke) typically require therapy. Therapy is also needed to assist students with clefts of the palate or lip if they cannot produce speech sounds or sound combinations correctly. Therapy may also be needed to help a student with a hearing loss who is experiencing difficulty in correctly producing speech sounds because he cannot hear the sounds clearly.

Apraxia of Speech. **Apraxia** is a motor speech disorder that affects the way in which a student plans to produce speech. The preferred term for children is childhood apraxia of speech (CAS) (American Speech-Language-Hearing Association, 2007b). Apraxia can be acquired as the result of a trauma such as a stroke, a tumor, or a head injury, or with other disorders. Apraxia can also occur early in life in isolation without trauma or other disorders.

Students with apraxia have difficulty with the voluntary, purposeful movements of speech even though they have no paralysis or weakness of the muscles involved in speech. They have difficulty positioning the articulators and sequencing the sounds. Students with apraxia may be able to say the individual sounds required for speech in isolation or syllables, but they cannot produce them in longer words and sentences. They may be able to say sounds and words correctly when there is no pressure or request to do so but not when there is.

Some characteristics of apraxia are errors in production of vowels, inconsistent speech errors, more errors as words or sentences get longer, voicing errors (for example, /b/ for /p/ or /g/ for /k/), and stress on the wrong syllables, also referred to as prosody. These errors are not usually present in students who have traditional articulation disorders. Students with apraxia need frequent therapy that focuses on repetition, sound sequencing, and movement patterns (American Speech-Language-Hearing Association, 2007b; Caruso & Strand, 1999). When individuals have significant difficulty with coordinating motor movements for sound production, as Kylie does, they usually benefit from evaluation for an AAC device while they continue to work on their speech.

Voice Disorders. Each person has a unique voice. This voice reflects the interactive relationship of pitch, duration, intensity, resonance, and vocal quality. Pitch is determined by the rate of vibration in the vocal folds; men tend to have lower-pitched voices than women do. **Pitch** is affected by the tension and size of the vocal folds, the health of the larynx, and the location of the larynx. **Duration** is the length of time any speech sound requires.

Intensity (loudness or softness) is based on the perception of the listener and is determined by the air pressure coming from the lungs through the vocal folds. Rarely do individuals believe that their voices are too loud. Rather, they may seek professional voice therapy because their voices are too soft.

Resonance, the perceived quality of someone's voice, is determined by the way in which the tone coming from the vocal folds is modified by the spaces of the throat, mouth, and nose. Individuals with an unrepaired cleft palate may experience resonance problems because the opening from the mouth to the nasal cavity may be too large or differently shaped. This type of resonance trait is an example of **hypernasality**, in which air is allowed to pass through the nasal cavity on sounds other than /m/, /n/, and /ng/. Sometimes

IEP TIP

Unless everyone on a student's IEP team has heard the student try to communicate, team members would be wise to observe him or her before drafting the IEP.

Students can learn pragmatics by working together; each can become a coach for the others to communicate in a particular environment.

students have another type of resonance problem; they may sound as if they have a cold or are holding their noses when speaking. This is referred to as **hyponasality** because air cannot pass through the nose and comes through the mouth instead. These students may need speech therapy to learn how to produce non-nasal sounds.

The quality of the voice is affected by problems of breath support or vocal-fold functioning as well as resonance. You might have experienced short-term vocal-quality problems after cheering at a football game. Repeated abuse of the vocal folds may cause vocal nodules, growths that result from the rubbing together of the vocal-fold edges. When the folds cannot vibrate properly or come together completely, the sound of your voice will change temporarily until the vocal nodules heal. This short-term problem usually heals because the vocal-fold abuse is not constant. If, however, nodules develop and persist, therapy may help a student learn to talk in a way that is less abusive to the vocal mechanisms. In most cases, nodules disappear after rest and/or voice therapy. If vocal nodules are the result of an organic problem, therapy alone may not resolve them, and surgery may be required (Justice, 2010).

Fluency Disorders. Normal speech requires correct articulation, vocal quality, and **fluency** (rate and rhythm of speaking). Fluent speech is smooth, flows well, and appears to be effortless. Fluency problems are characterized by interruptions in the flow of speaking, such as atypical rate or rhythm, as well as repetitions of sounds, syllables, words, and phrases.

All children and adults have difficulties with fluency on occasion. They hesitate, repeat themselves, or use fillers such as "umm" at one time or another. In other instances, dysfluency is considered stuttering, which is frequent repetition and/or prolongation of words or sounds. More males than females stutter (American Speech-Language-Hearing Association, 2011b).

Language Impairments

Students may have language disorders that are receptive, expressive, or both. Their language impairment may be associated with another disability, or it may be a **specific language impairment**—not related to any physical or intellectual disability. Despite their causes, language impairments have a substantial effect on classroom participation and learning.

Phonology. Students with phonological disorders may be unable to discriminate between differences in speech sounds or sound segments that signify differences in words. For example, the word *pen* may sound no different from *pin*. Their inability to differentiate sounds, as well as similar, rhyming syllables, may cause reading and/or spelling difficulties (Apel & Swank, 1999; Lombardino, Riccio, Hynd, & Pinheiro, 1997). Phonological difficulties are common in children with language impairments and may affect reading (McCormick & Loeb, 2003). You should be sensitive to these phonological disorders as young children develop early literacy skills (Gillon, 2007).

Morphology. Children with morphological difficulties have problems using the structure of words to get or give information. They may make a variety of errors. For example, they may not use *-ed* to signal past tense, as in *walked,* or *-s* to signal plurality. When a child is unable to use morphological rules appropriately, the average length of her utterances is sometimes shorter than expected for the child's age because plurals, verb markers, and affixes may be missing from her statements (McCormick & Loeb, 2003). Students with morphological difficulties are unable to be as specific in their communication as others are. For example, if they do not use verb markers such as *-ed,* it is difficult to know if they are referring to past or present tense.

Morphology errors can be associated with differences in dialects as well as with a variety of other conditions, including intellectual disability (Chapter 9), autism (Chapter 11), hearing loss or deafness (Chapter 14), and expressive language delay. Incorrect use of morphology is also associated with specific language impairment.

Syntax. Syntactical errors are those involving word order, such as ordering words in a manner that does not convey meaning to the listeners (e.g., "Where one them park at?"), using immature structures for a given age or developmental level (e.g., a four-year-old child using two-word utterances, such as "Him sick"), misusing negatives (e.g., a four-year-old child saying, "Him no go"), or omitting structures (e.g., "He go now"). As with phonology and morphology, differences in syntax sometimes can be associated with dialects and other conditions.

Semantics. Children who experience difficulty using words singly or together in sentences may have semantic disorders. They may have difficulty with multiple-meaning words and have restricted meanings for words (McCormick & Loeb, 2003). Some students with semantic disorders may have problems with words that express time and space (e.g., *night, tiny*), cause and effect (e.g., "Push button, ball goes"), and inclusion versus exclusion (e.g., *all, none*). Sometimes students with semantic language disorders rely on words with fairly nonspecific meanings (e.g., *thing, one, that*) because of their limited knowledge of vocabulary. Difficulty with semantics can impact both understanding and expressing concepts in the classroom.

Pragmatics. Pragmatics focuses on the social use of language—the communication between a speaker and a listener within a shared social environment. Pragmatic skills include adapting communication to varied situations, obtaining and maintaining eye contact, using appropriate body language, maintaining a topic, and taking turns in conversations.

Pragmatic disorders are reflected in many different ways. A student who talks for long periods of time and does not allow anyone else an opportunity to converse may be displaying signs of a pragmatic disorder. Similarly, a student whose comments during class are unrelated to the subject at hand or who asks questions at an inappropriate time may be exhibiting a pragmatic disorder (American Speech-Language-Hearing Association, 2010b). Students who have difficulty with pragmatics include those with autism (Chapter 11) and traumatic brain injury (Chapter 13).

DETERMINING THE CAUSES

There are two types of speech and language disorders, each classified according to its cause: (1) **organic disorders**, those caused by an identifiable problem in the neuromuscular mechanism of the person; and (2) **functional disorders**, those with no identifiable organic or neurological cause.

The causes of organic disorders are numerous; they may originate in the nervous system, the muscular system, the chromosomes, or the formation of the speech mechanism. They may include hereditary malformations, prenatal injuries, toxic disturbances, tumors, traumas, seizures, infectious diseases, muscular diseases, and vascular impairments (Gillam & Gillam, 2011). Neuromuscular disabilities may result in difficulties with clear speech-sound production. The speech disorder would then have an organic origin and be classified as an organic speech disorder.

A functional speech and/or language disorder is present when the cause of the impairment is unknown. An articulation disorder with no known physical cause is regarded as functional in nature.

Communication disorders can be classified further according to when the problem began. A disorder that occurs at or before birth is referred to as a **congenital disorder**. A disorder that occurs well after birth is an **acquired disorder**. For example, an acquired communication disorder may be present after a severe head injury (Chapter 13). A functional disorder may be congenital or acquired. Some causes have both organic and functional origins. In addition, portions of the communication disorder may have been present at birth, and other parts may have been acquired later in life.

Evaluating Students with Communication Disorders

DETERMINING THE PRESENCE OF COMMUNICATION DISORDERS

Under IDEA, a speech or language impairment is a communication disorder, such as stuttering, impaired articulation, a language impairment, or a voice impairment, that adversely affects a child's educational performance. Educators, early intervention specialists, and speech-language therapists try to meet the physical, cognitive, communication, social, or emotional and adaptive needs of infants and toddlers ages birth through two and young children ages three through five who have communication disorders.

They start by conducting a screening (an intervention also called problem solving and prereferral), a referral for evaluation, or both. Many school districts use interventions as the first step to determining if a referral is needed (American Speech-Language-Hearing Association, 2010a). The emphasis of the intervention or prereferral is to begin to explore the relationship between communication abilities and a student's participation in the school environment. Box 6.1 describes the evaluation process.

During interventions, after a referral for an assessment, or both, the speech-language pathologist gathers information from sources such as school records, parent and teacher interviews, hearing and vision screenings, observations, speech samples, language samples, classwork samples/portfolios, checklists, standardized tests, non-standardized tests, and curriculum-based assessments. Having completed the assessment, the speech-language pathologist determines if a communication impairment/disorder is present and if it affects the child's learning. Depending on the area of speech and/or language being assessed, the speech-language pathologist may obtain certain types of information using the assessment tools shown in Box 6.1 and described in more detail here.

Speech Assessments

Speech assessments determine the presence of articulation, voice, or fluency problems.

Articulation. Articulation assessments evaluate a student's abilities to produce speech sounds in single words, sentences, and conversation. Speech-language pathologists listen, noting the phonemes in error, the pattern of the error, and the frequency of the error. Test items include use of consonants in the initial, middle, and final positions of words (e.g., for /p/, students might name a "pig," a "zipper," and a "cup"). An **oral motor exam**, which is the examination of the appearance, strength, and range of motion of the lips, tongue, palate, teeth, and jaw, is also typically conducted.

Voice. Voice evaluations include information about the onset and course of the voice problem, environmental factors that might affect vocal quality, and typical voice use (Verdolini, 2000), including pitch, intensity, and nasality.

Fluency. When completing a fluency assessment, the speech-language pathologist measures the amount of dysfluency as well as the type and duration of dysfluencies while the student is speaking. The SLP also notes associated speech and nonspeech behaviors such as eye blinking or head movements (Haynes & Pindzola, 2012).

Language Assessments

Language assessments focus on specific components of language such as phonology, semantics, morphology, syntax, pragmatics, and overall expressive and/or receptive language. Students who are nonverbal or use nonconventional means of communication require more descriptive than standardized assessment measures (Downing, 2005). The SLP documents the communicative forms (conventional and nonconventional) and the

BOX 6.1

NONDISCRIMINATORY EVALUATION PROCESS

Determining the Presence of Communication Disorders

Observation	**Medical personnel observe:** The child is not achieving developmental milestones related to communication skills, or there is a change in a child's communication skills.
	Teacher and parents observe: The child has difficulty understanding or using language. The child may also have difficulty speaking clearly.
Screening	**Assessment measures:**
	Classroom work products: The child may be hesitant to participate in verbal classroom work. Written classroom projects may reflect errors of verbal communication or, in some instances, be a preferred avenue of expression for the student.
	Vision and hearing screening: The child may have a history of otitis media (middle-ear infection). Hearing may be normal, or the student may have hearing loss. Limited vision may impact language skills.
Prereferral	**Implementation of suggestions from a school-based team:** The teacher models speech sounds, expands language, asks open-ended questions, etc.
	If the child has been identified before entering school, the parents may implement suggestions from the school-based team.
Referral	If, in spite of interventions, the child still performs poorly in academics or continues to manifest communication impairments, the child is referred to a multidisciplinary team. The team may continue with more in-depth interventions.
Nondiscriminatory evaluation procedures and standards	**Assessment measures:**
	Speech and language tests (articulation, phonology, language sample, speech sample, oral motor functioning, receptive language, and expressive language): The student performs significantly below average in one or more areas.
	Anecdotal records: The student may have genetic or medical factors that contribute to speech or language difficulties. Some students with other disabilities are at risk for having speech and language disorders.
	Curriculum-based assessment: A speech and/or language difficulty may affect progress in the curriculum.
	Direct observation: The student experiences difficulty in communicating.
Determination	The nondiscriminatory evaluation team determines that the student has a communication disorder and needs special education and related services. The student's IEP team proceeds to develop appropriate education options for the child.

functions these forms serve by observing the child in different environments and with various communication partners (Downing, 2005). For example, the SLP might observe this interaction: John looks at a friend's snack and then at his friend. He repeats this behavior several times. When the friend gives John some of his snack, John smiles. The SLP then notes the communication functions observed and the form the student used, including that John initiated a communication interaction, requested an item, and expressed a social interaction (e.g., *thank you* or *please*). John's forms of communication included eye contact (to gain attention to initiate communication), eye gaze (to request), and facial expression (a smile as thanks). The SLP then determines how to shape and expand on John's communication forms (e.g., speech, pointing to pictures, voice output, etc.).

Bilingual and bidialectical skills make this speech-language pathologist especially effective, but note that she and her student also communicate by a semi-universal sign.

Multicultural Considerations

Sometimes a student will need specialized speech or language assessment, as when the student is bilingual or multilingual. The SLP must be particularly skilled when assessing the communicative capabilities of students for whom English is not the primary language. Fair, unbiased evaluation is difficult for a student who is **bilingual** (uses two languages equally well) or **bidialectal** (uses two variations of a language) or for whom language dominance (the primary language of the student) is difficult to determine.

To assess such a student, the SLP should not merely translate test items into the child's primary language. The SLP must determine whether a bilingual student should be tested in the student's first language or in English (Paradis, Genesee, & Crago, 2011). Then the SLP tests the student in the dominant language with appropriate diagnostic tools to determine whether a language difference or a disability exists. The SLP determines a student's language strengths and preferences using appropriate assessment tools and learns about the student's communicative abilities and needs using alternative rather than standardized measures (Roseberry-McKibbin & O'Hanlon, 2005). Having observed a communication disorder or disability, the SLP then can plan appropriate therapies using culturally sensitive standardized measures whenever possible.

DETERMINING THE NATURE OF SPECIALLY DESIGNED INSTRUCTION AND SERVICES

Language occurs throughout the school day and is the vehicle for teaching the curriculum (Howell & Nolet, 2000; Losardo & Notari-Syverson, 2001). Curriculum-based assessment enables you and your colleagues to determine a student's present strengths and needs in school and then to develop strategies to help the student progress within the general education curriculum (Losardo & Notari-Syverson, 2001). Curriculum-based assessments use tasks and materials that relate to the general education curriculum and depend on partnerships to be accomplished (Nelson, 2010). Whether the student is asked to discuss a topic verbally, answer questions, read language, write language, or work with others cooperatively, he is practicing language throughout the entire curriculum.

During curriculum-based assessment, the student's teaching team determines the nature of specifically designed instruction by data-based performance modifications and by assisting the student to complete portions of the assessment instrument (Howard & Nolet, 2000). This portion of the assessment usually begins after the team identifies the student's problem and her degree of discrepancy from her peers. The SLP then develops theories aimed at decreasing the discrepancy, tests the theories systematically, and monitors the student's performance by collecting data.

Because speech and language occur throughout the day and data collection may need to be undertaken in multiple settings, the SLP may need other members of the team to assist in data collection; the classroom teacher often collects data because that teacher is generally with the student for more of the day than other educational staff are. The SLP then analyzes the data and makes decisions about instruction based on them (Howard & Nolet, 2000). This procedure is called data-based performance modification (Howard & Nolet, 2000). Assisted assessment is the process of determining what strategy or supports the student may need to accomplish the task that is being monitored (Howard & Nolet, 2000). Both of these procedures help define the instruction that best suits a student and the supports he may need to be successful in communicating in school.

IEP TIP

As helpful as school-based assessment is, the IEP team should also consider conducting home- and community-based assessments to gain a thorough understanding of how the student communicates.

Designing an Appropriate IEP

PARTNERING FOR SPECIAL EDUCATION AND RELATED SERVICES

Collaboration is critical when planning and providing services for students with communication disorders. Communication occurs throughout the day, so it is important for everyone who works with the student to have a good understanding of how she best understands and/or expresses information. For instance, the lunchroom and recess staff may need to understand strategies to help her initiate requests from others, take turns, and use AAC systems. Those staff members also could be an excellent resource for anecdotal information regarding progress toward the student's goals in a natural context with her peers. Furthermore, collaboration may help lighten everyone's workload (Giangreco, 2000; Sandall & Schwartz, 2002).

The American Speech-Language-Hearing Association (2003) has identified four different types of activities (called activity clusters) that SLPs use in schools: direct services to students, indirect services to implement students' education programs, indirect services to support students in the general education curriculum, and activities as members of the community of educators. Each requires a high level of collaboration with teachers and families.

Direct service involves direct contact between the student and the SLP. Historically, direct services have constituted the majority of an SLP's workload. By contrast, indirect services consist, for example, of designing and programming a student's augmentative communication device and training paraeducators in how to use it. Indirect activities also include meeting and planning with teachers and paraprofessionals to align the student's IEP goals with the standards for the general curriculum and designing instructional strategies so the student can make progress in the general curriculum. Activities that SLPs engage in as members of a community of educators include staff meetings, school committees, and other duties expected of all educators.

Teachers can expect SLPs to move away from the more traditional model of individual and group-pullout direct services and instead participate in more collaborative consultation, curriculum-based intervention programs, and classroom-based direct services (American Speech-Language-Hearing Association, 2003). SLP collaboration includes supportive teaching, complementary teaching, consultation, and team teaching. Each requires a high level of collaboration with teachers and families, as exemplified in Boxes 6.2 and 6.3.

DETERMINING SUPPLEMENTARY AIDS AND SERVICES

Assistive technology (AT) includes any piece of equipment, commercial or hand-made, that assists an individual to perform various functions, such as communication. One form of AT is an augmentative and alternative communication (AAC) system. AAC systems consist of integrated components that supplement the communication abilities of individuals who cannot meet their communication needs through speaking (Beukelman & Mirenda, 2005). An AAC system may include an AAC device, a physical object to transmit or receive messages, and other types of communication such as gesturing, speaking, and/or writing. AAC devices include communication books, communication/language boards, communication charts, mechanical or electronic voice output equipment, and computers.

An AAC device contains a set of symbols. A *symbol* is a visual, auditory, gestural, and/or tactile

Assistive technology can be as simple and universal as a handheld personal assistant, and even that device can be specially tailored for a designated user.

BOX 6.2
MY VOICE

Carrie Lauds Joey's Educators

Literacy skills are important for all children but especially so for Joey because he uses written text instead of oral discussion to learn new information and to learn speech. As his mother Carrie explained, "Joey has been reading words since he was two."

Joey participates in guided reading groups with his second-grade classmates. Determining his comprehension of grade-level text, however, is another issue. At first, "it was hard for the teachers to figure out what he knew as he is not good at answering oral questions." So, Carrie said, "to have a better understanding of what Joey was getting out of the stories, Joey's teachers typed out the questions" and provided multiple-choice answers. Usually he gets 70 to 75 percent correct. "If he doesn't get the answer correct, they go back to the page that relates to that question, talk about the picture, and give him the question again." Carrie noted, "They really do a great job of making him part of the class. The other kids talk to him and help him and he even helps them with reading."

But spelling challenges Joey. Once he has experience with a word, he generally is able to spell it; so spending time rewriting words he already knows does not engage him. He also has trouble writing with a pencil. So Joey's educators administer a pretest when presenting a new list of words to the class. Joey studies the words he missed and types them. His teachers and SLP then assess the definitions and comprehension purposes of those words so that they can teach them to Joey.

Carrie said, "I like that the teachers work on social skills with Joey. They understand that play is important, so they encourage play with him. When he goes to the resource room, one or two of his peers go with him." The teachers provide words, phrases, and questions in text form for Joey to use while playing. "Now he is starting to say these things on his own and getting more creative with his toys, and this draws other kids to him."

Carrie's favorite idea was to send a digital camera to school with her children. Joey's teachers take pictures through the day so when Joey and his sister Kylie get home off the bus they can discuss what happened at school, thus giving Carrie and her husband Paul a point of reference to build upon and a way to practice communication. "This is great because Joey can't really answer the question 'What did you do today?'"

BOX 6.3
PARTNERSHIP TIPS

Three Partnership Options

There are three usual ways for teachers and speech-language pathologists (SLPs) to work with each other (American Speech-Language-Hearing Association, 2003):

- *Consultation.* Consultation involves activities such as meeting with the classroom teacher to discuss lessons and to develop adaptations and accommodations for the student in the classroom. Let's consider Cristena, a ninth grader with autism. She loves science, music, and drama. The science curriculum presents many challenges for her, so her SLP works with her classroom teacher to adapt text materials, handouts, and tests so that they match Cristena's language abilities. The adapted science handouts also benefit students who need visual presentations of the content.

- *Supportive teaching.* Supportive teaching occurs when the teacher and the SLP plan lessons together. The SLP completes some pre- and post-activities related to the lesson with the student, and the teacher and SLP co-teach the lesson. Andrew, for instance, is a second grader with Down syndrome. His class is studying the life cycle of the frog. His SLP and teacher meet to plan for the unit and determine what extra supports Andrew will need to participate. They also discuss what responsibilities each will take during class.

The SLP works with Andrew individually to preteach vocabulary and then teaches part of the unit to the whole class. She may meet individually with Andrew again to clarify any information he did not understand.

- *Complementary teaching.* Complementary teaching occurs when the SLP and the teacher co-teach material for the lesson in ways that reflect their levels of expertise. Beth, for example, is in the fifth grade. She has language learning difficulties that include auditory processing weaknesses, and she has a hard time taking notes during social studies. So her SLP takes notes while the teacher teaches. He also prepares study guides, teaches small groups that need more adaptation, and on occasion teaches organizational skills to the whole class.

Speech-language pathologists can help students succeed in the general education curriculum. They need to be aware of curriculum plans and upcoming instructional opportunities the student may be involved in. Meeting with the general educator on a regular basis can be beneficial. Team members should define their roles and responsibilities to avoid confusion and misunderstanding, which will also leave them more time to focus on the student's outcomes.

representation of a concept (American Speech-Language-Hearing Association, 2004). Symbol sets include photographs, pictographs (symbols that look like what they represent), ideographs (more abstract symbols), printed words, objects, partial objects, miniature objects, braille, textures, or any combination of these symbols. Symbols that may be part of the AAC system, but not part of the symbol set for a physical device, include gestures, manual sign sets/systems, and/or spoken words.

A team approach is helpful when determining what assistive technology may be needed because so many areas need to be considered. Input from the parents as well as information regarding the student's vision skills, fine-motor skills, gross-motor skills, hearing, and curriculum requirements all help educators and SLPs recommend the features the AAC system should have and whether the student needs additional forms of AT. Once the student is trying out or using an AAC device, the student's educational team will develop a plan to monitor its benefits and to provide the appropriate vocabulary.

If the student is using an AAC device, individualized vocabulary will have to be added to it. There are a variety of comprehensive vocabulary sets available commercially that offer a range of frequently used vocabulary in both high- and low-tech versions and that may be customized for the student. Many of the high-tech devices also come with software so that the programming/editing can be completed on a separate computer and transferred to the student's device.

Students, especially those who are beginning to use symbols, depend on others to make vocabulary available for them to communicate. That is why you should carefully consider how to make vocabulary available throughout the school day. Focus on vocabulary that occurs frequently instead of vocabulary used only once or twice a day: For example, choose high-frequency core words such as *like, go, more, want,* etc. In addition, the ability to express a variety of communication functions (i.e., questions, comments, directives, and requesting) is also important. Without vocabulary, students cannot express their thoughts or discuss the topics that are being shared in their environments. The selection of a device, its features, and the degree of a student's needs and capacities all figure into establishing an AAC system.

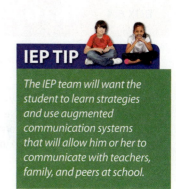

IEP TIP

The IEP team will want the student to learn strategies and use augmented communication systems that will allow him or her to communicate with teachers, family, and peers at school.

PLANNING FOR UNIVERSAL DESIGN FOR LEARNING

When planning universal design for learning for students with communication disorders, you must answer two questions: "How can I assure that my student understands what I am teaching?" and "How can I assure that my student can express what she knows?" Remember that universal design for learning includes modifications to how content is presented as well as options for expression. When you use only one or two methods to teach, especially if you only use verbal methods, some students with communication disorders, as well as some students without disabilities, are not able to access the material.

To assist, you can vary the format for relaying the information, such as by using both audio and text formats, visual representations with verbal information, graphics, graphic organizers, and controlled vocabulary. Similarly, you can vary the ways in which students demonstrate their knowledge. For instance, instead of assigning only a written report, also allow PowerPoint presentations, demonstrations with visual supports, taped oral reports, or dramatic performances. These and the facilitative language strategies described in Box 6.4 provide access to the general curriculum. Box 6.5 provides further examples of universal design, as described by a parent.

PLANNING FOR OTHER EDUCATIONAL NEEDS

Students with communication disorders may need support in building social relationships because they are at risk for difficulties in social communication (Rice, 1993). Social interactions are important; they increase classroom participation and build social relationships. Most children learn social skills with no instruction or support. However, other students may have difficulty recognizing social cues, initiating a conversation, maintaining a conversation, or determining how to verbally express emotions.

BOX 6.4

INTO PRACTICE

Facilitative Language Strategies

The facilitative language strategies described here have been validated in preschool settings (Bunce, 2008; Bunce & Watkins, 1995; Rice & Wilcox, 1995), but they can be used in any adult-child interaction in any context and provide many natural teaching and learning opportunities.

Focused contrast. Here, an adult highlights the difference between the child's speech or language and the adult's. This can occur as feedback or a model. During feedback, when the child says, "Otey," for "Okay," the adult could say, "Oh, you said 'Otey,' and I said, 'Okay.'" During a modeled focused-contrast approach, the adult provides many examples for the child. Thus, if the focus is on the past-tense marker *-ed*, the adult, while playing house, may say, "She is walking," while moving the doll and then stop the movement and say, "She walked to the door." The adult then repeats this strategy with numerous actions during play.

Modeling. Modeling helps a child learn a language or speech structure he doesn't yet use. If the structure is the plural marker *-s*, the adult may use it to describe the plurals in the ongoing activity, highlighting them with extra emphasis or stress.

Event casts. Event casts provide an ongoing description of an activity, just as a sports broadcaster might. The events can be what the child or adult is doing. For example, during dress-up play, the adult may say, "You are putting on the hat. Now you are putting on blue shoes."

Open questions. Questions that have a variety of possible answers are open questions. Examples include "What should we do next?" and "What do you think happens next?"

Expansions. The adult repeats the child's utterance, filling in the missing components. For example, if the child says, "Two horse," the adult expands with "Two brown horses."

Recasts. When recasting, the adult keeps the child's basic meaning but changes the structure or grammar of the child's utterance. For example, if the child says, "He has juice," the adult can say, "Yes, he is drinking juice now."

Redirects and prompted initiations. These strategies encourage children to interact with each other. When a child approaches an adult and makes a request that could be made to another child, the adult redirects him to ask a classmate: "You could tell Tom, 'I need a blue crayon.'" When a child does not make a request to an adult but has the opportunity to interact with another child, he might be prompted to ask another child to play or request some item.

To be able to use the facilitative language strategies described, follow these steps:

- Know the child's goals and objectives.
- View every interaction as an opportunity to use the strategies.
- Identify the goals and objectives that relate to specific activities of the day.
- Identify teaching strategies to be used during specific activities.
- Decide when to use strategies to emphasize targets within the activity.
- Use the strategies identified during the activity.
- Document the child's response.

BOX 6.5

UNIVERSAL DESIGN FOR PROGRESS

Graphic Organizers

When might graphic organizers be helpful?

- *During a lecture.* Use a graphic organizer to help students learn information and understand how parts of a lesson are related to each other (Boon, Burke, Fore, & Spencer, 2006), as a reference during discussion to help a student answer comprehension questions after discussion, and as a study guide for later testing.
- *During reading.* Use a graphic organizer to help students organize information (Cunningham & Allington, 2007). For example, if the purpose for reading is to compare and contrast two characters within a story, ask all members of the class to use a Venn diagram while reading and to write the qualities of each story character within the organizer as they read.

- *During the development of reference material.* Use an organizer to display data and information a student collects (Cunningham & Allington, 2007). The student can use the graphic organizer later as a reference tool. For example, in a math lesson students may survey others about a topic and graph the responses. In an English lesson, students may need to brainstorm a variety of describing words during a group discussion. Because some of the words may be unfamiliar to some of the students, they may need synonyms and/or pictures. All the information can be placed within a graphic organizer for reference.
- *During writing.* Use a graphic organizer to help students with writing activities (Sturm & Rankin-Erickson, 2002). The graphic display can help students sequence their thoughts and be a visual highlight of where they may need additional information.

Active listening is a life skill. In order to actively listen, one must comment, ask questions, and maintain a conversation as well as initiate topics within a natural context with peers (Musselwhite & Maro, 2010a, 2010b, 2010c). For instance, if students share good news or bad news that occurred over the weekend, others can focus on the importance of this news by commenting, "Awesome!" or "Oh, gross!" or "What happened next?" (Musselwhite & Maro, 2010a, 2010b, 2010c). These comments let the communication partner know that the other person is listening. As a learning strategy, active listening helps students increase their use of communication systems and offers an opportunity for the whole class to learn and practice social interactions skills.

Using Effective Instructional Strategies

EARLY CHILDHOOD STUDENTS: FACILITATIVE LANGUAGE STRATEGIES

Most early education programs facilitate language development. Because communication is social in nature and is learned across all parts of a child's day, the child's communication partners should use strategies to promote his speech and language development. The strategies you learned about in Box 6.4 were developed, researched, and refined in the Language Acquisition Preschool at the University of Kansas (Bunce & Watkins, 1995; Rice & Wilcox, 1995). In the preschool classroom, the adults provide the intervention with no additional pullout therapy, so children do not receive individual therapy. These strategies rest on several foundations: Language intervention is best when provided in a meaningful social context, language facilitation occurs across the preschool curriculum, language begins with the child, language is learned through interaction, valuable teaching occasions can arise in child-to-child interactions, and parents are valuable partners in language intervention programming.

ELEMENTARY AND MIDDLE SCHOOL STUDENTS: GRAPHIC ORGANIZER MODIFICATIONS

When children leave early childhood programs, they move into a curriculum in the early elementary grades that focuses on teaching them to read and write. Then in the later elementary and middle school years, they work on reading and writing to learn. Making these transitions can be difficult for students with communication disorders.

Graphic organizers are a form of advance organizer, which you first learned about in Chapter 5. They assist students to comprehend and write more effectively (Cunningham & Allington, 2007; Sturm & Rankin-Erickson, 2002). Graphic organizers provide a visual representation in an organized framework, and they are especially useful for students with Down syndrome, autism spectrum disorders, and language-learning disabilities (Kumin, 2001; Myles & Simpson, 2003; Nelson & Van Meter, 2004), as well as students who are learning English as a second language. Graphic organizers can be hand-drawn or computer-generated.

When using graphic organizers, you should first determine which organizer will best meet the desired curriculum outcome (Cunningham & Allington, 2007). You might choose a web design, a

Graphic organizers are simple yet effective methods for helping students with receptive language disorders remember information.

story map, a feature matrix, or data charts. You also should consider how students will participate when completing and using a graphic organizer and what adaptations they may need.

For example, if a student with a receptive language delay or disorder needs to learn and remember information for a science unit on insects, you may provide a web design using pictures to organize the insects' anatomical makeup, what the insects eat, what animals eat the insects, what habitats the insects live in, and so on. As you learned in Box 6.5, the information in a graphic organizer visually links together groups of important information for the student.

How Are Organizers Created?

You can create a graphic organizer template on most classroom computers, using standard drawing tools found in word processing software or in the computer's accessory tools. You can also draw them by hand. Further, you can locate premade organizers by searching the Web for graphic organizers or obtaining books with premade organizers. Some textbooks come with online companions that have graphic organizer ideas. There are also commercial programs that can be purchased that create graphic organizers on the computer.

What to Consider When Using Graphic Organizers

You should consider the student's past experience with graphic organizers. Students may not necessarily know how to fill out a graphic organizer or how to use the information within one to answer questions. You may need to provide examples, model how to complete them, and model how to find information using them (Cunningham & Allington, 2007).

You should consider how the student feels about writing. If he is concerned about making mistakes, reluctant to rewrite information, or hesitant to correct information, he might choose to write ideas on sticky notes instead of directly onto a standard, prepared organizer, thus giving himself the option to easily change the information or its placement (Foley & Staples, 2000). To assist some students, teachers can provide concepts, facts, ideas, and/or events. Then the students choose the information they want to display and place it into the organizer (Foley & Staples, 2000) or create their own organizer. The teacher may also use photos, drawings, symbol sets, or a combination, as Figure 6.2 demonstrates.

SECONDARY AND TRANSITIONAL STUDENTS: AUGMENTED INPUT

AAC systems enable students to participate in the curriculum. But learning to use communication symbols requires a team effort from the student's familiar and frequent communication partners. AAC instructional strategies should focus on teaching communication rather than solely teaching the student to operate AAC systems. AAC is a means to an end, the end being communication and participation. The students will need to have a comprehensive vocabulary in order to learn and express a wide range of daily communication functions. The students will also need to be able to explain the strategies and equipment that benefit them. They will need further instruction and support to meaningfully integrate their AAC communication systems into new communication environments.

One instructional strategy for modeling how to use AAC is the **system for augmenting language (SAL)** (Romski & Sevcik, 1988). SAL focuses on augmented input of language. Using SAL, communication partners augment their speech by activating the student's communication device in naturally occurring communication interactions at home and school and in the community, encouraging but not requiring the student to use the device (Romski & Sevcik, 2003). For example, during a literacy discussion, you could introduce the task by saying, "We will read this story. Then you will tell what happened first, second, third, and last in the story." While activating buttons on the device for "read," "story," "then," "tell," "first," "second," "third," and "last," the student has not only a model of what symbol vocabulary to use in that situation but also a model of how to use the vocabulary in conversation.

Although the SAL strategy was developed for use with electronic communication devices, augmented input can also be used if students have communication books or

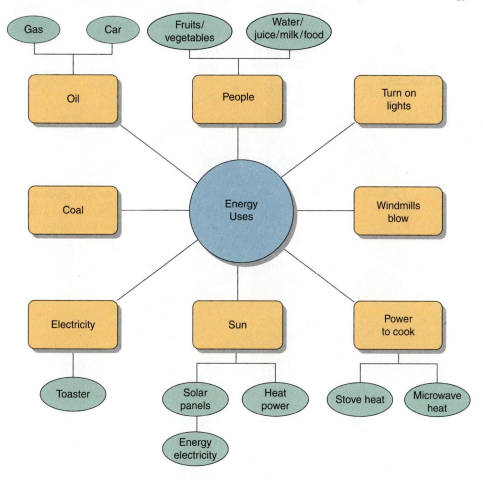

boards or sign language. It is sometimes called *aided language stimulation* when focusing on communication books or boards (Elder & Goossens, 1994; Goossens, Crain, & Elder, 1992). When the student uses sign language, the term *total communication* applies. Aided input can be effective with toddlers as well as students between the ages of six and twenty, regardless of whether a student is using SAL or the aided language stimulation strategy with a device (Romski & Sevcik, 1992, 1996; Romski, Sevcik, & Forrest, 2001).

The success of the augmented input instructional strategy depends on training the student's frequent and significant communication partners. Blackstone, Hunt-Berg, Nygard, and Schultz (2004) have developed a tool called Social Networks to identify these important partners. A student's communication partners should receive instruction about the importance of input with respect to the physical operation of the device as well as practice in providing input, feedback, and coaching in natural settings (Romski & Sevcik, 2003). Other, less familiar partners may need training only in the operation of the device and how to model input (Blackstone, 2006).

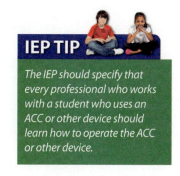

IEP TIP

The IEP should specify that every professional who works with a student who uses an ACC or other device should learn how to operate the ACC or other device.

Including Students with Communication Disorders

According to the U.S. Department of Education (2011), 86 percent of the children who receive speech and language services spend 80 to 100 percent of their time in the general education classroom (see Figure 6.3). That is so, in part, because effective teachers use some of the tips that you will find in Box 6.6.

Students who do not develop speech and language skills early in life will have a difficult time acquiring these skills later (Downing, 2005). In addition, students who do not

FIGURE 6.3 *Educational placement of students with speech and language impairments: School year 2008–2009*

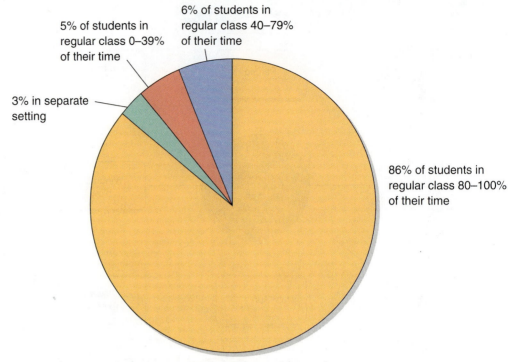

5% of students in regular class 0–39% of their time

6% of students in regular class 40–79% of their time

3% in separate setting

86% of students in regular class 80–100% of their time

Source: U.S. Department of Education. (2011). *Data accountability center: Individuals with Disabilities Education Act (IDEA) data.* Retrieved on February 12, 2011, from https://www.ideadata.org.

Note: Percentages have been rounded and collapsed across categories.

have a conventional communication system may use inappropriate, aggressive, or ineffective means to meet their needs (Downing, 2005). Other students may become passive. Language is also the basis for reading and writing skills; indeed, 50 percent or more of children with a language impairment in preschool or kindergarten have reading disabilities in primary or secondary grades (Catts & Kamhi, 1999).

Assessing Students' Progress

MEASURING STUDENTS' PROGRESS

Progress in the General Curriculum

There are many different tools for measuring a student's progress, but curriculum-based assessment is commonly used because it focuses on a student's progress in the general curriculum (Howell & Nolet, 2000; Losardo & Notari-Syverson, 2001). So you should consider using a data-based performance modification procedure to monitor a student's progress and make decisions about instructional strategies. Here's how that measurement system works: With input from the educational team, the SLP teams with the student's teachers to try to reduce the discrepancy between the student's current communication skill level and the curriculum standard against which the student's progress is assessed. For example, if a student exhibits atypical dysfluencies (or stuttering) and if the dysfluencies negatively affect her participation in class, interaction with other students, or both, the SLP might set a goal of monitoring the amount of class participation that occurs as a result of the student's improved fluency, give the teacher and the parents suggestions that may be helpful when speaking with someone who stutters, work with the student to teach different fluency strategies, observe in class to monitor the use of the strategies in the classroom and the student's class participation, and ask the teacher to rate the student's fluency during the day and tally class participation at agreed-upon times.

BOX 6.6

INCLUSION TIPS

	What You Might See	What You Might Be Tempted to Do	Alternative Responses	Ways to Include Peers in the Process
Behavior	The student appears shy and reserved. He may not participate in large-group settings. It may take him time to compose a response when speaking in front of the class.	Encourage him to hurry or avoid calling on him in large groups.	Provide a multiple-choice response option. Write the questions on the board, giving students time to compose their answers before calling on specific children. Allow for small-group discussion and reporting.	Provide multiple-choice response options or alternate response options for all students, along with other types of question formats.
Social interactions	She is alone during unstructured times. She does not ask friends to play. She does not join peer interactions.	Assume she is happy alone, and let her be.	Demonstrate that you value her contributions. Provide a model to help her learn to interact with other students.	Encourage peer buddies within the classroom for all of the students to help model and encourage interactions with other children.
Educational performance	He produces syntactically incomplete sentences verbally and in writing. He avoids writing tasks.	Constantly correct him. Decrease the occurrence of writing assignments.	Provide visual and verbal models of complete sentences. Continue to provide lots of opportunities for writing. Provide positive feedback.	Allow small-group interactions with assigned roles that rotate to every student. The students can then provide models for each other.
Classroom attitudes	She expects the teacher to intercede when she has difficulty with other students. She might rely on the teacher to initiate interactions with other students.	Tell her to go play with others. Assume the children will work it out on their own.	Teach all the students ways to interact and solve problems.	Provide opportunities for the students to practice independent interactions with one another, offering assistance when needed.

Progress in Addressing Other Educational Needs

Ecological inventories are another helpful tool for monitoring communication progress. You will learn more about ecological inventories in Chapter 9 and how they apply to students with intellectual disabilities, but those inventories can also assist you to determine what communication expectations exist in natural environments (Downing, 2005).

When you conduct an ecological inventory, your first step is to collaborate with the SLP and others to determine what interactions occur within the natural environment. For example, assume a student needs to summarize current-events articles for a social studies class. You, the SLP, and others analyze the steps or components of the task, such as announcing the title, describing the main idea, including some of the facts disclosed, stating the conclusion, and offering an opinion.

This team then observes one of the student's peers completing the task and monitors the degree to which the peer is independent. Was the peer completely independent; did equipment need to be set up first; were verbal cues needed?

Now the student completes the task, and the team records the steps that the student needed assistance with or was not yet able to complete. The team then compares those data with the peer's data to determine the student's degree of discrepancy and target the areas of discrepancy for instruction, strategies, and possibly supplementary aids.

Subsequent assessments based on the ecological inventory enable the team to determine whether the instruction, strategies, and/or supplementary aids are helping the student decrease the discrepancy in the performance observed. For instance, the student may need new vocabulary to be added to an AAC device, picture cues for the steps, pages of pictures of line drawings (called topic boards), or role playing and practice with others.

MAKING ACCOMMODATIONS FOR ASSESSMENT

Many students with communication disorders do not need accommodations for assessment. Others may need additional time for tests or access to a word processor and computer software when writing. When assessing a student with more significant speech and language impairments, you should ask, "What is being assessed, how does the student best receive information, and how does the student best express himself?" You should consider the focus of the assessment in order to reduce the chances that the student will be assessed in more than one area at one time. For instance, if the student's augmentative voice-output communication system is new or unfamiliar and he uses it during a science test, you may not be accurately assessing the student's understanding of science but the student's knowledge of the communication system. In other words, you may be finding it difficult to differentiate between whether the student did not answer a question correctly because he did not know how to find the answer with the new system or did not answer correctly because he did not know that particular science concept.

Similarly, if a student who exhibits difficulty understanding written complex language structures takes a science test but the test format is not adapted for him, then you may be assessing the student's ability to read complex sentence structures as well as his knowledge about science. If you want to assess the student's understanding of complex language structures, then you should make sure that the test consists of complex structures. If, however, you are assessing science, you may need to take into account the student's preferred manner of receiving information. When the assessment is isolated, the student may concentrate solely on what he knows about science.

You should present information in a manner that assists the student's comprehension of the assessment directions and questions. For instance, if your student finds it difficult to receive written information, you should explain it verbally or use visual supports. If a student has difficulty understanding complex sentence structures, you should adjust the language and sentence structure, use visual supports, or both.

If a student has difficulty expressing herself verbally or in written form, you should use an assessment format that does not require long verbal or written output. For example, a multiple-choice or true-false format may be helpful. She may then only need to respond with a one-word answer, a switch activation, or a gesture indicating the correct answer. This change in format may decrease the probability that the student will not provide the answer because of the length of the response needed, an inability to clearly express an answer verbally, or both.

The format should complement the student's most common means of expression. For instance, if the student has begun to explore a new communication system, such as a device using a computer screen, you should use the more familiar previous system for assessment until he has had time to learn the new system.

ADDRESSING THE PROFESSIONAL STANDARDS

The following Council for Exceptional Children (CEC) Common Core Knowledge and Skills are addressed in this chapter through the content and concepts we discuss. See the Appendix for a full listing of these Knowledge and Skill statements:

ICC2K1, ICC2K2, ICC2K4, ICC2K5, ICC2K6, ICC4S3, ICC4S4, ICC4S5, ICC5S3, ICC5S4, ICC5S9, ICC6K4, ICC6S1, ICC6S2, ICC7S1, ICC7S3, ICC7S6, ICC7S9, ICC8K3, ICC8S2, ICC8S6, ICC8S8, ICC10S2, ICC10S4, ICC10S5

Summary

IDENTIFYING STUDENTS WITH COMMUNICATION DISORDERS

- Communication disorders include both speech and language impairments.
- A speech disorder is an impairment of one's articulation of speech sounds, fluency, or voice.
- A language disorder reflects problems in receiving information; understanding it; and formulating a spoken, written, or symbolic response.
- Communication differences that are related to the culture of the individual are not considered impairments.
- Language is a shared system of rules and symbols for the exchange of information. It includes rules of phonology, morphology, syntax, semantics, and pragmatics.
- Communication impairments can affect a student's academic, social, and emotional development.

EVALUATING STUDENTS WITH COMMUNICATION DISORDERS

- The speech-language pathologist is the professional who determines the presence and extent of a speech and/or language impairment.
- Assessments include the use of informal and formal measures. They should occur in settings that are comfortable and natural for the student.

DESIGNING AN APPROPRIATE IEP

- The collaborative participation of students, their teachers, speech-language pathologists, and parents to enhance communicative development results in students' language objectives being targeted in many settings and situations.

- When planning universal design for learning for students with communication disorders, a teacher must answer two questions: "How can I assure that my student understands what I am teaching?" and "How can I assure that my student can express what she knows?"

USING EFFECTIVE INSTRUCTIONAL STRATEGIES

- Students with communication disorders benefit from language facilitation strategies in early childhood.
- Graphic organizers and story webs can be helpful for elementary and secondary students with communication disorders.
- Students transitioning to community-based instruction will need instruction and support to meaningfully integrate their AAC systems into this new environment.
- One instructional strategy that has been effective is the system for augmenting language (SAL).

INCLUDING STUDENTS WITH COMMUNICATION DISORDERS

- According to the U.S. Department of Education, 86 percent of the children who receive speech and language services spend 80 to 100 percent of their time inside general education.

ASSESSING STUDENTS' PROGRESS WITH COMMUNICATION DISORDERS

- Curriculum-based assessment can help monitor students' progress in the general education curriculum.
- Ecological inventories can be helpful for assessing and monitoring progress in and outside the classroom.

MyEducationLab

Go to Topic #13: Communication Disorders in the MyEducationLab (http://www.myeducationlab.com) for *Exceptional Lives*, where you can do the following:

- Find learning outcomes for Communication Disorders along with the national standards that connect to these outcomes.
- Complete assignments and activities that will help you more deeply understand the chapter content.
- Apply and practice your understanding of the core teaching skills identified in the chapter with the Building Teaching Skills and Dispositions learning units.
- Examine challenging situations and cases presented in the IRIS Center Resources.
- Access video clips of CCSSO National Teachers of the Year award winners responding to the question, "Why Do I Teach?" in the Teacher Talk section.
- Check your comprehension on the content covered in the chapter with the Study Plan. Here you will be able to take a chapter quiz, receive feedback on your answers, and then access review, practice, and enrichment activities to enhance your understanding of chapter content.
- Use the Online Lesson Plan Builder to practice lesson planning and integrating national and state standards into your planning.

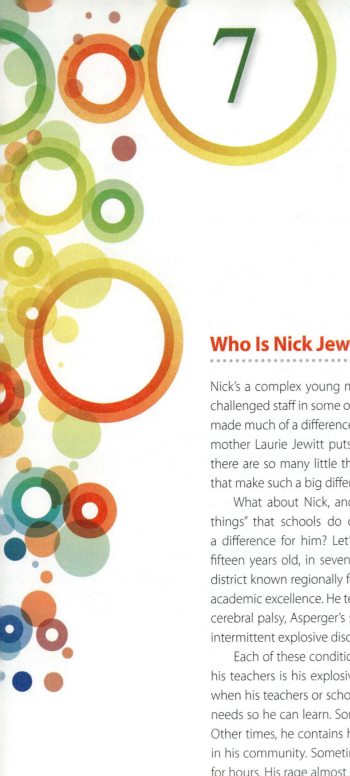

7 Understanding Students *with* Emotional *or* Behavioral Disorders

Who Is Nick Jewitt?

Nick's a complex young man. That fact alone has challenged staff in some of his schools but has not made much of a difference in other schools. As his mother Laurie Jewitt puts it, "To me, it's just that there are so many little things the school can do that make such a big difference."

What about Nick, and what about the "little things" that schools do or do not do to make a difference for him? Let's start with Nick. He is fifteen years old, in seventh grade in a suburban district known regionally for its rigorous pursuit of academic excellence. He tells you he has a learning disability, but Laurie clarifies that he also has cerebral palsy, Asperger's syndrome (a form of autism), an obsessive compulsive disorder, and intermittent explosive disorder.

Each of these conditions poses its own challenges, but the greatest challenge to Nick and his teachers is his explosive behavior. These behaviors occur when he becomes frustrated or when his teachers or school administrators refuse to listen to what he is saying about what he needs so he can learn. Sometimes Nick erupts right at the moment he is pushed to the brink. Other times, he contains his rage and later lets it all come out, whether in school, at home, or in his community. Sometimes his rages last for less than twenty minutes. Sometimes they last for hours. His rage almost always provokes teachers and administrators to intervene—properly or not.

Some principals and assistant principals have made it clear that they do not want Nick and other students like him in their buildings, so they relegate him and others to separate buildings or even special schools. Some of his teachers are simply unprepared to teach him. They tell him to calm down, they shout in his face, and they try to restrain him, pushing him down to the floor and sitting on his hands and legs and sometimes his chest. When he resists, they panic, call the police, and press criminal charges against him when, in fact, they have escalated his behaviors rather than diffused them.

Other school administrators and teachers take an entirely different approach with Nick and Laurie. They believe in him and his potential and accommodate his needs. For example, they allow Nick to keep his school books in their classrooms rather than in his school locker, thereby making it possible for him to walk (he walks slowly because of his cerebral palsy) from one class to another without stopping at his locker. Or they give him a key to the faculty elevator or let him leave class early or arrive a few minutes late without being counted as tardy. The school he attends now has disallowed iPods and cell phones, but his principal and teachers allow him to have a calculator so he can do his math. He cannot, however, use it when he is taking the state assessments of math proficiency because state regulations prohibit calculators. When it comes time for Nick to have appointments with psychologists, psychiatrists, speech-language pathologists, or cerebral palsy specialists, his teachers give him time to make up his work, and they welcome any of those specialists' input into Nick's IEP. And, in the best of worlds, they also allow Nick's lawyer, Nancy Huerta, to attend his IEP meetings without also involving the school's lawyer. In a word, these administrators and teachers are creative ("little things make the difference"), experienced and competent, and eager to join a team—Nick himself, his mother Laurie, three physicians, several other health experts, and a lawyer—to wrap services around him.

The consequence is as predictable as it is remarkable: Nick is enrolled in three honors courses, has two hours of resource room assistance from a special educator, has far fewer explosive incidents and receives positive behavioral support for them when necessary, and has a goal for life after high school: the information technology profession, which he will study for at an institution of higher education.

Little things, done by big people, make a huge difference for Nick and Laurie and, of course, for his teachers and their administrators.

- You will learn about the characteristics that define what IDEA calls *emotional disturbance*: the traits that once made Nick Jewitt the object of criminal charges but that now do not impede him from being an honors-level student.

- You will learn about specific emotional or behavioral disorders, including anxiety disorders, mood disorders, oppositional defiant disorder, conduct disorder, and schizophrenia.

- You will learn about externalizing and internalizing behaviors.

- You will learn that students with emotional or behavioral disorders are often quite intelligent and that, with support such as Nick has had, they can progress in the general education curriculum.

- You will learn about biological and environmental contributors to emotional or behavioral disorders.

- You will learn how to evaluate students and develop an IEP for students with emotional or behavioral disorders, using various rating scales.

- You will learn how to provide wraparound supports, classwide self-management, and classroom-centered interventions such as conflict-resolution training.

Identifying Students with Emotional or Behavioral Disorders

DEFINING EMOTIONAL OR BEHAVIORAL DISORDERS

IDEA uses the term *emotional disturbance* to refer to a condition that is accompanied by one or more of the following characteristics over a long time and to a marked degree and that adversely affects a child's educational performance:

- An inability to learn that cannot be explained by intellectual, sensory, or health factors
- An inability to build or maintain satisfactory interpersonal relationships with peers and teachers
- Inappropriate types of behavior or feelings under normal circumstances
- A general, pervasive mood of unhappiness or depression
- A tendency to develop physical symptoms or fears associated with personal or school problems

Emotional disturbance includes schizophrenia but does not apply to children who are socially maladjusted unless they also meet the other criteria for having an emotional or behavioral disorder.

Gender and ethnicity influence the prevalence of emotional or behavioral disorders (EBD). Three fourths of high school students identified as having EBD are male, and 25 percent are African American (compared to 16 percent in the general population) (Wagner & Davis, 2006; Wagner, Kutash, Duchnowski, Epstein, & Sumi, 2005). The prevalence of EBD is higher for girls during adolescence (Rice, Merves, & Srsic, 2008).

In fall 2008, approximately 7.1 percent (418,068) of all students ages six through twenty-one in special education were classified as having an emotional or behavioral disorder (U.S. Department of Education, 2011). Experts disagree about whether the official figure accurately reflects the number of students with this disability. A national study of special education services reported that 14 to 22 percent of students in the school population were identified as having EBD (Wagner et al., 2006).

DESCRIBING THE CHARACTERISTICS

Not all students who have EBD receive services under IDEA. Students with EBD may be underidentified or the disorder may not interfere with their educational progress. Nick Jewitt's explosive behaviors do interfere with his learning. A student with a phobia of heights, however, may not need special education services or specially designed instruction. But a student who has a phobia of school will likely need special education services under IDEA.

Emotional Characteristics

The *Diagnostic and Statistical Manual of Mental Disorders* (DSM-IV-TR) (American Psychiatric Association, 2000) describes the standard classification system for mental illness and EBD. It identifies five disorders that can lead to students' being classified as having an emotional or behavioral disorder: (1) anxiety disorder, (2) mood disorder, (3) oppositional defiant disorder, (4) conduct disorder, and (5) schizophrenia. Of these, Nick has anxiety about school, moodiness, defiance, and conduct challenges. Some of these may be exacerbated because of the physical difficulties he experiences because of cerebral palsy and speech limitations.

Anxiety Disorder. **Anxiety disorder** is one of the most common childhood disorders (Robb & Reber, 2007; Southam-Gerow & Chorpita, 2007). It is characterized by excessive fear, worry, or uneasiness. Specific anxiety disorders include the following (Appleton, 2008):

- **Separation anxiety disorder:** excessive and intense fear associated with separating from home, family, and others with whom a child has a close attachment.

- **Generalized anxiety disorder:** excessive, overwhelming worry not caused by any recent experience.
- **Phobia:** unrealistic, overwhelming fear of an object or a situation.
- **Panic disorder:** overwhelming panic attacks resulting in rapid heartbeat, dizziness, and/or other physical symptoms.
- **Obsessive-compulsive disorder:** obsessions manifesting as repetitive, persistent, and intrusive impulses, images, or thoughts (e.g., repetitive thoughts about death or illness) and/or compulsions manifesting as repetitive, stereotypical behaviors (e.g., handwashing or counting)
- **Post-traumatic stress disorder:** flashbacks and other recurrent symptoms following exposure to an extremely distressing or dangerous event, such as witnessing violence or a hurricane.

The American Academy of Child and Adolescent Psychiatry describes the impact of anxiety disorders on children:

> Children with anxiety disorders may present with fear or worry and may not recognize their fear as unreasonable. Commonly they have somatic complaints of headache and stomachache. The crying, irritability, and angry outbursts that often accompany anxiety disorders in youths may be misunderstood as oppositionality or disobedience, when in fact they represent the child's expression of fear or effort to avoid the anxiety-provoking stimulus at any cost. A specific diagnosis is determined by the context of these symptoms. (Connolly & Bernstein, 2007, p. 268)

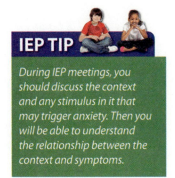

IEP TIP

During IEP meetings, you should discuss the context and any stimulus in it that may trigger anxiety. Then you will be able to understand the relationship between the context and symptoms.

Mood Disorder. A **mood disorder** involves an extreme deviation in mood in either a depressed or an elevated direction or sometimes in both directions at different times (Rudolph & Lambert, 2007; Youngstrom, 2007). Depression can occur at any age, including childhood. Students experiencing major depression may experience changes in the following:

- *Emotion.* They may feel sad and worthless, cry often, or appear tearful.
- *Motivation.* They may lose interest in play, friends, and schoolwork, with a resulting decline in grades.
- *Physical well-being.* They may eat or sleep too much or too little, disregard hygiene, or make vague physical complaints.
- *Thoughts.* They may believe they are ugly and unable to do anything right and that life is hopeless.

The prevalence of depression has increased over the past several decades; the highest rate occurs in adolescent females (Garber & Carter, 2006). Major depressive episodes typically last seven to nine months for individuals who receive clinical treatment (Rudolph & Lambert, 2007), and depression frequently recurs. Youth who experience depression are twice as likely as peers without depression to engage in substance use (SAMHSA, 2007), which often interferes with treatment for depression (Goldstein et al., 2009).

Suicide is the third leading cause of mortality among individuals ages fifteen to twenty-four and the fourth leading cause for individuals ages ten to fourteen (Centers for Disease Control and Prevention, 2010). Approximately half of all suicides are caused by firearms and almost one fourth by hanging/strangulation. Approximately three fourths of individuals who commit suicide have a diagnosis of depression.

Each student with emotional or behavioral disorders has a unique combination of strengths and needs, and each teacher should seek out and build on those strengths.

Understanding Students with Emotional or Behavioral Disorders   **153**

Bullying can be a catalyst for suicide. Research has examined early experiences with bullying and later thoughts about committing suicide, suicide attempts, and completed suicides. There is an association between being a bullying victim and suicide among females but not among males (Heibron & Prinstein, 2010; Klomek et al., 2009). Victimization often leads to feelings of hopelessness. This hopelessness can be buffered to some extent by social support from families (Bonanno & Hymel, 2010).

If a student tells you she is having suicidal thoughts, take her seriously by referring her to a mental health center for treatment. Also seek advice from the school principal or district special education director about other procedures you should follow. School districts often have written guidelines; you need to learn and follow them. Not all students who are significantly depressed will talk about suicide, but you should not assume that not talking about it means that they are not thinking about it.

A **bipolar disorder** is a category of mood disorders in which individuals experience recurrent and extreme mood episodes referred to as mania and depression (Meyer & Carlson, 2010). Mania includes an atypically elevated mood with episodes of euphoria, increased activity, self-confidence, racing thoughts, decreased need for sleep, irritability, and an exaggerated sense of strength. Depression includes the same symptoms as described in the previous section. To be diagnosed as having a bipolar disorder, the student must experience the symptoms of mania for at least a week and the episodes of depression for a minimum of two weeks (American Psychiatric Association, 2000).

Oppositional Defiant Disorder. **Oppositional defiant disorder** causes a pattern of negativistic, hostile, disobedient, and defiant behaviors (American Psychiatric Association, 2000). Students must have some of the following behaviors for at least six months: loss of temper, arguments with adults, refusal to cooperate with adult requests, frequent rule breaking, deliberate annoyance of others, blaming others for mistakes, misbehavior, low self-esteem, low threshold for annoyance, expressed resentfulness and anger, and tendency toward vindictiveness (American Psychiatric Association, 2000). Oppositional defiant disorder typically is diagnosed during the elementary school years and is often a precursor to conduct disorders and depression (Burke, Hipwell, & Loeber, 2010).

Conduct Disorder. **Conduct disorder** consists of a persistent pattern of antisocial behavior that significantly interferes with others' rights or with schools' and communities' behavioral expectations (American Psychiatric Association, 2000). There are four categories of conduct disorders: (1) aggressive conduct, resulting in physical harm to people or animals; (2) property destruction; (3) deceitfulness or theft; and (4) serious rule violations, such as truancy and running away (American Psychiatric Association, 2000).

Unlike students with oppositional defiant disorder, students with conduct disorders have severe aggressive and antisocial behavior; they often infringe on other students' rights and demonstrate a lack of empathy (McMahon & Frick, 2007; Sterzer, Stadler, Poustka, & Kleinschmidt, 2007). Although anger and aggression can emerge in infancy and through-out the early childhood years, it is typically during elementary school years that students, especially boys, are identified as having conduct problems. Children who are diagnosed during the elementary years with conduct disorders typically have more serious problems with emotional regulation and impulsivity as compared to students who are diagnosed during adolescence (Dandreaux & Frick, 2009). Males are two to four times more likely than females to experience conduct disorders and ten to fifteen times more likely than females to have persistent challenges (Eme, 2007).

Students who have conduct disorders are often placed into juvenile correction programs. Almost half of students who are in juvenile correction programs have been identified as having an emotional or behavioral disorder—probably conduct disorders, although the studies did not specify this (Krezmien, Mulcahy, & Leone, 2008; Quinn, Rutherford, Leone, Osher, & Poirier, 2005). Approximately two thirds of incarcerated students are African American, and African American students are more likely to be committed to a long-term correction setting as contrasted to having a short-term placement in a detention center (Krezmien et al., 2008).

Let's consider Nick Jewitt for a moment, in light of the definitions of the types of emotional-behavioral disorders we have just described. We have said that he has anxiety—that's natural, given the challenges he has faced in school and the effects of his physical limitations on his ability to learn. We have also said he is moody, but his moodiness is not the true challenge he faces. Instead, his greatest challenges, it can be argued, come from being oppositional and defiant—his conduct disorder.

In light of what you know about Nick's history in school, to whom, if anyone, do you attribute his school problems? In his case, some of the problems arose from the ways in which some adminstrators dealt with him. But some of the solutions to his school problems came from other administrators and teachers. It is always best to consider what seems to contribute to a student's school challenges as well as what mitigates those challenges and to then use the strategies we describe in this chapter, and even in Nick's story, to forestall problems that professionals may cause and instead to create solutions that professionals may use.

Intensive family and community support can keep many students out of the criminal justice system.

Schizophrenia. The DSM-IV-TR classifies people as having **schizophrenia** if they experience

- One of the following: highly unusual delusions; an auditory hallucination of one voice that provides commentary on the individual's characteristics, behavior, and/or feelings; or auditory hallucinations with multiple voices conversing.

- At least two of the following: delusions, hallucinations, disorganized expressive language, disorganized or **catatonic behavior** (behavior that lacks typical movement, activity, and/or expression).

- Other negative symptoms characterized by a loss of contact with reality. (American Psychiatric Association, 2000)

The symptoms associated with schizophrenia must result in challenges associated with interpersonal and academic success and must be present for at least six months. Schizophrenia occurs in phases. There are precursors associated with atypical behavior, followed by an acute phase in which symptoms are most pronounced. The person then enters a recovery phase and, finally, a residual phase during which there are no symptoms. Most individuals with schizophrenia have multiple cycles, but some may have only one cycle (McDonell & McClellan, 2007). Children with schizophrenia have an average age of onset of eleven, are twice as likely to be male than female, have an average IQ, and have moderate educational challenges that require special supports in school (Frazier et al., 2007).

Behavioral Characteristics

Students with EBD tend to have one or both of two easily identifiable behavioral patterns: externalizing or internalizing.

Externalizing Behavior. **Externalizing behaviors**—persistently aggressive or acting-out and noncompliant behaviors—often are associated with conduct and oppositional defiant disorders, as they are with Nick (Teeter et al., 2009). Teachers have reported that, compared to students with other disabilities, students with EBD are twice as likely to fight with other students (Wagner et al., 2006). One of the early risk factors associated with later problem behavior is property destruction (e.g., the child destroys his toys), a type of externalizing behavior (Nelson, Stage, Duppong-Hurley, Synhorst, & Epstein, 2007). In a large national study of children with externalizing behavior, parents and caregivers/teachers reported the following (Miner & Clark-Stewart, 2008):

- Children's externalizing behavior declined in frequency from the ages of two to nine years.

- When mothers and caregivers/teachers rated the same children, the mothers rated them as having higher levels of externalizing behaviors.

- Caregivers/teachers identified African American children as having higher levels of externalizing behavior, but mothers reported the reverse.

IEP TIP

Students with externalizing behaviors are subject to zero tolerance policies that allow educators to expel a student who exhibits violent behavior. However, IDEA protects them against total cessation of their education if they receive special education services (see Chapter 1).

Bullying is a form of externalizing behavior. It can consist of verbal abuse—calling a student by a stigmatizing name; cyberabuse—using online forums or networks to attack a student's behavior or characteristics; or physical abuse of any amount or degree, including sexual abuse. Approximately 13 percent of the school population exhibits bullying characteristics, and students with disabilities are perpetrators of bullying more often than are their counterparts without disabilities (Rose, Monda-Amaya, & Espelage, 2010). One interpretation is that they are more frequently victimized and that the vulnerability associated with victimization leads to more aggressive characteristics.

Internalizing Behavior. **Internalizing behavior** includes withdrawal, depression, anxiety, obsessions, and compulsions. Students with internalizing behavior display sadness or depression—key indicators of internalizing behavior—approximately three times more frequently than students with other types of disabilities (Wagner et al., 2006). Yet teachers typically refer students with anxiety disorders for evaluation less often than they refer students with disruptive behavior. Students with anxiety disorders are less likely to receive special education services than are their peers with externalizing behaviors (Schoenfeld & Janney, 2008).

Some researchers believe that females' lower rate of being identified as having EBD is because their internalizing behaviors are often overlooked. "The girls are much more quiet on the surface but they hold a lot of things in and they like to walk away. That's their mechanism of coping . . . is to walk away versus becoming physically aggressive. . . . Boys' behavior is much more overt and acting out and calls for attention, more obvious, than the girls who may be going through the same crisis and will retreat and sit quietly" (Rice et al., 2008, p. 556).

Adolescents with EBD reported being more dissatisfied with their quality of their life than were their peers without EBD (Sacks & Kern, 2008). The researchers suggest that "it may be that focus on QoL [quality of life], rather than (or in addition to) focusing on discrete problem behaviors will result in a more enduring resolution of behavioral problems. . . . QoL is an important aspect of students' well-being" (Sacks & Kern, 2008, p. 125).

Cognitive and Academic Characteristics

Students with EBD may be gifted or have an intellectual disability, but most have IQs in the low-average range (Wagner, Kutash, Duchnowski, Epstein, & Sumi, 2005). Nick has above-average intelligence and is enrolled in three honors courses. In a national study of elementary/middle school students, parents reported that about 1 percent of their children with an emotional or behavioral disorder also have an intellectual disability and that approximately 2.5 percent are gifted. Almost two thirds of parents indicated that their child also experienced AD/HD. A national profile of cognitive and academic characteristics of students with EBD revealed the following (Wagner et al., 2005):

- Slightly less than two thirds of the students had reading scores in the lowest 25 percent of all students in the school population, and 43 percent were reported to be in the bottom 25 percent of scores in mathematics. This finding is consistent with other research, which documents that students with EBD at the elementary and secondary level typically fall below the twenty-fifth percentile on reading, math, and written expression (Lane, Barton-Arwood, Nelson, & Wehby, 2008).

- Among elementary and middle school students with EBD, 22 percent were reported to have been held back in a grade, as were 38 percent of secondary students with EBD—twice the rate of the general population.

- Almost two thirds of students with EBD also have expressive and/or receptive language disorders.

- Only 38 percent of students with EBD graduate with a regular diploma as compared to 55 percent of all students with disabilities. The dropout rate for students with EBD is 52 percent as compared to 31 percent for students without disabilities (U.S. Department of Education, 2009).

DETERMINING THE CAUSES

Typically, there is no single cause of an emotional and behavior disorder (Situ et al., 2009; Willcutt & McQueen, 2010). Nick's physicians cannot point to a single cause. A cooking analogy offers a way to think about how multiple factors interact to produce outcomes.

> Both the raw ingredients and the manner in which they are combined are important. Timing also matters. In the cooking analogy, the raw ingredients represent the many genetic and environmental influences, while cooking represents the biological and psychological processes of development. Nobody expects to find all the separate ingredients represented as discrete, identifiable components in a soufflé. Similarly, nobody should expect to find a simple correspondence between a particular gene (or a particular experience) and particular aspects of an individual's behavior or personality. (Bateson & Martin, 1999, p. 9)

Let's apply the cooking analogy to bipolar disorder. A review of genetic and environmental contributions to bipolar disorder suggests that "bipolar disorder is a heterogeneous condition that arises from the additive and interactive effects of multiple genetic and environmental risk factors at different points in development" (Willcutt & McQueen, 2010, p. 245).

Biological Causes

Biological causes of EBD relate primarily to brain functioning and heredity (Breedlove, Watson, & Kosenweig, 2010). For example, the brains of people with schizophrenia have distinct characteristics, including a lower volume of gray matter (Boos, Aleman, Cahn, Pol, & Kahn, 2007; Borgwardt et al., 2007). A reduced volume of gray matter has also been identified in adolescents who have a conduct disorder (Sterzer, Stadler, Poustka, & Kleinschmidt, 2007). A lower volume of gray matter is correlated with lower levels of empathy.

Research on EBD suggests that genetics influence a child's temperament. **Temperament** refers to behavioral tendencies that are biologically based (Posner & Rothbart, 2009; Sheese, Voelker, Posner, & Rothbart, 2009). For example, a child's temperament might naturally be impulsive and resist guidance or supervision from others. Because temperament is biologically based, it interacts with numerous environmental factors within the family, neighborhood, school, and community to produce more positive or more negative outcomes. When problems with temperament interact with environmental challenges, it is more likely that behaviors will become extreme and lead to an emotional or behavioral disorder. A child who is impulsive and resists others' guidance and supervision may establish behaviors that in time lead to oppositional defiant or even conduct disorder (Stringaris, Maughan, & Goodman, 2010). Children who have early separation anxiety, emotional intensity, less adaptability, and more negativity have been shown to have a higher likelihood of a later diagnosis of bipolar disorder (West, Henry, & Pavuluri, 2007). The child's temperament, even if biologically based, can be negatively and positively affected by his environment, family, neighborhood, school, and community.

Environmental Considerations

School and family factors can contribute to EBD.

School factors. Often school systems and educators have not been adequately prepared to provide a quality education to students with EBD (Wagner et al., 2006):

- One half to three fourths of students with EBD have a behavioral intervention plan, but fewer than 40 percent actually receive behavioral intervention or mental health services.
- Schools identify 14 to 22 percent of students as having an emotional or behavior disorder, but only 9 percent of these students have an IEP.
- Only one fourth to one third of teachers believe they possess adequate training to teach students with EBD.

It is essential for teachers to develop competence in addressing problem behavior in a way that facilitates students' progress within classroom settings.

A national study compared 850 teachers of students with EBD to special education teachers generally (Billingsley, Fall, Williams, & Tech, 2006). Teachers of students with EBD were the least-qualified special educators. They were less likely to be certified to teach in their specialty (EBD), they more frequently needed to take certification tests more than once, and they were less likely to be certified in core academic areas. Nick's history involves administrators and teachers who had negative attitudes and poor skills as well as administrators and teachers who had high expectations and excellent skills. The former refused to do the "little things" that made a difference for Nick in school; the latter searched for and applied the "little things." More than that, they brought Nick's health team and his lawyer into the IEP planning process. They wanted assistance, were humble enough to know they needed it, and welcomed it when Laurie and Nick's health team at the local children's specialty hospital offered it.

Family Factors. Families of students with EBD, as well as the students themselves, experience special challenges (Wagner et al., 2005):

- Slightly more than one third of elementary students with EBD live in a single-parent household, compared to about one fourth of students overall.

- Approximately one fourth live in households in which the head of the family is unemployed. The head of household in these families is two times less likely to be a high school graduate than are the heads of household in the general population.

- Students are more likely to have an additional family member with a disability than are their peers with other disabilities.

- Approximately twice as many elementary/middle school students with EBD live in poverty as compared to students in the general population.

Many parents of children with EBD believe that other people blame them for their child's problems. Laurie remembers bitterly that when Nick enrolled in preschool and then elementary school in a school district different from the one he attends now, the administrators and teachers—but especially the administrators—accused her of having a syndrome in which she wanted Nick to be sick when there really was nothing wrong with him (according to them). They might not have been explicitly blaming her for whatever disabilities Nick had, but they certainly were joining the large chorus of professionals who believe that a child's disability is powerfully linked to his or her parents. As you discovered in the section on causes, researchers are beginning to discover genetic and environmental contributors to EBD. Blaming parents impairs partnerships with families and does nothing to solve problems.

Experts emphasize how important it is for teachers to develop partnerships with the student's family and use a strengths-based approach when working with students and families (Huang et al., 2005). Nevertheless, parents of students with EBD are significantly more likely to be dissatisfied with schools, teachers, and special education services than are parents of students with other disabilities (Wagner et al., 2005). Their rates of dissatisfaction are triple that of parents of students in the general population. They also are more likely to spend time helping their child with homework five or more days a week and to attend parent-teacher conferences. But they are less likely to volunteer at school and to attend school or class events. Laurie and Nick's father (they are soon to be formally divorced from each other) have committed themselves deeply to Nick. From his very early years, they paid out of pocket—without insurance reimbursement—for occupational, physical, speech, aquatic, and horse-riding therapies.

Although you should avoid blaming parents for their children's emotional or behavioral disorder, you also should recognize that family factors can play a role:

- Maternal depression and marital problems are associated with an increase in child adjustment problems (Miner & Clarke-Stewart, 2008; Nelson, Stage, Duppong-Hurley, Synhorst, & Epstein, 2007).

- Parents' family history and their emotional expression and regulation affect how children learn to express and regulate their own emotions (Morris, Silk, Steinberg, Myers, & Robinson, 2007; Saarni, Campos, Camras, & Witherington, 2006).

- Problems with parent-child interaction, including overprotectiveness, critical and harsh parenting styles, and insecure attachment, are related to the development of EBD (Button, Lau, Maughan, & Eley, 2008; Connolly & Bernstein, 2007).

- Conflict between a child's temperament and a parent's temperament can escalate any challenges the child might have (Morris et al., 2007; Nelson et al., 2007).

Interestingly, when parents were asked to rate the causes of their child's emotional or behavioral disorder, African American families were less likely to see causes related to the family and more likely to see causes related to prejudice (Yeh, Forness, Ho, McCabe, & Hough, 2004). Latino parents also tended to have this view, although the perception was not reported as strongly.

Evaluating Students with Emotional or Behavioral Disorders

DETERMINING THE PRESENCE OF EMOTIONAL OR BEHAVIORAL DISORDERS

Assessment guidelines for specific emotional or behavioral disorders (EBD) have been outlined by specialists in each disorder (Rudy & Levinson, 2008; White, Jellinek, & Murphy, 2010). Box 7.1 describes the standard nondiscriminatory evaluation process for students with EBD. Although various evaluation measures help teachers and other professionals identify students with EBD (Flick, 2011; Severson, Walker, Hope-Doolittle, Kratochwill, & Gresham, 2007), few align with or take into account IDEA's description of the five characteristics of EBD—namely, inability to learn, inability to build or maintain satisfactory relationships, inappropriate behavior, unhappiness or depression, and physical symptoms or fears.

Researchers have developed and established the reliability and validity of a scale that specifically measures these five elements: the Scale for Assessing Emotional Disturbance (Cullinan, 2007; Epstein, Cullinan, Ryser, & Pearson, 2002). This norm-referenced scale has five subscales, each of which corresponds directly to one of the five elements in the IDEA definition. It also has a sixth scale that focuses on social maladjustment, with a particular emphasis on the student's involvement in antisocial behaviors in environments outside the school. This scale includes forty-five items, each of which is rated between 3 and 0 (3 equals a severe problem; 0 equals no problem). For example, three of the items on the relationship subscale ask the evaluator (who should know the student well and can be a teacher, parent, or other adult) whether any of the following applies to the student:

- Does not work well in group activities
- Feels picked on or persecuted
- Avoids interacting with people

After completing the scale, the evaluator sums the subscale scores and converts them to percentiles, obtaining an overall indication of the student's emotional or behavioral functioning. The scale takes only about ten minutes to complete and includes items to help identify a student's resources, competencies, and other assets (for example, family support).

DETERMINING THE NATURE OF SPECIALLY DESIGNED INSTRUCTION AND SERVICES

Educators usually determine whether a student qualifies for IDEA services before they identify her areas of strengths and needs and build an IEP around them. But tools exist that allow you to identify a student's strengths.

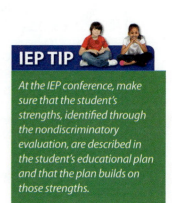

IEP TIP

At the IEP conference, make sure that the student's strengths, identified through the nondiscriminatory evaluation, are described in the student's educational plan and that the plan builds on those strengths.

BOX 7.1 **NONDISCRIMINATORY EVALUATION PROCESS**

Students with Emotional or Behavioral Disorders

Observation

Teacher and parents observe: The student may be unable to build and maintain satisfactory interpersonal relationships, may engage in aggressive behaviors, or may have a pervasive mood of unhappiness or depression. The student acts out or withdraws during classroom instruction and independent activities. Problematic behavior occurs in more than one setting.

Screening

Assessment measures:

Classroom work products: The student may require one-to-one assistance to stay on task. The student has difficulty following basic classroom behavioral expectations during instruction or assignments, resulting in incomplete or unsatisfactory work products.

Group intelligence tests: Most students perform in the low-average to slow-learner range. Performance may not accurately reflect ability because the emotional/behavioral disorder can prevent the student from staying on task.

Group achievement tests: The student performs below peers or scores lower than would be expected according to group intelligence tests. Performance may not be a true reflection of achievement because the student has difficulty staying on task as a result of the emotional/behavioral disorder.

Vision and hearing screening: Results do not explain behavior.

Prereferral

Teacher implements suggestions from school-based team: The student is not responsive to reasonable adaptations of the curriculum and positive behavior-support techniques.

Referral

Nondiscriminatory evaluation procedures and standards

Assessment measures:

Individualized intelligence test: Intelligence is usually, but not always, in the low-average to slow-learner range. The multidisciplinary team makes sure that the results do not reflect cultural difference rather than ability.

Scale for assessing emotional disturbance: As described in the chapter, this scale is specifically tailored to IDEA's definition of emotional or behavioral disorders and is especially helpful in diagnosis in this area.

Individualized achievement test: Usually, but not always, the student scores below average across academic areas in comparison to peers. The evaluator may notice acting-out or withdrawal behaviors that affect results.

Behavior rating scale: The student scores in the significant range on specific behavioral excesses or deficiencies when compared with others of the same culture and developmental stage.

Assessment of strengths: Using the Behavioral and Emotional Rating Scale (as described in the text) enables evaluators to identify student strengths.

Assessment measures of social skills, self-esteem, personality, and/or adjustment: The student's performance indicates significant difficulties in one or more areas according to the criteria established by testing and in comparison with others of the same culture and developmental stage.

Anecdotal records: The student's problem behavior is not of short duration but has been apparent throughout time in school. Also, records indicate that behaviors have been observed in more than one setting and are adversely affecting the student's educational progress.

Curriculum-based assessment: The student often is experiencing difficulty in one or more areas of the general curriculum.

Direct observation: The student is experiencing difficulty relating to peers or adults and in adjusting to school or classroom structure or routine.

Determination

The nondiscriminatory evaluation team determines that the student has emotional or behavioral disorders and needs special education and related services.

The Behavioral and Emotional Rating Scale—Second Edition (BERS-2) is a companion to the Scale for Assessing Emotional Disturbance and assesses strengths in interpersonal capacity, family involvement, intrapersonal competence, school functioning, and affective ability (Buckley, Ryser, Reid, & Epstein, 2006; Epstein, 2004). It includes a total of fifty-two items across these five scales. Each item is scored on a four-point scale ranging from "not at all like the child" to "very much like the child." Teachers, parents, or other adults who know the student well can complete the Behavioral and Emotional Rating Scale in approximately ten minutes. It can be used with children ages five to eighteen. Research on the scale's reliability and validity shows it has strong psychometric properties and measures students' emotional and behavioral strengths (Benner, Beaudoin, Mooney, Uhing, & Pierce, 2008; Epstein, 2004; Uhing, Mooney, & Ryser, 2005). Assessment information is collected from three perspectives: child (Youth Rating Scale), teacher (Teacher Rating Scale), and parent (Parent Rating Scale). A Spanish version is also available (Sharkey, You, Morrison, & Griffiths, 2009).

Designing an Appropriate IEP

PARTNERING FOR SPECIAL EDUCATION AND RELATED SERVICES

Students with EBD have both educational and mental health needs. Nick Jewitt also has physical health needs related to his cerebral palsy. The best practice, known as **wraparound**, is to provide services that address all of those needs. Wraparound services are family-driven, collaborative, individualized, culturally competent, and community- and strengths-based (Winters & Metz, 2009). Just as the word itself suggests, school, community, mental health, and other services are wrapped around the student instead of being compartmentalized by field or agency. That is how it works with Nick: He has a team of three physicians from the same hospital, a team of educators, and his lawyer.

Key principles for implementing the wraparound approach include voice and choice, team process, natural supports, collaboration, flexible funds, family orientation, individualization, strengths-orientation, partnerships, and outcome-based (Winters & Metz, 2009). Box 7.2, Partnership Tips, highlights the four phases of wraparound and tasks within each phase (Quinn & Lee, 2007; Walker & Schutte, 2004).

BOX 7.2   PARTNERSHIP TIPS

Implementing the Four Phases of Wraparound

In the wraparound process, the individual with an emotional or behavioral disorder, family members, representatives of agencies providing services, and other key people who are part of the support team come together to engage in collaborative planning. There are four major phases of wraparound, and the tasks associated with each phase must be carried out in partnership in order to achieve success.

- *Phase 1: Engagement and team preparation*
  - ✓ Orient the student's family.
  - ✓ Plan crisis responses.
  - ✓ Identify long-term goals.
  - ✓ Assemble the team.
  - ✓ Schedule meetings.

- *Phase 2: Initial plan development*
  - ✓ Develop an initial wraparound plan.
  - ✓ Develop a crisis plan.
  - ✓ Plan logistics and how to disseminate information.

- *Phase 3: Implementation*
  - ✓ Implement the plan.
  - ✓ Update the plan.
  - ✓ Build cohesiveness and trust.
  - ✓ Organize logistics.

- *Phase 4: Transition*
  - ✓ Terminate one or more wraparound services when appropriate.
  - ✓ Plan and implement closure activities.
  - ✓ Remain available.

Although a process as dynamic and individualized as the wraparound approach is extremely difficult to research (Bruns, Walrath, & Sheehan, 2007), evidence does suggest that the implementation of wraparound leads to improved child and family outcomes (Farmer et al., 2008; Stambaugh et al., 2007). Yet as effective as the wraparound approach is, some students may not remain with their families and may enter a state's foster-care system, either permanently or temporarily. In Box 7.3, you will read how the two systems—special education and foster care—can cause conflict for the student and the student's family.

DETERMINING SUPPLEMENTARY AIDS AND SERVICES

Determining the role of peers in the educational programs of students receiving special education services is one aspect of determining supplementary aids and services. Peers can play an important role in supporting students with EBD to self-regulate their behavior and improve academic performance. For example, Riccomini, Witzel, and Robbins (2008) used peer mediated instruction to enable students with EBD to improve their performance in mathematics.

One evidence-based peer-mediated practice that supports students with EBD to have positive peer interactions is classwide peer tutoring (CWPT). CWPT enables teachers to

---

BOX 7.3 | **MY VOICE**

Caught 'Twixt and 'Tween

My son, now age eighteen, spent thirty-three months of his life between the ages of ten and fourteen in foster placements. His and my experiences are all too common and deplorable, given how valuable education is.

Child welfare involvement is based on whether agencies believe a risk of abuse or neglect exists—and children with special needs are considered to be at higher risk than other children are. Many disabilities, including emotional disturbances and learning disabilities, have biological components, so the parent of a child with a disability may also be struggling with the impact of his or her own disability on the family's life.

For special education to work well, it must rely on the values of the disability rights movement: participation in both society and individual planning. Systems may not always live up to those values, but at least they are written into special education law. Unfortunately, they are not written into child welfare laws, where "the best interest of the child" may have nothing to do with parent or child preferences and where "safety is paramount." Additionally, the judicial systems that oversee child welfare decisions are separate from the special education system.

Special ed parents may feel outnumbered by school personnel on IEP teams, but they still know they are the child's parents. When a child with a disability is in foster care, figuring out "who is the parent?" gets murky. Parents, foster parents, caseworkers, and the courts all have some degree of parental authority—whether they share it or fight over it.

Parental rights also get shared—and possibly fought over—in the education of a foster child. My son entered foster care in the middle of an ongoing dispute with the school about whether he needed special education services. First, he was moved to a different school farther away.

While in foster care, he attended four different schools in two states. When we could get evaluation started, he would be moved before it was completed. When eligibility was refused and we attempted due process, the school disputed my parental rights—but by then he was in yet another school system, so we started over. There were so many school and foster-care records but so little education. Our lives were documented, not lived.

Now, at eighteen, my son has four of twenty-two credits required by his high school for a diploma. Many young adults who spend time in foster care, especially those who need special education, face the same future. But my son has his own kind of persistence. He has continued to show up at the schoolhouse door. Finally, too, he has found an academic subject (algebra) about which he can say, "I found out I like it, and I'm good at it." Any student who can say that has found value beyond measure, no matter what price has been paid. There has been educational benefit.

I've seen another kind of education benefit. In my son's IEP meetings, he's the decision maker. His school, like many, values student compliance over student self-advocacy. Many times students with disabilities can claim their independence only by rejecting what the school has to offer. But as the person who needs the services, my son is in a good position to focus on what he believes he needs and wants the most. He's not just a self-advocate; he's his own lobbyist.

Imagine what a young adult like that could do with a better education.

—*Sheri McMahon*
North Dakota

differentiate learning. Teachers organize the class into tutoring dyads that include a student with a disability and a same-aged peer (Kamps et al., 2008). There are seven basic operational components of CWPT (Maheady & Gard, 2010):

- *Multimodal learning.* Students hear, see, say, and write responses.
- *Reciprocal and distributed practice.* Each student gets to serve as both the tutor and the tutee.
- *Immediate error correction and feedback.* Errorless learning occurs (see Chapter 8).
- *Games and competing teams.* Students are motivated to engage in learning.
- *Built-in reinforcement.* Peer and teacher reinforce learning.
- *High-mastery levels.* Differentiation of work and learning objectives is based on student capacity.
- *Measured outcomes.* Pre- and postintervention assessments and data are collected daily.

IEP TIP

If you believe the student's peers can support the student to learn, then the student's IEP should identify the peer-mediated learning strategies and peer-tutoring strategies that are necessary as supplementary aids and services.

Bowman-Perrott (2009) documented the benefits of CWPT in science classes with students with EBD, including a positive effect on student behavior, peer interactions, and inclusion. Students exhibited fewer inappropriate or off-task behaviors during CWPT instruction and more time on task. In addition to learning science skills, they also learned lifelong skills of cooperative learning and working with peers.

PLANNING FOR UNIVERSAL DESIGN FOR LEARNING

Computer-based programs can support students to self-regulate behavior. Box 7.4 introduces one such UDL support, the KidTools support system. Tools such as KidTools can support students to learn to solve problems and regulate their actions, leading to better academic, behavioral, and self-determination outcomes (Miller, Fitzgerald, Koury, Mitchem, & Hollingshead, 2007). And once students learn to navigate the system, they can use computer-based instruction (CBI) tools with minimal support from teachers or other adults. As you can see in Box 7.4, the KidTools system encourages and supports students to self-regulate learning through multiple means—from self-monitoring, to goal setting, to problem solving. A qualitative analysis of the KidTools system with high school students with autism, learning disabilities, and EBD documented positive academic, behavior, and transition-related outcomes for all students (Mitchem, Kight, Fitzgerald, & Koury, 2007). Students with EBD indicated that the tools assisted them in recognizing and managing their own behavior. Nick uses a computer and a calculator in school and at home.

PLANNING FOR OTHER EDUCATIONAL NEEDS

Dropping out of school will almost always create, not solve, students' problems, yet studies and reports consistently document that more than 50 percent of youth with EBD drop out. A report from the National High School Center (2007) indicated that 61 percent of youth with EBD dropped out in a given year. The next closest was students with learning disabilities, at 35 percent. What are the consequences of dropping out? Students who drop out of school have unemployment rates approximately 40 percent higher than those of students who complete school. Of people who are incarcerated, 80 percent dropped out of high school, and 73 percent of youth with EBD who drop out of high school are arrested at least once (Lehr, Johnson, Bremer, Cosio, & Thompson, 2004). These data give teachers a strong message: Try to prevent your students from dropping out. As you know, Nick aspires to higher education, and his teachers, parents, and even his physicians and lawyer reinforce him in his path to college.

Students with EBD leave school for many reasons—problems at home, substance abuse, frequent discipline problems, or referrals—but generally because they are not interested in what is being taught and feel negative about school in general. But other reasons exist.

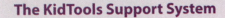

BOX 7.4   UNIVERSAL DESIGN FOR PROGRESS

The KidTools Support System

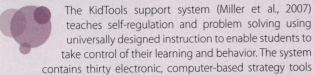

The KidTools support system (Miller et al., 2007) teaches self-regulation and problem solving using universally designed instruction to enable students to take control of their learning and behavior. The system contains thirty electronic, computer-based strategy tools that can be used in classrooms and by the student and his or her family at home (Miller et al., 2007). The software is designed and validated for use with elementary and middle school students. It provides cognitive, behavioral, and academic supports and includes templates to create the following:

- *Contracts* that students develop with their teacher to agree upon what the student will do and consequences that accrue when the contract is or is not completed

- *Checking contracts* that allow students to compare their contract-based performance with a teacher's evaluation

- *STAR plan forms,* which support students to Stop, Think, Act, and get Results" (e.g., STAR) when confronting a problem and to make a plan to address that problem

- *"Am I working?" card templates* to help students self-monitor their attention and on-task behavior in classrooms

- *Monitoring card templates* to support students to check their performance as part of a self-monitoring plan

- *Class, period, or picture point cards* that give students a way to track what they need to do in class

The middle school version of KidTools includes the above tools and adds the following:

- *Goal contract form* that gives students a way to set a behavioral goal and check their progress toward that goal

- *Homework contract form* to enable students to establish expected performances on homework completion and submission

- *Costs/payoffs card template* to support students to think about positive and negative consequences of actions before choosing how to act

- *Thinking/feeling/doing plan template* to assist students to evaluate how their actions in the past worked and to consider what might happen the next time the situation occurs

KidTools is a server-based application, so it runs from a school computer; and it incorporates features of both UDL and computer-based instruction (CBI).

Several studies have linked poverty to school failure (Christle, Jolivette, & Nelson, 2007). Reschly and Christenson (2006) identified *student engagement*—defined as a student's involvement in curricular and extracurricular activities and feelings of belonging within the school—as a significant predictor of whether students with learning and emotional or behavioral disabilities would drop out or remain in school. Stout and Christensen (2009) identified three groups of risk factors associated with dropping out:

1. Students' social background, including race and ethnicity, socioeconomic status, mobility, and growing up in a single-parent home

2. Students' educational experiences, including grade retention, absenteeism, and disciplinary problems

3. School characteristics, such as school size and lack of teacher support (p. 17)

Christenson, Reschly, Appleton, Berman, Spanjers, and Varro (2008) identified key components for reducing dropout:

1. Students experience some success at school.

2. The school has a positive social/interpersonal atmosphere.

3. Students take courses relevant to their lives and future goals.

4. Supports are available for students who are experiencing personal problems.

One evidence-based intervention to improve graduation and reduce dropout rate is the Check and Connect program (Stout & Christensen, 2009). Check and Connect includes mentoring, regular checking in on student progress, maintaining student connections to school, and partnering with families. As we have pointed out, a student's ethnicity and family make a difference in whether he or she is classified as having an emotional or behavioral disorder and how you work with the student's family as a partner. Being an effective partner with families from diverse backgrounds requires you to be culturally competent, as you learned in Chapter 3.

Using Effective Instructional Strategies

EARLY CHILDHOOD STUDENTS: MULTICOMPONENT INTERVENTIONS TO PREVENT CONDUCT DISORDERS

As early as first grade, a student's aggressive behavior can predict "later substance use, antisocial behavior, and criminality" (Bradshaw, Zmuda, Kellam, & Ialongo, 2009, p. 927). That is why early intervention to prevent these challenges is essential. Complex behavioral problems require complex solutions. Two rules of thumb are particularly important: Begin early, and use all the tools available in your toolbox.

Researchers at Johns Hopkins University have created strategies to intervene against poor academic achievement and aggressive and shy behavior (Bradshaw et al., 2009). **Classroom-centered intervention** combines mastery learning and the Good Behavior Game (which we describe later in this section). Classroom-centered (CC) intervention involves enhancing the curriculum, applying specific behavior management strategies, and providing additional supports for students who are not performing adequately. The enhanced curriculum consists of critical thinking, composition, listening, and comprehension skills. The behavior management strategies include once-weekly class meetings to develop social problem-solving skills and opportunities to play the Good Behavior Game. The Good Behavior Game is a whole-class intervention in which students are assigned to teams, which "win" by not exceeding a specified level of off-task, disruptive, or aggressive behaviors.

Bradshaw and colleagues (2009) conducted a longitudinal study of the CC intervention beginning in the fall of 1999 with more than 600 students in the first grade, 574 of whom were assessed again when they entered grade 12. When compared to students in a control group, boys who received the CC intervention during elementary school showed improvements in reading and general academic achievement, high school graduation, and college attendance. For girls, the effect was for high school graduation only. All in all, though, the message is clear: As we've already said, begin early, and use all the tools available in your toolbox.

IEP TIP

Complex behaviors and problems often require complex solutions. It's likely that no single intervention will be sufficient for students with EBD, so you and your colleagues on the IEP team should use multicomponent interventions.

ELEMENTARY AND MIDDLE SCHOOL STUDENTS: SERVICE LEARNING

Increasingly, students in public schools are engaging in service learning activities. **Service learning** refers to instructional activities that integrate teaching activities with community service. Service learning is usually designed to teach civic responsibility, reinforce lessons learned in the classroom in the context of real life, and improve communities. Students who participate in service learning show improved school attendance, greater self-esteem, enhanced leadership and communication skills, and increased awareness of community and governmental issues. They also report having greater social responsibility, career awareness, and acceptance of cultural diversity (Dymond, Renzaglia, & Chun, 2007). For example, students can engage in service learning by participating in a community cleanup. That activity teaches them about individual responsibility for other members of their community; it also teaches other community members that students with EBD can contribute to the community and are able to do so in any number of jobs within the community. Nick volunteers as an aide in a horseback therapy program for students with autism. This service learning teaches him valuable civic skills while also allowing him to ride, as he did as a young child.

SECONDARY AND TRANSITION STUDENTS: CONFLICT RESOLUTION

Unfortunately, conflict between youth with EBD and peers, family members, educators, and other authority figures is all too common. In Chapter 11, you will learn more about using positive behavior support (PBS) to change the environmental factors that contribute

IEP TIP

If a student is prone to conflict, you should make sure that the student's IEP includes strategies to teach the student social problem-solving and anger-management skills.

Service learning helps students with emotional or behavioral disorders develop positive character traits.

to problem behavior. PBS is not the only effective approach for students in secondary programs. When you instruct your students about how to resolve conflicts, you reduce their inappropriate behaviors. You can teach students to use three skills for resolving conflicts: effective communication, anger management, and taking another's perspective (Johns, Crowley, & Guetzloe, 2005).

Problem solving and successful decision making are also important conflict-resolution skills, especially because these strategies can help students avoid backing down or acting out when confronting problems. You should help your students identify the nature of the problem they face, brainstorm and evaluate the pros and cons of various solutions, determine which of several solutions seems likely to be most effective to resolve the problem, and make a plan to carry out that solution. In addition, you should instruct your students in negotiation skills that help them find solutions that benefit everyone and allow others to save face so that they will not oppose the solution. Box 7.5 provides tips on how you can teach conflict-resolution skills.

Including Students with Emotional or Behavioral Disorders

Figure 7.1 sets out the percentage of students with emotional or behavioral disorders in each of several educational placements. Students with EBD are at great risk for not being included in the general education classroom and of being educated in a segregated setting: 23 percent of students spend less than 40 percent of their time in general education classrooms, and almost 20 percent are educated in separate schools, residential facilities, private schools, correctional facilities, or hospitals/home environments (U.S. Department of Education, 2011). Nevertheless, inclusion is entirely feasible, consistent with IDEA, as Box 7.6 shows.

FIGURE 7.1 *Percentage of students with emotional or behavioral disorders in educational placement: School year 2008–2009*

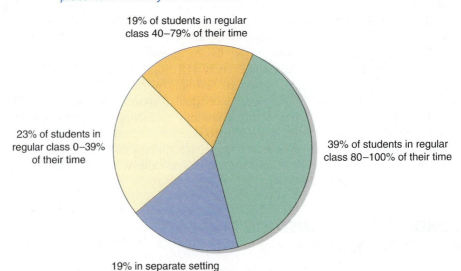

19% of students in regular class 40–79% of their time

23% of students in regular class 0–39% of their time

39% of students in regular class 80–100% of their time

19% in separate setting

Source: U.S. Department of Education. (2011). *Data accountability center: Individuals with Disabilities Education Act (IDEA) data.* Retrieved February 12, 2011, from https://www.ideadata.org.

Note: Percentages have been rounded and collapsed across categories.

BOX 7.5   **INTO PRACTICE**

Strategies for Teaching Conflict Resolution

Several strategies are helpful in resolving conflicts. After reviewing the research literature to identify strategies educators often use to teach conflict resolution, Bullock and Foegen (2002) found the following to be effective:

Cooperative learning. Cooperative learning involves teaching students in small groups in which they focus on a common learning task or activity (see Chapter 13). Students must learn how to communicate with one another, negotiate, and work collaboratively. You can teach conflict resolution using cooperative learning strategies as you teach any content area.

Structured (or cooperative) controversy. This strategy is a small-group, debate-like process in which students learn to explore and present positions on both sides of a controversial topic or issue (D'Eon, Proctor, & Reeder, 2007). Teachers assign a topic that has clear opposing views; but unlike typical debate formats, in which students are assigned or choose one side of that topic, students here study and present information about all the opposing views. In this way, they learn persuasion skills and understand that there are at least two sides to every story.

Mediation. Mediation strategies teach students conflict resolution through the use of a neutral party. Johns and colleagues (2005) suggest nine steps to implement a mediation session:

1. Bring together two students who have a conflict. Have them sit at a table facing one another, with you or another mediator at the head of the table. It can be useful to have another adult or, even better, a student serve as a mediator.
2. Open the session by introducing yourself (or having the mediator introduce herself) and having the participating students introduce themselves.
3. Emphasize the confidentiality of the session and ensure that participants understand that outcomes must be discussed.
4. Emphasize active listening and turn taking.
5. Characterize the process as a fact-finding process: getting information from both sides.
6. Assist students to state issues in neutral terms by providing summaries and clarifications.
7. Once both sides have been stated and summarized, identify and emphasize common interests that will benefit from a solution to the conflict, and ask students to generate potential solutions.
8. Help students expand, clarify, and decide upon an agreeable resolution.
9. Write up the agreed-upon resolution and ask each student to sign it.

Negotiation. Negotiation is an integral part of virtually any conflict-resolution process. It can be taught as a primary strategy, using these approaches:

1. *It's about being prepared.* To negotiate successfully, both students have to know what they want out of a negotiation and also what others might want. They have to think through not only their interests but also the interests of others.
2. *It's about timing.* Students need to understand that there are good times to bring up a topic and bad times to do so. Negotiations occur in the context of conversations, so learning and applying some basic conversational skills—such as not interrupting someone else, staying on topic, and listening—are important to the negotiation process.
3. *It's about persuasion, not aggression.* Students should learn that, to achieve their goal, they'll need, in part, to convince someone else to change his mind and be willing to give up elements of their own goal as well. Bullying and aggressive behaviors never achieve that outcome. Instead, students need to learn the skills of persuasion. First, teach students how to let people know they understand what another person is saying by restating what that person has said. Second, teach them to emphasize how the other person could achieve the same goal in a different way—one that is, of course, more closely aligned with their own goal! Third, teach students to calmly and systematically tell others about the advantages of their own plan or idea.
4. *It's about compromise.* Finally, students should learn that they may be more successful in achieving their ultimate goal if they settle for incremental steps toward that goal instead of expecting it to be fully achieved all at once.

Group problem solving. Problem solving is a critical strategy for resolving conflicts. There are three steps for teaching problem solving:

1. Teach students to identify and communicate the problem to be solved.
2. Teach students to generate potential solutions to the problem.
3. Teach students to select one solution that best fits the problem.

Problem-solving instruction should occur in the context of real-world problems that students might face.

More than 134,000 teenagers are in juvenile correctional facilities (Sickmund, 2002). It is estimated that 30 to 70 percent of those youth have disabilities (Leone, Meisel, & Drakeford, 2002). Typically, these teenagers are boys from culturally and linguistically diverse backgrounds who experience poverty and have substantial learning and/or

BOX 7.6   **INCLUSION TIPS**

	What You Might See	What You Might Be Tempted to Do	Alternate Responses	Ways to Include Peers in the Process
Behavior	The student refuses to follow directions and uses inappropriate language.	Respond in anger and send her out of the classroom. Place her in time-out for extended periods.	Include her in conflict-resolution instruction and capitalize on her strengths in this instruction.	Involve classmates in the conflict-resolution instruction so that all students have an opportunity to work closely and constructively with each other.
Social interactions	He fights with other students and is always on the defensive.	Seat him as far away as possible from the students with whom he is fighting.	Teach appropriate social skills, using modeling, videos, and social skills programs.	Pair him with different students who can model and help him practice social skills and responses.
Educational performance	She is rarely on task and appears to have an inability to learn.	Give her poor grades and require her to remain after school until all her work is done.	Create an opportunity for her to engage in service learning based on her interests, which will enable her to make contributions to others.	Develop a buddy system in implementing service learning so that students work together collaboratively.
Classroom attitudes	He is sad all the time and does not speak or interact with others.	Discipline him for nonparticipation and instruct him to cheer up.	Recognize the warning signs of depression. Partner with the school counselor to get professional help.	Encourage all students to affirm each others' strengths by giving positive feedback to each other.

behavior problems (Leone et al., 2002). Although incarcerated youth have been reported to have academic achievement one to several years below grade level, they tend to receive special education services two thirds less often in correctional facilities than they would in public schools (Foley, 2001). Without a skilled lawyer (who also had been trained in special education), Nick may well have found himself trapped in the juvenile justice system, the victim of incompetent teachers.

Assessing Students' Progress

MEASURING STUDENTS' PROGRESS

Progress in the General Curriculum

In *mastery learning* or *mastery training* instruction, teachers frequently assess their students' mastery of content, determining whether it is time to move to the next concept or activity. They offer more instruction to those students who do not show mastery, and then they assess these students again.

Mastery learning makes it possible for all students to master the content, even if they do so at different rates. Mastery training has been used with students with disabilities, including students with emotional or behavioral disorders (Vannest, Temple-Harvey, & Mason, 2008), and is a useful way to ensure student progress in the general curriculum.

You will recall that the classroom-centered intervention for young children with EBD incorporated mastery learning as a major component of the intervention. To monitor students' progress toward mastery, you will need to do the following (King-Sears & Mooney, 2004):

- *Ask questions of the whole class.* Ask all of the students in the class to indicate what they think the correct answer is. Ask them to raise their hands to answer a question. Some students will feel intimidated and will not participate. But technology-based response systems allow greater anonymity. There, students have remote-control devices and respond by pressing a button. The responses, when presented on the screen, are anonymous, but you can obtain data on each student's response.

- *Use a cooperative learning strategy such as "think-pair-share."* Create small groups of students, ask each group to *think* about a question, *pair* the student with a disability with a peer in the group, and ask each of them to *share* their responses to your question. Be sure that at least one student has the correct responses. You will learn more about how students can teach each other (cooperative learning) in Chapter 13.

Progress in Addressing Other Educational Needs

Students with EBD usually need to learn social skills, and teachers need to know how to chart their students' progress in learning those skills. A commonly used social skills rating scale, validated for use by students with EBD, is the Social Skills Improvement System (SSIS) (Gresham, Elliott, Cook, Vance, & Kettler, 2010). It includes a screening guide as well as monitoring and feedback components, and it can be used across ages. One important component of the SSIS is its classwide intervention component, which lends itself to use in inclusive settings.

MAKING ACCOMMODATIONS FOR ASSESSMENT

As you have read, students with EBD are more likely than other students with disabilities to be served in alternative schools. Gagnon and McLaughlin (2004) conducted a survey of private and public day treatment and residential schools for elementary school students with EBD to evaluate whether the students were given the opportunity to progress in the general curriculum and to participate in district accountability systems. The researchers also investigated whether these alternative schools offered accommodations for state and district assessments. Nearly 20 percent of the schools had no accommodation policy. Of the 80 percent that did have such a policy, most simply adopted the school district's policy. The results of this research are disappointing. Students need opportunities to progress in the general education curriculum so they are not behind when they return to their neighborhood schools.

State education agencies increasingly take into account students' emotional anxiety when determining whether to provide accommodations in statewide assessments. Because of their anxiety problems, students with EBD may have more difficulties completing tests than other students do. Accommodations to address this difference can include extended time to take the tests, individual administration of the tests, and testing with breaks. Nick benefits from extended time and breaks.

ADDRESSING THE PROFESSIONAL STANDARDS

The following Council for Exceptional Children (CEC) Common Core Knowledge and Skills are addressed in this chapter through the content and concepts we discuss. See the Appendix for a full listing of these Knowledge and Skill statements:

ICC2K1, ICC2K2, ICC2K3, ICC2K4, ICC2K5, ICC2K7, ICC3K1, ICC3K2, ICC5K5, ICC5K6, ICC5S2, ICC5S3, ICC5S4, ICC5S5, ICC5S6, ICC5S10, ICC5S11, ICC7S3, ICC7S7, ICC8K3, ICC8S2, ICC8S6, ICC8S8, ICC9S2, ICC9S3, ICC9S5, ICC10K3, ICC10S3

Summary

IDENTIFYING STUDENTS WITH EMOTIONAL OR BEHAVIORAL DISORDERS

- Students with emotional or behavioral disorders manifest emotional, behavioral, social, and/or academic characteristics that are chronic and severe and adversely affect their educational performance.
- Students may exhibit characteristics of anxiety disorder, mood disorder, oppositional defiant disorder, conduct disorder, and/or schizophrenia.
- Students may exhibit externalizing (aggressive, acting-out, noncompliant) behaviors and internalizing (withdrawn, depressed, anxious, obsessive, compulsive) behaviors.
- Students with emotional or behavioral disorders typically have normal intelligence, but they have significant challenges related to academic achievement and social skills.
- Approximately 7 percent of all students with disabilities have emotional or behavioral disabilities, although there are estimates that the percentage is much larger than that.
- Emotional or behavioral disorders are caused by interactions between biological (for example, brain functioning and genetics) and environmental factors (for example, stressful living conditions and child maltreatment).

EVALUATING STUDENTS WITH EMOTIONAL OR BEHAVIORAL DISORDERS

- The Scale for Assessing Emotional Disturbance is a norm-referenced scale tied directly to the five elements of the IDEA definition of EBD; it adds the element of social maladjustment.
- The Behavioral and Emotional Rating Scale—Second Edition, a norm-referenced tool with strong psychometric properties, is designed to identify students' strengths and needs as a basis for educational planning.

DESIGNING AN APPROPRIATE IEP

- The wraparound planning model is a process linking school, community, and mental health services to provide a family-driven, collaborative, individualized, culturally competent, and strengths-based planning approach.
- Complex problems require thoughtful planning and multicomponent interventions, such as the classwide, peer-assisted, self-management approach described in this chapter.

- An important universal design feature for all students, including those with emotional or behavioral disorders, involves modifications to the ways in which students respond to the curriculum and provide evidence of their knowledge, either orally or through multimedia presentations.
- It is important to implement multiple dropout-prevention strategies, such as linking youth with a mentor and involving them in extracurricular activities.

USING EFFECTIVE INSTRUCTIONAL STRATEGIES

- Two rules of thumb need to be in place for preventing conduct disorders: Begin early, and use all the tools available.
- Service learning strategies provide a means for students with emotional or behavioral disorders to learn important skills and to contribute to their communities.
- Students with emotional or behavioral disorders need to acquire conflict-resolution skills, including negotiation, compromising, problem-solving, and decision-making skills, if they are to succeed as adults.

INCLUDING STUDENTS WITH EMOTIONAL OR BEHAVIORAL DISORDERS

- Students with emotional or behavioral disorders have one of the lowest rates of inclusion in general education classrooms.
- Students with emotional or behavioral disorders are at risk for being served in separate schools, private schools, correctional facilities, residential settings, hospitals, or homes.

ASSESSING STUDENTS' PROGRESS

- Mastery evaluation takes a different approach to evaluation and is intended to provide information on student progress that teachers can use to modify instruction.
- Interventions to promote social skills are important for students with emotional or behavioral disorders.
- Students with emotional or behavioral disorders need access to the general curriculum. A critical component of assessing the progress of students with EBD in the general curriculum is the provision of accommodations, such as extended time, individual administration, and testing with breaks.

8

Understanding Students *with* Attention-Deficit/ Hyperactivity Disorder

Who Is Will Sims?

Will Sims is a seventeen-year-old eleventh grader who has attention-deficit disorder. He was in fourth grade when he and his mother, Leigh Ann, first learned that he has the disorder. He had been ill on the day when his school administered the state-required examination of students' proficiency, so he took his makeup examination in a room alone, not in a room with other students, as he would have done if he had not been ill. On that day, his teacher noticed how well Will was able to concen-

trate on the examination. "Isolation," she declared, "is a way to help him." She then wondered if this need for isolation was a clue that he might have attention-deficit disorder: In a room with other students, Will became distracted; but in a room by himself, he focused intensely on his work.

Will's attention-deficit disorder does not prevent him from taking his classes in the general education classroom. But he does receive accommodations, including testing in a room by himself; and he spends one class period per day in a resource room, where he receives help on his schoolwork from a special educator. Will is happy to declare that has brought up his grades, first to a 2.9, then to a 3.0 (on a 4.0 scale), while annually reducing the types and extent of the accommodations he receives.

Will's success has not come easily. After his fourth-grade teacher noticed how well he

performed when he was alone, his mother asked his school administrators to test him for a disability. They said they could but that they had to arrange for the school psychologist to observe him over a period of six to eight weeks. "That was just too long," said Leigh Ann, "so we went and had him independently tested by an expert. He confirmed the diagnosis, and then when the school psychologist had finished his round of observations, he came to the same conclusion."

Leigh Ann adds that, not only did she have to pay for the independent evaluation, but she also had to pay for "learning remediation. That was another huge expense, almost $15,000 for getting him additional tutoring at a private center, four hours a week for nine months."

In addition to his attention-deficit disorder, Will has hearing loss in one ear, so he works with a speech therapist appointed by his school, reading and then speaking a sentence over and over again until he can say the words so well that he cannot be misunderstood.

Will is proud of his progress in school, but he is not satisfied with himself, even now. The accommodations and special services in school "helped me out a lot because they made me more responsible [for learning]. Now, it's like I have more responsibility to the point where I have to study a lot longer. I might have to study a lot longer than other peers in my classes do, but I can definitely understand the material more when I get all the help through my IEP and through my family too."

In addition to his daily hour in the resource room and his speech therapy, what help does Will get? His accommodations include taking practice tests at home, using a school online site called "Study Island" where he answers twenty questions at a time and instantly learns his score as well as which answers were correct or incorrect. "I take all the help I can get," he says. And despite the increasing difficulty of his curriculum, "every year my IEP has been reduced and reduced. It's getting a lot harder now, so I take control of my grades now. I want to go to college and I want to be successful. I just want to get all my time done and just put forth all the effort I can into my schoolwork so I can improve everything."

Both Will and Leigh Ann have had to confront the fact that Will, like many students with an attention-deficit disorder, needs more than classroom accommodations. Throughout his school years, he has taken three different kinds of medication; but he now has finally found the one that suits him best—the one that allows him to concentrate but does not affect him so much that he is unable to learn.

Will characterizes himself as "athletically active." He quickly adds, "I want to get out of high school, graduate, and go to business school for four years and

OBJECTIVES

- You will learn about three types of attention-deficit/hyperactivity disorder (AD/HD): predominantly inattentive, predominantly hyperactive-impulsive, and combined.

- You will learn how to evaluate a student to determine if she has AD/HD using the Conners's Rating Scales—Revised and how to determine the nature and extent of special education services needed using the Attention Deficit Disorders Evaluation Scale—Third Edition.

- You will learn how to accommodate students with AD/HD by taking simple steps such as rearranging a classroom, posting daily schedules, helping students organize their work, and partnering with families or school nurses on medication management.

- You will learn that multiple interventions often are necessary to develop effective instruction and include students in the general curriculum.

- You will learn about how to use goal attainment scaling to assess progress on educational goals and about the accommodations students with AD/HD might need on statewide assessments to assess their progress in the general education curriculum.

then after that I want to go to a maintenance school, like a car place, so I can get my car degree and then eventually open up my own car shop and redo cars." Are Will's goals realistic? He thinks so, and so does Leigh Ann. He knows what accommodations he needs. He has learned what medication works. He has become responsible for his own learning. He has ambition. Finally, he has a strategic plan for his future. Asked if he is self-confident, he answers, "Yes, I am." And he has good reason to be self-confident: Special education services have boosted his abilities and his confidence.

Identifying Students with AD/HD

DEFINING ATTENTION-DEFICIT/HYPERACTIVITY DISORDER

Instead of listing AD/HD as a separate disability category, IDEA includes it as a subcategory of "other health impairments" (see Chapter 12). Under the IDEA definition, a student with other health impairments has limited strength, vitality, or alertness, including a heightened alertness to environmental stimuli, that results in limited alertness with respect to the educational environment, that

- is due to chronic or acute health problems such as asthma, attention deficit disorder or attention deficit hyperactivity disorder, diabetes, epilepsy, a heart condition, hemophilia, lead poisoning, leukemia, nephritis, rheumatic fever, sickle cell anemia, and Tourette's syndrome; and
- adversely affects a child's educational performance.

AD/HD accounts for slightly more than two thirds of students identified in the category of other health impairments (Schnoes, Reid, Wagner, & Marder, 2006). Because of coexisting disabilities, students with AD/HD often are also served through IDEA in the categories of learning disability, emotional or behavioral disorders, and intellectual disability. You will learn more about coexistence with these other disabilities later in the chapter.

Because IDEA does not specifically define AD/HD, most professionals adhere to the definition offered by the American Psychiatric Association (APA) (2000) in the *Diagnostic and Statistical Manual of Mental Disorders* (DSM-IV-TR): "The essential feature of Attention-Deficit/Hyperactivity Disorder is a persistent pattern of inattention and/ or hyperactivity-impulsivity that is more frequently displayed and severe than is typically observed in individuals at a comparable level of development" (p. 85).

The criteria for persistence, frequency, and severity are important. Everyone is forgetful and absentminded at times, especially during periods of stress. Also, some people are simply more or less active or energetic than others. Unless those characteristics are persistent, frequent, and severe, the person does not meet the APA criteria. And a student whose educational performance is not adversely affected will not qualify for IDEA services. Will's teachers first suspected he might have attention deficit when he was required to take a two-day standardized state assessment given to all fourth graders. He took the first day of the test in a classroom with his peers. He missed the second day of the test so took the makeup in the quiet and uncrowded school library. The differences between the scores were remarkable: The classroom scores were much lower than the library scores were, yet the classroom scores were typical of the scores Will had been receiving for several years. The discrepancy caused his school's principal and his teacher to think that Will might have attention-deficit disorder.

The APA criteria also require that the symptoms must persist for at least six months, be present in at least two settings, and not be attributable to another disability. The symptoms must occur before the age of seven, although studies show that approximately one third of children and one half of adults with AD/HD have an onset after that age (Barkley, Fischer, Smallish, & Fletcher, 2006). Of children identified as having

AD/HD, 26 to 46 percent persist in displaying the disorder into adolescence (Bussing, Mason, Bell, Porter, & Garvan, 2010; Molina et al., 2009).

In the United States, 6 to 9 percent of children and youth and 3 to 5 percent of adults are identified as having AD/HD (Dopheide & Pliszka, 2009). Estimates suggest that rates have doubled or tripled since 1990 (Stevens & Ward-Estes, 2006). Roughly 50 percent of preschoolers who are diagnosed with AD/HD no longer exhibit a disorder once they begin school. Due to the increase of students identified as having AD/HD, the category of other health impairments has increased significantly over the past decade. Autism is the only other category of disability that has had similar increases.

In a national study of elementary-aged students, students with AD/HD were found to be disproportionately male—approximately four times as many males as females. African American students are not overrepresented (as they are in several other categories, such as emotional or behavioral disorders and intellectual disability), and Hispanic students are underrepresented (Schnoes et al., 2006).

DESCRIBING THE CHARACTERISTICS

Diagnostic Criteria for AD/HD

Under the DSM-IV-TR diagnostic criteria (APA, 2000), there are three subtypes of AD/HD: predominately inattentive, predominately hyperactive-impulsive, and combined. Accordingly, the abbreviation AD/HD features a slash, indicating inclusion of all three subtypes: attention-deficit disorder, hyperactivity disorder, and a combination. For all three subtypes, the characteristics must have been present for at least six months and fall outside the range of adaptive behavior.

Predominately Inattentive Type. A student must exhibit six or more of the following characteristics to be classified as having the predominately inattentive type (APA, 2000, p. 92):

- Often fails to give close attention to details or makes mistakes in schoolwork, work, or other activities
- Often has difficulty sustaining attention in tasks or play activities
- Often does not seem to listen when spoken to directly
- Often does not follow through on instructions and fails to finish schoolwork, chores, or duties in the workplace (not due to oppositional behavior or failure to understand instructions)
- Often has difficulty organizing tasks and activities
- Often avoids, dislikes, or is reluctant to engage in tasks that require sustained mental effort (such as schoolwork or homework)
- Often loses things necessary for tasks or activities (e.g., toys, school assignments, pencils, books, or tools)
- Often is easily distracted by extraneous stimuli
- Often is forgetful in daily activities

Will has many of these characteristics, such as not paying close attention to details, making mistakes in schoolwork, and being easily distracted. But like many students with attention-deficit disorder, he has no single characteristic but a combination of them.

Because students with the inattentive type of AD/HD usually are not as disruptive as those with hyperactivity-impulsivity, their needs may be overlooked. These students often display a slow tempo in their approach to academic tasks, boredom, lack of motivation, and self-consciousness (Adams, Derefinko, Milich, & Fillmore, 2008). The inattentive type has a higher ratio of girls to boys than do the other two types (Glanzman & Blum, 2007a). Students with the inattentive diagnosis typically are identified later than students with hyperactivity.

Many children with AD/HD have difficulty learning from their experiences and cannot remember routines and procedures, so they are often corrected.

Without a specific diagnosis and appropriate interventions, these students are at risk for long-term academic, social, and emotional difficulties. They usually have difficulty working in distracting environments, absorbing large amounts of new information, shifting flexibly from one task to another, or linearly linking a series of cognitive operations. That is why you should (1) make sure that your students with the inattentive type of AD/HD have enough time to shift from one activity to another, (2) teach them techniques for organizing their thoughts and materials, (3) offer them flexible time limits for finishing their assignments or examinations, and (4) simplify tasks that have multiple steps. It helps Will greatly to have flexible time for finishing his examinations. Flex time does not give him a special advantage over students who do not need it; instead, it allows him to show what he knows, and that is what examinations are all about—allowing a student to prove he or she has learned the curriculum.

Predominately Hyperactive-Impulsive Type. A student must have six or more of the following characteristics of hyperactivity or impulsivity to be classified as having the predominately hyperactive-impulsive type of AD/HD (APA, 2000, p. 92):

Hyperactivity

- Often fidgets with hands or feet or squirms in seat
- Often leaves seat in classroom or in other situations in which remaining seated is expected
- Often runs about or climbs excessively in situations in which it is inappropriate (in adolescents or adults, may be limited to subjective feelings of restlessness)
- Often has difficulty playing or engaging in leisure activities quietly
- Often is on the go or acts as if driven by a motor
- Often talks excessively

Impulsivity

- Often blurts out answers before questions have been completed
- Often has difficulty waiting to take turns
- Often interrupts or intrudes on others (e.g., butts into conversations or games)

Problems associated with hyperactivity and impulsivity typically start when a child is young, several years before problems with the inattentive type of AD/HD emerge (Brock, Jimerson, & Hansen, 2009). These students are often described as displaying fidgetiness and being in constant motion. It is especially important for students with hyperactivity or impulsivity to have opportunities to take breaks, have extended time for assignments, and participate in instructional activities that enable them to move around the classroom. Although hyperactivity tends to decrease with age, impulsivity typically persists into adolescence and adulthood.

Combined Type. The third classification describes students who have features of both inattention and hyperactivity-impulsivity; the literature refers to the combined type as ADHD (without the slash). A key characteristic is distractibility (Adams et al., 2008). Most students with AD/HD have combined ADHD, and the majority of research is done on this group of students (Glanzman & Blum, 2007b).

Intellectual Functioning and Academic Achievement

Experts disagree about extent to which students with AD/HD have impairments in intellectual functioning. One research study found an average IQ of 95 in a sample of students with AD/HD (Scheirs & Timmers, 2009). Other studies have found students with AD/HD have scores on intelligence tests that are approximately nine points lower than the scores of their age peers (Brock et al., 2009). Barkley (2003) reported that IQ ranges of students with AD/HD tend to be seven to ten points below the norm (IQ 100). Approximately 21 percent of elementary students with AD/HD have also been identified as having intellectual disability, which, as you will learn in Chapter 9, means that they have an IQ score of approximately 70 or below as well as limitations in adaptive behavior (Schnoes et al., 2006).

Academic Achievement

Although the majority of students with AD/HD have typical intelligence, as Will does, they frequently have problems achieving academically. Research on the academic achievement of students with AD/HD reveals the following:

- Students with AD/HD, compared to typical peers, have lower standardized achievement scores in reading and math, are more likely to experience grade-level retention, and are more likely not to graduate from high school (Bussing et al., 2010).
- Students with AD/HD often have impairments associated with motivation, memory, goal-directed behavior, processing environmental cues, and incorporating feedback to improve performance (Adams et al., 2008; Smith et al., 2007). Will has none of these difficulties.

Despite their academic challenges, students with AD/HD have a variety of strengths. In Box 8.1, Chris Fraser, an adult who has experienced both personal and professional success and who has grown up with AD/HD, shares his perspectives on ways to capitalize on strengths. Note that he, like Will, confronts his challenges and has found ways to overcome them and find a satisfying life.

Behavioral, Social, and Emotional Characteristics

Many students with AD/HD have behavioral, social, and emotional challenges. A high overlap exists between the categories of AD/HD and emotional or behavioral disorders. For example, 30 to 50 percent of students identified as having AD/HD also have been identified as having oppositional defiant disorder and/or conduct disorder (Armenteros, Lewis, & Davalos, 2007), and about one half have been identified as having an anxiety disorder (Bowen, Chavira, Bailey, Stein, & Stein, 2008). Will has had some challenges with his behavior, but all derived from Adderal, the medication he first used after being formally diagnosed as having attention deficit disorder. Especially as he entered adolescence, his moods, influenced by the medication, made him especially sensitive among his peers. Yes, he was able to concentrate on his academics; but when peers tried to speak with him or accidentally bumped into him, he sometimes became angry. His present medication does not affect his moods nearly as much. As he said, "each pill changes who you are."

Among children with AD/HD, 50 to 80 percent experience peer rejection (Hoza, 2007). Sleep problems are frequent in this group of students, and the resulting fatigue can affect behavior (Cortese, Lecendreux, Mouren, & Konofal, 2006). Other common behavioral, social, and emotional challenges include the following:

- Difficulty in perceiving social cues, accurately estimating one's abilities and performance, and adjusting behavior in light of feedback (McQuade & Hoza, 2008)
- Difficulty in interpreting and processing emotions (Da Fonseca, Seguier, Santos, Poinso, & Deruelle, 2009)
- Higher rates of tobacco use (Upadhyaya & Carpenter, 2008)

BOX 8.1　MY VOICE

Chris Fraser

I've been waiting to have my voice heard for many years. I feel so happy and fortunate to be able to share what has been in my mind and heart regarding AD/HD. I have found that one of my life's greatest assets and greatest teachers has been growing up and living with attention-deficit disorder paired with a learning disability. Don't get me wrong: As you can imagine, I obviously haven't felt this way for the majority of my life. Rather, this has been a gradual realization that I have felt growing in my heart ever since I was a young child. Therefore, my personal perception of AD/HD is that describing it as a disorder is a matter of perspective.

As an adult, I work as a therapist in a community mental health center and share with children and their families an empowering and hopeful perspective about AD/HD: that it is a collection of adaptive mechanisms and temperament traits that are more suited to some societies and tasks than to others.

I share this information because I wish I had been told this as a young child and because I came up with the concept on my own in high school. I can remember specifically a conversation with my friend Jawn, who was also struggling through the academic confines of traditional academia, in which we agreed that if we had lived in a different time in the past, we would have survived while most National Merit Scholars would have perished. Since then, many publications and articles have been written about this very topic. As I began to discover these articles and research my findings in graduate school, I saw confirmation of a concept that I had already come up with and had used as a source of energy. I enjoy looking at AD/HD as an inherited set of skills, abilities, and personality tendencies that I can use to my benefit to be successful. For me, this has been a very healing and empowering way of looking at things.

I have a number of tips about how people with AD/HD can survive in a world that doesn't automatically accommodate some of our personality characteristics. I have developed these tips on my journey through academia and life as a person with AD/HD.

Tip 1: Use your resources and advocate for your needs. I was very sensitive about other people thinking I was not intelligent, and I didn't want to be seen as different in any way. Therefore, I was embarrassed to go to the resource room each day in elementary school, and in high school I didn't even use available resources. I didn't learn that it was okay and smart to use those resources until after I suffered my way through high school.

Tip 2: Find your joy or bliss and follow it. In college I found that, like other students with AD/HD, I have the ability to hyperfocus and excel in subjects I have a passion for. This acknowledgment of my strengths and interests gave meaning to the frustrations I endured in academia and gave me a sense of hope for the future.

Tip 3: Work on acknowledging your growth areas and develop your own special ways of dealing with them. In college I also found out that the real world was not going to accommodate to me, so I needed my own bag of tricks to survive in it. This was a difficult realization: I figured out how to deal with my growth areas through trial and error. I confess that I still am disorganized occasionally and that I still have difficulty managing time. But I deal with this growth area by making lists. I write things down before I forget them. I find that even if I don't refer back to the list, the process of writing things down helps me remember them better.

Tip 4: Never give up on your dreams, and view your mistakes as learning opportunities rather than personal failures. To this day, I am still developing my own tips for learning how to compensate for my growth areas and to use my capabilities as a person with AD/HD.

Overall, my family has made all the difference in the way I have learned to view my challenges. My father also grew up with AD/HD traits and at the end of high school was told that he was not college material. But he went on to get a bachelor's degree, a master's degree, and a doctorate in psychology. Hence, I grew up knowing that my father had experienced the same struggles I had. He ingrained in me the idea that I was capable of doing whatever I put my mind to. My mother was always a strong student and now works as a remedial reading and gifted teacher. Therefore, I was doubly fortunate because my parents had both personal experience and professional knowledge about AD/HD. I am also fortunate to have a wife who has special traits that compensate for my growth areas, with the result that I become more functional each year we spend together.

My journey as a person with AD/HD has involved continuous learning, struggle, toil, frustration, realization, and finally peace. Along the way I obtained a bachelor's degree in social work and sociology with a psychology minor and a master's degree in social work. But most important, by learning about how to help myself, I am now in a position to pass on this information and help others who live with AD/HD.

- Substantially higher likelihood of involvement with the juvenile justice system (Bussing et al., 2010)
- Increased risk-taking behavior (Flory, Molina, Pelham, Gnagy, & Smith, 2006)
- Compared to other students who receive special education services, a significantly higher likelihood of receiving behavior management programs, mental health services, social work services, and in-school family counseling (Schnoes et al., 2006)

DETERMINING THE CAUSES

Do you agree or disagree with each of these statements?

- AD/HD stems from a lack of will or self-control.
- AD/HD is caused by parents who don't discipline their children.
- AD/HD results from watching too much television or playing too many video games.
- AD/HD results from dietary issues, such as eating too much sugar.
- AD/HD results from living in a fast-paced, stressful culture (Harman & Barkley, 2000).

If you had agreed with any of these statements, you would have been wrong. There are three causes of AD/HD: heredity, structural differences in the brain, and other biological causes.

Heredity

Family, twin, and adoption studies suggest that genetics strongly contributes to AD/HD (Brock et al., 2009). Children who have a parent with AD/HD have a 40 to 57 percent risk of having AD/HD, and siblings of children with AD/HD are five to seven times more likely to have AD/HD than are children whose siblings do not have AD/HD (Barkley, Murphy, & Fischer, 2007; Wilens et al., 2005). Identical twins have AD/HD in 55 to 92 percent of cases (Faraone et al., 2005). Twins have highly stable AD/HD symptoms during elementary and secondary years, and the stability and similarity of their characteristics is mainly genetically based (Larsson, Larsson, & Lichtenstein, 2004). When asked what has caused Will's attention-deficit disorder, Will's mother Leigh Ann says that she believes heredity plays a role. She suspects that Will's father has attention deficit, though he has not been formally diagnosed, and her sister (Will's aunt) was formally diagnosed as an adult.

Structural Differences in the Brain

Researchers have identified structural and functional differences in the brains of people who have AD/HD, particularly in the frontal lobes, cerebellum, and basal ganglia (Mahone & Wodka, 2008; Vaidya & Stollstorff, 2008). The frontal lobes play a key role in controlling cognitive, emotional, and motor responses, whereas the cerebellum and basal ganglia are central to motor planning, motivation, and behavioral inhibition. Structural differences appear to result from reduced brain volume in children with AD/HD (Bush, 2008). When comparing individuals with AD/HD to typical peers, scientists have found that their brain volume is 3 to 8 percent lower (Kieling, Goncalves, Tannock, & Castellanos, 2008).

Environmental Causes

Prenatal factors (e.g., prenatal exposure to cigarette smoking, lead, and alcohol), perinatal factors (e.g., complications with labor and delivery), and postnatal causes (e.g., environmental toxins) also have a role in AD/HD (Brock et al., 2009). However, the evidence is much weaker for environmental causes. Environmental factors appear to interact with genetic factors rather than act as primary causes in and of themselves.

As in Chris Fraser's family, AD/HD is often multi-generational, suggesting a genetic link. Enjoying a family ski trip, Chris Fraser, a master's level licensed independent social worker, is pictured here with his father, J. Scott Fraser, a full professor at Wright State University.

Evaluating Students with AD/HD

DETERMINING THE PRESENCE OF AD/HD

Children can be accurately diagnosed with AD/HD starting around two years of age, but four- and five-year-olds are more likely to meet the criteria than are toddlers (Egger, Kondo, & Angold, 2006). Although early diagnosis is possible, other students with AD/HD may not be identified until they enroll in school or even until they are in adolescence. Often children with AD/HD encounter challenges in general education classrooms, and general education teachers may be the first people to develop concerns and initiate the referral process. As you may recall, it was Will's teacher who first suspected he had attention-deficit disorder. Would it have been proper for the teacher to suggest that Will should use medication? No. Under IDEA, an educator may not require or recommend medication but may suggest a student be evaluated by a physician or psychologist. The purpose of the referral is to receive expert assistance in performing IDEA's mandatory nondiscriminatory evaluation (see Box 8.2). School-based special education teams, pediatricians, family doctors, psychiatrists, clinical psychologists, and neurologists often provide the expert assistance.

The process described in Box 8.2 begins after the student's parent or parents agree to the nondiscriminatory evaluation. When a medical evaluation is warranted as part of the AD/HD evaluation, the school district is responsible for paying for it. If you suspect that a student has AD/HD, you will need to document her behavior, referring to the characteristics that define AD/HD. The effect of medicine can be positive and dramatic. But medicine alone does not always do the trick. No single "silver bullet" exists; that's why the nondiscriminatory evaluation must be based on a variety of assessments.

The nondiscriminatory evaluation seeks to answer three questions (Smith, Barkley, & Shapiro, 2007): (1) Does the student have AD/HD, and can the evaluators rule out other disabilities? (2) Do other disabilities exist simultaneously with AD/HD? (3) What should the student's IEP contain? The four most frequently used evaluation tools include behavior rating scales, interviews, psychological testing, and behavioral observations (Brock, Jimerson, & Hansen, 2009). Of these four techniques, the most frequently used is rating scales.

For the initial evaluation of whether a student has AD/HD, many psychologists use the Conners's Rating Scales—Revised (Conners, 1997). The Conners's Rating Scales is available in a long and short version for teachers (for students ages three to seventeen), parents (for students ages three to seventeen), and students themselves (ages twelve to seventeen). The long version for teachers contains thirteen subscales (for example, Oppositional, Hyperactivity, Social Problems) and takes fifteen to twenty minutes to complete. The short version for teachers contains only four subscales and requires five to ten minutes to complete.

Researchers compared the properties of five frequently used AD/HD rating scales. They concluded that the Conners's is substantially more comprehensive than the other four, and a national survey of school psychologists found that the Conners's is also the most frequently used. Approximately 80 percent of school psychologists use it (Demaray, Schaefer, & DeLong, 2003).

DETERMINING THE NATURE OF SPECIALLY DESIGNED INSTRUCTION AND SERVICES

After determining that a student has AD/HD, the evaluation team must decide whether the student needs special education and related services. Many teams use the Attention Deficit Disorders Evaluation Scale—Third Edition (ADDES-3) because it is better than other available rating scales at identifying interventions for students with AD/HD (Demaray, Elting, & Schaefer, 2003). The ADDES-3 has three main scales:

- Attention Deficit Disorders Evaluation Scale—Third Edition (ADDES-3)
- Early Childhood Attention Deficit Disorders Evaluation Scale
- Attention Deficit Disorders Evaluation Scale—Secondary-Age Student

BOX 8.2	# NONDISCRIMINATORY EVALUATION PROCESS

Students with AD/HD

Observation

Teacher and parents observe:

Predominantly inattentive type: The student makes careless mistakes, has difficulty sustaining attention, doesn't seem to be listening, fails to follow through on tasks, has difficulty organizing, often loses things, is easily distracted, or is forgetful.

Predominantly hyperactive-impulsive type: The student is fidgety, leaves his seat when expected to be seated, runs or climbs excessively or inappropriately, has difficulty playing quietly, talks excessively, blurts out answers or comments, has difficulty taking turns, or acts as if always on the go.

Combined type: Characteristics of both are observed.

Screening

Assessment measures:

Classroom work products: Work is consistently or generally poor. The student has difficulty staying on task, so his work may be incomplete or completed haphazardly.

Group intelligence tests: Tests may not reveal true ability because student has difficulty staying on task.

Group achievement tests: Performance may not be a true reflection of achievement because the student has difficulty staying on task.

Medical screening: The physician does not find a physical condition that could cause inattention or hyperactivity-impulsivity. Medication may be prescribed.

Vision and hearing screening: Results do not explain academic difficulties.

Prereferral

Teacher implements suggestions from school-based team:
The student still experiences frustration, inattention, or hyperactivity despite reasonable curricular and behavioral accommodations.

Referral

The child should be referred to a multidisciplinary team for a complete evaluation if prereferral intervention is not successful.

Nondiscriminatory evaluation procedures and standards

Assessment measures:

Psychological evaluation: A psychiatrist or psychologist determines that the student meets DSM-IV-TR criteria for AD/HD.

Individualized intelligence tests: The student's intelligence may range from below-average to gifted.

Individualized achievement tests: The student's performance on achievement tests may suggest that his educational performance has been adversely affected by the condition.

Behavior rating scales: The student scores in the significant range on measures of inattention or hyperactivity-impulsivity.

Teacher observation: The student's educational performance has been adversely affected by the condition. The behaviors have been present in more than one setting, were first observed before age seven, and have lasted for more than six months.

Curriculum-based assessment: The student may be experiencing difficulty in one or more areas of the curriculum used by the local school district because the behaviors have caused the student to miss important skills.

Direct observation: The student exhibits inattention or hyperactivity-impulsivity during the observation.

Determination

The nondiscriminatory evaluation team determines that the student has AD/HD and needs special education and related services. The student's IEP team develops appropriate education options for the student.

The ADDES-3 is based on the American Psychiatric Association definition of AD/HD and includes both the inattentive and the hyperactive-impulsive type. The ADDES-3 is suitable for evaluating students who are between four and eighteen years old. It has both a home and a school version for parents and teachers. The ADDES-3 also includes the following:

- Technical manual
- Prereferral checklist
- Intervention manual with IEP goals, objectives, and interventions
- Parent guide (includes practical strategies for helping the child at home)
- Computer program for quick scoring
- Spanish language version
- Diagnostic tool for comparing the student's ADDES-3 score with DSM-IV-TR eligibility criteria

Designing an Appropriate IEP

PARTNERING FOR SPECIAL EDUCATION AND RELATED SERVICES

Not every student with AD/HD qualifies for IDEA services. As you learned at the beginning of this chapter, AD/HD must adversely affect a student's educational performance in order for the student to qualify for services. Many students with AD/HD can function well in a general classroom with modifications and accommodations that do not require specially designed instruction. Will's attention-deficit disorder affects his educational performance; he has an IEP entitling him to specially designed instruction.

If a student does not qualify for special education and related services under IDEA, does that mean he cannot get modifications and accommodations? No. In fact, another option is to develop what educators call a *504 plan*. As you learned in Chapter 1, the Americans with Disabilities Act (ADA) and Section 504 of the Rehabilitation Act Amendments of 1973 both prohibit discrimination against students with AD/HD or other disabilities if their disabilities substantially limit one or more major life activities. To comply with these laws, schools offer 504 plans (named after the antidiscrimination section of the Rehabilitation Act) to students who are not classified into the IDEA "other health impairments" category and provided with IDEA benefits. As you will recall from Chapter 1, the Rehabilitation Act of 1973 is a broad civil rights law that identifies individuals with a disability as those who have substantial limitations in one or more major life activities, have or have had a disability, or are regarded by others as having a disability. This is a functional definition of disability, as contrasted to IDEA's categorical definitions. In Chapter 1 you also learned that Congress amended ADA to include "concentrating," "reading," and "thinking" as major life activities. These are life activities that can be particularly challenging for many students with AD/HD.

To assist students with AD/HD who do not qualify for special education and related services under IDEA, educators usually include in the student's 504 plan a list of reasonable accommodations (Holler & Zirkel, 2008; Zirkel, 2009). Box 8.3, Partnership Tips, outlines a three-step process for creating a 504 accommodation plan.

One of the roles of either the 504 or IEP team is to plan educational supports that can accompany the use of medication for students with AD/HD. You will learn later in the chapter about the effectiveness of medication with students who have AD/HD. You and other members of 504 or IEP teams should never do what Will's elementary school principal and teacher did, which was to suggest to his parents that he should be on or off medication. Only a physician can make that determination. You may suggest to parents that they should have a medical evaluation because, as you have learned, AD/HD is linked to physiological conditions. However, IDEA prohibits educators from requiring a student to take medication as a condition of attending school.

BOX 8.3

PARTNERSHIP TIPS

Creating a 504 Accommodation Plan

Bonita Blazer is an expert on classroom accommodations for students with AD/HD. She advocates a three-step process for creating 504 accommodation plans.

Step 1
Engage in collaborative problem solving to identify preferred classroom accommodations and formalize a Certificate of Accommodations.

- Initiate conversations with parents and students (starting as young as five years of age) about the types of accommodations that would make school easier.
  - ✓ Hold a first meeting with the parents and then a follow-up meeting with the student.
  - ✓ Share a list of instructional strategies and invite their input on what they think would work best.
  - ✓ Explain the relationship between accommodations and academic and social success.
  - ✓ Encourage students unable to communicate verbally about accommodations that would allow them to draw pictures or use computer-assisted means of communication.
- Ask the student to list preferred classroom accommodations on a first draft of a Certificate of Accommodations.
  - ✓ Use the formal certificate to enable the parent and student to recognize their rights to meaningful instructional accommodations.
  - ✓ Have ongoing conversations with students and parents about the certificate.
- Once agreement is reached, be sure the student, parents, teachers, and principal sign the certificate to formalize it.
  - ✓ Allow the student to keep the certificate in a notebook as a constant reminder.
  - ✓ Encourage the student to use a plastic sheet protector, color folder, or other aid to protect the certificate and make it easy to locate.

Step 2
Reach team agreement on a formal written 504 accommodation plan.

- Meet with the school-based team to describe the certificate and to gain members' input into accommodations that will be implemented for the student.
- Based on team input, develop a more comprehensive written list of 504 accommodations.
- Add a rating scale to the accommodation plan as a way to access the ongoing implementation of each accommodation.
- Include space in the plan for teacher reflections on the quality of implementing the plan.
- Engage in ongoing communication with the student, parent, and team about the implementation of the accommodations.
- As more information is available on accommodations that do and do not work, develop an annual classroom accommodation review based on the data from the rating form.

Step 3
Implement the 504 plan.

- Send a copy of the Annual 504 Classroom Accommodation Form to the person within the school district who is responsible for 504 implementation.
- Bear in mind that you and the educational team, working collaboratively with the student and parent, are responsible for completing rating scales on a periodic basis to ensure that the instructional accommodations are being implemented.
- Teach the student self-determination skills focusing on communicating with teachers in a constructive way if required accommodations are withheld.
- Ensure that the 504 plan is placed in the student's permanent confidential file.

Source: Based on information from Blazer, B. (1999). Developing 504 classroom accommodation plans: A collaborative, systematic parent-student-teacher approach. *Teaching Exceptional Children, 32*(2), 28–33.

DETERMINING SUPPLEMENTARY AIDS AND SERVICES

You want to take into account a variety of classroom factors when designing students' IEPs or reasonable accommodations. You will recall from Chapter 2 that supplementary aids and services involve modifications to aspects of the classroom environment. These include student seating arrangements, classroom furniture arrangement, and lighting and auditory features.

Box 8.4 sets out various classroom and educational program modifications that might benefit students with AD/HD. You may find it disturbing that Will's elementary school evaluation team took nearly two months to evaluate him. Unwilling to wait for the school's evaluation, his parents secured an independent evaluation within a much shorter period of time and had to pay for it themselves. Also while waiting for the school evaluation and a plan of accommodation (under Section 504) or special education services (under IDEA),

BOX 8.4 **INTO PRACTICE**
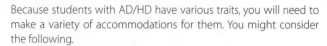

Accommodations for AD/HD

Because students with AD/HD have various traits, you will need to make a variety of accommodations for them. You might consider the following.

For students who display inattention:

- Seat them in quiet areas, at desks that are far apart, near students who model appropriate class behavior, or near peers who study with them.

- Give them more time to complete their work, reduce the amount of work you ask them to do (focus on the essentials), divide long assignments into smaller parts and ask for completion of each part and then of the whole, require fewer correct answers to receive a passing grade, or use cues (such as private signals to stay on task) and oral and written instructions simultaneously.

For students who are impulsive:

- Ignore their mildly inappropriate behaviors, reward them promptly when they behave correctly, acknowledge the correct behavior of other students so that the impulsive students understand and model that behavior, correct them gently, supervise them closely when they transition from one activity to another, and enter into a behavior contract.

For students with excessive motor activity:

- Let them stand while in class, ask them to run errands and use their energy physically, and break for a short while between assignments to allow them and the other students to do something physical (a "stretch break").

For students who have mood characteristics:

- Reassure and encourage them, speak gently, and review your assignments.

- Meet with their parents and ask how their child wants to communicate.

- Be on the alert for unusual moods, especially frustration or anger, so you can modify your expectations at those times, provide support, and contact the student's parents.

- Help them learn anger-control strategies or refer them to professionals who can teach those strategies.

For students who have academic challenges:

- In reading, offer more time for them to complete reading assignments, reduce the amount of reading, using texts that are less "dense" (i.e., have fewer words on a page), and don't have them read aloud in front of peers.

- In speaking, accept nearly every spoken response to encourage them to speak out, allowing them to develop a display of what they have read and learned, and ask them to speak about topics that interest them.

- In writing, accept displays or oral projects as substitutes for some written work, allow students to use a voice recorder or a computer, reduce their written workload, and use multiple-choice or similarly formatted questions.

- In mathematics, allowing them to use a calculator or graph paper to space numbers, give more time to complete an assignment, and frequently model the proper process for doing a calculation.

For students who have problems organizing and planning:

- Ask them to use notebooks, dividers, smartphones, computer programs, or other tools that help them remember what to do and when and how to do it.

- Provide daily or weekly reports to students and parents regarding organizational tools and devices and the work you require.

For students who have difficulty complying:

- Praise appropriate behavior, provide immediate feedback, ignore minor misbehaviors (pick your issues), use a behavior contract for individuals and for the entire class, and help them learn how to monitor their own behaviors.

For students who have socialization challenges:

- Praise their appropriate behavior, monitor their social interactions, use behavior contracts, provide small-group study and cooperative learning and social skills opportunities, and publicly reward leadership or participation.

Source: Based on information from Parker, H. C. (1992). ADAPT accommodation plan form. *ADD Warehouse.* Retrieved on August 9, 2011, from http://www.addwarehouse.com.

his parents enrolled him in a private tutoring program, four days a week for nine months, at the unreimbursed cost of $15,000.

If a student has the predominately hyperactive-impulsive type of AD/HD, she may, for example, have difficulty sitting for long periods of time and may need some classroom modifications to address these issues. Those modifications can be as simple as allowing the student to stand during work periods (rather than sit) or to get up from the chair every five or ten minutes. Classroom arrangements that minimize distractions can also be beneficial, as can instructional activities that involve movement, such as role plays and strategies derived from multiple intelligences theory (see Chapter 16).

Another characteristic of many learners with AD/HD is their lack of organization skills. In the next section you will learn about goal setting and organizational skills that can support students with AD/HD to be more organized and engage with the general education curriculum. There are also classroom organization features that can help. You can establish clearly marked locations for students to store materials. Sometimes color-coding those areas can help students remember where materials belong. You can also provide clearly marked locations for students to store personal items, such as coats, backpacks, lunchboxes, and athletic gear. Minimizing the amount of clutter in a classroom can reduce student confusion about where materials and personal effects belong.

PLANNING FOR UNIVERSAL DESIGN FOR LEARNING

Classroom modifications are only the first steps to enabling students with AD/HD to succeed in the general education classroom. Teaching students organizational and goal-setting skills augments the curriculum and supports students to engage effectively with the general education curriculum. As you learned in Chapter 2, curriculum augmentations involve expanding or adding to the general curriculum to teach students learning-to-learn or self-regulation strategies that enable them to learn more effectively.

Students who are organized are more likely to know what tasks they need to accomplish and what homework needs to be completed. Often, parents need to help the student follow through at home. Students can also apply organizational skills to improve their study habits. One component of effective study skills is setting goals for the completion of academic work. Whether it is setting a goal to study for a set amount of time each night or to get a certain percentage of problems correct on a quiz, students who set goals perform more effectively.

Classroom modifications such as those listed in the previous section help students learn organization skills. Teaching students to be responsible for their classroom modifications can be helpful—for example, learning to organize their notebooks by using folders of different colors, with each color indicating a different course or topic.

Because they are easily distracted, students with AD/HD may have difficulty being neat. This is a common problem for all students but can be particularly problematic for students with AD/HD. Students need to be taught effective work skills (for example, making sure numbers in a math equation are lined up appropriately) and note-taking skills. Using strategies like self-instruction and self-monitoring (described in Chapter 11), students can develop the habit of checking their work to make sure it meets the standard set by the teacher.

Goal-setting and organization skills go hand in hand to promote better outcomes. If a student sets a goal, he is more likely to perform behaviors related to that goal. Goal setting is one of the critical predictors of success in adulthood for students with AD/HD or learning disabilities. A coaching intervention that incorporated self-monitoring and goal setting improved the homework completion and accuracy of students with AD/HD (Konrad, Fowler, Walker, Test, & Wood, 2007; Merriman & Codding, 2008).

Within educational settings, promoting goal-setting skills involves helping students learn to do the following:

1. Identify and define a goal clearly and concretely.

2. Develop a series of objectives or tasks to achieve the goal.

3. Specify the actions necessary to achieve the desired outcome.

At each step, students must make choices and decisions about the goals they wish to pursue and the actions they wish to take to achieve their goals. You can incorporate goal setting into a variety of educational activities and instructional areas as well as into educational planning. By involving a student in his IEP or transition-planning meetings, you can provide multiple opportunities to practice setting goals and give the student a sense of involvement in and control over her educational experiences.

Goals should be challenging for the student, but not so challenging that he cannot reach them, as this will lead to frustration. However, they must provide enough challenge to motivate the student to work to attain them. If goals are too easy, students will not be motivated to engage in the work necessary to reach them, nor will they experience a feeling of accomplishment after achieving them. Finally, while it is preferable for students to participate in setting their own goals at whatever level is appropriate, given the nature of their disability, this is not always possible. If goals need to be set by teachers, then you should incorporate the student's preferences and interests into the goal to increase her motivation. Goals that have personal meaning are more likely to be attained (Meltzer, 2010).

Ever since he was in the fourth grade, when he was first diagnosed, Will has attended his IEP team meetings, usually coming into them just as they conclude so that he has a summary of the goals and objectives. At his and Leigh Ann's suggestion, the team has decided to remove gradually some of the accommodations he has used. "I want to remove some of those crutches," Will says, "but I know it will be harder for me to learn, and I will have to work harder so I can improve each year." He makes the point that it is not always wise for a student with AD/HD to depend permanently on IEP-based accommodations. Colleges and employers cannot be counted on to do for him what his present school does.

Students with AD/HD may have a difficult time attending to multiple goals. Several strategies are available to address this challenge. For example, you should break complex goals into smaller subgoals that the student can complete in a shorter amount of time with fewer steps. You should assist students to make a list of their goals so they have a concrete, easy-to-find visual reminder. And you should use the strategies to promote the student-directed learning that we discuss in Chapter 11, enabling students with AD/HD to self-monitor their progress toward goals.

PLANNING FOR OTHER EDUCATIONAL NEEDS

Medication is often an important component of a student's multimodal educational program. (You'll learn more about multimodal treatments in the next section.) In addition, monitoring the effects of medication can be an area of educational need for students with AD/HD.

When you teach students who are taking medicine to treat AD/HD, you should be familiar with the types, effects, and side effects of frequently used medications, such as Ritalin, Dexedrine, and Adderall. Side effects include sleep and appetite disruption, stomachaches, headaches, dizziness, irritability, anxiety, and sadness/unhappiness (Davis-Berman & Pestello, 2010). The American Academy of Child and Adolescent Psychiatry (2007) recommends that students treated with any type of medication have their height and weight monitored, as weight loss and growth reduction can be side effects of some medications. Will certainly experienced some unwanted effects of Adderall—a tendency to become aggressive. Having now used three different medications, he has found an effective one that has no undesirable side effects.

Obviously, it is important for you to help monitor the impact of medications on a child. Students who are drowsy may have fewer behavior problems in the classroom, but trading hyperactivity or impulsivity for drowsiness does not ensure the student's educational progress. The student's IEP should stipulate what training you need to ensure an appropriate education program. It will be difficult for you to be effective for a student with AD/HD unless you know about the student's medication: the name of the drug, its purposes,

IEP TIP

When you and other members of an IEP team are working with a student who takes medicine for AD/HD, be sure to solicit and take into account all information the student's parents or physician gives you about the medicine. Ask the student's parents to secure that information from the physician. You will want to know the purpose of the medicine and its effects so you can accommodate to any of its effects.

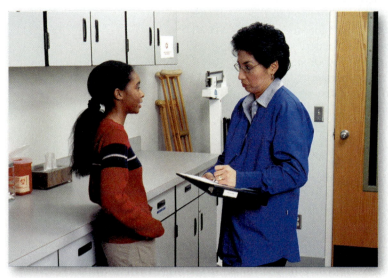

Consistent administration of medication, even at school, helps some children manage the symptoms of AD/HD.

its effects (positive and other), and when the student must take it (at home or at school, and, if at school, when).

You also should assess systematically the effects of medication for students with AD/HD. Simple checklists of student behavior patterns and behavior states throughout the day can provide useful information. Students can learn to self-monitor and self-evaluate their behaviors and feelings by using student-directed learning strategies such as those we discuss in Chapter 11. Finally, the IEP teams should consider teaching students to self-manage their medication process, increasing the likelihood that medicine will be taken as prescribed.

Using Effective Instructional Strategies

EARLY CHILDHOOD STUDENTS: MULTIDISCIPLINARY DIAGNOSTIC AND TRAINING PROGRAM

The most effective strategies for children with AD/HD throughout their life spans involve multimodal treatments. This does not simply mean using multiple intervention components, such as the multicomponent interventions you learned about in Chapter 7. **Multimodal treatments** involve multiple interventions or treatments across modes or types of therapies (e.g., medical, behavioral, psychological).

Common components of multimodal treatment include medication, parent training, behaviorally oriented treatments, and classroom behavior management (Hoza, Kaiser, & Hurt, 2007). Kern and colleagues (2007), for example, evaluated a multicomponent intervention that combined parent education and an individualized, assessment-based intervention program conducted in both home and daycare settings. The multicomponent intervention included student-focused behavioral interventions to address behavior problems, preacademic readiness skills, and child safety skills. These interventions included functional behavioral assessments, a focus on early literacy, and a token reinforcement system. The parent education content paralleled these areas, teaching parenting skills and strategies related to behavior management, preacademics, and child safety at home. Students who received the multicomponent intervention showed significant improvement in behavior and preacademic skills.

ELEMENTARY AND MIDDLE SCHOOL STUDENTS: ERRORLESS LEARNING

Errorless learning is an instructional strategy that minimizes the mistakes students make when learning a new task. The idea behind errorless learning is that learning without mistakes is more effective and lasts longer. With trial-and-error learning, students run the risk of learning something that is wrong or learning to do something incorrectly; they then have to unlearn and relearn the correct information or process.

When using errorless learning, teachers present a discriminative stimuli to the student and arrange the delivery of prompts in such a way that the student can give only correct responses (or only a few incorrect responses) (Alberto & Troutman, 2008). The discriminative stimulus, called the S^D, is a specific event or environmental condition that elicits a desired response. This stimulus acquires control over the desired response when the response is paired with a reinforcer. Prompts are any additional stimuli that increase the chances that the S^D will elicit the desired response.

These are technical terms for some fairly simple concepts. When you ask a student to perform a task, you are providing an S^D. For example, you might ask a third-grade student, "Tell me what time it is." That S^D ("Tell me what time it is") should result in the student's telling the time (the response). Let's say, though, that the student does not provide the correct response, no matter how many times you repeat the instruction. Once you know this, you might again ask the student, "Tell me what time it is," and then point to the clock on the wall. The pointing gesture is a prompt; it is an additional stimulus intended to increase the chance that the S^D will elicit the desired response.

There are several kinds of prompts, including physical, verbal, and visual prompts. Taking a student's hand to help him shape a piece of clay is a physical prompt. Verbal prompts can be questions ("Does this have four sides?" in response to the S^D, "Find the square."), instructions ("Find the shape with four sides), or hints ("This box is a square. Does anything on the worksheet look like the box?"). Visual prompts include pictures or gestures that provide information to students, but they also can include written instructions (a list of the classroom rules posted on the wall) or even the way a room or furniture is arranged.

Errorless learning begins by identifying a task the student can reasonably perform without a prompt. Let's say you are teaching a third-grade student with AD/HD how to add fractions. Unless that student has mastered basic addition skills, there is no reason to believe he will be ready for adding fractions. If, however, he knows basic addition skills, it is likely he can learn to add simple fractions.

Having identified the task, you then must determine how best to present the S^D, what level of prompt to use, and when to present the prompt. You should base your decisions on what it will take to ensure that the student can give the correct response. If the student has never added fractions, for example, the probability that she will respond correctly may increase if the problem is written instead of just given verbally. Once you present the S^D, you then determine what level of prompt to use and when to deliver that prompt.

In errorless learning, you typically use a most-to-least prompting strategy. That is, you begin with prompts that are, on a continuum, more intrusive but also more likely to ensure the correct response. Physical prompts are often the most intrusive for students, followed by visual and then verbal prompts. Sometimes you will combine prompts—for example delivering both a visual and a verbal prompt together. Finally, you have to determine how soon after the S^D to deliver the prompt. Prompts that are delivered almost immediately after the S^D and that are of sufficient intensity to ensure that the response will occur tend to ensure errorless learning.

Let's consider the examples we've presented. In the case of the student responding to the S^D, "Tell me what time it is," you might have provided the visual prompt (pointing at the clock) immediately following the instruction. In teaching addition of fractions, you might present the S^D ("Add these fractions") and then immediately present the problem visually using an overhead projector and provide a verbal prompt. ("If the bottom numbers in each fraction are the same, just add the top numbers."). Once students begin to master the tasks, you should begin to fade the prompt, moving from more intrusive to less intrusive prompts and lengthening the time between the presentation of the S^D and the prompt.

SECONDARY AND TRANSITION STUDENTS: COMPUTER-ASSISTED INSTRUCTION AND VIDEO SELF-MODELING

Computer-assisted instruction (CAI) refers to the use of computer technology to deliver instruction. CAI is often used for drill-and-practice exercises, and using it for independent practice and review activities with students with AD/HD improves student motivation and achievement in reading and mathematics (Jitendra, DuPaul, Someki, & Tresco, 2008). CAI has also been used to teach self-management and goal-setting skills. Mazzotti, Wood, Test, and Fowler (2010) used CAI to teach students with AD/HD and learning disabilities to set academic goals using the *Self-Determined Learning Model of Instruction,* which you will learn more about in Chapter 9. Students had decreased levels of disruptive behavior and increased knowledge of the goal-setting process after CAI.

Another computer-based technology useful for promoting outcomes such as goal setting and self-management for students with AD/HD is video self-modeling (VSM). In VSM, students watch videos of themselves performing skills correctly. Box 8.5 discusses the use of VSM to promote self-regulation and self-monitoring.

BOX 8.5

UNIVERSAL DESIGN FOR PROGRESS

Video Self-Modeling

When you use video self-modeling (VSM), you record and have students watch videos of themselves performing skills correctly. Not only does VSM have proven effectiveness, but it is also a strategy that you and any other teacher with access to basic technology can implement, using these simple steps.

1. *Select a recording technology.* Creating a self-modeling image begins by recording the image to be viewed by the student. Up until recently, the simplest way was to use a video camera to record the image onto a videotape that could be played on a VCR. This may still be the easiest route for a few teachers, but the increased availability of digital technology and personal computers allows for the development of images that can be viewed on a computer, cell phone, or camera.

2. *Create a self-modeling image.* This step sounds obvious; after you figure out how you will record the student performing the desired behavior, you just film it, right? But ask yourself this: If the purpose of VSM is to have students view images of themselves engaged in a behavior you want them to master, how can you film them performing the behavior at that mastery level before they actually achieve it? There are two primary ways to meet this challenge (Buggey, 2007). The first is to have students role-play or imitate the desired behavior. In this case,

you must script the role-play situation and provide support to have the student perform the behavior while recording. Another option is that if the desired behavior is performed occasionally but not consistently, you can film the appropriate behavior when it does occur. Most self-modeling videos are no more than two or three minutes long.

3. *Have students view the video image and imitate or repeat the desired behavior.* Students should view the self-modeling image six to ten times during a two- to three-week period, either at home or school or both. You (or the student's parent if the student is watching the video at home) should view the video with the student and, for the first few viewings, point out some of the features of the behavior you want the student to attend to.

4. *Record student progress in mastering the behavior.* As when teaching any behavior, you must assess student progress. You need to determine the best way to collect data, based on the type of behavior you are teaching.

5. *Use the video for occasional booster sessions.* The video can be used to remind students how to perform the behavior you are targeting after more intensive intervention has been completed.

Including Students with AD/HD

Because AD/HD is not a separate category under IDEA, the U.S. Department of Education does not provide data on the extent to which students with AD/HD participate in general education classrooms. Box 8.6 provides some inclusion tips useful for students with AD/HD.

Many students with AD/HD face particular challenges in making friends. Peers, teachers, and others often rate students with AD/HD as having poor social skills (Makami, 2010); indeed, more than half of elementary-age students with AD/HD have been rejected by peers. Friendship interventions for students with AD/HD should include (1) careful selection of potential friends, (2) focus on specific friendship behaviors in key situations, and (3) high parental involvement (Makami, 2010). Matching peers based upon shared interests is an important way to select potential friends.

Assessing Students' Progress

MEASURING STUDENTS' PROGRESS

Progress in the General Curriculum

In Chapter 5 you learned about curriculum-based measurement as a means of tracking progress in the general education curriculum. One of the advantages of CBM over standard pencil-paper measurements is that you collect data on an ongoing basis and use the information to modify instruction.

BOX 8.6

INCLUSION TIPS

	What You Might See	What You Might Be Tempted to Do	Alternate Responses	Ways to Include Peers in the Process
Behavior	*Inattentive type:* The student is inattentive, withdrawn, forgetful, a daydreamer, and/or lethargic. *Hyperactive-impulsive type:* He is restless, talkative, impulsive, and/or easily distracted. *Combined type:* The student has features of both.	*Inattentive type:* Overlook him. *Hyperactive-impulsive type:* Be critical and punitive.	*Inattentive type:* Consider changing the student's seating arrangement and providing daily schedules of activities. *Hyperactive-impulsive and combined types:* Teach the student organization and goal-setting skills.	Model acceptance and appreciation for him. Then peers are more likely to do the same.
Social interactions	*Inattentive type:* She withdraws from social situations. *Hyperactive-impulsive type:* She bursts into social situations and may be gregarious or inappropriate and annoying.	*Inattentive type:* Call attention to her isolation in front of other students; try to force her to play. *Hyperactive-impulsive type:* Pull her out of social situations for inappropriate behavior.	Role-play friendship skills. Help the student discover her strengths and encourage group participation in those activities. Start with small groups. Encourage membership in a support group for students with AD/HD.	For projects, pair her with another student who has similar interests and tends to be accepting. The initial goal is achieving one close friend.
Educational performance	His work is incomplete, full of errors, and sloppy.	Assign failing grades to the student.	Use errorless learning procedures to present discriminative stimuli and arrange prompts that will enable him to be successful.	Model for peers good prompting strategies that they can also use in peer-tutoring interactions.
Classroom attitudes	Her motivation is inconsistent or lacking.	Send frequent notes to parents about your disappointment in their daughter's motivation.	Use goal attainment scaling (discussed in this chapter) as a way for the student to see her progress. Provide rewards on a periodic basis when she accomplishes her goals.	Enable the student to teach another member of the class about how to document her progress through goal attainment scaling.

IEP TIP

Goal attainment scaling goes hand in hand with teaching students goal-oriented behavior. That is why you and your IEP team members should consider a program in which the student learns the goal attainment scaling process and evaluates his or her progress toward IEP goals.

Another means of determining student progress within the general education curriculum involves *goal attainment scaling.* Most students with AD/HD and other disabilities have goals pertaining to all aspects of their educational program, including general curriculum content. Unfortunately, comparing goals across students or goals for an individual student can be difficult. Some goals are easier to reach than others, and some goals address areas that are very different from one another.

The **goal attainment scaling** process allows you to compare goals and quantify student goal attainment. You begin this process by identifying a goal (Roach & Elliott, 2005). Having set a goal, you then must identify five potential outcomes of instruction. These five outcomes range from a least-effective outcome to a highly effective outcome. The first outcome quantifies what the least-positive outcome would be, usually indicating no progress toward the goal. The second outcome would be better but still less than expected. The third outcome reflects what the teacher would consider an acceptable outcome, one that he would be satisfied to have the student achieve. The fourth outcome identifies an outcome that is better than expected, and the fifth outcome identifies an outcome that far exceeds expectations.

Having identified the outcomes, you instruct the student. When the student has completed the instructional program, you then return to the rubric of outcomes created at the start and identify the outcome closest to the one the student has achieved. From least to most effective, you award scores ranging from −2 to +2, with 0 being the middle outcome (the one that was viewed as an acceptable outcome).

You can graph these scores across multiple goals to determine student progress or can transform the raw scores into a standardized t-score (which ranges from 0 to 100, with 50 as the middle or acceptable point), using tables published by Kiersuk, Smith, and Cardillo (1994). In most cases, however, simply graphing the goal attainment will suffice. Graphing allows you to compare a student's progress on different goals and compare progress across multiple students to determine the effectiveness of an intervention.

Progress in Addressing Other Educational Needs

Sometimes you can track progress in areas such as social skills, self-control, and medication management (areas important to students with AD/HD) by using T-charts or checklists. A **T-chart** is laid out in the form of a capital letter *T*. The chart allows teachers to track two aspects of a behavior. Stanford and Reeves (2005) created a T-chart to help students figure out what appropriate behavior "looks like and sounds like" (p. 20), listing visual cues that reflect appropriate behavior on one bar of the *T* and the auditory sounds on the other (e.g., sounds like using "please" and "thank you").

You also may use checklists. They are easier to design and involve breaking the task into discrete steps, listing them, and identifying ways of marking or quantifying progress, often using check boxes.

MAKING ACCOMMODATIONS FOR ASSESSMENT

The most common areas of accommodations for students with AD/HD pertain to attention and concentration. Students with AD/HD who have a difficult time sitting still and concentrating for long periods of time may qualify for an accommodation to take extra breaks during assessments. Students for whom extra break times are not sufficient may request multiple testing sessions instead of a single session. Another possibility would be for students to request a reduced-distraction testing environment (e.g., fewer students in the testing room).

ADDRESSING THE PROFESSIONAL STANDARDS

The following Council for Exceptional Children (CEC) Common Core Knowledge and Skills are addressed in this chapter through the content and concepts we discuss. See the Appendix for a full listing of these Knowledge and Skill statements:

ICC2K1, ICC2K2, ICC2K3, ICC2K4, ICC2K5, ICC2K7, ICC4S2, ICC4S3, ICC4S4, ICC4S5, ICC5K5, ICC5S4, ICC5S5, ICC5S6, ICC7S1, ICC7S3, ICC7S6, ICC7S9, ICC8K3, ICC8S6, ICC8S8, ICC10S2, ICC10S3, ICC10S4, ICC10S5

Summary

IDENTIFYING STUDENTS WITH AD/HD

- The DSM-IV-TR (American Psychiatric Association, 2000) identifies three subtypes of AD/HD: (1) predominately inattentive, (2) predominately hyperactive-impulsive, and (3) combined.
- Under IDEA, students with AD/HD are served under the "other health impairments" category.
- Although prevalence of AD/HD varies according to gender, age, and ethnicity, approximately 6 to 9 percent of children and youth are identified as having AD/HD.
- Other common characteristics of students with AD/HD include intellectual functioning in the average range; impaired academic achievement; and challenges associated with behavioral, social, and emotional functioning.
- AD/HD has multiple causes associated with heredity, structural differences in the brain, and environmental causes.

EVALUATING STUDENTS WITH AD/HD

- Diagnosis of AD/HD by a psychologist, a psychiatrist, or a physician often occurs outside the school system. The person who makes the diagnosis becomes part of the evaluation team.
- A frequently used evaluation tool to identify AD/HD is the Conners's Rating Scales—Revised, which come in teacher, parent, and adolescent versions.
- A particularly helpful evaluation tool for determining the nature and extent of specially designed instruction is the Attention Deficit Disorders Evaluation Scale—Third Edition (ADDES-3) because it prescribes more interventions than other available rating scales do.

DESIGNING AN APPROPRIATE IEP

- Students with AD/HD who do not qualify for special education services might still benefit from a Section 504 accommodation plan that enables them to receive some of the instructional supports they need to succeed in school.
- A number of classroom environment variables can benefit students with AD/HD, including arranging student seats to reduce distractibility, posting daily schedules, and arranging the classroom to facilitate smooth transitions.
- Teaching students with AD/HD organization and goal-setting skills gives them strategies to better interact with the general education curriculum.
- Many students with AD/HD take medication, so it is important for the IEP team to address teacher knowledge about medicine use and potential side effects as well as student self-medication strategies.

USING EFFECTIVE INSTRUCTIONAL STRATEGIES

- Young children with AD/HD can benefit from multi-modal treatments—that is, multiple treatments across multiple fields or disciplines (e.g., medicine and behavioral programming).
- Errorless learning involves arranging the presentation of stimuli and the provision of prompts to ensure that students acquire new skills without errors associated with trial-and-error learning.
- Computer-assisted instruction and video self-modeling are effective tools to teach self-regulation and other skills.

INCLUDING STUDENTS WITH AD/HD

- The U.S. Department of Education does not provide data on the extent to which students with AD/HD participate in general education classrooms.
- A particular challenge associated with inclusive placements for many students with AD/HD is making friends.

ASSESSING STUDENTS' PROGRESS

- Goal attainment scaling allows teachers to assess student progress in the general education curriculum and can be used to compare progress across students and, for a particular student, across goals.
- Simple T-charts or checklists can be excellent ways to supplement more standardized data collection and to document progress in areas of other educational need.
- To address problems with attention and concentration, students with AD/HD may need testing accommodations that include extra breaks, multiple sessions, and distraction-free testing environments.

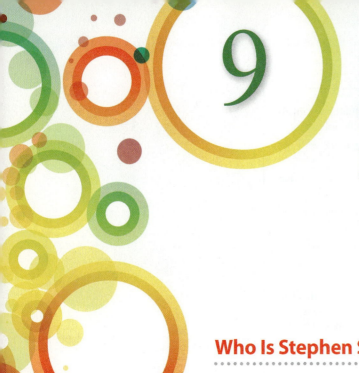

9 Understanding Students *with* Intellectual Disability

Who Is Stephen Sabia?

Ownership: It's as simple as that.

Meet Stephen Sabia, who has Down syndrome. One winter morning, he arrived at his middle school, ready to attend class, just as he had been doing for two years. Instead, he found himself in the middle of a fire emergency. Something was burning in the school. In the dim light of early morning, students were exiting from buses and buildings and forming into groups on the football field, far away from the buildings. Fire engines were arriving. Controlled chaos was the order of the morning.

Caught up by the crowd, Stephen made his way to the football field. Amid the noise caused by nearly 1,700 excited and anxious students, he heard his classmates shouting his name as they searched for him. "Stephen, Stephen Sabia, where are you?" Having found him, they huddled together; Stephen clearly belonged to this particular group of students.

Who were they? They were the members of the J.V. football team. Why did they seek him out? Because he was the team's manager. Because he had some responsibility for them. Because from the very beginning of Stephen's association with the team, the team's coach, Bryan Walker, had made it clear that Stephen was a valued member of that team.

These students owned Stephen, not in the sense of commanding his obedience or having

a person whom they possessed, but in the sense of being responsible for him. Just as he is responsible for them in football.

Ownership is evident in other ways. Stephen attends Andrew White's ninth-grade honors-level American history class, where he sits in the front row. There Andrew can easily supervise Stephen's work, making sure that he identifies, on the map in his textbook and on the larger map hanging in front of the class, the islands of the Philippines and Japan as Andrew explains why the Japanese invaded Pearl Harbor in Hawaii and not the American bases in the Philippines. Including Stephen in the class discussion, Andrew asks, "Stephen, what day did the Japanese invade Pearl Harbor?" Stephen's answer is correct: "Sunday, December 7, 1941."

Shifting from the start of World War II, Andrew asks the class to consider President Franklin D. Roosevelt's Arsenal of Democracy speech, an articulation of why, other than in self-defense, America was fighting.

"Class, go to page 312 of your textbook. Tell me what President Roosevelt's Four Freedoms are."

With his paraeducator, Nate Wiles, beside him for this lesson, Stephen turns to that page, listens to his classmates respond to their teacher, and answers, in his turn, "Speech." Other students have given other correct answers: freedom of worship, freedom from fear, and freedom from want.

Military strategy, self-defense, and the fundamentals of democracy are not challenging concepts for the students in an honors course. Nor are they for Stephen, at least not if the essence of each is what he needs to learn. The essence constitutes Stephen's appropriate education.

Essence is accessible when Andrew applies the principles of universal design for learning. It is accessible when Stephen's mother, Ricki, boils down his homework and rehearses the objectives of tomorrow's lessons with him. It is accessible when Ricki uses summer vacation time to support Stephen to read the books he will use when school resumes or when she takes him to a museum to see artifacts of World War II. Or when she and his father, Peter, take him to the theater to view dramatic portrayals of the lessons he must master in school.

Stephen's appropriate education, his preparation for the jobs he wants when he graduates or for the junior college he may attend, is accessible when a common vision and commitment rest on universally designed learning—adapted curricula and individualized methodologies.

Appropriateness also occurs when Stephen, along with his teachers and his mother, holds himself accountable for coming to class prepared to participate. This lesson bears repeating: IDEA favors the participation of students with intellectual disability,

OBJECTIVES

- You will learn about the characteristics that define intellectual disability and the pattern of strengths and limitations that students with intellectual disability experience.

- You will learn about the causes of intellectual disability, specifically biological and environmental causes.

- You will learn how to assess student's intelligence and adaptive behavior, including how to use the Adaptive Behavior Scale, developed by the nation's leading professional association in the field of intellectual disability.

- You will learn how to develop an appropriate IEP and how general educators adapt their curricula to include students like Stephen, even in honors courses.

- You will learn about prelinguistic milieu teaching for early childhood students, about self-determination for students in elementary school, and about transition and community-based instruction for students in secondary school.

- You will learn about the value of including students in the general curriculum and how to assess progress in that curriculum.

like Stephen, in the general education curriculum, and the Elementary and Secondary Education Act (ESEA) holds educators accountable for their students' learning.

Accessible education and appropriate education are linear; the zero reject rule (access to school) leads to an evaluation that underlies appropriate education in the general curriculum and in extracurricular activities for each student. But how do they relate to ownership? The answer lies in understanding what ownership means in Stephen's life.

Ownership is not merely the result of an accessible and appropriate general and special education. It is the goal for teachers and students in general and special education and for the nation. It's what history teacher Andrew White, special education director Christine Genua, paraeducator Nate Wiles, and J.V. football coach Bryan Walker strive for. It's what Stephen's previous teachers also adopted—those

at his elementary school (Maria Dummann, Dianne Chupka, and John Vigna) and those at his middle school (Kristen Andre, Kimberly Johnson, and Diane Filmore). For Stephen, inclusion, high expectations, and ownership began early and have endured.

The J.V. football players sensed that when they sought out Stephen on the morning of the fire emergency. In a very real sense, they, together with Stephen's teachers and Ricki, proclaimed that we are all responsible for each other. Ricki and Peter have said that their goal for Stephen is the same as their goal for his older brother: to maximize his potential so that he can maximize his opportunities in all aspects of life.

That's where ownership enters the picture. Unless everyone involved with Stephen understands, as the J.V. football players did, that they are responsible for each other, the goal—maximized potential and opportunities—will be elusive.

PEARSON
myeducationlab

Visit the MyEducationLab (www.myeducationlab.com) for *Exceptional Lives* to enhance your understanding of chapter concepts with a personalized Study Plan. You'll also have the opportunity to hone your teaching skills through video- and case-based assignments and activities, IRIS Center Resources, and Building Teaching Skills and Disposition lessons.

Identifying Students with Intellectual Disability

DEFINING INTELLECTUAL DISABILITY

What do you know about the term *intellectual disability?* What about the term *mental retardation?* What connotations do you associate with the term *mental retardation*, and what do you associate with the term *intellectual disability?* Perhaps your answer acknowledges the stigma that is attached to *mental retardation*. If so, you may easily understand why a major shift in terminology is occurring for the students whose education is the focus of this chapter.

Over the past fifty years, the term used most often to describe this disability, including in IDEA, has been *mental retardation*. But in 2010, President Obama signed a law changing the term to *intellectual disability* in federal laws, including IDEA. IDEA defines *intellectual disability* as "significantly subaverage general intellectual functioning, existing concurrently with deficits in adaptive behavior and manifested during the developmental period that adversely affects a child's educational performance." The American Association on Intellectual and Developmental Disabilities (AAIDD) introduced the term *intellectual disability* in its *Manual for Definition, Classification, and Systems of Support* (Schalock et al., 2010) and defines it as "significant limitations both in intellectual functioning and in adaptive behavior as expressed in conceptual, social, and practical adaptive skills. This disability originates before age 18" (p. 5).

This shift in terminology occurred, partly, because the term *mental retardation* has stigmatized many people with this disability, their families, friends, and the professionals who work with them. Another reason for the shift, however, is that intellectual disability is now regarded less as an inherent limitation *within* an individual than as an outcome of the interaction between a person's capacities and the context in which the person wants to function (Schalock et al., 2010). You will understand that point by studying Figure 9.1. It lists the five assumptions of the AAIDD definition and shows how they apply to Stephen. Note that assumptions 4 and 5 call for professionals, teachers, family, and community members to support people with an intellectual disability to function more competently in

FIGURE 9.1

Assumptions regarding the definition of intellectual disability and their application to Stephen Sabia

Five Assumptions	Applications to Stephen
1. Limitations in present functioning must be considered within the context of community environments typical of the individual's age, peers, and culture.	Stephen's limitations are intellectual (although he prospers with support), but not behavioral, because he has sufficient social skills to be included in school and community activities with his peers and family.
2. Valid assessment considers cultural and linguistic diversity as well as differences in communication, sensory, motor, and behavioral factors.	Stephen has good skills in understanding what people say (receptive communication), but he struggles in using written and oral expressive language.
3. Within an individual, limitations often coexist with strengths.	Stephen's assessments reveal his limitations, such as in mathematics, as well as his strengths, such as self-direction, a sense of responsibility, self-esteem, and following rules.
4. An important purpose of describing limitations is to develop a profile of needed supports.	Stephen's supports are academic (he has a paraeducator and his general and special educators adapt curriculum for him) and social (from his peers on the football team; his paraprofessional, Nate; and, at home, his brother, David, and David's friends); the degree of those supports varies according to his environments (he is fairly independent in daily living skills but not as self-directed as usual if he is in a new situation that does not generalize to ones he already has mastered).
5. With appropriate personalized supports over a sustained period, the life functioning of the person generally will improve.	Stephen has benefited from inclusive education and extensive community experiences and, with the supports his teachers and family provide, has gained and is continuing to gain skills to work, use public transportation independently, and walk about in his neighborhood (although his parents worry about this and provide privately paid training for him to become more conscious that he must look both ways when crossing a street and not wander off from his friends or family while he is in the community).

Source: MENTAL RETARDATION DEFINITION CLASSIFICATION AND SYSTEMS OF SUPPORTS by Ruch Luckasson. Copyright 2002 by American Association on Intellectual Developmental Disabilities. Reproduced with permission of American Association in Intellectual Developmental Disabilities in the formats Textbook and Other book via Copyright Clearance Center.

everyday environments. **Supports** are the services, resources, and personal assistance that enable a person to develop, learn, and live effectively (Schalock et al., 2010; Thompson et al., 2009).

Stephen Sabia receives various kinds of supports at various levels of intensity at his school. In his honors and other general education classes, the special education director, Christine Genua, has selected general education teachers who have the skills best suited for teaching Stephen; and using Stephen's IEP, she helps them modify and adapt their curriculum and methods of teaching. Some of Stephen's teachers adapt homework from texts other than the one they use in class, some use videos that relate to the class textbook developed by the book's publisher, and all play to his strengths—namely, his ability to learn by studying graphics (maps, tables, figures, and illustrations with captions). Stephen's only separate special education class is mathematics; there his support is different than but no less intense than in his honors and general education classes. He also receives ninety minutes of speech therapy each week in school and an hour of extra help in study hall. In short, Stephen benefits from pervasive (constant) support in his academic program.

You are beginning to learn about the characteristics of people with intellectual disability. As you do, you may ask, How many people are there who, like Stephen, have an intellectual disability? It is difficult to obtain an accurate prevalence rate for intellectual disability. Factors that influence prevalence include age (intellectual disability is diagnosed most frequently during school years), gender (more males than females are diagnosed), and socioeconomic status (poverty is strongly related to intellectual disability) (Emerson, 2010).

IEP TIP

When you and your colleagues develop an IEP for a student with an intellectual disability, be sure to take into account what her parents teach her, and then factor these strategies into the IEP or suggest other strategies, especially universal design for learning and assistive technology, which you will learn about later in this chapter.

The Centers for Disease Control (CDC) have concluded that the prevalence of intellectual disability is 12 per 1,000 children (Avchen, Bhasin, Braun, & Yeargin-Allsopp, 2007). The CDC study found that the prevalence rate for European American students was 7.4 per 1,000 and 19.7 per 1,000 for African American students. In fall 2008, approximately 8.1 percent (476,131) of students ages six through twenty-one receiving special education services and supports were classified as having an intellectual disability (U.S. Department of Education, Office of Special Education Programs, 2011b).

DESCRIBING THE CHARACTERISTICS

The two major characteristics of intellectual disability are limitations in intellectual functioning and limitations in adaptive behavior (Schalock et al., 2010).

Limitations in Intellectual Functioning

Intelligence refers to a student's general mental capability for solving problems, paying attention to relevant information, thinking abstractly, remembering important information and skills, learning from everyday experiences, and generalizing knowledge from one setting to another. Educators measure a student's intelligence by administering tests such as the Wechsler Intelligence Scale for Children—IV (see Chapter 5). Among the general population, 95 percent have intellectual functioning that falls within two standard deviations below and above the mean. Students with intellectual disability have an IQ score approximately two standard deviations below the mean—namely, an IQ of 70 or below on the Wechsler scale. Approximately 85 percent of students with intellectual disability have an IQ ranging from 50–55 to 70. The DSM-IV-TR (American Psychiatric Association, 2000) classifies mental retardation according to IQ levels (and the next version of the DSM will use the term *intellectual disability* instead of *mental retardation*):

- Mild mental retardation: IQ 50–55 to approximately 70
- Moderate mental retardation: IQ 35–40 to 50–55
- Severe mental retardation: IQ 20–25 to 30–40
- Profound mental retardation: IQ below 20–25

Stephen has had only one IQ test, when he was five years old. He was asked to repeat words, testing his memory. Because of his language difficulties, he could not express clearly enough what he had learned; therefore, the resulting IQ score showed little about his intellectual abilities. But IQ does not limit Stephen as much as you may imagine. He was the first student with an intellectual disability in each of his schools to be fully included in the school's academic program, beginning with preschool and continuing through ninth grade. As his teachers learned what he was able to accomplish, they became more invested in his academic performance. Simultaneously, Stephen developed the self-confidence and then the ability to work alongside peers without a disability, to be independent, and to solve problems. These are highly functional skills for him in school, and they will serve him well after he leaves school.

Regardless of their IQ score, students with intellectual disability typically have needs in three areas related to intellectual functioning: memory, generalization, and motivation.

Memory. Individuals with intellectual disability have impairments in memory, especially short-term memory and working memory (Schuchardt, Gebhardt, & Mäehler, 2010; Van der Molen, Van Luit, Van der Molen, & Jongmans, 2010). **Short-term memory**

Students with intellectual disability often can achieve positive outcomes, such as competitive employment, after they graduate if their educational program is based on their strengths and preferences.

refs to the ability to recall information that has been stored for a few seconds to a few hours, such as the step-by-step instructions teachers give their students. **Working memory** refers to the ability to use information that has been retained in order to carry out a task. Students with intellectual disability have impairments in both types of memory, and the impairment increases as the degree of intellectual disability becomes more severe (Jarrold, Purser, & Brock, 2006).

Generalization. **Generalization** refers to the ability to transfer knowledge or behavior learned for one task to another task (for example, identifying the main idea of a paragraph in a novel and in a history textbook) and to make that transfer across different settings or environments (for example, knowing how to add dollars and cents in the classroom and at the movie theater). Individuals with intellectual disability often have difficulty generalizing skills they learn in school to home and community settings. The cues, expectations, people, and environmental arrangements of one setting are usually very different from other settings.

Home and community settings often have greater complexity, more distractions, and more irrelevant stimuli than classrooms do. Individuals with intellectual disability experience challenges in using their working memory in novel situations, especially ones with high complexity, as compared to familiar situations (Van der Molen et al., 2010). One way to overcome the challenges associated with generalizing learning from the classroom to community settings is to provide instruction in typical community settings. Community-based instruction is successful in supporting students with intellectual disability to learn shopping, banking, daily living, recreation, and vocational skills (Walker, Uphold, Richter, & Test, 2010). When students learn skills in the settings in which they will use the skills, they do not need the extra step of learning to generalize from classroom to community settings.

Motivation. No single profile of motivation applies to all people with intellectual disability, any more than any single profile applies to all people without intellectual disability (Switzky, 2006). But students with intellectual disability are often externally oriented (Shogren, Bovaird, Palmer, & Wehmeyer, in press; Tassé & Havercamp, 2006). Many tend to wait for other people to prompt them before acting and believe that they have little control over outcomes in their day-to-day lives (Wehmeyer & Mithaug, 2006). That helps explain why they can be less hopeful about the future than, for example, their peers with learning disabilities or those without disabilities (Shogren et al., in press).

As a teacher, you can promote student motivation. For instance, Stephen's parents and teachers challenge him to be independent. The school's special education director, Christine Genua, allows him to choose his elective classes. Ricki and Peter expect him to choose what to pack for lunch and to go to bed at the agreed-upon hour. It helps that Stephen is motivated to please others, but the "others" also have to teach, expect, and respond to his choices.

IEP TIP

When you and your colleagues develop an IEP for a student with an intellectual disability, you will want to consider carefully her home and community environments and teach skills that enable the student to be effective in them. This is because the student needs to generalize the school curriculum to her home and community environments and to adapt to them. To know about those environments, you need to learn from the student's parents; their participation in the IEP conferences is essential.

Limitations in Adaptive Behavior

Adaptive behavior refers to the "collection of conceptual, social, and practical skills that have been learned and are performed by people in order to function in their everyday lives" (Schalock et al., 2010, p. 43). There are three domains of adaptive behavior (Schalock et al., 2010):

- Conceptual skills include language (receptive and expressive), reading and writing, money concepts, and self-direction.
- Social skills include responsibility, self-esteem, gullibility, and rule following.
- Practical skills include activities of daily living, occupational skills, and maintenance of safe environments.

By definition, people with intellectual disability have significant limitations in adaptive behavior. A significant limitation occurs when a student scores at least two standard deviations below the mean on (1) one of the three types of adaptive behavior: conceptual, social, and practical skills or (2) an overall score on a standardized measure that includes conceptual, social, and practical skills (Schalock et al., 2010).

Students' adaptive behavior relates to contextual considerations such as their culture, environment, and age (Borthwick-Duffy, 2007). Students with intellectual disability will almost always fall below the norm of their typically developing peers. The causes of their significant limitations may include not knowing how to perform a skill, not knowing when to perform a skill, and motivational factors that influence whether or not skills are performed.

DETERMINING THE CAUSES

There is no single cause of intellectual disability. In fact, researchers have identified a number of different risk factors that contribute to the occurrence of intellectual disability. The timing of these risk factors also makes a difference, both in the occurrence and extent of intellectual disability. It should be noted, however, that even though risk factors have been identified, the exact cause of intellectual disability can be difficult to determine. In approximately half of all cases, especially when a person has mild or moderate intellectual disability, the cause is unknown (McDermott, Durkin, Schupf, & Stein, 2007).

Timing

Timing refers to when the causal factors occurred and whether these factors affected the parents of the person with intellectual disability, the person with intellectual disability, or both (McDermott et al., 2007; Percy, 2007):

- Prenatal (before birth, such as chromosomal disorders and disorders of brain formation)
- Perinatal (during the birth process, such as prematurity and birth injury)
- Postnatal (after birth, such as traumatic brain injury and infections)

Risk Factors

Four main risk factors have been identified that can cause intellectual disability (Schalock et al., 2010):

- *Biomedical factors* relate to biologic processes, such as genetic disorders and nutrition.
- *Social factors* relate to social and family interaction, such as stimulation and adult responsiveness.
- *Behavioral factors* relate to potentially causal behaviors, such as dangerous activities and maternal substance abuse.
- *Educational factors* relate to the availability of educational supports that promote development of adaptive skills.

Biomedical Causes. Biomedical causes typically originate early in a child's development (Einfeld & Emerson, 2008). An example of a biomedical cause is a chromosomal disorder that occurs at or soon after conception. When the egg and sperm unite during conception, they bring together genes from the mother and the father. These genes determine the personal characteristics of the developing embryo and are found on threadlike structures called **chromosomes**. Chromosomes direct each cell's activity. Humans have twenty-three pairs of chromosomes in each cell, with one chromosome in each pair coming from the mother and one from the father. A chromosomal disorder occurs when a parent contributes either too much genetic material (an extra chromosome is added) or too little (all or part of a chromosome is missing).

The most common autosomal chromosomal disorder is Down syndrome, which typically occurs when there is an extra twenty-first chromosome. An individual with Down syndrome has forty-seven individual chromosomes rather than forty-six. Stephen has Down syndrome; the cause of his disability is biological, and it occurred during the prenatal period.

In Box 9.1, My Voice, Margaret Muller shares her perspectives about experiencing Down syndrome. Margaret wrote this essay with assistance and conducted some of her own research, including interviews with her pediatrician.

Social, Behavioral, and Educational Causes. Social, behavioral, and educational risk factors interact with each other and with biomedical risk factors to influence whether intellectual

Margaret's Guide to Down Syndrome

Today I'd like to tell you about Down syndrome. My purpose for talking about this is to be able to say, "Yes, I have Down syndrome. Sometimes I have to work harder to learn things, but in many ways I am just like everyone else." I would like to tell people that having Down syndrome does not keep me from doing the things I need to do or want to do. I just have to work harder.

Down syndrome is a condition and not a disease. You cannot catch Down syndrome like you can catch a cold or virus. It is something you are just born with—like blond hair and blue eyes. If you have Down syndrome when you are born, you will have it your whole life.

People without Down syndrome have 46 chromosomes, which carry all the genetic information about a person, in each of their cells. People with Down syndrome have one extra chromosome. So a person with Down syndrome has a total of 47 chromosomes in each cell. Doctors and experts are not really sure what causes it, but they say it occurs in about 1 of every 700 babies. This happens randomly, like flipping a coin or winning the lottery.

Everyone with Down syndrome is a totally unique person. The extra chromosome makes it harder for me to learn. Sometimes I need someone to say, "Settle down and get busy!" Also, it's really easy for me to be stubborn, so I don't mind if you say, "Hey, Margaret, please stop."

Even though I have one extra chromosome, the rest of my chromosomes carry information from generation to generation just like yours. Chromosomes control certain genetic characteristics, like eye color, skin color, height, and some abilities like music, art, or math.

For example, I get my blue eyes from my father, my fair skin and freckles from my mother, my blond hair from my grandmother, my long, thin feet from both my mom and my dad, and my need to wear glasses from both my grandparents and my parents. I like to concentrate on the ways that I am like everyone else.

I am very lucky to be alive today rather than 50 years or even 20 years ago because back then the doctors and experts believed that people with Down syndrome were not capable of learning. But now we know that people with Down syndrome are capable of doing many different things.

I personally am doing things that some people didn't think I could do. When I was born, somebody told my mom that it was too bad that I was named "Margaret" because I would never even be able to say my name. That person might never have expected that I could win four medals in Special Olympics swimming, be a green belt in karate, cook a pizza, read a novel, run half a mile, or get up in front of the class and give a speech! With a lot of hard work and encouragement, I have been able to do all these things.

I am not sad about the fact that I have Down syndrome. It is just part of me. I have a great brother (most of the time) and parents who love me a lot. I have wonderful friends who enjoy hanging out and having fun with me. I have teachers who help me keep on learning new things. I am glad to be a student at Lincoln Middle School because it is a great school and almost everyone is really nice. Down syndrome has not stopped me from having a worthwhile life.

—*Margaret Muller*
Cape Cod, Massachusetts

Source: By Margaret Muller, from www.patriciaebauer.com <http://www.patriciaebauer.com/>. Originally printed in the *Washington Post,* September 14, 1999.

disability exists and, if so, the extent of intellectual disability (Einfeld & Emerson, 2008). In examining social, behavioral, and educational risk factors, researchers have found that an influencing factor is poverty and the multiple challenges associated with it. Poverty is more associated with intellectual disability than it is with any other disability (National Research Council, 2002). Poverty during childhood creates risk factors for intellectual disability, including lower educational attainment, poorer physical and mental health, and increased mortality (Emerson, 2010; Fujiura & Parish, 2007). Elementary and secondary school students who live in families with incomes in the lowest 20 percent of the population are four times more likely to have intellectual disability than are those in the top 20 percent (Emerson, Graham, & Hatton, 2006).

Other social, behavioral, and educational risk factors include the following:

- Low maternal education is the strongest predictor of having a child with an intellectual disability when the child does not have a serious neurological condition (Avchen et al., 2007).

- By three to four years of age, children raised by adolescent mothers have been found to have difficulties with self-regulation, academic achievement, and language development (Borkowski et al., 2004).

- Risk factors for fetal alcohol syndrome include amount and time of alcohol consumption during pregnancy, poverty, smoking and drug use, and inadequate care during pregnancy (Ismail, Buckley, Budacki, Jabbar, & Gallicano, 2009).

IEP TIP

When there is an obvious connection—or even a suspicion of a connection—between the student's intellectual and adaptive functioning, such as inadequate nutrition, health care, and rest, you and related service providers such as a school social worker should develop an IEP that addresses these factors to the maximum extent you can in the general curriculum, and you should connect the student's family to appropriate school and community resources.

Evaluating Students with Intellectual Disability

DETERMINING THE PRESENCE OF INTELLECTUAL DISABILITY

To determine whether a student has intellectual disability, teachers and other professionals evaluate the student's intellectual functioning and adaptive behavior; you will recall that these are the two major characteristics of intellectual disability (Dixon, 2007; Tylenda, Beckett, & Barrett, 2007). The evaluation process includes observation, screening, and the IDEA nondiscriminatory evaluation process (see Box 9.2) (O'Reilly et al., 2007).

Evaluators use IQ tests, such as the Wechsler scale, to assess intellectual functioning. Evaluators must also assess a student's adaptive behavior. They need to know whether students have conceptual, social, and practical adaptive skills that are appropriate to their age and

---

BOX 9.2 | **NONDISCRIMINATORY EVALUATION PROCESS**

Determining the Presence of Intellectual Disability

Observation

Medical personnel observe: The student does not attain appropriate development milestones or has characteristics of a particular syndrome associated with intellectual disability.

Teacher and parents observe: The student (1) does not learn as quickly as peers, (2) has difficulty retaining and generalizing learned skills, (3) has low motivation, and (4) has more limitations in adaptive behaviors than do peers in the general education classroom.

Screening

Assessment measures:

Medical screening: The student may be identified through a physician's use of various tests before the child enters school.

Classroom work products: The student has difficulty in academic areas in the general education classroom; reading comprehension and mathematical reasoning/application are limited.

Prereferral

Teacher implements suggestions from school-based team: The student still performs poorly in academics or continues to manifest impairments in adaptive behavior despite interventions. (If the student has been identified before entering school, this step is omitted.)

Referral

If, in spite of interventions, the student still performs poorly in academics or continues to manifest impairments in adaptive behaviors, the child is referred to a multidisciplinary team.

Nondiscriminatory evaluation procedures and standards

Assessment measures:

Individualized intelligence test: The student has significantly subaverage intellectual functioning (bottom 2 to 3 percent of population) with IQ standard score of 70 to 75 or below. The nondiscriminatory evaluation team makes sure the test is not culturally biased.

Adaptive behavior scales: The student scores significantly below average in two or more adaptive skill domains, indicating deficits in skill areas such as communication, home living, self-direction, and leisure.

Anecdotal records: The student's learning problems cannot be explained by cultural or linguistic differences.

Curriculum-based assessment: The student experiences difficulty in making progress in the general curriculum used by the local school district.

Direct observation: The student experiences difficulty or frustration in the general classroom.

Determination

The nondiscriminatory evaluation team determines that the student has an intellectual disability and needs special education and related services. The student's IEP team proceeds to develop appropriate education options for the child.

---

environments and typical of their community. The AAIDD is developing the Diagnostic Adaptive Behavior Scale (DABS), a new standardized measure of adaptive behavior. The DABS will be based on the three components of conceptual, social, and practical skills that you learned about previously in the chapter. It will determine a cutoff point for significant limitations in adaptive behavior that is approximately two standard deviations below the mean of individuals without intellectual disability who are between four and twenty-one years of age.

The DABS is being normed on the general population; this means that the range of scores in the general population will be identified and used to determine significant limitations in adaptive behavior. In the past, adaptive behavior measures were normed only with people with impairments in adaptive skills. However, adaptive behavior should be evaluated based on what is typical or expected in the general population. The DABS should be available for use in 2013.

Until the DABS is available, an alternative is the American Association on Mental Retardation's (now AAIDD) Adaptive Behavior Scale—School. This norm-referenced scale is appropriate for evaluating students ranging in age from three to twenty-one (Dixon, 2007) and has adequate reliability and validity (Stinnett, Fuqua, & Coombs, 1999; Watkins, Ravert, & Crosby, 2002). Part 1 of the scale assesses personal independence in daily living and includes nine behavior domains: physical development, economic activity, language development, numbers and time, independent functioning, prevocational/vocational activity, self-direction, responsibility, and socialization. Part 2 concentrates on social behaviors in seven domains: social behavior, conformity, trustworthiness, stereotyped and hyperactive behavior, self-abusive behavior, social engagement, and disturbing interpersonal behavior. The domains of the Adaptive Behavior Scale—School were developed before AAIDD categorized adaptive behavior into the three domains of conceptual, social, and practical; so while it is useful, it is not current.

DETERMINING THE NATURE OF SPECIALLY DESIGNED INSTRUCTION AND SERVICES

When a student is in secondary school, the student's IEP will concentrate on the skills needed to be successful at work and in the community as an adult. (You will learn more about transition services later in this chapter.) A useful procedure for determining the strengths and needs of older students and planning services and supports for them is the Transition Planning Inventory (Clark, 2007; Clark & Patton, 2006). The inventory is appropriate for students ages fourteen to twenty-five. It focuses on nine areas of adulthood: employment, further education/training, daily living, living arrangements, leisure activities, community participation, health, self-determination, communication, and personal relationships. Within each area, the inventory identifies the knowledge, skills, or behaviors that are associated with successful postsecondary outcomes.

The inventory has student, home, and school versions as well as a form for profiles and further assessment recommendations. Students, parents (or other family members or guardians), and a school representative independently complete a five-point rating scale (strong disagreement to strong agreement) for each transition-related item. A Spanish version of the home form of the inventory also has validity and reliability (Stevens, 2006).

The inventory's senior author created a practical guide, *Assessment for Transitions Planning,* that instructs educators on how to use the inventory (Clark, 2007). Research documents that the use of the inventory during transition planning results in IEPs that have more transition-related goals as well as greater parental satisfaction with the IEP process (Rehfeldt, Clark, & Lee, 2010).

Designing an Appropriate IEP

PARTNERING FOR SPECIAL EDUCATION AND RELATED SERVICES

Despite the availability of tools such as the Transition Planning Inventory and the importance of a curriculum that takes into account a student's age and transition needs, students with

IEP TIP

The Transition Planning Inventory enables the IEP team to comply with IDEA's requirement that transition planning be based on the student's needs, strengths, preferences, and interests.

Community-based instruction teaches student to generalize skills to everyday settings.

intellectual disability typically experience some of the least positive postschool outcomes of students with disabilities in postsecondary education, employment, and productive engagement in the community (Newman, Wagner, Cameto, & Knokey, 2009).

An area of critical importance for effective transition is interagency collaboration (Noonan, Morningstar, & Erickson, 2010). Teachers, however, are too often not adequately involved in making interagency links; thus, the level of interagency communication is not sufficient (Bambara, Wilson, & McKenzie, 2007; Li, Bassett, & Hutchinson, 2009).

Box 9.3 provides partnership tips for interagency collaboration based on a national study of exemplary school districts.

DETERMINING SUPPLEMENTARY AIDS AND SERVICES

You know that special education is a team enterprise and that many different professionals are involved (see Chapter 1). Among them are paraprofessionals, sometimes called paraeducators. Paraprofessionals are school staff included under the IDEA term *supplementary*

BOX 9.3 **PARTNERSHIP TIPS**

Improving Interagency Collaboration

Sometimes it can feel beyond the scope of your responsibility as a teacher to contribute to interagency collaboration; however, each and every teacher can make a difference in the success of such collaborations. First, you should know best practices and encourage your team members to use them. Second, you should use these practices yourself.

Researchers identified twenty-nine high-performing school districts to determine what strategies they used to develop interagency collaborations (Noonan et al., 2010). Eleven key strategies were identified, but a major theme was that schools should have a transition coordinator whose job it is to build interagency collaborations. The strategies are as follows:

- Develop personal relationships with staff in community organizations who have responsibilities related to transition.

- Invite members of community agencies to come to IEP and other transition planning meetings; consider their scheduling preferences in arranging the time for the meetings.

- Ensure that school staff network within community settings.

- Anticipate that students and families will need support after graduation and share information with them about workshops, websites, and parent-to-parent connections.

- Recognize that administrative support is critical to flexible scheduling, compensation time, substitute teachers, and paid summer training.

- Recognize that interagency collaboration involves shared funding from multiple agencies, including government benefits for employment and housing.

- Seek technical assistance and continuing education from the state education agency, universities and colleges, and other professional development sources; encourage staff from community agencies to take advantage of continuing education opportunities.

- Partner with school, community, and state transition personnel in providing practical information and educational opportunities for students and families relating to all the key aspects of adult life planning.

- Find out about the availability of any interagency groups such as a community-wide transition council, learn who from your district is attending those meetings, and ask if that person will keep you informed about the decisions that are made.

Source: Information from Noonan, P. M., Morningstar, M. E., & Erikson, A. G. (2008). Improving interagency collaboration: Effective strategies used by high performing local districts and communities. *Career Development for Exceptional Individuals, 31*(3), 132–143.

aids and services. They often are IEP team members. Stephen Sabia's paraeducator adapts materials and assessments and provides direct support in the general education classroom. In other areas, such as transition between classes, participation in specialty classes (such as art, physical education, and keyboarding), managing lunchtime, and riding the bus, Stephen needs no assistance.

As you learned in Chapter 2, paraprofessionals enable students to be educated with their nondisabled peers and progress in the general education curriculum. Paraprofessionals can play an important role in instruction pertaining to literacy (Causton-Theoharis, Giangreco, Doyle, & Vadasy, 2007); physical education (Lytle, Lieberman, & Aiello, 2007); learning strategies (which you learned about in Chapter 5) (Keller, Bucholz, & Brady, 2007); social stories (Quilty, 2007); and reading skills, including phonological awareness (Lane, Fletcher, Carter, Dejud, & Delorenzo, 2007), alphabetic skills (Vadasy, Sanders, & Peyton, 2006a), and structural analysis (Vadasy, Sanders, & Payton, 2006b). The U.S. Department of Education estimated in 2007 that there were approximately 373,972 paraprofessionals providing special education supports and services to students with exceptionalities ages six through twenty-one who were being served in general and special education classrooms (U.S. Department of Education, 2011a).

Appropriate roles for paraprofessionals include providing individualized instruction to groups of students with and without disabilities, facilitating friendships among students with and without disabilities, supporting peer tutors, using state-of-the-art technology, teaching in community settings, and assisting students with personal care (e.g., bathroom care and feeding). Most paraprofessionals provide direct instruction to students for at least three quarters of the time they are on the job (Riggs & Mueller, 2001). That role certainly assists students to progress in the general curriculum. It also enables general educators and special educators to concentrate on other students—those with and without disabilities—and on their progress in the general curriculum.

However, some educators and researchers have expressed concerns about how paraprofessionals support students in general education classrooms (Giangreco & Broer, 2007). Although paraprofessionals can add appropriate and meaningful support for students with disabilities as well as their classmates, they may sometimes isolate students with disabilities. Ferguson (1995) referred to this as the "Velcroed effect" (p. 284). Here is how a student without a disability described the Velcroed situation of one of her classmates: "Whenever you try to talk to her you can't because her aides are there and they just help her say what she's trying to say and you want to hear it from her. They do it for her, and then they say, 'Is that right?' It's like you're having a three-way conversation and [the aide] is the interpreter and it is not right that way. . . . It just doesn't work" (Martin, Jorgensen, & Klein, 1998, p. 157).

Giangreco and Broer (2007) developed a sixteen-item screening tool that IEP teams can use to determine the extent to which the student's educational program relies too much on paraprofessionals. The tool examines whether students spend an excessive or unnecessary amount of time in close proximity to a paraprofessional, if students receive their primary instruction from paraprofessionals, if classroom teachers are minimally involved in instruction with students who are in their class as a result of the presence of a paraprofessional, and so forth.

PLANNING FOR UNIVERSAL DESIGN FOR LEARNING

In Chapter 12 you will learn about Digital Talking Books, which provide a variety of supports for reading and literacy instruction. A simpler UDL support for reading that will be useful for many students with intellectual disability involves e-readers. You are probably familiar with many of the commercially available e-readers, such as Amazon's Kindle and Barnes and Noble's Nook. The Apple iPad also has e-reader capabilities. In addition to functioning simply as e-readers, all of these devices also have the capacity to also read the text aloud to the user. However, like many off-the-shelf devices, their operation can be too complex for users with intellectual disability, and the actual read-aloud quality of such devices can be poor. To solve these problems, developers at AbleLink Technologies in Colorado Springs, Colorado, have developed a cognitively accessible e-reader, called Rocket Reader, which you can learn about in Box 9.4.

IEP TIP

As you develop an IEP, be sure to include any involved paraprofessionals and the supports they will provide. (These are supplementary aids and services.) If the student needs but does not have a paraprofessional, write into the IEP the services the student needs and then affirm that the IEP team has concluded the student needs a paraprofessional in order to participate in and make progress in the general curriculum.

BOX 9.4   UNIVERSAL DESIGN FOR PROGRESS

Computer-Based Reading Supports

Buck did not read the newspapers, or he would have known that trouble was brewing, not only for himself, but for every tidewater dog, strong of muscle and with warm, long hair, from Puget Sound to San Diego.

So begins Jack London's classic American novel, *The Call of the Wild*. Buck is a mixed-breed dog, part Saint Bernard, living comfortably in a home in California when suddenly he is stolen from a life of domestic tranquility and transported to the frozen tundra of Alaska, where he is put to work as a sled dog. Buck's adventures have thrilled adolescent readers since the book's publication in 1903; and this classic novel, as well as others, such as *Huckleberry Finn*, and *Charlotte's Web*, are staples of childhood reading and memories. Difficulty in reading should not prevent adolescents with intellectual disability from knowing the thrill of the chase, whether it be across the Alaskan tundra or across the ocean in search of the white whale.

In the past, one solution for students with intellectual disability and limited reading abilities was to get audiotaped versions of the book, typically on cassette tapes. E-readers provide a more modern and flexible format for listening to content from the classics to classwork. Unfortunately, most e-readers are not accessible to students with intellectual disability because the devices on which they operate often require a number of complex actions for operation. In response to this problem, AbleLink Technologies in Colorado Springs, Colorado, has developed a cognitively accessible e-reader called Rocket Reader.

Rocket Reader software can be operated on either a handheld computer device or a personal computer. What the user sees on the screen is highly visual and provides auditory feedback to maximize usability and simplicity. As you can see from the images in this box, the selection screen is simple and graphic. When any book is selected, either by touching the screen or using a mouse, the Rocket Reader software "reads" the title of the book and instructs the user to "touch this picture again" if she wants to read the book. Thus, users with limited reading skills can tap each picture until they identify the book they want to read.

All of the audio prompts can be customized and recorded by the student's teacher or parent. Once the student selects the book he wants to read by tapping on the picture of the book cover a second time, the book opens. If it is the first time the student has read the book, the book begins reading at the beginning. If the book has been listened to previously, the audio presentation begins where the user last left off reading. The software provides a progress meter showing how far into the book the user has read. Operation is simple, as you can see in the following picture, with a speaker icon present if the book is currently being read and three operation buttons—restart, stop, and read/pause—available.

Users with intellectual disabilities made fewer errors and required fewer prompts when using Rocket Reader than when using two other commercially available e-readers (Davies, Stock, King, Woodard, & Wehmeyer, 2008). Electronic versions of classic books, such as *The Call of the Wild*, are readily available through sources such as http://audible.com and http://bookshare.org. An exciting feature of Rocket Reader is that educators can also create their own recorded content. Lee, Wehmeyer, Palmer, Williams-Diehm, Davies, and Stock (in press) recorded sections of a student-directed transition-planning program for use with the Rocket Reader and found that students who used this teacher-created audiobook showed increased transition-planning knowledge and self-determination compared to students who used the same transition-planning program without Rocket Reader.

It's important to remember that reading is about more than just learning. Reading is a valued leisure activity that enriches the lives of many people. The simple adoption of e-readers such as Rocket Reader can enhance the quality of life of people with intellectual disability and open doors for socialization.

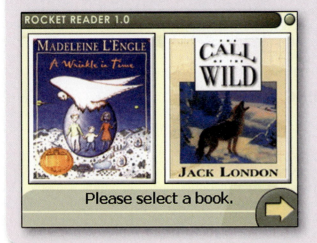

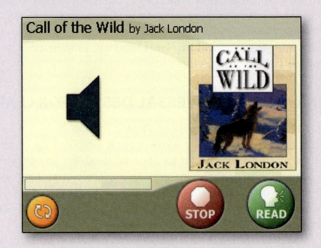

BOX 9.5   MY VOICE

The O'Halloran Outcome

He's nineteen years old, a senior at North Fort Myers High School in Florida. But he's a whole lot more than just a senior.

He's a member of the student council, having earned the requisite grade-point average and secured the required number of signatures to run for senior-class representative. He's served as the manager of the varsity wrestling team for three straight years and is a big-ticket fundraiser at school. He's a greeter-employee at the local Gap store, and he's also a busboy, dishwasher, and counter man at Daddy Dee's Ice Cream Parlor. He's a Boy Scout who is working on the "Life" badge (the next-to-highest rank possible) and has been admitted to the exclusive Order of the Arrow at Troop 82 in Cape Coral. He's a member of the youth group at the local Methodist church and serves as an altar boy and a volunteer at the children's liturgy for his church, Saint Cecilia's Catholic Community.

He's Casey O'Halloran, the all-American kid. The youngster most apt to flirt with all the girls but who singled out one for the junior-senior prom. The buddy of a hometown hero who represented the United States as a pentathlete in the summer 2000 Olympics and who inspires him to stay fit. The "knows no strangers" guy.

His course work consists of English and math, with a one-on-one tutor so he will learn real applications of the course content; a special education developmental speech class, where he focuses on articulation in his expressive speech; a leadership development class (for elected class officers and other student leaders), where he refines his social and self-determination skills; and an advanced weightlifting class. He's headed to Edison Community College in Fort Myers to sample some community development courses after graduation. In addition, he will continue his tutoring in academic subjects and work with a job coach.

What's Casey's secret? There is none. Combine community-based instruction with inclusion plus education in subjects that will make a difference in his life. Add the types of community-based activities that other young men undertake. Throw in two jobs. Set high expectations—better yet, let Casey set them for himself. And, then, just watch it happen.

But remember this. The "O'Halloran Outcome"—the one that IDEA envisions—would not have occurred without two things. The first is family: a mother, father, and older brothers who would not take no for an answer when it came to inclusion and who knew their way around their community. The second is a school system that has responded in creative, flexible, and individualized ways to meet Casey's unique needs as well as IDEA's implied promise. Remember the promise? It is that the outcomes of education will be equal opportunity, full participation, independent living, and economic self-sufficiency. In North Fort Myers, let's call it the "O'Halloran Outcome."

PLANNING FOR OTHER EDUCATIONAL NEEDS

To address students' limitations in intellectual functioning and adaptive behavior and to teach students to function successfully in their community, teachers need to support students to master skills that are sometimes more applied or functional than is the content of the general education curriculum. These skills include applied money concepts, applied time concepts, community mobility and access, grooming and self-care, leisure activities, health and safety, and career education (Snell & Brown, 2011). In many cases, such skills need to be taught where they will be used.

To what extent should a functional curriculum be taught to students with intellectual disability in typical community environments rather than classroom settings? The answer is that when students with intellectual disability are unable to generalize skills to typical community settings such as home, places of worship and recreation, and work sites, their instruction should occur in some or all of those settings (Walker et al., 2010). You can read about the results of effective community-based special education in Box 9.5.

Using Effective Instructional Strategies

EARLY CHILDHOOD STUDENTS: PRELINGUISTIC MILIEU TEACHING

All preschool-age children need to acquire language, but many children with intellectual disability struggle to do so (Brady, Warren, & Sterling, 2009). Prelinguistic milieu teaching is an effective language-acquisition instructional strategy for these children (Brady & Bashinski, 2008; Warren, Fey, Finestack, Brady, Bredin-Oja, & Fleming, 2008).

Prelinguistic milieu teaching (PMT) teaches children with intellectual disability who do not speak to make frequent, clear requests or comments with gestures or sounds while looking at the person with whom they are communicating. The steps in prelinguistic milieu teaching are simple and straightforward, as Box 9.6 shows. While following these steps, teachers should keep in mind a few basic principles. First, follow the child's lead. Children focus best on things that they are interested in. Observe the child and begin teaching only when you see what he is interacting or playing with. Then talk with the child, face to face at eye-level, about the object he is interacting or playing with.

Second, set the stage for communication. By putting a favorite toy in the room but out of reach, you encourage the child to ask for it. By putting objects out of order in a room, you may elicit a comment from the child.

Third, be strategic when using games like Pat-a-Cake and Peek-a-Boo. Children learn the game ritual; when you interrupt or change the ritual, the child will

---

BOX 9.6 | **INTO PRACTICE**

Steps to Prelinguistic Milieu Teaching

Prelinguistic milieu teaching (PMT) is an evidence-based, early intervention strategy for teaching young children with intellectual disability and other disabilities important prelinguistic skills, such as gesturing, vocalizing, and making eye contact. These skills serve as the foundation for language development. PMT has several advantages. It is implemented in children's natural environments; involves activities and routines that are based on the child's preferences and interests; enlists a child's natural communication partners, including parents and teachers; and creates opportunities for teachers and speech-language pathologists to be partners.

Prelinguistic milieu teaching improves language acquisition outcomes for children with intellectual disability, but it requires educators to follow these steps in carrying it out (Yoder & Warren, 2001):

Step 1: *Prompt the child to communicate.* To begin the training session, the trainer, whether a teacher or the child's parent, conveys through words or gestures an expectation that the child should communicate or use a particular communicative behavior to obtain a preferred object or engage in a preferred activity. The trainer might ask, for example, "What do you want?" or say, "Look at me," or provide a gesture, such as upturned or extended palms, to indicate a question and request. These prompts are specific to the child's preferred object or activity.

Step 2: *Prompt the child to initiate.* Next, the trainer provides a verbal prompt to the child to imitate a sign or a word, such as "Say, 'Ball,'" with reference to a preferred activity (playing with a ball) or "Do this," while modeling the sign for "more" (obtaining more of something the child likes).

Step 3: *Vocally imitate the child's resultant vocalizations.* When the child responds to the prompt, the trainer provides an exact, reduced, or expanded imitation immediately following the child's vocalization. So, for example, if the child responds to the "Say, 'Ball,'" prompt in Step 2 with the vocalization "Ba," the trainer immediately

imitates the vocalization, saying, "Ba." When the child repeats the "Ba" vocalization, the trainer expands that, saying, "Ball."

Step 4: *Comply with the child's request.* The child's vocalizations in Step 3 were the result of prompts in Steps 1 and 2 related to the preferred object or activity. In Step 4, the trainer complies with the intended or apparent request by the child ("Ba" to play with the ball). So when the child says, "Ba," the trainer repeats the vocalization and gives the child the ball.

Step 5: *Recode the child's communication act.* In the context of complying with the child's request, the trainer recodes or interprets the child's communication in the form of a question or statement. Thus, as the child is reaching for the ball and looking at the trainer, the trainer says, "Ball," or "Do you want the ball?"

Step 6: *Acknowledge the child's communicative act.* In a reinforcing manner, the trainer tells the child she did what was required. So when the child obtains the ball, the trainer should say, "You asked for the ball!"

Step 7: *Talk to the child.* To continue the interaction and further reinforce the child, the trainer should continue to talk to her, saying "Good, you are playing with the ball," or "You asked for the ball!"

You can put these strategies to work for progress in the general curriculum:

1. Conduct an online search for "prelinguistic milieu teaching" and summarize five tips that you learn from this search.

2. Imagine that you have a child in your classroom who could benefit from prelinguistic milieu teaching. How might you and a speech-language pathologist partner in order to provide instruction?

3. What do you see as the advantages of teaching communication within natural environments and typical routines as contrasted to having language instruction in specialized therapy sessions?

Source: Based on information from Yoder, P. J., & Warren, S. F. (2001). Relative treatment effects of two prelinguistic communication interventions on language development in toddlers with developmental delays vary by maternal characteristics. *Journal of Speech, Language, and Hearing Research, 44,* 224–237.

communicate in order to keep playing. Pat-a-Cake and Peek-a-Boo also reinforce face-to-face contact and require give and take, like a conversation. Further, PMT is consistent with the concept of self-determination, which you'll read about next, because its philosophy is that children will learn if their instruction matches their interests and abilities.

ELEMENTARY AND MIDDLE SCHOOL STUDENTS: THE SELF-DETERMINED LEARNING MODEL OF INSTRUCTION

Promoting self-determination has become an important educational focus for students receiving special education services. One empirically validated instructional model to promote self-determination is the *self-determined learning model of instruction (SDLMI)*. The SDLMI builds on the principles of self-determination (Wehmeyer, Agran, Hughes, Martin, Mithaug, & Palmer, 2007) and promotes middle school students' progress in achieving educational goals (Mithaug, Mithaug, Agran, Martin, & Wehmeyer, 2007), including goals related to the general education curriculum (Palmer, Wehmeyer, Gipson, & Agran, 2004).

The model involves three phases. In each, the teacher presents the student with a problem to solve. In Phase 1, the problem is "What is my goal?" In Phase 2, it is "What is my plan?" In Phase 3, it is "What have I learned?" The student learns to solve the problem in each phase by answering a series of four questions. Although the questions vary in each phase, each question represents one of four steps in a typical problem-solving process: (1) identify the problem, (2) identify potential solutions to the problem, (3) identify barriers to solving the problem, and (4) identify consequences of each solution. Figure 9.2 shows each of the twelve questions.

These questions connect to a set of teacher objectives. In each phase, the student is the person who makes the choices and takes actions, even as the teacher remains in

IEP TIP

Because transition services must be based on the student's preferences and interests, you should use the self-determined learning model of instruction with elementary and middle school students in the general education curriculum, thereby giving them a head start on learning to practice self-direction in transition-related planning conferences and in all aspects of their lives in school and after they leave it.

FIGURE 9.2

Student questions in the self-determined learning model of instruction

Phase 1 Problem: What Is My Goal?

Student question 1	What do I want to learn?
Student question 2	What do I know about it now?
Student question 3	What must change for me to learn what I don't know?
Student question 4	What can I do to make this happen?

Phase 2 Problem: What Is My Plan?

Student question 5	What can I do to learn what I don't know?
Student question 6	What could keep me from taking action?
Student question 7	What can I do to remove these barriers?
Student question 8	When will I take action?

Phase 3 Problem: What Have I Learned?

Student question 9	What actions have I taken?
Student question 10	What barriers have been removed?
Student question 11	What has changed about what I don't know?
Student question 12	Do I know what I want to know?

Source: Wehmeyer, M. L., Agran, M., Palmer, S. B., & Mithaug, D. (1999). *A teacher's guide to implementing the self-determined learning model of instruction (adolescent version).* Lawrence: University of Kansas, Beach Center.

Supporting students to take a meaningful role in their educational and transition planning results in improved transition outcomes and increased self-determination.

charge of the teaching. Each phase includes a list of educational supports that teachers can use to enable students to direct their own learning.

Some students will learn and use all twelve questions exactly as they are written. Other students will need to have the teacher reword the questions. Still other students will need to have the teacher explain what the questions mean and give examples of each question.

The outcome of Phase 1 is that students set an instructional goal based on their preferences, interests, abilities, and learning needs. The outcome of Phase 2 is that they design a plan for achieving their goal and self-monitor their progress toward the goal. The outcome of Phase 3 is that they evaluate data from their self-monitoring and, if necessary, alter their action plans or change their goal.

Are students successful in setting and attaining their goals? Yes. Wehmeyer and Agran (2010) have documented numerous studies in which students with intellectual disability have set and achieved academic, behavioral, transition, and functional goals when provided with instruction using the model. Recently, Shogren, Palmer, Wehmeyer, Williams-Diehm, and Little (2011) found in a randomized-trial, control-group study that intervention with the SDLMI results in enhanced student transition and academic goal attainment and greater access to the general education curriculum. Wehmeyer, Shogren, Palmer, Williams-Diehm, Little, and Boulton (in press) found that instruction with the SDLMI resulted in enhanced self-determination.

SECONDARY AND TRANSITION STUDENTS: COMMUNITY-BASED INSTRUCTION

"Learn it where you'll need to do it." That's good advice for any student with intellectual disability who experiences challenges in generalizing and adapting to community expectations.

"Teach it where you want your students to practice it." That's good advice for teachers, especially those whose students struggle with memory and with generalizing skills to the community.

To address these issues, teachers can use *community-based instruction (CBI)*, a technique that special education teachers have reported to be highly beneficial in increasing the likelihood that students will achieve positive postschool outcomes (Kim & Dymond, 2010). Because students with intellectual disability typically learn fewer skills than do their peers without disabilities, it is critical that they learn functional skills that are relevant to the community.

Students with intellectual disability in high school and, particularly, those who are ages eighteen through twenty-one and who are still receiving special education services should receive instruction in their communities. Best practice in community-based instruction includes the following:

> *High-quality educational services are provided in an age-appropriate environment that allows for social interaction and promotes community inclusion.* During high school, this can be the high school campus. But because the high school is no longer an age-appropriate environment for students ages eighteen through twenty-one, educational supports should be provided in environments that are age-appropriate and promote interaction with same-age peers, such as a community or a junior college. In fact, there is a growing network of two- and four-year

colleges and universities that provide postsecondary education for students with intellectual disability (Grigal & Hart, 2010).

High-quality educational services are ecologically valid and community-based. As students grow into adulthood, they should receive more of their instruction in community-based settings that approximate the environments in which they might live, work, learn, or play as adults.

High-quality transition services are results-oriented. IDEA requires transition services to be results-oriented, especially with respect to employment, independent living, postsecondary education, and community participation. Transition programs are effective when students obtain competitive work, are integrated into and participate in their community, live where they prefer with needed supports, and engage in a full array of leisure and recreation activities.

Academic instruction in quality programs is functional and focused on outcomes. Students continue to need academic instruction, so educators need to teach academic and functional skills in inclusive settings, such as community and junior colleges.

Quality services emphasize person-centered planning and active family involvement. Education leads to employment when families and community leaders, not just the school team, are involved.

Adult service providers actively participate in planning and implementing quality services. IDEA requires interagency collaboration in transition planning, especially with agencies that serve adults with and without disabilities and community businesses where students may someday work or become customers.

Quality transition services implement best practices. Among the best practices are job shadowing, job sampling, and leisure training.

Community-based instruction is most effective when based on an ecological inventory. To conduct such an inventory, teachers should

1. Select the instructional domain (e.g., vocational, recreation-leisure, independent living, etc.)
2. Identify current and future environments in this domain where the student needs to learn skills to succeed
3. Prioritize the need for instruction in specific subenvironments in each environment
4. Identify activities within each subenvironment
5. Task-analyze the priority activities into their component skills

For example, if a student wants to work with animals, the ecological inventory should identify a specific environment (e.g., pet store) and subenvironments within that environment (e.g., stock room, checkout counter, animal cages); prioritize the subenvironments in which the student will most likely work; identify tasks within prioritized subenvironments (e.g., cleaning cages, feeding animals, cleaning windows); and conduct a task analysis to use in teaching each task. After completing an ecological inventory, ask yourself the following questions when picking appropriate instructional strategies to teach the identified skills (Walker et al., 2010):

1. Will you train in a natural or simulated setting?
2. How can you plan for generalization?
3. What chaining procedure will you use?
4. What prompting procedure will you use?
5. Will you train individually or in a group?

Like any other type of instruction, community-based instruction can be heavily teacher-directed, or it can become heavily student-directed. Given the importance of self-determination for successful outcomes for students with intellectual disability, consider these guidelines:

Goal setting and instructional planning should be student-directed. Student-directed learning strategies (Chapter 10) and the self-determined learning model of instruction you learned about in this chapter can ensure that students have a meaningful voice in planning for their future.

Instructional goals should be based upon student preferences, interests, and strengths. The rule of thumb is that students should not see any difference between their final day of school and the first day of the rest of their lives. That outcome can be achieved when students learn skills in environments in which they will work or live. Obviously, if the student's preferences, interests, and strengths do not significantly influence teachers' decisions, students are unlikely to use the skills they have learned.

Job development should begin with the student. Although high-quality transition programs focus on more than employment, employment affects the student's life in a great many ways. Using a student-directed approach, job development begins with student preferences and interests.

The challenge comes in aligning these community-based instructional approaches with the goals of inclusion. If students with disabilities are in the community but not at school, how can they also be included in the general education curriculum with students who do not have disabilities? Some schools are demonstrating how to make community-based learning an important part of the curriculum for all students. Like universally designed learning, community-based instruction is good for all students, not just students with intellectual disability.

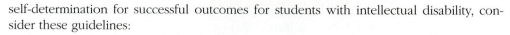

IEP TIP

Although involving adult support providers, such as potential employers, in transition planning is a good idea at any time during secondary education, it is especially important for students ages sixteen through twenty-one so that their community-based instruction curriculum becomes embedded in their community.

Including Students with Intellectual Disability

To what extent are students with intellectual disability included in general education classes? Figure 9.3 illustrates where students with intellectual disability were educated during the 2008–2009 school year.

FIGURE 9.3   *Educational placement of students with intellectual disability: School year 2008–2009*

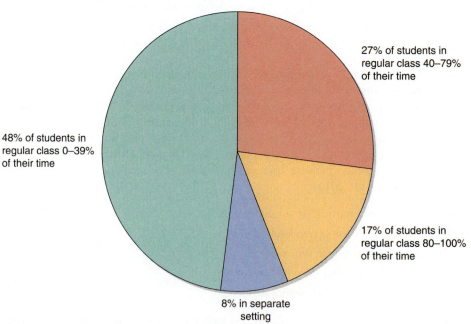

27% of students in regular class 40–79% of their time

48% of students in regular class 0–39% of their time

17% of students in regular class 80–100% of their time

8% in separate setting

Source: Information from U.S. Department of Education. (2011). *Data accountability center: Individuals with Disabilities Education Act (IDEA) data.* Retrieved February 12, 2011, from https://www.ideadata.org.

Note: Percentages have been rounded and collapsed across categories.

BOX 9.7

INCLUSION TIPS

	What You Might See	What You Might Be Tempted to Do	Alternate Responses	Ways to Include Peers in the Process
Behavior	The student demonstrates potentially distracting behavior such as loud laughter.	Tell her to stop the behavior (laughter) and be quiet or leave the room.	Teach skills to enable students to self-regulate their behavior. For example, you could teach her to self-monitor loud laughter.	Encourage peers to ignore inappropriate behavior and praise classmates when they regulate their own behavior.
Social interactions	On his job-training sites, he feels very shy around co-workers.	Tell him he will never get a job unless he learns to interact with others on the job.	Include social skills as an important component of transition instruction.	Gather information from co-workers about preferences for social interactions at work.
Educational performance	She shows an apparent lack of interest and boredom with class activities.	Discipline her for lack of cooperation.	Create opportunities for community-based instruction.	Include other class members as part of community-based instruction.
Classroom attitudes	He demonstrates learned helplessness with new activities.	Let him be excused from the activity.	Encourage him to identify motivational strategies that have worked in the past and incorporate them into the activity.	Pair him with a partner who needs help in an area of his strength (e.g., music).

Data from the federal government show that students with intellectual disability now spend more time in general education classes than in years past. That is probably because more educators are using strategies like those that Stephen's teachers use (graphics, UDL, DVDs, book summaries) as well as those we explain in Box 9.7. However, work still needs to be done to improve the number of students with intellectual disability who are included in general education classes. Almost 50 percent of students with intellectual disability spend less than 40 percent of their day in general education classes.

Assessing Students' Progress

MEASURING STUDENTS' PROGRESS

Progress in the General Education Curriculum

An important and time-tested means for monitoring a student's progress is to observe how well she has mastered certain skills and then to record those observations (Snell & Brown, 2011). Figure 9.4 illustrates the steps in this type of data-based decision making. Teachers regularly collect different types of data, including the following (Brown, Lehr, & Snell, 2011):

1. *Response-by-response data*. How well has a student learned a task that has been broken down into discrete steps or subtasks?

2. *Instructional and test data.* How well does a student perform under teaching and nonteaching conditions? Instead of collecting data strictly on each step in a task, teachers collect data on the student's independent performance of the task as a whole.

3. *Error data.* How many errors are there, what kind are they, and how does a student make them when performing a task?

4. *Anecdotal data.* What other student performance information has the teacher collected?

As Figure 9.4 points out, teachers must collect data continuously and systematically; otherwise, the data will not yield meaningful information about the student's progress.

Progress in Addressing Other Educational Needs

Teachers can assess a student's progress in community-based instruction using the ecological inventory process (Brown et al., 2011) described previously in the chapter. Teachers collect data using the ecological inventory process to design effective community-based instruction. They can continue to collect data about how the student functions in current and prospective environments to assess progress. This is called the **life space analysis**. Figure 9.5 describes the steps.

MAKING ACCOMMODATIONS FOR ASSESSMENT

To demonstrate their competencies on state- or districtwide assessments, most students will require one or more accommodations. IDEA requires a student's IEP team to set out in the IEP the accommodations the student will receive. Accommodations for students with intellectual disability typically include the following (Kleinert & Kearns, 2010):

- Dictating responses to a scribe
- Having extended time to complete an assessment
- Having test items read to them
- Securing clarification of test items

FIGURE 9.5 *Steps in life space analysis*

Gather information. The first step in a life space analysis is to gather information about the student's daily environments, such as home and living, employment, school and education, recreation and leisure, and community integration. Who is present with the student, what activities are involved in those environments, and what skills does the student need to be successful in them? Teachers, family members, and others use the answers to these questions to determine how many subenvironments a student is involved in, the choices the student is making or can make to be involved in various activities common to all of the environments, the skills the student needs to succeed in these environments, and whom the student interacts with. They then use this information to determine what other environments the student might access and what unaccessed environments might be appropriate for community-based instruction.

Conduct ecological inventories. The second step in life space analysis involves conducting **ecological** inventories in each of the environments where teaching will occur and comparing those inventories with ecological inventories for peers who are the same age as the student but do not have a disability. These ecological inventories identify the subenvironments in which students function, the activities involved in them, and the skills needed in them. For example, a student may have a preferred fast-food restaurant (environment) in which community-based instruction might occur. Within that restaurant, there are several subenvironments (for example, the counter where food is ordered, the dining area, and the restrooms) in which different sets of skills are needed.

Conduct discrepancy analysis. Having completed ecological inventories for the student and for nondisabled peers, the evaluation team members then conduct a **discrepancy analysis**, examining where and how the two ecological inventories differ and whether the points of difference can be the basis for instruction or can be addressed through other means, such as assistive technology.

Analyze tasks. Once they have identified the specific activities and skills the student needs to function in each of the natural environments, team members perform an activity task analysis, identifying each step the student needs to master and the goals for community-based instruction.

Measure progress. At this point, the activity task analysis ceases to be a planning tool and becomes a means for measuring the student's progress. The team members use data-based decision-making procedures to measure the frequency of the student's behavior, percentage correct, level of prompts necessary, duration information, and error data. Then the team determines just how effective it has been in teaching the student to master the skills needed in those environments.

ADDRESSING THE PROFESSIONAL STANDARDS

The following Council for Exceptional Children (CEC) Common Core Knowledge and Skills are addressed in this chapter through the content and concepts we discuss. See the Appendix for a full listing of these Knowledge and Skill statements:

ICC2K1, ICC2K2, ICC2K4, ICC2K5, ICC2K6, ICC4S1, ICC4S2, ICC4S3, ICC4S4, ICC4S5, ICC4S6, ICC5S2, ICC5S3, ICC5S4, ICC5S9, ICC7S1, ICC7S3, ICC7S6, ICC7S9, ICC8K3, ICC8S2, ICC8S6, ICC8S8, ICC10S2, ICC10S3, ICC10S4, ICC10S5

Summary

IDENTIFYING STUDENTS WITH INTELLECTUAL DISABILITY

- Intellectual disability consists of significant limitations in both intellectual functioning and adaptive behavior. It originates before age eighteen.
- In fall 2008, 476,131 students ages six through twenty-one were classified as having an intellectual disability.
- The two major characteristics of intellectual disability are limitations in intellectual functioning (including memory, generalization, and motivation) and limitations in adaptive behavior (including conceptual, social, and practical skills).
- The causes of intellectual disability are classified according to timing and type. Timing classifications include prenatal, perinatal, and postnatal. Type classifications include biomedical, social, behavioral, and educational.

EVALUATING STUDENTS WITH INTELLECTUAL DISABILITY

- AAIDD proposes a comprehensive assessment that involves diagnosing intellectual disability; classifying and describing the student's strengths, weaknesses, and need for supports; and developing a profile that includes intensities of needed supports.
- The AAIDD Adaptive Behavior Scale—School assesses school-aged children's adaptive behavior. A soon-to-be-published new adaptive behavior tool is the Diagnostic Adaptive Behavior Scale.
- The Transition Planning Inventory assesses nine knowledge, skill, and behavior areas to provide level-of-performance information related to transition needs.

DESIGNING AN APPROPRIATE IEP

- Interagency collaboration is a critical feature of successful transition for students with intellectual disability.

- Paraprofessionals can be a valuable resource in enabling students with intellectual disability to make progress in the general curriculum.
- Assistive technologies include software that provides audio and video resources to improve students' literacy skills.
- A functional curriculum is important for teaching skills for independent living.

USING EFFECTIVE INSTRUCTIONAL STRATEGIES

- Preschool and early-education students benefit from prelinguistic milieu teaching to elicit communication and language from them.
- Elementary and secondary students can develop their self-determination skills in school and postschool environments using the self-determined learning model of instruction.
- Students in transition programs benefit from community-based instruction.

INCLUDING STUDENTS WITH INTELLECTUAL DISABILITY

- Students are not often included in general education programs.
- Students achieve higher academic and social gains when they are included in general education classes.

ASSESSING STUDENTS' PROGRESS

- Data-based decision-making strategies document students' progress in the general curriculum.
- The ecological inventory process is useful both for planning community-based instruction and assessing students' attainment of community-based instructional goals.
- Students' IEPs must describe the accommodations to which they are entitled, such as dictating responses, having questions read to them, having more time, and having items clarified for them.

10 Understanding Students *with* Multiple Disabilities

Who Is Sally Ridgely?

Sally Ridgeley, age six, is a rarity and a paradox. Why a rarity? Because the incidence of Smith-Magenis syndrome (SMS), with which Sally was born, is estimated at 1 in 25,000 children.

Why a paradox? Because she has seemingly contradictory qualities. Let's begin with her intellectual abilities. Her parents, Jack and Ida, describe her as a bookworm, always absorbing information from the printed page or her computer-assisted toys. Her teachers say that she is on grade level with her kindergarten peers without disabilities, has made progress in the general education curriculum, and should be included with her nondisabled peers for first grade rather than placed in a self-contained classroom.

The paradox is created by some of Sally's other traits, some of which are characteristic of children with SMS. She engages in self-injurious behaviors that include head banging, hand biting, and picking at her skin and sores. She experiences emotional meltdowns and has temper tantrums. She constantly has something in her mouth that doesn't belong there, including her hands, clothing, toys, and small objects. She has not yet learned to use the toilet independently; that's because her bladder and bowels do not send signals to her brain. She frequently demands the attention of adults (often to the exclusion of peers in her kindergarten class or her brother and two sisters at home). At school, she experiences daytime sleepiness and requires frequent short naps and a few longer

ones: Like other children with SMS, she does not have a great deal of stamina because her sleep cycle is opposite that of children without the syndrome. Sally has an inverted circadian rhythm caused by inverted secretion of melatonin, a hormone that regulates the sleep-wake cycle. She awakens frequently during the night, usually four to five times, and she almost always is awake by 5:00 A.M. She is physically small for her age yet strong enough to hurt herself.

Her gross- and fine-motor challenges require several accommodations from her teachers; her one-to-one educational aide; and her physical, occupational, and speech therapists.

A rarity? Yes. Who would have expected Sally to have SMS, given how unusual the condition is? Like other people with SMS, her genes were the cause of the syndrome, which you will learn more about in this chapter.

A paradox? Yes. Most people would not have expected her to have made such progress in school; to have earned the pro-inclusion support of her general education teacher, special education teacher, and principal; and to have gained the affection of her peers.

Sally's teachers and principal are committed to her. The paradox is that their commitment simply reinforces her behaviors—those that demand adults' attention and result in meltdowns when she does not get her way. They are drawn to her, and she in turn absorbs them, gaining even more attention from them.

Sally needs to learn to be more independent, not just for the sake of her future in school and as an adult, but also for her teachers' sake, so that they can attend to other students. To teach her how to become more independent, her teachers had to learn how to depend on each other; for both of them have responsibilities in Sally's classroom, which includes seventeen students without disabilities and two (including Sally) who have disabilities. Here, too, is another paradox: Two highly qualified teachers—one an expert in general early childhood education, the other an expert in early childhood special education—must learn to be partners and depend on one another to teach a student to depend less on them.

OBJECTIVES

- You will learn the meaning of the term *severe and multiple disabilities* and discover that children with multiple disabilities vary in their strengths and limitations but share common characteristics related to their intellectual, adaptive, motor, sensory, and communication support needs.

- You will learn about the biological and the genetic causes of these disabilities and how to assess these students, including how physicians use the Apgar test to screen newborns.

- As you learn how to plan for these students' education and develop an IEP, you will learn about assistive technology, including augmentative and alternative communication, person-centered planning (MAPs), peer tutoring, and handheld computers (an example of universally designed learning).

- You will learn about effective instructional strategies, including the Children's School Success program for preschoolers, the principle of partial participation, basic methods of task analysis, and student-directed learning strategies.

- You will learn about assessing students using portfolio-based assessment, field observations, time sampling, and event recording.

Given her disabilities, Sally's inclusion in a general education classroom is itself a rarity in many school districts across the country. Yet she has made so much progress in her kindergarten year that her teachers, together with her parents, have successfully advocated for her to be included in the typical first-grade classroom with her nondisabled peers. The partnership among Sally's teachers and principal on the one hand and her parents on the other is essential to her education.

One other facet of Sally's education is also worth mentioning: Her success in the general education setting is a function of the collaboration between her special and general educators to provide specially designed instruction and curriculum modifications that enable her to succeed. For example, the long-term task of teaching Sally to become a more independent person, less dependent on adults, and less prone to self-injury and behavioral meltdowns, began with a simple, immediate, curriculum-adaptation strategy—the picture book—which her teachers designed based upon an analysis of why Sally behaves as she does.

Sally needs consistency and predictability in her life and has difficulty communicating, which is part of why she acts out. She can acquire consistency and predictability each day at school and home by using her picture book to see what she will be doing that day; she can understand both the pictures and her teachers' and parents' directions and supports. There was a time when Sally would engage in tantrum-like behavior whenever an adult asked her to do something she did not want to do. Yet it is in the nature of education itself that adults do and should direct students. So the challenge was to provide her with consistency and predictability, direct her without causing her to experience an emotional crisis, and teach her how to secure additional consistency and predictability on her own.

The picture book does all that, but it is no substitute for consistent behavior from her teachers and parents. Sally's education is a twenty-four-hour-a-day enterprise. She needs to practice at home what she learns at school. And that, in turn, requires her teachers and parents to follow through on each other's instruction and to communicate regularly via a communication log.

Sally's picture book illustrates the activities of her school day. Because she is a bookworm, always absorbing information through the printed page, a book is an ideal mode of communication. A simple response to a complex challenge, based on Sally's own strengths and preferences and on adults' analysis of why she behaves as she does, has become a powerful and effective form of intervention.

Let's return to the question, Who is Sally Ridgely? She is a rarity, in large part because she has a rare syndrome and is among the smallest population of students receiving special education services. She is a paradox because her gifts and challenges are so seemingly contradictory and because the ways in which her teacher and parents respond—including her in the general education classroom, partnering to capitalize on the talents and resources of each team member, and using simple methods to address complex needs—are a rarity in practice.

Yet these educators' response to Sally has produced a result that IDEA seeks: education that benefits, is inclusive, and leads to the outcome of independence.

Identifying Students with Multiple Disabilities

DEFINING MULTIPLE DISABILITIES

No single definition covers all the conditions associated with multiple disabilities. Schools sometimes use a compound of two terms, *severe disabilities* and *multiple disabilities*, as a single category for students who need intensive support to address their intellectual, adaptive, motor, sensory, or communication needs. These students' impairments often occur in combination with each other. Some of these students have average or above-average intelligence, although their physical and communication limitations may mask it. This is the case for Sally, who reads at grade level but has physical, communicative, and behavioral support needs. Her coexisting abilities and disabilities present another challenge: How should educators classify her? What type of disability does she have?

The answer is found in the federal regulations implementing IDEA, which refer to the fact that a student has more than one disability ("multiple disabilities") and to the extent of those disabilities, in combination with each other ("severe educational needs"): Multiple disabilities means concomitant impairments (such as intellectual disability–blindness or intellectual disability–orthopedic impairment), the combination of which causes such severe educational needs that they cannot be accommodated in special education programs solely for one of the impairments. Sally exemplifies the definition; she has more than one disability and severe educational needs; but as you know, she also has strengths.

In fall 2008, approximately 2.1 percent (124,073) of students ages six through twenty-one receiving special education services were classified as having these disabilities (U.S. Department of Education, Office of Special Education Programs, 2011).

Students with multiple disabilities have complex support needs associated with intellectual functioning, adaptive skills, motor development, sensory functioning, and communication skills.

DESCRIBING THE CHARACTERISTICS

Given the different impairments associated with severe and multiple disabilities, it is difficult to describe accurately all characteristics of all students classified as having these disabilities. These students are a widely heterogeneous group in terms of their characteristics, capabilities, and educational needs. They are as diverse as people who do not have disabilities, with interests, preferences, personalities, socioeconomic levels, and cultural heritages as varied as those of any of their peers (Giangreco, 2011). Nevertheless, students with multiple disabilities generally have specific characteristics related to their intellectual functioning, adaptive skills, motor development, sensory functioning, and communication skills.

Intellectual Functioning

Most students with multiple disabilities have significant impairments in intellectual functioning; their IQ scores are approximately thirty-five or more points below the norm—that is, an IQ of 65 or lower (Batshaw, Shapiro, & Farber, 2007). However, students with a higher IQ still may be classified as having multiple disabilities because of their adaptive, motor, sensory, or communication impairments. No one yet knows exactly what Sally's intellectual capacity is; she reads and is progressing in kindergarten, yet a nondiscriminatory evaluation has revealed she has an intellectual disability.

It is not easy to determine the capabilities of students such as Sally. As you read in Chapter 5, schools typically measure a student's intellectual functioning by administering an intelligence test. Yet these traditional methods are inappropriate for many students with multiple disabilities (Brown, Snell, & Lehr, 2011). This is so for four reasons. First, students with multiple disabilities usually are not included in the normative samples of standardized intelligence tests. Second, the information generated from these tests has limited utility when designing appropriate educational programs. Third, these students have not been exposed to some of the academic content on tests that are used to measure basic cognitive abilities. Fourth, most intelligence tests rely primarily on verbal abilities, and many students with multiple disabilities have language and communication impairments that limit their capacity to respond verbally, as Sally does.

Students with multiple disabilities vary widely in their academic abilities. Many students develop functional academic skills in literacy and math as well as skills for home and community living, including how to count money, find items in a grocery store, and read basic vocabulary (Bambara, Koger, Bartholomew, & Browder, 2011; McDonnell & Copeland, 2011). Sally's academic prospects are bright for learning functional academic skills, including some literacy skills. Other students with the most severe intellectual impairments will focus on learning how to make eye contact, track objects with their eyes, and respond to stimuli around them.

Adaptive Skills

As you learned in Chapter 9, adaptive skills include conceptual, social, and practical competencies for functioning in typical community settings in an age-consistent way. Self-care skills are especially important for students with multiple disabilities. Sally's parents and teachers are unanimous about their goals for her: They want her to understand when she should go to the bathroom and how to take care of herself there. Most students and adults with multiple disabilities attain some level of independence in caring for their own needs (Snell & Delano, 2011). School programs typically include instruction in self-care skills such as dressing, personal hygiene, toileting, feeding, and simple household chores as part of the focus on students' other educational needs. It is especially important to make sure that these skills generalize to home and community settings. That is why the student's parents and other caregivers should be highly involved in developing the IEP. In addition, teachers need to communicate with parents and caregivers about the school-based training, including how to carry it out at home and where to get support to do so (for example, from nonschool professionals, family friends, members of the family's spiritual community, and parent associations such as the parent training and information centers you read about in Chapter 4).

Motor Development

Students with multiple disabilities usually have significant motor and physical challenges (Campbell, 2011; Frey, 2007). Sally's petite size and low stamina impede her ability to get around in school as quickly as other students do and to use a pencil without tiring. Students with multiple disabilities often have motor impairments that produce abnormal muscle tone. Some have underdeveloped muscle tone; they may have difficulty sitting and moving from a sitting to a standing position. Others have increased muscle tension and extremely tight muscles, causing spasticity. Any abnormal muscle tone can interfere with a student's ability to perform functional tasks such as eating, dressing, using the bathroom, and playing with toys. Nevertheless, many students learn to perform these skills, with supports.

Sensory Functioning

Hearing and vision impairments are common among individuals with multiple disabilities (Silberman, Bruce, & Nelson, 2004). Because of the unique educational needs of students who experience deafness and blindness, the IDEA regulations include a separate category of disability, called deaf-blindness, and define it as follows: "Deaf-blindness means concomitant hearing and visual impairments, the combination of which causes such severe communication and other developmental and educational needs that they cannot be accommodated in special education programs solely for children with deafness or children with blindness."

It is inaccurate to assume that all students classified as deaf-blind are completely unable to hear or see. They have various combinations of vision and hearing impairments. Their impairments in each of these senses, however, are so severe that they need specially designed instruction, especially in developing meaningful communication, including how to recognize and respond to tactile and gestural cues (Rowland & Schweigert, 2003). For example, a student might learn a simple touch cue: A classmate might wave good-bye very close to the student's face so that the hand and air movements that this action generates signal the student and elicit a response (Engleman, Griffin, Griffin, & Maddox, 1999). A comprehensive review of research focusing on individuals with deaf-blindness documented multiple research-based strategies for teaching students with deaf-blindness behavior, communication, daily living, and vocational skills (Parker, Davidson, & Banda, 2007).

Communication Skills

Almost all students with multiple disabilities, not just those who are deaf-blind, have communication impairments (Downing, 2011). Students may have limited or no functional speech. Teachers will often instruct students with multiple disabilities to use facial expressions, informal gestures, and rudimentary vocalizations to communicate (Schlosser, Sigafoos, Rothschild, Burke, & Palace, 2007). Many students with multiple disabilities use augmentative and alternative communication (AAC) systems, which you learned about in Chapter 6. AAC enhances the student's communication abilities (Fossett & Mirenda, 2007). Sally's teachers and parents believe that many of her behavior problems occur because she can speak only a few words; they regard her disruptive or inappropriate behaviors as communication and are teaching her appropriate behaviors to communicate her wants and needs.

DETERMINING THE CAUSES

Sometimes the cause of a student's disability is simply unknown; often, however, the cause is easy to pinpoint. In approximately three quarters of all children who have severe intellectual impairments, there is a biological cause—typically, a prenatal biomedical factor (Batshaw et al., 2007). Complications during birth (perinatal causes) and after birth (postnatal causes) also account for some severe disabilities (Percy, 2007).

Specific genetic factors cause particular types of impairments because of gene or chromosome abnormalities. These genetic factors may occur spontaneously through basic alterations in genes, or they may be inherited. More than 7,000 genetic disorders have been identified; slightly more than one third of those are associated with intellectual disability (Moser, 2004).

For example, Fragile X syndrome is caused by a single gene mutation on the X chromosome that is associated with the absence of a protein (Mastergeorge, Au, & Hagerman, 2010). (**Syndrome** refers to a group of concurrent signs or symptoms that are related to a particular condition.) Fragile X syndrome typically manifests itself as an intellectual disability, multiple disabilities, and/or autism. As the most commonly known inherited cause of intellectual disability, the prevalence of Fragile X is approximately 1 in 4,000 males and 1 in 9,000 females (Mazzocco & Holden, 2007; Tartaglia, Hansen, & Hagerman, 2007). Typically males with Fragile X have a more significant intellectual disability than do females with Fragile X (Saul & Tarleton, 2010). Although not typical, some individuals with Fragile X do not have an intellectual disability.

Smith-Magenis syndrome (SMS) is the genetic disorder that Sally experiences. It is caused by a deletion of genetic material on chromosome 17 (Smith et al., 2010). Children with SMS typically experience intellectual disability, behavior challenges, vocal chord impairments, speech and communication delays, sleep disruption, and hearing loss (Gropman, Smith, & Duncan, 2010). Like Sally, their height is usually below the typical range for their age, and they have distinct facial features. Also similar to Sally, children with SMS frequently experience self-injurious behavior such as self-hitting, self-biting, and putting foreign objects into their mouths (Smith et al., 2010).

Evaluating Students with Multiple Disabilities

As you know, IDEA's nondiscriminatory evaluation process determines whether the student has a disability and requires specially designed instruction and, if necessary, the student's special education and related-service needs. Box 10.1 describes this process for students with multiple disabilities.

DETERMINING THE PRESENCE OF MULTIPLE DISABILITIES

The **Apgar test** is a way to screen the health of a newborn (Gaitatzes, Chang, & Baumgart, 2007) and can be the first indicator of an impairment leading to disability. When using this test, a physician ranks the child on five physical traits (skin color, heart rate, respiratory

NONDISCRIMINATORY EVALUATION PROCESS

Determining the Presence of Multiple Disabilities

Observation	**Physician/medical professionals observe:** The newborn may have noticeable disabilities associated with a syndrome or may have medical complications that are often associated with severe disabilities.
	Parents observe: The child has difficulties nursing, sleeping, or attaining developmental milestones.
Screening	**Screening measures:** Apgar scores are below 4, indicating the possibility of severe disabilities.
Prereferral	Prereferral is typically not used for these children because the severity of the disability indicates a need for special education and related services.
Referral	Children with severe and multiple disabilities should be referred by medical personnel or parents for early intervention during the infancy/preschool years. Many states have Child Find organizations to make sure these children receive services. The child is referred upon reaching school age.
Nondiscriminatory evaluation procedures and standards	**Assessment measures:**

Genetic evaluations: Evaluation leads to identification of a genetic cause.

Physical examinations: Medical procedures, including vision and hearing tests, blood work, metabolic tests, spinal tests, etc., reveal the presence of a disabling condition.

Individualized intelligence test: The student scores at least two standard deviations below the mean (i.e., 70 to 75 or lower), indicating that intellectual disability exists. Most students with severe and multiple disabilities have IQ scores that are significantly below 70, indicating severe cognitive impairment.

Adaptive behavior scales: The student scores significantly below average in two or more areas of adaptive behavior, indicating severe deficits in skills such as communication, daily living, socialization, gross- and fine-motor coordination, and behavior.

Assistive technology assessment: The student receives a comprehensive assessment for assistive technology needs in all of the environments in which the student participates. This evaluation should be consistent with IDEA's definition of assistive technology device and assistive technology service. The student's IEP team develops an IEP for the student.

---

effort, muscle tone, and reflex irritability when stimulated) at one minute and five minutes after birth. The newborn receives a score of 0, 1, or 2 for each trait. Apgar scores provide a quick overall impression of the newborn's condition. When Apgar scores are low (less than 4), a more thorough evaluation is indicated. This evaluation is more precise and focuses on identifying the nature of the disability, its possible causes, and the extent of the disabling conditions. Professionals often use neuroimaging to create anatomical pictures of the brain. There are three techniques (Percy et al., 2007):

- Computed tomography (CT) scans, which use a computer to create a sophisticated picture of the brain's tissues and structures
- Magnetic resonance imaging (MRI), which use a combination of magnetic fields and radio waves, instead of radiation, to create a picture of the brain
- Magnetic resonance spectroscopy (MRS), which is a type of imaging that reveals levels of particular substances

Students with multiple disabilities are typically identified at birth or in their early years; physicians, not educators or psychologists, usually make the initial diagnosis.

FIGURE 10.1 *Questions to use in implementing the SETT (Student, Environment, Tasks, Tools) framework for making evaluation decisions*

Questions about student training:

1. What specific technology use skills will the student need to learn?
2. How much training does the student require?
3. What kind of support will the student need in order to use the device in a functional manner?
4. Who will provide the training and support to the student?

Questions about equipment:

1. Who will provide the device(s), tools, and supplies needed?
2. How will the device be made available in each environment where it is needed?
3. Where will the device be located when the student needs to use it?
4. Who will be responsible for maintaining the device, making repairs, and reordering supplies?

Questions about training for staff, family, and others:

1. What will staff and family members need to know about the device and how it works?
2. Which adults in the child's environments will require training in the use of the device?
3. Who will provide the needed training for these people?
4. Who should be called if technical assistance is needed?

Questions about the general environment:

1. Are changes needed to ensure accessibility?
2. Is additional support needed?

Source: Zabala, J., Bowser, G., & Korsten, J. (2004/2005). SETT and ReSett: Concepts for AT implementation. *Closing the Gap, 23*(5), 1–4.

DETERMINING THE NATURE OF SPECIALLY DESIGNED INSTRUCTION AND SERVICES

Students with multiple disabilities often benefit from assistive technology. That is because assistive technologies can help students overcome functional limitations. Sally uses a laptop computer and software toys and games to supplement her classroom instruction.

Assistive technology evaluations typically are multidisciplinary: Assistive technology specialists, speech-language pathologists, orientation and mobility specialists, and occupational and physical therapists usually are involved. The student's family members and the student should participate to the maximum extent possible. Together, all professionals and family members should evaluate how assistive technology can enhance communication, seating/positioning, and fine-motor skills (e.g., hand and grip strength).

A helpful guide for an assistive technology evaluation is the SETT framework. It considers the Student's needs, interests, and abilities; the Environment in which the technology will be used; the Tasks for which the technology will be needed; and then the Tools that might be needed to meet the student's needs (Zabala, 2005; Zabala, Bowser, & Korsten, 2004/2005). Figure 10.1 identifies questions to ask while implementing the SETT framework.

Designing an Appropriate IEP

PARTNERING FOR SPECIAL EDUCATION AND RELATED SERVICES

It is increasingly common for teachers to design IEPs for students with multiple disabilities by using person-centered planning (Vlaskamp & van der Putten, 2009). When using person-centered planning, you seek the active participation of everyone involved in the

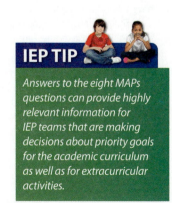

IEP TIP

Answers to the eight MAPs questions can provide highly relevant information for IEP teams that are making decisions about priority goals for the academic curriculum as well as for extracurricular activities.

student's life (family, teachers, administrators, and, of course, the student), focus on the student's and family's dreams and visions, and seek school and community inclusion (Brown, Galambos, Poston, & Turnbull, 2007; Holburn, Gordon, & Vietze, 2007). You also should consider the family's cultural values and implement person-centered planning so that it responds to these values (Trainor, 2007).

One of the most popular person-centered planning approaches is the MAPs process. It customizes students' educational programs to their specific visions, strengths, and needs (Falvey, Forest, Pearpoint, & Rosenberg, 2002; Potvin, Prelock, & Snider, 2008; Xu & Filler, 2008). It is especially effective in planning transitions from school to postschool activities (Mount & O'Brien, 2002). Box 10.2 provides tips for how to implement the MAPs process.

DETERMINING SUPPLEMENTARY AIDS AND SERVICES

Supplementary aids and services can consist of support from teachers, paraprofessionals, and peers. **Peer tutoring** involves pairing students one on one or in small groups so that students who have already developed certain skills can help teach other students. Can peer tutoring be successful for students with multiple disabilities? The answer is yes. Peer tutoring can lead to increased academic outcomes, enhanced social skills, stronger personal relationships, and greater school inclusion for students with multiple disabilities (Carter, Cushing, & Kennedy, 2009).

BOX 10.2 | **PARTNERSHIP TIPS**

Implementing the MAPs Process

You may incorporate the MAPs process into a student's IEP meeting, or you may incorporate it independently of the IEP. If you incorporate it into the IEP meeting, you will need to make sure that everyone sets aside sufficient time to complete the MAPs process and incorporate its contents into the IEP.

Whether you do the MAPs process while developing a student's IEP or not, you will follow the same general process. You, or perhaps a facilitator who has done MAPs planning before, should guide the discussion, infuse it with positive energy, and encourage brainstorming to generate as many creative ideas as possible. You and the other people involved in the MAPs process will want to think outside the box, ask yourselves what makes the student tick, identify how you can build on the student's strengths to facilitate his well-being in school and community, identify what stands in the way, and decide how to overcome those barriers.

You need to have the right people participate in the MAPs process. This includes the student, his family members, and friends who have formed an emotional bond with the student and who have taken the time to know what is most important in his life.

The facilitator should lead the meeting participants through the following questions (Turnbull et al., 2011):

- *What is MAPs?* At the beginning of the meeting, the facilitator explains the purpose of the process, the type of questions to be asked, and the ground rules for open-ended and creative problem solving. The facilitator creates an upbeat, energized, and relational ambience.

- *What is your history or story?* Typically, the student and his family talk about what they regard as their successes and triumphs as well as the challenges still facing them, especially those impeding the student's visions, expectations, strengths, and preferences.

- *What are your dreams?* The student and family members share their great expectations for the future. The MAPs team members use these to customize academic and extracurricular activities.

- *What are your nightmares?* Because students with disabilities and their families often have major fears that may cloud their great expectations, identifying those fears—their nightmares—lets everyone know them and plan to respond to them. Some fears are realistic, but others can be addressed through support for the student and family.

- *Who are you?* The MAPs team members use as many adjectives as it takes to avoid the student's disability label. Instead, they describe the student's noncategorical traits. For example, instead of identifying the student as having severe, multiple disabilities, they say she is curious, misbehaving at times, eager to please, or hard to understand.

- *What are your strengths, gifts, and talents?* Often teachers, friends, family members, and others can lose sight of the fact that the student has strengths on which to build. So the MAPs team members identify them.

- *What do you need?* What will it take to make the student's and family's great expectations come true? What barriers stand in the way? Identifying these lays the foundation for planning for the student's participation in academic, extracurricular, and other school activities.

- *What is the plan of action?* A plan of action includes the specific steps required to accomplish the great expectations. The plan of action should identify the people, tasks, timelines, and resources that will help the student and family realize their expectations.

There are critical features of effective peer supports for students with multiple disabilities. You should clarify the roles of all involved, match students with peer tutors, and provide supports to the peer (Hughes & Carter, 2008). Box 10.3 identifies the steps you should follow to implement peer tutoring with students with multiple disabilities.

Relying too much on students without disabilities to support their classmates who have disabilities can lead to relationships that tend to be one-way rather than reciprocal. There is nothing wrong with help; friends often help each other. Help, however, is not and should never be the only basis for friendship. You need to support all your students to do something for each other, such as giving a compliment or nominating another student for a class honor.

Peer tutoring, promotes inclusion, academic responding, social interactions, and self-determination.

INTO PRACTICE

Peer Buddies

Suppose you could accomplish several goals with a single effort. For example, you could effectively integrate the educational programs of students with severe and multiple disabilities into the general education curriculum, remove them from their separate and self-contained classrooms for at least one class period a day, help them learn functional academic and employment skills, and increase the number of genuine friendships they have with students who do not have disabilities. Would you be interested in adopting that program in your school? Probably.

What if that same strategy could simultaneously benefit students without disabilities in three or four different ways? Give them academic credit? Teach them how to be good citizens? Still interested? Definitely. After all, this is a win-win proposition for everyone.

The strategy we are talking about is called peer buddies, and it was designed by researchers at Vanderbilt University to promote social relationships among students with severe disabilities and their same-age peers without disabilities. In the large urban school district of Nashville, Tennessee, nine of eleven comprehensive high schools paired 200 students with severe disabilities with 115 students who had no disabilities. The program was a great success (Hughes & Carter, 2008).

How does the peer buddies strategy work? Pretty simply, if you follow these steps:

Step 1: *Introduce a one-credit course.* Many high schools already require students to engage in service learning. The peer buddies model fulfills the requirements for service learning.

Step 2: *Recruit peer buddies.* Recruit students who hold high-status roles to serve as peer buddies: student government leaders, sports and cheerleading standouts, and high academic performers. These high-status students add credibility to the program process.

Step 3: *Establish a screening process.* Peer buddies must be responsible and reliable students, such as those who have a good attendance record and have shown they can juggle extracurricular activities and academic demands. Once an initial screening has been completed, allow a potential peer buddy to observe existing peer buddy activities and allow her to ask questions to get a better idea about the purpose of the activities.

Step 4: *Train the students.* Topics include people-first language and disability, awareness of effective communication strategies, sample activities in which to engage with students with severe disabilities, and how to deal with inappropriate behavior effectively but respectfully.

Step 5: *Establish expectations and evaluate progress.* Observe peer buddies, provide feedback and reinforcement on their interactions, and answer questions. Establish regularly scheduled times for the peer buddies to meet and discuss what worked for them and what did not. This is also a good venue to teach peer buddies skills related to time management and organizational and scheduling strategies.

Now put these ideas to work for progress in the general curriculum:

1. What do you see as the benefits of participating in a peer buddies program for students with and without disabilities?

2. The peer buddies strategy was set up at the high school level. Do you think the program could be adapted to the elementary level? If so, what changes would you recommend for using this program with younger children?

3. What might be some concerns of students without disabilities when interacting with Sally and her teachers?

PLANNING FOR UNIVERSAL DESIGN FOR LEARNING

Many new advances in technology make it possible to include students with multiple disabilities in the general education curriculum. Among the most promising types of technologies involve the use of smartphones, an iPad, or a tablet PC.

Assume you are teaching three high school students with severe disabilities to get jobs in their communities. One student needs to learn how to set the tables in a restaurant; another to wash, dry, and fold laundry in a fitness club near his home; the third to deliver the mail from a central mailroom to the offices of the judges and clerks of court in a county courthouse. Assume you have only one paraprofessional to assist you. How do you teach all three students, especially if they go off campus daily, to learn how to perform their duties?

You should consider teaching your students to use prompting technologies that run on a smartphone, the iPad, or a tablet PC. These prompting technologies share common features. Digital photographs that fit the student's task or activity can be uploaded, and digital instructions or prompts can be recorded. In Chapter 2 we pointed out that UDL modifies how teachers present and represent the curriculum that a student must learn. Using smartphone, iPad, or tablet PC computer technology, you can display digital pictures or video clips that show the student performing each step in a learning task.

Smartphones, iPads, and tablet PCs are ideal for introducing UDL features into instruction. They are unobtrusive, easily portable, and can incorporate (or often already incorporate) other devices, including digital cameras and global positioning satellite (GPS) devices. Researchers are even developing smartphone programs that use GPS data to help people with intellectual disability use public buses equipped with transmitters.

PLANNING FOR OTHER EDUCATIONAL NEEDS

You have already learned that students with multiple disabilities experience communication challenges. People rely on communication skills for many important things, from learning to making friends. Fortunately, one form of assistive technology, augmentative and alternative communication, enables students who cannot communicate verbally or through other formats, such as sign language, to do so through the use of technology. You learned a little about AAC in Chapter 6; but because those devices are so important for students with multiple disabilities, it's worth learning more about them here.

AAC refers to the devices, techniques, and strategies used by students who are unable to communicate fully through natural speech and/or writing (Schlosser, 2003). AAC frequently involves technology in the form of voice-output communication aids (VOCA) and synthesized speech, but it may also involve a wide array of other low-tech options such as message boards, symbols, and pictures. Blackstone, Williams, and Wilkins (2007) identified basic principles underlying research and practice in AAC:

- AAC fosters the abilities, preferences, and priorities of individuals with complex communication needs, taking into account motor, sensory, cognitive, psychological, linguistic, and behavioral skills, strengths, and challenges.
- AAC recognizes the unique roles communication partners play during interactions.
- AAC enables individuals with complex communication needs to maintain, expand, and strengthen existing social networks and relationships and to fulfill societal roles. (p. 192)

Like other forms of assistive technology, AAC devices are supplementary aids and services. AAC is important for literacy learning and promoting access to the general education curriculum (Light & McNaughton, 2009). It also increases autonomy and self-sufficiency and promotes self-determination (McNaughton & Beukelman, 2010). When making decisions about appropriate AAC devices, IEP teams need to identify features that meet the student's needs, especially the symbols the device uses (how meanings are represented), the way the device displays information (fixed or dynamic), the device's selection options (scanning or direct selection), and its method for outputting information.

IEP TIP

Electronic and information technologies, such as the Visual Assistant shown in Box 10.4, are becoming less expensive and more powerful. IEP teams should consider what off-the-shelf technologies can be modified to meet students' unique needs rather than looking only at expensive disability-related assistive devices.

IEP TIP

IEP teams should remember that among the special factors they are required to consider for every student receiving special education services are communication needs and the need for assistive technology. Alternative and augmentative communication devices address both of these areas.

BOX 10.4

UNIVERSAL DESIGN FOR PROGRESS

The Visual Assistant Digital Prompting System

The Visual Assistant system provides powerful step-by-step support for students with severe and multiple disabilities to complete tasks. Educators set up tasks by recording spoken instructions and taking digital pictures of each step in the task. Preferably the pictures will be of students completing each step in a real-world environment. The Visual Assistant is ideal for complex or multistep tasks where the addition of a picture can increase accuracy. Setting up the Visual Assistant is easy and uses the principles of universal design.

Pocket Compass—an instructional media task-prompting system from AbleLink Technologies.

When the student initiates the Visual Assistant program by tapping on the Visual Assistant icon, the software opens to a screen showing all the tasks set up for the person. Each task has an individualized icon or a picture.

So, for example, if Dan, a student with severe disabilities, wants to use the Visual Assistant to make coffee, he taps on the icon of the coffee maker.

This opens a screen with a larger picture of the coffee maker and initiates an audio message saying, "Dan, if you want to make a pot of coffee, tap on the *Next* button."

When Dan taps on the *Next* button, it opens another screen, which has a picture of the first step in the coffee-making process and two buttons, one that reads *Play* and one that reads *Done*. Dan's teacher has already taught Dan to tap the *Play* button when he sees it. When Dan does so, an audio message in the teacher's voice says, "First, fill the glass coffee pitcher with water up to the ten-cup line."

Dan can play that message as often as he needs. If Dan needs more assistance, he can zoom in on the picture or more steps can be included, such as a picture of Dan himself filling the coffee pitcher at the sink.

When Dan completes the task depicted in the picture and described in the audio message, he taps the *Done* button. Tapping on that button takes him to the next screen, with a picture of the next step in the process and the *Play* and *Done* buttons.

The Visual Assistant is a "see it" (visual image), "hear it" (spoken voice), "do it" (job being done and then finished), universally designed device! Recently, AbleLink Technologies developed an instructional media standard (AIMS) that creates common computer language standards for use in the development of digital prompting systems. That means that organizations can create libraries of tasks that teachers can access easily. You can access one such library at the AIMS website (http://www.aimsxml.com).

Visual Assistant—an instructional media task-prompting system from AbleLink Technologies, Inc.

Source: Images reproduced with permission of AbleLink Technologies© 2005. All Rights Reserved.

FIGURE 10.2 *A communication board: Example of a fixed display*

Source: Photo reprinted with permission of DynaVox Technologies, Pittsburgh, PA (http://dynavoxtech.com).

A fixed display offers an unchanging symbol arrangement. The pictures on the communication board in Figure 10.2 are in a fixed display; all of the pictures remain the same. Dynamic displays enable students to make choices that change the display on the device screen. More and more, AAC devices resemble computers; and the various dynamic displays are similar to displays presented on a computer screen, which users can modify or customize to their preferences.

AAC devices typically offer two major types of selection options: scanning or direct selection. Scanning involves pointing or using a cursor to scan an item at a time, a row of items, or a block of items and is useful for students with extensive motor impairments. Sophisticated systems allow users to "point" to a symbol or word without having any physical contact, such as by looking at the symbol, using light pointers, or using head- or mouth-controlled pointers.

The student's IEP team needs to include and work closely with speech-language pathologists in selecting AAC devices. As you have learned, instruction related to AAC is complex. Students will need to learn how to use the device in different communicative situations and with different partners as well as how to care for the equipment. They also must learn some of the basics of communication. Those include how to maintain and sustain conversations (e.g., taking turns and showing interest in others) and when to use different kinds of messages (e.g., keeping secrets or telling jokes). Designing AAC to promote progress in the general curriculum is more than just buying a device; it involves thoughtful planning and effective instruction.

Using Effective Instructional Strategies

EARLY CHILDHOOD STUDENTS: CHILDREN'S SCHOOL SUCCESS

What exactly, you may ask yourself, is the general education curriculum for preschoolers? That's an excellent question. Researchers at several universities are collaborating to answer it and to develop strategies for educators to use to include preschoolers with severe, multiple disabilities in the general education curriculum. They have named their collaboration the Children's School Success (CSS) curriculum (Lieber, Horn, Palmer, & Fleming, 2008).

As we have stressed, access to the general education curriculum occurs when students with disabilities are educated with their nondisabled peers in the general education classroom. The same is true for preschool children, and the CSS model presumes that

IEP TIP

IEP teams must have representation and active involvement from professionals from different disciplines, including speech-language therapy, assistive technology, and, possibly, physical or occupational therapy, to identify an AAC device that meets a student's communication and quality of life needs.

preschool children are attending preschools with their nondisabled peers (Odom, 2009). The model seeks to reduce the educational gap for students who are at risk for poor school performance, prepare children for school entry, support individualization, and promote evidence-based practices. It addresses content areas such as math, literacy, and science by using developmentally age-appropriate activities. The model rests on five key assumptions:

1. Children are active, self-motivated learners who learn best from personal experience.
2. They learn best when they have opportunities to practice skills in the context of meaningful activities.
3. They construct knowledge by participating with others using problem-solving and self-evaluation skills.
4. They should be allowed to exercise choice in their learning environments.
5. They learn best through a curriculum that presents information in an integrated fashion.

The CSS model emphasizes an integrated general education curriculum. At some times during the school day, students may work on only one content area, such as reading or math; but most of the time, instruction on these core content areas is integrated across activities. When you focus on active learning and constructing knowledge through problem solving and self-evaluation skills, you teach young children the critical self-regulation skills they will need to learn more effectively once they enter elementary school. The CSS model emphasizes four steps in the problem-solving process (Odom et al., 2010):

1. *Reflect and act.* Preschoolers learn to reflect on what they know about the problem and what they need to find out more.
2. *Plan and predict.* Based upon information from the first phase, children make predictions about what they think will happen next and use these predictions to create a plan.
3. *Act and observe.* Children implement their plan and test out their predictions.
4. *Report and reflect.* Children report the solution they have identified via multiple means, such as drawing a picture.

Students receiving instruction with the CSS model make academic and social gains (Lieber et al., 2008). Of course, none of this should be new to you. Look at the key assumptions and the problem-solving process again; notice anything familiar? You should notice the following: universal design for learning (multiple means for providing content and for having students respond to the content); self-determination and student involvement (student-directed learning strategies, choice opportunities, problem solving); inclusion and integration with nondisabled peers; high expectations (emphasis on core academic content for all students); and scientifically based strategies. Good instructional practices are good for all students, no matter how young they are.

ELEMENTARY AND MIDDLE SCHOOL STUDENTS: THE PARTIAL PARTICIPATION PRINCIPLE

Several important principles govern the education of students with multiple disabilities. The first is the principle of maximal participation (Baumgart et al., 1982), which asserts the right of students with multiple disabilities to participate to the maximum degree possible in activities that contribute to the quality of their lives. The goal of the principle of maximal participation is, quite simply, to maximize participation in one's life.

A related principle is that of **partial participation** (Baumgart et al., 1982; Ferguson & Baumgart, 1991).This principle holds that students with multiple disabilities should not be denied access to general education and other inclusive activities solely because of their intellectual, adaptive, skill, motor, sensory, and/or communication support needs (Snell & Brown, 2011). The principle rejects an all-or-none approach under which students either

function independently in a given environment or not at all. Instead, students with multiple disabilities should participate, even if only partially, in age-appropriate environments. Students can often learn and complete a task if it is adapted to their strengths. Under the partial participation principle, students are not kept out of the activities that benefit them simply because they cannot perform all of the activities without support (Bambara, Koger, Bartholomew, & Browder, 2011). Teachers like you should ask themselves three questions to implement partial participation:

- What noninstructional supports does the student need for meaningful participation?
- How much does the student wish to participate?
- How can teachers enhance the student's independence, especially partial independence?

Once you have answered these questions, you need to observe the student performing a task and use well-developed observational methods (such as the ones we discuss below) to determine what parts of the task the student can do or can learn to do.

The principle of partial participation enables students with multiple disabilities to learn and participate in self-care and other functional skills (Snell & Delano, 2011); but it also applies to instruction in literacy (Copeland & Keefe, 2007), math, and science (Courtade, Spooner, & Browder, 2006). To determine what a student can do or needs to learn to do, you should conduct a task analysis. A task analysis identifies the individual steps that, in combination, are required to perform a skill or activity. According to Snell and Brown (2011), a task analysis follows these steps:

1. Define the target skill or task.
2. Perform the task yourself and observe the student's peers performing the task.
3. Identify the steps in the activity.
4. Write these steps on a data collection form. Make sure each step is
   - Stated in terms of observable behavior.
   - Ordered in a logical sequence.
   - Written in second-person singular so it can serve as a verbal prompt (if used).
5. Observe the student performing the task and identify steps that he or she can or will be able to
   - Perform independently.
   - Learn to perform.
   - Use technology or other supports to perform if needed.

SECONDARY AND TRANSITION STUDENTS: STUDENT-DIRECTED LEARNING STRATEGIES

Consider this question: "If students were floated in life jackets for 12 years, would they be expected to swim if the jackets were suddenly jerked away?" (Martin, Marshall, Maxson, & Jerman, 1993, p. 4). The obvious answer is "Of course not." Students would sink without specific instruction about how to swim. Depending on a life jacket does not ensure success once the life jacket is removed. Unfortunately, "the situation is similar for students receiving special education services. All too often these students are not taught how to self-manage their own lives before they are thrust into the cold water of post-school reality" (Martin et al., 1993, p. 4). In Box 10.5, you will read what self-management means, and you will find that being "his own man" is Madeleine Will's great expectation for her son Jon.

To avoid the life-jacket situation, you can use **student-directed learning strategies**. These strategies teach students with and without disabilities to modify and regulate their own learning (Wehmeyer et al., 2007). The educational supports that you should use to implement the Self-Determined Learning Model of Instruction (Chapter 9) include many student-directed learning strategies, but three are particularly important for students with severe disabilities: picture prompts or antecedent cue regulation, self-instruction, and self-monitoring.

Madeleine Will

With a little reflection, I decided that what I really wanted for Jon was for him to dream big dreams, his own dreams. I wanted him to be his own man, a man with a disability who could and would define himself. Most importantly, I wanted him to become an adult who would know himself well enough to understand his own needs and assume responsibility to the greatest extent possible for his own happiness.

In my imaginary world of care and education for people with disabilities, the emphasis on making and maintaining friends would grow more pronounced in the adolescent years, especially as nondisabled friends went off to college or became preoccupied with job responsibilities. A job, an apartment or a house, and various material goods do not constitute a fulfilled existence for any of us. What matters most to people are their families and loved ones and the quality of those relationships. This fundamental human need should be reflected throughout every phase of education.

Source: Reprinted from *Journal of Vocational Rehabilitation, 3*(2), M. C. Will, "The Question of Personal Autonomy," pp. 9–10, 1993, with kind permission from Elsevier Science Ireland Ltd., Bay 15K, Shannon Industrial Estate, Co. Clare, Ireland.

Picture Prompts or Antecedent Cue Regulation Strategies

You learned a little about these strategies when you read about the Visual Assistant software program earlier in this chapter. This software provides visual and audio prompts for students to successfully complete multistep tasks. The antecedent cue regulation strategy involves a similar approach: providing visual and/or audio cues to support students to regulate their own behavior and to complete assigned tasks. The visual cues include photographs, drawings and illustrations, video clips, and even actual items involved in the task. Audio cues are instructions or directions recorded on a CD-ROM, a smartphone, or an MP3 player. Technology platforms such as desktop or smartphone/iPad/tablet PC formats provide both video and audio cues, just as the Visual Assistant software does.

Given the potential for multimedia devices to present cues in multiple formats, the term *antecedent cue regulation* is preferable to *picture prompts* because many cues are not visually oriented. *Antecedent* means "occurring before," so antecedent cue regulation simply means giving visual or auditory cues before a task to help students regulate their own behavior.

Antecedent cue regulation has three benefits. First, it reduces your students' reliance on others to complete a task. Second, it supports those who cannot remember the steps or sequence in a multistep task. Third, it can be a temporary support, not a permanent one, and thus promote learning.

Self-Instruction Strategies

Self-instruction strategies involve teaching students to use their verbal or other communication skills to direct their learning. Like the antecedent cue regulation strategies, students use self-instructions as cues for what they need to do next to perform the task. Self-instruction strategies are often more flexible than antecedent cue regulation strategies are because students use something they have with them at all times: their means of communication (Wehmeyer et al., 2007). Several research-based templates for self-instruction exist, including the following (Wehmeyer et al., 2007):

- In traditional problem-solving self-instruction, students learn to verbally instruct themselves to identify the problem ("What do I do next in this task?"), identify a solution to the problem ("I place the silverware in the napkin."), evaluate the effectiveness of the solution ("Does this look right?"), and reinforce themselves ("Yes, that looks good!").

- In the task sequencing, or "did-next-now," strategy, students learn self-instruction statements related to the step they just completed ("I placed the silverware in the napkin."), the next step ("I need to roll the silverware in the napkin."), and when they will perform the next step ("I'll do the next step now.")

- In the "what-where" strategy, students learn statements about what they need to do ("I need to roll the silverware in the napkin.") and where they will do it ("I roll the silverware in the napkin at my workstation in the restaurant."), which helps them remember the context in which they engage in certain activities.

- In the interactive, or "did-next-ask," strategy, students learn self-instruction statements similar to the task-sequencing strategy but complete the statement by instructing themselves to ask someone about the next step or about some aspect of the task. It is helpful to teach this in conjunction with the task-sequencing strategy in case students forget the next step.

Self-Monitoring Strategies

One of the most effective student-directed learning strategies involves teaching students to monitor their own behavior or actions. Essentially, when using **self-monitoring strategies**, students learn to collect data on their progress toward educational goals. They can do this through traditional formats, such as charting their progress on a sheet of graph paper or completing a checklist. For students with multiple disabilities, however, there are simpler ways to monitor themselves. They can place a marble in a jar each time they complete a task successfully or move a poker chip from one container to another. Once they fill the jar or move all of the chips from the original box, they learn that they have completed their specific goals. And even when students are not entirely accurate, there are benefits to the use of self-monitoring. Wehmeyer and colleagues (2007) provide these suggestions for implementing self-monitoring strategies:

- Implement self-monitoring strategies after the student has already learned to do the task that is being monitored.

- Teach the self-monitoring strategy to the student before implementing the strategy.

- Build in checks to determine the accuracy of the student's self-monitoring.

Including Students with Multiple Disabilities

Leaders in the field of multiple disabilities have advocated for inclusive education (Downing, 2008; Jorgensen, McSheehan, & Sonnenmeier, 2010; Munk & Dempsey, 2010; Snell & Brown, 2011). The major professional organization in the field of multiple disabilities, TASH (formerly the Association for Persons with Severe Handicaps), has had a long-term commitment to inclusive education. Nevertheless, Figure 10.3 shows that most students with multiple disabilities still spend most of their time outside the regular classroom.

Advocacy alone does not ensure inclusion. Research into the application of evidence-based practices is also necessary. There is convincing evidence that students with multiple disabilities can be successfully included in the general education classroom as well as extracurricular and other school activities (Jackson, Ryndak, & Wehmeyer, 2010). This research has shown several consistent characteristics of successful inclusion for students with multiple disabilities:

- Collaborating among teachers and parents at classroom, building, and systems levels, as Sally's teachers, principal, and parents do

- Teaching new skills in general education classrooms

- Promoting friendships in inclusive settings, as Sally is doing in her general education classroom

- Facilitating positive outcomes for classmates without disabilities

- Adapting the students' curriculum, as Sally's teachers adapt the curriculum to her need for sleep, difficulty holding a pencil, and picture book

Box 10.6 offers tips for promoting inclusion.

FIGURE 10.3 *Educational placement of students with multiple disabilities: School year 2008–2009*

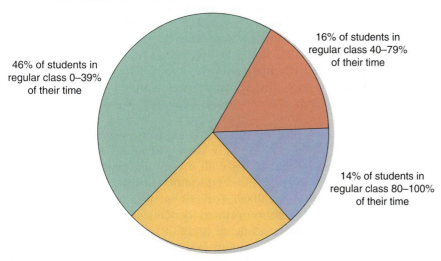

46% of students in regular class 0–39% of their time

16% of students in regular class 40–79% of their time

14% of students in regular class 80–100% of their time

24% in separate setting

Source: U.S. Department of Education. (2011). *Data accountability center: Individuals with Disabilities Education Act (IDEA) data.* Retrieved February 12, 2011, from https://www.ideadata.org.

Note: Percentages have been rounded and collapsed across categories.

BOX 10.6

INCLUSION TIPS

	What You Might See	What You Might Be Tempted to Do	Alternate Responses	Ways to Include Peers in the Process
Behavior	He has temper tantrums and hits himself or others.	Discipline and isolate him from the rest of the class.	Learn to identify cues that trigger positive behavior. Reward appropriate behavior.	Support the peers closest to him and teach them to recognize and give cues that encourage positive behavior in a way that is respectful of him.
Social interactions	She is unable to communicate needs or wants using words.	Allow her to remain a class observer rather than a participant.	Use assistive technology to enable her to communicate her needs and wants.	Teach peers to communicate with her using her assistive technology.
Educational performance	He is not able to read or write, and his functional skills are extremely limited.	Give up and let him color or do something quiet.	Create opportunities for him to benefit from peer tutoring.	Arrange for peers to assist him with task completion. Support them to be friends as well as peer tutors.
Classroom attitudes	She appears bored or unresponsive and often sleeps during class instruction.	Ignore her and focus on other, more attentive students.	Use times of alertness to teach self-instruction strategies to enable her to engage in more proactive learning.	Encourage peers to prompt her to use her preferred self-instruction strategies.

Given that educators know how to include students with severe disabilities, why do 46 percent of students spend less than 40 percent of their time in general education, and why do 24 percent of students spend their entire day in a separate school, residential setting, or at home or in the hospital? Jackson and colleagues (2010) identify several reasons. Particularly at the high school level, many teachers still believe that students with multiple disabilities cannot be appropriately served in general education classes or even in their neighborhood schools. Other teachers believe they are not prepared to teach those students. Unfortunately, many parents also believe that general educators are not well prepared for inclusion (Turnbull, Turnbull, Erwin, Soodak, & Shogren, 2011).

Yet there are effective practices that support students with multiple disabilities in the general education classroom, as we have discussed in this chapter. More research is emerging that documents that students with severe and multiple disabilities can be involved with and progress in the general education curriculum (Jackson et al., 2010; Lee, Soukup, Little, & Wehmeyer, 2009; Lee, Wehmeyer, Soukup, & Palmer, 2010). Finally, parents have reported that the primary benefit of inclusion is that their child has a greater chance to learn more academic and functional skills in general education classes because there are higher expectations in those classes than in special education classrooms (Turnbull et al., 2011).

Assessing Students' Progress

MEASURING STUDENTS' PROGRESS

Progress in the General Education Curriculum

Many students with multiple disabilities are unable to take typical paper-pencil assessments that measure their progress in core curriculum areas. Some cannot take these tests even with accommodations. Furthermore, curriculum-based measurement techniques that we discussed in Chapter 5 have not been validated with students with multiple disabilities. So how can you track students' progress in the general curriculum? You should use two strategies that resemble curriculum-based measurement techniques and that have been developed for students with multiple disabilities. We discussed one of them, data-based decision making, in Chapter 9. The second strategy is portfolio-based assessment (Kleinert & Kearns, 2010).

Portfolio-based assessment requires teachers to accumulate permanent products that exemplify the student's work. These products are indicators—evidence—of student performance, do not require continuous observation (as do the observational methodologies we discuss later), and allow for ongoing analysis **(formative analysis)** and comparisons between less and more mature products **(summative evaluation)** (Brown & Snell, 2011). Portfolios should include a range of products that reflect a student's progress, including the data-based and performance data discussed in Chapter 9; graphs of student progress; student, peer, and parent reflections; student products; and video or audiotapes of a student's work (Kleinert & Kearns, 2010).

Progress in Addressing Other Educational Needs

While student work in academic content areas often results in products, many areas of instruction, particularly those that fall outside the realm of core content areas, do not yield permanent products. For example, when assessing progress in learning communication skills, the only way to measure progress toward this goal is to observe a student's behavior and record data. You can also use observations to compile evidence of the student's involvement and progress in the general curriculum and in other school settings.

Observational methodologies are just what their names imply: ways of collecting data by watching or observing student behavior. You can carry out these observations by watching the student (live observation) or by watching videotapes of the student.

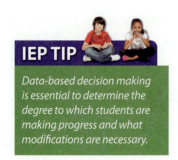

IEP TIP

Data-based decision making is essential to determine the degree to which students are making progress and what modifications are necessary.

Observational methods include field observations, time sampling, and event recording. **Field observations** involve simply observing and recording, in a quick anecdotal format, what the student is doing. Those anecdotal records are often the first step in collecting observational data because they identify the specific behaviors or events that warrant more systematic observation.

Time sampling and event recording enable teachers to collect samples of a student's behavior. It is almost impossible to observe across the entire school day, so these two strategies are especially useful.

When **time sampling**, an observer, such as yourself, records the occurrence or nonoccurrence of specific behaviors during short, predetermined intervals. For example, if you want to know whether a particular intervention increases communication skills, you may set up three ten-minute observation times daily, selected randomly or according to the periods when the behavior is most likely to occur. During the observation, the teacher has a list of behaviors in which the student might be engaged, including the communication skill. During each ten-minute observation period, you observe for twenty seconds and then spend ten seconds checking off on the list the behaviors that occurred at any time during the twenty-second period. The entire ten-minute session yields data for twenty unique twenty-second observation intervals. You count the frequency of the intervals in which the communication skill occurred and then tally those frequencies across time as more ten-minute observations occur. By contrast, when you use **event recording**, you record every occurrence of a behavior during an observation period instead of using the yes/no recording per interval that is characteristic of time sampling.

Now consider the types of data collected through observational methods. Frequency counts involve literal counts of the number of times a behavior occurred or the number of intervals in which a behavior occurred. Frequency counts of intervals can be converted to percentage data by dividing the number of intervals in which a behavior occurred by the total number of intervals observed. With event recording, frequency counts cannot be converted to percentage data, but they can be converted to rate data—an average of the frequency over a specific period of time.

Another measure involves collecting duration data. This method requires you to use a stopwatch or timer to record the length of a behavioral event. Still another measure involves collecting latency data, the time that lapses from one point to another—typically, the lapsed time between a direction or an instruction and the student's response.

Most teachers who rely on observational methods collect data using all or most of these methods. They do so because collecting observational data is inexpensive and provides detailed information about students' performance.

MAKING ACCOMMODATIONS FOR ASSESSMENT

Many students with disabilities receive accommodations in assessments and testing. Many students with multiple disabilities, however, will not be able to take state accountability assessments, even with accommodations. In Chapter 2, you learned that IDEA allows states to create alternate assessments for use with students with the most significant cognitive disabilities or other students who are identified by IEP teams as unable to take the regular assessment, even with accommodations.

Alternate assessments must be aligned with the state's academic content standards. They serve the same purpose as the typical accountability assessment—namely, to determine how well a student has mastered content that is aligned with standards. Increasingly, alternate assessments are being aligned with alternate achievement standards. Researchers at the National Center on Educational Outcomes (http://www.cehd.umn.edu/NCEO) have identified several formats for alternative assessments (Snell & Brown, 2011):

- *IEP-linked body of evidence*. You collect student products, similar to portfolio assessment, but link them to IEP goals and objectives.
- *Performance assessment*. You use the data collection procedures described in Chapter 9.

- *Checklist.* You identify a student's skills and abilities on a checklist.
- *Portfolio-based alternate assessment.* You rely on samples of student products that are related to a state's standards. You score these portfolios by relying on rubrics for determining the quality and quantity of a student's performance and the students independence in showing how he or she has acquired academic skills that are linked to the state's standards.

Alternate assessment also relies on scoring criteria. When scoring a portfolio, you must have examples of high-quality work so that you will be able to distinguish high-quality from poor-quality portfolios. Many states are still struggling with developing alternate assessments that are comparable with other state accountability procedures, but it is clear that this is the goal under federal law.

ADDRESSING THE PROFESSIONAL STANDARDS

The following Council for Exceptional Children (CEC) Common Core Knowledge and Skills are addressed in this chapter through the content and concepts we discuss. See the Appendix for a full listing of these Knowledge and Skill statements:

ICC2K1, ICC2K2, ICC2K4, ICC2K5, ICC2K6, ICC4S1, ICC4S2, ICC4S3, ICC4S4, ICC4S5, ICC4S6, ICC5S2, ICC5S3, ICC5S4, ICC5S9, ICC5S12, ICC5S15, ICC6K4, ICC6S1, ICC7K5, ICC7S1, ICC7S3, ICC7S6, ICC7S7, ICC7S9, ICC8K3, ICC8S2, ICC8S6, ICC8S8, ICC10S2, ICC10S3, ICC10S4, ICC10S5

Summary

IDENTIFYING STUDENTS WITH MULTIPLE DISABILITIES

- The term *multiple disabilities* defines a diverse group of people whose common characteristic is the severity of their educational needs.
- Students with multiple disabilities have impairments in intellectual functioning, adaptive skills, motor development, sensory functioning, and communication skills.
- The primary causes are tied to biological considerations, particularly genetic ones occurring during prenatal development.
- Fewer than one half of 1 percent of all students ages six through twenty-one with disabilities have multiple disabilities.

EVALUATING STUDENTS WITH MULTIPLE DISABILITIES

- Physicians use screening tests such as the Apgar to determine whether a newborn might have a disability.

- The evaluation process usually begins right after birth and may continue throughout a student's school career.
- The SETT framework provides an outline of questions helpful in conducting evaluations for appropriate assistive technology.

DESIGNING AN APPROPRIATE IEP

- Person-centered planning procedures, such as the MAPs process, are effective tools for planning services and supports for students with multiple disabilities.
- Peer tutoring has been used successfully to improve students' achievement.
- New and emerging technologies such as Visual Assistant offer greater access to universally designed learning.
- Many students require AAC systems. The IEP team must identify the device and establish instructional goals related to language use and communication skills.

USING EFFECTIVE INSTRUCTIONAL STRATEGIES

- Access to the general education curriculum for preschool students with multiple disabilities is possible when teachers ensure inclusion and infuse content information into the typical preschool social environment.
- Partial participation enables students with multiple disabilities to participate to the maximum extent possible in school, home, and community environments.
- Student-directed learning strategies such as antecedent cue regulation, self-instruction, and self-monitoring are research-based ways to teach students to self-regulate learning; they contribute to enhanced inclusion, generalization, and student empowerment.

INCLUDING STUDENTS WITH MULTIPLE DISABILITIES

- Almost half of all students with multiple disabilities spend the majority of their day outside general education, and 24 percent spend their day in separate settings.

- Students with multiple disabilities can learn new skills, be involved and make progress in general education classrooms, and experience meaningful friendships.
- Preparing general educators to work with all students is a critical step in promoting inclusive practices.

ASSESSING STUDENTS' PROGRESS

- Using portfolios to assess the progress of students with multiple disabilities involves collecting examples of permanent products for students.
- Observational methodologies such as field observations, time sampling, and event recording enable teachers to collect data on behavioral frequency, percentage, rate, duration, and latency.
- Students who cannot take the state's general assessment even with modifications can still be involved in accountability decisions through alternate assessment procedures such as portfolios, performance assessments, IEP-linked content data, and checklist data.

MyEducationLab

Go to Topic #17: Multiple Disabilities and Traumatic Brain Injury in the MyEducationLab (www.myeducationlab.com) for *Exceptional Lives*, where you can do the following:

- Find learning outcomes for Multiple Disabilities and Traumatic Brain Injury along with the national standards that connect to these outcomes.

- Complete assignments and activities that will help you more deeply understand the chapter content.

- Apply and practice your understanding of the core teaching skills identified in the chapter with the Building Teaching Skills and Dispositions learning units.

- Examine challenging situations and cases presented in the IRIS Center Resources.

- Access video clips of CCSSO National Teachers of the Year award winners responding to the question, "Why Do I Teach?" in the Teacher Talk section.

- Check your comprehension on the content covered in the chapter with the Study Plan. Here you will be able to take a chapter quiz, receive feedback on your answers, and then access review, practice, and enrichment activities to enhance your understanding of chapter content.

- Use the Online Lesson Plan Builder to practice lesson planning and integrating national and state standards into your planning.

11 Understanding Students *with* Autism

Who Is Shawn Jackson?

There have been two kinds of hurricanes in nine-year-old Shawn Jackson's life. One has always been part of his life. It is called autism. The other came and went, but its effects, both immediate and longer-term, were devastating to Shawn. It was called Katrina.

Shawn's mother, Donnica, first suspected that Shawn was different than other young boys when he was three years old. At home, he would try to hide in the refrigerator or use bookcases, tables, or beds as platforms for his leaps into space. Flour and sugar fascinated him; opening a bag and playing with its ingredients pleased him to no end. He was drawn to gadgets of all kinds—computers, TV sets, Nintendo controls. He was more than a mischievous boy.

He would not speak words; gibberish and babble were his means of communication. Trips to Target or Wal-Mart triggered tantrums, screaming, and global meltdowns. Donnica's family was puzzled. Wasn't she raising him properly? To which she had to respond, politely: "You can't discipline autism out of a boy."

When Shawn was four, Donnica—a single parent trying to break into journalism after having graduated from Southern University in New Orleans—took him to Charity Hospital, seeking answers to her question: Why is my son the way he is? The evaluation results were conclusive. Shawn acquired a label: autism. And Donnica acquired a mission: to make sure that Shawn would have an effective education so that he would one day be a productive adult.

When Shawn entered school at age six, Donnica expected results. "I didn't send him to school to be baby-sat." Results, however, were not forthcoming, at least not in his first several years. Shawn's language did not improve, and his behaviors deteriorated. He would hit himself and other students to get attention or to express his frustration about not being able to communicate what he wanted.

And then came Katrina in September 2006. Like thousands of others, Donnica and Shawn escaped to Houston. Shawn went to school there for a year but without benefit. Indeed, his ability to read, which had first become evident in the year before Katrina hit,

vanished. His placement in the Houston schools was comparable to his placement in the New Orleans schools: a segregated classroom for students with autism and other disabilities. The word *bleak* hardly describes any hope for Shawn's future when he returned to New Orleans and the state-operated school system.

However, after a year in fourth grade Shawn began to prosper. Under the guidance of skilled educators, *bright* replaced *bleak*. Richard Hubbard, a special educator, and Edna Crawford, a paraeducator, collaborated with two general educators, Geraldine Myers (reading and social studies) and Rochella Mitchell (math and science). They were aided by related service providers: Kirk Ealing, a speech-language trainer, and Miss Maxwell, an occupational therapist.

Did this team of six experts convert Shawn's dismal prospects into opti-

mistic ones? Yes, but they didn't do it alone. The decision of the school leaders to use schoolwide positive behavior support and the omnipresence of Shawn's mother in all decision making contributed greatly to his progress. And so did his classmates, those with and those without disabilities.

Identifying Students with Autism

DEFINING AUTISM

Autism is a developmental disability that significantly affects a student's verbal and non-verbal communication, social interaction, and educational performance and often manifests in children by the age of three (Lord, 2010). Children with autism often engage in repetitive activities and stereotyped movements, resist environmental change or changes in daily routines, and display unusual responses to sensory experiences.

Autism is a severe form of a broader group of disorders referred to as **pervasive developmental disorders** (Ozonoff, 2010; Wolf & Paterson, 2010). The Diagnostic and Statistical Manual of Mental Disorders (DSM-IV-TR) includes, as part of pervasive development disorders, five discrete conditions that have their onset in childhood (American Psychiatric Association, 2000): autistic disorder, Rett's disorder, childhood disintegrative disorder, Asperger's disorder, and pervasive developmental disorder not otherwise specified. Educators often use the term **autism spectrum disorder** when referring to some or all of these disorders.

In this chapter we will concentrate on the condition known as *autistic disorder,* or simply *autism,* because it has the highest prevalence of the five discrete conditions. Shawn is typical of students with autism. In fall 2008, approximately 5 percent (292,818) of all students ages six through twenty-one served by IDEA were classified as having autism (U.S. Department of Education, 2011).

Recent prevalence figures report that one out of 70 boys and one out of 315 girls are identified as having autism spectrum disorders, with an overall rate of one in 110 children (Autism and Developmental Disabilities Monitoring Network, 2007). A review of sixty-one studies worldwide related to prevalence reported that prevalence rates have increased in most countries and are likely largely due to changes in definition, public understanding, availability of services, enactment of new policies, and the way in which research studies have been designed (Saracino, Noseworthy, Steiman, Reisinger, & Fombonne, 2010). The review's authors concluded that the increase may not just be associated with circumstantial factors but may also represent a substantiated increase in the incidence of autism spectrum disorders. Unlike students with many other types of disabilities, students who are African American, Latino, or another race/ethnicity are less likely than European American children to be diagnosed with an autism spectrum disorder (Mandell et al., 2009).

Another autism spectrum disorder is **Asperger syndrome**. The term describes individuals who have significant challenges in social functioning but do not have significant delays in language development or intellectual functioning (Bade-White, Obrzut, & Randall, 2009). The prevalence rate for Asperger syndrome is far less than for autism. Although prevalence studies of Asperger syndrome are reported to be imprecise, experts estimate that the ratio of individuals with autism to individuals with Asperger syndrome is about three or four to one (Fombonne, 2009).

DESCRIBING THE CHARACTERISTICS

The six distinct characteristics of autism are (1) atypical language development, (2) atypical social development, (3) repetitive behavior, (4) problem behavior, (5) sensory and movement disorders, and (6) differences in intellectual functioning.

Atypical Language Development

Students with autism have a broad range of language abilities, ranging from no verbal communication to quite complex communication (Llaneza et al., 2010). Approximately one third to one half of students with autism do not develop sufficient communication through natural speech to meet environmental expectations (Noens, Berckelaer-Onnes, Verpoorten, & VanDuijn, 2006). Approximately one quarter of individuals with autism are nonverbal (Tager-Flusberg, Paul, & Lord, 2005).

Communication of children with autism is often characterized by the following attributes (Eigsti, de Marchena, Schuh, & Kelley, 2011; Llaneza et al., 2010):

- Interrupting when others are communicating and experiencing difficulty in knowing when it is appropriate to speak
- Focusing attention on one topic only
- Limiting a communication topic to fewer than a couple of interactions
- Reversing pronouns (e.g., the student may look at his teacher and say, "You want have a snack now," meaning that he, not the teacher, wants a snack)
- Repeating or echoing other people's language **(echolalia)**

Shawn's language development is typical of many young students with autism. He can form sentences to make himself understood: "Momma, I want more chicken wings," and "Get dressed to go to the store," are examples of Shawn's ability to use words and grammar correctly to express what he wants. But Shawn is "lazy," says Donnica, and will resort to gestures, babble, and gibberish to communicate. His speech-language interventionist, Kirk Ealing, takes him aside for individual therapy and advises his teachers about how to challenge him to speak in full sentences.

Of course, Donnica won't put up with gibberish; she commands, "Speak in words, Shawn." Together, his teachers, related service providers, and mother are helping him generalize his ability to speak. The problem comes, says Donnica, with Shawn's peers. "They like him so much they let him get away with being lazy. I've got to work on them and so do his teachers." Generalizing skills means getting everyone—even a student's peers—to use the same approach all the time and in all places.

Atypical Social Development

Another hallmark of autism is atypical social development: delays in social interaction and social skills (McConnell, 2002; National Research Council, 2001; Thompson, 2007, 2008). The American Psychiatric Association (2000) has four criteria for diagnosing atypical social development in individuals with autism:

- Impaired use of nonverbal behavior
- Lack of peer relationships
- Failure to spontaneously share enjoyment, interests, and achievements with others
- Lack of reciprocity

One explanation for delayed social development is **theory of mind**. Individuals with autism do not understand that their own beliefs, desires, and intentions may differ from those of others (Colle, Baron-Cohen, & Hill, 2007; Sodian & Kristen, 2010; Williams, 2010). They have difficulty comprehending others' feelings, preferences, and emotions even when other people directly say what their feelings are, and they often do not infer and intuit others' social cues and nonverbal signals. Students with autism also have difficulty empathizing with others' feelings and emotions (Baron-Cohen, 2009).

Students with Asperger syndrome often have difficulty making friends, interpreting social signals, understanding unwritten rules, responding to questions and tasks without prompts, being relaxed in social situations, and being aware of their social challenges (Cederlund, Hagberg, & Gillberg, 2009; Kaland, Mortensen, & Smith, 2011; Lee & Park, 2007). A strengths-based approach builds on students' special interests (which are often topics around which students have intense interests) to motivate them to make social connections and converse with their peers (Winter-Messiers et al., 2007). An intervention with students with Asperger syndrome reveals that, when they had conversations about their special interests, their "global organization abilities—physical, intellectual, oral, and social—came almost immediately into sharper focus and showed improvement for the duration of the . . . discussions" (Winter-Messiers et al., 2007, p. 73).

An insightful view of the social development of individuals with autism is provided through a number of autobiographies that have been written by adults with autism. An analysis of these autobiographies reveals a strong desire to interact socially with peers but

IEP TIP

Because students with autism are challenged socially, you and your IEP team colleagues should make sure that a student's IEP includes goals for social development, not just academic goals.

Time-out removes this student from the much-needed opportunities to learn. Rather than putting him into time-out, teachers should use positive behavioral supports and the other strategies we describe in this chapter.

significant confusion about appropriate social behavior (Causton-Theoharis, Ashby, & Cosier, 2009). These first-person accounts emphasize the critical importance of providing supports and instruction for students with autism to be more confident and competent in social interactions as the basis for developing a sense of belonging within their classrooms and schools.

Shawn has been slow to develop socially. As a younger child, he was aggressive to other students. Donnica thinks he was that way because he wanted attention, not because he was angry at them. Because he has acquired language, and because he is (in his mother's words) "a ladies' man," a charmer, he has learned not to be aggressive but to be affectionate—sometimes, however, giving too many hugs to those who may want simply a high five.

He also has learned about himself. Because he cannot communicate as well as his classmates, he senses, Donnica says, that he is different. Yet with her and his teachers' support, he is learning how to make friends, to "read" them. The proof of that is his circle of support from his classmates, which includes boys and girls alike, with and without disabilities. This year, he received his very first invitation to another student's birthday party.

Repetitive Behavior

Repetitive behavior involves repeated movements and verbalizations. These include hand and finger mannerisms or motor movements (e.g., hand flapping), repeating the same phrase over and over, persistent attention to parts of objects (e.g., the movable bolt in a door's deadbolt lock), and strict adherence to routines (Kim & Lord, 2010). Repetitive behaviors also include an insistence on sameness (Richler, Huerta, Bishop, & Lord, 2010). Students often use their repetitive behaviors as ways to communicate boredom and agitation and/or to regulate their levels of awareness (Carr et al., 1994). Obviously, these behaviors can interfere with their ability to learn and be included in typical school, work, and community settings. Simply decreasing students' repetitive behaviors, however, is not sufficient; increasing their appropriate communication and social skills and leisure activities is the state-of-the-art approach (Bellini, Peters, Benner, & Hopf, 2007).

Predictability and structure provide security to many individuals with autism (Freeman, Paparella, & Stickles, 2009; Thompson, 2008). When their predictability and structure are interrupted by events such as school vacations, overnight stays with friends or extended family, holiday celebrations, changes in television schedules, or movement from one classroom to another, students can become highly anxious. In addition, having things in their usual place means a great deal to some students. Most of us do not think much about whether the telephone is straight on the desk, whether the cosmetics are always in the same place on the bathroom counter, or whether a door is open or closed. However, disruptions in these seemingly insignificant environmental patterns disturb many students and impede their ability to learn.

Shawn prizes his routines, and Donnica has learned to accommodate them. Upon arriving home from school, Shawn changes his clothes; shorts and t-shirts replace the school garb. He turns on nearly every electronic device in the house. TV, Nintendo, computer, and radio: All must be on, at high volume, all the time. Eschewing his former favorite channel, the Spanish-language one, Shawn locks onto the Shopping Channel. Using his computer, he downloads and watches the same three movies, over and over again.

When bedtime comes, he puts everything in order throughout the rest of the house but leaves his school clothes scattered around his bedroom and insists on having a bottle of water near his bed. Having established some dominion over his environment and expressed his preferences, Shawn is ready to sleep.

Problem Behavior

IDEA requires educators to consider using positive behavior support (which we discuss later in this chapter) when students engage in behavior that impedes their or other students' learning. Students with autism may exhibit any of four categories of problem behavior: self-injurious behavior, aggression, tantrums, and property destruction. We will focus on the first two.

Self-Injurious Behavior. Some individuals engage in self-injurious behavior, such as head banging, biting, or scratching. Males are more likely than females to display self-injurious behavior. First symptoms often occur during the preschool years and can manifest through daily self-biting or chewing directed toward the hand or arm (Symons, Byiers, Raspa, Bishop, & Bailey, 2010). These behaviors often persist into adulthood. Individuals with severe self-injurious behaviors may permanently injure themselves; sometimes (but fortunately for relatively few people) self-injurious behaviors are life-threatening. One of those life-threatening behaviors is called *pica:* eating inedible items.

Aggression. Aggressive behaviors are similar to self-injurious behaviors, but the behavior is directed toward others. The most common types of aggression include hitting, biting, kicking, pinching, and scratching (Brosnan & Healy, 2011). Behavioral interventions have been highly successful in decreasing and eliminating aggression. By using positive behavior support, teachers enable students to learn a wider repertoire of appropriate behaviors. Once students learn appropriate alternative behaviors, they often stop using aggressive behaviors.

Problem behavior typically serves a communicative function, enabling students to obtain something positive, avoid or escape something unpleasant, and/or increase or decrease sensory stimulation (Dunlap & Carr, 2007; Matson et al., 2010). Given the functions that problem behavior serves, you will want to teach your students other ways to communicate (Carr, 2007; Fossett & Mirenda, 2007).

As you have already read, Shawn has had serious problem behavior: aggression toward other students and some self-injurious behavior, primarily hitting his sides with his hands and elbows. But as you also know, those behaviors have dissipated as a result of speech-language training and positive behavioral supports at school and at home.

Sensory and Movement Disorders

Children and youth with autism frequently experience sensory disorders related to food selectivity, sleep problems, toe walking, taste/smell, tactile sensitivity, and/or visual/auditory sensitivity (Klintwall et al., 2010; Wiggins, Robins, Bakeman, & Adamson, 2009). Some have under- or overresponsiveness to sensory stimuli, although more have overresponsiveness.

Movement disorders also are an element of autism (Staples & Reid, 2010). Examples include abnormal posture; abnormal movements of the face, head, trunk, and limbs; abnormal eye movements; repeated gestures and mannerisms; and awkward gait (Donnellan, Hill, & Leary, 2010). Motor clumsiness and disorders are present in the majority of individuals who have Asperger syndrome (Lee & Park, 2007).

Differences in Intellectual Functioning

Autism occurs in children with all levels of intelligence, ranging from students who are gifted to students classified as having intellectual disability. Approximately 75 percent of children and youth with autism have an intellectual disability (Fombonne, 2005; Klinger, O'Kelley, & Mussey, 2009). The strongest predictor of the severity of autism symptoms is IQ (Mayes & Calhoun, 2010). This means that autism symptoms are more severe when individuals have lower IQs. Although Shawn's primary diagnosis is autism, he, like many students with that classification, has an intellectual disability. As much as he loves to read, he is two years below grade level. Poor education before Katrina and then the enforced removal to Houston explain why he is at that level when, earlier, he had been only one grade level below. That is about the right level, Donnica and his teachers think, and that's their goal: to improve Shawn's reading and thereby his intellectual capacities to levels closer to those of his age-peers.

IEP TIP

Under IDEA, a student's IEP team must consider using positive behavior intervention and support if the student's behavior impedes his or her or others' learning. The question is "Why not use positive behavior intervention as a means to prevent impeding behavior?" The answer is "Always use the intervention."

Individuals with Asperger syndrome, however, tend to have higher intellectual functioning than do individuals with other types of autism. Their IQ scores tend to fall in the average range and to reveal a frequency distribution similar to that of the general population (Bade-White et al., 2009).

Some people with autism also display the unusual **savant syndrome**, which consists of extraordinary talents in areas such as calendar calculating, musical ability, mathematical skills, memorization, and mechanical abilities. For example, a student with savant syndrome may be able to recite the baseball game scores and the batting averages of all players who ever participated in the major leagues or have a calendar range of 6,000 years in being able to describe weather and to answer questions such as "What date was the second Sunday in October in 1947?" The same students who can answer these questions may not be able to add or subtract. Currently, an analysis of research on students with savant skills is serving as the basis for studying various forms of giftedness and the neuroscience of giftedness (Wallace, 2008). But a student's unusual ability in these areas occurs in conjunction with low ability in most other areas.

DETERMINING THE CAUSES

Historical Perspective on Causes

When autism was first diagnosed and described in the early 1940s, parents of children with autism were often regarded as intelligent people of high socioeconomic status who were also "cold." At that time, incredibly, some professionals referred to mothers of children with autism as "refrigerator mothers" (Bettleheim, 1967).

By the 1970s, however, researchers had established that autism is caused by brain or biochemical dysfunction that occurs before, during, or after birth and that it is totally unwarranted to blame parents. In 1977 the National Society for Autistic Children (now known as the Autism Society of America) asserted, "No known factors in the psychological environment of a child have been shown to cause autism." Today parents are not seen as the cause of problems; they are seen as partners with educators, contributing to solving their children's problems.

Biomedical Causes

Significant progress has been made in understanding the cause of autism. However, scientists have not yet been able to pinpoint the definitive cause (Schroeder, Desrocher, Bebko, & Cappadocia, 2010). It has been established that autism is primarily biological in origin and that multiple biological factors are implicated, including genes, brain structure, and neural pathways.

With respect to genetic causation, identical twins have an 82 to 92 percent chance of both having autism, whereas nonidentical twins have a 1 to 10 percent chance (Freitag, 2007). Genetic research has established that the cause of autism is not limited to one specific gene. At least ten genes are currently suspected as possibly contributing to autism (Toro et al., 2010). Current genetic studies have identified a breakdown in the early production of protein that is necessary for typical brain growth and maturation.

With respect to brain growth, the brains of children with autism grow at an accelerated rate during the first few years of life. A recent longitudinal study of brain growth in toddlers reported that toddlers with autism have brain overgrowth by 2½ years of age and that females with autism have more overgrowth than males (Schumann et al., 2010). The primary regions of the brain that contribute to overgrowth continue to grow at an accelerated rate throughout early childhood. It is important to recognize, however, that brain overgrowth occurs more frequently in children with autism as compared to children without this diagnosis but that overgrowth does not occur for all children with autism.

In addition to the structural difference in brains in terms of overgrowth, left and right hemispheres of the brains of people with autism often do not communicate in proper ways (Anderson et al., 2010). This lack of communication is associated with key areas of the brain related to facial recognition, social functioning, and motor skills. To study this issue, Anderson and colleagues (2010) used MRI as their diagnostic tool for identifying

IEP TIP

You almost always will destroy any partnership you have with a child's parents if you accuse them, in an IEP meeting or at another time or occasion, of causing their child's autism. The view that parents cause autism is an erroneous perspective.

brain dysfunction, which underscores the potential benefit of using MRI as an early, objective, and quick diagnostic tool.

Aside from biological factors, environmental contributions to autism include toxic exposure to chemicals (e.g., lead, methylmercury, arsenic) and exposure in early pregnancy to thalidomide, valproic acid, and prenatal rubella infection (Landrigan, 2010). Although there has been much publicity on the possible link between childhood immunization and autism, studies conducted in the United States, the United Kingdom, Europe, and Japan have consistently found no credible evidence of this link (Landrigan, 2010). It is important to promote this scientific finding, given that some parents refuse to immunize their children against deadly diseases because they fear that immunizations will cause autism.

Overall, research on the causes of autism is one of the most heavily funded areas across the entire disability field. Although the prevalence of autism is increasing, researchers are optimistic that the scientific commitment to discovering the cause of autism is also on an upward trajectory.

Evaluating Students with Autism

DETERMINING THE PRESENCE OF AUTISM

Many children receive the initial diagnosis of autism from an interdisciplinary evaluation team, typically during their early childhood years (Shea & Mesibov, 2009). Shawn was evaluated when he was four years old. Evaluators usually administer some of the same tests given to students with intellectual disability and students with severe and multiple disabilities (Goldstein, Naglieri, & Ozonoff, 2009). Box 11.1 highlights the standard techniques used for observations, screening, and nondiscriminatory evaluation.

Various diagnostic tools can detect the presence of autism (Risi et al., 2006). A medical diagnosis of autism requires that a physician or a psychologist administer the evaluation according to the criteria of the DSM-IV-TR. One of the common tests is the Autism Diagnostic Interview— Revised (Rutter, Le Couteur, & Lord, 2003). It consists of three domains: Language/ Communication; Reciprocal Social Interactions; and Restricted, Repetitive, and Stereotyped Behaviors and Interests. Only specially trained professionals administer and score the interview because scoring is based on clinical judgment regarding the caregiver's description of the child's development and behavior. The interview consists of ninety-three questions and takes about 1½ to 2½ hours to complete. The professional conducting the interview

The Autism Diagnostic Interview—Revised is a semistructured interview consisting of 93 items. It is administered by a professional to caregivers of children and adults who might have autism.

BOX 11.1

NONDISCRIMINATORY EVALUATION PROCESS

Determining the Presence of Autism

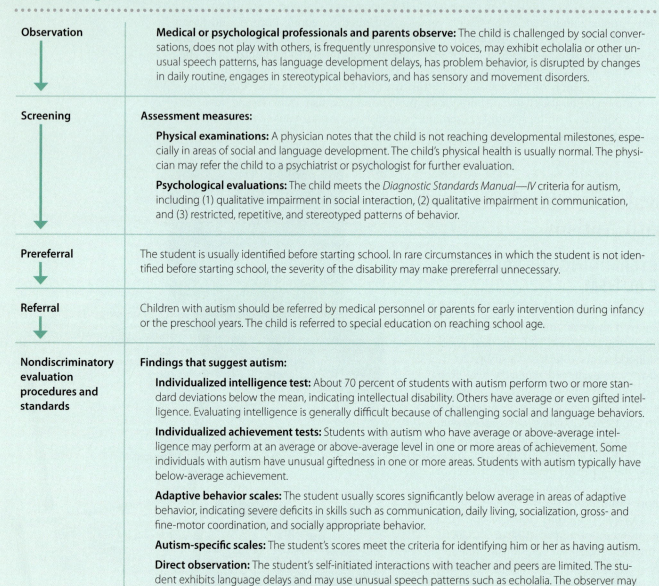

Observation ↓	**Medical or psychological professionals and parents observe:** The child is challenged by social conversations, does not play with others, is frequently unresponsive to voices, may exhibit echolalia or other unusual speech patterns, has language development delays, has problem behavior, is disrupted by changes in daily routine, engages in stereotypical behaviors, and has sensory and movement disorders.
Screening ↓	**Assessment measures:** **Physical examinations:** A physician notes that the child is not reaching developmental milestones, especially in areas of social and language development. The child's physical health is usually normal. The physician may refer the child to a psychiatrist or psychologist for further evaluation. **Psychological evaluations:** The child meets the *Diagnostic Standards Manual—IV* criteria for autism, including (1) qualitative impairment in social interaction, (2) qualitative impairment in communication, and (3) restricted, repetitive, and stereotyped patterns of behavior.
Prereferral ↓	The student is usually identified before starting school. In rare circumstances in which the student is not identified before starting school, the severity of the disability may make prereferral unnecessary.
Referral ↓	Children with autism should be referred by medical personnel or parents for early intervention during infancy or the preschool years. The child is referred to special education on reaching school age.
Nondiscriminatory evaluation procedures and standards	**Findings that suggest autism:** **Individualized intelligence test:** About 70 percent of students with autism perform two or more standard deviations below the mean, indicating intellectual disability. Others have average or even gifted intelligence. Evaluating intelligence is generally difficult because of challenging social and language behaviors. **Individualized achievement tests:** Students with autism who have average or above-average intelligence may perform at an average or above-average level in one or more areas of achievement. Some individuals with autism have unusual giftedness in one or more areas. Students with autism typically have below-average achievement. **Adaptive behavior scales:** The student usually scores significantly below average in areas of adaptive behavior, indicating severe deficits in skills such as communication, daily living, socialization, gross- and fine-motor coordination, and socially appropriate behavior. **Autism-specific scales:** The student's scores meet the criteria for identifying him or her as having autism. **Direct observation:** The student's self-initiated interactions with teacher and peers are limited. The student exhibits language delays and may use unusual speech patterns such as echolalia. The observer may notice that the student has difficulty with changes in routines and manifests stereotypical behaviors. **Anecdotal records:** Records suggest that performance varies according to moods, energy level, extent and pile-up of environmental changes, and whether or not individual preferences are incorporated.

calculates summary scores for each domain and compares scores to a cutoff metric that then determines the presence of autism spectrum disorder (as contrasted to a discreet focus on autism). The reliability and validity of this tool has been carefully established (Naglieri & Chambers, 2009).

DETERMINING THE NATURE OF SPECIALLY DESIGNED INSTRUCTION AND SERVICES

As you have already read, some students with autism have problem behaviors. To reduce or eliminate those behaviors, teachers and other professionals often use positive behavior

BOX 11.2 **INTO PRACTICE**

Functional Behavioral Assessment

A functional behavioral assessment (FBA) is a systematic process for gathering information that helps teachers and related service providers determine why a student engages in problem behaviors and how teachers can influence events and circumstances to change these behaviors. As we've discussed, there are a few basic steps teachers can use to conduct an FBA. Shawn's school-based team used these steps to create this functional behavioral assessment and the behavior intervention plan that follows the assessment. This plan is incorporated into his IEP and will allow him to interact with his peers and teachers in the general education classroom in more socially acceptable ways.

FUNCTIONAL BEHAVIORAL ASSESSMENT (FBA)

Student: *Shawn Jackson*   **Grade:** *4*   **School:** *John Dibert*   **Date:** *November 19, 2012*
FBA/BIP developed for: Programming purposes   **IEP requirement**   **Participants:** _____

In your own words, describe the behavior that prompted this FBA	**ANTECEDENTS**	**CONSEQUENCES**
	Ask yourself: What is likely to set off (precede) the problem behavior? *Directions to academic work.*	Ask yourself: What payoff does the student obtain when she/he demonstrates the problem behavior?
	WHEN is the problem behavior most likely to occur?	The student GAINS:

Issues with off-task behavior; e.g.	Morning Approximate times(s)✔
	Afternoon Approximate times(s)✔
	Before/after Lunch/recess
	  school
		✔ Teacher/adult attention
		  Peer attention
		  Desired item or activity
		✔ Control over others or the situation

	WHERE
	✔Reg. Ed Classroom Hallway
	  Spec. Ed Classroom Cafeteria
		The student AVOIDS or ESCAPES:
		✔ Teacher/adult interaction
		  Peer interaction
		✔ Nonpreferred activity, task, or setting
		  A difficult task or frustrating situation

	During what SUBJECT/ACTIVITY is the problem behavior most likely to occur?	
PROBLEM BEHAVIOR	Subject(s) *R/LA, Soc. stud. & Science*	What has been tried thus far to change the problem behavior?

If the above explanation addresses multiple behaviors, identify the ONE BEHAVIOR to be targeted for intervention.	✔ Seatwork Classmates
	  Group Activities Other
	  Lesson Presentation peers
		Implemented rules and consequences for behavior as posted
		Implemented behavior or academic contract

Avoiding an unpreferred activity by resting head on desk and covering ears.	Are there OTHER EVENTS or CONDITIONS that immediately precede the problem behavior:
	✔ A demand or request
	  Unexpected changes in schedule or routine
	  Consequences imposed for behavior
	  Comments/teasing from other students
		Implemented home/school communication system
		Adapted curriculum. How? *Picture symbols, one on one.*

The behavior I have targeted for intervention is: ✔ ✔ OBSERVABLE MEASURABLE		Modified instruction. How? *Smaller lessons*
	When is the student most successful? When DOESN'T the problem behavior occur? *When performing an academic task he enjoys.*	Adjusted schedule. How? Conferenced with parents: Dates: Sent to office: Dates:

(continued)

support. Before offering that support, they conduct a functional behavioral assessment of the student. A **functional behavioral assessment (FBA)** identifies specific relationships between a student's behaviors and the circumstances that trigger those behaviors, especially those that impede the student's or others' ability to learn (Furniss, 2009; Love, Carr, & LeBlanc, 2009; Scott, Alter, & McQuillan, 2010). Although a functional behavioral assessment is helpful for many students who do not have autism, it is particularly apt for students with autism. Box 11.2, Into Practice, includes a functional behavioral assessment of a fourth-grade student with autism.

BOX 11.2 **INTO PRACTICE (continued)**

Functional Behavioral Assessment

FUNCTION OF PROBLEM BEHAVIOR Ask yourself: Why is the student behaving this way? What function/need is being met by the student's behavior? Complete the following preliminary analysis by summarizing information from the three columns on part one of the **FUNCTIONAL BEHAVIORAL ASSESSMENT**. When: *Teacher has asked Shawn to perform academic work he cannot do.* (summarize antecedents) This student *will at times lower head onto desk & cover ears.* (identify the problem behavior) In order to *avoid doing work he cannot perform (temporarily).* (summarize payoff)	**REPLACEMENT BEHAVIOR** Ask yourself: What alternative behavior would meet the same function/need for the student? Complete the following: Rather than: *Tuning out, lowering head, covering ears.* (identify the problem behavior) I want this student to: *Attempt to perform his academics or explain to teacher that work is too difficult for him.* (Note: This replacement behavior should represent an IEP goal) This definition is: OBSERVABLE MEASURABLE
EXAMPLES: 1. When in the halls before school, after school, and during transitions, this student pushes other students and verbally threatens to beat them up in order to gain status and attention from peers. 2. When working on independent seatwork during his regular education math class, this student puts his head on his desk in order to escape work that is too difficult/frustrating.	**EXAMPLES:** 1. Rather than pushing students and threatening to beat them up, I want this student to walk in the halls with his hands to his side and say "hello" to those with whom he wishes to interact. 2. Rather than putting his head on his desk because he doesn't know how to do the problem, I want this student to raise his hand for help and move onto the next problem while waiting for my assistance.

Behavior Intervention Plan

Name: *Shawn Jackson*
Date of Implementation: *11/19/12*
Behavior:
Avoidance of work
Challenging academics
Preventative Measures:
Determine Shawn's correct academic levels at all times!
Quietly redirect Shawn to complete his work.

Hypothesis:
From observation of antecedents, Shawn appears to display this behavior to avoid academic work which he cannot (or will not) do.

Reinforcement Schedule:
Computer time, 10 minutes per "successful" day. For a successful week, 20 minutes at the end of the week, Friday afternoon.

You will use these basic steps when you conduct a functional behavioral assessment (Chandler & Dahlquist, 2010):

1. Through careful observation, describe as precisely as you can the nature of the behaviors that are impeding the student's or others' ability to learn.

2. Gather information from teachers, related service providers, family members, the student, and any other individuals who have firsthand knowledge about the circumstances regularly associated with the student's problem behavior. Determine as specifically as you can the events that occur before, during, and after the student's appropriate and inappropriate behavior.

3. Determine why the student engages in the problem behavior. What is the student trying to accomplish or communicate? Does the student want to obtain something positive, avoid or escape something unpleasant, or increase or decrease certain sensory stimulation?

IEP TIP

Members of the team that conducts the student's functional behavioral assessment should be members of the team that develops the student's IEP; if that is not practicable, then there should be overlap between the two teams.

4. Hypothesize the relationship between the problem behavior and the events occurring before, during, and after the behavior.

5. Incorporate the functional assessment information into the student's IEP. Focus on changing the environmental events and circumstances so that the student does not need to use problem behavior to accomplish an outcome.

6. Help the student develop alternative behaviors and new skills to accomplish the same outcome in more socially acceptable ways.

Designing an Appropriate IEP

PARTNERING FOR SPECIAL EDUCATION AND RELATED SERVICES

Partnerships among educators, related service providers, and family members are essential to assure that students benefit from special education. As members of the IEP team, these individuals must rely on the nondiscriminatory evaluation to develop and use a common curriculum, instructional strategies, and positive behavior support in school, home, and community settings. It is therefore especially important to have a person on the evaluation and IEP team who has conducted or can interpret the functional behavioral assessment and can guide the team in developing a positive behavior supports plan.

Shawn's team consists of a special educator (Richard Hubbard), a paraeducator (Edna Crawford), two general educators (Geraldine Meyers and Rochella Mitchell), a speech-language specialist (Kirk Ealing), and an occupational therapist (Miss Maxwell). In Box 11.3, Partnership Tips, you will read about Rosie Mack, a young child with autism, and how educators at the University of New Hampshire and Rosie's family adapted the Individual Support Program to implement positive behavior support. Rosie experienced dramatic improvement in a very short time.

Shawn's positive behavior support plan targets his communication and behaviors alike because the former affects the latter.

DETERMINING SUPPLEMENTARY AIDS AND SERVICES

In implementing positive behavior support (PBS), a student's IEP team should consider supplementary aids and services that address access, classroom ecology, and task modifications. These aids and services improve the student's access to an effective learning environment by modifying the community, campus, building, or classroom. They also provide "behavioral access" by promoting positive behavior and minimizing disruptive behavior. Shawn benefits from two kinds of PBS interventions: His school uses schoolwide PBS, and Shawn has his own PBS plan. Equally important, he has a paraeducator (Edna Crawford) and an occupational therapist (Miss Maxwell). Edna helps him with his reading and behaviors; Miss Maxwell shows him how to use simple technologies, such as raised paper to write on, a pencil with a rubberized grip, and, for those times when sensory overload threatens to invoke tantrums, vibrating tools that establish predictability, mimic his use of many electronic devices at home, and are not so obvious as to call great attention to his needs.

The student's IEP team should also consider other campus or building modifications. The lunchroom is a place where problem behaviors occur frequently. It's noisy, there is not as much direct supervision as there is in the classroom, and there is constant movement. Modifications to the lunchroom environment can decrease problem behavior. Consider replacing long rows of tables that accommodate many students with round tables around which fewer students congregate or rotating lunch periods to reduce the number of students in the cafeteria at any one time. Modifications before and after school and in the hallways between classes also can decrease problem behaviors.

Some students have behavioral problems because they can't see or hear well. Simply modifying the classroom arrangement can ensure better visual and acoustic access and

BOX 11.3   **PARTNERSHIP TIPS**

Implementing Positive Behavior Supports

It took only six months, an amazingly short period, for three-year-old Rosie Mack to change dramatically—so dramatically that "progress in the general curriculum" was not just a phrase but a reality. The challenge was to help Rosie behave in such a way that she could be included in a preschool with students who do not have disabilities. What stood in the way was Rosie's erratic behavior: she was alternatively hyperactive and withdrawn and sobbing. Rosie's behaviors were typical for a preschooler with autism. She needed to learn appropriate behavior, such as how to calm down, how to comply with safety instructions and other directions ("Don't touch the hot stove"), and how to express her needs and choices other than by acting out ("Tell me what you want, Rosie"). By approaching the challenge step by step, Rosie and her team had remarkable success, but only because they acted as a team.

Step 1: *Create a team.* The partners consisted of Rosie's mother, Kathy; Kathy's parents, Lorraine and John Mack; Ann Dillon of the University of New Hampshire's Jump Start program (where positive behavior support is linked to family support and person-centered planning); Ann's graduate students; and the teachers and therapists in Rosie's early intervention program and elementary school.

Step 2: *Conduct an FBA and develop a PBS plan.* Under Ann's direction but with Kathy's diligent participation, the team began by conducting a functional assessment of Rosie's behavior; then they developed and carried out a plan for positive behavior support for Rosie. The plan included social stories (with graphic design by Kathy and photographs by Rosie's grandmother, Lorraine). At Ann's suggestion, Kathy or Ann's students read the stories to Rosie before she went to different places (e.g., the preschool or elementary school, the swimming pool, and the theater) or engaged in various activities (e.g., being a patient at a dentist's or physician's office). The stories prepped her for what lay ahead, gave her a sense of predictability, and helped her be calm when places changed and people entered her life.

Step 3: *Support the family.* Again under Ann's guidance, the team engaged in family support. Following the guidance of Kathy, Lorraine, and John, they developed a shared vision for Rosie, which was for her to be included in general education and to have friends—including both those who do and those who do not have disabilities. They also helped Kathy find child care, learn how to advocate for Rosie's inclusion in school and the community, and meet some of Rosie's needs for strenuous physical activity. Grandfather John himself built Rosie's swing-set.

Step 4: *Embed the plan.* Finally, the team worked with Rosie's teachers in the preschool and the elementary school to help them learn how to deliver positive behavior support to Rosie.

The results were remarkable. Rosie's problem behavior is a thing of the past. She progressed through the preschool and is now fully included, with support, in a typical first-grade classroom. She uses words and phrases to express her choices. If she doesn't know a word, she tells herself, "I will be okay," and uses hand signals, not acting-out behaviors, to communicate. She is fully included in her elementary school (with an aide), has friends who have and don't have disabilities, and has progressed from no literacy skills to knowing how to read and being a regular visitor to the community library. Rosie's favorite book is her well-worn copy of *The Tale of Peter Rabbit*.

Even though Ann pointed her team members in the right direction, everyone participated equally in leading and following. As in all the best partnerships, a teacher can jump-start the process, but everyone has to be a leader. Their comments recognize this shared leadership. As Kathy said, "We wouldn't be so much in control of our lives without Jump Start." Ann replied, "It's about the family and in turn about Rosie."

The key in partnerships, as Rosie's story illustrates, is to

- Involve family members other than just the student's parents (remember how we defined *family* in Chapter 4?).
- Involve all school-based personnel and other professionals who work for the student.
- Seek and apply what researchers and their students know about interventions.
- Carry out a functional behavioral assessment, make it the basis for a positive behavior intervention plan, and implement the plan diligently and across all settings and times.
- Support each other, not just the student but also the student's family and teachers.

Put these tips to work for progress in the general curriculum:

1. Provide a rationale of why it is important to conduct a functional assessment and implement positive behavior support in multiple settings.

2. Identify related service providers who might be available to assist you as a teacher in providing family support. What types of assistance would you expect from each related service provider that you identify?

3. How can you involve family members to address problem behavior and enhance student outcomes?

help decrease problem behaviors. By contrast, some seating arrangements can precipitate problem behavior, so teachers should consider changing where they seat a student or limiting how many students interact with each other at any given time. Teachers also can create visual schedules for students to follow, thereby reducing off-task time and curtailing the times when problems may occur. Finally, problem behavior may arise because students become frustrated at being unable to complete required tasks. IEP teams should consider modifications, such as extended time, to address this situation.

PLANNING FOR UNIVERSAL DESIGN FOR LEARNING

Up to this point we have discussed the characteristics of autism that contribute to students' problems in learning and development. Paradoxically, some characteristics associated with autism spectrum disorders, particularly Asperger syndrome, are strengths and can be foundations for adaptations and augmentations to a student's curriculum. Some students may be able to focus their attention on detailed information for a long period of time, while others may excel in areas of the curriculum that are not language-based, such as math or science. As we noted in Chapter 2, curriculum adaptations modify either the way in which teachers present or represent curriculum content or the way in which students respond to the curriculum, while curriculum augmentations expand the general curriculum to teach students "learning-to-learn" strategies that will enable them to succeed in the general curriculum. Simpson, Ganz, and Mason (2012) identified cognitive learning strategies and social decision-making strategies, both forms of curriculum augmentation, as important for students with ASD. Similarly, Wehmeyer, Shogren, Zager, Smith, and Simpson (2010) identified self-directed learning strategies as effective for students with ASD.

Mnemonic Strategies

Some students with Asperger syndrome are skilled in memory tasks that can form the basis for curriculum adaptations and augmentations; you should take these students' memory strengths into account when planning for universally designed instruction. One such curriculum modification involves mnemonic strategies (Lee, Wehmeyer, Soukup, & Palmer, 2010). **Mnemonic**, or memory, strategies help students learn and retain information.

Keyword. **Keyword strategies** teach students to link a keyword to a new word or concept to help them remember the new material. The keyword is a word that sounds like the word or concept in question and can be easily pictured (Scruggs, Mastropieri, Berkeley, & Marshak, 2010). For example, to remember the three bones in the inner ear, you might use the following keyword strategies:

- *Malleus* sounds like mallets, and you can picture an image of hitting a bell with a mallet and causing it to ring (i.e., make sound).
- *Incus* sounds like ink, and you can picture an image of a large ear holding an ink pen and writing the word "incus."
- *Stapes* sounds like staple, and you can picture an image of a stapler with ears.

Pegword. The **pegword strategy** helps students remember numbered or ordered information by linking words and numbers that rhyme. The visual images help students remember a number or number sequence. There are standard pegwords that have come to represent numbers, such as the pegword "bun" representing the number one, the pegword "shoe" representing the number two, and so forth.

Letter. **Letter strategies** employ acronyms or a string of letters to help students remember a list of words or concepts. Recalling the acronym helps them recall the list or sequence. The fact that IDEA stands for Individuals with Disabilities Education Act helps you remember the law's name. Another common letter strategy uses the acronym HOMES to help people remember the list of the Great Lakes (Huron, Ontario, Michigan, Erie, Superior). Another letter strategy involves acronyms that do not form recognizable words. The letter mnemonic for the notes that fall on the lines of the musical staff of the treble clef is EGBDF, which is not a useful mnemonic in and of itself. However, forming an acrostic (that is, using each letter to identify a word in a sentence) helps: The acrostic letter strategy for remembering the notes on the treble clef is "*Every Good Boy Deserves a Favor*."

PLANNING FOR OTHER EDUCATIONAL NEEDS

The most common characteristics of autism are impairments in language development and social development. We discussed language development in Chapter 6, so we will focus here on social development for children with autism.

When a student participates in solving problems facing her, she is more likely to own the solution and overcome the problem itself.

Impairments in social skills and social interactions can result in problems in many areas, but for students with autism, none may be more problematic than the impact of poor social skills on developing friendships. Sadly, teachers ranked student friendships as only eleventh in importance among twenty potential outcomes for students with autism; they rated the likelihood of that outcome even lower (Ivey, 2007).

Promoting Friendships

We all know what friends are: people we like to be around and who like to be with us. Having friends is important at all points in life, perhaps especially during the school years. But difficulties with communication, poor social skills, and problem behavior too often cause students with autism to be isolated from their peers with and without disabilities (Kasari, Locke, Gulsrud, & Rotheram-Fuller, 2010).

While you probably knew immediately what we were talking about when we mentioned the word *friend,* you may not know quite as intuitively how one goes about planning for and teaching friendship skills. These are skills that most children—but not students with autism—learn through typical play activities and, of course, with the guidance of their parents or brothers and sisters. The first step toward promoting friendships involves including students with autism in general education classrooms and in extracurricular and nonacademic activities such as school clubs, plays, sporting events, dances, and field trips (Boutot, 2007). The peer buddy program you learned about in Chapter 10 links same-age peers with and without intellectual disability in a wide array of activities, including those outside the classroom, and can be equally useful for students with autism.

As we discussed in Chapter 10, however, you have to support students without disabilities to interact with and respond appropriately to students with disabilities. Simply placing students in the proximity of their peers without disabilities will not be sufficient. You will need to do more than ensure that your students with autism interact with their classmates in general education settings. Using person-centered planning models (described in Chapter 10) that involve peers is a good first step. A second step is to identify the interests and abilities of your students with autism and then to connect those students with others who share their interests and abilities. Third, focusing on social and communication skills will be an important element of friendship building (Frankel, Myatt, Sugar, Whitham, Gorospe, & Laugeson, 2010).

Obviously, planning for promoting friendship involves setting goals for instructional activities. Your students' IEPs should address the following instructional areas (Kluth, 2008):

IEP TIP

A student's IEP team should address the student's social skills by prescribing peer tutoring, social skills groups, student-directed learning strategies, person-centered planning, and social stories.

- *Trustworthiness and loyalty:* teaching your students how important it is to be a loyal friend by keeping secrets and promises, standing up for one's friends, and supporting friends' rights
- *Conflict resolution:* teaching your students how to resolve conflicts between and among friends and acquaintances and how to help their peers to do so
- *General friendship skills:* teaching your students how to act around a friend, such as by taking turns speaking, asking about the well-being or feelings of a friend, and asking questions about hobbies and areas of shared interest
- *Positive interaction style:* teaching your students to be active listeners, give positive feedback, ask questions, and respond to the needs of others
- *Taking the perspective of others:* teaching your students to consider others' needs, feelings, and interests; to compromise on activity choices; and to listen to others' ideas

BOX 11.4

UNIVERSAL DESIGN FOR PROGRESS

Teaching Emotion Recognition to Students with Autism and Asperger Syndrome

One reason that students with autism have problems with social interactions is that they sometimes have difficulty comprehending others' feelings, preferences, and emotions. Think about it. If you deduce that someone is angry by noticing that the person's face is red from emotion and she's frowning, you can modify how you approach and communicate with the person based upon this knoweldge. If you do not notice, it might lead to an uncomfortable exchange. This is the dilemma faced by many people with autism, and it certainly contributes to difficulty in making friends and maintaining friendships.

Simon Baron-Cohen and his colleagues have developed a multimedia software program called *Mind Reading: The Interactive Guide to Emotions* (Baron-Cohen, Golan, Wheelwright, & Hill, 2004) designed specifically to address these difficulties in determining emotion. This software program has three main sections: an Emotions Library, a Learning Center, and a Games Zone. The Emotions Library presents photographs, video clips, and audio of people who are expressing any one of 412 different emotions, grouped into twenty-six overarching groups. For example, the emotions depicted in the "excited emotions" group are adventurous, alert, ardent, aroused, enthusiastic, excited, exhilarated, hysterical, inspired, invigorated, keen, lively, refreshed, spirited, titillated, and vibrant. For each of these emotions, there are six images of people ranging across ages and ethnic groups, stories showing how the emotion is used in a social situation, voices of people whose voice patterns depict the emotion, and additional information about the emotion. The Emotions Library is a good example of universal design for learning using technology because it uses both video and audio output to represent content information (e.g., what a person looks and sounds like when expressing an emotion).

The Learning Center was designed specifically for use by people with autism spectrum disorders and provides lessons on emotions, followed by a quiz. Again conforming with UDL principles, the difficulty of lessons can be adjusted to ensure that students with varying cognitive abilities and ages can progress in the lessons, and the lessons are presented using both audio and video content.

The Game Zone provides a chance for students to play video games that incorporate emotion recognition features. For example, in the Hidden Face game, students are presented with a grid of nine squares. As they select each square, it reveals a portion of a photograph of a person's face. As more and more of the face is revealed, students can choose from among a selection of ten possible emotions what emotion they believe the person is showing. Points are awarded for correct answers and deducted for incorrect answers. An audio feature provides audio instructions for playing the game.

Golan and Baron-Cohen (2006) found that British children with autism using the Mind Reading software for up to fifteen weeks in a home-based intervention improved their emotion recognition capacity and were able to generalize these gains to new audio and video representations of emotion. LaCava, Golan, Baron-Cohen, and Myles (2007) used the Mind Reading program with eight students from the United States with Asperger syndrome in both home and school settings and, as in the British sample, found that after ten weeks of use students improved their face and voice emotion recognition, including recognition of more complex emotions.

You can learn more about the Mind Reading software by going to the product's web page at http://www.jkp.com/mindreading/.

Because students with autism have difficulty recognizing emotions from others' facial or vocal patterns, they sometimes have problematic social interactions (LaCava, Golan, Baron-Cohen, & Myles, 2007). Box 11.4 provides information about addressing this issue by way of universally designed technology.

Using Effective Instructional Strategies

EARLY CHILDHOOD STUDENTS: SOCIAL STORIES

Early intervention and education, with special attention to your students' communication and social competence, are important for launching your students toward IDEA's four outcomes and for supporting their families (Cardon, 2007; Simpson & Myles, 2008). Early intervention and preschool programs use different approaches, including the following:

- Applied behavior analytic techniques, such as discrete trial training (which we discuss later in this chapter), that emphasize assessment, programming, systematic reinforcement of appropriate behavior, and generalization of skills and behavior across settings (places) and people (Simpson & Myles, 2008)

- Incidental teaching in natural environments, such as the child's home, a child-care center, and the community (McGee, Morrier, & Daley, 1999)
- Communication, sensory processing, motor planning, and shared affect with caregivers and peers (Cardon, 2007; Koegel, 2007)

Social stories are useful for preschool and older children with autism. That is because students with autism and Asperger syndrome often need to learn how to interact appropriately with others in social situations: knowing what is cool and uncool behavior, understanding others' perspectives, and knowing the unwritten codes of conduct—what educators call the "hidden curriculum" (Simpson & Myles, 2008). **Social stories** are written by educators, parents, or students and describe social situations, social cues, and appropriate responses to those cues. These stories usually consist of four different types of sentences (Gray, 1998, pp. 178–179):

- Descriptive sentences define where a situation occurs, who is involved, what they are doing, and why.
- Perspective sentences describe a person's internal physical state or desire. They also describe another person's thoughts, feelings, beliefs, and motivations.
- Directive sentences define what is expected as a response to a cue or in a particular situation.
- Control sentences identify strategies students may use to recall the information in a social story, reassure themselves, or define their responses.

The goal of social stories is to expose the student to a better understanding of an event and to encourage alternative, and appropriate, responses (Ryan, Hughes, Katsiyannis, McDaniel, & Sprinkle, 2011). Ryan and colleagues identify several tips for successful implementation:

- Social stories should be presented (typically) to the child before a situation occurs so as to allow the student to rehearse the situation.
- A story should include both positive and problem behaviors.
- Using illustrations may help students with autism who are younger or have cognitive limitations.

At Shawn's school, teachers develop positive behavior support plans for him by also developing a positive plan for his peers.

ELEMENTARY AND MIDDLE SCHOOL STUDENTS: SCHOOLWIDE POSITIVE BEHAVIOR SUPPORT

Schoolwide positive behavior support (SWPBS) is a systems-level and evidence-based method for improving valued social and learning outcomes for all students, not just students with autism. It is proactive, oriented toward problem solving, and data-based; it elicits appropriate behavior and contributes to academic, social, and communication outcomes throughout a school building (Janney & Snell, 2008).

Because students' problem behavior often results from someone else's failure to provide individualized and comprehensive support (Janney & Snell, 2008), positive behavior support seeks to tailor students' environments to their preferences, strengths, and needs. It rearranges school environments and changes school systems to discourage students from engaging in problem behaviors in the first place.

SWPBS involves interventions at three levels: universal support, group support, and individualized support, as needed. The primary goal of universal support is to create a positive learning context for all students. You can carry out this goal by setting clear expectations for student behavior in all places and activities in a school (cafeteria, hallways, bathrooms, library, and playgrounds), making sure the students agree to those expectations, giving them many opportunities to meet these expectations, and rewarding them when they do. You will succeed in implementing universal support when you do the following:

- *Clearly define behavioral expectations.* These expectations are defined simply, positively, and succinctly.
- *Teach behavioral expectations.* Each expectation should be explicitly taught so that students know exactly what is expected of them.
- *Frequently acknowledge appropriate behaviors.* A rule of thumb is to have at least four times as many positive affirmations as negative sanctions.
- *Evaluate problems and make adaptations on an ongoing basis through a team approach.* A student's IEP team should review data on behavioral incidences, attendance rates, detentions, and suspension rates and then implement proactive strategies to discourage negative behavior and reward positive behavior.
- *Target support to address students who need more intense skill development and practice than is offered through universal support.* The targeted support might relate to particular behavior in the hallways or cafeteria, social skills, conflict resolution, and/or communication training.

Group support is the second component of positive behavior support (Janney & Snell, 2008). Group support addresses problem behavior that is occurring with at least ten to fifteen students, each of whom has received universal support but has not yet learned appropriate behavior. To provide group support, you typically will need to

- Observe students individually and as a group.
- Interview those who are having problem behaviors.
- Develop hypotheses that deal with the behaviors of all of the members of the group.
- Teach the specific skills that all of the students need to eliminate their problem behaviors.

Group support often occurs where students have higher rates of problem behaviors, such as hallways, lunchrooms, and playgrounds.

The most intense level of positive behavior support is individual support. Individual support is for students who are not able to sufficiently eliminate their problem behavior through universal and group support; it often includes students with autism and other significant disabilities (Dunlap et al., 2010). To provide individual support, begin with a functional behavioral assessment, as described in Box 11.2. The functional behavioral assessment becomes the foundation for IEP goals that target reducing problem behavior, teaching appropriate behavior, and maximizing positive outcomes through communication and social skills.

Shawn's school uses SWPBS. Its system is community-referenced, seeking to teach students behaviors they will need in their schools and communities by using reinforcements that are quintessentially American. The school has printed faux money. Each student receives a fixed allowance of dollars. Students earn more of these faux dollars when they behave well and lose some when they do not. Simply having "cash" to spend at the school store teaches a lesson about earning and productivity: The more you do to behave, the more you will earn, and vice versa.

There's a powerful element of peer reinforcement, too. The students who earn more receive their peers' approval; those who are penalized may lose their peers' approval but more often receive their support to redeem their losses. Finally, getting and losing money teaches the math skills of adding and subtracting. SWPBS at Shawn's school combines economics, peer interaction, math skills, and community-referenced behaviors. It exemplifies the comprehensive approach that research supports: Generalize across settings and make behaviors durable across time.

SECONDARY AND TRANSITION STUDENTS: DISCRETE TRIAL TEACHING

You have learned that positive behavior support is important for many students with autism. The techniques underlying positive behavior support emerged from strategies and techniques referred to as applied behavior analysis. **Applied behavior analysis (ABA)** uses the principles of operant psychology to reduce problem behavior or increase positive behavior. ABA is the "process of applying sometimes tentative principles of behavior to the improvement of specific behaviors and simultaneously evaluating whether or not any changes noted are indeed attributable to the process of application" (Baer, Wolf, & Risley, 1968, p. 91).

ABA principles undergird instructional techniques and strategies that are essential to students' success. One of those strategies is discrete trial teaching. **Discrete trial teaching** uses three elements: the discriminative stimulus, the response, and the reinforcing stimulus or consequence.

- The *discriminative stimulus* is a specific event or environmental condition that elicits the response you want your student to give. The stimulus, such as an instruction or command to perform a task, controls the desired response when your student's response is paired with a reinforcer that you provide.
- The *response* is the behavior your student performs when you present the discriminative stimulus. The response is the behavior you are trying to teach the child.
- The *reinforcing stimulus,* or reinforcer, is an event or action that follows your student's response and increases the possibility that your student will exhibit that same response again.

Let's consider a simple example of these principles. You want to teach an adolescent with autism ("Jane") the steps in a vocational task, such as sorting silverware into bins. To do that job, Jane must distinguish each type of utensil (spoon, fork, knife). So you lay a spoon, a fork, and a knife in front of her and provide a discriminative stimulus by saying, "Jane, show me the spoon." Most likely, Jane will point to or touch one of the utensils or, if she is not certain, not respond at all. If she points to the spoon, you immediately praise her, saying, "Great job, Jane! That's right; that's the spoon." Your praise constitutes the reinforcing stimulus. If she points to a different utensil or to none of them, she does not get your reinforcer (verbal praise). Instead, you prompt her again to identify the spoon. Eventually, if you reinforce ("Great job!") her correct response (pointing to the spoon) to your discriminative stimulus ("Show me the spoon"), while ignoring or not reinforcing her other responses, Jane will respond more consistently to the stimulus with the appropriate response.

Discrete trial training is, then, a single instructional trial consisting of the following elements:

- Presentation of a discriminative stimulus, sometimes called a cue
- Presentation of a prompting stimulus, if needed
- The response
- Presentation of a reinforcing stimulus, if appropriate

In discrete trial teaching, this trial is followed by a brief interval, called the intertrial interval, before the sequence is repeated. You will notice that we have added a step to the original three steps—a prompting stimulus. If your student is learning a brand-new concept, she may need a variety of levels of prompts to be able to exhibit the correct response. A prompting stimulus is any stimulus that, when paired with the discriminative stimulus, increases the probability that the student will exhibit the correct response.

Let's go back to our example of sorting utensils. If Jane does not know what a spoon is, the probability is one in four that she will choose the right utensil. That means there is a three in four probability that she will not select the right utensil and will instead point to the fork or knife or simply not respond. If, however, when you present the discriminative stimulus ("Show me the spoon") you also provide a prompt (pointing to the spoon yourself, taking her hand and placing it on the spoon, looking at the spoon), you increase the probability that Jane will give the appropriate response.

Discrete trial teaching is particularly useful for teaching students with autism new forms of behavior (behaviors not previously in the child's repertoire) and how to discriminate among events and activities (DeBoer, 2007). It has been used to improve communication outcomes for students with autism (Ryan et al., 2011) and has reduced their stereotyped behaviors (Dib & Sturmey, 2007).

Including Students with Autism

Although research demonstrates that students with autism can be effectively included in general education classes, these students have low rates of inclusion. As illustrated in Figure 11.1, only 36 percent of students with autism spend more than 80 percent of their time inside general education classes, and 10 percent of students are educated in separate settings (U.S. Department of Education, 2011). Donnica is candid about Shawn's inclusion: It was nil or noneffective during first through third grades. Either he was in a class designed solely for students with autism, or he was simply taking up a seat in a general education class and not benefiting at all.

Just as she criticizes what the schools did in the past—"I didn't send Shawn to be baby-sat at school"—so she praises the staff at his school for what it does now. Shawn participates in general education classes in math, science, reading, and social studies, with support from both general and special educators and his paraeducator, Edna Crawford. He does so because IDEA prefers inclusion to separation.

But he also is included because Donnica prepared a storyboard about Shawn before enrolling him at school, met with his IEP team, and demonstrated, using the storyboard, how Shawn learns—principally by using symbols or pictures to understand the text he has to read and by using a computer program that combines text with pictures. She persuaded his team that, because he had been reading only one grade level below his peers before Katrina and the move to Houston, he would be capable of making progress, moving from being two grade levels behind his peers to one grade level behind them. His team agreed with her, and his goals now are both academic and behavioral.

Shawn benefits from other supports, principally a Dynavox that assists him as he spells out words and makes sentences that he cannot vocalize. (In Chapter 6 you learned about other forms of assistive technology that help students communicate.) Box 11.5 offers suggestions for promoting successful inclusion for students with autism.

FIGURE 11.1 *Educational placement of students with autism: School year 2008–2009*

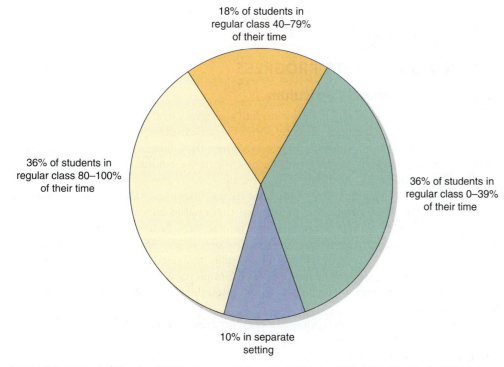

Source: U.S. Department of Education. (2011). *Data accountability center: Individuals with Disabilities Education Act (IDEA) data.* Retrieved February 12, 2011, from https://www.ideadata.org.

Note: Percentages have been rounded and collapsed across categories.

BOX 11.5 | **INCLUSION TIPS**

	What You Might See	What You Might Be Tempted to Do	Alternate Responses	Ways to Include Peers in the Process
Behavior	She often rocks back and forth over and over during class activities she's not interested in.	Ignore her behavior or tell her to stop.	Conduct a functional behavioral assessment to understand why rocking is occurring.	Help peers to understand her behavior. Encourage and support their acceptance of her.
Social interactions	On the playground she is almost always left out of group interactions.	Assume that being alone is how she prefers to spend her time.	Teach her to ask if she can be included and to develop the skills to participate in play with one or two peers.	Pair her with students who understand her preferred communication method.
Educational performance	She learns very slowly and needs a great deal of extra help to learn simple concepts.	Expect less and make the requirements less structured.	Use visual images and music to teach abstract concepts.	Provide opportunities for peer tutoring with visual images and music.
Classroom attitudes	She becomes antagonistic during activities in which there is noise or confusion.	Remove her from class activities to work alone in the library.	Use social stories to help her learn ways to concentrate in noisy environments.	Teach peers to write social stories that include all students. Have small groups, including the student, revise and work out different scenarios.

Assessing Students' Progress

MEASURING STUDENTS' PROGRESS

Progress in the General Curriculum

Most of the procedures for measuring a student's progress in the general curriculum are assessment strategies. Educators often combine them with other strategies to get a more robust understanding of a student's progress. When they bundle assessment strategies with other strategies, they create a holistic assessment or evaluation system. There are several such systems in use in the field of autism.

The Autism Screening Instrument for Educational Planning (ASIEP-2) (Krug, Arick, & Almond, 1993) has five components or subtests that enable educators to evaluate a student's capacity across communication, social interactions, behavior, academic content, and other domains. The most frequently used subtest of the ASIEP-2 is the Autism Behavior Checklist, which is a screening tool to identify the need for further assessment to determine whether the student has autism. The Sample of Vocal Behavior subscale and the Social Interaction Assessment help teachers track their students' progress in areas of other educational needs.

Of particular relevance to tracking students' progress in the general curriculum is the Educational Assessment subscale of the ASIEP-2. Although designed for screening and planning activities, the Educational Assessment subscale also has been administered to determine students' progress in school and at home (Arick et al., 2003).

Progress in Addressing Other Educational Needs

Just as teachers measure their students' academic outcomes, so they also measure the outcomes of schoolwide positive behavior interventions and supports. Measurement strategies such as the data-based measurement techniques you read about in Chapter 9 are effective for measuring each student's behavioral changes. Because positive behavior support involves multiple levels, however, it is necessary to measure all students' behavioral change at the school and district levels.

What types of data do educators need to determine the effectiveness of schoolwide positive behavior interventions? Some data are direct counts of problem behavior, including the number of office referrals for the school or district on a weekly or monthly basis or the types of problem behavior reflected in those office referrals. Other data involve problem behavior reported by environment or time of day. Some data are indirect indicators of success, including student absences or attendance rates as a function of student enrollment. All of these data can be collected by hand or can be collected and analyzed using an online data collection system called the School-Wide Information System (May et al., 2003).

Another data collection tool is the School-Wide Evaluation Tool (SET) (Horner et al., 2006). It assists educators in assessing and evaluating the features of schoolwide behavior support across the academic year and from year to year. Finally, the Self-Assessment of Contextual Fit in Schools (Horner, Salentine, & Albin, 2003) enables educators to assess the need for and impact of the types of supplementary aids and services we have already discussed, such as access and classroom ecological modifications.

More recently, researchers at the University of South Florida have introduced an instrument, the School-wide Benchmarks of Quality (BoQ) (Kincaid, Childs, & George, 2005), to measure the implementation of SWPBS. The BoQ is a fifty-three-item rating scale yielding data in ten areas of interest when implementing SWPBS: PBS team, faculty commitment, effective discipline procedures, data entry, expectations and rules, reward system, lesson plans, implementation plans, crisis plans, and evaluation. Cohen, Kincaid, and Childs (2007) validated the use of the BoQ in a study in 105 schools in two states.

IEP TIP

SWPBS requires the IEP teams for all students receiving positive behavioral supports to collect data about each student, using tools such as the SET and BoQ, and then to determine how to improve the delivery of positive behavioral supports to each IEP-based student and indeed to other students as well.

MAKING ACCOMMODATIONS FOR ASSESSMENT

Accommodations improve students' outcomes on standardized assessments. One particular accommodation differs from typical test modifications because it considers not the test itself but the examiner giving the test and his or her interactions with the student. Students with autism can benefit if this examiner is someone familiar to them. The presence of a familiar person minimizes the students' anxiety and stress associated with testing, and students with autism frequently have difficulty during times of transition or stress. Typically, on days during which students complete standardized testing, the normal schedule is not followed. Between disruption of the schedule and the stress associated with testing, particularly high-stakes testing, teachers and school administrators must do whatever they can to reduce the anxiety that students normally will experience, including providing a familiar examiner.

Like every other student in Louisiana, Shawn must take the state assessment of academic progress, LEAP (Louisiana Education Assessment Program). He is scheduled to receive an important accommodation: The questions will be read to him. He also is scheduled to make progress toward a certificate of attendance, not a diploma. That goal disquiets Donnica. Her goal, and that of Shawn's present IEP team, is to assure that he passes his academic assessment, moves forward with his peers to the next grade, and then shifts from the certificate track to the diploma track.

They believe that it would not be good for Shawn to have to repeat a grade and be in "LEAP remediation" (as Louisiana requires) if he does not pass his assessment. They also believe that the diploma, more than the certificate, will signify to others—future employers especially—that Shawn can be the man Donnica and his teachers want him to be: a productive citizen of a recovered city.

ADDRESSING THE PROFESSIONAL STANDARDS

The following Council for Exceptional Children (CEC) Common Core Knowledge and Skills are addressed in this chapter through the content and concepts we discuss. See the Appendix for a full listing of these Knowledge and Skill statements:

ICC2K1, ICC2K2, ICC2K4, ICC2K5, ICC2K6, ICC4S1, ICC4S2, ICC4S3, ICC4S4, ICC4S5, ICC4S6, ICC5S2, ICC5S3, ICC5S4, ICC5S9, ICC5S12, ICC5S15, ICC7K5, ICC7S1, ICC7S3, ICC7S6, ICC7S7, ICC7S9, ICC8K3, ICC8S2, ICC8S6, ICC8S8, ICC10S2, ICC10S3, ICC10S4, ICC10S5

Summary

IDENTIFYING STUDENTS WITH AUTISM

- Autism is a developmental disability significantly affecting verbal and nonverbal communication and social interaction. It is generally evident in children before age three and adversely affects educational performance. Other characteristics include repetitive activities, stereotyped movements, behavioral challenges, need for environmental predictability, unusual responsiveness to sensory stimulation, and differences in intellectual functioning.
- Autism is part of a broader group of disorders called pervasive developmental disorders. Also in that group is the disorder known as Asperger syndrome.
- The current prevalence of autism is one in 110, which represents a substantial increase in prevalence.
- The majority of people with autism function intellectually as though they have an intellectual disability. Some have the savant syndrome.
- Autism is caused by biological (i.e., genes, brain overgrowth, neural pathways) and environmental factors (i.e., exposure to toxins in the environment and during prenatal development).

EVALUATING STUDENTS WITH AUTISM

- The Autism Diagnostic Interview—Revised is a psychometrically sound assessment tool that frequently is used to determine whether children have autism.
- A functional behavioral assessment identifies specific relationships between environmental events and a student's problem behavior. It is used to tailor an intervention plan aimed at helping students to function as successfully as possible.

DESIGNING AN APPROPRIATE IEP

- Planning to implement positive behavior support requires a team effort, with particular emphasis on creating an effective partnership among families, general and special educators, administrators, and behavior specialists.
- Implementing positive behavior support involves ensuring that issues pertaining to behavioral accessibility are addressed, including building and classroom supports that promote positive behavior.
- Mnemonic strategies are effective curriculum adaptations and augmentations that enable students with autism to succeed in the general curriculum.

USING EFFECTIVE INSTRUCTIONAL STRATEGIES

- Social stories are effective ways to teach young children with autism a number of skills, particularly social interaction skills.
- Positive behavior support, including schoolwide, group, and individual strategies, has been shown to decrease problem behavior and improve opportunities for learning.
- Discrete trial teaching is one strategy derived from applied behavior analysis; it applies learning principles from operant psychology to provide an effective way of teaching skills to students with autism.

INCLUDING STUDENTS WITH AUTISM

- Relative to other students with disabilities, students with autism have low rates of inclusion in general education classes.

ASSESSING STUDENTS' PROGRESS

- Some systems and assessment packages, such as the Autism Screening Instrument for Educational Planning, provide teachers with organized ways to collect data on student progress, including progress in the general curriculum, across multiple domains.

- There are multiple means for collecting data on progress as a function of the implementation of positive behavior supports, most of which focus on collecting data on school referrals, types of problem behavior, and changes in absenteeism or tardiness.

- For students with autism, having a familiar person administer standardized tests may reduce test and schedule anxiety and improve their performance.

MyEducationLab

Go to Topic #14: Autism in the MyEducationLab (www.myeducationlab.com) for *Exceptional Lives*, where you can do the following:

- Find learning outcomes for Autism along with the national standards that connect to these outcomes.

- Complete assignments and activities that will help you more deeply understand the chapter content.

- Apply and practice your understanding of the core teaching skills identified in the chapter with the Building Teaching Skills and Dispositions learning units.

- Examine challenging situations and cases presented in the IRIS Center Resources.

- Access video clips of CCSSO National Teachers of the Year award winners responding to the question, "Why Do I Teach?" in the Teacher Talk section.

- Check your comprehension on the content covered in the chapter with the Study Plan. Here you will be able to take a chapter quiz, receive feedback on your answers, and then access review, practice, and enrichment activities to enhance your understanding of chapter content.

- Use the Online Lesson Plan Builder to practice lesson planning and integrating national and state standards into your planning.

12

Understanding Students *with* Physical Disabilities *and* Other Health Impairments

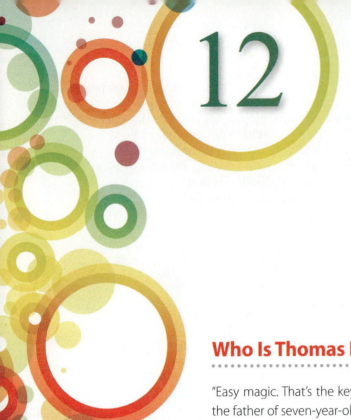

Who Is Thomas Ellenson?

"Easy magic. That's the key," says Richard Ellenson, the father of seven-year-old Thomas Ellenson.

The key to what? To being with Thomas, to entering into his life, to educating him, and especially to including him in school and in life outside school.

And why does Thomas need a key? Because he has cerebral palsy. That condition makes it extremely difficult for him to move from place to place. It also greatly impedes his ability to speak.

So how might a typical person understand Thomas, communicate with him, hear what is in his head? Without mobility and reciprocity in communication, Thomas could be cut off from others, whether in school or elsewhere. The answer, according to Richard, lies in "perspective."

Richard looks at his son's life from his own unique perspective as a successful New York advertising executive. To be an effective ad man, he tries to understand how prospective buyers will respond to his ads.

Richard headed up an advertising campaign for United Cerebral Palsy of New York City. It consisted of four simple words: "See me. Not CP." Look at Thomas. What do you see? Richard does not hesitate to answer, "The killer smile." When people see it, "they get that moment of personality."

A killer smile. That's the easy magic, and it is invaluable. Richard believes that when people understand a killer smile or any engaging characteristic as an indicator of ability or personality, they don't simply feel sympathy or, at best, empathy for a person's disability. Instead, they see the light that shines from inside it. "You need to find the easy magic that will open that door for people quickly. After that, people will do the work for themselves. Once people have taken an interest, building a relationship is much easier."

Richard, Lora (Thomas's mother), and Thomas have built relationships, advocating to school officials to create an innovative new program that did not exist within the current school system. Richard says, "You have to give all those kids [with disabilities] the benefit of the doubt. Frankly, when you do that, you will be developing techniques for better teaching for everyone. You will be gaining insights into delivering curriculum to an increasingly broad group of students. That's benefiting everyone. In short, the benefit of the doubt benefits everybody." He adds, "The joy of all of this is that we don't have to convince people. Thomas convinces the kids, and the kids convince everyone else."

"The fact is, you always need to learn how to best communicate with a person," says Richard. "If you become sensitive to that, your life will open up and, you know, that's the joy." You'll also find that there's an easy magic in it, too. As Richard puts it, "Find that one thing that is simple now and just build on it."

Building on a student's strengths. It makes sense. It's what education is all about.

Who Is Jarron Shaffer?

For Jarron Shaffer and his family, everything is falling into place. This idea—that everything will fall into place—is the motto his family lives by.

Jarron is nine years old; and like his father and uncle, he has asthma. Jarron had his first asthma attack when he was three years old. He had to spend the night in the hospital and adjust to using a nebulizer and inhalers on a regular basis. But he adjusted and has thrived: Everything has fallen into place. Jarron received nebulizer treatments each morning and evening until he was eight, and it became part of his routine. His mom, LaShorage, would read him books while he did his treatments; he even learned to fall asleep with his nebulizer mask on. His sister, Victoria, who is eight years older than Jarron, learned what to listen for at night so that she could help him if he were having an attack. His father, Eric, who is in the military, was deployed to Iraq when Jarron was younger. He is currently stationed about two hours away from where the family lives, is home on the weekends, and helps Jarron learn to manage his asthma while not letting it hold him back.

Jarron is now able to recognize the signs of a possible attack (such as cold weather or heavy exercise) and use his inhaler independently to control his breathing. Every day he carries his inhaler with him in his book bag or his

jacket and uses it when he needs to at home and school. He even tells his dad to use his inhaler when his dad sounds like he is having difficulty breathing, usually after he mows the grass. Jarron's friends do the same for him. According to LaShorage, when Jarron is outside playing with the kids in his neighborhood, they often ask him if he needs his inhaler after a particularly taxing game of baseball or tag. Even at birthday parties, his friends have told other kids, "He'll be fine in a few minutes. He has asthma, and he just needs his inhaler."

Jarron is learning about himself, and everything is falling into place for him among his peers. He has a network of friends who know he has asthma but see it as just a part of who he is, like having brown eyes or hair. Things are falling into place at school as well. LaShorage, a former teacher and current doctoral candidate in special education, is always available if Jarron needs her at school. She works to arrange before-the-school-year meetings with his teachers so they know he has asthma and carries an inhaler with him, and so that they will understand signs of trouble. One year, a teacher

took the inhaler from Jarron and put it in the office, thinking that it would be safer there. LaShorage had to explain to the teacher that Jarron might not have enough time to get to the office if his breathing gets bad; he needs to keep it with him. She also explained that Jarron knows how to use the inhaler and that he is aware of how to take care of his needs. As a result of this conversation, the teacher let Jarron keep the inhaler in his book bag, recognizing the inhaler is a lifeline for him.

Jarron is learning to advocate for himself. LaShorage still steps in when she needs to but says that he is learning that asthma is part of who he is. He knows that he has to take care of his health because, if he can't breathe, he won't be able to participate in school or in activities with his friends.

Jarron has an IEP at school, not for his asthma but because he has experienced some delays in his speech and language. LaShorage does not know if some of the early issues that he experienced (e.g., low muscle tone in his jaw, articulation delays, speech delays) had anything to do with his asthma; but with support from speech therapists, additional tutoring in reading, and great teachers in third and fourth grade, Jarron is making outstanding progress. As his mother says, everyone has strengths in different areas. Jarron excels in math and design/building; his mom thinks he could go into engineering or architecture. However, he is working on his language and literacy, learning about how to apply literacy to his everyday life through conversations and interacting with books. When talking about Jarron's future, LaShorage says that everything will fall into place. He has many opportunities open to him and she has no doubt that he will take advantage of all of them.

PEARSON
myeducationlab

Visit the MyEducationLab (www.myeducationlab.com) for *Exceptional Lives* to enhance your understanding of chapter concepts with a personalized Study Plan. You'll also have the opportunity to hone your teaching skills through video- and case-based assignments and activities, IRIS Center Resources, and Building Teaching Skills and Disposition lessons.

Identifying Students with Physical Disabilities and Other Health Impairments

Unlike previous and subsequent chapters, this one discusses two categories of exceptionality: physical disabilities and other health impairments. We begin, as in the other chapters, by providing an overview of these categories. Because there are common educational issues involving students with physical disabilities and other health impairments, we address these issues in common throughout the chapter.

Physical Disabilities

DEFINING PHYSICAL DISABILITIES

IDEA refers to physical disabilities, such as Thomas's cerebral palsy, as *orthopedic impairments* and defines the term as follows: "'Orthopedic impairment' means a severe orthopedic impairment that adversely affects a child's educational performance. The term includes impairments caused by congenital anomaly, impairments caused by disease (e.g., poliomyelitis, bone tuberculosis, etc.), and impairments from other causes (e.g., cerebral palsy, amputations, and fractures or burns that cause contractures)."

Although IDEA uses the term *orthopedic impairments,* educators typically use the term *physical disabilities*. So there are two terms in use, the IDEA term and educators' term. But special educators also sometimes refer to students with severe and multiple disabilities (see Chapter 10) or traumatic brain injury (see Chapter 13) as having physical disabilities. The term *physical disabilities* is typically used to refer to a large group of students who experience conditions that are quite different from each other, even though most students may experience mobility limitations. We focus in this section on two physical disabilities: cerebral palsy and spina bifida.

Because physical disabilities often occur in combination with other disabilities, it is hard to determine their prevalence. Nevertheless, some data are available. In fall 2008, approximately 1.1 percent (62,371) of all students ages six through twenty-one receiving special education services and supports were classified as having an orthopedic impairment (U.S. Department of Education, 2011).

CEREBRAL PALSY: DESCRIBING THE CHARACTERISTICS AND DETERMINING THE CAUSES

What Is Cerebral Palsy?

Cerebral refers to the brain. *Palsy* describes the lack of muscle control that affects a student's ability to move and to maintain balance and posture. That is why Thomas Ellenson uses a wheelchair. The term **cerebral palsy** refers to a group of neurological disorders that affect movement and posture and occur before birth or during infancy (Pakula, Braun, & Yeargin-Allsopp, 2009). Cerebral palsy is a lifetime condition, but it is not a disease. It is inappropriate to consider children and youth with cerebral palsy to be sick.

The prevalence of cerebral palsy is 3.6 cases per thousand people (Yeargin-Allsopp et al., 2008). The prevalence is slightly higher in males than females. The prevalence is highest among African American children and lowest among Latino children.

There are multiple types of cerebral palsy; each refers to a person's specific movement patterns (Pellegrino, 2007):

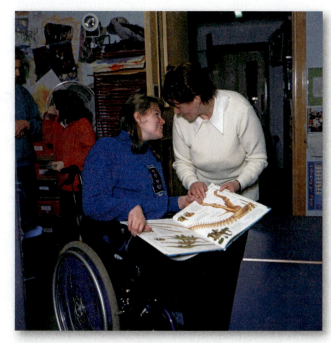

Wheelchairs are just another type of chair. They aren't barriers to learning, as this photograph shows.

- **Spastic** is characterized by tightness in one or more muscle groups and affects 70 to 80 percent of individuals with cerebral palsy.

- **Dyskinetic** involves impairments in muscle tone affecting the whole body.

- **Athetoid** involves abrupt, involuntary movements of the head, neck, face, and extremities, particularly the upper ones.

- **Ataxic** involves unsteadiness, lack of coordination and balance, and varying degrees of difficulty with standing and walking.

FIGURE 12.1 *Topographical classification system*

Monoplegia: one limb
Paraplegia: legs only
Hemiplegia: one half of body
Triplegia: three limbs (usually two legs and one arm)
Quadriplegia: all four limbs
Diplegia: more affected in the legs than the arms
Double hemiplegia: arms more involved than the legs

- **Mixed** combines two or more movement patterns when one type does not predominate over another.

In addition to characterizing cerebral palsy by the nature of a person's movement, professionals also refer to the part of the person's body that is affected. In this **topographical classification system**, the specific body location of the movement impairment correlates with the location of the brain damage (O'Shea, 2008). Figure 12.1 describes the topographical classification system.

What Other Conditions Are Associated with Cerebral Palsy?

Many health and developmental problems may accompany cerebral palsy. More than half of children and youth with cerebral palsy have an intellectual disability, between 22 and 40 percent have epilepsy, more than 70 percent have low visual acuity, and about 25 percent have problems with controlling their bladder and bowels (Pakula, Braun, & Yeargin-Allsopp, 2009). Some students with cerebral palsy, however, have few associated challenges.

What Are the Causes of Cerebral Palsy?

Cerebral palsy is caused by *prenatal* (e.g., gestational infection, brain malformation before birth, prematurity), *perinatal* (e.g., stroke, lack of oxygen or infection during birth), or *postnatal* (e.g., brain injury or meningitis after birth) factors (Nelson & Chang, 2008; Warchausky, White, & Tubbergen, 2010). The most common causes are problems during prenatal development, including prematurity.

SPINA BIFIDA: DESCRIBING THE CHARACTERISTICS AND DETERMINING THE CAUSES

What Is Spina Bifida?

Spina bifida, which means "open spine," refers to a malformation of the spinal cord prior to birth (Taylor, Landry, English, & Barnes, 2010). The spine is made up of separate bones called vertebrae, which normally cover and protect the spinal cord. In a person with spina bifida, the spinal column does not close completely and cover the spinal cord, usually resulting in a protrusion of the spinal cord, its coverings, or both. A saclike bulge may occur in any part of the person's spine, from neck to buttocks. The higher on the spinal column the impairment appears, the more severe the person's loss of function. Typically, the impairment occurs in the lower region of the spine and causes loss of skin sensation and complete or partial paralysis of the person's lower extremities.

Spina bifida is not a progressive condition and has three common forms (see Figure 12.2) (Liptak, 2007):

- **Spina bifida occulta**. An opening occurs in one or more bones of the spinal column, with no damage to the spinal cord. This is the mildest and most common form.

FIGURE 12.2   *Types of spina bifida*

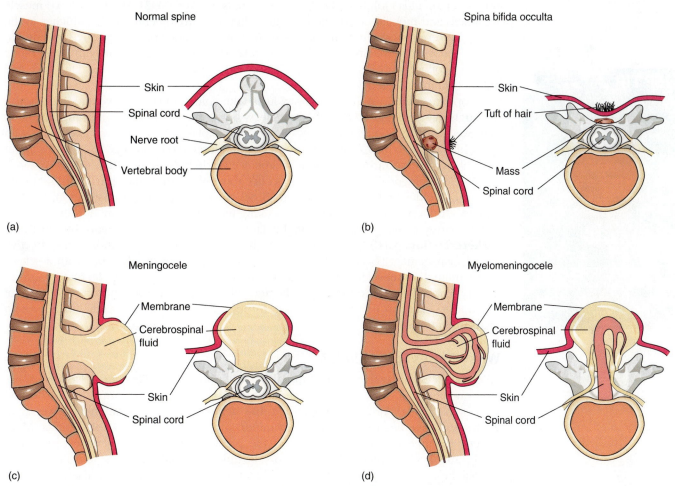

Source: From Umbreit, John. *Physical Disabilities and Health Impairments: An Introduction,* 1e. Published by Allyn and Bacon, Boston, MA. Copyright © 1983 by Pearson Education. Reprinted by permission of the publisher.

- **Meningocele**. The covering of the spinal cord, but not the cord itself, protrudes through the opening created by the defect in the spine. This more serious form can be repaired through surgery and usually does not lead to mobility impairments.

- **Myelomeningocele**. The spinal cord's covering and a portion of the spinal cord or nerve roots protrudes or forms a sac that protrudes through the opening created by the defect in the spine. This is the most serious form and results in alterations in brain development during the early stages of gestation that lead to physical and cognitive impairments. The term *spina bifida* typically is used to refer to myelomeningocele.

Spina bifida belongs to a larger group of malformations associated with the spinal cord, brain, and vertebra that are referred to as **neural tube defects**. The prevalence of spina bifida in the United States is two out of 10,000 individuals, and this rate has been declining over the past several decades (Au, Ashley-Koch, & Northrup, 2010). Later in the chapter you will learn that one of the major contributors to this decrease in prevalence is daily vitamin supplements containing folic acid. There is increased risk for spina bifida in households with low socioeconomic status and with mothers who are over age forty or under age nineteen. African Americans have a slightly reduced risk as compared to other racial groups.

What Are Other Conditions Associated with Spina Bifida?

The extent of mobility and sensory loss in children and youth with myelomeningocele depends upon the location of the spinal impairment (Fletcher & Dennis, 2010). In a study of approximately 350 adolescents and young adults with myelomeningocele, 57 percent used wheelchairs, approximately one-third used braces, and approximately one-fourth used walking aids (Johnson, Dudgeon, Kuehn, & Walker, 2007). More extensive muscle weakness and mobility impairment occurs when the myelomeningocele is higher in the spine; however, most children and youth with myelomeningocele typically have significant mobility impairments. Other mobility-related issues that co-occur with spina bifida include scoliosis, hip disorders, knee pain, and impairments associated with feet and ankles (Thomson & Segal, 2010).

Approximately 75 percent of individuals with spina bifida have average intelligence, although many of these students struggle with attention, abstract reasoning, memory, and executive functioning (Holmbeck et al., 2010; Liptak, 2007). Children and youth with spina bifida tend to have challenges in social development often related to concerns about their physical appearance and social acceptance (Holmbeck et al., 2010).

Myelomeningocele almost always occurs above the part of the spinal cord that controls the bladder and bowels (Clayton, Brock, & Joseph, 2010). Constipation, bladder paralysis, urinary tract infections, and resulting incontinence are common. Kidney failure can also result. Many students can be taught the technique of **clean intermittent catheterization (CIC)** (inserting a tube into the urethra for urination) and effective bowel management (Best, Heller, & Bigge, 2010). Teachers should work with a school nurse trained in these techniques. Most children with spina bifida learn to perform intermittent catheterization between the ages of eight and twelve, and up to 90 percent are able to maintain urinary continence through clean intermittent catheterization and medication (Clayton et al., 2010).

What Causes Spina Bifida?

Spina bifida occurs within the first month of gestation (Yeates, Fletcher, & Dennis, 2008). Environmental and genetic factors interact to cause the spinal malformations associated with spina bifida. Although more than 100 genes have been examined, fewer than 20 percent have been found to have a minor impact on the risk of spina bifida. More genetic research is needed to pinpoint the precise nature of the genetic causes (Au et al., 2010). Environmental contributors include maternal exposure to valproic acid (Depakote), acne medication (Accutane), and hyperthermia (excessive use of saunas); maternal diabetes; and obesity (Liptak, 2007).

A woman who uses daily vitamin supplements containing folic acid reduces the risk that her baby will have spina bifida. Folic acid is a B vitamin that enables bodies to build healthy cells. Beginning in 1998, the federal Food and Drug Administration required breads and enriched cereal-grain products to be fortified with synthetic folic acid. Research in Canada evaluated rates of neural tube defects before and after folic acid fortification (De Wals, Tairou, Van Allen, & Uh, 2007). This study found a 46 percent reduction in the prevalence of neural tube defects after a large variety of cereal products were fortified with folic acid.

Other Health Impairments

DEFINING OTHER HEALTH IMPAIRMENTS

The regulations implementing IDEA define students with other health impairments as those "having limited strength, vitality or alertness, including a heightened alertness to environmental stimuli, that results in limited alertness with respect to the educational environment, that:

1. is due to chronic or acute health problems such as asthma, attention deficit disorder or attention deficit hyperactivity disorder, diabetes, epilepsy, a heart condition, hemophilia, lead poisoning, leukemia, nephritis, rheumatic fever, and sickle cell anemia; and

2. adversely affects a child's educational performance."

IEP TIP

Because students often can learn to attend to their physical needs using techniques such as clean intermittent catheterization, you should be sensitive about ways to discuss CIC with the student's parents and the student and, if they consent, ensure that the student's IEP provides for instruction in CIC, probably from the school nurse. The instruction will promote the student's dignity and independent living.

The word *other* in the categorical name *other health impairments* distinguishes these from conditions such as multiple disabilities (Chapter 10), physical disabilities (this chapter), and traumatic brain injury (Chapter 13). To be served under the "other health impairments" category, the student's health condition must limit his or her strength, vitality, or alertness to such a degree that the student's educational progress is adversely affected.

As you also learned in Chapter 8, AD/HD falls into the category of other health impairments. In terms of the criteria of limitations in strength, vitality, or alertness, students with AD/HD, such as Will Sims (see Chapter 8), generally experience difficulty only with alertness.

Under the current IDEA definition, a student may have a chronic or an acute condition creating a health impairment. A chronic condition develops slowly and has long-lasting symptoms. Students with diabetes, one chronic condition, have lifelong medical needs. An acute condition, on the other hand, develops quickly with symptoms that last for a relatively short period of time. Students with pneumonia may need temporary special education services; however, once they recover from this acute condition, they may no longer be eligible for special education services.

In fall 2008, approximately 11 percent (648,398) of all students ages six through twenty-one receiving special education services were classified as having other health impairments (U.S. Department of Education, 2011). In this chapter, we focus on two relatively prevalent health conditions: epilepsy and asthma.

EPILEPSY: DESCRIBING THE CHARACTERISTICS AND DETERMINING THE CAUSES

What Is Epilepsy?

Epilepsy is a condition characterized by recurrent and unprovoked **seizures**, which are temporary neurological abnormalities that result from unregulated electrical discharges in the brain, much like an electrical storm (Shorvon, Andermann, & Guerrini, 2011). Figure 12.3 provides information about general and partial seizures and their subtypes. If a person has seizures only once or temporarily, perhaps from a high fever or brain injury, he does not have epilepsy. To be classified as having epilepsy, an individual must have at least two seizures that are unprovoked on separate days at least twenty-four hours apart (Berg, 2006). Approximately 1 to 2 percent of school-aged children and youth have epilepsy, and the onset is before five years of age for approximately one half of this group (Felix & Hunter, 2010).

As illustrated in Figure 12.3, there are two types of seizures: partial seizures and generalized seizures (Westerveld, 2008). **Partial seizures** begin in one side of the cerebral hemisphere and typically involve only one motor or sensory system. Simple partial seizures usually involve motor symptoms such as uncontrollable bending and flailing. Complex partial seizures involve an alteration of consciousness involving mood, memory, typical behavior patterns, and/or personality traits. Children and youth with complex partial seizures are more likely to have stereotypic, repetitive movements such as pursing or smacking their lips or moving in a repetitive way such as marching.

FIGURE 12.3 *Overview of seizure types and subtypes*

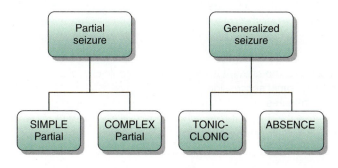

IEP TIP

You and other IEP team members should specify, in the IEP, the first aid procedures that educators should apply if a student has seizures, and you should make sure that all educators working with the student are familiar with and know how to use these procedures.

The second type of seizure is primary **generalized seizures**. As contrasted to partial seizures, primary generalized seizures involve both cerebral hemispheres. An alteration of consciousness is a primary characteristic, and the seizure affects both sides of the body (partial seizures typically affect only one side of the body). Primary generalized seizures can be further classified into tonic-clonic seizures and absence seizures. Figure 12.4 describes first aid procedures for people having seizures.

Tonic-clonic seizures (once known as *grand mal*) cause the student to lose consciousness and go back and forth through rigid extensions of extremities (tonic phase) and rhythmic contractions of extremities (clonic phase) (Fisch & Olejniczak, 2006). Students may make unusual noises during tonic-clonic seizures, have a bluish hue, lose bladder control, and require sleep or rest after the seizure. Students typically have no memory of the seizure.

During **absence seizures** (formerly known as *petit mal*), the student also loses consciousness but only for a brief period lasting about ten seconds (Benbadis & Berkovic, 2006). Frequently students also have motor movements such as blinking their eyes or

---

FIGURE 12.4

First aid for seizures

Seizure Type	Characteristics	First Aid	Possibility of Injury
General seizures			
Tonic-clonic	Uncontrolled jerking Loss of consciousness Disorientation Violent reactions Cessation of breathing Vomiting Loss of continence	Lay the person on side. Move potentially dangerous or fragile objects. Place pillow under her head. Never attempt to restrain her or place anything in her mouth.	Fairly high; person often bumps into objects during seizure.
Tonic	Sudden stiffening of muscles Rigidity Falling to ground	Reassure the individual. Provide a place to lie down afterward. Stay calm.	Quite high; person may strike an object while falling
Atonic	Sudden loss of muscle tone resulting in a collapse on ground	Reassure the individual. Provide a place to rest.	High; person may fall into an object.
Absence	Very brief interruption in consciousness Appearance of momentary deja-vu	Reassure the individual following the event.	Fairly low
Partial seizures			
Simple partial	Twitching movements Sensation of deja-vu	Reassure the student.	Fairly low
Complex partial	Altered state of consciousness Psychomotor movements	Provide verbal reassurance during occurence.	Fairly low unless there is increased physical activity.

Seek medical attention immediately if . . .

- There is no previous history of seizures, especially if the student is experiencing a tonic-clonic seizure.
- Several tonic-clonic seizures follow one another in rapid succession.
- A tonic-clonic seizure lasts for more than 2 to 3 minutes.

Source: INTERVENTION IN SCHOOL AND CLINIC by Spiegel, G. L., Cutler, S. K., & Yetter, C. E. Copyright 1996 by Sage Publications Inc. Journals. Reproduced with permission of Sage Publications Inc. Journals in the formats Textbook and Other book via Copyright Clearance Center.

changing the position of their head. The student, teachers, and peers might not realize a seizure has taken place. Absence seizures can occur hundreds of times a day and can severely affect learning.

What Other Conditions Are Associated with Epilepsy?

Research on the impact of epilepsy on intelligence indicates that approximately three fourths of individuals with epilepsy have normal intelligence, 5 percent have borderline intelligence, and 20 percent have an intellectual disability (Berg et al., 2008). Intellectual functioning is influenced by the age of onset and the particular location in which seizures originate in the brain (Westerveld, 2010). Even students with epilepsy with typical intelligence sometimes experience learning challenges associated with memory, attention, and learning disabilities (Bennett & Ho, 2009). Research has also documented a higher prevalence of emotional and behavioral disorders, including both externalizing and internalizing behaviors (Plioplys, Dunn, & Caplan, 2007).

What Are the Causes of Epilepsy?

Epilepsy is caused by a combination of genetic and environmental factors (Weinstein & Gaillard, 2007). For approximately 40 percent of individuals with epilepsy, there is a clear genetic component (Gardiner, 2000). For the remaining 60 percent, genetic causes are unclear. Environmental causes of epilepsy include prenatal brain infections, birth trauma, poisoning, stress, fatigue, and sleep deprivation. However, in approximately three fourths of individuals with epilepsy, the precise cause of the brain insult that triggered the epilepsy is unknown (DePaepe, Garrison-Kane, & Doelling, 2002).

ASTHMA: DESCRIBING THE CHARACTERISTICS AND DETERMINING THE CAUSES

What Is Asthma?

Asthma is a chronic lung condition characterized by airway obstruction, inflammation, and hyperirritability of the bronchial tubes (Adams, 2007). You probably have heard about asthma attacks, but you may never have been in the presence of someone who is experiencing an attack. Usually, asthma attacks are characterized by a shortness of breath with signs of struggles such as heaving of the chest and using neck muscles to breathe (Adams, 2007). Wheezing and coughing are often present, and individuals struggle so hard to breathe that they may not be able to talk or respond to questions. The symptoms and severity of asthma vary widely from person to person and are generally classified in the following ways (Heller, Forney, Alberto, Best, & Schwartzman, 2009):

- Intermittent (asthma attacks two or fewer days per week or two or fewer nights a month)
- Mild persistent (asthma attacks more than two days per week, three to four nights a month)
- Moderate persistent (asthma attacks daily, more than one night per week)
- Severe persistent (asthma attacks are continual and interfere with physical activity)

Asthma is the most common chronic disease among children in the United States. Approximately 7 to 10 percent of the general childhood population has a diagnosis of asthma (Bellenir, 2006). Approximately one half of children with asthma outgrow this condition as they reach their teenage years. Approximately one fourth of children with asthma are African American and Latino, and one third live in families who experience poverty (Kim, Kieckhefer, Greek, Joesch, & Baydar, 2009; Vasquez et al., 2009). Children that experience poverty have the lowest levels of checkups and medication use for asthma. If one of your students has an asthma attack, you may be reassured to know there are guidelines to follow to help you know when to seek emergency care as described in Figure 12.5.

FIGURE 12.5 *When to seek emergency care for asthma*

- Symptoms worsen, even after the medication has had time to work (generally five to ten minutes).
- The student cannot speak a sentence without pausing for breath, has difficulty walking, and/or stops playing and cannot start again.
- Chest and neck are pulled or sucked in with each breath.
- Peak flow rate lessens or does not improve after bronchodilator treatment or drops below 50 percent of the student's personal best.
- Lips and fingernails turn blue: emergency care is needed immediately!
- A second wave occurs after an episode subsides; the student is uncomfortable and having trouble breathing but does not wheeze.

IEP TIP

The IEP of a student who has asthma should describe the supports and accommodations the student needs in school, including procedures that help the student catch up on material missed when out of school.

What Other Conditions Are Associated with Asthma?

Children and youth who have asthma often experience fatigue from waking during the night because of breathing difficulties, and they are frequently absent from school due to symptoms. Jarron sometimes has to miss school because of severe asthma attacks. A review of sixty-six research studies of students with asthma concluded that, although students with asthma have a high rate of absenteeism, there are no measurable differences in their academic achievement when compared to that of students who do not have asthma (Taras & Potts-Datema, 2005). Not surprisingly, students with asthma who adhere to a prescribed medical treatment plan had less school absenteeism. Students with asthma who experience lower achievement tended to have more severe and persistent symptoms and to have more sleep interruptions.

Research differs on the link between psychological characteristics and asthma. Some research indicates a stronger association between children with asthma and internalizing disorders (Alati et al., 2005), and other research refutes this link (Tibosch, Verhaak, & Merkus, 2010). What is clear, however, is that high levels of stress are associated with an increased risk of new asthma attacks (Tibosch et al., 2010).

What Are the Causes of Asthma?

Individuals with asthma have airways that are especially sensitive. Asthma attacks have been linked to environmental and genetic factors (Castro-Giner et al., 2009). Environmental factors include air pollution associated with many factors, including traffic, industry, and smoke (Bellenir, 2006; Clark et al., 2010). In addition, genes can increase susceptibility to inflammation from environmental pollutants, which increases the chances that an asthma attack will occur (Castro-Giner et al., 2009). Jarron has a family history of asthma, although the exact genetic factors are unknown.

Evaluating Students with Physical Disabilities and Other Health Impairments

DETERMINING THE PRESENCE OF PHYSICAL DISABILITIES AND OTHER HEALTH IMPAIRMENTS

Boxes 12.1 and 12.2 highlight the nondiscriminatory evaluation processes for determining the presence of physical disabilities and other health impairments, respectively. In both cases, a physical examination from a physician is often the first step in determining whether or not the student has a disability

This student is using an inhaler to prevent debilitating effects of an acute attack of asthma. School nurses can supervise the students and the students' IEPs should provide for a health care plan as well as an education program.

BOX 12.1 NONDISCRIMINATORY EVALUATION PROCESS

Determining the Presence of Physical Disabilities

Observation

Parents or teacher observe: The student has difficulty with moving in an organized and efficient way; with fine-motor activities; with gross-motor activities; with activities of daily living, such as dressing; with postural control; and with speaking.

Physician observes: The child is not passing developmental milestones. Movement is better on one side of the body than the other. Muscle tone is too floppy or stiff. The child has problems with balance or coordination or has neurological signs that suggest a physical disability.

Screening

Assessment measures:

Developmental assessment: The child is not meeting developmental milestones or shows poor quality of movement on measures administered by a physician, physical therapist, occupational therapist, and psychologist.

Functional assessment: Activities of daily living are affected.

Prereferral

Prereferral is typically not used with these students because of the need to quickly identify physical disabilities. Also, most children with physical disabilities will be identified by a physician before starting school.

Referral

Students with physical disabilities who are identified before starting school should receive early intervention services and a nondiscriminatory evaluation upon entering school. Because some physical disabilities may develop after a student enters school, teachers should refer any student who seems to have significant difficulty with motor-related activities.

Nondiscriminatory evaluation procedures and standards

Assessment measures:

Individualized intelligence test: Standard administration guidelines may need to be adapted because the student's physical disability interferes with the ability to perform some tasks. Results may not be an accurate reflection of ability. The student may be average, above average, or below average in intelligence.

Individualized achievement test: The student may be average, above average, or below average in specific areas of achievement. Standard administration guidelines may need to be adapted to accommodate student's response style. Results may not accurately reflect achievement.

Motor functioning tests: The student's differences in range of motion, motor patterns, gaits, and postures may present learning problems. Also, length and circumference of limbs and degrees of muscle tone or muscle strength may affect his or her ability to learn specific skills.

Tests of perceptual functioning: The student is unable or has difficulty in integrating visual/auditory input and motor output in skills such as cutting and carrying out verbal instructions in an organized manner.

Adaptive behavior scales: The student may have difficulty in self-care, household, community, and communication skills because of the physical disability.

Anecdotal records: Reports suggest that the student has functional deficits and requires extra time or assistance in mobility, self-care, household, community, and communication skills because of the physical disability.

Curriculum-based assessment: The student's physical disability may limit accuracy of curriculum-based assessments.

Direct observation: The student is unable to organize and complete work or has difficulty doing so.

Determination

The nondiscriminatory evaluation team determines that the student has a physical disability and needs special education and related services.

Understanding Students with Physical Disabilities and Other Health Impairments

275

BOX 12.2

NONDISCRIMINATORY EVALUATION PROCESS

Determining the Presence of Other Health Impairments

Observation	**Parents or teacher observe:** The student may seem sluggish or have other symptoms that suggest illness. The parent takes the student for a medical examination.
	Physician observes: During a routine physical or a physical resulting from symptoms, the physician determines why the student needs further medical assessment. Some health impairments are detemined before or shortly after birth.
Screening	**Assessment measures:**
	Battery of medical tests prescribed by physician and/or specialists: Results reveal that the student has a health impairment. A physician makes the diagnosis.
Prereferral	Prereferral may or may not be indicated, depending on the severity of the health impairment. Some students function well in the general classroom. A decision may be made to serve the student with a 504 plan if accommodations are needed solely to monitor medications and/or to make sure the faculty knows what to do if the student has a medical emergency.
Referral	Students with health impairments that adversely affect their learning or behavior need to be referred for educational assessment.
Nondiscriminatory evaluation procedures and standards	**Assessment measures:**
	Medical history: Completed jointly by parents and medical and school personnel, the history yields information needed to develop a health care plan.
	Individualized intelligence test: The student's condition or treatment may contribute to a decrease in IQ.
	Individualized achievement test: The student's medical condition and/or treatment regimen may affect achievement.
	Behavior rating scales: The student is not mastering the curriculum in one or more areas as a result of the condition, treatment, and/or resulting absences.
	Curriculum-based assessment: The student is not mastering the curriculum in one or more areas as a result of the condition, treatment, and/or resulting absences.
	Direct observation: The student may experience fatigue or other symptoms resulting from the condition or treatment, detrimentally affecting classroom progress.
Determination	The nondiscriminatory evaluation team determines that the student has an "other health impairment" and needs special education and related services.

(Robb & Brunner, 2010). Although medical exams are individualized according to the particular symptoms of each student, a neurological exam is frequently administered when there is any concern about the brain's involvement in a particular condition. **Neuroimaging** provides detailed pictures of various parts of the brain. Neuroimaging is exceedingly helpful in determining the presence of cerebral palsy, spina bifida, and epilepsy (O'Shea, 2008; Weinstein & Gaillard, 2007). Neuroimaging is typically not needed for students who have symptoms associated only with asthma.

DETERMINING THE NATURE OF SPECIALLY DESIGNED INSTRUCTION AND SERVICES

Physical therapists and occupational therapists test a student's functional competence. A test of functional competence for elementary students with disabilities is the School Function Assessment. It has three parts:

- "Participation" evaluates students' level of participation in school activities and environments.
- "Task Supports" evaluates the extent to which students need supplementary aids and services to participate in school activities and environments.
- "Activity Performance" evaluates students' ability to complete functional activities requiring cognitive and physical skills.

The School Function Assessment is criterion-based. The items in each of its three parts ask questions about a range of task and activities, from simpler to more complex. Educators who are very familiar with the student in school settings are the respondents. They usually can complete the entire instrument in five to ten minutes.

The reliability, validity, and psychometric characteristics of the School Function Assessment have been established (Davies, Soon, Young, & Clausen-Yamaki, 2004). Validity studies have demonstrated that it differentiates among the students with and without disabilities and also distinguishes between groups of students with different disabilities, such as those with cerebral palsy and learning disabilities (Coster & Haltiwanger, 2004; Hwang, Davies, Taylor, & Gavin, 2002).

Designing an Appropriate IEP

PARTNERING FOR SPECIAL EDUCATION AND RELATED SERVICES

Partnerships among teachers, school nurses, physicians, family members, and students are essential to assure that students' support needs related to physical disabilities and health impairments are addressed (Engelke, Guttu, Warren, & Swanson, 2008; Taras & Brennan, 2008). Some schools have set up school-based health centers to provide comprehensive support for children with health impairments (Clayton, Chin, Blackburn, & Echeverria, 2010; Soleimnpour, Geierstanger, Kaller, McCarter, & Brindis, 2010). These centers typically provide medical and mental health care at the school so that it is easier for students and families to access the care. Box 12.3 highlights a school-based health center that had a program specifically aimed to provide support to students with asthma.

We have emphasized how important it is for you to work with a student's family and physicians. Perhaps Box 12.4, My Voice, will give you insight into the life of parents of a young boy who has juvenile diabetes.

DETERMINING SUPPLEMENTARY AIDS AND SERVICES

You have already learned how important technology can be for students with disabilities. You have learned about word processors that promote students' written performance, PDAs that help students with sequencing tasks, digital talking books and e-text formats, and adapted and augmentative communication devices. Students with physical disabilities, particularly students with cerebral palsy, such as Thomas, will often benefit from the use of a variety of technologies, including AAC devices to help them overcome communication limitations. Powered or electric wheelchairs are another frequently used type of assistive technology for students with physical disabilities. Electric wheelchairs involve a combination of technology supports. There's the motorized chair itself as well as the switch that operates the chair. Many people incorporate other technologies, such as AAC,

This student is using two forms of technology to surmount his physical limitations. One is the wheelchair, and the other is a lap-held communication book. The student's IEP should provide for both of these, and for instruction in how to use them.

into the structure of the chair. When supporting students and their families to purchase a chair, keep the following issues in mind:

- *Consider transportation issues.* Power chairs are heavy and often require modified vehicles, including vans, to transport them.
- *Consider the size.* A power chair's size sometimes limits a student's opportunity to navigate in school environments.
- *Consider maintenance.* From charging the battery to replacing worn motor bearings to adjusting and replacing footrests, power chairs require maintenance.
- *Consider operation and navigation.* Chairs can be operated by joysticks, head switches, and other means, so consider which is best for the student.
- *Consider safety.* Power chairs are heavy and can be hazardous. They can be hard to stop or navigate. Training and maintenance of critical systems such as the brake system is critical.

In the past, another consideration might have been the stigma associated with wheelchair use. Fortunately, that stigma has decreased over time. Arbour-Nicitopoulos (2010) surveyed almost 3,000 adolescents without disabilities from seventh to twelfth grade about their attitudes toward peers who used wheelchairs and found that stigmatized attitudes were held only by a small proportion (5.5 percent) of these students. That's 5.5 percent too many, but it is still a dramatic improvement from past years!

Sometimes, though, simple is better when it comes to technology. Not every student needs high-end equipment. The only device that some students with physical disabilities may need as a supplementary aid is a simple switch to operate an educational tool such as a computer, mobility equipment such as an electric wheelchair, or a device that the student uses to record teachers' lessons. Switches come in all shapes and sizes and vary in how they operate. Some

BOX 12.4	MY VOICE

Diane Lorenzo

When our then fifteen-month-old child was diagnosed with juvenile diabetes (Type I), we thought, "Oh—we can handle this—he just can't have any sugar." After he was hospitalized for one week, we realized we were drastically wrong. We were told what this disease was and how hard it would be to maintain. We were trained on how to give insulin injections (three times a day), how to test his blood sugar by drawing blood from his finger with a needle (six times a day), how to count every gram of carbohydrate that entered his body, and how to monitor his exercise to keep him from dangerously low blood sugars that could lead to seizures and/or a coma. We also had to learn how to avoid high blood sugars that could lead to a coma and very serious long-term effects such as blindness, kidney failure, heart disease, and amputations. When we left the hospital, we felt completely alone and afraid to be unsupervised in taking care of our own son.

Austin is now five years old, and he has bravely faced more than 2,555 insulin injections and 7,665 blood tests since he was diagnosed. I have had people comment that they would never know from looking at Austin that there was anything wrong. In reality, diabetes is wearing down every organ in his body, and every day is a battle to keep his blood sugar at the right level to avoid immediate danger.

As he gets older, he is becoming more aware of his special needs and that he is different from most kids. There are days where he embraces the fact that he is "special," as he calls it, and performs his own blood tests, and there are days that he screams, "I hate diabetes!" when we try to give him his shots. We try to keep him focused on the things he likes—like Batman, and dinosaurs, and sugar-free chewing gum—and try to give him the most normal childhood he can possibly have facing these hourly medical responsibilities.

Being a parent of a child with Type I diabetes has its challenges. Every day I hope for a cure that will allow Austin the freedom to live without insulin injections, blood and urine testing, and having to eat regulated, scheduled meals. The freedom to play without interrupting him to test his blood because he might be low from too much activity. The freedom to eat when he is hungry and stop eating when he is full. The freedom to wake up each morning without being poked by needles. The freedom to sleep in when he is tired instead of woken up because he must follow the same daily schedule. Austin often wonders why he does not get to enjoy these normal freedoms of childhood. And we wonder if maintaining this rigid schedule will be enough to prevent him suffering from the devastating complications of diabetes such as blindness, amputations, and kidney and heart failure.

As a result of Austin's disease, we have become very involved with the Juvenile Diabetes Foundation (JDF). JDF was started in 1972 by parents of children with diabetes; their main goal is to find a cure through funding research. We were recently asked by JDF to travel to Capitol Hill and tell Congress what our son endures. As a result of many such efforts, Congress has for the first time formed a Diabetes Caucus, which currently has 250 representatives from across the country whose goal is to pass legislation for funding to help find a cure.

operate an on/off switch with pressure, others activate a timed sequence with pressure, and still others operate the device only as long as pressure is on. The joysticks on most power chairs operate in this manner.

Pneumatic switches operate when a student puffs air into a strawlike tube. More sophisticated switches detect movement, such as eye or head movement, to operate; others operate in response to sound. Standen, Camm, Battersy, Brown, and Harrison (2011) even used the nunchuk controller from a Nintendo Wii system as a switch to enable students with physical and cognitive disabilities to operate a computer device! Thomas benefits from assistive technology and uses computers and other technology on a regular basis to access the general curriculum.

PLANNING FOR UNIVERSAL DESIGN FOR LEARNING

In Chapter 2, you learned that the 2004 amendments to IDEA included provisions for a national standard for electronic text materials, called the National Instructional Materials Accessibility Standard (NIMAS). NIMAS establishes technical standards for electronic texts. Just as DVDs are standardized, NIMAS sets a standard so that all e-text materials are accessible to students with sensory or learning disabilities.

An e-text is created from a *digital source file*, a term that refers to computer files or programs written in some digital format. Digital text can range from formats used for word processors, to markup languages such as HTML or XML, to computer codes such as JAVA. Currently, XML (extensible markup language) and XSL (extensible stylesheet language) are the digital formats most commonly used to create electronic texts. The NIMAS standard is based on these digital formats.

After a digital source file is created, it can be read by commercially available media players. When a standard format is used, it can be read by different media players. These media players can then present the information in multiple ways. Media players can convert digital source files into audio and video media, flexible text, or electronic braille and can even create avatars (digitally created figures) that virtually present content in sign language. Think of these media players like web browsers, which take HTML (hypertext markup language) and convert it to output that includes text, pictures, graphics, audio, and so forth. Within a few years, most school textbooks will be available in a digital file format.

Until the NIMAS standard and media players become available to all students, there are other ways of accessing e-text and digital documents. For example, Tom Snyder Productions publishes a series of digital texts under its Thinking Reader series. Thinking Readers were designed by researchers at the Center for Applied Special Technology (CAST) and are digital talking book (DTB) formats of popular books such as *Tuck Everlasting*; *Bud, Not Buddy*; and *A Wrinkle in Time* that are often taught in middle or junior high school. The DTB versions of these classics allow learners who are not reading at grade level to access the book through audio and video outputs and through supports programmed into the software. This can benefit students who have severe physical impairments that limit their ability to use or see print materials. It can also benefit students with more severe cognitive disabilities who otherwise could not read the book.

You can also create your own electronic texts using programs such as Microsoft Word and PowerPoint. Many of the materials that teachers use are not subject to copyright or have been developed by the teacher or the school district and can be converted to electronic versions. Also, there are copyright-free digital audio and video materials that can be used to make content more accessible. Box 12.5 provides simple steps teachers can use to create electronic content materials. Sometimes using simple e-text options can allow students with physical and other disabilities, such as Thomas, to have access to general education content and provide evidence of their knowledge and skills.

PLANNING FOR OTHER EDUCATIONAL NEEDS

One area in which both students with physical disabilities and those with other health impairments may need IEP goals is the area of physical education. Students with these disabilities often experience limitations in the type, intensity, and duration of physical activities in which they can engage. Jarron loves swimming, baseball, basketball, and soccer; he just has to remember to use his inhaler when he needs it to allow him to breathe and participate.

IEP teams need to consider adapted physical education (PE) goals and supports. Adapted physical education is, as you would guess, physical education in which activities have been adapted or modified to enable students with disabilities to participate and benefit (Lytle, Lavay, & Rizzo, 2010).

Drum, Krahn, and Bersani (2009) documented the barriers that often limit access to physical activities for people with physical and other disabilities as well as the importance of physical activities for this population. Adapted physical education allows students with

IEP TIP

All students need exercise and physical activity, so IEP teams should consider accommodations and modifications to the curriculum that promote these activities.

BOX 12.5

UNIVERSAL DESIGN FOR PROGRESS

Creating Electronic Text

Teachers can create instructional materials that include the features embedded in digital talking books and other universally designed materials by following these simple processes:

1. *Use word processing programs such as Microsoft Word to create content.* You can create documents in word processing programs that can be read aloud by text-to-speech reader programs. You can also adjust the size and color of the letters and words to accommodate students who have visual impairments. Further, you can easily paste pictures into word processing documents as well as embed hyperlinks to access Internet content (see Step 3).

2. *Use presentation software such as Microsoft PowerPoint to create content.* Presentation software is a very powerful tool to present nontext content, such as pictures and videos, and to provide content through advanced or graphic organizers. As in word processing programs, you can modify the font size and color and embed Internet-based content through hyperlinks. You can also incorporate motion features when presenting text and pictures. It is simple to cut and paste pictures into presentations and to embed video and audio playback. Also, supporting students to create their own presentations is an excellent means to promote self-directed learning.

3. *Embed links to the Internet into content presentations.* Both word processing programs and presentation software readily support hyperlinks, so you can link to Internet-based content that expands on information you are presenting, defines key terms or ideas, presents content in video or audio format, or reinforces learned information. Web quests are frequently used to promote learning and generalization, and you can link to web quest sites quite easily. You can also use hyperlinks to link to other content on the computer's hard drive.

4. *Access existing electronic text.* It is important to remember that there are copyright restrictions on the types of content you can modify into electronic versions. The above activities are primarily geared toward teacher-generated content. In addition to commercially available digital talking books, such as the Thinking Reader software discussed in the text, there are several sources through which you can obtain electronic versions of texts that are in the public domain. Bookshare.org is a frequently used site from which you can download public domain books in DTB, digital braille, text, and HTML formats. Text and HTML formats can be played using a word processor, while DTB versions can be played using free media player software (see Step 5). Memberships to the Bookshare.org library are free to U.S. schools and students. Further, beginning in the 2008–2009 school year, Bookshare.org users can use a specially designed text-to-speech software program, Read:OutLoud (manufactured by Don Johnston Incorporated), as a text reader (http://www.donjohnston.com/products/rol_bookshare/index.html). Also, the CAST website has a library of electronic books that can be used by teachers (http://bookbuilder.cast.org/library.php).

5. *Download a digital talking book player.* There are a number of DTB players that are available for download and use for low or no cost. For example, the AMIS (Adaptive Multimedia Information System) software is an open source DTB player available for free download at http://www.amisproject.org/software/index.html. Once downloaded, you install the software on a Windows computer.

In addition, researchers and developers at CAST, a center that has led in the definition and application of universal design for learning, have provided numerous suggestions that assist teachers to create universally designed instructional materials. You can see sample UDL lesson plans and develop your own at the CAST UDL Lesson Builder website (http://lessonbuilder.cast.org/), as well examples of UDL books and instructions to create your own UDL book (http://bookbuilder.cast.org/).

---

a disability to participate in typical sports or physical activities. Adapted PE specialists may suggest modifying the environment in which the sport or physical activity will occur or providing or modifying equipment. For example, a student who is blind can participate in softball if a beeping softball is used: This is an ordinary softball with an auditory sound that enables the person with the visual impairment to hear, and thus sense, the approaching ball.

In addition to using modified equipment, adapted PE focuses on students' specific educational needs related to sensory awareness systems, reflexes, fine- and gross-motor skills, body image, locomotor skills, manipulation skills, muscular endurance, and agility or speed (Winnick, 2010). Enabling students with physical disabilities or other health impairments to participate in sports and recreation activities may link that student to a source of lifelong enjoyment.

Visual impairments do not limit all activities, especially those sports and recreation activities requiring hands-on participation.

Using Effective Instructional Strategies

EARLY CHILDHOOD STUDENTS: TOKEN ECONOMY SYSTEMS

A number of instructional strategies you've already read about in this text are useful for students across disability categories and ages. Indeed, some are useful across age ranges for all students with or without disabilities. One such strategy, the use of token economy systems, is useful in all classrooms.

In Chapter 8 you learned about errorless learning and using prompts to ensure learning. Another way to support student learning is to modify the reinforcer that students receive after they have responded. You can alter the schedule on which a reinforcer is delivered (e.g., every time the student performs a behavior, every other time, or intermittently) or modify the type of reinforcer provided (e.g., providing stickers or access to a preferred activity). In token economy systems, you provide students with tokens such as points, poker chips, or tickets after they engage in desired behaviors to increase the likelihood that the behavior will occur in the future. A reinforcer (or reinforcing stimulus) is anything that increases the probability that the desired response will be performed. How can points, poker chips, or tickets serve that function? Well, think about the most common token economy system, one that you use every day. What is that? Money! Money is a token that people receive for work that they use to purchase other items or activities that are reinforcing.

Tokens function like money. Students can use their tokens (e.g., points, poker chips, or tickets) to "purchase" something reinforcing. Tokens take on a reinforcing value because students can trade them for something they enjoy. Tokens are especially beneficial because it can be difficult and ethically questionable to use primary reinforcers such as food all of the time. Tokens provide an alternative that becomes reinforcing to students.

You should take the following steps to implement a successful token economy:

- Make sure that tokens keep their value. Allow your students to earn tokens on a frequent-enough schedule and give them frequent-enough opportunities to exchange tokens.

- Decide with students what they can purchase with the tokens they earn. Remember, students will only work for tokens if the tokens can be exchanged for something they want.

- Consider how you will fade the token economy system. You can do this by pairing the tokens with other forms of reinforcement, such as verbal praise, and then slowly increasing the number of tokens needed to earn reinforcers.

Token economy systems have the benefit of being easily used at both school and home, and thus are ideal for early childhood education. Parents frequently find that these systems are manageable and that using them provides consistency between home and school. Plus, they're effective! Plavnick, Ferreri, and Maupin (2010) found that a token economy system, combined with a self-monitoring program such as the one you learned about in Chapter 10, implemented with young children with physical and developmental disabilities resulted in enhanced academic readiness. Klima and McLaughlin (2007) found, similarly, that a token economy system was effective in improving social and academic behaviors of a young child with disabilities.

ELEMENTARY AND MIDDLE SCHOOL STUDENTS: SELF-AWARENESS

The middle school years are difficult for most students, with or without disabilities. Disabilities can adversely affect adolescent milestones, including the development of a student's self-awareness distinct from the disability, health condition, or disorder. The term *self-awareness* refers to one's understanding of oneself as a unique individual and is often used in conjunction with the notions of self-understanding and self-knowledge. This includes the process referred to as *disability awareness,* which involves understanding one's abilities as a function of a specific disabling condition.

Too frequently, the only time the issue of student self-awareness comes to the forefront in education is when people other than the student question the degree to which the student has accepted her disability or, in less positive terms, accepted what she cannot do because of the disabling condition. As a result, students with disabilities and other health impairments can easily begin to think of themselves only in the context of their disability (Wehmeyer, 2008). This frequently occurs for girls and young women with disabilities (Wehmeyer et al., 2009), though boys and young men with disabilities often have similar experiences. Promoting student self-awareness can be very effective within the context of career or vocational awareness activities. Wehmeyer, Parent, and colleagues (2009) and Lindstrom and colleagues (2008) both created model programs focused on self- and disability-awareness for girls and young women with disabilities in the context of career development and planning. Box 12.6 provides strategies for promoting healthy self-awareness.

The most important theme is that, in all such efforts, the student must be the catalyst for change. Students need to be actively involved in identifying their interests, abilities, strengths, and unique learning needs as well as in applying this knowledge to identify strategies and supports that can enable them to overcome limitations.

BOX 12.6 | **INTO PRACTICE**

Promoting Healthy Self-Awareness

Self-awareness for students with disabilities must extend beyond disability awareness. The following steps and strategies can be used to promote healthy self-awareness for students with and without disabilities:

- Do not regard a student's self-awareness as consisting only of accepting a limitation.

- Recognize that while disability-awareness is an important part of self-awareness, understanding one's disability and its effects should not be the goal of efforts to promote self-awareness.

- Emphasize every student's unique skills, abilities, and talents.

- Avoid overprotecting students with disabilities at any age but especially during early adolescence, when students want to fit in instead of standing out.

- Begin instruction in self-awareness by identifying a student's basic physical and psychological needs, interests, and abilities.

- Help students identify their physical and psychological needs and teach them how to meet those needs.

- Encourage role-playing and brainstorming activities that explore students' interests and abilities.

- Ask students to discuss common emotions, such as self-worth; their own positive physical and psychological attributes and how these attributes make them feel; how other people's

actions affect their feelings of self-worth, fear, love, hate, and sadness; how these feelings affect their and others' behavior; and how to cope with these emotions.

- Transition from emotional to basic physical awareness, teaching students about their physical selves and how their physical health and capacities affect their actions.

- Teach students that there are physical causes for the way they feel and that how they feel affects the way they behave.

- Use additional materials that teach about health, sexuality, and body systems.

- Help students explore others' perceptions of them, listing others' potential reactions and constructing a view of how others see them; discuss differences among people, including interests and abilities.

- Teach students how to give and accept praise and criticism appropriately and inappropriately, list the effects and purposes of praise and criticism, and offer strategies to give and receive both.

- Ask students to identify their own positive characteristics, how to express confidence in themselves, how to react to others' expressions of confidence, and how to appropriately make positive statements about themselves (Wehmeyer, 2008).

SECONDARY AND TRANSITION STUDENTS: DRIVER'S EDUCATION

You can probably remember the day you passed your driver's test and received your license. It's a big day in any young person's life. Having a driver's license is like having a license to freedom. You can go places without your parents, and you can do more things you want to do. Many people assume that students with disabilities cannot drive, but many people with physical disabilities are quite capable drivers. In fact, given the lack of accessible public transportation in many communities, a driver's license is key to getting to a job and earning the money needed to live independently.

How do you or another person teach driving to young people with physical disabilities? Mainly, this involves direct instruction using vehicle adaptations that enable a person with a physical disability to drive. The Association for Driver Rehabilitation Specialists (n.d.) has identified a number of adaptations that might assist a driver with cerebral palsy. For one, steering wheels can be fit with a spinner knob that allows students with limited motor control to grip and turn the wheel. Vehicles can be reconfigured with a left-foot accelerator, additional mirrors, additional room for wheelchair storage and access, hand controls for accelerating and braking, and even a joystick modification to allow steering with feet instead of hands.

Not all students with physical disabilities will be able to obtain a driver's license; but if schools provide direct instruction with modified vehicles, more students will be able to do so. Just as important, students with physical disabilities will have the opportunity to undergo a rite of passage for adolescence—driver's education and then a license!

Including Students with Physical Disabilities and Other Health Impairments

Figures 12.6 and 12.7 display the percentage of students with physical disabilities and other health impairments, respectively, in inclusive placements.

FIGURE 12.6 *Educational placement of students with physical disabilities: School year 2008–2009*

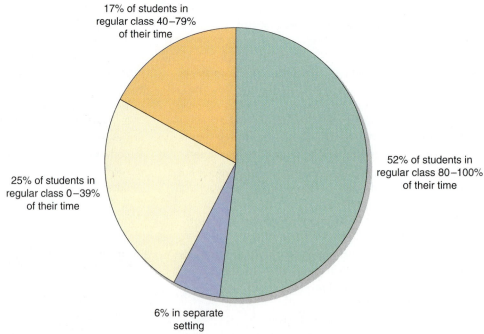

17% of students in regular class 40–79% of their time

52% of students in regular class 80–100% of their time

25% of students in regular class 0–39% of their time

6% in separate setting

Source: U.S. Department of Education. (2011). *Data accountability center: Individuals with Disabilities Education Act (IDEA) data.* Retrieved February 12, 2011, from https://www.ideadata.org.

Note: Percentages have been rounded and collapsed across categories.

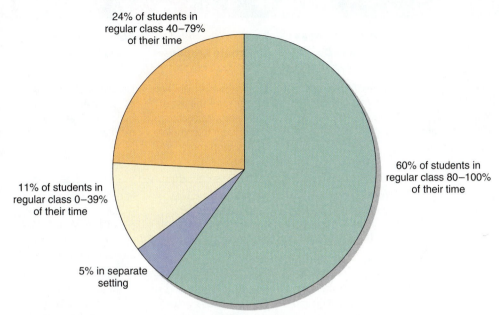

24% of students in regular class 40–79% of their time

11% of students in regular class 0–39% of their time

5% in separate setting

60% of students in regular class 80–100% of their time

Source: U.S. Department of Education. (2011). *Data accountability center: Individuals with Disabilities Education Act (IDEA) data.* Retrieved February 12, 2011, from https://www.ideadata.org.

Note: Percentages have been rounded and collapsed across categories.

Compared to students with other types of disabilities, students with orthopedic impairments have one of the highest rates of placement in home or hospital settings. Receiving an appropriate education while in the hospital or at home is important if students are to avoid grade retention, inappropriate special education placement, learned helplessness, or early dropout (Bessell, 2001b). Students often feel isolated by homebound services (Bessell, 2001a). The Committee on School Health (2000) emphasizes that "homebound instruction is meant for acute or catastrophic health problems that confine a child or adolescent to home or hospital for a prolonged but defined period of time and is not intended to relieve the school or parent of the responsibility for providing education for the child in the least restrictive environment" (p. 1154).

Parents, school administrators, teachers, and the student's primary care physician need to partner with each other to consider how to address the curriculum standards and IEP goals that the student would achieve if still in school, what the specific duration of the homebound services will be, and how to return the student to school as quickly and smoothly as possible. Dual enrollment in homebound and school-based instruction enables students to continue functioning as a classroom member, even if they cannot spend the whole day in the classroom (Bessell, 2001b). Box 12.7 offers suggestions for including students with other health impairments and physical disabilities in general education classrooms.

Assessing Students' Progress

MEASURING STUDENTS' PROGRESS

Progress in the General Curriculum

Many means of assessing progress in the general curriculum involve paper/pencil examinations. Students with physical disabilities often have fine- and gross-motor limitations that reduce their capacity to demonstrate their abilities on these assessments; similarly, students with other health impairments may lack the stamina required to complete them on time.

BOX 12.7

INCLUSION TIPS

	What You Might See	What You Might Be Tempted to Do	Alternate Responses	Ways to Include Peers in the Process
Behavior	The student becomes very anxious when he is not able to complete assignments at the same speed as his classmates.	Tell him to be realistic and face his own limitations.	Develop a 504 plan that incorporates the use of technology to enable the student to complete assignments more quickly.	Explore ways in which all class members can benefit from assistive technology.
Social interactions	She may be self-conscious or embarrassed, so she withdraws from others.	Allow her to work alone, assuming she is merely low on energy or needs to be by herself.	Work with the school counselor to provide the student with self-awareness instruction.	Recognize that all students deal with self-esteem issues and involve the class in self-awareness instruction.
Educational performance	Lack of strength and use of a wheelchair hinder his capacity for full participation in physical education.	Excuse him from physical education and have him attend a study hall instead.	Use curriculum-based assessment to evaluate the student's strengths and needs related to adapted physical education.	Explore opportunities for him to participate in a wheelchair basketball league.
Classroom attitudes	She appears to be overwhelmed by class activities when feeling fatigued.	Tell the student that her only choice is to deal with it.	In a 504 plan, specify the appropriate length of work and rest periods for her.	Have classmates serve as scribes for her and offer other support as needed.

An increasing number of alternatives to handwritten performance examinations make use of computer technology. For example, you and other teachers may use computer-based assessment to augment a curriculum-based measurement. As you learned in Chapter 5, curriculum-based measurement (CBM) involves frequent assessments of indicators that are tied to the curriculum, that are measured repeatedly, and that provide indicators of student improvement. You may make an obvious accommodation for your students by using a computer for CBM purposes. At the same time, you are able to assess the progress that all of your students make by using CBM (Tsuei, 2008).

Progress in Addressing Other Educational Needs

As you have learned, physical activity has important benefits for students with physical disabilities or other health impairments, and adapted physical education services can give these students the exercise they need. There are a variety of ways for you to track student progress in the area of physical education, including tracking students' correct performances of a physical task and measuring the frequency with which a student engages in an activity. Winnick (2010) suggests that measurement in adapted physical education also include the following:

- Cardiovascular function, including resting and target heart rate
- Body composition, mass, and weight
- Muscle strength and endurance
- Muscle and joint flexibility
- Posture evaluation
- Mobility

MAKING ACCOMMODATIONS FOR ASSESSMENT

You have already learned that computer-based assessment can be an important strategy for measuring progress in the general curriculum for students with physical disabilities and other health impairments. It is also an important accommodation to enable students to participate in standardized testing. Students with other health impairments may also require more frequent breaks or multiple test sessions in order to complete a test. If a computer-based assessment is not available, students with physical disabilities may need a scribe to record answers or extended time to complete the test.

You also have learned that there are many universal accommodations—those that benefit students with different disabilities. One particular accommodation that may be specific to students with physical disabilities, however, involves physical access to the testing environment. In many cases, concerns about ensuring security and minimizing the potential for cheating or disruption of the testing environment take priority over physical access. To make sure students with physical disabilities can participate in test situations, you should consider accessibility, such as the availability of an elevator and physical access to needed test materials.

ADDRESSING THE PROFESSIONAL STANDARDS

The following Council for Exceptional Children (CEC) Common Core Knowledge and Skills are addressed in this chapter through the content and concepts we discuss. See the Appendix for a full listing of these Knowledge and Skill statements:

ICC2K1, ICC2K2, ICC2K4, ICC2K5, ICC2K6, ICC3K1, ICC3K2, ICC4S1, ICC4S2, ICC4S3, ICC4S4, ICC4S5, ICC4S6, ICC5S2, ICC5S3, ICC5S4, ICC5S9, ICC5S12, ICC5S15, ICC7K5, ICC7S1, ICC7S3, ICC7S6, ICC7S7, ICC7S9, ICC8K3, ICC8S2, ICC8S3, ICC8S6, ICC8S8, ICC10S2, ICC10S3, ICC10S4, ICC10S5

Summary

IDENTIFYING STUDENTS WITH PHYSICAL DISABILITIES

- The term *physical disability* refers to a large group of students who, though quite different from each other, share the common challenge of mobility limitations.
- *Cerebral palsy* refers to a disorder of movement or posture occurring when the brain is in its early stages of development. The damage is not progressive or hereditary.

- *Spina bifida* is a malformation of the spinal cord. Its severity depends on both the extent of the malformation and its position on the spinal cord.
- Cerebral palsy is caused by prenatal, perinatal, or postnatal factors; and spina bifida is caused by an interaction of environmental and genetic factors.

IDENTIFYING STUDENTS WITH OTHER HEALTH IMPAIRMENTS

- *Other health impairments* are chronic or acute health problems that result in limitations of strength, vitality, or alertness and adversely affect a student's educational performance.
- *Epilepsy* is a condition characterized by seizures that can be classified into two major types: partial seizures and generalized seizures.
- *Asthma* is a chronic lung condition characterized by airway obstruction, inflammation, and increased sensitivity. It is the most common chronic disease among children in the United States.
- Both epilepsy and asthma are caused by a combination of genetic and environmental factors.

EVALUATING STUDENTS WITH PHYSICAL DISABILITIES AND OTHER HEALTH IMPAIRMENTS

- A physical examination, performed by a physician, is often the first step in determining whether or not a student has a physical disability or other health impairment.
- Sometimes a neurological examination is needed, and neuroimaging is a technique for that kind of examination.
- Prenatal screening assists in identifying some physical disabilities, including spina bifida.
- The School Function Assessment is a criterion-based measure of functional skills required of elementary students in school settings.

DESIGNING AN APPROPRIATE IEP

- Students with physical disabilities and other health impairments will benefit from a comprehensive health plan that specifies the health supports and accommodations that will enable them to experience successful inclusion.
- School-based health clinics can be helpful in providing comprehensive health care by an interdisciplinary team of health care providers and educators.
- IEP teams should consider the use of switches to provide greater access to the general curriculum for students with physical disabilities and other health impairments.
- Electronic or digital text formats enable educators to deliver core academic content in multiple ways.
- Physical exercise is important for *all* children. Adapted physical education provides students with opportunities for inclusion, exercise, and recreation.

USING EFFECTIVE INSTRUCTIONAL STRATEGIES

- Token economy systems use tokens to reinforce positive behavior and academic outcomes. They can be incorporated into the educational programs of young children with disabilities to promote positive outcomes.
- Students with physical disabilities and other health impairments may struggle to develop self-awareness distinct from the disability, health condition, or disorder. Teachers should include instruction on student self-awareness as part of the educational program.
- Driver's education is part of the transition to adulthood for most adolescents and should be for students with physical disabilities and other health impairments as well. Some students are able to learn to drive if they have instruction and are provided with vehicle modifications.

ASSESSING STUDENTS' PROGRESS

- Students with physical disabilities and other health impairments may perform more effectively on curriculum-based measurement if such measures are computer-based.
- There are multiple means to measure progress in physical education; teachers should focus on a wide array of health outcomes, including cardiovascular outcomes.
- Students with physical disabilities and other health impairments may need multiple accommodations for testing, such as extended time, a scribe, or computer administration. Physical access to the testing site is also important.

13 Understanding Students *with* Traumatic Brain Injury

Who Is Dylan Outlaw?

Graduation: One word.

One meaning? The awarding of an academic degree or diploma. Another meaning? Moving forward, just as IDEA envisions for students with disabilities and ESEA envisions for all students.

For twelve-year-old Dylan Outlaw, graduation has occurred six times. Yes, six. Each time, it has consisted of far more than the awarding of degrees or diplomas. Think of graduation as moving from one stage of life to another. Then apply that meaning to Dylan.

Dylan graduated from the category of students who do not have disabilities into the category of those who do when a two-ton refrigerator truck plowed into his family's car and caused a traumatic brain injury. Dylan was only four years old.

He graduated again by defying the dire prognoses of physicians after the accident. They had warned Dylan's mother, Renee, and her family that he might not survive the injury. He was evaluated as having the most severe form of brain injury. Shards of bone from his eye sockets and temples were floating in his cerebral fluids, near his optic nerves. To prevent them from moving, doctors placed him into an induced coma for five days. Seemingly miraculously—Renee attributes his recovery to prayer—Dylan's body digested the shards. Yet even though his many MRI scans revealed no bone residue, the brain injury nonetheless affected him.

Dylan graduated from the hospital's critical care unit to its rehabilitation unit in a near-record time of six weeks, and then graduated from that unit to rehabilitation at home. From there he went to kindergarten.

Through fifth grade, Dylan was classified as a student with a disability under IDEA and had the requisite IEP. When it came time for him to enter sixth grade, however, Renee attended a Partners in Policy Making training session sponsored by the state's council on developmental disabilities. There she learned about Section 504 of the Rehabilitation Act and its requirements for "reasonable accommodations." She told Dylan that, for

him, having those accommodations was like, for another boy, having a cast for a broken arm; it was no big deal to accept those benefits. Together, Renee and Dylan insisted that he receive Section 504 accommodations and that he graduate from his status as a student covered by IDEA. So instead of benefiting from the federal special education law (IDEA), Dylan now benefited from the federal antidiscrimination law.

Count up the graduations in Dylan's life: from nondisabled to having a disability, from near death to life, from critical care to center-based rehabilitation, from center-based to home-based rehabilitation, from home to IDEA benefits, and from IDEA to Section 504's protection. No student graduates without first having been educated. Often, the student learns from professionals, sometimes from family, and sometimes from peers. Dylan's teachers—in the broadest sense—were from each of those groups.

His physicians saved his life. Occupational therapists, speech-language therapists, and physical therapists restored most of his functional abilities. His mother, Renee, resigned from her job and stopped taking college courses to coordinate his care at home. His father, Bob, his aunt, Laura, and his grandmother, Ruby, delivered the therapies they had learned from professionals. Dylan's older brother, also named Bob, was Dylan's model: no matter his circumstances, Dylan was determined to follow Bob into kindergarten and then through the grades ahead.

Dylan's classmates in special education also played a role, however accidentally. By having an IEP and being educated with them, Dylan learned that he could do a lot more for himself than his teachers were allowing him to do. He learned the importance of high expectations. Armed with Renee's knowledge

about Section 504, Dylan decided that he would abandon his IDEA rights, the special education pullout programs, and (truth be told) the labeling that came with being in special education.

Dylan is bright enough to have understood something profound about himself: He wants to be more typical than not. He's determined enough to have persevered through physically challenging therapies and to have relabeled himself. And he's so value-driven that he, with his family wholly behind him and with support from his teachers (Patti Whipple and Kate Simsek at Tiller Middle School, a state-approved charter school), seeks inclusion and independence.

Yet he still needs therapy and accommodations. Because he injured the right side of his brain, he has functional limitations on the left side of his body. Occupational therapists target his fine-motor skills. He receives accommodations in taking tests and doing homework because traumatic brain

injury scrambles a person's executive functions: the ability to plan and to execute a plan.

Because he still has not fully recovered his strength, simply getting from one place to another in school exhausts him, often to the point that he physically cannot carry out his homework assignments as well as his classmates who do not have disabilities are able to do. Because academic demands, sparked by state and district assessments, increase from grade to grade, schoolwork is becoming more difficult, despite the fact that Dylan is an excellent reader.

Because all of this makes him realize that he still has a disability, he is offended when students call him names. He prefers the company of compassionate peers (usually girls), and he cannot easily hide his frustration and sadness.

His teacher Patti Whipple cautions us all: "Don't judge before you deal with the student. Traumatic brain injury is not a death sentence. Indeed, I'd love to teach a classroom of a thousand Dylans."

Identifying Students with Traumatic Brain Injury

DEFINING TRAUMATIC BRAIN INJURY

IDEA defines **traumatic brain injury (TBI)** as

an acquired injury to the brain caused by an external physical force, resulting in total or partial functional disability or psychosocial impairment, or both, that adversely affects a child's educational performance. Traumatic brain injury applies to open or closed head injuries resulting in impairments in one or more areas, such as cognition; language; memory; attention; reasoning; abstract thinking; judgment; problem-solving; sensory, perceptual, and motor abilities; psychosocial behavior; physical functions; information processing; and speech. Traumatic brain injury does not apply to brain injuries that are congenital or degenerative, or to brain injuries induced by birth trauma.

We call your attention to three aspects of this definition: First, TBI must be an **acquired injury** (occurring after a child is born). It is inappropriate to classify a student as having TBI if her brain injury was **congenital** (present at birth) or if it occurred at the time of delivery. Second, TBI must be caused by an external physical force. Thus, if a student had **encephalitis** (inflammation of the brain) and his brain was injured as a result of the inflammation, he would not be classified as having TBI. Finally, the term TBI applies to both open and closed head injuries (Kirkwood et al., 2008). An **open head injury** penetrates the bones of the skull, allowing bacteria to have contact with the brain and potentially impairing specific functions, usually only those controlled by the injured part of the brain. A **closed head injury** does not involve penetration or fracture of the bones of the skull. It results from an external blow or from the brain being whipped back and forth rapidly, causing it to rub against and bounce off the rough, jagged interior of the skull. Figure 13.1 illustrates how a closed head injury can occur in an automobile accident.

FIGURE 13.1 *Closed head injury accident*

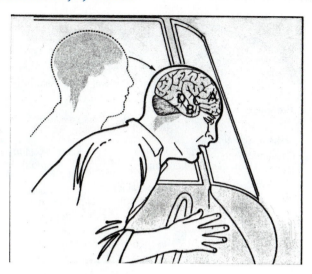

In fall 2008, approximately 0.4 percent (24,866) of all students ages six through twenty-one receiving special education services were classified as having a traumatic brain injury (U.S. Department of Education, 2011). The Centers for Disease Control and Prevention (Faul, Xu, Wald, & Coronado, 2010) report the following statistics:

- Approximately 1.7 million people annually sustain a TBI.
- Approximately one-third of all injury-related deaths in the United States are related to a TBI.
- Children from birth to age four, adolescents ages fifteen to nineteen, and senior citizens over age sixty-five are most likely to sustain a TBI.
- Males are approximately 1.4 times more likely to sustain a TBI than females are.
- Males from birth to age four have the highest rates of emergency room visits, hospitalizations, and deaths related to TBIs.
- African American children have about twice the rate of TBI from birth to age four. American Indian and Asian students have lower rates of TBI from ages ten to nineteen.

Between 2002 and 2006, there was a 14 percent increase in emergency room visits and a 20 percent increase in hospitalizations due to TBI (Faul et al., 2010). Dylan Outlaw certainly added to these data; emergency rooms and hospitalizations have been part of his young life.

DESCRIBING THE CHARACTERISTICS

Students with TBI differ in onset, complexity, and recovery (Lajiness-O'Neil & Erdodi, 2011). Their injuries may affect them in many areas of their functioning; however, they often share similar characteristics with students who have learning disabilities (Chapter 5), communication disorders (Chapter 6), emotional or behavioral disorders (Chapter 7), intellectual disability (Chapter 9), health impairments (Chapter 12), and physical disabilities (Chapter 12). Dylan's injury caused learning, communication, emotional, and physical challenges. Of those, the emotional challenges are the greatest, says his mother Renee. Interestingly, his teacher Patti downplays those challenges: "When any student has any emotional problem, we deal with it right then. It doesn't take long. All kids have problems, especially during puberty. Then we move along in class." She knows that Dylan is not so unlike other students and that a short deviation from lesson plans to address behaviors makes teaching easier and learning more effective.

Figure 13.2 illustrates the six areas of the brain (including the brain stem) and their related functions. The characteristics manifested by students who experience TBI are

FIGURE 13.2   *Areas of the brain and related general functions*

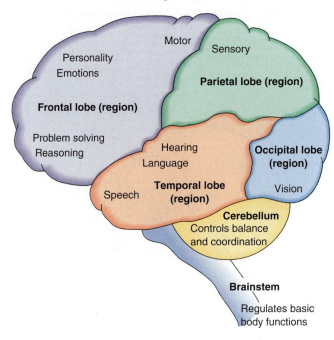

aligned with the particular site and extent of their injury (Johnson, DeMatt, & Salorio, 2009). Injuries are classified as mild, moderate, or severe. The extent of functional changes and the course of recovery depend largely on whether the injury was mild, moderate, or severe. Approximately 80–90% of TBIs are classified as mild (Lajiness-O'Neill & Erdodi, 2011).

Physical Changes

Coordination problems, physical weakness, and fatigue are common effects of TBI (Michaud et al., 2007), as they are for Dylan. Students who were previously athletic often find these changes to be especially frustrating. Fortunately, coordination and physical strength usually improve after the injury as students' brains heal and they undergo rehabilitation, especially occupational therapy, to reacquire their fine-motor skills. Dylan's injury was on the right side of his brain, so his left side is impaired; his occupational therapy targeted his left-side fine-motor skills (holding eating utensils, for example). Students' fatigue often lingers, though; and if occupational therapy and other rehabilitation interventions are not brought to bear, their muscles may **atrophy,** resulting in lost or reduced muscle strength.

Cognitive and Academic Changes

A ten-year follow-up study of individuals who sustained a TBI between birth and age seventeen reported long-term impairments in verbal learning and verbal IQ. As compared to people of the same age without a disability, individuals with TBI had particularly low verbal IQs as contrasted to their performance IQs. Verbal abilities

Students with traumatic brain injury often receive assistance from a school-based physical therapist. Here, the therapist is helping the student recover her sense of balance and her torso strength.

typically improved within the first twelve months of the injury, but there was limited improvement after twelve months. The authors concluded that "a brain injury in childhood not only has a direct effect on the brain but also affects the ongoing maturation process" (Horneman & Emanuelson, 2009, p. 912). Overall, the TBI group scored between one quarter and three quarters of a standard deviation below the mean of the group without disabilities.

The extent of injury, ranging from mild to severe, is an important determining factor of the extent of cognitive changes. When a TBI injury is mild, students usually do not face significant changes in their academic or language abilities; by contrast, students with moderate TBI often have variable outcomes that are influenced by the amount of time since injury and the specific skills being targeted. Children with moderate TBI tend to have an early small drop in academic skills that persists on a long-term basis, as contrasted with those children who have a less severe injury and are able to catch up academically after their injury (Vu, Babikian, & Asarnow, 2011). Finally, children with a severe TBI injury initially have the most significant impairments in academic and language performance. It is encouraging, however, to note that these students tend to show the most improvement over time in math, spelling, reading, and language. The cognitive impairments associated with severe TBI include difficulties with processing speed and recall of detailed new information.

The child's age at the time of injury is a second factor affecting cognitive functioning (Donders, 2008). Children injured under the age of four demonstrate greater rates of cognitive impairment as compared to children over the age of four (Freeman et al., 2008). Very young children have greater brain vulnerability, and the impairment often becomes more evident over time, especially as cognitive demands increase.

Undoubtedly, Dylan has improved cognitively. For a full month after his accident, he was unable to speak. His therapists elicited responses by asking him to play video games. By mastering one game and then another, he began to talk about himself and the games. They soon learned that Dylan was a competitive young boy. He was determined to succeed, as indeed he has.

Emotional, Behavioral, and Social Changes

Emotional, behavioral, and social changes can be especially problematic for children and youth with TBI. From time to time Dylan has meltdowns: His frustration gets the better of him when tasks he thinks he should be able to do elude him. One of Patti's accommodations is subtle; she allows him to leave the classroom, compose himself, give himself a pep talk, and return. Often he is out of the room for only a few minutes, so he does not lose much, if any, real instructional time and he regains his ability to learn.

Depending upon the extent and location of their injuries, students with TBI have an increased likelihood of experiencing a multitude of challenges:

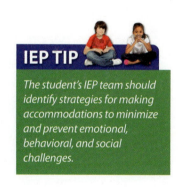

IEP TIP

The student's IEP team should identify strategies for making accommodations to minimize and prevent emotional, behavioral, and social challenges.

- Behavioral problems occur in 35 to 70 percent of children and adolescents with TBI (Slifer & Amari, 2009). Behavior problems can vary by the stage of rehabilitation. In the early stages, common problems are agitation, disinhibition, and aggression; in the later stages problems often include immature behavior, behavioral rigidity, and impaired social perception.
- One year after injury, students with TBI are more likely to show recovery in cognitive skills as compared to behavioral skills (Fay et al., 2009).
- Post-traumatic stress disorder includes symptoms such as depression, anxiety, irritability, and sleep disturbance. It can occur in response to the stress of the accident as well as to the stress associated with hospitalization and loss of a regular and predictable routine (Hajek et al., 2010). Approximately two thirds of children with TBI experienced post-traumatic stress disorder in the first three months, while only 10 percent experience the condition two years after injury (Max, 2005).
- Students with TBI have an increased likelihood for being diagnosed with obsessive-compulsive disorders, anxiety disorders, and depression (Grados et al., 2008).

DETERMINING THE CAUSES

There are four major causes of acquired TBI (Faul et al., 2010):

- *Falls* (accounting for 35 percent) are the number-one cause of TBI. They are most frequent among young children from birth to age four and adults ages seventy-five or older. Falls also account for the greatest number of emergency room visits and hospitalizations due to TBI.

- *Automobile accidents* (accounting for 17 percent) are the leading cause of death from TBI and occur most frequently among adults ages twenty to twenty-four years.

- *Being struck by or against something* (accounting for 17 percent) typically occurs in sports or recreation when a person collides with a moving or stationary object (for instance, sledding, skiing, snowboarding, diving, skateboarding, playing contact sports, or being hit by a baseball).

- *Assaults* (accounting for 10 percent) frequently involve firearms. Non-firearm assaults include child abuse that results in infant head injuries.

- *Unknown/other causes* account for 21 percent.

A review of data on the relationship between TBI and child abuse suggests that abuse is the most common cause of severe TBI in children under age one as well as a substantial percent of the TBI in children up to five years of age. Children with TBI from child abuse have a 30 percent rate of death and a 30 to 50 percent rate of having significant neurological impairments (Case, 2008). **Shaken baby syndrome** refers to TBI that results when a caregiver shakes a child violently, often in situations in which the caregiver is frustrated because of the child's crying (Altimier, 2008). This situation often occurs when caregivers have high stress levels, poor impulse control, negative childhood experiences including a history of abuse, and unrealistic child-rearing expectations. The National Center on Shaken Baby Syndrome has developed materials to educate parents about early infant crying and the danger of shaking babies (Barr et al., 2009).

Evaluating Students with Traumatic Brain Injury

The evaluation of students with TBI needs to be comprehensive (across the student's physical, cognitive, emotional-behavioral, and developmental support needs) and ongoing because children change (Kade & Fletcher-Janzen, 2009), just as Dylan changed after his injuries. Box 13.1 illustrates the evaluation process.

DETERMINING THE PRESENCE OF TRAUMATIC BRAIN INJURY

Immediately after a child experiences a head injury, the first steps are resuscitation, stabilizing the child, and, if necessary, performing surgery. The next step is to assess the extent of neurological impairment. The Glasgow Outcomes Scale is a standard scale for assessing the extent of neurological impairment. It classifies injuries into the following broad groups: "(1) death, (2) persistent vegetative state (i.e., no cerebral cortical function as judged behaviorally), (3) severe disability (conscious but dependent on 24-hour care), (4) moderate disability (disabled but capable of independent self-care), and (5) good recovery (mild impairment with persistent sequelae but able to participate in a normal social life)" (Kraus & Chu, 2005, p. 17). The scale focuses on the best response that an individual is able to make in terms of eye, verbal, and motor responses.

The Glasgow Outcomes Scale has a pediatric version that researchers believe has superior psychometric characteristics compared to other pediatric scales (Cheng, Khairi, & Ritter, 2006; Simpson, 2006). The items are as follows (Cheng et al., 2006):

- *Eyes open:* spontaneously, to speech, to pain, none (graded from 4 to 1)
- *Best verbal response:* coos/babbles, irritable, cries to pain, moans, none (graded from 5 to 1)
- *Best motor response:* normal spontaneous movement, withdraws to touch, withdraws to pain, abnormal flexion, abnormal extension, none (graded from 6 to 1)

BOX 13.1 **NONDISCRIMINATORY EVALUATION PROCESS**

Determining the Presence of Traumatic Brain Injury

Observation

Parents observe: The student receives a head injury from an accident, fall, sports injury, act of violence, or other cause.

Physicians observe: The student has an open or closed head injury caused by an external physical force.

Teacher observes: In the case of a mild head injury that might not have been treated by a physician, the teacher observes changes—physical, cognitive, communication, social, behavioral, and/or personality.

Screening

Assessment measures:

Scanning instruments: EEGs, CAT scans, MRIs, PETs, and other technology determine the extent of injury.

Neurological exam: A neurologist examines the student for indications of brain injury.

Coma scale: In instances of moderate to severe head injuries that induce comas, these scales provide some information about probable outcome.

Prereferral

Prereferral typically is not used with these students because the sudden onset and severity of the disability indicates a need for special education or related services.

Referral

Students with moderate to severe TBI should be referred to special education evaluation while still in rehabilitation. Teachers should refer students with mild head injuries if they notice any changes—physical, cognitive, communication, social, behavioral, and/or personality.

Nondiscriminatory evaluation procedures and standards

Assessment measures:

Individualized intelligence test: The student tends to score higher on the verbal section than on the performance section.

Individualized achievement tests: The student usually has peaks and valleys in scores. The student often retains skills in some areas, while other skills are affected adversely by the injury.

Adaptive behavior scales: The student may have difficulty in social, self-care, household, and community skills as a result of the injury.

Cognitive processing tests: The student may have difficulty in areas of attention, memory, concentration, motivation, and perceptual integration.

Social, emotional, and behavioral changes: The student may demonstrate difficulty relating to others and behaving in socially appropriate ways. The student may have problem behavior and/or emotional disorders.

Anecdotal records: The student's cognitive, communication, motor, and behavior skills appear to have changed from what was indicated in records before the accident.

Curriculum-based assessment: The student may have difficulty in areas of curriculum that were not problematic before the injury.

Direct observation: The student appears frustrated, has a limited attention span, tires easily, or lacks motivation to perform academic tasks. The student may have difficulty relating appropriately to others. Skills can improve rapidly, especially during the early post-injury stage.

Determination

The nondiscriminatory evaluation team determines that special education and related services are needed.

FIGURE 13.3 *Classroom observation checklist for students with TBI*

Functional Domain	Examples of Problems
Taking in/retaining information	__ Forgets things that happened even the same day
	__ Has problems learning new concepts, facts, or information
	__ Cannot remember simple instructions or rules
	__ Forgets classroom materials, assignments, and deadlines
	__ Forgets information learned from day to day (does well on quizzes but fails tests covering several weeks of learning)
Attention and maintaining activity	__ Confused by time (day, date), place (classroom, bathroom, schedule changes), or personal information (birth date, address, phone, schedule)
	__ Confused or requires prompts about where, how, or when to begin assignment
	__ Confused or agitated when moving from one activity, place, or group to another
	__ Stops midtask (math problem, worksheets, story, or conversation)
	__ Gives up quickly on challenging tasks
Language comprehension/expression	__ Unable to recall word meaning or altered meaning (homonym or homographs)
	__ Difficulty understanding complex or lengthy discussion
	__ Processes information at a slow pace
	__ Difficulty finding specific words (may describe but not label)
	__ Stammers or slurs words
	__ Difficulty expressing ideas fluently (speech disjointed, stops midsentence)
Awareness	__ Fails to correctly interpret nonverbal social cues
	__ Difficulty understanding the feelings and perspectives of others
	__ Does not understand strengths, weaknesses, or self-presentation
	__ Does not know when help is required or how to get assistance
	__ Denies any problems or changes resulting from injury

Source: Adapted from Waaland, P. K., & Bohannon, P. (1992). Traumatic brain injury checklist. In *Guidelines for educational services for students with traumatic brain injury*. Richmond: Virginia Department of Education. Reprinted with permission.

A severe injury is indicated by a score of fewer than 9 points, a moderate head injury by a score of 9 to 12, and a mild injury by a score greater than 12. The maximum number of points is 15, signifying the top score in each of the three areas.

IEP TIP

Results from the observation checklist can be shared in IEP meetings and serve as the basis for planning appropriate goals and objectives.

DETERMINING THE NATURE OF SPECIALLY DESIGNED INSTRUCTION AND SERVICES

Students with TBI need frequent reevaluation because of the nature of their recovery, especially in the first couple of years after the onset of injury. To evaluate frequently, teachers must make classroom observations of the key neurological skills affected by TBI. Figure 13.3 is a classroom observation checklist that includes the cognitive and academic domains frequently affected by TBI. Teachers can complete this checklist monthly during the first year after a head injury and less frequently thereafter.

Designing an Appropriate IEP

PARTNERING FOR SPECIAL EDUCATION AND RELATED SERVICES

One of the most challenging times for students who have traumatic brain injury is when they return to school after having been hospitalized or in a center-based rehabilitation program. Reentry IEPs usually result from the collaboration of special and general education teachers and related school personnel, physicians, other health care providers, and rehabilitation professionals (Slomine & Locascio, 2009). Physicians and rehabilitation professionals play specialized roles in describing a student's brain functioning and prognosis and in developing and implementing the student's IEP. Many rehabilitation centers realize the particular importance of the student's reentry to school and employ a hospital-school liaison (sometimes referred to as a school reentry specialist).

Dylan was in preschool at the time he was injured, so he had an entry plan (not a reentry plan) because he was moving from preschool to kindergarten. Thanks to intensive occupational, speech-language, and physical therapy at the hospital, in a rehabilitation center, and at home (where all the adult members of his family carried out therapy), Dylan "graduated" from preschool to kindergarten on time; he never missed a beat. In Box 13.2, you will find tips for creating partnerships for transitions such as Dylan's.

In many cases, teams formed for reentry remain intact to support the student in school. Some schools have designated a core team to foster partnerships. The team usually consists of general and special education teachers, parents, a speech pathologist, a physical therapist, an occupational therapist, and the school district's director of curriculum. Dylan's team consists of his teachers, including Patti Whipple; the school's director, Kate Simsek; a speech-language therapist; an occupational therapist; and a physical therapist. Kate coordinates

IEP TIP

Now that Dylan is twelve, he may decide to take part in some of the meetings his teachers hold to discuss his Sec. 504 plan. Those discussions are comparable to the ones that occur at an IEP team meeting.

BOX 13.2 | **PARTNERSHIP TIPS**

From Hospital-Based Rehabilitation to Successful School Reentry

Partnerships among various professionals and students with TBI and their families can make rehabilitation less traumatic for student and family. But collaboration is not always easy to achieve. For one thing, physicians and other health care providers have a focus different from that of other professionals. In some instances, they are intent on saving the student's life. If they are successful, then they focus on rehabilitation, a specialized field of medicine that involves not only physicians but also other professionals:

- Pulmonary therapists (to develop the student's lung and heart capacity)
- Physical therapists (to develop the student's muscle strength and stamina)
- Occupational therapists (to develop the student's ability to do the chores of daily living, such as brushing his teeth and tying his shoes)
- Psychologists or cognitive retrainers (to help the student learn how to think again)
- Speech-language therapists (to help the student regain the ability to communicate)

Whether these professionals work in a hospital or a rehabilitation center, they are trying to restore the student's ability to learn.

Educators, on the other hand, are teaching the student, working to move him to the next lesson and increase his cognitive abilities. Educators are also helping students cope with behavioral and social challenges that arise in school.

Finally, the student's family members are experiencing their own grief and shock over the sudden onset of the TBI. Their goals may include all of the goals of the professionals, but they also have to learn to alter their family routines to address the needs and challenges associated with the injury and rehabilitation as well as to reintegrate their child into their lives and family.

What Are Partnership Tips for Hospital-Based Rehabilitation?
- Keep the same long-term goals in mind.
- Identify short-term goals and how they will help achieve long-term goals.
- Show how one professional's techniques complement another's.
- Acknowledge that different professionals bring different but equally valuable strategies to partnership efforts, albeit at different times.
- Remember that the child and family are being launched into new territory and deserve the respect and support that will enable them to be as successful as possible.

What Are Partnership Tips for Hospital-to-School Transitions?
- Involve educators during the hospital stay.
- Keep school personnel updated on student medical progress.
- Make the period of homebound instruction as short as possible.
- Frequently monitor the student's progress after reentry.
- Assign someone to be the point person for coordinating the transition (Ylvisaker et al., 2001, p. 83).

What Key Abilities Predict a Student's Successful Reentry?
- Attending to the instructor and instruction
- Understanding and retaining information
- Reasoning and expressing ideas
- Solving problems
- Planning and monitoring his own performance (Semrud-Clikeman, 2001)

Traumatic brain injury can impede a student's memory and other executive functions, so the student will benefit from a simple hand-held device that jogs her memory or helps her know what tasks to complete and how and when to complete them. The student's IEP should provide for the student to use these devices.

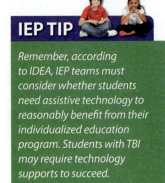

these services, in cooperation with Renee, Dylan's mother. They meet regularly, often monthly, to discuss how Dylan is developing and to consider how to respond to his academic, developmental, emotional-behavioral, and functional needs.

DETERMINING SUPPLEMENTARY AIDS AND SERVICES

Many of the classroom modifications discussed in Chapter 11, focusing on students with autism, also benefit students with TBI. There are also technology devices to support students with TBI, particularly to compensate for their impaired memory skills. Common school-related tasks, such as following a class schedule, being on time to classes, remembering to do and submit homework, and remembering to take medications, can become significant problems for students with memory impairments. Technology can help with these activities. Researchers have found that students with TBI were on time to class more often when using a smartphone or a device such as those highlighted in Chapter 10 than when using a paper checklist or a planner (Gillette & Depompei, 2008). IEP teams should consider the role of technology in providing memory support for students with TBI, as illustrated in Box 13.3.

Of course, universal design for progress doesn't always have to involve technology. Like many students with TBI, Dylan has short-term memory challenges. His daily planner—a three-ring spiral notebook—helps him stay on track. But so does Patti's approach:

> When Dylan can't remember something, I simply review what he needs to know, and review it again and again until it takes. He has a folder of schoolwork that he can refer to in order to trigger his memory. And his daily planner helps him with his executive skills, staying organized, and planning. When he does well, by being on time to class and completing his work, we put a stamp into his book. Each teacher does that with every other student, so we don't treat Dylan specially. The more stamps a student gets, the more special field trips the student goes on. Dylan likes the challenge and loves the rewards.

In addition, mnemonic strategies such as those you learned about in Chapter 11 can help students with TBI remember what they have learned.

PLANNING FOR UNIVERSAL DESIGN FOR LEARNING

A traumatic brain injury often makes it difficult for students to pay attention as teachers' present course content. Students also may have difficulty processing the information presented to them, particularly when it is presented in lecture format. Dylan faces this challenge. Indeed, he has traces of attention-deficit disorder (Chapter 8) and sometimes uses one kind of medication to regulate his hyperactivity and another to regulate his moods.

Universal design for learning modifies *how* teachers present information. Almost every IEP team should consider the "how" challenge. Renee and Patti have learned that simply redirecting Dylan works most of the time. When he is especially fatigued and wanders off mentally, Patti lets him lie down on the couch in her classroom. From there, he listens to her and his classmates so he does not completely miss out on instruction. When he is physically able, he retakes his place in the classroom. These short downtimes help him greatly: His mind is engaged while his body refreshes itself. Patti adds, "Of course, I would do that for any student." How better to describe *universal?*

BOX 13.3   **UNIVERSAL DESIGN FOR PROGRESS**

Electronic Aids for Memory Support

Throughout this text, you have learned how technology—from assistive, to electronic and informational, to educational—can promote student learning and independence. This is true for students with traumatic brain injury as well. In fact, there are multiple electronic aids that can support memory, organization, and scheduling. At the heart of all of these activities is memory support. Electronic memory aids range from simple to complex technologies. In some cases, the student does not need something as complex as a smartphone and may do fine with simpler devices to help her remember the time of an appointment, when to change classes, or when to take medication. In fact, when considering technology, the motto "simple is better" is worth keeping in mind. There is a tendency to want to get the latest and most fashionable technology, but in most cases a device's reliability, not its newness, is its most important feature. Quite simply, less complex devices usually require less maintenance and are more reliable than more complex devices.

You can support students with TBI to learn and function more effectively if you consider introducing some of these electronic memory aids:

Pagers. A pager (also called a beeper) is a small radio receiver that produces sounds (beeps, tones, buzzes) or visual stimuli (flashing lights, text messages) or vibrates when it receives a signal. The most common way to activate a pager is through a phone call, but any device that can send a radio signal can activate it. Like a cellular phone or an Internet account, pagers and digital beepers require a subscription service.

Digital watches. Simple and inexpensive (ten to fifteen dollars), electronic watches can also be used to provide audio prompts (beeps). Most of those watches have various functions, including a timer, a stopwatch, and an alarm. Some watches have a built-in pager. All of these functions can be used as memory aids. The downside is that they can be confusing to set up and use.

Medication reminder devices. Medication reminder devices provide prompts to remind people to take their medicine. Most are built into a pill tray or holder, where the appropriate dosage can be inserted and auditory sounds (beeps, chimes, rings) or vibrations can be scheduled for up to twelve times per day.

Digital mobile phones. Sometimes memory support can be both as complex and as simple as using a mobile phone. With the advent and wide adoption of text messaging, it is possible to provide prompts to students without the obtrusiveness of the ring of the phone.

Smartphone prompting systems. The Visual Assistant system you learned about in Chapter 10 is an example of a prompting system that operates on a smartphone. These systems can be very powerful, providing audio and video prompting supports. They are also relatively expensive. But if simpler prompting mechanisms don't work, they may be worth the investment.

Another universally designed modification is instructional pacing. This evidence-based strategy involves delivering course content in smaller increments or in packets of information and allowing students to respond to smaller chunks of information (Ylvisaker et al., 2001). Hall (2009) identified critical features of instructional pacing:

- *Appropriate instructional pacing.* Vary how fast you present information and how often you ask your students to respond, bearing in mind differences in attention, information processing, and cognitive ability.

- *Frequent student responses.* Ask for frequent responses and require your students to respond through different formats to actively engage them in learning.

- *Adequate processing time.* Allow students varying response times, taking into account processing capacity and giving some students more "think" time than others.

- *Monitoring responses.* Monitor the quality and nature of your students' responses to determine if they are mastering the content. If this monitoring suggests they are not, adjust your instruction immediately; do not wait until the lesson is over.

- *Frequent feedback.* Provide supportive and specific feedback to students on correct and incorrect responses, and correct the latter immediately instead of waiting until after the lesson.

Chapter 7 (on emotional and behavioral disorders) discussed mastery assessment and mastery learning as a way to ensure ongoing progress. Appropriate pacing incorporates a mastery learning approach, one in which teachers assess their students' knowledge frequently and pace their instruction accordingly.

IEP teams should consider both instructional pacing strategies and technology to deliver content. For example, watching a DVD may have the benefit of visual input, but in many cases information presented in video format is paced briskly. Students may have a difficult time paying attention throughout an entire DVD and processing the information it presents. You can pause the DVD to pace the video presentation, using that time to solicit student responses and assess student mastery.

PLANNING FOR OTHER EDUCATIONAL NEEDS

The long-term effects of TBI in children and adolescents require interventions to address present and anticipated future needs. As you know from reading about Dylan, students with TBI, particularly those in middle school and high school, need to develop or refine their self-management, learning, thinking, and problem-solving skills. That is especially true when students are planning their transition from school to adulthood, including the transition to college.

It can be challenging and even frightening for a student with TBI to transition from high school to a college or university. In Box 13.4, you will read about Megan Kohnke and her experiences in rehabilitation. A gifted student and soccer player, she had plans to attend Pepperdine University on a full athletic scholarship. After her intensive rehabilitation, Megan entered Pepperdine a semester late. To prepare for her entry, Megan and her mother met with her rehabilitation team. Her neuropsychologist mapped out strategies and modifications that Megan would need to be successful.

Immediately after arriving at Pepperdine, Megan met with each professor, introduced herself, and explained her disability. To illustrate her injury, she brought pictures of herself immediately after the accident, showing her bald head and a scar reaching from ear to ear. She wasn't seeking sympathy; rather, she used the pictures to show the professors what had happened to her. Her hair had grown back and covered the scar; but she wanted them to know that, even though she looked fine, she had significant challenges because

---

BOX 13.4 **MY VOICE**

Megan's Story

Four days after graduation, my friends Dan, Elizabeth, Sundance, and I went on a fishing trip for steelhead at C. J. Strike Reservoir outside of Boise, Idaho. We were driving down a dirt road when our vehicle was in a head-on collision with another vehicle. Dan and Sundance suffered many external injuries and were flown by helicopter to a local air force base. Elizabeth was a lifesaver; she managed to get herself free and with a broken arm ran to the nearest house, which was a few miles away. Guided only by a porch light, she made a sling for her arm out of her shirt as she ran along the road. Covered in blood, Elizabeth arrived at the house and called for help. Within twenty-five minutes a Life Flight crew had arrived and transported me to Saint Alphonsus Hospital for immediate surgery.

I received multiple injuries, but the one that was the most severe was to my head. At Saint Alphonsus, I immediately underwent a craniotomy. Dr. Michael Henbest repaired my skull, correcting a posterior displacement of the cranial vault. My skull was basically destroyed, and it took titanium mesh and plates to piece my skull back together. During surgery, a priest administered last rites, figuring that it was unlikely I would live through the night. A day after

the surgery, I was transported to the Elk's Rehabilitation Center, where I remained in a coma for a week. My prognosis was not good, and the chance of a full recovery was very slim.

After nearly two weeks in a coma, I awoke at the Elk's Rehabilitation Center, where my family and the Brain Injury Program's staff had already begun my rehabilitation. My parents, brothers, and friends were by my side twenty-four hours a day, assisting in shifts, talking to me, holding my hands, and letting me know what was happening. Although I didn't respond (nor do I remember this), the Elk's staff explained to me that this interaction served as the beginning of the slow road of recovery for me. After I came out of the coma, I began a more strenuous rehabilitation. Although I cried a lot and was often frustrated, I approached it as I had other athletic endeavors and simply figured I was preparing for next season. Each day I worked with a series of staff members, working my way through a series of physical and mental exercises designed to build my physical strength and mental acuity.

—*Megan Kohnke*

of this injury. She also brought information about her high school grades and about the rehabilitation she had recently completed. Megan explains,

> I wasn't looking for a handout but, instead, I wanted my professors to know what I had been through. I let them know that I was going to try extra hard, but without accommodations I wouldn't succeed. This wasn't easy for me. I used to be a very social person; but like most people who suffer from a TBI, I had lost confidence in myself and was uncomfortable talking with people, especially about myself. However, I met with every professor and told them what my neurologist suggested and how I would need additional time to complete tests, I would need to tape every lecture, I would benefit from any type of handout that would further illustrate the lecture, and I would need the assistance of the writing center.

Megan's first semester at Pepperdine included a number of other hurdles. One of the first involved attending to her basic needs and being independent. Unfortunately, simple activities such as selecting food at the cafeteria proved to be a challenge. Her mother explains,

> I went to Pepperdine with Megan and spent the first week with her. The first morning, we went over to the cafeteria, and I told Megan to get something to eat. I left to allow her the opportunity to make the appropriate selection. After a long time, she returned to the room not having eaten a thing. With all the choices, Megan didn't know how to make a selection. I quickly learned she needed direct instruction in how to select food items from the cafeteria if she was going to eat in this environment. So we went through the various lines and reviewed what a balanced meal would include and selected various items. This involved further demonstration and practice before Megan was comfortable and able to eat on her own.

When her classes began, Megan, armed with a tape recorder, recorded every lecture. At the end of the day, she returned home and transcribed these lectures by hand. Next, she reviewed her handwritten transcription and created another outline that would help her study. This was exceedingly time-consuming but necessary for Megan's learning needs. On test days, Megan was allowed to arrive early and begin the test thirty to sixty minutes ahead of the rest of her peers. As Megan explains, "I was the first person there and the last to leave for every one of my tests." Megan's hard work and postsecondary accommodations have paid off. She successfully completed her undergraduate degree.

In Chapter 5, we discussed the importance of teaching students with learning disabilities the self-advocacy skills they need to transition from high school to college. These skills are equally important for students with TBI, as Megan so clearly demonstrates. Students with TBI need to be equipped with the knowledge and skills required to succeed in postsecondary education. It is important that the IEP team identify the assistance that students will need and the support strategies that will enable them to achieve a positive transition to the next level of education, including college.

Using Effective Instructional Strategies

EARLY CHILDHOOD STUDENTS: COLLABORATIVE TEAMING

When you think of instructional strategies, you probably think of methods a teacher uses when teaching students. But you have already learned about strategies that involve students teaching other students and students teaching themselves, so it is obvious that not all instructional strategies focus on the teacher-student interaction. Collaborative teaming is an important strategy that focuses on the role of teachers in promoting inclusive practices for all students with disabilities, from early childhood to high school. Simply, collaborative teaming involves two or more people working together to educate students

with disabilities. Thousand, Villa, and Nevin (2007) identified a collaborative team as a group of people who

- Partner to achieve a shared goal
- Believe that all team members have unique and needed expertise and skills and value each person's contribution
- Distribute leadership throughout the team

Snell and Janney (2005) have identified five principal components of collaborative teaming. We describe them below.

Building Team Structure

This involves creating school policies that support team teaching, defining the core team (those team members who are most directly responsible for the student's education) and the entire team (core team plus members who might occasionally teach the student), and identifying time to plan together for instruction.

Learning Teamwork Skills

To succeed, team members need to learn and practice teamwork skills such as active listening, negotiation and compromise skills, and role-release skills (turning over some of one's own responsibilities to other team members). Teams should discuss and agree on shared values and a shared goal related to a student's progress.

Taking Team Action

Teams begin by problem solving, creating an action plan, determining a schedule for program delivery, and identifying assessment and program evaluation components.

Teaching Collaboratively

After the groundwork has been laid, teaching collaboratively feels more natural and effective. Co-teachers learn one another's areas of instructional strength and how to best use those strengths to all students' benefit.

Improving Communication and Handling Conflict

Along with experience comes more open communication, stronger (and more effective) partnerships, and trust (as we pointed out in Chapter 4). In some circumstances, however, conflicts can arise; so it is important that team members treat one another with respect and practice effective conflict-resolution skills, especially when the student with a traumatic brain injury participates in team meetings.

Collaborative teaming is important across all age levels, including early childhood, and across content areas from academic to behavioral. Collaborative teaming has benefits for students: for example, preschool children with disabilities have shown more positive on-task behavior during circle time when collaborative teaming is used (Hundert, 2007). An innovative means to support collaborative teaming and to improve instruction is the use of "bug-in-ear" technology—essentially a wireless microphone and earphone combination that allows you to communicate unobtrusively during class sessions (Scheeler, Congdon, & Stansbery, 2010).

ELEMENTARY AND MIDDLE SCHOOL STUDENTS: COOPERATIVE LEARNING

One of the most important strategies to ensure progress in the general education curriculum for students with disabilities, including those with TBI, involves the use of cooperative learning strategies in which small groups of students focus on a common learning task or activity. Successfully implementing cooperative learning, however, involves much more than simply putting students together in small groups and giving them an assignment. A haphazard approach to group learning can result in a few students doing most of the work and, indeed, most of the learning.

Early seminal work in cooperative learning by Johnson and Johnson (1991) identified the primary characteristics of cooperative learning groups, two of which are very important: positive interdependence and individual accountability.

Positive Interdependence

Positive interdependence refers to "linking students together so one cannot succeed unless all group members succeed" (Johnson, Johnson, & Holubec, 1998, p. 4). In essence, students are compelled to support and enable their fellow group members in order to succeed. Positive interdependence is created by assigning each group member tasks that are critical to the overall goal and are individualized to the student's ability level. Students engage in different levels of learning and their tasks vary, as is the case in universally designed learning, but each task is essential to the overall success of the group.

Individual Accountability

In haphazardly created learning groups, all students benefit or are punished equally by the group outcome, not necessarily by their individual contribution. One student may do all the work and the group may earn an *A,* but other students may not have deserved that grade. Similarly, one student may perform her portion of the task at a high-quality level, but the overall quality of the product may be dragged down by other students' performances; that one student is unfairly punished with a grade lower than she deserved.

By assigning each student in cooperative learning groups discrete, identifiable tasks that contribute to the whole, teachers can individually assess students on the quality of their component task. However, most important to the implementation of cooperative learning is that students understand that each group member has a role and that the group as a whole will be accountable for the quality of the product.

Johnson and colleagues (1998) identified several ways to structure cooperative learning groups to ensure both individual and group success. One factor is group size: The smaller the group, the easier it is to fairly distribute tasks and to individualize those tasks to the unique needs of students. A second factor is detailing each student's individual task, providing examples of quality outcomes pertaining to that task, and making sure the student understands the contribution of his task to the group's task or goal. Instead of waiting until the group is finished, you should use frequent assessments of what each group member is doing and learning. Additionally, peers can hold one another accountable. For instance, you might assign one group member to be a "checker" and to question other group members to ensure that everyone understands the task (Johnson et al., 1998).

IEP TIP

Remember, cooperative learning involves more than just grouping students together. Each student must have a unique role that contributes to the outcomes of the learning activity, and the activity itself must depend upon each student completing his or her task.

SECONDARY AND TRANSITION STUDENTS: PROBLEM-SOLVING AND DECISION-MAKING INSTRUCTION

Even after a student has recuperated from a traumatic brain injury, he or she may still have difficulties in executive function. Executive functioning includes higher-level brain or intellectual functions that govern complex activities such as making plans and decisions, solving problems, and setting goals. Impairments in executive function are not easily detected, at least not until the student is called upon to perform one of these tasks. You should provide students with systematic instruction that will enable them to improve their executive functioning skills, including problem-solving and decision-making skills.

A *problem* is a "task, activity, or situation for which a solution is not immediately identified, known, or obtainable" (Wehmeyer, Palmer, Agran, Hughes, Martin, & Mithaug, 2007, p. 35). Teaching problem-solving skills requires you to teach students to identify a solution that resolves the initial perplexity or difficulty. The skills typically involved in problem solving are (1) problem identification, (2) problem explication or definition, and (3) solution generation.

Problem Identification

The first step in solving a problem is to recognize that a problem exists. Wehmeyer and colleagues (2007) suggest that, as part of this step, students should address the following questions: (1) Is the problem caused by me or someone else? and (2) How important is the problem? Students should also learn to estimate the time needed to solve a problem.

Problem Explication or Definition

In many cases, students are too global in their definition of the problem. That is, they attribute the problem to broad factors ("That teacher is mean.") rather than the real problem at hand (failing a class, not meeting class deadlines, or arriving late). So you should teach students to narrow the problem down to one that is solvable.

Solution Generation

Once a student has defined the problem she must solve, she will need to learn how to generate potential solutions. Initially, you should allow students to generate as many solutions as possible, even if they do not adequately address the problem. Discuss with students why a solution does or does not solve the problem and whether or not the solution can be implemented.

At this point students are ready to make a decision about the best option available, selecting the option that best fits their needs, circumstances, and capacity. When teaching problem solving, you should use real-world situations. Adolescents face a myriad of problems, from relationship troubles to tobacco and alcohol use; using these problems as examples can enable students to learn problem-solving strategies and also can provide a way for students to address issues in adolescence.

As we have noted, the problem-solving process ends with making a decision: choosing the best solution to the problem from among several possible solutions. Many people view problem solving and decision making as one and the same. But this is not accurate. Problem solving requires students to identify potential solutions. Decision making involves selecting the best potential solution.

Just as the typical problem-solving process ends with making a decision, the typical decision-making process begins with problem solving. Teaching students to make decisions involves a number of steps:

Identify relevant alternatives or options. If students already know their options, this step is straightforward: Have them write down the solution. But more often than not, students do not know all of the options or alternatives available to them, so they need to problem-solve and identify all of the alternatives or options.

Identify consequences of alternatives. One characteristic of many students with disabilities (indeed, many adolescents in general) is their tendency to act impulsively or without considering the consequences of their actions. In certain circumstances, such as taking drugs, their impulsivity can be more than just exasperating; it can be life-threatening. So you should teach your students to think through the possible consequences of each alternative.

Identify the probability of each consequence. You need to be clear about the consequences of a student's behavior. Consequences range from positive to neutral to negative. They also range from highly likely to occur to unlikely to occur. Students with TBI should learn to weigh the relative risk of each alternative against the relative likelihood that it will occur and against its potential benefits. The potential risks of some activities (cancer from smoking or AIDS from unprotected sex) are so negative that the slightest possibility that they could occur should prompt the student to discard that option.

IEP TIP

Problem solving and other executive function and self-regulation skills are critical to learners with TBI and should be a part of virtually all IEPs for this population.

BOX 13.5 INTO PRACTICE

Ready, Set, . . . Study! Teaching Study Skills

Teaching problem solving is one strategy to teaching effective study skills. But many students with TBI require more intensive instruction to learn how to study efficiently (Lambert & Nowacek, 2006). Like other complex tasks, learning to study involves learning the stages of studying: preparing to study, studying across content areas, and following up after studying (Lambert & Nowacek, 2006).

Ready, Set . . .
Key steps in teaching skills related to preparing to study involve teaching students to think about when, where, and how to study. Encourage students to do the following:

- *Find a place to study that is free from distractions.* Ecological accommodations, such as preferential seating, are supplementary aids and services, as you have learned.

- *Find a time to study that isn't too late.* As Lambert and Nowacek (2006) note, the most effective study times are during the day and not too late at night.

- *Establish a study routine.* Like most actions, when something is automated and routine, it is more likely to occur.

- *Gather together all needed study materials.* Stopping the study session to get a textbook or sharpen a pencil disrupts the continuity of a study session and quickly becomes a strategy for avoiding studying.

- *Determine what to study.* Establish an agenda, use study guides, and prioritize study content based upon deadlines and assignments.

. . . Study!
- *Teach students to focus on discrete tasks for planned periods of time.* Lambert and Nowacek (2006) suggest that students should plan study times in one-hour blocks, with the last ten minutes of each hour set aside for a break.

- *Teach study strategies.* Teach students to use or develop advance organizers to identify big ideas in the reading.

- *Teach comprehension skills.* Teach students what to do when they reach content they have a difficult time understanding or remembering. Use mnemonic strategies such as those we discussed in Chapter 11 and the learning strategies you read about in Chapter 5 to provide ways for students to tackle difficult content areas.

- *Teach students to summarize what they have learned.* This can be through written summaries, outlines, graphic organizers, or questions derived from the reading.

Students with TBI can learn self-regulation skills that enable them to become more effective at studying, and focusing on these skills is time well spent by teachers.

Determine the value of each option or alternative. You should support your students to consider the risks, benefits, and consequences of each option. Their values, preferences, and interests should come into play and often will become the dominant factors in reaching a decision. Cultural, ethical, and religious factors can also play a role in their decisions.

Integrate values and consequences to select a preferred option. Finally, you should support your students to choose one option based on all the factors considered. As Laatsch and colleagues (2007) noted, students with TBI (and AD/HD) are at increased risk for impairments in executive functioning skills and benefit from instruction in these areas.

An additional benefit of teaching problem solving, decision making, and other executive functioning skills is that they can be applied to issues that limit the success of students with TBI in school, including study skills. Box 13.5 provides steps to teach students important study skills.

Including Students with Traumatic Brain Injury

Figure 13.4 indicates the educational placement of students with TBI, and Box 13.6 provides tips for increasing their success in general education classrooms. Among students with TBI, 45 percent spend more than 80 percent of their day in general education classes. However, 9 percent are educated in a separate setting, including at a hospital or at home.

FIGURE 13.4 *Educational Placement of Students with Traumatic Brain Injury, School year 2008–2009*

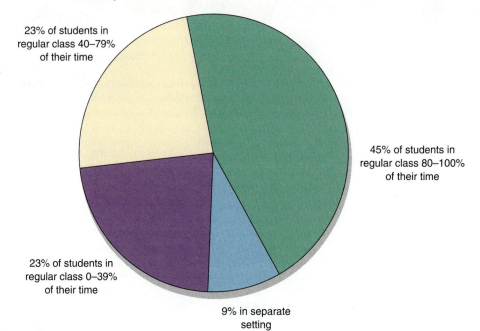

23% of students in regular class 40–79% of their time

45% of students in regular class 80–100% of their time

23% of students in regular class 0–39% of their time

9% in separate setting

Source: U.S. Department of Education. (2011). *Data accountability center: Individuals with Disabilities Education Act (IDEA) data.* Retrieved February 12, 2011, from https://www.ideadata.org.

Note: Percentages have been rounded and collapsed across categories.

BOX 13.6

INCLUSION TIPS

	What You Might See	**What You Might Be Tempted to Do**	**Alternate Responses**	**Ways to Include Peers in the Process**
Behavior	The student shows behavior and personality changes, such as temper outbursts, anxiety, fatigue, or depression.	Respond with strong disapproval to her new behavior.	Teach problem-solving strategies to reduce frustration that is associated with problem behavior.	Give her time to work in natural settings with peers who will encourage appropriate behavior yet show acceptance during the relearning stage.
Social interactions	He has forgotten social skills and experiences social misunderstandings because of his new identity struggles.	Ignore his social difficulties and hope they go away.	Partner with both the speech-language pathologist and the school counselor to plan the best ways to teach successful language and social skills.	Allow friends with whom he feels secure to role-play social activities. Structure many opportunities for successful interactions. Use videotapes for self-evaluation.
Educational performance	Learning new information is difficult for her, or it takes her much longer to process information.	Require extra work in areas of difficulty.	Use cooperative learning groups to aid her in organization, memory, and cognitive processes.	Have her brainstorm and work with her peers/friends to practice skills as well as to plan future projects and educational aspirations.
Classroom attitudes	He is confused about exactly what is expected on assignments.	Excuse him from assignments.	Use analytic rubrics as a way to delineate expectations for assignments.	Pair him with a partner and friend who can help him focus and participate meaningfully during instruction.

Assessing Students' Progress

MEASURING STUDENTS' PROGRESS

Progress in the General Curriculum

One strategy for measuring progress in the general education curriculum is the use of analytic rubrics (De la Paz, 2009). A rubric is a scale developed by a teacher (or others) as a guide to scoring a student's performance. To create an analytic rubric, teachers identify specific outcomes linked to a standard, rank them from less to more positive, and assign a score (typically from 0 or 1 to 4 or 5) to each outcome. For example, an analytic rubric for a first-grade writing standard might set the following outcomes:

1 = handwriting not legible; cannot be read by adult

2 = some words legible, but most are not

3 = most words legible; some cannot be read

4 = all words legible

Tips for developing rubrics include the following (De La Paz, 2009):

- Focus on only one dimension of student performance (e.g., legibility).
- Include enough points in the scale to adequately judge performance.
- Focus on specific outcomes rather than a process.
- Provide students with information about the rubrics and examples of high-quality performance.

Progress in Addressing Other Educational Needs

Traumatic brain injury can often result in perceptual and motor impairments. Perceptual-motor skills are those that coordinate visual and sensory input with motor activities. For example, many students may have difficulty with handwriting due to poor eye-hand coordination. You may recall that Dylan has fine-motor challenges and works with an occupational therapist to learn, for example, how to hold a pen.

There are a number of widely used tests of perceptual-motor skills. The Bender-Gestalt Visual Motor test provides a relatively quick way to measure children's visual-motor functioning, visual-perception skills, and the impact of brain injury on these functions. The test presents nine geometric designs, one at a time, to the student and asks him to reproduce the designs. Like many such standardized tests, the administration of the Bender-Gestalt test should be performed by a school psychologist.

On a more applied level, you can assess student progress in specific perceptual-motor areas through collaborations among special and general educators and occupational or physical therapists. For example, evaluating students' handwriting is a common activity performed by occupational therapists. Working with special educators, occupational therapists can determine whether a student's handwriting difficulties are a function of visual impairments, perceptual difficulties, eye-hand coordination problems, motor-tone problems, hand-grasping or pinching difficulties, or general hand functioning. In turn, the teacher and occupational therapists can create an instructional program to improve the student's handwriting or, if necessary, identify assistive writing devices, including adaptive word processors (such as those discussed in Chapter 7).

MAKING ACCOMMODATIONS FOR ASSESSMENT

Students with TBI may have trouble concentrating and attending for long periods of time. Like students with AD/HD, they will benefit from the accommodations discussed in Chapter 8. In addition, as you have learned in this chapter, problems with memory and retention are often barriers for students with TBI, so testing situations present special challenges. One accommodation involves the way in which test items are constructed.

Students with TBI may perform better on exams with multiple-choice or true-false questions than on tests that rely on memory and recall and include short-answer or essay questions. While it is not always a reasonable accommodation to reword items from one format to another, the use of a scribe (someone who writes the answer for the student) can also help students with TBI. Having someone write the answer allows the student to focus or concentrate on recalling information. You may remember that Patti gives Dylan extra time to take tests, permits him to mark in his textbook, allows him to leave the room to compose himself, and lets him rest on the couch in her classroom if he is particularly tired. These simple accommodations do not give Dylan any special advantage relative to other students; they simply allow him to demonstrate what he knows.

ADDRESSING THE PROFESSIONAL STANDARDS

The following Council for Exceptional Children (CEC) Common Core Knowledge and Skills are addressed in this chapter through the content and concepts we discuss. See the Appendix for a full listing of these Knowledge and Skill statements:

ICC2K1, ICC2K2, ICC2K4, ICC2K5, ICC2K6, ICC3K1, ICC3K2, ICC4S1, ICC4S2, ICC4S3, ICC4S4, ICC4S5, ICC4S6, ICC5S2, ICC5S3, ICC5S4, ICC5S9, ICC5S12, ICC5S15, ICC7K5, ICC7S1, ICC7S3, ICC7S6, ICC7S7, ICC7S9, ICC8K3, ICC8S2, ICC8S6, ICC8S8, ICC10S2, ICC10S3, ICC10S4, ICC10S5

Summary

IDENTIFYING STUDENTS WITH TRAUMATIC BRAIN INJURY

- The IDEA definition of TBI includes acquired injuries to the brain caused by an external force but does not include brain injuries that are congenital, degenerative, or induced at birth.
- Closed head injuries and open head injuries are the two types of brain injuries included under the IDEA definition.
- Students with TBI often experience physical; cognitive; and emotional, behavioral, and social changes.
- Severity of the injury and age of onset are two critical factors in determining the severity of the disability and the prognosis for improvement.
- The four major causes of TBI are falls, automobile accidents, events of being struck by or against, and assaults.

EVALUATING STUDENTS WITH TRAUMATIC BRAIN INJURY

- The pediatric Glasgow Outcomes Scale is often used initially to measure the severity of injury.
- On an ongoing basis, teachers can use a classroom observation guide to pinpoint a student's precise cognitive functioning.

DESIGNING AN APPROPRIATE IEP

- It is critical that educators partner with medical and other rehabilitation professionals to ensure student success when transitioning back to school.
- Simple technologies such as pagers, alarms, and watches can provide the support students need to be more independent and to minimize memory impairments.
- The rate at which teachers present content information impacts student success when they have attention and processing difficulties. Instructional pacing is important to consider.
- Many students with TBI can succeed in college if appropriate planning occurs and the student is prepared to advocate for accommodations.

USING EFFECTIVE INSTRUCTIONAL STRATEGIES

- Collaborative teaming involves two or more educators working together to meet shared goals for student achievement.
- Cooperative learning groups are critical to the success of inclusive classrooms. Teachers need to be sure, however, that all students have a meaningful role in the process and contribute to the outcome.

- Problem-solving and decision-making skills are important for students with TBI, whose injuries often result in lifelong difficulties in these areas of executive function.

INCLUDING STUDENTS WITH TRAUMATIC BRAIN INJURY

- Among students with TBI, 45 percent spend more than 80 percent of their day in general education classes.

ASSESSING STUDENTS' PROGRESS

- Rubrics provide a way for teachers to quantify student progress in the general curriculum.
- A variety of perceptual and motor-skills assessments may help teachers who are working with students with TBI. Teachers should focus on assessing perceptual and motor skills because, for example, they directly impact handwriting.
- The use of a scribe and different types of test questions are accommodations for students with TBI who have memory impairments.

MyEducationLab

Go to Topic #17: Multiple Disabilities and TBI in the MyEducationLab (www.myeducationlab.com) for *Exceptional Lives*, where you can do the following:

- Find learning outcomes for Multiple Disabilities and TBI along with the national standards that connect to these outcomes.
- Complete assignments and activities that will help you more deeply understand the chapter content.
- Apply and practice your understanding of the core teaching skills identified in the chapter with the Building Teaching Skills and Dispositions learning units.
- Examine challenging situations and cases presented in the IRIS Center Resources.
- Access video clips of CCSSO National Teachers of the Year award winners responding to the question, "Why Do I Teach?" in the Teacher Talk section.
- Check your comprehension on the content covered in the chapter with the Study Plan. Here you will be able to take a chapter quiz, receive feedback on your answers, and then access review, practice, and enrichment activities to enhance your understanding of chapter content.
- Use the Online Lesson Plan Builder to practice lesson planning and integrating national and state standards into your planning.

14 Understanding Students *with* Hearing Loss

by Sally L. Roberts, University of Kansas

Who Are Cameron, Zander, and Alina Symansky?

What is the one factor that binds people to each other? That makes it possible for parents and children who hear to interact with each other? That makes it possible for parents and children who are deaf to participate with those who have hearing and those who do not?

Ask Kim Symansky, who is deaf, and you will learn that, for her and others who are deaf, the answer is "language." Without language, there can be no communication. Without communication, there can be no common ground. Without common ground, there can be no community.

What is the significance of Kim's argument? It is that education for deaf children, whether in general schools and environments or in separate schools or environments, should emphasize the children's language over everything else.

Kim knows whereof she speaks. She herself is deaf and the daughter of hearing parents, but she has deaf grandparents. Because Kim's mother grew up with deaf parents, her first language was American Sign Language (ASL), which she used with Kim from birth. Kim's husband, Ron, is also deaf, but his parents were not. All three of their children are deaf. One, Cameron, is twelve

and was born to South Korean hearing parents. His younger brother, Zander, ten, is from China, and so is their sister Alina, nine.

Kim's own education and her children's education have convinced her that language is the key. Her parents were teachers at a state school for the deaf. Kim attended that school and later earned her undergraduate degree and a master's degree in special education in universities in which ASL is the only mode of communication. Although she did take some postgraduate courses in which English was the only language used in teaching and learning, she did so with an interpreter. Ron teaches in the interpreter training program at a community college.

All of their children spent their early years in general education and now attend the state school for the deaf where Kim works. Cameron attended a regular school and was enrolled in the general education curriculum until the third grade. He did well academically, but he chose to attend the state school for subsequent grades because he was socially isolated in general education. At the state school, he says he feels normal, implying that he did not feel that way as he was about to enter the fourth grade.

Zander also felt isolated in general education and wanted to attend the state school. There, his self-confidence has grown.

Similarly, Alina was in a general education program in preschool and kindergarten but now attends the state school, despite having much stronger English-language skills than her brothers do.

Isolation brought each child to the state school. The hearing world communicated in only one language: spoken English. But at the state school, they found communication, common ground, and community because the school had two languages: ASL and English.

You have already learned that, among special educators, the abbreviation LRE usually stands for "least restrictive environment." But for Kim and her children, as well as for other parents and children who are deaf, the initials stand for "language rich environment." When language is absent, as it sometimes has been for Kim, Ron, and their children, no environment that hearing people regard as "general" or "regular" is "least restrictive." Instead, it is "most restrictive" because there can be no common ground and no community without communication.

The degree of deafness is measured by the decibels a person cannot hear; and according to that measurement, Cameron and Zander are 100 percent deaf. Alina, on the other hand, has a hearing loss of 75 percent in one ear and 50 percent in the other. And unlike them, she has improved her hearing by means

OBJECTIVES

- You will learn about the categories of hearing loss.

- You will learn how people hear and about the anatomy of the ear.

- You will learn how to design an IEP that conforms to the IDEA provision that students with hearing impairments may learn with each other as well as from deaf adults.

- You will learn about the various modes of communication used by students with hearing loss.

- You will learn how to evaluate students for hearing loss and academic progress.

- You will learn about the Deaf community and Deaf culture, an important aspect of identity for a child with hearing loss.

of a surgical procedure known as cochlear implantation, the placement of auditory receptors inside the cochlea in each ear. Yet each child uses American Sign Language to communicate while also learning to use written English. In other words, they are bilingual: ASL and English are their languages.

The use of cochlear implants is controversial among deaf people. Some favor them because the implants enable hearing to occur and thus create two channels for language: spoken English and signed language. Others dislike them because the implants imply that the deaf person is medically impaired and in need of repair. Like her deaf peers, Kim rejects the medical approach. She does not have an impairment and refuses to accept the term *hearing impaired*. She simply communicates using another language. And with that challenge comes the challenge of finding a common ground with hearing peers.

But Kim is also glad that her children spent some time attending a regular school and being in a general education program. There they began to learn English and came into early contact with the majority population—those of us who are hearing. In time, she expects Cameron, Zander, and Alina to attend the state school and a local high school simultaneously. That is because the state school cannot offer the same broad curriculum as the local high school does. Kim's approach is to mix the benefits of both programs, always matching them with her children's needs.

Kim and Ron have succeeded in both the hearing and deaf worlds. They expect their children to be equally successful in achieving the four policy goals of IDEA and ADA: equal opportunity, independent living, full participation, and economic self-sufficiency. With language and equal opportunities, they have enjoyed independent living, been fully included, and been economically productive. With language, they are full citizens. With language, her children will be too.

Identifying Students with Hearing Loss

DEFINING HEARING LOSS

Two terms, *deaf* and *hard of hearing*, describe hearing loss. The term *deaf* is often overused to describe all individuals with hearing loss. The current regulations implementing IDEA define *deafness* as a hearing impairment that is so severe that the student is impaired in processing linguistic information through hearing (with or without amplification) and the student's educational performance is adversely affected. Two terms, **unilateral** and **bilateral**, describe whether the loss occurs in one or both ears.

The severity, or level, of a student's hearing loss determines whether she will be classified as deaf or as hard of hearing. To be considered **deaf**, a person must have a hearing loss of 70 to 90 decibels or greater and be unable to use hearing, even with amplification, as the primary means for developing language. Figure 14.1 illustrates the degrees of hearing loss. By contrast, a person is considered to be **hard of hearing** if he has a hearing loss in the 20 to 70 decibel range, benefits from amplification, and communicates primarily through speaking. **Congenital deafness** (hearing loss is present at birth) is a low-incidence disability affecting a small number of people. The majority of the people with whom this group interacts are hearing, including most of their family members.

Although some people use the term *hearing impaired* to describe a student with a hearing loss, special educators prefer to use person-first language (student who is deaf) when referring to students with hearing loss. In addition, the **Deaf community** believes that the term *impaired* has negative connotations and prefers *deaf child*. Members of the Deaf community particularly resist the term *hearing impaired* because it implies a condition in need of correction or repair. Members of the Deaf community do not view themselves as needing to be fixed or cured but as a distinct cultural and linguistic group

FIGURE 14.1

Degrees of hearing loss

Frequency (Hz)

	125	250	500	1,000	2,000	4,000	8,000

Loudness (dB)	
0 10	(0–15 dB) *Normal*—There is no impact on communication.
20	(16–25 dB) *Slight*—In noisy environments, faint speech is difficult to understand.
30	(26–40 dB) *Mild*—Faint or distant speech is difficult to hear even in quiet environments. Classroom discussions are challenging to follow.
40 50	(41–55 dB) *Moderate*—Conversational speech is heard only at a close distance. Group activities in a classroom present a challenge.
60	(56–70 dB) *Moderate-severe*—Only loud, clear conversational speech can be heard, and group situations present great difficulty. Speech is intelligible, though noticeably impaired.
70 80	(71–90 dB) *Severe*—Conversational speech cannot be heard unless it is loud; even then, many words cannot be recognized. Environment sounds can be detected, though not always identified. Speech is not always intelligible.
90 100 110 120	(91+ dB) *Profound*—Conversational speech cannot be heard. Some loud environmental sounds may be heard. Speech is difficult to understand or may not be developed at all.

(Padden & Humphries, 2005). That is one reason they and we capitalize *Deaf*—signifying its equivalence to, for example, Hispanic. The other reason is that the language by which Deaf individuals communicate is itself a separate language and thus merits a capital letter, as, for example, English does (when referring to the language in which this book is written).

Prevalence

Compared to other groups of students with disabilities, students with hearing loss are a relatively small group: 1.2 percent of the total population of students with disabilities served under IDEA. In 2008–2009, 70,781 students with hearing impairments received special education services and supports (U.S. Department of Education, 2011).

The Hearing Process

Before you can understand hearing loss, you must first understand what is involved in hearing sound. The hearing process is called **audition**. When we hear sounds, we are really interpreting patterns in the movement (vibration) of air molecules. Sounds are described in terms of their pitch or frequency (very low to very high) and intensity or loudness (very soft to very loud). Frequency is measured in **hertz (Hz)**, named in honor of Heinrich Hertz, and loudness is measured in **decibels (dB)**, named in honor of Alexander Graham Bell. Speech has a mix of high and low frequencies and soft and loud sounds.

Most of the sounds we hear every day occur in the 250 to 6,000 Hz range. Conversational speech is usually at about 45 dB to 50 dB of loudness. A whisper is about 20 dB, and a shout can be as loud as 70 dB. Vowel sounds such as "o" have low frequencies; consonant sounds such as "f" and "sh" have higher frequencies. An individual who cannot hear high-frequency sounds will have a very hard time understanding speech.

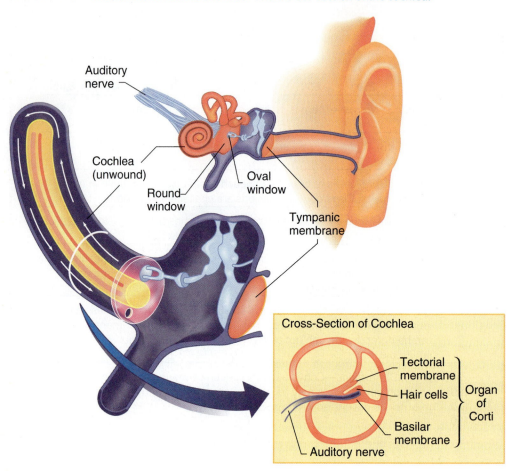

Cross-Section of Cochlea

Tectorial membrane

Hair cells

Organ of Corti

Basilar membrane

Auditory nerve

The Hearing Mechanism

To understand what can go wrong with the hearing process, begin with the anatomy of the hearing mechanism, which consists of three parts: the outer, middle, and inner ear. Figure 14.2 illustrates the structure and anatomy of the ear. Look at it as you read the next few paragraphs.

The outer ear consists of the **auricle**, or **pinna**, and the **ear canal**. Its purpose is to collect the sound waves and funnel them to the tympanic membrane, or eardrum. The vibrating air molecules hit the eardrum and cause it to vibrate.

The middle ear is behind the eardrum and consists of three little bones: the **malleus**, **incus**, and **stapes**. Because of their shapes, you may know them as the hammer, anvil, and stirrup. The vibration of the eardrum transfers energy to the middle ear bones causing them to vibrate and transmit the sound through the middle ear cavity.

Also found in the middle ear is the **eustachian tube**. It extends from the throat into the middle-ear cavity, and its primary purpose is to equalize the air pressure on the eardrum when you swallow or yawn. Unequal air pressure is why your ears can feel plugged in the mountains or when you are in an airplane that is landing.

The inner ear contains the cochlea and the vestibular mechanism. The cochlea is just beyond the **oval window**, the membrane that separates the middle and the inner ear. The **cochlea** is a snail-shaped bony structure that houses the actual organ of hearing (**organ of Corti**) and the **vestibular mechanism**, the sensory organ of balance. The cochlea has multiple rows of delicate hair cells that are connected to the auditory nerve. These hair cells are sensory receptors for the auditory nerve. The vibration of the middle-ear bones transfers the sound waves to the oval window, moving the fluid in the cochlea across the hair cells. This movement generates impulses to the auditory nerve.

The other structure in the inner ear, the vestibular mechanism, is a group of semicircular canals that controls balance. These canals are filled with the same fluid found in the cochlea. This fluid is sensitive to head movement, allowing the vestibular mechanism to help the body maintain its equilibrium. It is sensitive to both motion and gravity.

Sound moves from the inner ear to the temporal lobe of the brain by way of the auditory nerve. The route from the ear to the cochlea passes through at least four neural relay stations on its way to the brain. Think of this transfer of sound as a train trip that has stops at several stations along the route. Once sound reaches the auditory cortex, it can then be associated with other sensory information and memory, allowing us to perceive and integrate what we have heard (Gilbert, Knightly, & Steinberg, 2007).

DESCRIBING THE CHARACTERISTICS

Hearing loss impairs the development of spoken language, but the IQ range of students who are deaf or hard of hearing is much the same as it is in the general population (Nikolaraizi & Makri, 2004/2005). Most often, their academic problems are related to difficulties in speaking, reading, and writing, not to cognitive challenges (Antia, Jones, Reed, & Kreimeyer, 2009).

Speech and English-Language Development

Children are born with an innate ability and desire to communicate. Normal language acquisition for hearing children follows a predetermined sequence that is similar across most languages and cultures. Children will usually become native speakers of at least one language just by being exposed to it. They typically do not need direct instruction.

The language development of children who are born deaf or hard of hearing will also follow this sequence. However, their language delays will range from mild to severe. These delays are a direct result of their inability to process auditory information or their lack of exposure to a visually encoded language. Their delays will vary, depending on the level of hearing loss and the amount of visual and auditory input they receive (Spencer, 2004; Blackorby & Knokey, 2006; Nicholas & Greers, 2006).

Even the speech of a student with a moderate loss may be affected. Although the student may be able to hear speech sounds, crucial information will elude him. By contrast, a child born deaf will be unable to hear most speech sounds, even with amplification. Her receptive speech will be significantly impaired unless she is an exceptional **speech reader** (able to interpret words by watching the speaker's lips and facial movements without hearing the speaker's voice), and her expressive speech will most likely show problems with articulation, voice quality, and tone, making her difficult to understand.

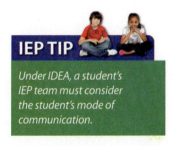

IEP TIP

Under IDEA, a student's IEP team must consider the student's mode of communication.

Communication Options

Professionals commonly use one of three approaches to teach communication skills to students with hearing loss: oral/aural, manual, or total communication. There is a long history of controversy over which approach is the most appropriate. There is, however, probably no one single method that meets the needs of *all* students. That is why IDEA provides that a student's IEP team must consider the languages and communication modes that the student who is deaf or hard of hearing might use in the educational setting.

Oral/Aural Communication. This approach includes two primary teaching techniques. The **oral/aural format** encourages early identification and subsequent amplification or cochlear implant. It emphasizes the amplification of sound and helping the child use what hearing remains (residual hearing). Auditory training enhances the student's listening skills and stresses using speech to communicate. This approach also emphasizes the use of amplified sound to develop oral language. In contrast to a strict auditory-verbal approach, however, this method allows for the use of visual input—speech reading—to augment auditory information. Unfortunately, this skill is extremely difficult to master because such a small amount of what is being said is visible on a speaker's lips.

Manual Communication. The **manual approach** to teaching communication stresses the use of some form of sign language. This approach makes use of the student's intact sight to receive information. Manual communication includes several different sign systems, each with its own proponents. **Sign language** uses combinations of hand, body, and facial movements to convey both words and concepts rather than individual letters.

Fingerspelling uses a hand representation for each of the twenty-six letters of the alphabet. Figure 14.3 shows you the accepted forms of manual communication for the letters of the alphabet.

American Sign Language (ASL) is the most widely used sign language among deaf adults in North America. Although some individual ASL signs may have comparable English words, its signs are meant to represent concepts rather than single words. For example, the sign for "look" is made by pointing the index and middle fingers in the shape

FIGURE 14.3 *Chart of the manual alphabet*

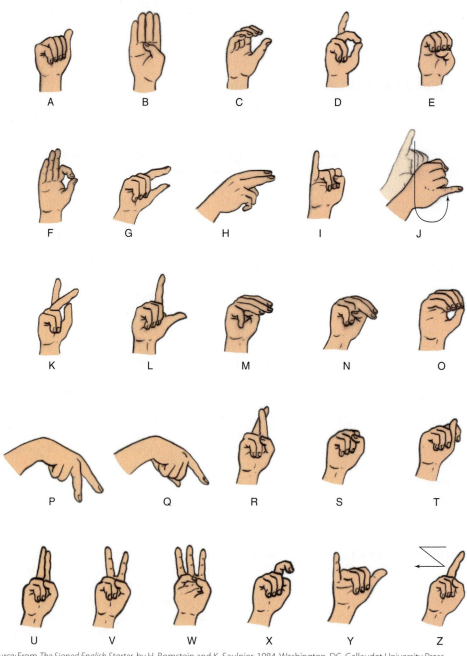

Source: From *The Signed English Starter*, by H. Bomstein and K. Saulnier, 1984, Washington, DC. Gallaudet University Press. Copyright 1984 by Gallaudet University Press. Reprinted with permission.

of a *V* at the eyes and then turning the hand to point forward. If the *V* moves from the eyes and then points upward, that small change indicates that the person is looking up.

Manually coded English sign language systems differ from ASL in that they are designed to be a visual representation of the English language. The primary sign systems used in the United States are **Pidgin Sign English (PSE); Seeing Essential English, Signing Exact English (SEE2); and Conceptually Accurate Signed English (CASE)**.

Total or Simultaneous Communication. This approach combines as many sources of information as possible, including simultaneous communication of both sign and spoken language and support for residual hearing. Amplification, speech reading, speech training, reading, and writing are all used in combination with signs. Total communication is somewhat out of favor. One reason is that it is unrealistic to expect a student to use every available communication technique and mode. Teachers typically emphasize speech and audition at the expense of sign language, or vice versa. And students often attend more to one mode than to the other.

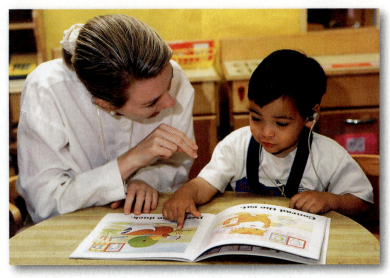

This teacher uses sign language to supplement the student's assistive technology hearing aid.

A second reason for total communication's decreasing popularity is that it uses speech and sign language simultaneously, an approach called *SimCom*. It is nearly impossible to speak and use ASL at the same time, so teachers use either manually coded English or Pidgin Sign English (Bishop, 2010; Moores, 2008a; Tevenal & Villanueva, 2009).

The three Symansky children are good examples of individuals who use various communication options. All three learned sign language as their first language. As a result of Alina's residual hearing and cochlear implant, she is able to use a combination of oral and manual communication (total communication). Even with her cochlear implant, however, she is more comfortable using ASL, both receptively and expressively, because it is the language of her family.

Academic Achievement

The academic achievement of students with hearing loss depends on their individual characteristics as well as the characteristics of their parents, teachers, and school programs. Most of these children have specific educational challenges in the areas of reading and writing (Blackorby & Knokey, 2006; Karchmer & Mitchell, 2003). Because educational curricula are so language-based, communication and learning are strongly linked.

Two issues have confounded researchers who have attempted to identify the causes of the relatively low academic achievement of students who are deaf and hard of hearing. The first concerns the effects of inclusive education settings versus segregated ones. Much research has shown that students with hearing impairments who are in general education classrooms demonstrate higher academic achievement than do comparable students who are in self-contained classrooms or segregated settings (Shaver, Newman, Huang, Yu, & Knokey, 2011). But research does not always prevail when placement decisions are being made. Sometimes families and students themselves want to be with other students who have hearing impairments, believing that their communication and learning will prosper when they are with others who have the same impairments.

IDEA recognizes the issue of integrated versus less integrated placements. Thus, when an IEP team is developing a student's IEP and making a placement decision for any child, not just a child who has a hearing impairment, the team must consider the child's communication needs. If the child is deaf or hard of hearing, the team must consider the child's language and communication needs, opportunities for direct communications with peers and professionals in the child's language and communication mode, the child's academic level, and the child's full range of needs, including opportunities for direct instruction in the child's language and communication mode. If the IEP team strictly follows this provision, it may decide that the child's academic and other development will prosper more if he is educated with others who have hearing impairments (because the child then would have opportunities for direct instruction in his language and communication mode) than he would in an integrated general education program.

Kim and Ron Symansky have chosen to place Cameron, Zander, and Alina in a state school for the deaf. While all three have been educated in regular public education classrooms in the past, each ultimately chose to continue their education in the school for the deaf, where they believed they would have greater access to natural communication and social interaction with their deaf peers. The choice seems to be a good one because all three are happy and finding academic success.

The second issue involves the rising numbers of students with hearing loss who are from diverse racial, ethnic, and linguistic backgrounds. There has been a change in relative size among racial/ethnic groups of deaf children in the United States, beginning with the 1973–1974 academic year. White deaf youth made up about 75 percent of the school-age population in 1974 but only 52 percent in 2008–2009, with Hispanic and Latino students making up 25 percent of the total population of students with hearing loss. There is a critical need to meet the educational needs of deaf children and youth who are from diverse racial, ethnic, or cultural backgrounds (Andrews & Covell, 2007; Gallaudet Research Institute, 1973/1974–2007/2008).

Families and teachers struggle to find appropriate methods for improving language and literacy for students with hearing loss. For students with a hearing loss whose families do not use English as their primary language, educational opportunities and outcomes appear to be even bleaker (Marschark, Sapere, Convertino, Mayer, Wauters, & Sarchet, 2009; Mayer & Leigh, 2010; Wolbers, 2002).

Academically, students who are hard of hearing are still among the least appropriately served groups. The issues and challenges of students with mild and moderate hearing losses are complex and have significant implications for their academic and social success. Their needs are often overlooked and misunderstood. Because these students can hear some sounds, they may not be immediately referred for services. Accumulated years of misunderstanding what they are hearing can result in grade retention and a gap between ability and academic achievement. They are also at risk socially because they may miss the small social nuances in schools' hallways, cafeterias, and gyms (Easterbrooks & Baker, 2002; Wake, Hughes, Poulakis, Collins, & Rickards, 2004).

These students—some but not all of whom have a hearing impairment—are communicating by sign language and by using assistive devices for their ears.

Social and Emotional Development

The communication barriers that result from the difficulty of acquiring oral language, compounded by preconceived ideas of deafness held by the hearing world, significantly affect a student's psychosocial development. The average hearing person has difficulty communicating with a person with hearing loss, and deaf students soon become aware of these communication problems as they try to make their wants and needs known.

Four factors affect deaf students' social and emotional development. First, parent-child interaction plays a fundamental role in every child's development. Hearing parents may very early find it difficult to communicate with their child who is deaf or hard of hearing. This difficulty will affect their interactions as well as parent-child bonding.

Second, peers and teachers play a significant role in a student's social development. When communication is easy, students learn social norms, rules of conversation, appropriate ways of responding in various situations, and how to develop relationships. If, however, there is a communication barrier among a student, teachers, and peers, the resulting lack of interaction is likely to hamper the student's development of a positive self-concept as well as close friendships.

Third, developing a social presence involves awareness of social cues. These cues are most often spoken; and while a student with hearing loss may pick up on some visual cues to appropriate social behaviors, he may miss the auditory ones.

Finally, deaf children can feel an increasing sense of isolation and loneliness as they realize that others may not be comfortable interacting with them (Cole, Cutler, Thobro, & Hass, 2009; Jacobs, 2010; Scheetz, 2004; Wauters & Knoors, 2007). They may even begin to see themselves through the eyes of society and develop a feeling of being outsiders in a hearing world.

IEP TIP

Social integration of deaf children in inclusive settings depends on the child's peer acceptance, social competence, and friendships. The student's IEP team should consider the child's social skills when developing the IEP.

DETERMINING THE CAUSES

Determining the cause of hearing loss is often complicated by a delay in diagnosis, and many causes remain unknown. When a hearing loss is present at birth, the proper term is **congenital** loss, regardless of the cause. Losses that occur after birth are described as **acquired**. A number of factors can result in hearing loss. They include hereditary or genetic causes, an event or injury during pregnancy (prenatal), or injury at or just following birth. Trauma, disease, and exposure to excessive noise can also cause hearing loss.

Genetic Causes

Hereditary loss occurs in approximately one in 2,000 children. Most hereditary hearing loss is a result of an inherited autosomal recessive gene (80 percent) and is not associated with any type of syndrome. There are more than seventy documented inherited syndromes associated with deafness; they can result in either a conductive, a sensorineural, or a mixed loss (Batshaw, Pellegrino, & Roizen, 2007).

Prenatal Causes

Exposure to viruses, bacteria, and other toxins before or after birth can result in hearing loss. During delivery or in the newborn period, a number of complications, such as lack of oxygen (**hypoxia**), can damage the hearing mechanism, particularly the cochlea.

The major cause of congenital deafness is infection that occurs during pregnancy or soon after the baby is born. Before the development of a vaccine, **rubella** was one of the leading causes of deafness. The rubella epidemic in the United States in 1964–1965 resulted in a huge increase in the incidence of deafness. Due to the use of an anti-rubella vaccine, the incidence has decreased considerably. **Toxoplasmosis**, **herpes virus**, **syphilis**, and **cytomegalovirus (CMV)** are also prenatal infections that can cause hearing loss.

Premature infants, particularly those weighing less than 1,500 grams (3⅓ pounds), have an increased susceptibility to hypoxia, **hyperbilirubinemia**, and **intracranial hemorrhage**, all of which have been associated with sensorineural hearing loss (Gilbert et al., 2007).

Postnatal Causes

Infections in infancy and childhood also can lead to a sensorineural hearing loss. For example, a child with **bacterial meningitis** has a 10 percent risk of hearing loss from damage to the cochlea. The most common cause of hearing loss in young children is middle-ear disease, or **acute otitis media** (ear infection). As a teacher, you will want to be aware of the fluctuating conductive hearing loss that can occur in your students who have middle-ear infections; those students might be missing important information while they have an ear infection. You should be aware of any signs (such as inattention or cocking the head) that might indicate that the child is not hearing what you are saying.

Postlingual Causes

A blow to the skull can cause trauma to the cochlea and may lead to a sensorineural hearing loss. It can also damage the middle-ear bones, resulting in a conductive loss. Mild to moderate sensorineural hearing loss can occur as a result of being around excessive noise such as firecrackers and air guns. Using headphones at high-intensity levels or attending rock concerts where noise levels can reach 100 to 110 dB may be damaging. In fact, any sustained exposure to sound levels of 90 dB or greater is potentially harmful to the cochlea and should be avoided (Batshaw et al., 2007).

Evaluating Students with Hearing Loss

DETERMINING THE PRESENCE OF HEARING LOSS

Diagnostic Assessment

The earlier hearing loss is identified, the more quickly intervention can begin. Figure 14.4 illustrates a recommended infant hearing screening process. Most states now have an early hearing detection and intervention (EHDI) system that

1. Screens all newborns for hearing loss before one month of age, preferably before leaving the hospital

2. Refers all infants who screen positive for a diagnostic audiologic evaluation before three months of age

3. Provides all infants identified as having a hearing loss with appropriate early intervention services before six months of age

The diagnosis of a hearing loss is made by a combination of professionals, including the child's doctor, an **otologist** (a physician who specializes in diseases of the ear), and an **audiologist**. Audiologists have special training in testing and measuring hearing and are able to evaluate the hearing of any child at any age. Audiologists also have the skills to participate in the child's rehabilitation and treatment and to prescribe and evaluate the effectiveness of hearing aids and cochlear implants.

Hearing Aids

Audiologists provide assistance in selecting and using hearing aids. Hearing aids amplify sound but do not correct hearing. In other words, they make sound louder but not necessarily clearer.

The behind-the-ear aid is probably the most common type of hearing aid used by both children and adults. The case holding all of the components of the hearing aid is worn behind the ear, and the signal is delivered through a tube into the ear using an earmold. For children, this type of aid has the advantage of durability. Behind-the-ear hearing aids are larger than the hearing aids worn inside the ear, making them easier to keep track of and better able to withstand the daily wear and tear that young children usually create.

In addition, behind-the-ear aids provide flexibility. As the child grows, the size of the ear also increases. When this happens, the earmold may no longer fit. With a behind-the-ear aid, accommodating growth means simply replacing the earmold rather than the entire hearing aid. Children can wear this type of aid behind one or both ears.

Cochlear Implants

A **cochlear implant** is an electronic device that is surgically implanted under the skin behind the ear and contains a magnet that couples to a magnet in a sound transmitter that is worn externally. A surgeon inserts an electrode array into the cochlea to provide direct stimulation to the nerve fibers. A speech processor that can be worn on the body or behind the ear is connected to a headpiece by a cable. The receiver delivers electrical stimulation to the appropriate implanted electrodes in the cochlea, and then this signal is carried to the brain through the auditory nerve.

FIGURE 14.4   *Infant hearing screening process*

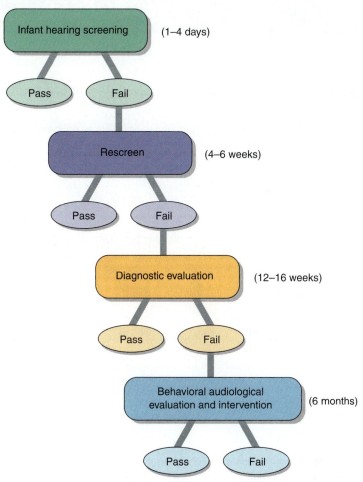

Infant hearing screening (1–4 days)

Pass   Fail

Rescreen (4–6 weeks)

Pass   Fail

Diagnostic evaluation (12–16 weeks)

Pass   Fail

Behavioral audiological evaluation and intervention (6 months)

Pass   Fail

Source: From "Universal Newborn Hearing Screening Using Transient Evoked Otoacoustic Emissions: Results of the Rhode Island Hearing Assessment Project," by K. R. White. B. R. Vohr, and T. R. Behrens, 1993. *Seminars in Hearing.* 14(1). pp. 18–29. Copyright 1993 by Thieme Medical Publishers. Reprinted with permission.

The cochlear implant does not restore normal hearing or amplify sound. Rather, it provides a sense of sound to individuals who are profoundly deaf and cannot otherwise receive auditory signals. It "gets around" the blockage of damaged hair cells in the cochlea by bypassing them and directly stimulating the auditory nerve (National Institute on Deafness and Other Communication Disorders, 2011).

DETERMINING THE NATURE AND EXTENT OF SPECIALLY DESIGNED INSTRUCTION AND SERVICES

Educational Evaluation

As we pointed out in Chapter 2, nondiscriminatory evaluation has two purposes: to determine whether a student has a disability and, if so, to determine an appropriate program and placement for the student. The test for eligibility for special education services for students with hearing loss is usually their initial assessment, the hearing test. Box 14.1 illustrates the evaluation process.

How Hearing Is Tested

Audiologists measure the type and severity of a hearing loss. The simplest test of hearing ability is pure tone audiometry. Audiologists use a machine called an **audiometer** to test hearing. It measures hearing threshold (the softest level at which sound can first be detected) at various sound frequencies.

BOX 14.1

NONDISCRIMINATORY EVALUATION PROCESS

Determining the Presence of a Hearing Loss

Observation

Medical personnel observe: The baby does not show a startle reflex to loud noises. As the child matures, speech and language are delayed.

Teachers and parents observe: The child (1) does not respond to sound; (2) does not babble or engage in vocal play; and (3) experiences communication misunderstandings, speech difficulties, and inattention.

Screening

Assessment measures:

Newborn screening: Most states require newborn screening for hearing loss.

Auditory brain stem response: Results may show inadequate or slow response to sound.

Transient evoked otoacoustic immittance: Results may show that measurement of sound in the ear is lower than normal.

Behavioral audiological evaluation: Hearing thresholds are higher than 15 dB.

Prereferral

Prereferral is typically not used with these students because of the need to identify hearing loss quickly.

Referral

Children receive nondiscriminatory evaluation procedures as soon as they enter school. Intervention should occur as soon as the child is diagnosed. Students with mild hearing loss may be referred.

Nondiscriminatory evaluation procedures and standards

Assessment measures:

Audiological reassessment: Recent audiograms may indicate that the student's hearing loss has stabilized or is worsening. Testing for hearing aid function is a regular need.

Speech and language evaluation: The student may have significant problems with receptive and expressive language. The student's speech is usually affected.

Individualized intelligence test: The student's scores show a discrepancy between verbal and nonverbal measures. Nonverbal tests are considered the only reliable and valid measures of intelligence for this population.

Individualized achievement test: The student may score significantly lower than peers.

Adaptive behavior: The student may score below average in communication and possibly in other areas of adaptive behavior.

Anecdotal records: The student's performance may indicate difficulty with reading, writing, or language arts.

Curriculum-based assessment: The student may be performing below peers in one or more areas of the curriculum because of reading and/or language difficulties.

Direct observation: The student may be difficult to understand and may misunderstand others.

Determination

The nondiscriminatory evaluation team determines that the student has a hearing loss and needs special education and related services. The student's IEP team proceeds to develop appropriate education options for the child.

Infants up to six months of age can be screened for hearing loss in two ways: evoked otoacoustic emissions (EOAE) and screening auditory brain stem response (SABR). EOAE is a fast and noninvasive test for a newborn that assesses how well the baby's cochlea is functioning and transmitting sound to the brain. The ear canal is sealed with a plastic probe, and clicks or tones of various frequencies are introduced into the ear canal. A computer records responses that are evoked from the cochlea.

The other newborn screening method, SABR, assesses more than the child's cochlea. It tests the child's auditory neural pathway as well. Electroencephalography (EEG) sensors are placed in various places on the baby's scalp. Using an external or inserted earphone, tones or clicks are presented separately to each ear, stimulating neural activity along the path. The electrodes detect sound, and the computer averages the responses.

Finally, diagnostic auditory brainstem response (ABR) audiometry is a highly sensitive test for both hearing loss and problems in the neural pathway. The ABR generates waveforms composed of three distinct waves (I, II, and III); the absence of waveform at a given intensity suggests a hearing loss, whereas the complete absence of a particular wave suggests an abnormality at a particular location along the brain pathway (Batshaw et al., 2007).

Behavioral audiological evaluations are appropriate for testing the hearing of older children. This test requires children to listen to a series of beeps called pure tones and indicate when they hear a sound.

The responses are recorded on an **audiogram**, a picture of what is heard. Figure 14.5 is an example of an audiogram showing a profound hearing loss, the type of loss Cameron and Zander have. It shows how much the hearing varies from normal if there is a loss (severity) and where the problem might be located in the auditory pathway (type). The vertical lines on an audiogram represent pitch or frequency (Hz), and the horizontal lines represent loudness or intensity (dB). The top of the audiogram on the left side shows 125 Hertz, a very low-pitched sound. As you look across, each line represents a higher and higher pitch. The critical pitches for speech are 500 to 3,000 Hz.

FIGURE 14.5 *Audiogram showing a profound hearing loss in both ears*

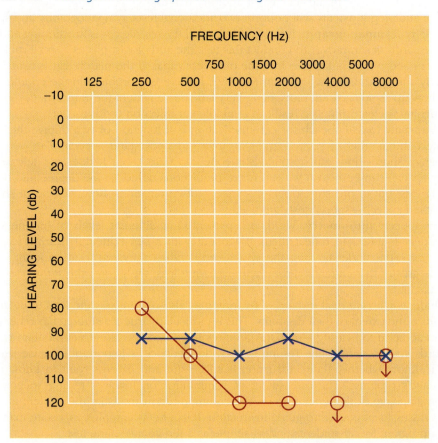

Audiologists retest the hearing of children with suspected or known hearing loss four times a year until age 3, twice a year until age 6, and annually after 6 years of age.

When you read down the left side of the audiogram, you can see the increasing loudness of sound represented by decibels. The first number listed is minus 10 dB because there is never a complete absence of sound in our world. Moving downward, each number represents a louder and louder sound, as if the volume were being turned up on a stereo. Responses to sound are plotted on the graph in terms of how loud a sound must be at each frequency before it is heard. Every point on an audiogram represents a different sound.

The audiologist tests the student's hearing by using air conduction (through earphones) and marks the hearing threshold on a graph with an *O* (for the right ear) and an *X* (for the left ear). The sound leaves the earphones, traveling through the air in the ear canal, through the middle ear, and to the cochlea in the inner ear.

The audiologist tests the sensitivity of the student's cochlea by using bone conduction through a small vibrator placed on the bone behind the ear. Sounds presented this way travel through the bones of the skull directly to the cochlea and auditory nerve, bypassing the outer and middle ear. When a bone-conduction vibrator is used to test for thresholds, a < symbol or a [symbol is used for the right ear and a > symbol or a] symbol is used for the left ear.

By comparing the headphone thresholds with the bone conduction thresholds at each pitch, the audiologist can determine whether a hearing loss is conductive, sensorineural, or mixed. If the air-conduction thresholds show a hearing loss but the bone-conduction thresholds are normal, then the individual has a conductive loss. If the hearing thresholds obtained by bone conduction are the same as by air conduction, there is no blockage of sound in the outer or middle ear, and the hearing loss is caused by a loss of sensitivity in the cochlea or auditory nerve.

The audiologist usually will perform two additional tests: tympanography and speech audiometry. **Tympanography** is a test of how well the middle ear is functioning and how well the eardrum can move. To conduct this test, the audiologist places a small rubber tip in the ear and pumps a little air into the outer ear canal. If the middle ear is functioning properly, the air causes the eardrum to move. If there is a problem in the middle ear, it may show up as no eardrum movement. Very little movement of the eardrum may indicate fluid behind the eardrum as a result of a middle-ear infection (otitis media).

The ability to use speech for communication is a function of two things: the ability to detect the sounds of speech and the ability to understand speech. The pure tone audiogram shows how much sound someone can detect, but it does not tell us how clearly speech can be heard. We can make predictions based on the degree and type of hearing loss; but to measure a person's speech discrimination—how well he or she can understand speech—special tests are used.

For speech **audiometry**, words are presented at different levels of loudness, and the student is asked to repeat them. A student with a sensorineural hearing loss may have a problem understanding the words, even when they are loud enough. Generally, the greater the student's sensorineural hearing loss, the poorer the student's speech discrimination.

Students who are deaf or hard of hearing may also require specific tests to determine the nature and extent of their disability. This is particularly true if a student has other problems in addition to hearing loss. IDEA requires increased attention to curriculum content standards and accountability. Testing to provide feedback is important because teachers need to know whether their instruction is successful and parents want to know about their child's progress. The assessment of communication involves testing speech and/or sign language skills depending on the communication modality the student is using. Finally, assessment is used to guide instruction. It can be as complex as a state-mandated testing program for all students and as simple as a ten-item spelling test.

Designing an Appropriate IEP

PARTNERING FOR SPECIAL EDUCATION AND RELATED SERVICES

Special and general educators, speech-language pathologists, audiologists, interpreters, paraprofessionals, family members, friends, and community members often become partners to contribute to a student's language, academic, and social development. In many school districts, an itinerant deaf educator—a professional who covers several schools in the same district—often becomes the key member and most informed advocate for the child. It is important to bear in mind that IDEA recognizes the contributions to the child's development that can be made by peers and professionals who can communicate directly with the child in the child's language and mode of communication. As we pointed out earlier in this chapter, the law does so by requiring the IEP team to consider the child's language and communication needs, opportunities for direct communication (that is, not-interpreted communication) with peers and professionals in the child's language, and communication mode. Beyond peers and other professionals, the increased use of cochlear implants means that any professionals who implant and maintain a child's cochlear implant should be members of the IEP team as well. Their participation on the IEP team is particularly important because IDEA provides that a surgically implanted medical device, such as the cochlear implant, is not a related service. The school is not responsible for providing or maintaining the device; that's the role of the implant team. Box 14.2 gives you tips on how partners educate a student who has a profound hearing loss.

BOX 14.2	INTO PRACTICE

Strategies for Vocabulary Development

As you have already learned, regardless of how effectively a child with hearing loss can comprehend complex concepts presented from teacher to student, reading about these concepts requires that he be able to manipulate English sentence structure, which is an especially daunting task for children who are not proficient in English. Consider the challenge facing Ben, age ten, who has a profound hearing loss and is in social studies and science classes. Linda is his classroom teacher, Katie is his deaf educator, Todd is his friend and can hear, John is his interpreter, and Ken and Sarah are his parents.

Linda and Katie use the following strategies with Ben and several other students during small-group time in the resource room:

1. *Semantic mapping* builds on a student's prior knowledge. Semantic maps are diagrams that show the connections between different categories of a topic. You begin with a brainstorming session that encourages students to think about concepts they know and then to see graphically how these concepts relate to the new information they are trying to learn. Students can learn the meanings and uses of new words, see words they already know from a new perspective, and, ultimately, see how the words connect to each other.
   - Write the new word to be learned in a circle in the middle of the white board.
   - In the brainstorming session, have the students think of as many words as they can that relate to the new word.
   - As the students give their words, write them on the board. Then have students categorize the different words by asking questions such as "What is it? What is it like?" Label the

categories, and then have students group their words into the categories.
   - Remember to pace your instruction and pause for interpretation. John, Ben's interpreter, reminds Linda to pause between calling on children because the lag time between Linda's question and John's interpreting means that Ben is a few seconds behind the other children in "hearing" the question.

   For example, Linda writes the new word, *journey,* on the board and draws a circle around it. The students suggest other words—*trip, vacation, travel, car, airplane, Disney World*—and the teacher categorizes these words into the categories of "Types of Journeys," "Places to Go," "How to Travel." Then the students come up with other words that fit into each category. Ben has been to Disney World and traveled by airplane to get there. He now understands that a "journey" can be a trip and to go on a journey, he must have some means of travel.

2. The teachers use the K-W-L approach: *know, what, learn.*
   - Before reading, they ask the children to brainstorm what they know about the topic.
   - They write all the ideas on the computer, project the display through an LCD projector, and then ask students to put their ideas into categories.
   - After this group activity, the teachers ask the students to create individual questions regarding what they want to learn about the topic.
   - Assign the text material for homework.

(continued)

BOX 14.2   INTO PRACTICE (continued)

Parents can use this strategy too. For instance, Ben's parents, Ken and Sarah, set aside a few minutes every evening so that Ben can show them his vocabulary questions and the answers he has found. The next day, Linda asks her students to discuss what they have learned. She focuses their responses on answering the questions they have written the previous day. She also draws their attention to similarities and differences between what they had previously known about the topic and what they have learned by reading the assignment.

3. *Thematic organization* promotes language development, critical thinking, independence, and collaboration among students. To be effective, thematic instruction must have meaning and purpose for students. It must also be relevant and interesting. So Linda's students choose the theme and the projects that will be part of a unit. Another important aspect of thematic organization is that it should build on students' prior knowledge, such as from their experiences, their families' cultures, and their understanding of themselves and others. There should be opportunities for students to use language and literacy, collaborate with others, and help to guide all aspects of the process. Finally, use a multi-subject approach incorporating the theme across all academic areas—mathematics, social studies, science, reading, etc.

   - Identify a theme. Linda's class chose "chocolate" as their theme.
   - Have students create an outline or flow chart of major concepts and vocabulary they will encounter in completing the different activities around the theme.
   - Develop a variety of lessons around the theme. Linda and Katie had the class read the book *Chocolate Touch*; write descriptive paragraphs using the five senses on paper shaped like Hershey's Kisses; learn about Hershey, Pennsylvania, find it on the map, and identify the state's capital; create twelve words out of the words *chocolate* and

Hershey; and answer the question "If a candy bar snitcher took 12 of your 30 bars, how many would you have left? Now write this number as a fraction."

   - Provide supports that Ben needs. Todd and Ben share ideas about the lessons. Todd often helps explain a concept in a way that is understandable to Ben.

   Ben has been able to keep up with his fourth-grade peers in comprehending the content material assigned as homework. His teachers and parents realize, however, that as text material becomes more difficult, Ben will be increasingly challenged to be independent in reading material written at grade level. In the future, Ben's teachers may wish to find supplementary material written at his reading level.

4. A *Venn diagram* strategy compares and contrasts objects. It can be used with either expository or narrative text.
   - Write two target words (e.g., *computer* and *brain*) on the white board.
   - Have students list as many characteristics as they can under each word: for instance, *computer*—out in the open, nonliving, can talk, hard, dry, many forms, made of plastic, solves problems, remembers things, cannot do things without being programmed, can be damaged; *brain*—enclosed, living, soft, made of tissue, warm, one form, solves problems, remembers things, can talk, can be damaged. Ben works with a small group of his friends during this stage.
   - Draw two overlapping circles on the board (the Venn diagram). Ask students to determine which characteristics the two words have in common and write those in the overlapping part of the two circles; then have them write the unique characteristics for each word in the parts of the circles that don't overlap. Katie, Ben's deaf educator, helps him write a short paper comparing and contrasting the two.

Interpreter services, illustrated here and consisting of the translation of the spoken word into signs and signs into the spoken word, are now a related service under IDEA.

Using Interpreters in Educational Settings

Related services under IDEA Part B (ages three through twenty-one) include interpreting services. Educational interpreters provide an essential service to both students and teachers. They translate the spoken word into signs for students with a hearing loss. Some perform additional duties within the school or classroom, such as tutoring, general classroom assistance, educational planning, and sign language instruction (Marschark, Sapare, Convertino, & Seewagen, 2005; Schick, Williams, & Kupermintz, 2006). The educational interpreter is often a student's communication bridge to the hearing world around him. Box 14.3 provides tips for using an educational interpreter in the classroom.

The National Deaf Education Project (NDEP), a collaborative project of the American Society

Using an Educational Interpreter in the Classroom

Grace, a student in the Mrs. Burke's fourth-grade class, has a profound hearing loss. She uses a behind-the-ear hearing aid and has language, speech, and auditory IEP goals. Her primary communication mode, however, is American Sign Language. She uses an interpreter, Jan, to access the general education curriculum. Jan facilitates communication between Grace and Mrs. Burke and other students in the class. Jan wears clothing that makes it easy for Grace to see her signing (e.g., solid-colored tops) and doesn't wear any jewelry when she's working.

Jan helps Grace communicate inside and outside of the classroom, accompanying her to after-school clubs and programs. Jan also is teaching sign language to the students in Grace's class so they can communicate directly with her. When Grace can't understand Mrs. Burke's explanation of a subject, Jan clarifies the information by rephrasing or repeating it. If Grace still needs clarification, Jan and Mrs. Burke will ask Grace's IEP team to determine alternate strategies and additional supports for her. Mrs. Burke makes sure that Jan has access ahead of time to all of the materials and lesson plans she will use that day. Together they determine what vocabulary and concepts will need to be pretaught to Grace before each lesson.

Educational interpreters use an inverted pyramid of responsibility to determine the support provided to the student with hearing impairment. While in elementary school, Grace will need a significant amount of support. Later she will be expected to do more and more of her work independently and communicate as much as possible herself. For now, Grace sits at a table located at the front of the class, facing Mrs. Burke and the whiteboard and screen. Jan stands by the board near Mrs. Burke. Both of them have made sure that Grace's seat allows her full view of the classroom and is away from the noisy hallway.

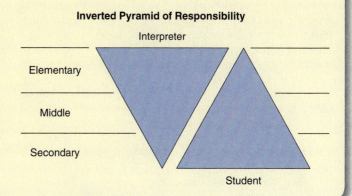

Inverted Pyramid of Responsibility

Interpreter

Elementary

Middle

Secondary

Student

for Deaf Children, the Conference of Educational Administrators of the Deaf, Gallaudet University, the National Association of the Deaf, and the National Technical Institute for the Deaf, advocates for a deaf or hard-of-hearing student's unlimited access to communication. According to this group, direct, multidimensional communication is much more efficient and dynamic than receiving communication through a third party (that is, an interpreter). When direct communication isn't possible, however, they believe that it is critical to maintain a high level of standards for the quality of educational interpreter skills (Siegel, 2000). Access to direct communication was a determining factor in Kim and Ron's decision to educate their children in the state school for the deaf.

DETERMINING SUPPLEMENTARY AIDS AND SERVICES

Managing the Listening Environment/Acoustics

When a classroom is equipped with a **sound-field amplification system**, the teacher transmits his voice by using a lavaliere microphone and ceiling- or wall-mounted speakers. These in turn amplify his voice to 8 to 10 dB above the ambient room noise. This can be useful because noisy environments, such as many classrooms, blunt the effects of hearing aids.

A student's hearing aid also allows access to **loop systems**. These involve closed-circuit wiring that sends FM signals from an audio system directly to an electronic coil in the student's hearing aid. The receiver picks up the signals much as a remote control sends infrared signals to a television. These systems allow students with residual hearing to participate in a variety of educational settings.

Assistive Technology

Just as a caption in a book is the text under a picture, **closed-captioned technology** translates dialogue from a spoken language to a printed form (captions) that is then

BOX 14.4

UNIVERSAL DESIGN FOR PROGRESS

Real-Time Captioning in Classrooms

Undoubtedly, you have seen movies in which a court stenographer is recording what judges, lawyers, and witnesses say. The stenographer is making a record that participants in the trial can consult later. Now technology takes that service to a new level, making the words instantly available to students who are deaf or hard of hearing.

Communication Access Realtime Translation (CART) is a technology that instantly converts the spoken word into English text, using a stenotype machine, a notebook computer, and real-time software. An individual types the spoken word into the stenotype machine, and a software program converts the shorthand into text that then appears on a computer monitor. The real-time captionist is a related service provider, just like the student's educational interpreter is. The regulations implementing the Americans with Disabilities Act recognize CART as an assistive technology that affords "effective communication access." Thus, communication access is what truly distinguishes CART from real-time reporting in a traditional courtroom sense. Real-time captioning in a classroom can give deaf and hard-of-hearing students instant access to a teacher's and peers' communications. Its power to advance students' inclusion is staggering.

Deaf students have had access to captioned movies and videos for many years, and captioning increases students' comprehension and their reading skills (Caldwell, 1973; Marschark et al., 2006; Robson, 2004). In fact, captions help both deaf and hearing students, particularly in classroom environments with poor acoustics (e.g., a large room or noisy conditions), where even hearing students have difficulties in hearing everything that is said.

What are the benefits of using real-time captioning in your classroom?

- *Independent learning.* With CART, the responsibility for your student's education rests with the student. The student will have a verbatim record of the class discussion and can determine what is important. Using the highlighting or annotating features of the computer software, she can pick out exactly what she needs to study.

- *Full participation.* Because CART provides information in real time, the student with hearing loss has the opportunity to participate in the class just like his classmates do. Besides getting the text of the lecture, CART allows for the inclusion of classroom banter, discussion, and questions asked by other students. This gives him full access to the classroom experience, not just to notes of the lesson's content provided after class.

How do you secure CART services for students with hearing loss? As with interpreters, there is a shortage of people skilled in this form of real-time captioning. Some companies, such as Caption First, provide CART services both locally and nationally through remote technology.

- When an IEP team has determined that a student will benefit from real-time captioning as a related service, the IEP should include the following specifics:
  a. Communication Access Realtime Translation (CART) will be provided by a court reporter who can write at a minimum speed of 225 words per minute.
  b. An electronic copy of the notes will be given to the student immediately after each class so the student can make her notes at home.
  c. Same-day substitutes will be provided when needed.
  d. The student will be allowed to follow the CART feed on a laptop computer on her desk.

The National Court Reporters Association (NCRA) has an online CART directory at http://www.cartinfo.org that you can use to find CART providers in your area.

---

inserted at the bottom of the television, movie, or videotape. Captioning increases deaf or hard-of-hearing students' ability to comprehend a speaker and understand the information presented (Cambria, Silvestre, & Leal, 2009). Box 14.4 provides you with tips on how real-time captioning in a classroom benefits students who are deaf or hard of hearing.

Computers and the Internet

Personal computers provide students with hearing loss access to information in remarkably innovative ways. They can provide instructional support and can even assist students in learning sign language. A computer system (C-print) developed by the National Technical Institute for the Deaf (NTID) provides students who use software-equipped laptop computers with real-time translations of the spoken word. Students with hearing loss can attend a lecture, watch an interpreter without having to look down to take notes, and view the simultaneous written text of what is being said.

PLANNING FOR UNIVERSAL DESIGN FOR LEARNING

Children who are deaf or hard of hearing typically communicate in one of three ways: oral/aural, manual (ASL or English system), or simultaneous communication.

Communication

Speech-language pathologists are responsible for carrying out instruction in speech and aural habilitation (teaching children to use their remaining hearing). Because many students with significant hearing loss do not hear speech or do not hear it without distortion, it is difficult for them to produce speech and to monitor their own speech without assistance. Their problems can include trouble with volume, pitch, and nasality. The speech-language pathologist helps them develop breath control, vocalization, voice patterns, and sound production.

The speech-language pathologist also usually educates students with hearing loss to use even their minimal residual hearing effectively. The pathologist teaches the student about awareness of sound, localization of sound, discrimination of sound differences, recognition of the sound, and, ultimately, comprehension of others' speech.

Here, both the student and the teacher wear an assistive technology device (a transmitter and receiver), but neither relies on it alone to communicate.

A Bilingual/Bicultural Model

One method of communication that interests both deaf and hearing parents of students with hearing loss is the bilingual/bicultural (bi-bi) program. This model is a bilingual/English-as-a-second-language (ESL) model for deaf students acquiring and learning two languages: ASL and English. Remember that ASL is a distinct language; it is not just a visual representation of the English. The bi-bi model takes theories and knowledge from ESL research and applies them to deaf education (Moores, 2008a). The student learns ASL as a first language and English as a second language.

Lesson Planning for Speech and Language

Collaboration is critical when preparing instruction for students who are deaf or hard of hearing. To account for the gap between the child's language and the linguistic demands of the lesson, the lesson plan should include a section for language, a section for speech, and a section for auditory goals in addition to the concepts to be taught. The teacher may choose to focus initially on the concept to be taught and then follow up with practice on language, speech, and auditory goals. Instruction may involve a general education teacher, a teacher of the deaf, and a paraprofessional in collaboration with a speech-language pathologist. There should be four levels of planning: (1) concept planning, (2) language goals planning, (3) speech goals planning, and (4) auditory goals planning. Each participant should have input and responsibility for every aspect of planning and instruction.

PLANNING FOR OTHER EDUCATIONAL NEEDS

When the majority of students with hearing loss attended residential schools for the deaf, they were exposed to the culture of deafness as a normal part of their lives. The school played an integral part in the Deaf community. Deaf adults spent large amounts of time at the schools, attending sports events and social affairs, serving as role models for the students, and providing them with direct access to the critical elements of Deaf culture. This included information about Deaf history, the arts, and stories about their lives. The schools contained a treasure trove of photos, trophies, and artwork from the past.

Today most students with hearing loss attend public school programs, so deaf immersion is not an option (Blackorby & Knokey, 2006; Miller, 2010). As a result, schools and communities must purposefully provide students with a study of their native language (ASL) and Deaf culture and make sure that they have opportunities to socialize with deaf adults. Making Deaf studies an indispensable part of a student's educational program is essential to the growth and development of the student's identity, awareness of diversity, and self-esteem. The successful deaf adult is likely to function in both the hearing and the Deaf worlds, so deaf children need to be taught about both communities (Nowakowski, Tasker, & Schmidt, 2009).

Using Effective Instructional Strategies

EARLY CHILDHOOD STUDENTS: FACILITATIVE LANGUAGE STRATEGIES

Early Intervention

Early intervention for children with hearing loss and their families is critical for developing children's language, social, and academic skills. Programs should provide young children with similar peers, role models, appropriate developmental skills training, and support for acquiring communication and language. Early intervention programs also should help parents understand their child's needs so they can make informed decisions about issues that will affect their child's and the family's future (Joint Committee on Infant Hearing, 2007). Implementation of universal newborn hearing screening has had a positive impact on the number and age of young children with hearing loss who are enrolled in early intervention programs (Halpin, Smith, Widen, & Chertoff, 2010).

Early access to a language-rich environment is critical. This means better education for parents on strategies to enhance communication with their deaf or hard-of-hearing children, whether they use spoken or sign language. Getting and maintaining attention, labeling and commenting on objects, and explaining events are important components of a child's early language, social, and cognitive development. Hearing parents need to learn the effective visual communication techniques that are typically used by deaf parents (Marschark, Lang, & Albertini, 2002).

Shared Reading

The Shared Reading Project, another appropriate program for young children with hearing loss, is based on how deaf adults read to deaf children and depends heavily on use of ASL, fluency in signing, and a knack for reading signs. Dramatization, connection of English sentences with how they are signed in ASL, and engagement of children in the reading process are emphasized. This project was found to be of particular benefit to families who were not sharing books before their training and to those who spoke a language other than English. The Shared Reading Project is effective in helping parents learn to share books with traditionally underserved deaf and hard-of-hearing children (Swanwick & Watson, 2007).

ELEMENTARY AND MIDDLE SCHOOL STUDENTS: GRAPHIC ORGANIZER MODIFICATIONS

Because students with hearing loss suffer in the academic areas of reading and writing, teachers give high priority to instruction in these content areas. Students should be given hands-on experiences and taught the relationships among concepts and the multiple meanings of words. Visual aids can show links between words and their categories (e.g., *animal–dog–golden retriever*).

Use Authentic Experiences

Students acquire language and knowledge only when they are presented in ways that are meaningful to the students. Often traditional language programs for students who are deaf or hard of hearing are limited because these programs have no connection to the students' real-world or authentic experiences (Luckner & Cooke, 2010).

A list of sentences in a book is relevant only if the student has had experiences related to what the sentences describe. Authentic experiences are particularly important for students with hearing loss because they may not have had the same experiences as their hearing peers or have had them in the same way. For example, we explain to hearing children why they must put on mittens to go outside ("It's below freezing today, and your hands will turn blue!"). For a child with hearing loss who lacks the language for this explanation, parents may just put the mittens on without explanation. When the child later encounters a written sentence about freezing temperatures, she will have had no authentic experience with that situation.

Integrate Vocabulary Development

The integration of vocabulary occurs when teachers show that words are parts of related concepts, are presented in context, and are everywhere. Words occur in bunches, and their contexts help define them and their meanings. *Spring* is a season of the year, a coiled piece of metal, a jump, a small body of water, and many other things. Words are everywhere. There is writing on toys, on clothing labels, and even on cereal boxes. In an integrated approach to vocabulary development, words appear on charts, bulletin boards, and objects in the room. As a teacher, you may find yourself using one of the standard models for increasing your students' language proficiency, the Cummins model, which Box 14.5 describes.

BOX 14.5 | INTO PRACTICE

Using the Cummins Model of Language Proficiency

James Cummins (1988, 1992, 2003, 2009) used two terms to describe the two dimensions of language: conversational and academic. His terms are (1) BICS (basic interpersonal communicative skills) and (2) CALP (cognitive academic linguistic proficiency). For a student to be successful socially and academically, both dimensions must be developed: BICS + CALP = academic success. The Cummins model can help team members analyze tasks, write objectives, and plan appropriate mediated activities for students with hearing loss. Here's how it works.

The Cummins Model is a continuum along which a student's progress from conversation to dealing with challenging material is increased (from simple to complex and visual to language dependent). The model has four quadrants:

Quadrant A: activities and tasks that are hands-on and visual, such as art, music, and physical education

Quadrant B: more complex activities that are visual but tied to a context, such as math computation, science experiments, and social studies projects

Quadrant C: activities that are much more abstract and dependent on language, such as written instructions without examples, which demand a much higher cognitive level for comprehension to occur

Quadrant D: activities that require language competence and the ability to deal with abstract concepts

How can you use this model for students who are deaf and hard of hearing?

- Improve listening skills.
  a. Add context to listening skills by improving the room's acoustics, repeating directions two or three times, adding gestures,

using a graphic support such as a picture or a drawing, or providing a word clue (e.g., "It rhymes with moon").
  b. Use the model to remind the team to be aware of one student's need to reduce some cognitive demands while recognizing that others may be ready for higher-level thinking skills.
- Add language comprehension skills.
  a. Include cognitively undemanding, context-embedded questions in Quadrant A: "What color is this table?" "Who is sitting by you?" "Which one is red?"
  b. Include cognitively undemanding, context-reduced questions in Quadrant B: "Where is your sister's classroom?" "What color is your house?" "What is your teacher's name?"
  c. Have more cognitively demanding questions in Quadrant C but keep the context embedded: "What do you think this story is about?" "Why are shoes made of leather?" "How does electricity make a lamp go on?"
  d. The most cognitively demanding, context-reduced language level is in Quadrant D: "How is a state different from a country?" "What is similar about a horse and a cow?" "Is a mile longer than a kilometer?"
- Identify levels of student support.
  a. Quadrant A includes directly teaching the necessary subskills with mediation (e.g., define key words using terms "Joe" knows; provide a picture or diagram).
  b. Quadrant B involves directly teaching the substeps to the objective (e.g., have Joe paraphrase the main ideas of the instructions or construct a graphic organizer of the steps).
  c. Quadrant C activities are teacher-led rather than teacher-directed (e.g., assist Joe in verbalizing his thought process by using open-ended questions—"What does 'identify the subject' mean?").
  d. Quadrant D lists a skill that is difficult for the student (e.g., Joe will understand the written directions in his textbook).

Create Opportunities for Self-Expression

Self-expression is a large part of a student's learning process. Teachers provide students with opportunities to practice their verbal skills and to define and refine ideas. They allow students to convert information into other forms and then express it. Self-expression shows how deeply and for what purposes a student has processed certain information.

Provide Deaf Role Models

Students with hearing loss should have the opportunity to meet and interact with deaf adults. A role model can be a positive example of adult behavior and show students what they can become. If the only adults in their world have hearing, it may be difficult for students with hearing loss to visualize their capabilities and to create future goals (Miller, 2010).

Teach about Deaf Studies

IEP TIP

Students with hearing loss should have knowledge of Deaf culture and the Deaf community. IEP team members should identify strategies for providing this information to the child.

Learning about deafness, the Deaf community, Deaf history, and famous deaf adults should be a part of the curriculum for students with hearing loss (McDonald, 2010). Teachers can incorporate this information into social studies, health, and science content for all students, but for their deaf and hard-of-hearing students in particular. Just as teachers provide students with information about diverse ethnic and racial cultures, so they should provide them with information about deafness. The subject matter should include the basics for interacting with people with hearing loss, sensitivity activities, ASL as a language, Deaf social interaction norms, Deaf history and organizations, Deaf literature and arts, and Deaf values.

SECONDARY AND TRANSITION STUDENTS: PLANNING FOR THE FUTURE

In the early years of deaf education, schools for the deaf typically prepared their students to get a job. A few students went on to college, but the majority graduated expecting to join the workforce. Today advances in technology in America have changed the nature of postsecondary education, jobs, and employment.

Transition Planning

The result is that all schools must prepare their students with hearing loss for postsecondary education and training rather than for a specific job. This is particularly critical for deaf people because they experience higher unemployment and underemployment than do their hearing counterparts (Hanks & Luckner, 2003; Newman, Wagner, Cameto, Knokey, & Shaver, 2010; Punch, Creed, & Hyde, 2006).

To prepare students with hearing loss for the world after school, you should inform them about the employment, education, and living opportunities that will be available when they graduate. Beyond providing this information, you should actively engage your students in meaningful, goal-oriented activities that will prepare them for the future. This means that IEP teams must plan for an extensive evaluation of each student, coordinate a number of educational and employment experiences, and help students match their experiences to their knowledge, experience, and preferences.

In the transition process, the student's reading level has implications for the future. Imagine a sixteen-year-old student who is reading at a fifth-grade level. His IEP has continually focused on increasing that level by one year. But this goal is inappropriate and probably unrealistic when planning for transition. Let's say that the student wants to enter a particular vocational program that requires a ninth-grade reading level. The questions to ask are "Is this student a good candidate for this program?" and "With sufficient support, such as help in learning the course's written materials and an interpreter to help with in-class communication, could this student succeed in this career?"

The Americans with Disabilities Act requires employers to offer reasonable accommodations for deaf employees, such as installing a telecommunications device for the deaf (TDD). This device consists of a keyboard, a display screen, and a modem. The user types into the machine, and the letters are converted into electrical signals that can travel over regular phone lines. When the signals reach another TDD, they are converted back into letters that appear on a display screen so that the individual with hearing loss can read them. Employees are also using pagers and interpreters for meetings and training.

Postsecondary Education

During the past few years, many colleges and universities have experienced a growth in the numbers of students who are deaf or hard of hearing. This increase has made the transition from high school to postsecondary education easier because students with hearing loss now may have a small community of supportive peers in attendance. In addition, most colleges and universities provide direct support through on-campus offices for students with disabilities. These offices often provide counselors, interpreters, tutoring, and training for professors who will have the students in their classes. They also make arrangements for note takers and even real-time captioning of lectures.

The Postsecondary Education Programs Network (PEPNet) provides resources and expertise to enhance educational opportunities for students who are deaf or hard of hearing. Through four regional centers, the organization offers consultation, training, professional development, and technical assistance to secondary education, two- and four-year colleges and universities, community rehabilitation, continuing education, and vocational and technical training programs. An example of their support is *iTransition*, a series of four online trainings created to assist students who are deaf or hard of hearing transition successfully from high school to postsecondary education or work. The training activities help students learn more about themselves, their career goals, and the skills they will need to be successful (http://www.pepnet.org).

Including Students with Hearing Loss

EDUCATIONAL QUALITY

When the Commission on the Education of the Deaf (1988) assessed the quality of all educational services provided to students with hearing loss, it concluded that the present status of education for persons who are deaf in the United States was unsatisfactory. The commission recommended promoting English language development and recognizing the unique needs of students who are deaf. It requested that service providers take these needs into account when developing IEPs and urged the U.S. Department of Education to reconsider how the fourth principle of IDEA, placement in the least restrictive environment, should apply to deaf and hard-of-hearing students. It also requested that educators focus on the appropriateness of placement, taking into consideration the student's need to be taught by and be able to interact with others who use the same mode of communication (Commission on Education of the Deaf, 1988).

In direct response to the commission's report, the federal government issued new policy guidelines relative to the education of students who are deaf. The guidelines pointed out that "any setting, including a regular classroom, that prevents a child who is deaf from receiving an appropriate education that meets his or her needs, including communication needs, is not the LRE (least restrictive environment) for that child" (U.S. Department of Education, 1992, p. 49275). Educators have understood these guidelines to mean that the least restrictive environment for students who are deaf or hard of hearing may not be the general education classroom. Accordingly, teachers balance appropriateness (that is, the student's opportunity to benefit) against placement (that is, inclusion) and place the priority on appropriateness when there is a conflict between it and an inclusive placement.

This approach seems defensible. When Congress reauthorized IDEA in 2004, it directed the IEP team for a student who is deaf or hard of hearing to consider the student's language and communication needs, opportunities for direct communications with peers in the student's language and mode of communication, and full range of needs, including opportunities for direct instruction in the student's language and mode of communication.

Box 14.6 illustrates the great expectations possible for students who are deaf or hard of hearing, and Box 14.7 provides you with tips for including deaf or hard-of-hearing students in your classrooms.

EDUCATIONAL PLACEMENT

Access to communication should drive decisions about educational placement for students with hearing loss, but access and placement for many students can be in the general curriculum. More and more students with hearing loss are educated in general education

IEP TIP

The IEP team should identify strategies to facilitate a student's success in the general education classroom, including appropriate interaction with an educational interpreter.

BOX 14.6 **MY VOICE**

Great Expectations Plus

I wear two hats. I am a former teacher of the deaf and now am a university professor in deaf education. And I have two adopted daughters, Mary Pat and Marcy, who are deaf. Both were honors students in public school; both are honors students at Rochester Institute for Technology in New York, a university for the deaf and hearing-impaired. Both have helped me teach or do volunteer work in Japan, Taiwan, and Mexico; and one, Marcy, has volunteered in Africa and even returned to her place of birth, Bulgaria, and the orphanage she lived in until we adopted her at age four.

Except for the fact that they are adopted and deaf, these two daughters are not unlike other young women: public school and college/university education; athletic-team participation; music lessons; after-school work (albeit at a state school for the deaf); summer camp (yes, at a camp for the deaf); marriage (at age nineteen, Mary Pat married a young man who is deaf); age-appropriate use of at least two languages (spoken English and sign language); and post-college/aspirations career (Mary Pat as a teacher of the deaf and Marcy as a public policy specialist).

What made the difference for them? Undeniably, it helped that they grew up as daughters of a deaf-education specialist (me) and in a family (husband, wife, and other daughters) who learned how to use sign language and held them to high standards, for we had high expectations for them. Family makes a difference.

Being in separate-school, after-school, and camp programs for the deaf and hearing impaired also was helpful. That's where they honed their signing skills, met other students with hearing challenges, and learned that they proudly belonged to a cultural minority in America: those who are deaf or have hearing impairments. Separation is not necessarily restrictive; it is different but beneficial.

But both also participated in the general curriculum with hearing students of their own age; benefited from a collaborating team of general and special educators, signing interpreters, and speech-language specialists; and had academic as well as extracurricular and social engagement with hearing peers. Inclusion had and continues to have huge academic and social benefits, not just for my daughters but for their hearing peers too.

Both had hearing aids and both later had cochlear implants. Two types of technology, like two types of teaching (separate and included), opened up the hearing world to them, just as two languages (spoken English and sign language) opened up two cultures (hearing and deaf) to them. My daughters are at home in any environment and any place. They have well-deserved self-confidence.

Sometimes teachers only see children for a year and never know what becomes of them as adults. I am thankful to all the people who helped to raise my children: It took a village. And I want others to know what can be done when great expectations combine with family, professional, and technological support.

—Barbara Luetke
Visiting Professor, Texas Women's College
Author, One Mother's Story *(Modern Sign Press, 1996);*
Contributor, Deaf Students Can Be Great Readers
(Modern Sign Press, 2003); Facebook-enrolled family

BOX 14.7	**INCLUSION TIPS**

	What You Might See	**What You Might Be Tempted to Do**	**Alternate Responses**	**Ways to Include Peers in the Process**
Behavior	The student does not participate in cooperative learning activities.	Tell her in front of the rest of the class to participate appropriately.	Be sure she understands the activity and what is expected of her beforehand.	Use a buddy system to foster greater participation.
Social interactions	His speech is difficult to understand, and the other students do not know how to sign, limiting his ability to interact during small-group discussions.	Randomly assign him to a group; assume the group will work out roles and participation.	Discuss the situation with the deaf educator and the educational interpreter. The deaf educator can work on making sure he is prepared for small-group discussions. The interpreter can encourage the other students to follow the teacher's rules for turn taking.	Arrange instruction for peers to learn more sign language. Use a student to facilitate a more structured approach that allows comments and input from everyone. Practice taking turns with everyone.
Educational performance	She misses some things other students say and appears not to understand.	Tell her to ask her interpreter.	Ensure that the other students face her when they are talking. Make sure the other students raise their hand before speaking so she can visually orient to the speaker. Have the interpreter move to the student who is talking so she can see both the interpreter and the student who is talking. If the vocabulary in the cooperative learning activity is unfamiliar, provide a study guide.	Check the notes taken by the student note taker to be sure they are adequate. Arrange for peer tutoring of unfamiliar vocabulary.
Classroom attitudes	He appears bored or inattentive due to not hearing all that is said or not watching the interpreter.	Discipline him for inattentiveness.	Be sure his hearing aid or cochlear implant is working and that his interpreting needs are being met during cooperative learning activities.	Group him with peers who are helpful and caring but do not mother him.

classrooms: 54 percent of students with hearing impairments now spend more than 80 percent of their day in general education classrooms. They may be receiving special services in the general education classroom, including classroom amplification, audiological evaluation, speech-language therapy, resource support from a trained deaf educator, instructional accommodations, and an educational interpreter. Interpreting services include, but are not limited to, oral transliteration services, cued language services, and sign language interpreting.

Another placement option is a special classroom in the public school with other students who are deaf or hard of hearing. The teacher is usually a trained deaf educator, and the students may be included with their hearing peers for some academic subjects or for art, music, physical education, or other non-academic programs.

Yet another placement option is a segregated setting. Before the 1980s, most students with hearing loss (particularly those who were deaf) were educated in large residential schools for the deaf or in separate public or private day schools. They often entered those schools at age five, learned to communicate from their peers and deaf adults who worked

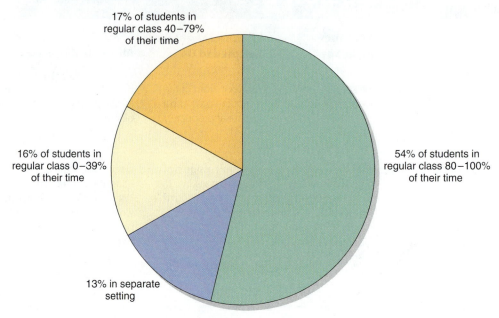

17% of students in regular class 40–79% of their time

16% of students in regular class 0–39% of their time

54% of students in regular class 80–100% of their time

13% in separate setting

Source: U.S. Department of Education. (2011). *Data accountability center: Individuals with Disabilities Education Act (IDEA) data.* Retrieved February 12, 2011, from https://www.ideadata.org.

Note: Percentages have been rounded and collapsed across categories.

at the schools, made lifetime friendships, met their spouse, and settled in the area to live and work. In fact, this educational setting was the basis for the development and perpetuation of the Deaf community and Deaf culture.

IDEA has changed the nature and prevalence of these residential and day programs. Given the wider range of placement options in public schools, enrollment in residential schools has declined and many have closed, although members of the Deaf community and some professionals in the field of deafness continue to advocate for the right to choose this placement option (Marschark, Richardson, Sapere, & Sarchet, 2010; Moores, 2009). slightly more than 13 percent of deaf students receive their education outside of their home school, in a separate school, residential school or alternate setting (see Figure 14.6).

The general education classroom, with supports, offers many opportunities for academic and social success for students who are deaf or hard of hearing.

Assessing Students' Progress

MEASURING STUDENTS' PROGRESS

To improve the quality of services for students with hearing loss, Moores (2008b) suggested that the field of deaf education consider implementing a form of the response to intervention (RTI) model. The continual progress monitoring that is an essential component of RTI allows professionals to identify students who are not making progress in a timely manner and make the necessary instructional changes based on individual need. The most common form of monitoring of students with hearing impairment is literacy assessment, and the second most common form assesses math facts. Some teachers use continuous monitoring to track amplification use. It is also critical to use data to compare the progress on state standards of students with hearing impairments with that of their general education peers. Progress monitoring that is student-centered allows students to be involved in documenting and charting their own progress and become motivated to achieve their individual goals.

The use of maze passages for reading comprehension can be successfully used with students with hearing impairment. The maze passages process involves using leveled narrative fiction passages that have been set up for progress monitoring assessment systems (such as http://www.edcheckup.com and http://www.aimsweb.com) or that have been developed by teachers. The passages are 140 to 400 words long, and the maze is a multiple-choice cloze task that students complete while reading silently (Rose & McAnally, 2008).

IEP TIP

As required by IDEA, the IEP team should consider what testing accommodations may be necessary so the student can participate in statewide testing.

MAKING ACCOMMODATIONS FOR ASSESSMENT

There are limitations to continuous monitoring. Teachers must make adaptations to the materials and assessments so they are accessible to students with hearing loss (such as use of sign language or visual phonics), use an interpreter, or require that a teacher of the deaf administer the assessment (Luckner & Bowen, 2010). Elliot, Kratochwill, and Schulte (1998) identified eight possible accommodations to state formats for students with disabilities. Using these categories, Stewart and Kluwin (2001) adapted the list and made the accommodations specific for deaf students. Their suggestions include providing assistance before testing to teach any new forms of test taking, providing a longer time period for the assessment, interpreting the directions, and even changing the format and content (rephrasing an item) if this can be done without altering the intent of the question. Accommodations allow for the greatest level of success for the students—the accurate measure of knowledge and performance on a level playing field (Cawthon, 2008).

ADDRESSING THE PROFESSIONAL STANDARDS

The following Council for Exceptional Children (CEC) Common Core Knowledge and Skills are addressed in this chapter through the content and concepts we discuss. See the Appendix for a full listing of these Knowledge and Skill statements:

ICC2K1, ICC2K2, ICC2K3, ICC2K4, ICC2K5, ICC2K6, ICC4S1, ICC4S3, ICC5S2, ICC5S3, ICC5S4, ICC5S6, ICC5S8, ICC5S9, ICC6K4, ICC6S1, ICC7S1, ICC7S2, ICC7S3, ICC7S6, ICC7S7, ICC7S9, ICC8K2, ICC8K3, ICC8K4, ICC8K5, ICC8S2, ICC8S6, ICC8S7, ICC10S2, ICC10S3, ICC10S4, ICC10S5, ICC10S6, ICC10S9

Summary

IDENTIFYING STUDENTS WITH HEARING LOSS

- Children are typically classified as deaf or hard of hearing.
- Conductive loss is caused by a problem in the outer and middle ear; sensorineural loss is caused by a problem in the inner ear or along the nerve pathway to the brain.
- Achievement levels, specifically in the areas of reading and writing, are primary concerns for students with hearing loss. They can be particularly problematic among children from diverse racial, ethnic, and linguistic backgrounds.
- Hearing loss in children is considered a low-incidence disability and is estimated at about 1.2 percent of students with disabilities.

EVALUATING STUDENTS WITH HEARING LOSS

- An audiologist diagnoses hearing loss using an auditory brain stem response or otoacoustic emissions test with infants and young children and behavioral audiological evaluation with older children.
- Hearing aids make sound louder but do not restore normal hearing; there is always some distortion of sound.
- Cochlear implants provide sound information by directly stimulating the functioning auditory nerve fibers in the cochlea. Cochlear implants do not make sound louder.
- Assessment of language, speech, speech reading, signing, academic achievement, and socialization are essential for providing an appropriate education for students who are deaf or hard of hearing.

DESIGNING AN APPROPRIATE IEP

- The increase in cochlear implants has resulted in increased input from the medical implant team.
- The educational interpreter is often the student's bridge to the hearing world around him.
- The various communication modes used by individuals with hearing loss include oral/aural, manual, and total communication.

- A bilingual/bicultural educational model combines the use of American Sign Language as the student's first language, English as her second language, and Deaf studies to teach the culture of deafness.

USING EFFECTIVE INSTRUCTIONAL STRATEGIES

- Intervention for young children with hearing loss includes access to a language-rich environment.
- Shared reading emphasizes the importance of reading to young children as they connect the English sentences in the book to how the sentences are signed in ASL.
- Real-world, or authentic, experiences are particularly important for students with hearing loss if they are to make a connection between what they know and what they read.
- Learning about deafness, the Deaf community, Deaf history, and famous deaf adults can be incorporated into social studies, health, and science curricula for all students.

INCLUDING STUDENTS WITH HEARING LOSS

- Access to communication is critical when deciding on placement for students with hearing loss.
- IDEA now includes interpreting services as related services; oral transliteration, cued speech, and sign language interpreting are part of interpreting.

ASSESSING STUDENTS' PROGRESS

- There may be problems in the assessment of a student with hearing loss if the student uses English as a second language (ASL being the first language), has unintelligible speech, or has difficulty with reading.
- Story retelling allows students to show that they understand what they have read, even though they may not have been able to sound out each individual word.

15 Understanding Students *with* Visual Impairments

by Sandra Lewis, Florida State University

Who Is Corbin Thornbury?

Imagine a bright, inquisitive, upbeat seven-year-old, actively involved in tae kwon do, swimming, music, cooking, nature exploration, school, and adventures with family and friends. Imagine a boy with a zest for living, and you have imagined Corbin Thornbury.

At seven, Corbin aspires to go to college and has mentioned an interest in several different occupations, including radio announcer, policeman, and firefighter. Recently, however, he told his mother, Lottie, "I am blind, so I won't have a job."

Taken aback, she responded that lots of people who are blind have jobs. She asked, "Why do you think that they don't?"

Corbin's reply was quick: "We can't drive. What do they do, ride horses?" This was a logical conclusion, certainly, as he loves riding ponies; and Lottie smiled as she explained the transportation options for people who are blind.

Blind since birth, Corbin functions quite well with the use of his cane and braille books. Recently, however, he has been curious about vision. He has expressed that he wishes he were not blind so that he could "see the ants coming" to avoid being bitten and that he wishes he

"could see color crayons like my friends." He doesn't dwell on differences for long, though, as he benefits from living with a busy family. They take trips to Disney World, playgrounds and parks, beaches, restaurants, grocery stores, and other public places. On a family campout, he helped pitch the tent, unroll sleeping bags, and set up battery-operated lanterns. This delightful event included his mom, Lottie, his dad, Nathan, as well as Corbin and his two-year-old brother, Ethan. The family told ghost stories, sang camp songs, and made s'mores.

Naturally inquisitive about nature and science, Corbin discovers and explores items often overlooked by sighted individuals and adds to his collections of cocoons, honeycomb, acorns, shells, and other objects he finds with his cane.

At the grocery store, Corbin loves to grind coffee beans. He puts the beans into the grinder, places the bag under the chute, and operates the machine. At home, he uses the talking microwave independently, sets the timer, and uses the timed cooking settings to prepare his own breakfast of waffles and bacon.

Each morning, Corbin and Lottie discuss what he needs for school. His tasks are listed in braille on a magnetic strip and are aligned on the left side of a divided magnet board. As he completes each task, he moves the strip to the right side of the

board. When finished, he receives a marble with Velcro on the back to attach to his chore chart on the refrigerator door. He also earns marbles for completing other chores, such as sweeping the floor, feeding his pet, wiping the table, or helping with the dishwasher. Corbin helped his mother organize his room so that he can find his toys, games, instruments, and books. He also has a system for organizing personal belongings, such as his cane, lunchbox, and backpack, so they are easily located and returned. He has learned to put things away, not just put them down! This has fostered responsibility through which his independence and confidence have grown.

Corbin begins his school days with a teacher of students with visual impairments (TVI). They work together on braille and on the Nemeth code, which he uses for mathematics. He goes to his general education class, where his teacher has learned the adaptations she needs to ensure that Corbin has access to all class activities. She collaborates with his TVI to accommodate the instructional materials so that he can do the same work and meet the same educational standards as her other pupils do. Assistive technology will continue to help Corbin maximize his potential.

With his orientation and mobility instructor, Corbin works on areas of the expanded core curriculum, emphasizing skills that will prepare him to become a fully participating member of society. He has studied traffic; grown and harvested vegetables; learned to do headstands; and explored faucets, fire extinguishers, thermostats, playground equipment, and other objects at the school. He visits the librarian, the custodial staff, and the cafeteria workers in their various work-places. He and his instructor purposely "get lost" and find their way back to their starting point, a game that increases Corbin's level of confidence.

Lottie and Nathan have never had a negative, limiting perspective about blindness. Lottie is a teacher and recognized in Corbin's infancy that it was important to challenge him every day, to have high expectations for him, and to take the role of being his first teacher very seriously. She has created unique materials to enhance new concepts, as when she molded clay representations of the life stages of a butterfly after Corbin received a caterpillar that formed a chrysalis and completed the transformation to a butterfly. Knowing that Corbin's peers in kindergarten would be opening snack packs and other food items independently, Lottie decided to pack his lunchbox during the summer before he started school, with the goal of helping him hone his skills at unpacking it. So every day, Corbin practiced opening the lunchbox, packages, and drink cartons. He learned strategies for opening the containers so that he could eat independently and then learned how to check his eating area for what needed to be discarded. Not surprisingly, he started school with confidence, having mastered the same skills in this area as his classmates had.

Nathan is helping Corbin understand football and soccer by playing ball with him. Corbin also helps his dad pump gas, check the oil, and do other routine mechanical work on the family car. The key to their interaction is that Nathan patiently answers Corbin's questions and demonstrates his responses through hands-on activities.

Corbin is increasingly independent: He visits friends after school and spends the night with his grandmother. His competence is blossoming. As an adult, he may not get around by riding horses, but he will definitely have a job. He will be able to live independently, to advocate for himself, and to communicate the clear message to the world that, although society often says blind people can't, Corbin *can!*

Identifying Students with Visual Impairments

DEFINING VISUAL IMPAIRMENTS

When you think about visual impairments and blindness, you might imagine someone such as Corbin, who sees almost nothing and must use adaptive techniques for tasks that typically require vision, such as braille for reading or a cane to detect objects when traveling. So it may surprise you to learn that most individuals with **legal blindness** have a great deal of useful vision and that most students who have visual impairments read print.

Two different definitions describe visual impairment. The legal definition of blindness is based on a clinical measurement of visual acuity. **Acuity** is determined by having an individual read the letters on a chart, each line of which is composed of letters written with a certain size of print. The ability to read the line that is composed of symbols with a measurement of 20 from a distance of 20 feet is typical: A person who can read at that line has 20/20 acuity. Individuals who from 20 feet can read only the top line, where the print size is 200 (the big *E*), even when using both eyes and wearing glasses, have 20/200 acuity; these people are legally blind. People are also legally blind if their **field of vision** (the area around them that they can visually detect when looking straight ahead) is less than 20 degrees (normal is 160 degrees), even if their visual acuity is normal. These individuals have **tunnel vision**. Figure 15.1 shows what people with various types of visual impairment might see.

The legal definition of blindness is an arbitrary clinical measure used to determine eligibility for federal Social Security benefits (Social Security Act, 2011). It does not provide reliable information about the way in which a person experiences and learns about the world (Corn & Lusk, 2010). But how a person experiences and learns about the world is at the core of the IDEA definition of visual impairments. The current regulations implementing IDEA define **visual disability (including blindness)** as "an impairment in vision that, even with correction, adversely affects a child's educational performance. The term includes both partial sight and blindness." Key to this definition is that the student has some kind of disorder of the visual system that interferes with learning.

FIGURE 15.1 *Estimate of how a view appears for (a) individuals with 20/20 vision, (b) reduced visual acuity, and (c) and (d) restricted fields of vision*

(a)

(b)

(c)

(d)

You should be cautious about these data. Because state and local educational agencies vary so widely in how they measure and report visual impairments, it is extremely difficult to count accurately the number of students with visual impairments who are served in schools (Kirchner & Diament, 1999). Best estimates indicate that approximately one to two students in 1,000 have a visual disorder that interferes with learning; those children are eligible to receive special education services (Nelson & Dimitrova, 1993; Wall & Corn, 2004).

Students with visual impairments have a wide range of visual abilities. Educators often classify these students by their tendency or need to use visual or tactile means for learning (Barraga & Erin, 2001; Lewis & Allman, 2000):

- **Low vision** describes individuals who read print, although they may depend on optical aids, such as magnifying lenses, to see better. A few read both braille and print; all rely primarily on vision for learning. Individuals with low vision may or may not be legally blind.

- **Functionally blind** describes individuals who typically use braille for efficient reading and writing. They may rely on their ability to use functional vision for other tasks, such as moving through the environment or sorting items by color. Thus, they use their limited vision to supplement a combination of tactile and auditory learning methods. Corbin is typical of a student who is functionally blind.

- **Totally blind** describes those individuals who do not receive meaningful input through the visual sense. These individuals use tactile and auditory means to learn about their environment, and they generally read braille.

Young children develop a "scheme" about tables through their experience with them. This incidental learning differs for a child who has always been visually impaired.

Every individual with visual impairment uses vision differently and in a way that is difficult to predict. So when you teach these students, observe carefully how the student functions and then present instructional activities to maximize the student's learning.

DESCRIBING THE CHARACTERISTICS

Students with visual impairments are surprisingly heterogeneous. They differ from each other in how they learn and in their visual functioning, socioeconomic status, cultural background, age of onset of visual impairment, presence of other disabilities, and cognitive abilities. Some are gifted or have special talents. A large number also have multiple disabilities (Huebner, 2000; Pogrund, 2002; Silberman, 2000). Yet each possesses a characteristic in common: limited ability to learn incidentally from the environment (Hatlen & Curry, 1987).

Almost from the moment they are born, children with good vision learn seemingly effortlessly through their visual sense. Their vision helps them organize, synthesize, and give meaning to their perceptions of the environment (Ferrell, 2000; Liefert, 2003; Lowenfeld, 1973). For example, a baby with unimpaired vision spends hours looking at his hand before that hand becomes an efficient tool. A young child will drop a toy repeatedly, watching its path to the floor until she learns to understand *down*. Through these recurring observations, the child is learning how to move her hands and the effects of her hands' movement on herself, the toy, and her caretakers. As similar and diverse experiences occur with various objects, she gradually learns about the properties of nature (sound, gravity, weight, etc.). This learning occurs almost exclusively through the power of observation without direct instruction from others.

Think about the way in which a young child learns the concept of *table*. Even before she has a name for that object, she has observed a variety of tables in her environment: in the kitchen, in the living room, at the homes of relatives and friends, and at preschool. Tables are everywhere, and the child with unimpaired vision begins to recognize that the objects people call *tables* have certain features in common. Soon she perceives a relationship between the object and the word. Later, after more visual experiences, she will distinguish among desks, counters, and other flat surfaces. Children learn this kind of conceptual information incidentally—that is, with little or no direct instruction.

Incidental learning is, however, problematic for all children with visual impairments (Ferrell, 2006; Hatlen & Curry, 1987; Liefert, 2003), so they need other forms of instruction. A child with limited visual access to her environment may need opportunities to explore carefully and completely, either visually at a close distance or through tactile means, every part of a variety of tables before she can acquire, organize, and then synthesize information about "tableness." But she certainly can achieve these levels of understanding.

Incidental learning also affects how children learn new skills. For example, most children need little training when they make toast for the first time. They have few problems with any of the steps involved because they have watched adults make toast. Without hands-on instruction, however, children with visual impairments may not be aware that a special machine is used in this task. Even youngsters with low vision, who may not see clearly beyond a distance of two or three feet, usually need special instruction and practice time to perform this and other tasks. Remember how Corbin's father instructed him about footballs and soccer balls? And how his mother teaches him skills for independent living?

Because it influences the important role of incidental learning, a visual impairment can influence the development of a student's motor, language, cognitive, and social skills. Generally, however, these influences are not long-lasting if the student receives appropriate interventions (Ferrell, 2000). Visual impairment primarily affects how students learn skills, but it does not prevent them from acquiring skills. Interventions must address the unique educational needs of students with visual impairments, including those that arise from limitations in range and variety of experiences, ability to get around, and ability to interact with the environment.

Limitations in the Range and Variety of Experiences

Vision allows a person to experience the world meaningfully and safely from a distance. Touch is not always an effective substitute for vision: Some objects are too big (skyscrapers, mountains), too small (ants, molecules), too fragile (snowflakes, moths), too dangerous (fire, boiling water), or too distant (the sun, the horizon) for their characteristics to be learned by touch (Lowenfeld, 1973). The other senses do not fully compensate for what can be learned visually. The song of a bird or the smell of baking bread may provide evidence that those

Young children with impaired vision need opportunities to explore a variety of environments to develop a healthy sense of competency.

objects are nearby but do not provide useful information about many of their properties. Individuals with visual impairment often have not shared the experiences of their peers with typical vision, so their knowledge of the world may be different.

Students with visual impairments also experience different social interactions because they cannot share common experiences with sighted friends. The student who has not seen the latest movie, played the newest video game, or taken a driver's training course has markedly different experiences from those of a sighted student. The potential for inadequate development of social skills and the related negative impact on self-esteem may have a lifelong impact (Lewis & Wolffe, 2006; Sacks, 2006; Wolffe, 2006). However, with appropriate instruction, social skills can develop, as Colin's have.

Similarly, career development can be limited. While individuals with visual impairments are employed in a variety of occupations, many young adults struggle with determining an appropriate vocation because they are unaware of the jobs that people with or without vision perform (Wolffe, 2000). That is why you will need to use alternative strategies to introduce careers to students. Corbin's parents and teachers expect that, through the collaboration of his TVIs and general educators, he will graduate from high school and pursue a career that he chooses for himself, based on his own understanding of his interests, strengths, and abilities.

Limitations in the Ability to Get Around

Individuals who are visually impaired are limited in their spontaneous ability to move safely in and through their environment. This restriction influences a child's early motor development and exploration of the world and thus affects the child's knowledge base and social development. The ability to move through the environment spontaneously is one area over which probably only moderate control can be exercised and is a continuing source of frustration for many adults (Lee & Ponchillia, 2010; Corn & Sacks, 1994) because it directly affects opportunities for experiences (Barraga & Erin, 2001). A child with impaired vision may not know what is interesting in the environment. Even if he is aware of something to explore, he may not know how to get to the desired object. These children can become passive and in turn have fewer opportunities for intellectual and social stimulation (Anthony, Bleier, Fazzi, Kish, & Pogrund, 2002; Pogrund, 2002). That is why you should support students to explore their environment and engage with objects they enjoy. In other words, do for your students what Colin's parents do for him.

Limitations in Interactions with the Environment

Knowledge about and control over the environment often are areas of concern for individuals with visual impairments. In some cases, their limited vision reduces their level of readily acquired information about their environment and their ability to act on that information. For instance, they cannot determine at a glance the source of a loud crash or a burning smell, so they cannot quickly determine an appropriate reaction. Similarly, they cannot adequately inform themselves about the effects of their actions on the people and things around them.

In young children, reduced vision correlates with poor motivation to move through the environment, manipulate toys, and initiate interactions (Ferrell, 2000; Sacks, 2006). Their tendency toward physical and social detachment (Wolffe, Sacks, & Thomas, 2000) and low motivation can have the long-lasting consequence of limiting their sense of competence and mastery. Individuals who have a poor sense of their ability to effect change in their lives are at risk for poor self-esteem, poor academic achievement, and reduced language and social skills (Lewis & Wolffe, 2006). Identifying alternative ways to enable students to acquire information from their environment from an early age is critical to reducing these negative outcomes. Again, Colin's life at home shows how well his family has helped him discover alternative ways to acquire necessary information for his independent living.

DETERMINING THE CAUSES

As Figure 15.2 illustrates, seeing involves both the eye and the brain. Damage to or malfunction of any part of the visual system can impair how a student functions.

Damage to the structures involved in the visual process can be the result of an event that happens during the development of the embryo, at or immediately after an infant's birth, or at any time during development. **Congenital** visual impairment occurs at birth or, in the case of blindness, before visual memories have been established. Corbin has a congenital visual impairment. That type of impairment can affect the child's earliest access to information and experiences. Students who acquire a vision loss after having unimpaired vision have an **adventitious** visual impairment. That is, their impairment results from an advent (e.g., loss of sight caused by a hereditary condition that has just manifested itself) or an event (e.g., loss of sight caused by trauma). Although the educational needs of students with adventitious and congenital visual impairments may be similar, even a short period of unimpaired vision can enrich the student's understanding of self, others, and the relationships among people, objects, and events in the environment (Scott, Jan, & Freeman, 1995).

Evaluating Students with Visual Impairments

DETERMINING THE PRESENCE OF VISUAL IMPAIRMENTS

Like students with other disabilities, a student with visual impairment receives a nondiscriminatory evaluation (see Box 15.1). However, evaluations of students with visual impairments have several highly specialized aspects. Medical specialists usually determine the presence of a disorder of a child's visual system. Physicians often detect a serious visual disorder when a child is very young or has just experienced a trauma. Their diagnosis generally is followed by a search for medical solutions to correct vision. When no such correction is possible, referrals to the schools occur.

When a school district receives a referral for services, the TVI will read the doctor's report to learn the cause, or **etiology**, of the visual disorder. Although a diagnosis of

FIGURE 15.2 *Anatomy of the eye*

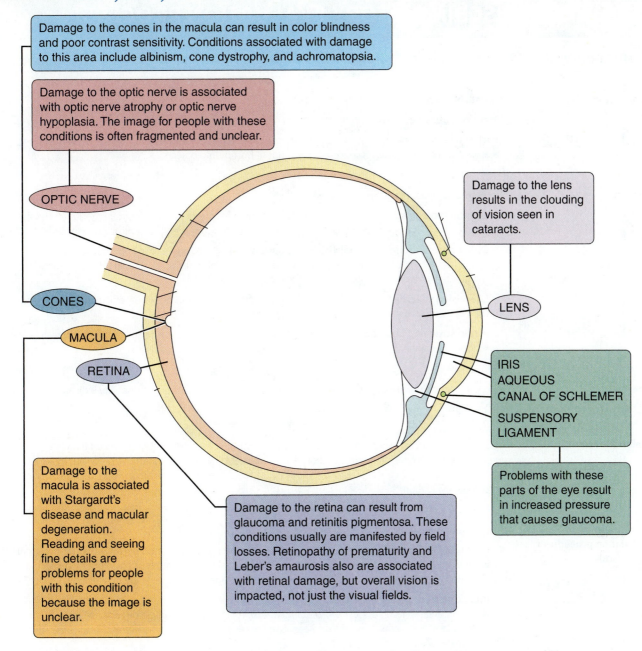

Damage to the cones in the macula can result in color blindness and poor contrast sensitivity. Conditions associated with damage to this area include albinism, cone dystrophy, and achromatopsia.

Damage to the optic nerve is associated with optic nerve atrophy or optic nerve hypoplasia. The image for people with these conditions is often fragmented and unclear.

Damage to the lens results in the clouding of vision seen in cataracts.

OPTIC NERVE

LENS

CONES

MACULA

RETINA

IRIS
AQUEOUS
CANAL OF SCHLEMER
SUSPENSORY LIGAMENT

Damage to the macula is associated with Stargardt's disease and macular degeneration. Reading and seeing fine details are problems for people with this condition because the image is unclear.

Damage to the retina can result from glaucoma and retinitis pigmentosa. These conditions usually are manifested by field losses. Retinopathy of prematurity and Leber's amaurosis also are associated with retinal damage, but overall vision is impacted, not just the visual fields.

Problems with these parts of the eye result in increased pressure that causes glaucoma.

the etiology may not provide accurate information about how much a student sees, an accurate diagnosis suggests typical characteristics associated with a particular eye condition, including probable lighting needs, a potential prognosis, and possible related medical disorders or learning problems. The next steps in the evaluation are to determine how the child uses any vision that is available and then whether she learns best using her visual or tactile sense.

Determining How a Student Uses Vision

Even given an accurate diagnosis and standard visual acuity measurements, teachers and family members will find it impossible to predict exactly how a student with a visual impairment will learn incidentally from the environment and to perform age-appropriate tasks. That is why TVIs work with a student and his family to determine the effects of the disorder on the student's visual functioning. To do so, they conduct a **functional vision assessment (FVA)** (Anthony, 2000; Erin & Topor, 2010; Lueck, 2004). While the results

BOX 15.1

NONDISCRIMINATORY EVALUATION PROCESS

Determining the Presence of Visual Impairments

Observation

Parents observe: The child may not respond to visual stimuli as expected.

Physicians observe: The newborn or infant may have an identifiable visual disorder.

Teacher observes: The student squints or seems to be bothered by light, the student's eyes water or are red, the student holds books too close, or the student bumps into objects.

Screening

Assessment measures:

Ophthalmological: Medical procedures indicate the presence of a visual disorder or reduced visual functioning that cannot be improved to typical levels through surgery or medical intervention.

Direct observation/functional vision evaluation: The TVI and orientation and mobility (O&M) specialist determine how the student uses vision to accomplish daily tasks and identify strategies that will facilitate increased efficiency in the student's use of vision.

Low vision specialist: A specialist evaluation indicates ways to improve visual efficiency through the use of low vision devices (magnifiers), electronic, and nonoptical approaches.

Vision screening in school: For students with low vision who have not been identified before entering school, screening indicates the need for further evaluation.

Prereferral

Prereferral typically is not used with these students because the severity of the disability indicates a need for special education or related services.

Referral

Students with visual impairments should be referred by medical personnel or parents for early intervention during the infancy/preschool years. Many states have child-find organizations to make sure these students receive services. Teachers should refer any students with possible vision impairments for immediate evaluation.

Nondiscriminatory evaluation procedures and standards

Assessment measures:

Individualized intelligence test: Standardization may need to be violated because the student's visual impairment interferes with the ability to perform some tasks. Therefore, results may not be an accurate reflection of ability. Students may be average, above average, or below average in intelligence.

Individualized achievement tests: The student may not achieve in concept development and academic areas at levels of peers. Also, standardization of these tests, unless developed for students with visual impairments, may have to be violated because of the visual impairment. Results may not accurately reflect achievement.

Adaptive behavior scales: The student may have difficulty in self-care, household, and community skills because of vision and mobility problems.

Anecdotal records: The student may not participate in age-appropriate self-help, social, and recreational activities in home, community, or school.

Curriculum-based assessment: The TVI and O&M specialist will assess a student's competence in all areas of the expanded core curriculum, including use of technology, independent living, self-determination, career education, recreation and leisure, sensory efficiency, social functioning, use of compensatory skills, and orientation and mobility.

Direct observation-learning media assessment: This involves determination of the most efficient method or methods that students with visual impairments will use to access general education materials.

Determination

The nondiscriminatory evaluation team determines that the student has a vision impairment or blindness and needs special education and related services.

Distant Vision

- Mimics teacher's facial expressions at _____ feet.
- Locates the drinking fountain at _____ feet.
- Recognizes own name, shapes, numbers at _____ feet.
- Identifies classmates at _____ feet.
- Locates personal possessions (lunchbox, jacket, backpack) in closet at _____ feet.
- Locates own cubby at _____ feet.
- Locates _____ of four dropped coins on a _____ (color) floor: quarter at _____ feet; nickel at _____ feet; dime at _____ feet; penny at _____ feet.
- Tracks and locates a _____ (size) moving ball at _____ feet.
- Avoids obstacles when moving a round P.E. apparatus. Yes _____ No _____
- Visually detects and smoothly navigates contour changes in surfaces such as ramps and steps. Yes _____ No _____

Near Vision

- Completes _____ (number of pieces) puzzle with head _____ inches from the board (describe how student performs task: e.g., trial and error, quickly, visually, tactually, etc.).
- Places pegs in pegboard at _____ inches from head _____ inches from pegs (describe how student performs task).

Source: From *Functional Visual Evaluation,* by the Los Angeles Unified School District, 1990. Copyright 1990 by the Los Angeles Unified School District. Adapted with permission.

of an examination by an eye specialist are reported in clinical terms (such as 20/120), the results of an FVA are reported in language that informs educators and others in more concrete ways. For example, an FVA report might read, "The student can see three-inch-high printed letters at a distance of no more than five feet," or "The student can pick up a raisin on a white table when seen from six inches." Figure 15.3 shows part of an FVA designed for preschoolers.

Functional vision assessments describe how a student uses vision in a variety of natural environments, such as under the fluorescent lights in a grocery store, on the playground in the glare of the midday sun, or in a dimly lit corridor leading to the school library. These assessments also consider the different activities that occur in these environments. For example, a student at a grocery store may be able to see the products on the shelves but not be able to read the aisle labels that hang directly below the bright lights or the value of paper money at the checkout counter. Obviously, information about how the student functions in various environments helps educators design relevant instructional strategies (Anthony, 2000; Erin & Topor, 2010).

Most youngsters with usable vision benefit from periodic evaluations by a **low vision specialist**, a person with special training who can prescribe optical and nonoptical devices appropriate to the individual's functioning (Lueck, 2004; Simons & Lapolice, 2000). Ideally, an FVA should occur before an examination by a low vision specialist so the TVI can share information about the student's functioning. If optical aids are recommended, a follow-up FVA may be necessary to describe the student's improved functioning while using these devices.

Determining the Appropriate Learning Medium

For students such as Corbin, it is easy for teachers to determine how educational materials should be presented. Because he can see very little, braille clearly is the appropriate learning medium for him. Remember, however, that most students who are visually impaired have some usable vision; determining the appropriate learning medium for them is more complex.

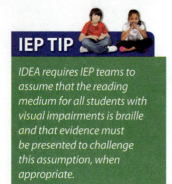
Learning medium describes the options for accessing literacy materials; these may include braille, print, audiotapes, and access technology. Many children who can read print do so at such slow speeds or with such inefficiency that they also benefit from using braille. Teachers determine the appropriate reading media for students by conducting a **learning media assessment (LMA)** (Koenig & Holbrook, 1993). The LMA begins with a functional vision assessment but also includes additional considerations, such as the student's use of touch and vision in new situations or environments, the stability of the eye condition, visual stamina, and motivation.

Like an FVA, the LMA needs to be repeated at regular intervals to determine whether circumstances or the student's skills have changed and whether additional instruction in a different reading medium is necessary. Students who use both braille and print have the advantage of being able to choose the reading medium that works best for them under different conditions—for instance, when they are in a dimly lit restaurant or when reading assignments are long and eye fatigue occurs.

DETERMINING THE NATURE OF SPECIALLY DESIGNED INSTRUCTION AND SERVICES

The provision of special education and related services must be based on a student's specific needs as identified through a comprehensive assessment of the student's current level of functioning and knowledge in both the general education curriculum and in the **expanded core curriculum** (Hatlen, 1996). The expanded core curriculum includes the following areas: compensatory and communication skills, social and interaction skills, **orientation and mobility (O&M)** skills, independent living skills, recreation and leisure skills, self-determination skills, use of assistive technology, sensory efficiency skills, and career/vocational skills (Brasher & Holbrook, 2006). Figure 15.4 describes the skills educators will evaluate in a complete assessment.

Assessment is best accomplished by a team of individuals with experience working with students with visual disabilities. In addition to those people who, under IDEA, must be included on the team, the team also should consist of an O&M specialist and a TVI. The outcome of a comprehensive assessment should be a description of the student's current level of functioning in all areas of the general and expanded core curriculum and the identification of skills to be addressed for that child to function optimally in current and future home, school, and community environments (Barclay, 2003; Pugh & Erin, 1999). Few teachers would consider it important to evaluate a straight-*A* high school student's ability to order a meal at a fast-food restaurant or to launder clothes, yet a student with a visual impairment who achieves at grade level may not function appropriately outside of the classroom. But many students with visual impairments lack these outside-school skills. Informal assessment techniques, including family and student interviews, the use of checklists, observation in natural environments, and authentic and performance assessments, are the most valuable methods for determining the level of functioning of students with visual impairments in the expanded core curriculum.

When assessing a student's needs, you should evaluate the age-appropriateness of a task from two perspectives. First, what are the student's peers doing? If Corbin's friends are at the stage of social development when participating in groups, such as Cub Scouts, is common, an assessment of Corbin's visual and social skills should be relevant to his potential to be a scout with his peers.

Second, because students with unimpaired vision are incidentally learning to perform some skills long before it is age-appropriate to expect mastery of them, you should evaluate a student's involvement in these tasks earlier than you might for sighted students. For example, while some students are not expected to launder clothes independently until their late teens, you should assess Corbin's participation in this task's component parts, such as scooping soap or folding freshly laundered towels and socks, because these skills are within the range of his capability now and are being learned visually by his peers.

FIGURE 15.4 Skill areas within the domains of the expanded core curriculum

Compensatory Skills, Including Communication Modes
- Concept development
- Listening and speaking skills
- Study and organizational skills
- Use of reference skills
- Determination of reading modes
- Communication modes for students with additional disabilities (such as tactile symbols, a calendar system, sign language, and recorded materials)

Social Interaction Skills
- Socialization
- Affective education
- Knowledge of human sexuality
- Knowledge of visual impairment

O&M Skills
- Development of body image
- Understanding physical environment and space
- Orientation to different environments
- Ability to travel in school and community environments
- Opportunities for unrestricted, independent movement and play

Daily Living Skills
- Personal hygiene
- Dressing
- Housekeeping
- Clothing care
- Food preparation
- Eating
- Basic home repair
- Money management
- Telephone
- Time and calendar
- Shopping
- Use of community services

Recreation and Leisure Skills
- Competitive sports
- Noncompetitive sports
- Hobbies and games
- Choosing recreational activities

Career/Vocational Skills
- Relationships between work and play
- Understanding value of work
- Job and career awareness
- Job acquisition skills (want ads, résumés, applications, interviews)
- Typical job adaptations made by workers with visual impairments
- Prevocational skills (work habits, attitudes, motivation)
- Awareness of vocational interests
- Work experience

Assistive Technology
- Keyboarding skills
- Braille access devices
- Visual assistive software and devices
- Auditory assistive software and devices
- Choosing appropriate options
- Device maintenance and troubleshooting

Visual Efficiency Skills
- Use of nonoptical low vision devices
- Use of optical low vision devices
- Use of a combination of devices
- Use of environmental cues and modifications
- Recognizing when not to use vision

Self-Determination Skills
- Knowledge of laws protecting people with disabilities, particularly visual impairment
- Assertiveness skills
- Negotiation skills
- Public interaction skills
- Management of readers and drivers

Source: Reprinted from Lizbeth A. Barclay, Expanded Core Curriculum: Education, in *Collaborative Assessment: Working with Students Who Are Blind or Visually Impaired, Including Those with Additional Disabilities,* Stephen A. Goodman and Stuart H. Wittenstein, Editors, pp. 98–99. New York: AFB Press, 2003.

You also should avoid making assumptions about a student's previously learned information. Because visual impairment often results in gaps in information, you should assess whether a student does in fact have knowledge common to his sighted peers. For example, one TVI was surprised to learn that her eighteen-year-old female student with low vision was unaware that men's sexual organs differ from her own. The TVI used the result of her assessment to work with the family to design an appropriate program to assure that the student graduated with this knowledge so critical to her social functioning.

Designing an Appropriate IEP

PARTNERING FOR SPECIAL EDUCATION AND RELATED SERVICES

Students with visual impairments often need additional supports to learn in the general education classroom. To include these students successfully in the general curriculum, there must be close partnerships among the general educator, the TVI, the O&M specialist, the student's parents or guardians, and other professionals involved in the student's education. In particular, these individuals must collaborate when designing the IEP to make important decisions about the following:

- Provision of instruction to support the child's success in the general education curriculum
- Nonacademic priorities on which the team will focus
- Location of special education and related services
- Ways in which partners will communicate to meet the student's needs

Providing Specialized Instruction

Because of the complex or highly visual nature of some academic areas, students with visual impairments may need specialized instruction to master the curriculum. For example, some students need specialized instruction to master writing braille with a **slate and stylus**; using the **abacus** for calculating; or developing listening, study, and organizational skills. For these purposes, special and general educators collaborate to provide appropriate learning experiences. As you read about how students who are blind learn braille, think about the level of interaction that must occur between the general and special educators.

Reading Instruction

Students who do not learn efficiently through their visual sense may access the academic curriculum through **braille**, a tactile method of reading. Like the print alphabet, braille is a code, a way of presenting spoken language in written form. As Figure 15.5 shows, there is one braille symbol for each of the twenty-six letters of the English alphabet. The early developers of braille used numerous shortcuts, called **braille contractions**, for writing common words or letter combinations. Because of the contractions, there is not a one-to-one correspondence between print and braille. In Figure 15.6, you can compare a print passage with its braille translation.

The use of braille contractions requires TVIs to collaborate closely with general educators to introduce the 169 braille symbols and the 450 rules for using them in a way that allows the student to become competent in literacy skills. Recent research (Emerson, Holbrook, & D'Andrea, 2009) has found that the early introduction of contractions correlates with better literacy skills, including performance in spelling, vocabulary, and general reading level.

This finding challenges educational teams who are serving students in the general education environment. The fast pace of whole- and small-group reading instruction often does not meet the needs of young braille learners, who typically benefit from an individualized approach to master initial literacy skills of identifying braille letters and contractions, using phonics, developing vocabulary, and reading connected text. Swenson (2008) suggests that a flexible approach that combines the strengths of individualized and general education instruction is most likely to be successful. As students develop basic skills, they can increase the time that they spend in class with peers. Before long, they can become full members of the classroom's reading and writing community, and the primary responsibility for teaching reading can shift to the classroom teacher. Corbin is in this period of transition now.

You can imagine that the situation becomes even more complex for students who are English-as-second-language learners. No curriculum exists for teaching literacy skills to students whose first language is not English (Conroy, 2005; Milian, 2000). Box 15.2 shows some strategies for teaching braille to these students.

FIGURE 15.5 *English braille symbols, including contractions*

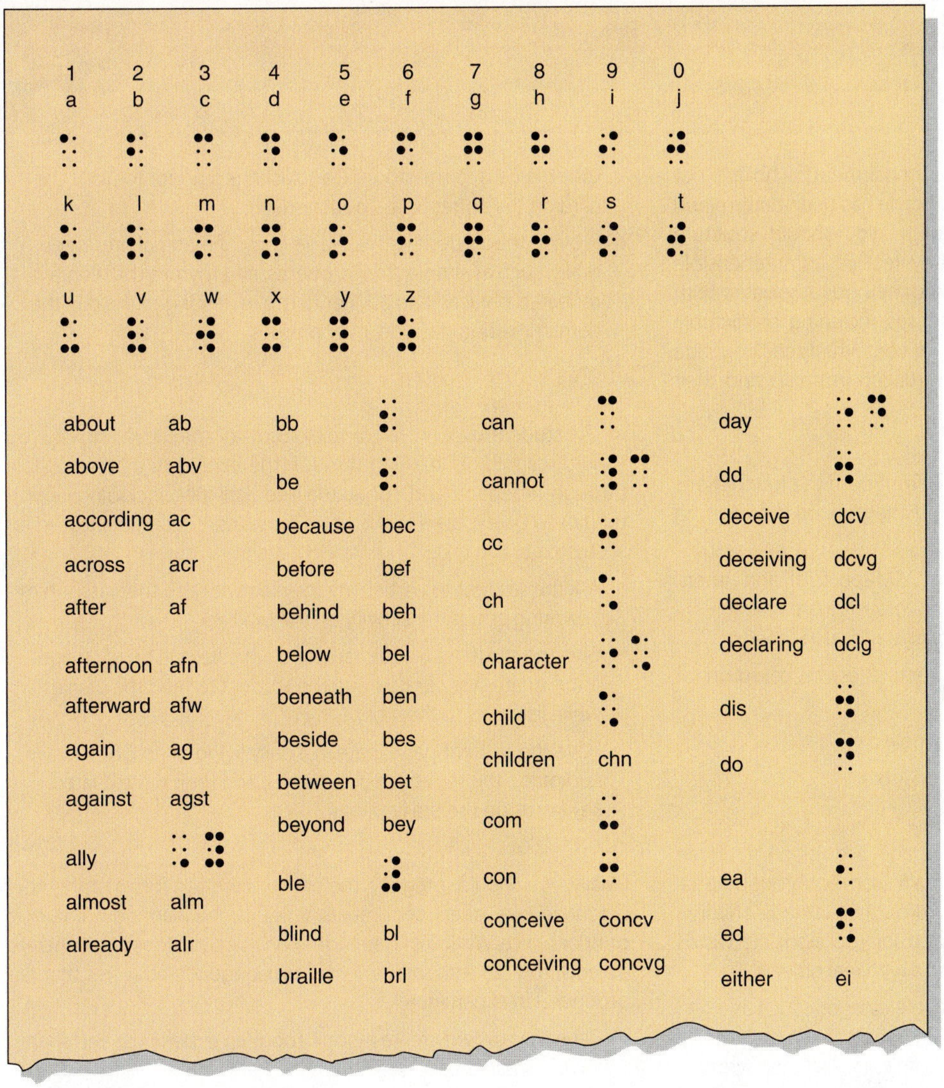

1	2	3	4	5	6	7	8	9	0
a	b	c	d	e	f	g	h	i	j

k	l	m	n	o	p	q	r	s	t

u	v	w	x	y	z

about	ab			can		day	
above	abv	be		cannot		dd	
according	ac	because	bec	cc		deceive	dcv
across	acr	before	bef			deceiving	dcvg
after	af	behind	beh	ch		declare	dcl
afternoon	afn	below	bel	character		declaring	dclg
afterward	afw	beneath	ben	child		dis	
again	ag	beside	bes	children	chn	do	
against	agst	between	bet				
		beyond	bey	com			
ally		ble		con		ea	
almost	alm			conceive	concv	ed	
already	alr	blind	bl				
		braille	brl	conceiving	concvg	either	ei

FIGURE 15.6 *Comparison of "Old Mother Hubbard" in braille and print*

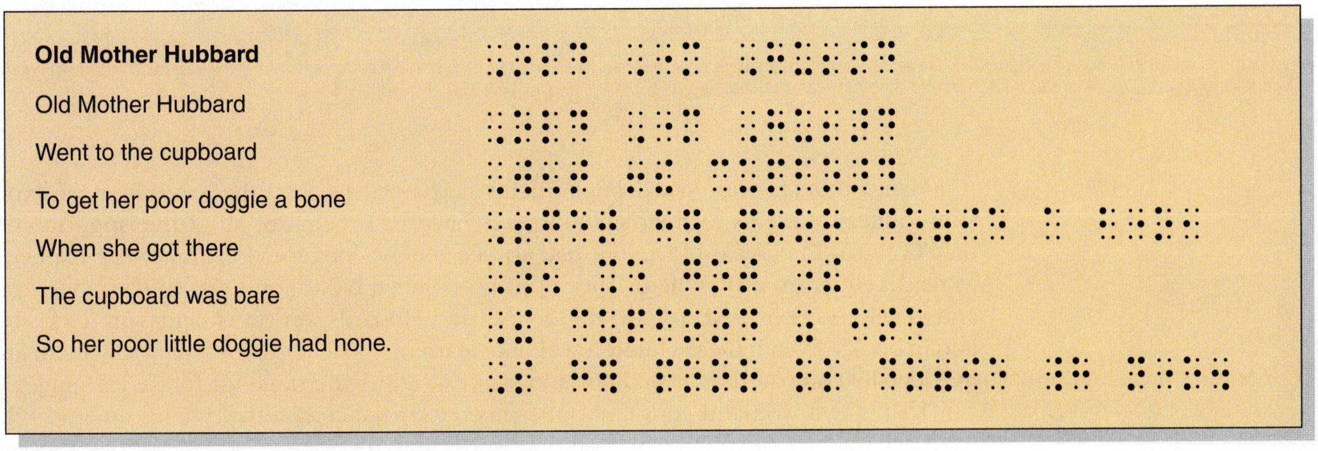

Old Mother Hubbard

Old Mother Hubbard

Went to the cupboard

To get her poor doggie a bone

When she got there

The cupboard was bare

So her poor little doggie had none.

BOX 15.2 **INTO PRACTICE**

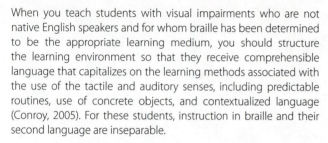

Strategies for Teaching Braille to ESL Students

When you teach students with visual impairments who are not native English speakers and for whom braille has been determined to be the appropriate learning medium, you should structure the learning environment so that they receive comprehensible language that capitalizes on the learning methods associated with the use of the tactile and auditory senses, including predictable routines, use of concrete objects, and contextualized language (Conroy, 2005). For these students, instruction in braille and their second language are inseparable.

General Strategies

General strategies for this process draw from both the foundations of teaching children who are blind and the principles of second language learning.

- Collaborate with the ESL teacher, the O&M specialist, and others involved with the student's education to coordinate teachers' activities and address students' language and visual needs.
- Sequence language activities and structure lessons based on the school district's ESL curriculum.
- Use real objects instead of visual examples.
- Use thematic instruction whenever possible.

Strategies for the Early Production Stage of Developing English

During the first stage in second-language acquisition, children develop receptive language skills, typically learned through visual association of words to objects or pictures. At this stage children who are blind must be given the opportunity to associate words presented both orally and in written form with real objects.

- Bring real objects that belong to a single category, such as fruits, to school. Make braille cards with words that match the objects. Assist the student in creating first oral and then written sentences using adjectives that describe the objects (e.g., "The orange is bumpy.").
- Create braille cards on which are written the names of classroom objects, such as *door*, *desk*, and *book*. Read each noun,

give the card to the student, and ask the student to place the card on the correct classroom item.

- Provide the student with a braille copy of material presented orally, such as simple stories, poems, and rhymes that contain repeated phrases, and ask her to move her fingers, held in the correct reading position, over phrases.

Strategies for the Emergence-of-Speech Stage of Developing English

As the student uses more complex forms of speech in English, you should scaffold his learning through the familiarity that is possible through repetition and contextualized activities, including opportunities to be exposed to the hand movement techniques used for accessing braille text.

- Ask the student to participate in an activity and then assist him in writing about the activity on the brailler.
- Give the student an audiotape and a braille version of an age-appropriate story. Encourage the student to read the braille while listening to the story.
- Have the student participate in a daily living or an O&M activity, audiotape the sequence of activities, and then write related keywords on the brailler.

Strategies for the Intermediate Fluency Level

Finally, you should integrate the oral and written forms of the new language in a variety of contexts, whether the learning medium is print or braille. While less dependent on real situations and concrete objects, this student still benefits from language activities that are grounded in experience.

- Have the student create a book about an experience and share it with classmates.
- Have the student keep a braille list of vocabulary words and a journal related to each of the content areas.
- Create meaningful activities that require the student to speak, listen, read, write, and interact with others.

Source: For more information about teaching braille to second language learners, refer to Milian, M. (1997). Teaching braille reading and writing to students who speak English as a second language. In D. P. Wormsley & F. M. D'Andrea (Eds.), Instructional strategies for braille literacy (pp. 189–230). New York: AFB Press.

Many students with visual impairments may not have had the same kind of exposure to literacy events as their sighted peers have had. Think of all the opportunities that Corbin's three-year-old peers had to see letters, long before they were expected to read. Letters are everywhere: They appear on cereal boxes, on toys, on the newspaper and envelopes delivered daily to the house, on billboards, on street signs, on television, and in books. Even if these children were not learning the letter names, they saw them and incidentally compared their outlines and shapes, setting the stage for future learning.

That is why you and your colleagues need to make certain that young students who have low vision are exposed to letters and words that can be seen clearly. For preschoolers who are blind, two essential components of an early literacy program include systematically introducing braille and flooding the environment with incidental opportunities to find braille, such as on labels, notes, books, schedules, and lunch menus.

Determining Nonacademic Priorities

As you reviewed Figure 15.4, you may have felt a bit overwhelmed by the list of areas in which a student with visual impairment may need specialized instruction. Once you assess a child's performance in these areas and identify any needs for instruction, the IEP team must prioritize those needs. Often, not all of the skills of the expanded core curriculum can be addressed every year. Nonetheless, the team should not ignore needed skills in these areas in favor of the academic skills that are the focus of statewide achievement and accountability testing. That is so because all are skills needed for success in adult life. Ideally, the team will identify some skills in each expanded core curriculum area for intensive instruction each year. The TVI must carefully monitor a student's acquisition and use of these skills so that by the time the student is ready to transition from school to adult life, she has the skills necessary for success.

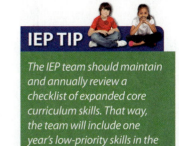

IEP TIP

The IEP team should maintain and annually review a checklist of expanded core curriculum skills. That way, the team will include one year's low-priority skills in the next year's list of skills to be developed.

Determining the Location of Special Education and Related Services

Having decided what is going to be taught, the IEP team then must determine where that instruction should take place. Sometimes it is more appropriate to provide initial instruction privately and then to practice emerging skills within the general education classroom. To meet other needs, such as the acquisition of skills related to human sexuality, cooking, or shopping, instruction in specialized environments is usually essential.

Communicating to Meet Students' Needs

For students who rely on adapted materials and who need increased opportunities for meaningful, hands-on activities, collaboration is essential. General educators need to feel confident that their lessons will be accessible to their students with visual impairments. Because these adaptations, especially of math, science, and social studies materials, require significant time to create, the TVI must receive the materials well in advance of the date of their intended use.

Close communication to meet students' needs is also necessary when determining modifications to assigned work. Corbin requires at least twice as much time as his peers do to complete a typical math assignment, in part because the braille math code is still unfamiliar to him. His teachers have discussed the possibility of reducing the length of his assignments, but it was obvious that, because of his lack of experience with numbers and math concepts, he needed additional opportunities in order to achieve at the level of his classmates. His IEP team had to deal with his competing needs for more time to complete the assigned work and more experiences to understand it thoroughly. They ultimately decided that his need for practice of these basic mathematical skills was critical to his long-term academic success and, as a result, did not recommend this modification.

Given that most math teachers have little background in visual impairment and limited understanding of how visual and spatial concepts can be presented to students who don't learn visually, they must rely on TVIs for support. Similarly, TVIs, who usually have limited knowledge of best practices in mathematics instruction, need assistance from students' mathematics teachers. To support the general educator who is teaching mathematics to a class in which a student with visual impairments is enrolled, the TVI should do the following:

- Preteach concepts or techniques before they are introduced in the general education class.
- Teach students specialized computation methods, such as finger math or use of an abacus.
- Teach students who are blind to use the Nemeth braille code for mathematics.
- Teach students to use tactile charts, diagrams, and graphs.
- Teach students to self-advocate and to ask questions when concepts or strategies are not understood.
- Provide opportunities to apply basic concepts and operations in real-life situations.

- Advise the math teacher on strategies for illustrating problems for students in a way that allows them to experience the principles being taught.
- Be present during math instruction to assist with students' understanding of the concepts.

Likewise, the math teacher can make instruction more accessible to the student by doing the following:

- Speak about mathematics consistently and unambiguously so that all students can understand.
- Verbalize whatever is written on the blackboard or overhead projector transparencies.
- Use manipulatives, real objects, and appropriate three-dimensional models for activities.
- Give advance copies of transparencies, assignments, and blackboard notes to the TVI so that they can be made available in the student's learning medium at the same time as peers receive them.
- Advise the TVI about key instructional principals when it is necessary to modify assignments and other materials.

DETERMINING SUPPLEMENTARY AIDS AND SERVICES

To participate in general education, many students who are blind or have low vision require curriculum modifications for accessing print as well as appropriate assistive technology.

Providing Adapted Materials

A variety of adapted materials are available for use by students with visual impairments, including braille and large-print maps, measuring devices, graph paper, writing paper, calendars, flash cards, and geometric forms. A good source of adapted materials is the American Printing House for the Blind (http://shop.aph.org).

TVIs often must adapt materials for assignments designed by general educators. Making these adaptations requires careful judgment by the TVI, who must determine what the primary and secondary purposes of the lesson are and what information can reasonably and meaningfully be represented in a tactile form. Adaptations can be simple, as when a child is given real coins instead of pictures of coins to complete a math assignment. Occasionally, meaningful adaptations are impossible to create, and alternative assignments that focus on the same skill must be prepared.

Students with low vision access print primarily through the use of optical devices, such as glasses, telescopes, and magnifying lenses. In some instances, they may read large-print books, though some researchers suggest that this practice does not lead to faster reading rates or more comfortable reading distances (Lussenhop & Corn, 2002). One of the advantages of magnification devices is that they allow the student access to printed materials not only at school but also at home, at work, and in the community.

Accessing Appropriate Assistive Technology

As you have learned, students with visual impairments often require alternative methods to ensure progress in the general education curriculum. Today, several types of devices make access to the curriculum much easier for people with visual impairment. Figure 15.7 describes some of these technologies.

Many students use these technologies in combination. For example, when he is older and is required to write an essay, Corbin will probably access the library's online catalog with JAWS, which speaks the text on the monitor aloud to him. He may take notes with his electronic braille note taker about which books and articles to check out of the library. Then, when he has copies of articles that aren't available electronically, he will scan them with his optical character reader, which will convert the print to an electronic form that he can either emboss in braille or read aloud using the computer's voice synthesizer. Corbin

IEP TIP

Although IDEA requires the IEP team to determine a student's needs before making a placement decision, all too often IEP teams will improperly decide on placement on the basis of the limited options in any district.

Students with visual impairments often need to use a variety of technologies to access print materials and to create the products expected of all students in the general curriculum.

- *When you have a student with low vision who needs to view a small object closely,* the student can use a handheld magnifier or a closed-circuit television (CCTV). CCTVs come in either handheld or desktop models that enlarge the image to the desired size and project it onto a television screen or computer monitor. The camera on some CCTVs can be adjusted to focus on a distant object, such as a demonstration or a whiteboard, thereby bringing the information to the computer screen directly in front of the student.

- *When you have a student who needs to scan a print document that is not available electronically,* the student can use an optical character reader (OCR) or scanner. Special software combined with an off-the-shelf scanner will increase the accuracy with which material is scanned. Some OCRs are specifically designed for people who are visually impaired and can even scan information in columns accurately.

- *When you have a student with low vision who needs to read information displayed electronically on a computer screen,* the student can use a screen enlargement and navigation system. These systems increase the size of the characters on the screen, the cursors, and the menu and dialogue boxes and provide features that allow easy access to displayed information.

- *When you have a student for whom electronic text on a computer screen is difficult to see,* the student can use a screen reader. Using synthesized speech, screen readers read the text aloud as the user moves the cursor (usually using keyboard strokes, not the mouse) or inputs from the keyboard.

- *When you have a student who needs to take notes in class,* the student can use a note-taking device. Several lightweight electronic note-taking devices (with either braille or qwerty keyboards) are available. The student can then download these notes to a computer for study or to be printed or embossed as braille. Most of these devices have audio output; some also create braille on an electronic display.

- *When you have a student who needs to create a personal braille copy of an assignment that has been created electronically,* the student can use a braille embosser, which, when connected to a computer and used in conjunction with braille translation software, will "print" a braille version of the text. Some braille embossers also print the ink-print translation on the same page.

no doubt will choose to emboss his last draft for proofreading and then will use braille translation software to print the final print copy to submit to his teacher.

These technologies create the opportunity for students with significant visual impairments to access and participate in the general education curriculum—as long as it remains print-based. There is a dark side to the technological revolution, however, particularly for students who are blind. As teachers supplement more and more of the general education curriculum with graphics-based sources, such as interactive software programs, they make it less likely that the curriculum will be accessible to students who cannot see the images on the screen. Already, vast areas of the graphics-based Internet are not accessible to students with visual impairments. Even if these materials are presented with audio descriptions, they may be meaningless to the student who is blind simply because he has limited or no experience with the concepts being described.

The challenge for classroom educators is to remain flexible, using interesting materials that are accessible to all students, including students with visual impairments. Through universally designed instruction, teachers can make a dark future bright.

PLANNING FOR UNIVERSAL DESIGN FOR LEARNING

Often students with visual impairments have difficulty understanding some of the ideas that their teachers are presenting because they have not directly experienced them. They may need many additional experiences to make up for their lack of incidental learning. Universally designed instruction provides these meaningful experiences and can benefit all students. For example, early reading books designed for children rely heavily on pictures to convey the meaning of the story. In addition, the pictures reveal to young readers information about the world that they may not have directly experienced. Not all new readers have been for a walk in a forest or have gone for a ride in a rowboat, but from pictures they can discern what the words in the story convey (Koenig & Farrenkopf, 1997). Even older students with visual impairments benefit from instruction that incorporates real experiences that employ a tactile/kinesthetic approach to learning. General educators of

BOX 15.3 UNIVERSAL DESIGN FOR PROGRESS

Transcribing into Braille

As you learned in Chapter 2, universal design for learning ensures that students with disabilities can access the general education curriculum through modifications achieved through technology and instruction. At this point in Corbin's schooling, UDL is achieved primarily through modifications to instruction and the instructional materials he uses. Later, technology will play a more important role. You also learned in Chapter 2 that UDL incorporates three elements: (1) multiple means of representation, (2) multiple means of action and expression, and (3) multiple means of engagement. Corbin's success in the classroom depends on his teachers applying these elements on a daily basis.

Because Corbin cannot see print materials, most instructional materials and activities must be modified for him. About a week in advance of her lesson, his teacher provides his TVI with copies of her lesson plans and any worksheets she plans to use in class. The TVI transcribes these worksheets in braille, staples the print version to the braille copy, and delivers it to the teacher to hand to Corbin in class. When pictures are involved, the TVI may need to create a tactile version of the worksheet. Usually, she doesn't try to replicate the picture because these often have little meaning to children who are blind. Instead, she determines (often in consultation with the classroom teacher) the primary educational purpose of the assignment and creates a slightly different worksheet that preserves the purpose. So instead of counting pictures of rabbits on a graph for a mathematics assignment, Corbin might count buttons on a tactile graph. The means of representation has changed, but the expectation of the student has not.

When Corbin's class was being introduced to expository writing, they studied facts about the earth, such as volcanoes, caves, and burrowing animals. Each student created an illustrated book, titled *Beneath My Feet*. Corbin's writing was done on the braillewriter. Most of his illustrations, though, were created by him using tangible materials, some of which were appropriate for all of the children in the class. For the illustration showing the layers of the earth's crust, his teacher had her students glue to their papers a strip of topsoil, a strip of waxy crayon (for the clay), a strip of sand, and finally, a strip of rocks. By using alternate means of action and expression, all students were able to demonstrate their knowledge of this concept. In this case, the UDL was built into the lesson, not provided as an accommodation for just one student.

In kindergarten, Corbin's class was studying the life cycle of plants. His O&M teacher used this unit to engage him in learning by doing, one of the most effective ways to create understanding of new concepts for students who are blind. Along with other students at Corbin's school with visual impairments, they planted a vegetable garden from seeds. They checked their plants' growth daily and finally harvested carrots, lettuce, and zucchini. When Corbin brought his crop to class for show-and-tell, his peers were surprised to see the leafy tops on the carrots and the drying flowers on the end of the zucchini. His teacher decided to bring in the roots and plants of several kinds of vegetables that she purchased at a whole-foods store for her students to explore. She also read the book *Tops & Bottoms*, by Janet Stevens, to the class. She instinctively was taking advantage of her students' interests and motivations by presenting new concepts through multiple means of engagement.

As valuable as the principles of universal design are, educators should be cautious about how they apply them to curriculum and instruction for students with visual impairments. Educators tend to underestimate these students' abilities and provide too much support, leading to learned helplessness. In general, educators should expect students with visual impairments to master the same content and meet the same performance standards as students with vision do, even though the students with visual impairments may use adapted methods to access the curriculum and demonstrate these standards. You can read about how teachers promote success in general education through high expectations and meaningful interaction with peers in Box 15.4.

students with visual impairments must provide more experiential activities in their classrooms to assure that all students understand the text. Box 15.3 describes an example of how Corbin's teachers collaborated to create a meaningful lesson for his class based on the principles of universal design. And Box 15.4 offers tips on including students with visual impairments in the general education classroom.

You might ask yourself how instruction in these areas affects the student's progress in the general education curriculum. When children with visual impairments have had the same experiences as their sighted peers and are encouraged to be autonomous and to make decisions for themselves, they are more interested and engaged in the content of the general curriculum and understand and appreciate it better. Mastery of these kinds of skills is critical to students' long-range educational and life outcomes. Students will need social, living, travel, and career skills to manage as competent adults and to apply the content and performance standards acquired in their general education programs. Typically, teachers need to focus on three areas in the curriculum of students with visual impairments: daily living skills, orientation and mobility, and self-determination.

BOX 15.4

INCLUSION TIPS

	What You Might See	What You Might Be Tempted to Do	Alternate Response	Ways to Include Peers in the Process
Behavior	She is a loner on the playground, choosing to play or walk by herself.	Allow her to stay in class and read or do homework.	Teach her board or card games.	Once she has mastered the games, set up a game table during recess where anyone who wants to play can do so.
Social interactions	He doesn't say hello to peers in hallways or acknowledge peers' presence when entering room.	Assume he is stuck up and unfriendly.	Have the entire class prepare autobiographies, including life history, special interests, and photos or objects for him and others to study.	Teach peers to say both his name and their own in greeting because he may not be able to recognize them from their voices alone.
Educational performance	She is completing her arithmetic assignments more slowly than her peers are.	Immediately shorten the assignment for her.	Assess to determine if she understands the arithmetical concepts. Provide concrete objects and manipulatives if they are necessary for mastery. Shorten the assignment if concepts are mastered.	Have her act as a cross-age tutor to younger students who benefit from use of concrete materials in learning.
Classroom attitudes	He seems bored or uninterested during class demonstrations or teacher-directed activities.	Assume the lesson is too difficult or simply ignore the inattention.	Make sure that he can "see" the teacher's materials by having copies of printed/brailled materials and real objects at his desk during the lesson.	Have him and peers help the teacher prepare a lesson by getting out materials and preparing overheads and hands-on materials for class use.

Daily Living Skills

Students with visual impairments require ongoing instruction in important skills of daily living, such as clothing management and kitchen skills. Generally, effective teaching strategies involve repeated visual or hand-over-hand kinesthetic demonstrations (or both), systematic instruction, gradual fading of assistance and prompts, and significant periods of practice (Koenig & Holbrook, 2000).

Often people do not think to include a child with visual impairment in simple activities of daily living. Involving the student in an activity and having high expectations that the skill can be acquired are critical factors in the acquisition of daily living skills. Because many adults think of people who are blind as helpless, they have low expectations for students with visual impairments. In addition, because adults may assume that students with low vision see more clearly than they

A student who is blind often needs hand-over-hand instruction to learn independent living skills.

These students work with an orientation and mobility specialist to learn how to move safely within their school neighborhood before tackling the challenge of a busy city street.

do, the adults do not show them how to perform some of the activities that sighted children learn incidentally, such as buttoning a shirt, holding a spoon correctly, or making a bed. When students do not spontaneously develop these skills, teachers may mistakenly think that the students also have cognitive disabilities and may reduce their expectations even more.

Low and inaccurate expectations of their abilities are students' worst enemies. Skilled teachers know to be constantly alert to what students are not doing for themselves. These teachers are prepared to challenge students to promote independence and self-motivation, just as Corbin's parents do with him.

Orientation and Mobility

O&M, an IDEA-related service, encompasses skills that people with visual impairments use to know where they are in their environment and how to move around that environment safely. Unlike sighted students, students with visual impairments must learn to listen to the flow of traffic; react to changes of street and road surfaces; and use their vision, other senses, and perhaps a cane or other mobility device to detect objects in the environment and to help them know where they are.

The development of O&M skills begins in infancy and continues until the student can reach a destination safely by using a variety of techniques. Young children concentrate on developing body image, mastering spatial and positional concepts, learning the layout of their homes and schools, and developing environmental awareness. Older students focus on crossing streets safely and negotiating travel in increasingly complex situations, such as a town's business district or a shopping mall.

Some blind adults learn how to travel with a guide dog. Primarily because of the responsibility associated with the care of these service animals, individuals under the age of eighteen who still attend local schools rarely learn to use a guide dog, but children can be prepared to use guide dogs by learning to care for animals as pets (Young, 1997) and by becoming proficient at orientation skills, which are necessary for efficient traveling.

Self-Determination

As adults, most people with visual impairments are required to explain their abilities and special needs to people they meet: bus drivers, prospective employers, landlords, restaurant workers, and flight attendants. Sometimes these explanations are simple, such as asking a bus driver to announce the name of every bus stop, but sometimes they require more detailed descriptions. For example, as a college student, Corbin may need to ask each of his teachers for permission to record lectures, explain that it will be necessary for them to say aloud what they write on the board, and describe special accommodations that he needs (e.g., a reader or additional time during testing). He may also need to convince each of his professors that he can do the work for the class. In brief, he will have to be an effective self-advocate.

Corbin has already begun developing self-advocacy skills. For now, he simply listens as his TVI explains his needs to his teachers; but soon he will be expected to participate in this task, taking responsibility for explaining the special tools that he uses to his general education teachers. As an adult, Corbin may need to advocate for his rights with landlords and, if he has a guide dog, for access to public buildings. His teachers will need to help him learn the laws (especially the Americans with Disabilities Act) and the communication techniques he can use to avoid confrontations (if possible) and to assert himself (as necessary). As part of Corbin's lessons in self-determination, his TVI is introducing him to successful adults who are blind.

Partnering Is Key

Meeting the academic, social, and functional life-skills needs of students with visual impairments frequently becomes a balancing act that demands considerable finesse, goal prioritization, and creative problem solving (Hatlen, 1996; Koenig & Holbrook, 2000; Pugh & Erin, 1999). Creativity is the answer to many questions: in scheduling, in instruction, in use of free time, and in collaboration among the many adults involved in each pupil's program. That is why IEP team members must assume responsibility for the instruction and practice of newly learned skills whenever the natural opportunity to do so occurs. Each member also must believe that successful adult functioning depends on the student's attainment of skills in all of the curriculum areas—that no one area is more or less important than the others. In Box 15.5, you can read about the collaboration of general and special educators to meet the needs of a student who wanted to participate in his school's band.

BOX 15.5 — PARTNERSHIP TIPS

Making Beautiful Music Together

Adults who are not familiar with the techniques that individuals with visual impairments use to accomplish tasks often have difficulty imagining that the students can participate at all. Frequently, effective problem solving to change attitudes and create practical answers requires both local and distant collaborators.

One such partnership occurred when Ja'dine, a saxophone player in his school's orchestra, mentioned to his mother that he wanted to participate in the school's marching band. This situation required extensive partnerships among many people. Several steps led to his participation:

1. *Adults responded to a desired goal expressed by the student.* His mother's first thought was that Ja'dine was asking for too much—that, because of his blindness, he was going to be disappointed. She called Eloisa Ramirez, Ja'dine's TVI, and asked for her advice.

2. *The student's TVI arranged a meeting with the partners involved in making the student's goal possible.* Eloisa was pleased that Ja'dine was interested in becoming involved in this extracurricular activity and wanted to support him. She recognized, though, that others at the school might have doubts about the wisdom of the idea, just as Ja'dine's mother did. She talked with the school principal, who, though not entirely supportive of the idea, was willing to meet with the individuals most likely to be involved in implementing the plan.

3. *The TVI and the student brainstormed potential benefits and obstacles to achieving the goal, which the student presented to the potential partners.* In preparation for this meeting, Eloisa and Ja'dine made two lists. The first set out the benefits he would experience as a member of the marching band. The second identified the adaptations that he might need. Before the meeting, Ja'dine practiced with Eloisa how he would present this information. Attending the meeting were the O&M specialist, the marching band director, the principal, Eloisa, and, of course, Ja'dine and his mother. Ja'dine persuasively presented his case for being involved in the marching band. Having decided that he was committed to the work that would be required to make his idea a reality, the group then began examining how it might be accomplished.

4. *Possible strategies for overcoming identified obstacles were discussed and assigned to specific partners for further investigation.* The collaborators identified two issues that had to be resolved. First, the principal was concerned that the district would use insurance liability as an excuse to prevent Ja'dine from marching. Eloisa offered to contact a state advocacy group of blind adults to get information that he could use to counter any arguments that the school district's insurance expert presented. The advocacy group even sent a representative to meet with district representatives. The marching band director voiced the second concern: How would Ja'dine be able to stay in step? The O&M instructor suggested that there might be several ways in which he could stay in formation with the rest of the band members. The band director still wasn't keen on the idea but agreed to allow the O&M specialist to attend band practice to work with him to identify the best solutions.

5. *The group worked as a team to resolve issues that arose; new partners were added as necessary.* During the summer, as the O&M specialist and the band director worked with Ja'dine and the other band members who were learning formations, other partners became involved. Eloisa had to contract with a faraway braillist who knew the braille music code and could emboss the needed braille sheet music. Ja'dine's peers in the band also became involved when his mother's work shift changed to early evenings and she was unable to get him to and from practice. Other band members had come to enjoy Ja'dine and his sense of humor as they practiced; they wanted to be with him and were willing to offer him rides.

6. *Successful collaboration and hard work resulted in the student's reaching his goal.* At the first game of the season, Ja'dine proudly marched with the band. Watching from the stands were the partners who had helped to make this night possible. Farther away, but also smiling, were the advocate and the braillist. Indeed, success for students with visual impairments can involve both distant and local collaboration.

Using Effective Instructional Strategies

EARLY CHILDHOOD STUDENTS: PROGRAMMING THAT FOCUSES ON REAL EXPERIENCES

Early intervention programs for young children with visual impairments generally are home-based, although many successful interventions, such as the BEGIN program at the Center for the Visually Impaired in Atlanta, also offer a center-based component in which parents of infants observe preschool children with visual impairments and meet the families of other youngsters who are blind or have low vision. The focus of early intervention is to help parents understand the effects of visual impairment on learning and to present effective methods that reduce the impact of these effects on development. These programs emphasize strategies that enhance children's acquisition of body image, language, self-help skills, sensorimotor skills, concepts, orientation, and early social interactions in home, school, and community environments where young children spend their time.

Preschool programs for children with visual impairments continue early intervention goals and provide many experiences that are the foundation for learning. Most of the activities are hands-on, meaningful, and related to real life. Students make their own snacks, wash their dishes, and find opportunities to change their clothes often, thereby practicing daily living skills. They collect tangible memories of their day and include them in braille or print experience stories dictated to their teachers. TVIs facilitate students' movement, meaningful language, exploration, and control of the environment to reduce the impact of visual impairment on development.

Many students with visual impairments are in heterogeneously grouped preschools and in preschools for children without disabilities. With the proper supports, these programs can be valuable learning environments for some children. It is easy to forget, however, that sighted children acquire many of the benefits of these programs through incidental learning. Although students with visual impairments participate, there is a possibility that they will fall behind others in the class unless they receive supplemental instruction.

A trip to the sculpture garden at the zoo provides a natural opportunity to encourage peer interactions.

ELEMENTARY AND MIDDLE SCHOOL STUDENTS: ACCOMMODATIONS TO DEVELOP BASIC SKILLS

Elementary school is a key time for sighted children to develop a positive self-image, lay a solid foundation in academic skills, and safely explore the world. For pupils who are blind or who have low vision, the focus of the educational program is the same as that for students with unimpaired vision; however, the techniques for accomplishing these goals may be different, requiring TVIs to teach or reinforce concepts presented in class.

TVIs spend much of their time adapting materials for students in elementary programs. TVIs who support inclusion of their students create braille sheet music for music class, provide maps with raised continents and tactilely different countries for social studies, and encourage peer-supported learning as students handle specimens in science.

In addition, and depending on the student's needs, the TVI emphasizes the development of recreation and leisure pursuits, career-awareness skills, social skills, knowledge of human sexuality, additional self-help skills, knowledge of the student's visual impairment, and early advocacy skills. At the same time, the O&M specialist may be increasing the environments in which the youngster can travel safely.

TVIs and O&M specialists monitor to ensure that their students are showing progress. Corbin's O&M specialist noticed that, in the middle of first grade, Corbin began to rely on peers to help him with tasks that he could do independently. For instance, he allowed students to guide him to the lunchroom and help him retrieve and put away materials more often than expected. He also began telling his O&M specialist that there were things he couldn't do because he was blind. Alarmed, the specialist met with Corbin's parents and teachers to discuss the matter. Guessing that Corbin was being reinforced by the peer attention he was receiving, they agreed on a plan that rewarded him for independent behavior, discouraged peers from helping excessively, and offered opportunities for him to spend time with peers engaged in activities of mutual interest. Corbin's O&M specialist even began taking one of his classmates on O&M lessons so that they could share that experience together.

SECONDARY AND TRANSITION STUDENTS: PREPARING FOR ADULT LIFE

For many students with visual impairments, the middle and high school years are a time to learn skills that students with good vision have been learning incidentally but that are not used until the teen years. TVIs generally spend more time with students to meet needs related to the expanded core curriculum while students are enrolled in general education classes to meet graduation requirements. Sometimes students choose to delay graduation in order to master all the skills needed for a successful transition to independent adult living.

Melissa Jorrey, an itinerant TVI and O&M specialist in Texas, works with her students on the transition skills they need. For example, one student, Eduardo Gonzalez, could not make a sandwich or clean a sink when he entered high school. At home, he had not been expected to help with general household tasks; and because of his visual impairment, he had not incidentally learned how to perform them. Melissa met several times with Eduardo's mother and persuaded her that he needed to learn to do more for himself at home—and that his educational program needed to focus on both his academic and functional needs.

Today Eduardo and Melissa are making a list of the utility services that he will need to contact when he moves into an apartment. Eduardo practices his note-taking skills as he contacts directory assistance to request the telephone numbers of the different utility companies and keys them into his electronic note taker. Later he will retrieve the numbers and call to request information about having the utilities started.

Recently, during O&M lessons, they have been exploring apartment complexes close to the vocational school where Eduardo will enroll next year. He knows he must spend many hours learning to negotiate safely the routes to use around the school's campus and to the grocery store, the mall, and other community areas he will be using.

Including Students with Visual Impairments

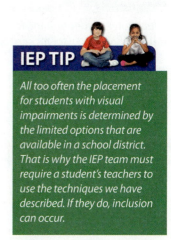

As you have already read, blindness and low vision do not affect what a student can learn as much as they affect *how* a student learns. In fall 2008, 62 percent of students spent 80 to 100 percent of their time in the general education classroom, as Corbin does. Another 14 percent were in general education for 40 to 79 percent of the school day (U.S. Department of Education, 2011). The percentage of students with visual impairments receiving most of their education in the general education class continues to rise. This change may reflect the increased access to the general education curriculum that has been made possible through new technologies. Figure 15.8 illustrates patterns of educational placement.

Corbin is included in a general education second-grade class and is expected to complete the same work as other students do. When appropriate, he occasionally leaves that

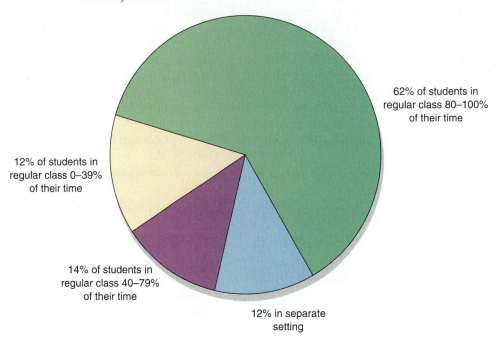

62% of students in regular class 80–100% of their time

12% of students in regular class 0–39% of their time

14% of students in regular class 40–79% of their time

12% in separate setting

Source: U.S. Department of Education. (2011). *Data accountability center: Individuals with Disabilities Education Act (IDEA) data.* Retrieved February 12, 2011, from https://www.ideadata.org.

Note: Percentages have been rounded and collapsed across categories.

Education includes training for job skills. Economic self-sufficiency is an obtainable goal for most people with visual impairments.

class to work with his TVI in another classroom or the community. Depending on the subject of instruction, however, there are times when his TVI will support Corbin in his general education class. This flexible approach to placement benefits many students with visual impairments. There are, however, some students who are best served in the general education classroom all day and who are never removed from that environment for special services. Still others receive educational benefit through placement at a school for the blind or in a special class.

The nature of visual impairment and the ways in which youngsters with visual impairments learn about the world mitigate against successful inclusion in all cases. Inclusion is successful when educators address both academic needs and those related to the expanded core curriculum. For students with visual impairments, inclusion in adult society is considered the goal of special education; but full inclusion in the general curriculum is not always the best means to that goal.

In Box 15.6, Donna McNear, a TVI in Minnesota, describes her role in creating learning communities in which students with visual impairments have the opportunity to succeed.

Assessing Students' Progress

MEASURING STUDENTS' PROGRESS

The progress of students with visual impairments is measured in both the general and the expanded core curriculum.

Donna McNear

"To teach is to learn twice" is a quotation by J. Joubert (1754–1824) that appears in my home, my notebook, and my office. As a teacher of children with visual impairments, I am continually traveling a path of learning. My work day is immersed in learning to create caring school communities and learning opportunities in which children can be successful.

As an itinerant teacher in seven rural school districts in east-central Minnesota, I begin my day in my car, traveling to see children in their home school districts. At the first school, I observe Chad, a preschool student with low vision, and assist the school staff in providing materials and arranging the classroom so he can easily see and participate in all activities.

I also stop at the high school to teach Tracy, who reads and writes in braille. I bring the worksheets the teachers have given me to put into braille and quickly visit with teachers between classes to answer questions and problem-solve. Mr. Johnson, the science teacher, and I discuss the possibilities of providing tactual materials in a genetics unit. He comes up with a great idea and benefits from my support, approval, and encouragement. I meet with Tracy who asks for help in learning new Nemeth code braille signs in the beginning algebra math unit and wants to review the route to the new girls' locker room for gym.

After an hour of reviewing information with Tracy, I travel to the next town and have lunch with the adapted physical education teacher. This gives us the opportunity to plan the physical education activities for Shannon, an eighth-grade student who is blind and now working on swimming goals. After lunch I go to my office to make phone calls and have a meeting with the braillist, Connie. She wants to discuss the format for braille music.

On my way to the next town, I make a brief stop at Cory's house. He is fourteen months old and has low vision. He just received glasses, and I spend a few minutes observing and assessing the difference his glasses make in how he uses his vision in daily activities at home. His parents also want to share new information from his ophthalmologist and ask a few questions.

My day ends with a mobility lesson with Annie, a high school student who is blind. I am dually certified as an O&M specialist, which allows children in rural areas to receive needed training. We review the route to the post office so Annie can pick up a package.

Sharing a description of my day with my family at dinner, I remember a statement attributed to Lewis Mumford: "It is not what one does, but in a manifold sense what one realizes that keeps existence from being vain and trivial." I do many things in a day for children, but what I realize about teaching and my students is what my work life is all about. I realize that I am a mirror, a window, and a doorway for my students: a mirror to reflect positively who they are and their capabilities, talents, and dreams; a window to show them their opportunities, possibilities, choices, and other ways of being; and, finally, a doorway for their future.

I have also realized my own mission in my work life. I see the meaning in my labor (beyond the reward of a paycheck); I see my abilities recognized and valued; I view myself as a craftsperson, creating something of beauty and value. I have a job that is large enough for my spirit, and I feel I am leaving the world better than I found it. Through my day-to-day teaching, I have learned love, fortitude, respectfulness, and humility. I have also learned to be delicate and to have passion for my time with children.

Progress in the General Curriculum

Because most students with visual impairments receive educational services in the general education classroom, their progress is measured alongside their peers: They take the same math, social studies, language arts, and science tests as do the other students in their class. Sometimes, of course, the TVI must transcribe print materials into braille or the student must use a magnifier when reading the test, but these accommodations are not designed to modify the purpose or difficulty of the test in any way. When students prepare their answers in braille, the TVI writes in print above the braille exactly what is written in braille. After the general educator has graded the interlined work, the TVI prepares the general educator's comments in braille for the student.

It is common, however, for students with visual impairments to take their tests in a separate classroom. Sometimes they must leave the general education classroom to use the assistive technology that is stored in another area; sometimes additional space is necessary to spread out their materials. Usually, these students also require extra time to complete tests because of the slow reading speed caused by their visual impairment.

Progress in Addressing Other Educational Needs

Teachers are also responsible for measuring students' progress in the expanded core curriculum, generally by using informal measures such as observation, evaluation of needed prompts, and curriculum-based tests prepared by the TVI. For example, after

Corbin completed a unit of study on his eye condition, his TVI prepared a test to determine his retention and understanding of the information taught. To measure Corbin's progress in learning to make a grilled cheese sandwich, however, his TVI used a checklist of the steps needed to complete this task and noted on the list the level of prompting that he required. For assessing progress in keyboarding, a computer-based test measured Corbin's speed and accuracy. In a word, educators must devise measurements of a student's progress in a variety of skill areas.

MAKING ACCOMMODATIONS FOR ASSESSMENT

Comprehensive assessments frequently include standardized and norm-referenced tests, which are often timed. Taking tests often requires complex use of vision, such as frequent eye movements between the test booklet and the answer sheet or scanning of multiple-choice answers and stimulus paragraphs. Because readers who use braille tend to have reading rates significantly below their peers with sight and because their system of reading is not conducive to efficient scanning, they may have difficulty with timed tests (Erin & Levinson, 2007). Therefore, the amount of time needed should be determined individually (Allman, 2004).

Other assessment accommodations include magnification devices, a reader (for the nonreading sections of the test), a scribe, or a computer; placement in a quiet testing area; and frequent breaks. Of course, these accommodations must be listed on the IEP and must be the types of accommodations typically used by the student to complete assignments.

ADDRESSING THE PROFESSIONAL STANDARDS

The following Council for Exceptional Children (CEC) Common Core Knowledge and Skills are addressed in this chapter through the content and concepts we discuss. See the Appendix for a full listing of these Knowledge and Skill statements:

ICC2K1, ICC2K2, ICC2K3, ICC2K4, ICC2K5, ICC2K6, ICC5S2, ICC5S3, ICC5S4, ICC5S6, ICC5S8, ICC5S9, ICC7S1, ICC7S2, ICC7S3, ICC7S6, ICC7S7, ICC7S9, ICC10S2, ICC10S3, ICC10S4, ICC10S5, ICC10S6, ICC10S8, ICC10S9

Summary

IDENTIFYING STUDENTS WITH VISUAL IMPAIRMENTS

- Legal blindness is a measurement used primarily for eligibility for government or private-assistance programs.
- Within education, visual impairment, including blindness, is defined as an impairment in vision that adversely affects a student's educational performance.
- Students with visual impairments have a limited ability to learn incidentally from the environment and must be directly exposed to or taught much of what they need to know.

EVALUATING STUDENTS WITH VISUAL IMPAIRMENTS

- Ophthalmologists determine the presence of a visual disorder, and optometrists and low vision specialists determine if a visual disorder can be corrected through lenses or optical devices.
- A functional low vision assessment determines how a student uses his vision in a variety of situations.
- A learning media assessment assists TVIs in determining the most efficient mode of reading and learning—for instance, with braille, magnification, or large print.

- Educators determine the effects of visual impairment on students' development of skills in the expanded core curriculum, including compensatory skills, orientation and mobility, career education, independent living, technology, self-determination, recreation and leisure, sensory efficiency, and social skills. They use observations, parent and student interviews, and other informal testing procedures.

DESIGNING AN APPROPRIATE IEP

- Students learn through meaningful involvement in activities from beginning to end. Often they need a hands-on approach that maximizes the use of all senses. Through practice, they have increased opportunities to develop new skills.
- Educators meet the academic needs of students through the principles of universally designed instruction.
- TVIs meet the functional and life-skill instructional needs of students to facilitate their eventual integration and full participation in adult society.
- Instruction must focus on the skills acquired incidentally by sighted students and those skills that are specific to students who have visual impairments.

USING EFFECTIVE INSTRUCTIONAL STRATEGIES

- In the early childhood years, TVIs emphasize teaching parents of young children with visual impairments to think like someone who can't see and teaching children to learn hands-on, real-life skills, such as changing clothes and making snacks.

- In the elementary years, the emphasis is on teaching compensatory skills (braille, raised maps, handling specimens) to access the general education curriculum, practicing social skills that facilitate inclusion, and developing orientation and mobility and self-advocacy skills.
- In the secondary and transition years, the focus is on transition from school to adulthood; from living at home with parents to living on one's own; on orientation and mobility training in the community; on choosing lifestyles, places of residence, and leisure activities; and on refining skills so that these choices can become realities.

INCLUDING STUDENTS WITH VISUAL DISABILITIES

- Most students with visual impairments are educated for most of the school day in general education classrooms.
- Special education services are provided by a TVI who is assigned to that school on either a part- or full-time basis.

ASSESSING STUDENTS' PROGRESS

- Progress in the general curriculum is measured through materials selected by the general education teacher that are adapted appropriately by the TVI.
- Progress in the expanded core curriculum is measured by the TVI and O&M specialist using informal assessment techniques, including interviews, teacher-made tests, and rubrics.
- Options for the use of accommodations on statewide tests are determined by the IEP team and often include different presentation (braille or print), additional time, a quiet setting, and use of a reader or scribe.

MyEducationLab

Go to Topic #16: Sensory Impairments in the MyEducationLab (www.myeducationlab .com) for *Exceptional Lives*, where you can do the following:

- Find learning outcomes for Sensory Impairments along with the national standards that connect to these outcomes.
- Complete assignments and activities that will help you more deeply understand the chapter content.
- Apply and practice your understanding of the core teaching skills identified in the chapter with the Building Teaching Skills and Dispositions learning units.
- Examine challenging situations and cases presented in the IRIS Center Resources.
- Access video clips of CCSSO National Teachers of the Year award winners responding to the question, "Why Do I Teach?" in the Teacher Talk section.
- Check your comprehension on the content covered in the chapter with the Study Plan. Here you will be able to take a chapter quiz, receive feedback on your answers, and then access review, practice, and enrichment activities to enhance your understanding of chapter content.
- Use the Online Lesson Plan Builder to practice lesson planning and integrating national and state standards into your planning.

16 Understanding Students Who *Are* Gifted *and* Talented

Who Is John Tabb

Ownership. This has been a key theme throughout John Tabb's life. His parents have worked to instill in him and his three older siblings a sense of ownership over their lives, their learning, and their decisions.

The Tabb family is unique. John's parents, Charles and Linda, were both identified as gifted. So were John's three older siblings: Rebecca, Natalie, and Charles, Jr. John followed in their footsteps, starting in the gifted program in elementary school. But even though all six members of his family are gifted, John has always made his own path. In fact, he's been encouraged to do so. As Linda says, "Our philosophy is to give the kids a lot of space, let them make a lot of choices, and give them a lot of credit to be able to do that. We've always encouraged them to be really independent and confident."

John has definitely carved out his own niche in his family and community. He chose to go to an elite boarding school for his freshman year, where he could play soccer and access a chal-

lenging academic curriculum. He joined the wrestling team in his senior year (even though he had never wrestled before), just to try something different. As he says, "I try to live life without regrets. . . . I don't want to live with any 'what ifs.'"

John has many gifts and talents, as shown by the fact that he recently received a perfect score on the math portion of the American College Test (ACT). Yet he feels that many aspects of his gifted education helped him develop his academic skills

and talents. In elementary school, he was in a self-contained gifted program, with fifteen to twenty other students who were also identified as gifted. He remembers that his teachers oversaw many hands-on projects, such as taking apart electronic devices. He feels that he really benefited from such unconventional teaching and from teachers who challenged him and his peers to achieve their full potential.

Middle school was a bit more of a challenge (which was one of the reasons why he chose to go to boarding school for his freshman year). John was no longer in a self-contained gifted program

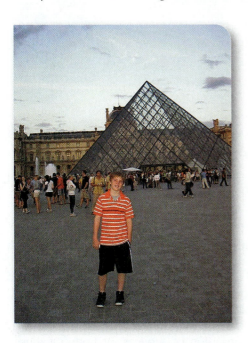

and sometimes did not feel challenged in his classes. He felt as if some teachers were trying to teach important life lessons while others just addressed problems and didn't teach very much. But he also felt that middle school taught him a lot about responsibility and taking ownership over this life. "Middle school is like a transition. You go from being in one class all day to switching classes. You have more responsibility, learn life lessons, and mature a lot."

John is also gifted in sports: He competed nationally in tennis when he was ten years old and is now playing competitive soccer. He has also played baseball and golf and, more recently, has wrestled. He's had to make decisions about which sports to play because of the challenges of balancing multiple sports and academics. Eventually he chose soccer because he not only excels at it but also enjoys its social aspects. Once again, John is owning his decisions and carving out the best path for himself.

John also considers his social skills a gift. He says, "I didn't have much to say in conversations when I was younger, but I was really observant. I'd pick up subtle things, people's emotions. I was always studying my parents' and siblings' emotions. I found them interesting." Now he wants to follow a career that lets him integrate his social abilities with his academic skills.

As the youngest child, John says that he always wanted to keep up with his brothers and sisters. "When your oldest sister goes off to one of the top universities in the country, you want to do well yourself; you don't want to be the straggler left behind." But he admits that much of the pressure is internal. "I have expectations for myself to do well and succeed." John knows that pressure, both internal and external, is a downside of being identified as gifted. But he also says that "IQ can only take you so far. You get to a point where you have to learn to manage things for yourself, and learn what is good and bad for you and work to live up to your potential."

John is taking ownership of living up to his potential. He is working hard, even in his senior year, and plans to major in business at a top college next year. While math is his strong suit, he wants to pursue a major that also allows him to use his social strengths and gives him options for the future. As he says, education is what you make of it.

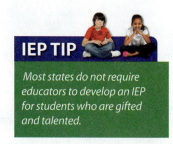

Visit the MyEducationLab (www .myeducationlab.com) for *Exceptional Lives* to enhance your understanding of chapter concepts with a personalized Study Plan. You'll also have the opportunity to hone your teaching skills through video- and case-based assignments and activities, IRIS Center Resources, and Building Teaching Skills and Disposition lessons.

IEP TIP

Most states do not require educators to develop an IEP for students who are gifted and talented.

Identifying Students Who Are Gifted and Talented

DEFINING GIFTED AND TALENTED

Unlike the laws benefiting students with disabilities, such as IDEA, Section 504, and ADA, there is no federal legislation that requires state or local educational agencies to offer special education to students who are classified as gifted or talented. State and local laws or regulations, however, may apply to these students. The National Association for Gifted Children (2009) surveyed states to identify the nature of state policy related to gifted education in the 2008–2009 school year. Thirty-two states have gifted and talented education policies that require identification of students, provision of services, or both. Of these states, five do not provide any funding. Six states describe their mandate as being fully funded.

Unlike the disabilities you have read about in this book, giftedness is not well or easily defined. Most states adopt (sometimes with modification) the definition the federal government introduced in 1978 (Stephens & Karnes, 2000):

> [T]he term "gifted and talented children" means children and, whenever applicable, youth, who are identified at the preschool, elementary, or secondary level as possessing demonstrated or potential abilities that give evidence of high performance capability in areas such as intellectual, creative, specific academic, or leadership ability, or in the performing and visual arts, and who by reason thereof, require services or activities not ordinarily provided by the school. (Gifted and Talented Children's Education Act, 1978)

Of the forty-seven states that responded to a survey asking how they define *giftedness,* forty-one reported that they do have a state-adopted definition (National Association for Gifted Children, 2009). However, only twenty-nine states require local school districts to follow that definition. Of the states that define giftedness, different ones recognize different attributes of giftedness:

- Thirty-four address intellectual giftedness.
- Twenty-six address creative giftedness.
- Twenty-five address giftedness in performing and visual arts.
- Twenty-three address academic giftedness.
- Seventeen address giftedness in leadership and specific academic areas.

The Davidson Institute for Talent Development maintains a website that provides information on each state's gifted education policies (www.davidsongifted.org/db/StatePolicy.aspx). Unfortunately, however, policy related to gifted education has been described as a "patchwork quilt" (Van Tassel-Baska, 2009, p. 1295).

To account for the fact that giftedness spans more than one area of human development and achievement, Gardner (1983) proposed a **multidimensional model of intelligence** that is broader yet more specific than the federal definition (Chen, Moran, & Gardner, 2009). This model includes eight specific intelligences found across cultures and societies: musical, bodily-kinesthetic, linguistic, logical-mathematical, spatial, interpersonal, intrapersonal, and naturalistic. Figure 16.1 lists the characteristics and distinctive features common in gifted individuals in each of these eight areas. Later in the chapter, you'll learn about how the multidimensional model of intelligence can be applied to education.

Gardner (2006) also described two predominant profiles of intelligences: searchlight and laser. Searchlight profiles—characteristic of politicians and businesspeople—involve a ready shifting among intelligences that are often comparably strong. Laser profiles—characteristic of artists, scientists, and scholars—demonstrate one or two powerful intelligences used in great depth that overshadow the other intelligences (Gardner & Moran, 2006).

It is difficult to identify how many students are gifted and talented because state and local educational agencies use so many different definitions and criteria for classifying a student as gifted and talented. The National Center for Education Statistics (2010) reports that there are approximately 3.2 million students, from prekindergarten through grade 12, who are academically gifted and talented. Most agencies apply an IQ score of 125 to 130 as a baseline for identifying these students. On that measure alone, the top 2 or 3 percent of the general population is gifted.

IEP TIP

As you work with the IEP team for gifted students who have a disability, you should address both the student's disability and her giftedness. The student's giftedness may not flourish unless you accommodate to her disability and her giftedness simultaneously.

In terms of demographics, females slightly outnumber males in gifted education placements (National Center for Education Statistics, 2009). There is a substantial and longstanding underrepresentation of students from certain racially and ethnically diverse backgrounds in programs for gifted and talented students (Castellano & Frazier, 2011; Ford, Grantham, & Whiting, 2008). The percentage of gifted students in elementary and secondary schools by race/ethnicity are as follows:

- Asian/Pacific Islander, 13.1 percent
- White, 8.0 percent
- American Indian/Alaska Native, 5.2 percent
- Hispanic, 4.2 percent
- Black, 3.6 percent

African American males have been identified as the group most vulnerable to not having their gifts and talents fostered (Whiting, 2009). Ford and colleagues (2008) recommend that culturally sensitive definitions and theories of giftedness be developed and aligned with culturally sensitive measures for identification. They underscore the need to examine policies and procedures to identify and eliminate bias in teacher referrals, cutoff scores, and criteria for admission to advanced placement classes.

DESCRIBING THE CHARACTERISTICS

It is difficult to identify the characteristics of all people who are gifted and talented. Indeed, "no one profile exists of a gifted child or a gifted education program" (Rizza & Gentry, 2001, p. 175). Nevertheless, those who are gifted and talented typically have one or more of these characteristics: high general intellect, specific academic

Students of color are disproportionately underrepresented in gifted and talented programs.

FIGURE 16.1

Potential areas of giftedness: An adaptation of Howard Gardner's eight areas of intelligence

Area	Gifted Person	Possible Characteristics of Giftedness	Early Indicators of Giftedness
Musical	Ella Fitzgerald Itzhak Perlman Ray Charles Carlos Santana Yo Yo Ma	Unusual awareness and sensitivity to pitch, rhythm, and timbre Ability may be apparent without musical training Uses music as a way of capturing feelings	Ability to sing or play instrument at an early age Ability to match and mimic segments of song Fascination with sounds
Bodily-kinesthetic	Michael Jordan Nadia Comĕneci Marla Runyon Jim Abbot	Ability can be seen before formal training Remarkable control of bodily movement Unusual poise	Skilled use of body Good sense of timing
Logical-mathematical	Albert Einsten Stephen Hawking John Nash	Loves dealing with abstraction Problem solving is remarkably rapid Solutions can be formulated before articulated: Aha! Ability to skillfully handle long chains of reasoning	Doesn't need hands-on methods to understand concepts Fascinated by and capable of making patterns Ability to figure things out without paper Loves to order and reorder objects
Linguistic	Virginia Woolf Maya Angelou Helen Keller Ralph Ellison Sandra Cisneros	Remarkable ability to use words Prolific in linguistic output, even at a young age	Unusual ability in mimicking adult speech style and register Rapidity and skill of language mastery Unusual kinds of words first uttered
Spatial	Pablo Picasso Frank Lloyd Wright I. M. Pei Maya Lin	Ability to conjure up mental imagery and then transform it Ability to recognize instances of the same element Ability to make transformations of one element into another	Intuitive knowledge of layout Able to see many perspectives Notices fine details, makes mental maps
Interpersonal	Martin Luther King, Jr. Madeleine Albright Rosa Parks Nelson Mandela	Great capacity to notice and make distinctions among people, contrasts in moods, temperaments, motivations, and intentions Ability to read intention and desire of others in social interactions; not dependent on language	Able to pretend or play-act different roles of adults Easily senses the moods of others; often able to motivate, encourage, and help others
Intrapersonal	Sigmund Freud Elizabeth Kubler-Ross	Extensive knowledge of the internal aspects of a person Increased access to one's own feelings and emotions Mature sense of self	Sensitivity to feeling (sometimes overly sensitive) Unusual maturity in understanding of self
Naturalist	Rachel Carson John James Audubon Jane Goodall Jacques Cousteau	Relates to the world around him or her In tune with the environment	Recognizes and differentiates among many types of an environmental item, such as different makes of cars Recognizes many different rocks, minerals, trees

aptitude, creativity and leadership ability, and visual or performing artistry. Paradoxically, high-ability students may also have language, hearing, visual, physical, or learning disabilities. Thus, giftedness can co-occur with disability (Hughes, 2011; Kalbfleisch & Iguchi, 2008).

High General Intellect

From its earliest conceptions, giftedness has been associated with high general intellectual ability. Today, thirty-four states (out of forty-seven reporting) include intellectual giftedness in their state definition (National Association for Gifted Children, 2009).

Typically an IQ score of 125 to 130 is the baseline for identifying giftedness. Students who have an IQ between 130 and 144 are considered to be moderately gifted, those with an IQ of 145 to 159 are considered to be highly gifted, and those with an IQ over 160 are considered to be exceptionally gifted (Clark, 2008). Although IQ tests typically can record scores as high as 160, scores of 180 to 200 have been estimated by other methods. This means that the IQ of people in the gifted population ranges from 125 to 200 and that students who are gifted are often very different from each other. Just look at John's family: Each member of the family had high general intellect, but all followed very different paths.

Exceptionally gifted individuals are sometimes referred to as prodigies. The term **prodigy** refers to a child who, before the age of ten, performs in a valued domain (such as the visual or performing arts or specific academic pursuits) at a professional level (Feldman, 2008). A child identified as a prodigy usually focuses on a specialized domain (e.g., music, chemistry) and exhibits highly developed giftedness within that domain. Box 16.1, My

---

BOX 16.1 **MY VOICE**

Michael Kearney, Age 9, Describes His College Experience

Thinking back on my years of college, I can see that I've dealt with many issues, such as the difficulty of development discrepancies, problems of conformity, and a general lack of understanding and support from the majority of people. I am constantly trying to maintain my emotional balance as I confront disbelieving educators and students. At the same time I am trying to be myself—a child who has the ability to learn and the desire to be educated.

Don't believe the myths that children like myself will not become achieving and well-adjusted adults. On the contrary, research shows that acceleration is beneficial, both academically and socially. Given appropriate education and personal support, children like myself will make a major contribution to the future.

To understand what life is like for someone like me, I must go back to the day I received my IQ results. Being told that I am not just somewhat different but dramatically different was both thrilling and terrifying. The thrill was being told that I am extremely bright, but the terror was knowing that society could never learn to put a square peg in a round hole.

Growing up, I have dealt with teachers who have never knowingly met, much less taught, someone like me. I had to deal with principals who doubted my test results, who disliked the word *gifted*, who were reluctant to make special accommodations for my needs, and who, if encouraged by law or policy, did so at a snail's pace.

In addition to struggles around decision making about school, I faced a general lack of understanding and support when it came time to attend my first day of college. I remember going through the hallways, looking at the faces of these students, and listening to them refer to me as "Doogie Howser." I thought to myself, I don't look anything like him, and I could never be a doctor. I hate the sight of blood and hospitals. Later, I came to realize that the general public is only aware of children like me through television. Well, any type of awareness is better than none.

Another issue that I had to deal with while attending college was the chatter of my classmates. They felt that my parents had pushed me. I beg to differ. My parents have done their best to see that I am a well-adjusted and a loving human being. For example, when I decided I wanted to go to college, they had to deal with the unexpected financial costs of early college attendance. They have been behind me 100 percent.

I started out at the age of six as a child who thrived on learning and craved a stimulating educational system that would enhance my academic spirit. At the University of South Alabama, I was allowed the freedom to think, act independently, and pursue my educational excellence even though I was only eight. These educators believed that children like myself have the potential to excel in an appropriate education.

After I graduate, I plan to travel and then work on a graduate degree in biochemistry to gain whatever knowledge is out there for me to grasp. My life captures the essence of the pursuit of excellence as a personal journey to overcome creative barriers imposed by the necessities of everyday college life. To be passionately in love with my work in college provides meaning for my existence.

A life of quiet desperation awaits those who will not strive for excellence. My journey is not over, but I have come a long way. My life experiences are quite different from most, and the wisdom I can share at this moment is that individual differences do exist in society and we must learn to accept and encourage those with such differences.

Voice, describes Michael Kearney, a prodigy who attended college when his age peers were in early elementary school.

Specific cognitive characteristics are associated with students who have high general intellectual ability. Those characteristics include superior functioning related to memory, concentration, abstraction, generalization, and reasoning (Hoh, 2008). Given these characteristics, students who are gifted typically develop vast knowledge in one or more areas. Sometimes, given the intensity of their curiosity, their particular interest can even be described as an obsession.

Creativity

Creativity has been defined as "the ability to generate ideas, products, or solutions that are considered novel and useful for a given problem, situation, or context" (Beghetto, 2008, p. 140). Creativity can be expressed in multiple ways (Clark, 2008):

- *Intuitive,* reflected in enhanced sensitivity and a rich fantasy life
- *Affective,* reflected in enhanced self-awareness and emotional expression
- *Physical/sensing,* reflected in creating new projects and having keen perceptions
- *Rational/reasoning,* reflected in enhanced divergent thinking

Leadership Ability

Key characteristics associated with leadership include the ability to engender others' trust (Burke, Sims, Lazzara, & Salas, 2007) and "wisdom in spontaneity—the ability to assess situations quickly and step forward or backward in taking direction for the benefit of the group" (Roach et al., 1999, p. 17).

Addressing issues related to values, ethics, and justice is a critically important type of leadership. Renzulli and Reed (2008) described characteristics of people who have "intelligences outside the normal curve" (p. 303) that enable them to use their gifts and talents to address the collective challenges of individuals and of communities at large. Characteristics that they highlight include optimism, courage, passion, sensitivity to the concerns of others, and a sense of vision or purpose about one's life contributions. Some gifted education programs focus on fostering the development and application of leadership skills (Lee, Olszewski-Kubilius, Donahue, & Weimholt, 2008; Newsom, 2010).

Talents in Visual and Performing Arts

The visual and performing arts include the areas of fine arts, music, dance, and theater (Worley, 2008). Families and peers are catalysts for nurturing interest in and commitment to the long-term development of artistic talents. Important types of support include encouragement, commitment to practice, financial support for lessons, and instrumental support related to transportation and performances. Clark (2008) suggests that the best way to determine giftedness in visual and performing arts is to have a panel of experts judge a student's performance in his area of talent. A number of states have developed residential schools with a particular focus on performing arts.

Emotional and Social Characteristics

Students who are gifted often experience significantly lower levels of anxiety as compared to their typical peers but do not differ with respect to depression (Martin, Burns, & Schonlau, 2010). It is encouraging that the self-concepts of elementary and secondary students who are gifted are relatively high across grades and gender; the lowest self-concept scores were found for older adolescents and females (Capper, Foust, Callahan, & Albaugh, 2009). However, this trend in self-concept scores (lower for older adolescents and females) has been documented with all students, not just those that are gifted (Harter, 2006). In terms of self-concept, a concern for many students who are gifted is their tendency to develop a sense of perfectionism that can lead to negative self-judgments. Factors that have been associated with the emergence of perfectionism are a lack of challenge in early school experiences, which can lead to the expectation of consistent success, and pressure from families to achieve consistently at a very high level (Neumeister, Williams, & Cross, 2009). John mentioned such pressures as a downside of being labeled as gifted; but he also felt that he often put more pressure on himself than his parents did and that this pressure could, at times, be helpful when he was going after goals.

In terms of emotional and social adjustment, being labeled as gifted can have an impact on students (Gates, 2010). Students identified as moderately and highly gifted identify positive aspects of the label, including greater opportunities for learning, not being bored in class, better teachers, and different curricula (Berlin, 2009). John felt that such options were an important aspect of being in a self-contained gifted program in elementary school. He believed that the program set students "on the right path" because they were challenged and held to high expectations from a young age.

Students, however, also identify negative aspects of the label, including greater parental expectations and pressure, more homework and schoolwork, teachers who have negative assumptions about giftedness, internal pressure to do well, and higher expectations from others (excluding parents and teachers). An encouraging finding was that students ranked feeling stereotyped by others and feeling punished by others for being smart as the lowest of all negative aspects of giftedness.

DETERMINING THE CAUSES

Whether giftedness originates from nature and/or nurture has long been debated (Dai, 2010). In terms of nature, neuroimaging techniques have enabled scientists to document differences in the structure of the brains and the neurological functioning of students who are gifted (Kalbfleisch, 2008). For example, the brains of extremely gifted individuals have some unique characteristics, such as dominance of right-hemisphere activity (Mrazik & Dombrowski, 2010). Additionally, the brains of gifted students have been found to have highly efficient and flexible neural functioning, which means there is greater connectivity among brain regions. This makes it easier for them to switch brain regions during a task and allows them to accomplish tasks with greater speed and accuracy (Newman, 2008).

Nurturing plays a role too. Families, mentors, teachers, and others can substantially influence accelerated development leading to giftedness (Callahan & Dickson, 2008; Schader, 2008). John feels that his home environment influenced him a great deal. "Being at home, you hear more big words, you hear more intelligent discussions; it's the environment you grow up in. I think it really influences you a lot in terms of how you progress. You almost learn more at home. It can influence you more than your schoolwork."

A recent study of parent perspectives on how they promote the academic motivation of their gifted children indicated the following (Garn, Matthews, & Jolly, 2010):

- Parents view themselves as the experts on their gifted children and seek to counteract their child's lack of challenge at school by modifying homework and increasing opportunities for the child to be academically motivated.

- Parents use techniques at home to increase academic motivation by instructing their child interactively, aligning homework with interest, providing structure for learning, and developing their child's intrinsic motivation.

- Parents use behavioral techniques (for example, rewards such as computer games, computer time, and money) to encourage their children to complete homework and to accomplish academic goals.

One of the early studies on the importance of nurture focused on the characteristics that propelled a group of young adults to achieve extraordinary success as artists, academics, and athletes. Families of these individuals had invested substantial time and financial resources into the development of their children's gifts and talents (Bloom, 1985).

Clark (2008) emphasizes the importance of both nature and nurture. The student's genetic patterns and environment interact because the environment enables the student to develop his abilities to the point at which he becomes gifted. Conversely, the environment can impede the student's development.

Evaluating Students Who Are Gifted and Talented

Box 16.2 describes a process for evaluating students who are gifted and talented in a way that is similar to what IDEA requires for the various categories of disability.

Because the category of gifted and talented is not included in IDEA, this specific process is not required, although Box 16.2 does incorporate the recommendations of leaders in the gifted education field (Borland, 2008; Van Tassel-Baska, 2008). A national survey of general education teachers, gifted education teachers, and administrators showed that most viewed standardized tests, teacher nominations, portfolios, performance assessments, and observations as effective but did not believe that parent nominations and peer nominations as effective (Schroth & Helfer, 2008).

DETERMINING THE PRESENCE OF GIFTEDNESS AND TALENTS

We will focus on alternative assessments for identifying giftedness among students from diverse backgrounds. Alternative assessments provide a different approach to identifying students who are gifted and talented as contrasted to traditional standardized measures such as IQ tests. Alternative assessments are especially important for the identification of students from diverse backgrounds who often are penalized due to the development and norming of traditional measures (Feng & Van Tassel-Baska, 2008; Ford, 2008).

DISCOVER (Discovering Intellectual Strengths and Capabilities through Observation While Allowing for Varied Ethnic Responses) is a performance-based and research-validated assessment for identifying giftedness in students from diverse backgrounds (Maker, 2001; Sarouphim, 2005, 2009). It requires the student to undertake problem-solving tasks in six of Gardner's domains of intelligence: spatial, logical-mathematical, linguistic, bodily-kinesthetic, interpersonal, and intrapersonal (Chen et al., 2009; Gardner, 2006). The tasks increase in complexity and openness as the assessment progresses. Assessments are available at four grade levels: K–2, 3–5, 6–8, and 9–12. Using DISCOVER, educators identify a higher proportion of students from diverse ethnic, socioeconomic, and linguistic backgrounds as gifted and talented (Sarouphim, 2002, 2004, 2009).

The DISCOVER instrument draws on Maker's (1993) definition of giftedness as "the ability to solve the most complex problems in the most efficient, effective, or economical ways" (p. 71). During the evaluation process, students work in small groups while highly trained observers use standard observation sheets, pictures, and a video camera to note their problem-solving processes and products. Over a 2½-hour period, observers accept all products, give helpful clues when asked, adopt a nonjudgmental attitude, and rotate regularly to minimize bias. Afterward, observers work as partners to rate the students' strengths on a scale of 1 to 5, from "no strength observed" to "definite strength observed." Students with superior problem-solver ratings are those with definite strength ratings in two or more activities.

In addition to using DISCOVER to identify children and youth who qualify for gifted education, an "exploring DISCOVER" curriculum has been developed that fosters students' multiple intelligences and problem-solving abilities. When implemented with preschoolers in an after-school enrichment program over three years, researchers found that children's problem-solving skills were enhanced (Kuo, Maker, Su, & Hu, 2010). Parents also reported their children's excitement about attending the program.

DETERMINING THE NATURE OF SPECIALLY DESIGNED INSTRUCTION AND SERVICES

In addition to measuring intellectual functioning, educators evaluate students' creativity. Having measures that specifically tap creativity are especially important, given the research finding that traditional IQ and academic achievement tests may miss students who are highly creative (Cramond & Kim, 2008). The Torrance Tests of Creative Thinking

BOX 16.2

NONDISCRIMINATORY EVALUATION PROCESS

Evaluating Whether or Not a Student Is Gifted, Using an IDEA-Like Process

Observation

Teacher and parents observe: The student may be bored with school or intensely interested in academic pursuits, has high vocabulary or specialized talents and interests, shows curiosity and frequently asks questions (especially *how* and *why*), is insightful, and has novel ideas and approaches to tasks.

Screening

Assessment measures:

Classroom work products: His work is consistently superior in one or more academic areas; or in the case of the gifted student who is underachieving, products are inconsistent, with only work of special interest being superior.

Group intelligence tests: Tests often indicate exceptional intelligence.

Group achievement tests: The student usually performs above average in one or more areas of achievement. (Cutoff for screening purposes is an IQ of 115.)

Prereferral

Generally, prereferral is not used for students who may be evaluated as gifted.

Referral

Schools vary on their procedures for referral; in some cases, referral will be handled very similarly to the process of referring students who have disabilities.

Nondiscriminatory evaluation procedures and standards

Assessment measures:

Individualized intelligence test: The student scores in the upper 2 to 3 percent of the population. Because of the cultural biases of standardized IQ tests, students from minority backgrounds are considered if their IQs do not meet the cutoff but other indicators suggest giftedness.

Individualized achievement test: The student scores in the upper 2 to 3 percent of the population in one or more areas of achievement.

Creativity assessment: The student demonstrates unusual creativity in work products as judged by experts or performs exceptionally well on tests designed to assess creativity. The student does not have to be academically gifted to qualify.

Checklists of gifted characteristics: These checklists are often completed by teachers, parents, peers, or others who know the student well. The student scores in the range that suggests giftedness as established by checklist developers.

Anecdotal records: The student's records suggest high ability in one or more areas.

Curriculum-based assessment: The student is performing at a level beyond peers in one or more areas of the curriculum used by the local school district.

Direct observation: The student may be a model student or could have behavior problems as a result of being bored with classwork. If the student is a perfectionist, anxiety might be observed. Observations should occur in other settings besides the school.

Visual and performing arts assessment: The student's performance in visual or performing arts is judged by individuals with expertise in the specific area. The student does not have to be academically gifted to qualify.

Leadership assessment: Peer nomination, parent nomination, and teacher nomination are generally used. However, self-nomination can also be a good predictor of leadership. Leadership in extracurricular activities is often an effective indicator. The student does not have to be academically gifted to qualify.

Case-study approach: Determination of a student's giftedness looks at all areas of assessment just described without adding special weight to any one factor.

Determination

The nondiscriminatory evaluation team determines that the student is gifted and needs special education.

are the most frequently used tools for assessing creativity. These tests were initially designed to foster the development of creativity and not simply assess students' creativity (Cramond & Kim, 2008). However, they can be used to assess creativity with both words and pictures. Thinking Creatively with Words focuses on students' verbal or linguistic creativity from kindergarten through adulthood. Six exercises assess fluency, flexibility, and originality with words. Thinking Creatively with Pictures evaluates students' figural and spatial creativity from kindergarten through adulthood. Exercises assess the five mental characteristics of fluency, elaboration, originality, resistance to premature closure, and abstractness of titles. For both tests, a manual is provided for scoring that includes national norms with standard scores and national percentiles by grade and age.

Designing an Appropriate Education

PARTNERING FOR SPECIAL EDUCATION AND RELATED SERVICES

IEP TIP

Differentiated instruction in all aspects of the curriculum and throughout the entire school day ensures high-quality educational experiences for students with and without disabilities, including students who are gifted.

Differentiated instruction is an effective strategy for teaching students who are gifted and talented as well as many students with disabilities in the general classroom. **Differentiated instruction** for students who are gifted focuses on implementing instruction that matches the strengths and needs of each gifted learner and offers opportunities for individualized responses (Tomlinson, 2008; Van Tassel-Baska, 2005). Linda says that John and her three other children have benefited from teachers who individualize instruction. She describes the best teachers as those who "sometimes go in a new direction to meet the needs of their students. They want their students to love to learn and structure learning in a way to make that happen."

Differentiated instruction requires partnerships not only among general education teachers and gifted education specialists but also with students and families. In Chapter 9, you learned about self-determination instruction for students with intellectual disability. Fostering self-determination is also critically important for students who are gifted; it prepares them to advocate for appropriately differentiated instruction. Box 16.3 describes an action research program focused on preparing gifted students to be partners in ensuring differentiated instruction.

The good news is that the research evidence is clear that students who are gifted improve their performance when appropriate individualization is implemented (Geisler, Hessler, Gardner, & Lovelace, 2009; Reis & Boeve, 2009). The bad news is that many classroom teachers believe that they do not have the time or expertise to implement a differentiated curriculum (Hertberg-Davis, 2009; Tomlinson, 2008).

DETERMINING SUPPLEMENTARY AIDS AND SERVICES

One of the most important decisions facing educators is how best to challenge a student in one or more content areas. Educators can achieve this goal through supplementary aids and services that modify the scope and sequence of the curriculum.

The first option is **acceleration**: Students "progress through educational programs either at rates faster than or at ages younger than one's peers" (Steenbergen-Hu & Moon, 2011, p. 39). That is what Graham does. He is an eighth-grader who is gifted and goes to the high school each morning to take honors geometry at the ninth-grade level. Then he returns to his middle school for the remainder of his educational program. In his school district, many students who are gifted and talented have IEPs, but this is not the case in all school districts. Graham's IEP team carefully considers the social effects of acceleration. Graham is mature and fits in fine at the high school; but if a student is physically, emotionally, or socially immature, it may not be in his best interest to be placed into classes with older students. Then the students' teachers need to consider other options. Box 16.4 shares some of Graham's experiences as he heads into high school

PARTNERSHIP TIPS

Students as Partners in Differentiating Instruction

A partnership among teachers, students, and families resulted in the implementation of a year-long program to prepare twenty-three seventh-grade students in a gifted education program to advocate for instructional differentiation that would match their individual needs. The program consisted of five introductory issue seminars facilitated by the gifted education coordinator. These one-class-period seminars focused on the nature of intelligence (for example, definitions, characteristics, and ways in which people of high intelligence may differ from others) and future planning (ways in which high intelligence affects planning for high school, college, career, and beyond). Students had opportunities to learn their rights and responsibilities, explore a range of educational options, meet advocates, and explore effective ways to advocate for their own needs. Additionally, some students were in a book club focusing on the book *The Gifted Kids' Survival Guide: A Team Handbook* (Galbraith & Delisle, 1996) and had individual conferences with the seminar leader.

Students and parents were surveyed before and after the self-advocacy program. Students reported

- Having a clearer understanding about their learning strengths and needs

- Having more knowledge of differentiated instruction options and more interest in participating in a variety of options

- Communicating with their parents more about their special needs

- Feeling more comfortable talking to teachers about their needs and asking a teacher to modify instruction

Douglas (2004) suggests that the program teaches the following lessons:

- Reminds students of their rights and responsibilities as they engage in problem solving about their instructional program on an ongoing basis

- Uses strategies such as casual hallway encounters and informal lunch discussions; reminds students that the gifted education staff and counselors are available to support them

- Provides information to parents about their advocacy role through a newsletter and group meetings; informs classroom teachers that parents are being encouraged to be advocates

- Ensures that teachers and counselors are responsive when students use their self-advocacy skills to request instructional modifications

- Works with students annually to assess their learning profiles and to compare and contrast results over time

Source: Information from Douglas, D. (2004). Self-advocacy: Encouraging students to become partners in differentiation. *Roeper Review, 26*(4), 223–228.

Steenbergen-Hu and Moon (2011) conducted a meta-analysis of the effect of acceleration on high-ability learners' outcomes and found that acceleration had a positive impact on academic achievement and a slightly lower but still positive effect on social-emotional development. Importantly, Lee, Olszweski-Kubilius, and Peternel (2010) found that acceleration in math was particularly beneficial to gifted minority students.

One way to accelerate students without moving them up a grade or class sequence is to **compact the curriculum**. Compacting involves identifying the aspects of the content that a student has already mastered and provide instruction only on the content that the student has not yet mastered (Rogers, 2007). A variation of compacting is the "most difficult first" strategy. Instead of doing all problems or activities on a task, students complete the most difficult tasks first (as identified in advance by the teacher). If they get the most difficult problems or activities correct, they move on to the next activity or task. If they do not, they complete the entire assignment. This variation allows for curriculum compacting on a day-to-day and lesson-to-lesson basis. Teachers often combine these modifications to the scope and sequence of the curriculum with universal design. Students' IEPs (as in Graham's school district) or their individualized programs should identify modifications and universal design features.

PLANNING FOR UNIVERSAL DESIGN FOR LEARNING

Two strategies that can effectively adapt or augment the curriculum for students who are gifted include (1) the use of curriculum extension techniques and (2) the application of cognitive taxonomies to the design of activity, lesson, and unit plans. **Curriculum extension** refers to efforts to expand the breadth and depth of coverage of a given topic.

BOX 16.4

MY VOICE

What It Means to Be Gifted

My name is Graham Wehmeyer. I'm in the ninth grade and I have been in the gifted education program since second grade. Being in this program has really helped me challenge myself, and it has opened me up to a lot of really good ideas and ways of thinking. I believe that every school should have some sort of a gifted program.

For me personally, being gifted means that I need something more from school than what is taught in the general classroom.

Graham Wehmeyer displays the electronic circuit board he created in his 8th grade curriculum-enrichment program.

I need to be challenged mentally so I can learn. Being in gifted education means that I can push myself sometimes, but I can still have fun at the same time. Also, the program is fun because we get to do a lot of neat projects, and the kids in the program usually have a lot of the same interests as me. I know that if I weren't in the gifted program, school would be a lot more boring than it already is.

Because I am in the gifted program, I get a lot of opportunities that other students don't. For example, in sixth grade, I got to test out of sixth-grade math and skip to seventh-grade math, along with about twelve other kids. This kept me a lot more interested in the work and prevented me from getting too bored in school. Additionally, I have had many opportunities to investigate careers that I might want to go into, so I am a lot more informed on that subject than most students are at my age. While I am in gifted education, I have an IEP, which sets year-long academic goals. These goals help me manage my time and learn how to set reasonable goals. Another opportunity is that in eighth grade I got the whole semester to investigate five colleges that I might want to go to. It helped me learn a lot more about the colleges I investigated and about the entire higher education system.

Personally, I really appreciate receiving gifted education services because they have made my experience at school a lot better. Additionally, I think that the gifted teachers, at least the teachers I have had, are really nice, fun, and well qualified for their position. So far, my experience in the program has been an immensely positive one, and I hope that the next four years will be too!

—Graham Wehmeyer

IEP TIP

Although a student's teacher will be the person who develops lesson plans using cognitive taxonomies, planning to use cognitive taxonomies to differentiate instruction begins with the IEP team or its equivalent. Teams can and should consider the design of content units using cognitive taxonomies.

Students who are gifted learn content more quickly than their peers do and do not need as much repetition, so curriculum extension activities should not simply repeat the same task but challenge them at a higher level.

Teachers can teach their students at a higher level using cognitive taxonomies. **Cognitive taxonomies** are ordered lists of cognitive skills or activities that can be used to differentiate expectations. The most familiar taxonomy is the one developed by Bloom and associates (1956). Bloom's taxonomy categorizes the cognitive skills that students use when achieving their learning goals. As students ascend Bloom's taxonomy, they face increasingly complex cognitive demands.

Teachers can differentiate what they expect from students by designing lesson and activity objectives that range from less to more complex. They also can extend the curriculum for gifted students by having students engage in activities that move up the taxonomy from "applying information and knowledge to solve novel problems" to "synthesizing information to create new patterns or structures." These activities will teach students the skills they need to be more creative and to develop effective thinking skills.

PLANNING FOR OTHER EDUCATIONAL NEEDS

It is not always easy being gifted. If schools do not plan for and implement practices such as differentiated instruction, acceleration, compaction, curriculum extension, and cognitive taxonomies, gifted students will be bored.

Autonomous Learning Model

Like problem-based learning, the autonomous learning model develops independent, self-directed learners who are not just exceptionally intelligent but also well developed in social, emotional, and cognitive domains. The model includes five areas in which students receive support and enrichment experiences:

1. *Orientation:* understanding giftedness, talent, intelligence, and creativity

2. *Individual development:* inter/intrapersonal skills, learning skills, technology, college and career involvement, organizational skills, productivity

3. *Enrichment:* explorations, investigations, cultural activities, service, adventure trips

4. *Seminars:* futuristic, problem-based, controversial, general interest, advanced knowledge

5. *In-depth study:* individual projects, group projects, mentorships, presentations, assessments

The strength of this program lies in its flexibility. As students and teachers work together, roles change and adapt. The teacher may become the student and the learner may become a facilitator of others' learning. By changing roles, all students develop and appreciate their own strengths and become independent learners.

There are other aspects of being gifted that educators should address to ward off potential social-emotional problems. As we have noted, students who are gifted tend to be perfectionists and highly competitive. Their advanced cognitive abilities may make their age-appropriate social-emotional skills seem immature.

One response to their needs is the **autonomous learner model (ALM)** (Betts & Kercher, 1999), which assists students in dealing with the social-emotional issues that might accompany their giftedness. This model is effective for helping elementary through secondary school students explore the social-emotional aspects of being gifted and enable them to become lifelong learners. Students involved with the ALM do the following (Betts & Kercher, 1999):

- Explore what it means to be gifted
- Explore what intelligence and creativity mean
- Explore aspects of their personal/social development
- Consider their strengths and limitations
- Learn organizational skills
- Engage in self-directed study about topics in which they are interested
- Learn the importance of autonomous lifelong learning

The activities in the autonomous learning model can benefit all students. Importantly, Betts and Carey (2010) have illustrated the fit between the ALM and response to intervention (RTI). As noted, the dimensions of the ALM can be infused into all tiers of an RTI framework, with the intensity of supports varying among the tiers. Both RTI and ALM focus on cognitive, academic, emotional, and physical needs of students and emphasize student autonomy and self-direction. Box 16.5 provides more detailed information about the ALM.

Using Effective Instructional Strategies

EARLY CHILDHOOD STUDENTS: MULTIPLE INTELLIGENCES

You've already examined Figure 16.1, which describes eight areas in Gardner's multidimensional model of intelligence and listed the typical characteristics and distinctive features common in gifted individuals. The theory of multiple intelligences (Gardner, 2011) has the potential to fundamentally reshape schools. Learning activities can reflect

The multiple intelligence theory encourages learning in real environments.

student strengths across the eight areas of potential giftedness. Instead of just presenting information in words through texts or lectures, teachers use physical and social experiences, music, and engagement with the natural world. Sounds a lot like universal design, doesn't it? In fact, in schools incorporating multiple-intelligences theory, there is a "school-community broker," a person who searches for educational opportunities for students within the wider community. In one school where the school day has been designed within this framework, students spend half of their day at school studying traditional subjects through project-oriented learning activities and the other half in the community exploring contexts in which they can apply what they have learned in school (Armstrong, 2009). John identified project-oriented learning as a key part of his learning and development in elementary school.

In Project Spectrum (Chen et al., 2009), Gardner and his colleagues applied his model to early childhood and early elementary education. There, teachers identify and serve different types of giftedness, ensuring that instruction and content correlate with their students' aptitudes, interests, and abilities and that assessment covers the spectrum of abilities (Chen & McNamee, 2007). The teachers look for different types of giftedness, plan activities specific to these areas, and then provide options for each child. Twice a year, they fill out a strengths checklist for each child.

For example, during a study of dinosaurs, children with a strong spatial orientation might want to know how big the dinosaurs were. To find out, educators might project enlarged pictures onto the school wall to help students grasp the concept of size. By contrast, children with a linguistic orientation might develop questions to ask a paleontologist. Children with artistic talents might use papier-mâché to make life-sized features of the dinosaurs, while students with a musical ability might write and sing songs about dinosaurs.

ELEMENTARY AND MIDDLE SCHOOL STUDENTS: SCHOOLWIDE ENRICHMENT

To address gifted students' unique cognitive characteristics and to promote their motivation, attention, and social-emotional development, teachers match the content of their courses to students' aptitudes, sophistication, and interests. Often they use enrichment strategies to engage students. The term *enrichment* refers to curricular and program delivery services that

- Add instruction in learning domains not found within the typical curriculum
- Use more challenging or complex material to present content
- Use an expanded range of instructional strategies
- Teach critical-thinking and problem-solving skills (Robinson & Campbell, 2010)

Renzulli and Reis (2010) developed and implemented an enrichment model known as the **schoolwide enrichment model (SEM)**. Its major goal is to promote challenging, high-end learning by creating services that can be integrated across the general education curriculum to assist all students, not just those who are gifted. There are three types of enrichment approaches within the schoolwide enrichment program. Type I enrichment exposes students to a wide variety of topics, disciplines, occupations, hobbies, people, places, and events that ordinarily would not be included in the general education curriculum. For example, Type I experiences may involve community speakers, demonstrations, performances, multimedia presentations, or other illustrative formats.

Type II enrichment focuses on resources that promote creative-thinking, problem-solving, and critical-thinking skills. This kind of enrichment consists of how-to-learn skills, including those for written, oral, and visual communication. Other Type II skills are specific to a students' particular talents and interests.

When a student becomes interested in pursuing a self-selected area of interest and commits the time necessary for this endeavor, Type III enrichment occurs. It consists of the following:

1. Providing opportunities for applying interests
2. Acquiring advanced-level understanding of the content and process used within particular disciplines
3. Developing authentic products
4. Developing self-directed learning skills
5. Empowering the student to control learning through organization and feelings of accomplishment

The Southeast Elementary School in Mansfield, Connecticut, has implemented the SEM model for fifteen years. Principal Norma Fisher-Doiron observes that in the era of school accountability it is even "more critical than ever to address the needs of high-ability students and to focus on the strengths and talents of all of our students" (Fisher-Doiron & Irvine, 2009, p. 26). She and enrichment teacher Susan Irvine particularly value the SEM focus on teaching critical-thinking and problem-solving skills and addressing student interests and talents. Sounds a lot like self-determination, doesn't it? "It is our strong belief," says Fisher-Doiron and Irvine, "that students will reach higher levels of success in their classrooms and on high stakes testing if we differentiate and enrich curriculum" and enable students to "think creatively, solve problems, and focus on their strengths and talents" (p. 26).

One of the tools that teachers use in SEM and other enrichment models is the Internet. Box 16.6 provides an overview of how to use the Internet to conduct WebQuests.

SECONDARY AND TRANSITION STUDENTS: PROMOTING CREATIVITY AND CRITICAL-THINKING SKILLS

Students who are gifted are highly original, independent, curious, motivated, and attracted to complexity. They are creative and effective critical thinkers. It would be wrong, however, for you to assume that students who are gifted are already highly skilled in creativity and critical thinking and do not need instruction in these areas. Instead, you should focus on enhancing your students' innate strengths by honing their creative talents and thinking abilities. According to Davis, Rimm, and Siegle (2010), you can promote their creativity by

- Fostering creative attitudes
- Improving student understanding of creativity
- Practicing and exercising creativity
- Teaching critical- and creative-thinking skills
- Engaging students in creative activities

McCollister and Sayler (2010) have suggested four useful ways to integrate critical thinking into day-to-day instructional activities. First, teachers should include problem-solving opportunities that allow gifted students to apply critical-thinking skills. Second, teachers need to develop skills related to critical questioning so that they can enhance the accuracy or clarity of students' responses without simply telling students what is correct. Questions such as "Could you elaborate on that point?" or "Could you express your point in a different way?" (McCollister & Sayler, 2010, p. 43) force students to apply critical-thinking skills to hone their responses and consider other options. Third, teachers need to teach their students to evaluate the sources from which they derive content information. You should teach your students to consider whether information comes from primary or secondary sources and, particularly in the Internet-age, to evaluate the credibility of the information. Finally, you should infuse opportunities for decision making into your

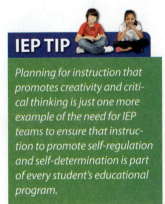

IEP TIP

Planning for instruction that promotes creativity and critical thinking is just one more example of the need for IEP teams to ensure that instruction to promote self-regulation and self-determination is part of every student's educational program.

BOX 16.6

UNIVERSAL DESIGN FOR PROGRESS

WebQuests

Today most schools and many homes have Internet connections. In classrooms all across the United States, teachers and students are integrating the content of web pages into their daily instruction. At the same time, educators often feel challenged by the amount of information available on the Internet and wonder how to apply specific resources as they teach.

What Is the Technology?

A WebQuest is an inquiry-oriented activity in which most or all of the information that students use comes from the web. WebQuests are designed to use students' time well; focus on using information rather than looking for it; and support students' analysis, synthesis, and evaluation skills. WebQuests are appealing because they provide structure and guidance for both students and teachers. The idea of promoting higher-level thinking skills by making good use of computer access resonates with many educators.

What Do We Do with It?

A WebQuest allows teachers and students to create activities around web-based resources. Instead of simply accessing or using a website, the student is shown how to interact with the site(s), what activities to undertake, and how to evaluate success with the site(s). Follow these steps:

1. Most WebQuests begin with an introduction to the purpose of the quest. For example, students working on a WebQuest pertaining to space exploration might navigate to pages that provide information about life on other planets, going on a mission to the moon or Mars, or mapping the course of Halley's comet.

2. Next the teacher assigns a task related to the content of the website(s). An outline tells the student how he will accomplish the task. For students working with a space exploration theme, tasks might identify how to prepare for a shuttle launch, lead an exploration team to discover which planet might be best for potential human settlement, or head a design team to place a robot on Mars.

3. The next links in the WebQuest describe the process to be used to complete the task (e.g., preparing for a shuttle launch) and the resources available. Using scaffolding (the process of building one skill on top of another), the student uses clear steps, resources, and tools for organizing information from the WebQuest.

4. Each WebQuest includes an evaluation component that identifies the specific criteria students must meet to satisfy performance and content standards.

5. Finally, the WebQuest conclusion brings closure to the task and encourages the student to reflect on her learning experience.

You can find more about WebQuests at http://webquest.org/. The website http://webquest.sdsu.edu/adapting/ provides helpful suggestions for adapting existing WebQuests for your use. As with other materials, it's important to seek permission to use existing resources such as WebQuests.

---

students' curriculum in order to promote their critical thinking and enable them to learn to "think like experts" (p. 47).

Including Students Who Are Gifted and Talented

Within the field of gifted education, there is an ongoing debate regarding student placement. On the one hand, IDEA's principle of the least restrictive environment (access to the general curriculum and inclusion) emphasizes student education in the general education classroom. Approaches such as the schoolwide enrichment model provide proven ways to educate students who are gifted in the general education classroom, to the benefit of all children (Renzulli & Reis, 2010). On the other hand, some leaders within the field of gifted education have expressed grave concern about the lack of curriculum breadth, depth, and specificity in many general education classrooms (Pfeiffer, 2003). They have underscored the need to consider a broad range of options:

- *Cluster grouping.* Assign three to six students who are gifted and talented to the same general education classroom so that they can work together.

- *All-school enrichment programs.* Address the top 20 percent of students in a school through special-interest groups, specialized instruction in small groups, and mentoring on individual projects (Renzulli & Reis, 2010).

- *Acceleration*. Students start kindergarten or college early, skipping one or more grades in order to experience higher levels of instruction, and/or attend a higher-grade-level program for part of the school day (National Association for Gifted Children, n.d.).

John's family has experienced multiple models of gifted education. His mom and dad, Linda and Charles, were both accelerated. John and his siblings have been in public- and private-school gifted programs and have received self-contained and integrated supports in the classroom. All have benefited from diverse options that can be individualized to each student's needs, strengths, and talents.

Box 16.7 provides tips about practices that will help you enhance your students' success in the general education classroom. As you read the tips, bear in mind that you must understand each student's needs in order to achieve the best match between his needs and the curriculum.

Co-teaching, which involves a general and special education teacher working together, is often an essential element of including students who are gifted in the general education classroom.

BOX 16.7	INCLUSION TIPS			
	What You Might See	**What You Might Be Tempted to Do**	**Alternate Responses**	**Ways to Include Peers in the Process**
Behavior	The student asks so many questions that there is time for nothing else.	Tell him to be quiet and pay attention to his work.	Begin a dialogue journal. Ask him to write down his questions. Then research and discuss some of the answers together.	Have an all-class "Challenge Box," where students can write questions they think are difficult. Enable the students who are gifted to work on these questions in small groups with their peers.
Social interactions	She is unable to see another person's perspectives.	Avoid calling on her in class in order to avoid potential conflict.	Build on her leadership skills by giving her responsibility for leading a class discussion of major concepts.	Have her work with small groups, teaching the other students to be discussion facilitators.
Educational performance	He is very bored in class and is refusing to do homework.	Discipline him for inattentiveness or give additional work to reinforce the lesson.	Modify the scope and sequence of the curriculum through acceleration or compacting to create more challenge.	Explore the possibility of this student attending one or more classes in the next grade.
Classroom attitudes	She is achieving slightly below grade level, but has unusual talents related to leadership and emotional intelligence.	Assume that she is being academically lazy and give her extra work to try to get her up to grade level.	Recognize her gifts and strengths and work with the school principal to find a school citizenship project for which she can provide leadership.	Identify other students with similar talents and get them involved in a cooperative citizenship project.

Assessing Students' Progress

MEASURING STUDENTS' PROGRESS

Progress in the General Curriculum

After identifying a student as gifted, you and other educators evaluate her progress by measuring performance on goals. In addition, you can place some of the evaluation responsibility on students themselves. For example, according to John, one of the most important lessons he learned in middle school and beyond was to take responsibility for his learning, his schedule, and ultimately his life.

Product Evaluation. Teachers commonly base academic assessment on written products of students' learning, which are often tests. The results of these tests can help teachers track grades and learning, but they do not provide teachers or students with tools for understanding students' learning processes. So you and other good teachers should use product measures not just for grading but also for helping students who are gifted record their own progress and compete with themselves rather than with classmates. In addition, use product measures to assess the thoroughness of your teaching, looking for areas that need additional or different instruction.

Process Evaluation. You should also evaluate a student's learning process, not just the product (McCollister & Sayler, 2010). When you do a process evaluation, you observe and learn from a student's comments or work to assess whether he is learning critical skills such as problem solving and critical thinking. This may require you to take notes on your students' strengths and weaknesses in solving problems and carrying out various learning activities. These notes become an excellent resource during parent-teacher conferences. Likewise, reflective assessment or evaluation involves teaching students to become aware of and monitor the process of their own learning. Figure 16.2 shows how teacher and student product and process assessments can work together on the student's behalf.

Progress in Addressing Other Educational Needs

One of the objectives of the autonomous learning model (which you learned about earlier in this chapter) is to teach students who are gifted to become independent thinkers and learners. Learning contracts can support this goal and help students evaluate their own progress toward achieving it.

FIGURE 16.2

Four areas of assessment

	Product	Process
Teacher uses	*Written Tests/Projects* • Teacher's grade book • Report card • How student compares	*Kid Watching: Teacher Portfolios* • Teacher's understanding of student • Teacher's instructional planning • Parent conferences
Student uses	*Written Tests/Projects* • Student understanding of what still needs to be learned • Review of material • How student compares to peers in the class	*Reflective Evaluation: Student Portfolios* • Active participation and responsibility in the assessment process • Development of self-monitoring strategies that use higher-order thinking skills

---

Learning contracts are agreements between a student and her teacher. They describe in detail the outcome of the student's learning, the product(s) that will provide evidence of that outcome, and, if necessary, the criteria for determining whether the products are of acceptable quality. The contracts also specify timelines, resources, and, importantly, reinforcement.

Learning contracts are effective with all students across many content areas. Their effectiveness derives in part from the fact that they are individualized and child-centered and promote independence and autonomy (Greenwood & McCabe, 2008). These contracts are important components of high-quality gifted education programs and are just as important as differentiated instruction, acceleration, and compacting.

As you know from reading this chapter, students from certain racial and ethnic groups are underrepresented in programs for gifted and talented students. Teachers should hold high academic and behavioral expectations for all students, guard against judging students and their families as a function of socioeconomic status or ethnicity, and incorporate multicultural and diversity issues into their classes whenever possible.

MAKING ACCOMMODATIONS FOR ASSESSMENT

Given that students who are gifted and talented achieve at high levels and have high general intellectual ability, they usually do not need assessment accommodations. That is not true, however, if they also have a disability, such as a learning disability, attention-deficit/hyperactivity disorder, or physical or sensory disability. Those students may need some of the same accommodations discussed in the chapters about those disabilities.

Although many students who are gifted do not need specific accommodations, they still warrant your special attention. As you have learned, they tend to be very competitive and expect to perform highly. They may feel additional pressure to do well on standardized tests and, as a result, may not perform as well as they could otherwise do. You can help your students keep the testing situation in perspective and reinforce that they should do as well as they can but not push too hard.

Among the standardized tests that gifted students will take are those used for college admission, typically the Scholastic Aptitude Test (SAT) or the American College Test (ACT). Students may feel extreme pressure to succeed on these examinations, particularly if they are working to qualify for exclusive colleges and scholarships. Whether a test is a state assessment or a college examination, you can teach your students skills such as deep breathing to help them relax and perform well. Basic preparation skills, such as pacing out study sessions instead of cramming all at once and being well rested before taking a test, are also important.

ADDRESSING THE PROFESSIONAL STANDARDS

The following Council for Exceptional Children (CEC) Common Core Knowledge and Skills are addressed in this chapter through the content and concepts we discuss. See the Appendix for a full listing of these Knowledge and Skill statements:

ICC2K1, ICC2K2, ICC2K4, ICC2K5, ICC2K6, ICC3K1, ICC3K2, ICC4S1, ICC4S2, ICC4S3, ICC4S5, ICC5K3, ICC5K4, ICC5S4, ICC5S7, ICC5S9, ICC7K2, ICC7K4, ICC7S3, ICC7S6, ICC7S9, ICC7S13, ICC8S2, ICC8S6, ICC8S8

Summary

IDENTIFYING STUDENTS WHO ARE GIFTED AND TALENTED

- Characteristics of students who are gifted include high general intellect, creativity, leadership ability, and visual or performing artistry. These students require special services not ordinarily provided by the public schools or covered under IDEA.
- Forty-one states have a definition of *gifted and talented,* and thirty-two states have a mandate to provide educational services and supports to students who are gifted and talented.
- High intellectual ability is the characteristic of gifted and talented students that most schools recognize.
- When IQ test scores are equated with giftedness, the top 2 to 3 percent of the general population is considered gifted.
- Students from certain racial and ethnic backgrounds are underrepresented in gifted and talented programs.
- Many students who are gifted show positive social and emotional adjustment.
- Giftedness originates from an interaction of environmental and biological factors.

EVALUATING STUDENTS WHO ARE GIFTED AND TALENTED

- Many gifted educators believe that it is appropriate to expand identification criteria beyond high intellectual ability to ensure cultural appropriateness for students from culturally and linguistically diverse backgrounds.
- DISCOVER is a performance-based, research-validated assessment for identifying giftedness in students, including those from diverse backgrounds.
- The Torrance Tests of Creative Thinking are a valid and reliable way to assess the strengths and needs of students in the area of creativity.

DESIGNING AN APPROPRIATE EDUCATION

- Students who are gifted benefit from differentiated instruction; however, many classroom teachers believe they do not have the time or expertise to implement a differentiated curriculum.

- Modifications to the scope and sequence of a student's educational program through acceleration and compacting can ensure that students who are gifted have access to a challenging curriculum.
- Extending the curriculum through the use of cognitive taxonomies can ensure that unit, lesson, and activity objectives are appropriate for students who are gifted or talented.
- Addressing the social-emotional needs of students who are gifted is critical to promoting their success. One useful strategy is the autonomous learning model.

USING EFFECTIVE INSTRUCTIONAL STRATEGIES

- Gardner's multiple intelligences theory has a direct and significant impact on education. As with universal design, schools that focus on the multiple intelligences can ensure that a wider array of students succeed, beginning as early as preschool.
- The schoolwide enrichment model provides an effective way to implement instructional strategies across a campus, ensuring that students who are gifted can be educated in the general education classroom.
- Even though students who are gifted are already ahead of their peers in many ways, they can still learn important skills related to creativity and critical thinking.

INCLUDING STUDENTS WHO ARE GIFTED AND TALENTED

- Leaders in gifted education disagree about the appropriateness of the general education classroom curriculum for students who are gifted and talented.

ASSESSING STUDENTS' PROGRESS

- Product and process evaluations and learning contracts are ways in which students who are gifted can be involved in evaluating progress in their educational programs.

Appendix

CEC Knowledge and Skill Base for All Beginning Special Education Teachers of Students in Individualized General Curriculums

These standards align most closely with a mild/moderate licensure framework. Implicit in all of the standards is their focus on individuals with disabilities whose education is based on an individualized general curriculum.

STANDARD I: FOUNDATIONS

ICC1K1:   Models, theories, philosophies, and research methods that provide the basis for special education practice.

ICC1K2:   Laws, policies, and ethical principles regarding behavior management planning and implementation.

ICC1K3:   Relationship of special education to the organization and function of educational agencies.

ICC1K4:   Rights and responsibilities of students, parents, teachers, and other professionals, and schools related to exceptional learning needs.

ICC1K5:   Issues in definition and identification of individuals with exceptional learning needs, including those from culturally and linguistically diverse backgrounds.

ICC1K6:   Issues, assurances and due process rights related to assessment, eligibility, and placement within a continuum of services.

ICC1K7:   Family systems and the role of families in the educational process.

ICC1K8:   Historical points of view and contribution of culturally diverse groups.

ICC1K9:   Impact of the dominant culture on shaping schools and the individuals who study and work in them.

ICC1K10: Potential impact of differences in values, languages, and customs that can exist between the home and school.

ICC1S1:   Articulate personal philosophy of special education.

GC1K1:   Definitions and issues related to the identification of individuals with disabilities.

GC1K2:   Models and theories of deviance and behavior problems.

GC1K3:   Historical foundations, classic studies, major contributors, major legislation, and current issues related to knowledge and practice.

GC1K4:   The legal, judicial, and educational systems to assist individuals with disabilities.

GC1K5:   Continuum of placement and services available for individuals with disabilities.

GC1K6:   Laws and policies related to provision of specialized health care in educational settings.

GC1K7:   Factors that influence the over-representation of culturally/linguistically diverse students in programs for individuals with disabilities.

GC1K8:   Principles of normalization and concept of least restrictive environment.

GC1K9:   Theory of reinforcement techniques in serving individuals with disabilities.

Skills   None in addition to Common Core

STANDARD II: DEVELOPMENT AND CHARACTERISTICS OF LEARNERS

ICC2K1:   Typical and atypical human growth and development.

ICC2K2:   Educational implications of characteristics of various exceptionalities.

ICC2K3:   Characteristics and effects of the cultural and environmental milieu of the individual with exceptional learning needs and the family.

ICC2K4:   Family systems and the role of families in supporting development.

ICC2K5:   Similarities and differences of individuals with and without exceptional learning needs.

ICC2K6:   Similarities and differences among individuals with exceptional learning needs.

ICC2K7:   Effects of various medications on individuals with exceptional learning needs.

GC2K1:   Etiology and diagnosis related to various theoretical approaches.

GC2K2:   Impact of sensory impairments, physical and health disabilities on individuals, families and society.

GC2K3:   Etiologies and medical aspects of conditions affecting individuals with disabilities.

GC2K4:   Psychological and social-emotional characteristics of individuals with disabilities.

GC2K5:   Common etiologies and the impact of sensory disabilities on learning and experience.

GC2K6:   Types and transmission routes of infectious disease.

Skills   None in addition to Common Core

STANDARD III: INDIVIDUAL LEARNING DIFFERENCES

ICC3K1:   Effects an exceptional condition(s) can have on an individual's life.

ICC3K2:   Impact of learners' academic and social abilities, attitudes, interests, and values on instruction and career development.

ICC3K3:   Variations in beliefs, traditions, and values across and within cultures and their effects on relationships among individuals with exceptional learning needs, family, and schooling.

ICC3K4:   Cultural perspectives influencing the relationships among families, schools, and communities as related to instruction.

ICC3K5:   Differing ways of learning of individuals with exceptional learning needs including those from culturally diverse backgrounds and strategies for addressing these differences.

GC3K1:   Impact of disabilities on auditory and information processing skills.

GC3S1:   Relate levels of support to the needs of the individual.

STANDARD IV: INSTRUCTIONAL STRATEGIES

ICC4K1:   Evidence-based practices validated for specific characteristics of learners and settings.

ICC4S1:   Use strategies to facilitate integration into various settings.

ICC4S2:   Teach individuals to use self-assessment, problem solving, and other cognitive strategies to meet their needs.

ICC4S3:   Select, adapt, and use instructional strategies and materials according to characteristics of the individual with exceptional learning needs.

ICC4S4:   Use strategies to facilitate maintenance and generalization of skills across learning environments.

ICC4S5:   Use procedures to increase the individual's self-awareness, self-management, self-control, self-reliance, and self-esteem.

ICC4S6:   Use strategies that promote successful transitions for individuals with exceptional learning needs.

GC4K1:   Sources of specialized materials, curricula, and resources for individuals with disabilities.

GC4K2:   Strategies to prepare for and take tests.

GC4K3:   Advantages and limitations of instructional strategies and practices for teaching individuals with disabilities.

GC4K4:   Prevention and intervention strategies for individuals at-risk for a disability.

GC4K5:   Strategies for integrating student initiated learning experiences into ongoing instruction.

GC4K6:   Methods for increasing accuracy and proficiency in math calculations and applications.

GC4K7:   Methods for guiding individuals in identifying and organizing critical content.

GC4S1:	Use research-supported methods for academic and non-academic instruction of individuals with disabilities.
GC4S2:	Use strategies from multiple theoretical approaches for individuals with disabilities.
GC4S3:	Teach learning strategies and study skills to acquire academic content.
GC4S4:	Use reading methods appropriate to individuals with disabilities.
GC4S5:	Use methods to teach mathematics appropriate to the individuals with disabilities.
GC4S6:	Modify pace of instruction and provide organizational cures.
GC4S7:	Use appropriate adaptations and technology for all individuals with disabilities.
GC4S8:	Resources and techniques used to transition individuals with disabilities into and out of school and post-school environments.
GC4S9:	Use a variety of nonaversive techniques to control targeted behavior and maintain attention of individuals with disabilities.
GC4S10:	Identify and teach basic structures and relationships within and across curricula.
GC4S11:	Use instructional methods to strengthen and compensate for deficits in perception, comprehension, memory, and retrieval.
GC4S12:	Use responses and errors to guide instructional decisions and provide feedback to learners.
GC4S13:	Identify and teach essential concepts, vocabulary, and content across the general curriculum.
GC4S14:	Implement systematic instruction in teaching reading comprehension and monitoring strategies.
GC4S15:	Teach strategies for organizing and composing written products.
GC4S16:	Implement systematic instruction to teach accuracy, fluency, and comprehension in content area reading and written language.

STANDARD V: LEARNING ENVIRONMENTS AND SOCIAL INTERACTIONS

ICC5K1:	Demands of learning environments.
ICC5K2:	Basic classroom management theories and strategies for individuals with exceptional learning needs.
ICC5K3:	Effective management of teaching and learning.
ICC5K4:	Teacher attitudes and behaviors that influence behavior of individuals with exceptional learning needs.
ICC5K5:	Social skills needed for educational and other environments.
ICC5K6:	Strategies for crisis prevention and intervention.
ICC5K7:	Strategies for preparing individuals to live harmoniously and productively in a culturally diverse world.
ICC5K8:	Ways to create learning environments that allow individuals to retain and appreciate their own and each others' respective language and cultural heritage.
ICC5K9:	Ways specific cultures are negatively stereotyped.
ICC5K10:	Strategies used by diverse populations to cope with a legacy of former and continuing racism.
ICC5S1:	Create a safe, equitable, positive, and supportive learning environment in which diversities are valued.
ICC5S2:	Identify realistic expectations for personal and social behavior in various settings.
ICC5S3:	Identify supports needed for integration into various program placements.
ICC5S4:	Design learning environments that encourage active participation in individual and group activities.
ICC5S5:	Modify the learning environment to manage behaviors.
ICC5S6:	Use performance data and information from all stakeholders to make or suggest modifications in learning environments.
ICC5S7:	Establish and maintain rapport with individuals with and without exceptional learning needs.
ICC5S8:	Teach self-advocacy.
ICC5S9:	Create an environment that encourages self-advocacy and increased independence.
ICC5S10:	Use effective and varied behavior management strategies.
ICC5S11:	Use the least intensive behavior management strategy consistent with the needs of the individual with exceptional learning needs.

ICC5S12:	Design and manage daily routines.
ICC5S13:	Organize, develop, and sustain learning environments that support positive intra-cultural and intercultural experiences.
ICC5S14:	Mediate controversial intercultural issues among students within the learning environment in ways that enhance any culture, group, or person.
ICC5S15:	Structure, direct, and support the activities of paraeducators, volunteers, and tutors.
ICC5S16:	Use universal precautions.
GC5K1:	Barriers to accessibility and acceptance of individuals with disabilities.
GC5K2:	Adaptation of the physical environment to provide optimal learning opportunities for individuals with disabilities.
GC5K3:	Methods for ensuring individual academic success in one-to-one, small-group, and large-group settings.

Skills

GC5S1:	Provide instruction in community-based settings.
GC5S2:	Use and maintain assistive technologies.
GC5S3:	Plan instruction in a variety of educational settings.
GC5S4:	Teach individuals with disabilities to give and receive meaningful feedback from peers and adults.
GC5S5:	Use skills in problem solving and conflict resolution.
GC5S6:	Establish a consistent classroom routine for individuals with disabilities.

STANDARD VI: COMMUNICATION

ICC6K1:	Effects of cultural and linguistic differences on growth and development.
ICC6K2:	Characteristics of one's own culture and use of language and the ways in which these can differ from other cultures and uses of languages.
ICC6K3:	Ways of behaving and communicating among cultures that can lead to misinterpretation and misunderstanding.
ICC6K4:	Augmentative and assistive communication strategies.
ICC6S1:	Use strategies to support and enhance communication skills of individuals with exceptional learning needs.
ICC6S2:	Use communication strategies and resources to facilitate understanding of subject matter for students whose primary language is not the dominant language.
GC6K1:	Impact of language development and listening comprehension on academic and non-academic learning of individuals with disabilities.
GC6K2:	Communication and social interaction alternatives for individuals who are nonspeaking.
GC6K3:	Typical language development and how that may differ for individuals with learning disabilities.
GC6S1:	Enhance vocabulary development.
GC6S2:	Teach strategies for spelling accuracy and generalization.
GC6S3:	Teach individuals with disabilities to monitor for errors in oral and written language.
GC6S4:	Teach methods and strategies for producing legible documents.
GC6S5:	Plan instruction on the use of alternative and augmentative communication systems.

STANDARD VII: INSTRUCTIONAL PLANNING

ICC7K1:	Theories and research that form the basis of curriculum development and instructional practice.
ICC7K2:	Scope and sequences of general and special curricula.
ICC7K3:	National, state or provincial, and local curricula standards.
ICC7K4:	Technology for planning and managing the teaching and learning environment.
ICC7K5:	Roles and responsibilities of the paraeducator related to instruction, intervention, and direct service.
ICC7S1:	Identify and prioritize areas of the general curriculum and accommodations for individuals with exceptional learning needs.
ICC7S2:	Develop and implement comprehensive, longitudinal individualized programs in collaboration with team members.

ICC7S3:	Involve the individual and family in setting instructional goals and monitoring progress.
ICC7S4:	Use functional assessments to develop intervention plans.
ICC7S5:	Use task analysis.
ICC7S6:	Sequence, implement, and evaluate individualized learning objectives.
ICC7S7:	Integrate affective, social, and life skills with academic curricula.
ICC7S8:	Develop and select instructional content, resources, and strategies that respond to cultural, linguistic, and gender differences.
ICC7S9:	Incorporate and implement instructional and assistive technology into the educational program.
ICC7S10:	Prepare lesson plans.
ICC7S11:	Prepare and organize materials to implement daily lesson plans.
ICC7S12:	Use instructional time effectively.
ICC7S13:	Make responsive adjustments to instruction based on continual observations.
ICC7S14:	Prepare individuals to exhibit self-enhancing behavior in response to societal attitudes and actions.
ICC7S15:	Evaluate and modify instructional practices in response to ongoing assessment data.
GC7K1:	Integrate academic instruction and behavior management for individuals and groups with disabilities.
GC7K2:	Model career, vocational, and transition programs for individuals with disabilities.
GC7K3:	Interventions and services for children who may be at risk for learning disabilities.
GC7K4:	Relationships among disabilities and reading instruction.
GC7S1:	Plan and implement individualized reinforcement systems and environmental modifications at levels equal to the intensity of the behavior.
GC7S2:	Select and use specialized instructional strategies appropriate to the abilities and needs of the individual.
GC7S3:	Plan and implement age and ability appropriate instruction for individuals with disabilities.
GC7S4:	Select, design, and use technology, materials and resources required to educate individuals whose disabilities interfere with communication.
GC7S5:	Interpret sensory, mobility, reflex, and perceptual information to create or adapt appropriate learning plans.
GC7S6:	Design and implement instructional programs that address independent living and career education for individuals.
GC7S7:	Design and implement curriculum and instructional strategies for medical self-management procedures.
GC7S8:	Design, implement, and evaluate instructional programs that enhance social participation across environments.

STANDARD VIII: ASSESSMENT

ICC8K1:	Basic terminology used in assessment.
ICC8K2:	Legal provisions and ethical principles regarding assessment of individuals.
ICC8K3:	Screening, pre-referral, referral, and classification procedures.
ICC8K4:	Use and limitations of assessment instruments.
ICC8K5:	National, state or provincial, and local accommodations and modifications.
ICC8S1:	Gather relevant background information.
ICC8S2:	Administer nonbiased formal and informal assessments.
ICC8S3:	Use technology to conduct assessments.
ICC8S4:	Develop or modify individualized assessment strategies.
ICC8S5:	Interpret information from formal and informal assessments.
ICC8S6:	Use assessment information in making eligibility, program, and placement decisions for individuals with exceptional learning needs, including those from culturally and/or linguistically diverse backgrounds.
ICC8S7:	Report assessment results to all stakeholders using effective communication skills.
ICC8S8:	Evaluate instruction and monitor progress of individuals with exceptional learning needs.
ICC8S9:	Develop or modify individualized assessment strategies.

ICC8S10:	Create and maintain records.
GC8K1:	Specialized terminology used in the assessment of individuals with disabilities.
GC8K2:	Laws and policies regarding referral and placement procedures for individuals with disabilities.
GC8K3:	Types and importance of information concerning individuals with disabilities available from families and public agencies.
GC8K4:	Procedures for early identification of young children who may be at risk for disabilities.
GC8S1:	Implement procedures for assessing and reporting both appropriate and problematic social behaviors of individuals with disabilities.
GC8S2:	Use exceptionality-specific assessment instruments with individuals with disabilities.
GC8S3:	Select, adapt, and modify assessments to accommodate the unique abilities and needs of individuals with disabilities.
GC8S4:	Assess reliable methods(s) of response of individuals who lack typical communication and performance abilities.
GC8S5:	Monitor intra-group behavior changes across subjects and activities.

STANDARD IX: PROFESSIONAL AND ETHICAL PRACTICE

ICC9K1:	Personal cultural biases and differences that affect one's teaching.
ICC9K2:	Importance of the teacher serving as a model for individuals with exceptional learning needs.
ICC9K3:	Continuum of lifelong professional development.
ICC9K4:	Methods to remain current regarding research-validated practice.
ICC9S1:	Practice within the CEC Code of Ethics and other standards of the profession.
ICC9S2:	Uphold high standards of competence and integrity and exercise sound judgment in the practice of the professional.
ICC9S3:	Act ethically in advocating for appropriate services.
ICC9S4:	Conduct professional activities in compliance with applicable laws and policies.
ICC9S5:	Demonstrate commitment to developing the highest education and quality-of-life potential of individuals with exceptional learning needs.
ICC9S6:	Demonstrate sensitivity for the culture, language, religion, gender, disability, socio-economic status, and sexual orientation of individuals.
ICC9S7:	Practice within one's skill limit and obtain assistance as needed.
ICC9S8:	Use verbal, nonverbal, and written language effectively.
ICC9S9:	Conduct self-evaluation of instruction.
ICC9S10:	Access information on exceptionalities.
ICC9S11:	Reflect on one's practice to improve instruction and guide professional growth.
ICC9S12:	Engage in professional activities that benefit individuals with exceptional learning needs, their families, and one's colleagues.
ICC9S13:	Demonstrate commitment to engage in evidence-based practice.
GC9K1:	Sources of unique services, networks, and organizations for individuals with disabilities.
GC9K2:	Organizations and publications relevant to individuals with disabilities.
GC9S1:	Participate in the activities of professional organizations relevant to individuals with disabilities.
GC9S2:	Ethical responsibility to advocate for appropriate services for individuals with disabilities.

STANDARD X: COLLABORATION

ICC10K1:	Models and strategies of consultation and collaboration.
ICC10K2:	Roles of individuals with exceptional learning needs, families, and school and community personnel in planning of an individualized program.
ICC10K3:	Concerns of families of individuals with exceptional learning needs and strategies to help address these concerns.
ICC10K4:	Culturally responsive factors that promote effective communication and collaboration with individuals with exceptional learning needs, families, school personnel, and community members.

ICC10S1: Maintain confidential communication about individuals with exceptional learning needs.

ICC10S2: Collaborate with families and others in assessment of individuals with exceptional learning needs.

ICC10S3: Foster respectful and beneficial relationships between families and professionals.

ICC10S4: Assist individuals with exceptional learning needs and their families in becoming active participants in the educational team.

ICC10S5: Plan and conduct collaborative conferences with individuals with exceptional learning needs and their families.

ICC10S6: Collaborate with school personnel and community members in integrating individuals with exceptional learning needs into various settings.

ICC10S7: Use group problem solving skills to develop, implement and evaluate collaborative activities.

ICC10S8: Model techniques and coach others in the use of instructional methods and accommodations.

ICC10S9: Communicate with school personnel about the characteristics and needs of individuals with exceptional learning needs.

ICC10S10: Communicate effectively with families of individuals with exceptional learning needs from diverse backgrounds.

ICC10S11: Observe, evaluate, and provide feedback to paraeducators.

GC10K1: Parent education programs and behavior management guides that address severe behavior problems and facilitation communication for individuals with disabilities.

GC10K2: Collaborative and/or consultative role of the special education teacher in the reintegration of individuals with disabilities.

GC10K3: Roles of professional groups and referral agencies in identifying, assessing, and providing services to individuals with disabilities.

GC10K4: Co-planning and co-teaching methods to strengthen content acquisition of individuals with learning disabilities.

GC10S1: Use local community and state and provincial resources to assist in programming with individuals with disabilities.

GC10S2: Select, plan, and coordinate activities of related services personnel to maximize direct instruction for individuals with disabilities.

GC10S3: Teach parents to use appropriate behavior management and counseling techniques.

GC10S4: Collaborate with team members to plan transition to adulthood that encourages full community participation.

Glossary

Abacus   is a tool composed of beads on vertical rods that is used by students with visual impairments to help them with mathematical calculations. The abacus is not a calculator but is similar to solving a math problem with paper and pencil.

Absence seizures   are a type of generalized seizure that cause the person to lose consciousness only briefly.

Academic content standards   define the knowledge, skills, and understanding that students should attain in academic subjects.

Acceleration   involves students' skipping one or more grades in order to experience higher levels of instruction and/or attending a higher-grade-level program for part of the school day.

Acquired   refers to hearing losses that occur after birth.

Acquired disorder   is a disorder that occurs well after birth.

Acquired injury   means that the injury occurred after a child was born.

Acuity   is a measure of the sharpness and clarity of vision. It is determined by having an individual stand at a specified distance to read a standard eye chart, each line of which is composed of symbols printed at a certain size.

Acute otitis media   is an infection in the middle ear that can result in conductive hearing loss.

Adaptive behavior   refers to the typical performance of individuals without disabilities in meeting the expectations of their various environments.

Additions   occur when students place a vowel between two consonants.

Adventitious visual impairment   means that the impairment results from an advent (e.g., loss of sight caused by a hereditary condition that has just manifested itself) or an event (e.g., loss of sight caused by trauma).

Alternate achievement standards   must align with the same academic content standards for all students so that these students will be able to make progress in the general curriculum.

Alternate assessment   means evaluating performance for students for whom test accommodations are not sufficient to enable them to participate in the typical state- or district-wide assessment.

Alternate assessments based on grade-level achievement standards (AA-GLAS)   enable students to demonstrate skills and knowledge on grade-level assessments, but the assessments are modified versions of the general assessment.

Alternate assessments based on modified achievement standards (AA-MAS)   are used for students across disability categories (other than primarily students with the most significant cognitive disabilities) who need both accommodations and some modifications to the grade-level standards.

American Sign Language (ASL)   is the most widely used sign language among deaf adults in North America.

Anxiety disorder   is characterized by overwhelming fear, worry, and/or uneasiness. The condition includes phobia, generalized anxiety disorder, panic disorder, obsessive-compulsive disorder, and post-traumatic stress disorder.

Apgar test   is a method for determining the health of a newborn immediately in transition to life outside the womb. The screening occurs in the first minute after birth and again at the fifth minute after birth.

Applied behavior analysis (ABA)   uses the principles of operant psychology to develop techniques that reduce problem behavior and/or increase positive behavior.

Appropriate education   is an IDEA principle that requires schools to provide an individualized educational program for students with disabilities that is appropriate to their educational strengths and needs.

Apraxia   is a motor speech disorder that affects the way in which a student plans to produce speech.

Articulation   is a speaker's production of individual or sequenced sounds.

Asperger syndrome   describes the traits of individuals on the autism spectrum who have significant challenges in social and emotional functioning but without significant delays in language development or intellectual functioning.

Asthma   is a chronic lung condition characterized by airway obstruction, inflammation, and increased sensitivity.

Ataxic cerebral palsy involves unsteadiness, lack of coordination and balance, and varying degrees of difficulty with standing and walking.

Athetoid cerebral palsy involves abrupt, involuntary movements of the head, neck, face, and extremities, particularly the upper ones.

Atrophy refers to lost or reduced muscle strength.

Audiogram is a graphic representation of an individual's response to sound in terms of frequency (hertz) and loudness (decibels).

Audiologist has special training in testing and measuring hearing.

Audiometer is a machine that measures hearing threshold, the softest level at which sound can first be detected at various sound frequencies.

Audiometry refers to a hearing test, using a device called an audiometer, which provides a graph showing hearing thresholds at various levels of pitch and loudness.

Audition is the hearing process.

Augmentative and alternative communication (AAC) refers to the devices, techniques, and strategies used by students who are unable to communicate fully through natural speech and/or writing.

Auricle or pinna is the top of the external ear; it channels sound into the ear canal.

Autism spectrum disorder refers to five types of pervasive developmental disorders, including autistic disorder, Rhett's disorder, childhood disintegrative disorder, Asperger syndrome, and pervasive developmental disorder not otherwise specified.

Autonomous learning model assists students in dealing with the social-emotional issues that might accompany their giftedness.

Bacterial meningitis is an infection of the meninges, the three membranes enveloping the brain and the spinal cord.

Behavioral audiological evaluations are hearing tests that require a child to respond to a series of beeps called pure tones to indicate that she hears a sound.

Bidialectal refers to someone who uses two variations of a language.

Bilateral is a hearing loss that occurs in both ears.

Bilingual refers to someone who uses two languages equally well.

Bipolar disorder refers to a condition in which a person experiences exaggerated mood swings—for example, sometimes feeling depressed and other times experiencing heightened activity, energy, and a sense of strength. (These latter experiences are sometimes referred to as mania.)

Braille is a method of writing that uses raised dots in specific configurations that can be read and interpreted by people who are blind (and who have received appropriate instruction) by running their fingers across the dots.

Braille contractions are shortcuts for writing letter combinations in braille. Intended to save space and reading time, these contractions may represent a whole word or part of a word. As a result, the braille version of printed material is usually composed of fewer symbols than the print version, even though both include the same words.

Bullying is a form of externalizing behavior. It can consist of verbal abuse—calling a student by a stigmatizing name; cyberabuse—using online forums or networks to attack a student's behavior or characteristics; or physical abuse of any amount or degree, including sexual abuse.

Catatonic behavior is behavior that lacks typical movement, activity, and/or expression.

Cerebral palsy refers to a lack of muscle control that affects a student's ability to move and to maintain balance and posture; it has a neurological basis.

Chromosomes direct each cell's activity and contain DNA and genes that determine a person's physical and mental condition.

Circle of friends refers to the individuals who surround a person with a disability with support that is consistent with the person's choices and that advances the person's self-determination, full citizenship, relationships, positive contributions, strengths, and choices.

Classroom-centered intervention refers to classroom-based strategies to intervene against poor academic achievement and aggressive or shy behavior.

Clean intermittent catheterization (CIC) refers to the procedure whereby a person or an attendant (a trained health aide) inserts a tube into the person's urethra to induce urination. It is "clean" because the procedure is done under sterile conditions, and it is "intermittent" because it is done as needed or on a regular schedule; the tube is not permanently placed in the person's urethra.

Cleft palate or lip describes a condition in which a person has a split in the upper part of the oral cavity or the upper lip.

Closed-captioned technology translates dialogue from a spoken language to a printed form (captions) that is then inserted at the bottom of a television or movie screen.

Closed head injury results when the brain whips back and forth during an accident, causing it to bounce off the inside of the skull. It does not involve penetration or a fracture of the bone of the skull.

Cochlea is a snail-shaped bony structure that houses the actual organ of hearing.

Cochlear implant is an electronic device that is surgically implanted under the skin behind the ear and contains a magnet that couples to a magnet in a sound transmitter that is worn externally.

Cognitive taxonomies are ordered lists of cognitive skills or activities that can be used to differentiate expectations for students.

Compacting the curriculum involves first testing students to identify the content they have already mastered and then teaching them only the concepts that they have not yet mastered.

Computer-assisted instruction (CAI) refers to the use of computer technology to deliver instruction.

Conceptually Accurate Signed English (CASE) is a sign system used in the United States that involves signing concepts rather than the literal English translation.

Conduct disorder consists of a persistent pattern of antisocial behavior that significantly interferes with others' rights or with schools and communities' behavioral expectations.

Congenital refers to an impairment that is present from birth or from the time very near birth; visual impairment occurs at birth or, in the case of blindness, before visual memories have been established.

Congenital deafness is a hearing loss that is present at birth.

Congenital disorder is a disorder that occurs at or before birth.

Cultural deficit theory blames the failure of students from culturally and linguistically diverse backgrounds on the disadvantages that they experienced within their own cultures.

Cultural difference theories also called cultural mismatch theories, contend that failure of students from culturally and linguistically diverse backgrounds in school cannot be attributed solely to their lack of assimilation into European culture.

Cultural reproduction theory holds that "racial and class inequity are reproduced over time through institutional and individual actions and decisions that maintain the status quo at the expense of less privileged groups."

Curriculum-based measurement (CBM) involves direct assessment of a student's skills in the content of the curriculum that is being taught.

Curriculum extension refers to efforts to expand the breadth and depth of the coverage of a given topic.

Cytomegalovirus (CMV) is a virus that may have very few symptoms in adults or might resemble mononucleosis. In a fetus, however, it can lead to severe malformations.

Deaf is a term used to describe a hearing loss greater than 70 to 90 decibels that results in severe oral speech and language delay or that prevents a person from understanding spoken language through hearing.

Deaf community is a group of individuals who are deaf; share a culture, attitudes, and a set of beliefs; and use American Sign Language to communicate.

Decibel (dB) is the unit used to express how loud sound is.

Dialect is a regional variation of a language, as when someone speaks English using terms or pronunciations common only in that region.

Differentiated instruction involves using different strategies such as flexible student instructional grouping, learning stations and learning centers, and two educators in the same classroom.

Discrete trial teaching is based on the three-term contingency outlined by applied behavior analysis: the discriminative stimulus, the response, and the reinforcer or consequence.

Distortions are modifications of the production of a phoneme in a word.

Domains of family quality of life include emotional well-being, parenting, family interaction, physical/material well-being, and disability-related support.

Duration is the length of time any speech sound requires.

Dykinetic cerebral palsy involves impairments in muscle tone affecting the whole body and changing throughout the day and week.

Dyslexia refers to the condition of having severe difficulty in learning to read.

Echolalia is a form of communication in which a student echoes other people's language by constantly repeating a portion of what he hears. It is either immediate or delayed.

Encephalitis refers to inflammation of the brain.

Errorless learning refers to a procedure that presents the discriminative stimuli and arranges the delivery of prompts in a learning situation in such a way as to ensure that the student gives only correct responses.

Etiology describes the cause or origin of a medical condition.

Eugenics refers to procedures to improve the human race by encouraging the birth of children with allegedly "good" hereditary qualities and discouraging or preventing the birth of those with allegedly "undesirable" hereditary qualities.

Eustachian tube is the structure that extends from the throat into the middle ear cavity; its primary purpose is to equalize the air pressure on the eardrum when a person swallows or yawns.

Event recording involves an observer recording every occurrence of a behavior during an observation period instead of using the yes/no recording per interval that is characteristic of time sampling.

Exclusionary standard refers to embedding particular exemptions within a definition. For example, in the IDEA definition of learning disabilities, learning disabilities do not include learning problems that primarily result from visual impairment; hearing loss; mental retardation; emotional disturbance; or environmental, cultural, or economic disadvantages.

Expanded core curriculum describes the areas of instruction in which students with visual impairments need additional instruction because of the impact of their visual impairment on incidental learning. It includes compensatory skills, orientation and mobility, social interaction skills, independent living skills, recreation and leisure skills, career education, use of assistive technology, visual efficiency skills, and self-determination.

Expressive language disorder   is characterized by difficulty in formulating ideas and information.

Externalizing behaviors   are behavior disorders comprising aggressive, acting-out, and noncompliant behaviors.

Family   means two or more people who regard themselves to be a family and who carry out the functions that families typically perform.

Family-professional partnerships   are relationships in which families and professionals collaborate, capitalizing on each other's judgments and expertise in order to increase the benefits of education for students, families, and professionals.

Family quality of life   refers to the extent to which the family's needs are met, family members enjoy their life together, and family members have the chance to do the things that are important to them.

Field observation   involves observing and recording, in a longhand, anecdotal format, what a student is doing.

Field of vision (visual field)   is the entire area of which an individual is visually aware when the person is directing her gaze straight ahead, typically 160 degrees.

Fingerspelling   uses a hand representation for all twenty-six letters of the alphabet.

Fluency   is the rate and rhythm of speaking.

Formative analysis   means that analysis is conducted on an ongoing basis.

Functional behavioral assessment (FBA)   is a process used to determine a specific relationship between a student's behaviors and the circumstances that triggered those behaviors, especially those that impede a student's ability to learn.

Functional disorders   are those with no identifiable organic or neurological cause.

Functionally blind   describes individuals who can use their available vision to some limited degree but acquire information about the environment primarily through their auditory and tactile senses.

Functional vision assessment (FVA)   is an evaluation of how an individual uses his vision to perform tasks. It results in a description of what an individual with a visual impairment does with his available vision, not an acuity measurement.

General education curriculum   refers to the curriculum used by nondisabled students.

Generalization   refers to the ability to transfer knowledge or behavior learned for doing one task to another task and to make that transfer across different settings or environments.

Generalized anxiety disorder   consists of excessive, overwhelming worry not caused by any recent experience.

Generalized seizures   involve both cerebral hemispheres. An alteration of consciousness is a primary characteristic, and the seizure affects both sides of the body.

Genetic deficit theories   typically support the notion that nonwhite people are genetically deficient when compared to white people.

Goal attainment scaling   is a process that enables teachers to compare goals and to quantify student goal attainment.

Hard of hearing   is a term used for individuals who have hearing loss of 25 to 70 decibels in the better ear, who benefit from amplification, and who communicate primarily through spoken language.

Herpes virus   is a virus leading to symptoms that range from cold sores, to genital lesions, to encephalitis; it causes disabilities in early infancy.

Hertz (Hz)   is the unit used to express the frequency of sound and is measured in terms of the number of cycles that vibrating sound molecules complete per second.

Hyperactivity   refers to behaviors associated with frequent movement, difficulty concentrating, and talking excessively.

Hyperbilirubinemia   results from an excess accumulation of bilirubin in the blood, which can result in jaundice, a yellowing of the complexion and the whites of the eyes.

Hypernasality   is when air is allowed to pass through the nasal cavity on sounds other than /m/, /n/, and /ng/.

Hyponasality   occurs because air cannot pass through the nose and comes through the mouth instead.

Hypoxia   is the lack of oxygen.

Impulsivity   refers to behaviors such as difficulty awaiting one's turn, interrupting or intruding on others, and blurting out answers before questions have been completed.

Incidental learning   occurs when an individual learns about a process or concept primarily through observation and without others knowingly providing instruction.

Inclusionary standard   refers to embedding certain criteria within a definition so as to clearly state the conditions that the definition covers. For example, in the IDEA definition of learning disabilities, perceptual disabilities, brain injury, minimal brain dysfunction, dyslexia, and developmental aphasia are included conditions.

Incus   is one of the small bones in the middle ear. It is sometimes called the *anvil* because of its shape.

Individualized education program (IEP)   is a written plan for serving students with disabilities ages three through twenty-one.

Individualized family services plan (IFSP) is a written plan for providing services to infants and toddlers, ages zero to three, and their families.

Intensity (loudness or softness) is based on the perception of the listener and is determined by the air pressure coming from the lungs through the vocal folds.

Internalizing behaviors are behavior disorders comprising social withdrawal, depression, anxiety, obsessions, and compulsions.

Intracranial hemorrhage is a neurological complication of extremely premature infants in which the immature blood vessels bleed into the brain.

Keyword strategies teach students to link a keyword to a new word or concept to help them remember the new material.

Language is a structured, shared, rule-governed symbolic system for communicating.

Language disorder is difficulty in receiving, understanding, and formulating ideas and information.

Learning media assessment (LMA) is an evaluation of students who have visual impairments to determine the learning medium in which they function most efficiently as well as to identify those media in which additional instruction may be necessary.

Learning medium is the term used to describe the format(s) of reading and literacy materials available to individuals who have visual impairments and may include braille, print, large print, audiotapes, and access technology.

Learning strategies help students with learning disabilities to learn independently and to generalize, or transfer, their skills and behaviors to new situations.

Least restrictive environment (LRE) is an IDEA principle that requires that students with disabilities be educated to the maximum extent appropriate with students who do not have a disability and that they be removed from regular education settings only when the nature or severity of their disability cannot be addressed with the use of supplementary aids and services.

Legal blindness is a term that refers to individuals whose central visual acuity, when measured in both eyes and when they are wearing corrective lenses, is 20/200 or whose visual field is no more than 20 degrees.

Letter strategies employ acronyms or a string of letters to remember a list of words or concepts.

Life space analysis is a process in which teachers collect two kinds of data: (1) baseline data about how well a student functions in certain community settings and (2) information about the student's current environments and prospective environments for community-based instruction.

Long-term memory involves storing information permanently for later recall.

Loop systems involve closed-circuit wiring that sends FM signals from an audio system directly to an electronic coil in a student's hearing aid. The receiver picks up the signals, much as a remote-control device sends infrared signals to a television.

Low vision is experienced by individuals with a visual impairment who can use their vision as a primary channel for learning.

Low vision specialist is an individual, usually an optometrist, who has specialized in the measurement of the basic visual skills of individuals with low vision and who is knowledgeable about and prescribes glasses and other assistive devices that facilitate visual functioning in people whose vision is impaired.

Malleus is a small bone in the middle ear. It is sometimes called the *hammer* because of its shape.

Manual approach involves teaching the use of sign language for communication.

Mean refers to an average.

Meningocele refers to the condition in which the covering of the spinal cord, but not the cord itself, protrudes through the opening created by the defect in the spine. This condition usually does not cause a person to experience mobility impairments.

Mixed cerebral palsy combines spastic muscle tone and the involuntary movements of athetoid cerebral palsy.

Mnemonic is a device such as a rhyme, formula, or acronym that is used to aid memory.

Mood disorder involves an extreme deviation in either a depressed or an elevated direction or sometimes in both directions at different times.

Morpheme is the smallest meaningful unit of speech.

Morphology is the system that governs the structure of words.

Multidimensional model of intelligence considers multiple domains of intelligence as contrasted to only intellectual ability or academic achievement.

Multimodal treatments involves multiple interventions or treatments across modes or types of therapies.

Myelomeningocele refers to a condition in which the protrusion or sac contains not only the spinal cord's covering but also a portion of the spinal cord or nerve roots. This condition results in varying degrees of leg weakness, inability to control bowels or bladder, and a variety of physical problems such as dislocated hips or club feet.

Neural tube defects a large group of malformations associated with the spinal cord, brain, and vertebrae.

Neuroimaging provides noninvasive detailed pictures of various parts of the brain that are helpful in determining the presence of a disability.

Nondiscriminatory evaluation is an IDEA principle that requires schools to determine what each student's disability is and how it relates to the student's education. The evaluation must be carried out in a culturally responsive way.

Norm group   is a comparison group usually representing an average standard of achievement or development for a specific age group or grade level.

Norm-referenced   achievement test compares a student with his or her age- or grade-level peers in terms of performance.

Obsessive-compulsive disorder   are obsessions manifesting as repetitive, persistent, and intrusive impulses, images, or thoughts (i.e., repetitive thoughts about death or illness) and/or compulsions manifesting as repetitive, stereotypical behaviors (i.e., hand washing or counting).

Omissions   occur when a child leaves a phoneme out of a word.

Open head injury   penetrates the bones of the skull, allowing bacteria to have contact with the brain and potentially impairing specific functions, usually only those controlled by the injured part of the brain.

Oppositional defiant disorder   causes a pattern of negativistic, hostile, disobedient, and defiant behaviors.

Oral/aural format   emphasizes the use of amplified sound to develop oral language.

Oral motor exam   is examination of the appearance, strength, and range of motion of the lips, tongue, palate, teeth, and jaw.

Organic disorders   are those caused by an identifiable problem in the neuromuscular mechanism of the person.

Organ of Corti   refers to the organ of hearing.

Orientation and mobility (O&M)   is a term used to describe the two components of travel: orientation (knowing where you are and where you want to go) and mobility (the safe, efficient, graceful movement between two locations). For students with visual impairments, instruction in O&M often is necessary.

Otologist   is a physician who specializes in diseases of the ear.

Oval window   is the membrane that separates the middle from the inner ear.

Panic disorder   involves overwhelming panic attacks resulting in rapid heartbeat, dizziness, and/or other physical symptoms.

Part B   refers to the section of IDEA that addresses the social education of students who range from three through twenty-one years of age.

Part C   represents the section of IDEA that addresses the needs of infants and toddlers ranging in age from birth through age two.

Partial participation   rejects an all-or-none approach under which students either function independently in a given environment or not at all. Instead, it asserts that students with severe and multiple disabilities can participate, even if only partially, and indeed can often learn and complete a task if it is adapted to their strengths.

Partial seizures   cause the student to lose consciousness and often to fall to the ground and have sudden, involuntary contractions of groups of muscles.

Peer tutoring   involves pairing students one on one so that students who have already developed certain skills can help teach those and other skills to less advanced students and also help those students practice the skills they have already mastered.

Pegword strategy   helps students remember numbered or ordered information by linking words that rhyme with numbers.

Pervasive developmental disorders   include five discrete disorders that are part of the autism spectrum, including autistic disorder, Rhett's disorder, childhood disintegrative disorder, Asperger syndrome, and pervasive developmental disorder not otherwise specified.

Phobia   consists of the unrealistic, overwhelming fear of an object or situation.

Phonemes   are individual speech sounds and how they are produced, depending on their placement in a syllable or word.

Phonological processing   refers to the ability to process written and oral information by using the sound system of language.

Phonology   is the use of sounds to make meaningful syllables and words.

Pidgin Sign English (PSE)   is a sign system used in the United States and employs a basic American Sign Language vocabulary in English word order.

Pitch   is affected by the tension and size of the vocal folds, the health of the larynx, and the location of the larynx.

Portfolio-based assessment   is a technique for assembling exemplars of a student's work, such as homework, in-class tests, artwork, journal writing, and other evidence of the student's strengths and needs.

Positive behavior support   is a proactive, data-based approach to ensuring that students acquire needed skills and environmental supports.

Post-traumatic stress disorder   refers to flashbacks and other recurrent symptoms following exposure to an extremely distressing and dangerous event such as witnessing violence or a hurricane.

Pragmatics   refers to the use of communication in context.

Prelinguistic milieu teaching (PMT)   is an effective language-acquisition instructional strategy based on the principle that children will learn if their instruction matches their interests and abilities.

Procedural due process   is the principle of IDEA that seeks to make the schools and parents accountable to each other through a system of checks and balances.

Prodigy   is a person who is gifted to the point of being unmistakably extraordinary.

Receptive language disorder   is characterized by difficulty in receiving or understanding information.

Repetitive behavior   involves obsessions, tics, and perseveration.

Resonance   is determined by the way in which the tone coming from the vocal folds is modified by the spaces of the throat, mouth, and nose.

Risk ratios   compare the proportion of a specific racial/ethnic group receiving special education services to the proportion among the total combined other racial/ethnic groups receiving special education.

Rubella   is a viral infection, also called German measles, that causes a mild fever and skin rash. If a woman in the first three months of her pregnancy gets this disease, it can lead to severe birth defects in her child.

Savant syndrome   is a condition in which individuals typically display extraordinary abilities in areas such as calendar calculating, musical ability, mathematical skills, memorization, and mechanical abilities.

Schizophrenia   is characterized by psychotic periods resulting in hallucinations, delusions, inability to experience pleasure, and loss of contact with reality.

Schoolwide enrichment model (SEM)   promotes challenging, high-end learning across a range of school types, levels, and demographic differences by creating services that can be integrated across the general curriculum to assist all students, not just students who are gifted.

Schoolwide positive behavior support (SWPBS)   is a systems-level and evidence-based method for improving valued social and learning outcomes for all students.

Seeing Essential English, Signing Exact English (SEE2)   is a sign system used in the United States that borrows signs from American Sign Language and then adds signs that correspond to English morphemes.

Seizures   are temporary neurological abnormalities that result from unregulated electrical discharges in the brain, much like an electrical storm.

Self-instruction strategies   involve teaching students to use their own verbal or other communication skills to direct their own learning.

Self-monitoring strategies   enable students to learn to collect data on their progress toward educational goals. They can do this through various formats, such as by charting their progress on a sheet of graph paper or completing a checklist.

Semantics   refers to the meaning of what is expressed.

Separation anxiety disorder   is excessive and intense fear associated with separating from home, family, and others with whom a child has a close attachment.

Service learning   is a method for students to develop newly acquired skills by active participation and structured reflection in organized opportunities to meet community needs.

Shaken baby syndrome   refers to a brain injury resulting from a situation in which a caregiver has shaken a child violently, often because the caregiver is frustrated by the child's crying.

Short-term memory   is the mental ability to recall information that has been stored for a few seconds to a few hours.

Sign language   uses combinations of hand movements to convey words and concepts rather than individual letters.

Slate and stylus   is a tool used by people who are blind to write short notes to themselves. It consists of a slate, a hinged metal template, and a stylus (a small awl) that is used to punch the dots of a message in braille on a piece of paper inserted in the slate.

Social interaction theories   emphasize that communication skills are learned through social interactions.

Social stories   are written by educators, parents, or students and describe social situations, social cues, and appropriate responses to those cues.

Sound-field amplification system   enables the teacher to transmit her voice by using a lavaliere microphone and ceiling- or wall-mounted speakers.

Spastic cerebral palsy   involves tightness in one or more muscle groups.

Specially designed instruction   refers to adaptations of the content, methodology, or delivery of instruction to address a student's unique needs and ensure that the student can participate and make progress in the general curriculum.

Specific language impairment   describes a language disorder with no identifiable cause in a person with apparently normal development in all other areas.

Specific learning disability   means a disorder in one or more of the basic psychological processes involved in understanding or using spoken or written language.

Speech   is the oral expression of language. The disorder may manifest itself in an imperfect ability to listen, think, speak, read, write, spell, or do mathematical calculations.

Speech disorder   refers to difficulty in producing sounds as well as disorders of voice quality (for example, a hoarse voice) or fluency of speech, often referred to as stuttering.

Speech reader   is someone who is able to interpret words by watching the speaker's lips and facial movements without hearing the speaker's voice.

Spina bifida   is a condition in which the person's vertebral arches (the connective tissue between one vertebra and another) are not completely closed; the person's spine is split—thus, spina (spine) bifida (split). Spina bifida is the most common form of neural tube defect.

Spina bifida occulta   refers to a condition in which the spinal cord or its covering do not protrude and only a small portion of the vertebra, usually in the lower spine, is missing. This is the mildest and most common form of spina bifida.

Standard deviation   is a way to determine how much a particular score differs from the mean (average).

Standards-based reform is a process that identifies the academic content (reading, mathematics) that students must master, the standards for the students' achievement of content proficiency, a general curriculum aligned with these standards, assessment of student progress in meeting the general curriculum and standards, and information from the assessments to improve teaching and learning and to demonstrate that the schools are indeed accountable to the students, their families, and the public.

Stapes is one of the small bones in the middle ear. It is sometimes called the *stirrup* because of its shape.

Student achievement standards define the levels of achievement that students must meet to demonstrate their proficiency in the subjects.

Student-directed learning strategies teach students with and without disabilities to modify and regulate their own learning.

Substitutions occur when a person substitutes one sound for another, as when a child substitutes /d/ for the voiced /th/ ("doze" for "those"), /t/ for /k/ ("tat" for "cat"), or /w/ for /r/ ("wabbit" for "rabbit").

Summative evaluation is an evaluation that occurs after a product or project is completed.

Supplementary aids and services are aids, services, and other supports provided in general education classes or other education-related settings to enable children with disabilities to be educated with nondisabled children to the maximum extent appropriate.

Supports are the services, resources, and personal assistance that enable a person to develop, learn, and live effectively.

Syndrome is a collection of two or more features that result from a single cause.

Syntax provides rules for putting together a series of words to form sentences.

Syphilis is a sexually transmitted disease that can cause an intrauterine infection in a pregnant woman and result in severe birth defects in her child.

System for augmenting language (SAL) focuses on augmented input of language.

T-Charts are charts that are laid out in the form of a capital letter *T;* they allow teachers to track two aspects of a behavior together.

Temperament refers to behavioral tendencies that are biologically based.

Theory of mind is an explanation of the delayed social development that suggests that individuals with autism do not understand that their own beliefs, desires, and intentions may differ from those of others.

Time sampling involves an observer who is recording the occurrence or nonoccurrence of specific behaviors during short, predetermined intervals.

Tonic-clonic seizures affect a student's motor control area of the brain, as well as sensory, behavioral, and cognitive areas. Tonic-clonic seizures can either occur in only one region of the brain or spread to other brain hemispheres.

Topographical classification system correlates the specific body location of a movement impairment with the location of the brain damage.

Totally blind describes those individuals who do not receive meaningful input through the visual sense.

Toxoplasmosis is an infectious disease caused by a microorganism that can cause severe fetal malformations.

Traumatic brain injury (TBI) is caused by an external physical force, resulting in impaired functioning in one or more areas. Educational performance is adversely affected. The injury may be open or closed.

Tunnel vision occurs when an individual's visual field is reduced significantly so that only a small area of central visual acuity remains. The affected individual has the impression of looking through a tunnel or tube and is unaware of objects to the left, right, top, or bottom.

Tympanography is not a hearing test but a test of how well the middle ear is functioning and how well the eardrum can move.

Unilateral is hearing loss in one ear only.

Universal design for learning (UDL) is the application of principles to the design of curricular and instructional materials to provide students across a wide range of abilities and from a variety of backgrounds with access to academic content.

Vestibular mechanism controls balance, helps a body maintain its equilibrium, and is sensitive to both motion and gravity.

Visual disability (including blindness) is an impairment in vision that, even with correction, adversely affects a child's educational performance. The term includes both partial sight and blindness.

Working memory refers to how students process information in order to remember it.

Wraparound refers to a philosophy of care that includes a definable planning process involving the child and family that results in a unique set of community services and natural supports individualized for that child and family to achieve a positive set of outcomes.

Zero reject is an IDEA principle that requires schools to enroll all students who have disabilities.

References

Chapter 1

Allday, R. A., Duhon, G. J., Blackburn-Ellis, S., & Van Dycke, J. L. (2011). The biasing effects of labels on direct observation by pre-service teachers. *Teacher Education and Special Education, 34*(1), 52–58.

American Association for Employment in Education. (2008). *Educator supply and demand in the United States.* Columbus, OH: Author.

CEC. (2008). CEC Code of Ethics and Standards for professional practice for special educators. *Exceptional Children, 74*(3), 389–393.

Chapman, C., Laird, J., & KewalRamani, A. (2010). *Trends in high school dropout and completion rates in the United States: 1972–2008* (NCES 2011–012). Washington, DC: U.S. Department of Education, Institute of Education Sciences, National Center for Educational Statistics. Retrieved March 1, 2011 from http://nces.ed.gov/pubsearch.

Donne, J. (1986). Meditation 17, *Devotions upon emergent occasions* (original work published 1624). In M. H. Abrams (Ed.), *The Norton Anthology of English Literature* (pp. 1107–1108). New York: Norton.

Goffman, E. (1963). *Behavior in public places: Notes on the social organization of gatherings.* Glencoe, IL: Free Press.

Lapadat, J. C. (1998). Implicit theories and stigmatizing labels. *Journal of College Reading and Learning, 29*(1), 73.

Mills v. Washington, DC, Board of Education. 348 F. Supp. 866 (D.DC 1972); contempt proceedings, EHLR 551: 643 (D.DC 1980).

National Association for Gifted Children. (2007). *State of the states in gifted education: 2006–2007.* Washington, DC: Author.

National Center for Education Statistics. (2011). *Grade 8 national results.* Retrieved April 4, 2011, from http://nationsreportcard.gov/math_2009 and http://nationsreportcard.gov/reading_2009/.

National Organization on Disability/Kessler Foundation and Harris Interactive. (2010). *The ADA, 20 years later.* West Orange, NJ: Author.

Newman, L., Wagner, M., Cameto, R., Knokey, A.M., & Shaver, D. (2010). *Comparisons across time of the outcomes of youth with disabilities up to 4 years after high school. A report of findings from the National Longitudinal Transition Study (NLTS) and the National Longitudinal Transition Study-2 (NLTS2)* (NCSER 2010-3008). Menlo Park, CA: SRI International.

Smith, P. (1999). Drawing new maps: A radical cartography of developmental disabilities. *Review of Educational Research, 69*(2), 117–145.

Turnbull, A. P., Turnbull, H. R., Erwin, E., Soodak, L., & Shogren, K. (2011). *Families, professionals, and exceptionality: Positive outcomes through partnerships and trust* (6th ed.). Upper Saddle River, NJ: Merrill/Pearson.

Turnbull, H. R., Shogren, K. A., & Turnbull, A. P. (2011). Evolution of the parent movement. In J. M. Kauffman & D. P. Hallahan (Eds.), *Handbook of special education* (pp. 639–653). New York: Routledge.

Turnbull, H. R., Stowe, M. J., & Huerta, N. E. (2007). *Free appropriate public education* (7th ed., revised printing). Denver: Love.

U.S. Department of Education. (2009). *28th annual report to Congress on the implementation of the Individuals with Disabilities Education Act, 2005* (Vol. 1). Washington, DC: Author.

U.S. Department of Education. (2010). *29th annual report to Congress on the Implementation of the Individuals with Disabilities Education Act, 2007* (Vo1. 1). Washington, DC: Author.

U.S. Department of Education. (2011). *Data Accountability Center: Individuals with Disabilities Education Act (IDEA) data.* Retrieved February 26, 2011, from https://www.ideadata.org.

Chapter 2

Aud, S., Fox, M. A., & KewalRamani, A. (2010). *Status and trends in the education of racial and ethnic groups.* Washington, DC: National Center for Education Statistics, Institute of Education Sciences. Retrieved February 11, 2011, from http://nces.ed.gov/pubs2010/2010015.pdf.

Bambera, L. M., & Kern, L. (2005). *Individualized supports for students with problem behaviors: Designing positive behavior plans.* New York: Guilford Press.

Brown, L., Udvari-Solner, A., Frattura-Kampschroer, E., Davis, L., Ahlgren, C., Van Daventer, P., & Jorgensen, J. (1991). Integrated work: A rejection of segregated enclaves and mobile work crews. In L. H. Meyer, C. A. Peck, & L. Brown (Eds.), *Critical issues in the lives of people with severe disabilities* (pp. 219–228). Baltimore: Brookes.

Bruns, D. A., & Mogharreban, C. (2007). The gap between beliefs and practices: Early childhood practitioners' perceptions about inclusion. *Journal of Research in Childhood Education, 21*, 229–239.

Byrd, E. S. (2011). Educating and involving parents in the response to intervention process: The school's important role. *Teaching Exceptional Children, 43*(3), 32–39.

Cole, C. M., Waldron, N., & Majd, M. (2004). Academic progress of students across inclusive and traditional settings. *Mental Retardation, 42*(2), 136–144.

Cormier, D. C., Altman, J., Shyyan, V., & Thurlow, M. L. (2010). *A summary of the research on the effects of test accommodations: 2007–2008.* (Technical Report 56). Minneapolis: University of Minnesota, National Center on Educational Outcomes.

Erlandson, R. F. (2008). Universal and accessible design for products, services, and processes. New York: CRC/Taylor & Francis.

Fairbanks, S., Sugai, G., Guardino, D., & Lathrop, M. (2007). Response to intervention: Examining classroom behavior support in second grade. *Exceptional Children, 73*(3), 288–310.

Gartner, A., & Lipsky, D. K. (1987). Beyond special education: Toward a quality system for all students. *Harvard Educational Review, 57*(4), 367–395.

Grosenick, J. K., & Reynolds, M. C. (1978). *Teacher education: Renegotiating roles for mainstreaming.* Minneapolis, MN: National Support Systems Project.

Grossen, B., Caros, J., Carnine, D., Davis, B., Deshler, D., Schumaker, J., et al. (2002). Big ideas (plus a little effort) produce big results. *Teaching Exceptional Children, 34*(4), 70–73.

Heinich, R., Molenda, M., Russel, J. D., & Smaldino, S. E. (1999). *Instructional media and technologies for learning*. Upper Saddle River, NJ: Prentice Hall.

Hoover, J. J., & Love, E. (2011). Supporting school-based response to intervention: A practitioner's model. *Teaching Exceptional Children, 43*(3), 40–48.

Jackson, L., Ryndak, D., & Wehmeyer, M. (2009). The dynamic relationship between context, curriculum, and student learning: A case for inclusive education as a research-based practice. *Research and Practice in Severe Disabilities, 34*(1), 175–195.

Jackson, L., Ryndak, D., & Wehmeyer, M. (2010). The dynamic relationship between context, curriculum, and student learning: A case for inclusive education as a research-based practice. *Research and Practice in Severe Disabilities, 34*(1), 175–195.

Janney, R., & Snell, M. E. (2008). *Behavioral support: Teachers' guides to inclusive practices*. Baltimore: Brookes.

Knowlton, E. (2007). *Developing effective Individualized Education Programs: A case-based tutorial* (2nd ed.). Upper Saddle River, NJ: Pearson Education.

Laurents, A., & Sondheim, S. (1979). *West side story*. New York: Heinemann.

Lazarus, S. S., Thurlow, M. L., Lail, K. E., & Christensen, L. (2009). A longitudinal analysis of state accommodations policies: Twelve years of change, 1993–2005. *Journal of Special Education, 43*, 67–80.

McGregor, G., & Vogelsberg, R. T. (1998). *Inclusive schooling practices: Pedagogical and research foundations: A synthesis of the literature that informs best practices about inclusive schooling*. Pittsburgh, PA: Allegheny University of the Health Sciences.

Munk, D. D., & Dempsey, T. L. (2010). *Leadership strategies for successful schoolwide inclusion: The STAR approach*. Baltimore: Brookes.

National Association of State Directors of Special Education (NASDSE). 2005. *Response to intervention: Policy considerations and implementation*. Retrieved July 7, 2008, from www.nasdse.org.

National Center on Educational Outcomes (n.d.). *Alternate assessments for students with disabilities*. Minneapolis: University of Minnesota. Retrieved February 28, 2011, from http://www.cehd.umn.edu/NCEO/TopicAreas/AlternateAssessments/altAssessTopic.htm.

Perie, M. (2010). *Teaching and assessing low-achieving students with disabilities: A guide to alternate assessments based on modified achievement standards*. Baltimore: Brookes.

Pugach, M. C. (1995). On the failure of the imagination in inclusive schools. *Jouranl of Special Education, 29*, 212–223.

Pugach, M. C., and Johnson, L. J. (2002). *Collaborative practitioners, collaborative schools* (2nd ed.). Denver, CO: Love.

Reynolds, M. C., Wang, M. C., & Walbert, H. J. (1987). The necessary restructuring of special and general education. *Exceptional Children, 53*, 391–398.

Rose, D. H., & Meyer, A. (2006). *A practical reader in universal design for learning*. Cambridge, MA: Harvard Education.

Sailor, W. (Ed.). (2002). *Building partnerships for learning, achievement, and accountability*. New York: Teachers College Press.

Sailor, W. (2009). *Making RTI work: How smart schools are reforming education through schoolwide RTI*. New York: Jossey-Bass.

Sailor, W., Stowe, M. J., Turnbull, H. R., & Kleinhammer-Tramill, P. J. (2007). A case for adding a social-behavioral standard to standards-based education with schoolwide positive behavior support as its basis. *Remedial and Special Education, 28*(6), 366–376.

Snell, M. E. (2009). Rethinking effective instructional practices: A response to Copeland and Cosbey. *Research and Practice in Severe Disabilities, 34*(1), 228–231.

Spooner, F., Baker, J. N., Harris, A. A., Ahlgrim-Delzell, L., & Browder, D. M. (2007). Effects of training in universal design for learning on lesson plan development. *Remedial and Special Education, 28*(2), 108–116.

Taylor, S. (1988). Caught in the continuum: A critical analysis of the principle of least restrictive environment. *Journal of the Association for Persons with Severe Handicaps, 13*(1), 41–53.

Thousand, J. S., Villa, R. A., & Nevin, A. I. (Eds.). (2002). *Creativity and collaborative learning* (2nd ed.). Baltimore: Brookes.

Thurlow, M. (2008). Assessment and instructional implications of the alternate assessment based on modified academic achievement standards (AA-MAS). *Journal of Disability Policy Studies, 19*(3), 132–139.

Turnbull, A., Turnbull, H.R., Erwin, E.J., Soodak, L.C., & Shogren, K.A. (2011). *Families, professionals, and exceptionality: Positive outcomes through partnerships and trust* (6th ed.). Upper Saddle River, NJ: Merrill/Pearson.

Turnbull, A.P. and Schulz, J.B. (1979). *Mainstreaming Handicapped Students: A Guide for Classroom Teachers*. Boston: Allyn and Bacon.

Turnbull, H. R., Turnbull, A. P., Wehmeyer, M. L., & Park, J. (2003). A quality of life framework for special education outcomes. *Remedial and Special Education, 24*, 67–74.

U.S. Department of Education. (2005a). *Alternate achievement standards for students with the most significant cognitive disabilities: Non-regulatory guidance*.

Retrieved January 9, 2008, from http://www.ed.gov/policy/elsec/guid/altguidance.pdf.

U.S. Department of Education. (2011). *Data accountability center: Individuals with Disabilities Education Act (IDEA) data*. Retrieved February 26, 2011, from https://www.ideadata.org.

U.S. Department of Education. (n.d.). *IDEA regulations: National instructional materials accessibility standard (NIMAS)*. Retrieved January 14, 2008, from http://idea.ed.gov/explore/view/p/%2Croot%2Cdynamic%2CTopicalBrief%2C12%2C.

Wehmeyer, M. L. (2011). Access to the general education curriculum for students with significant cognitive disabilities. In J. M. Kauffman & D. P. Hallahan (Eds.), *Handbook of special education* (pp. 544–556). New York: Routledge.

Will, M. C. (1986). Educating children with learning problems: A shared responsibility. *Exceptional Children, 52*, 411–416.

Chapter 3

Aguilera, D., & LeCompte, M. D. (2007). Resiliency in native languages: The tale of three indigenous communities' experiences with language immersion. *Journal of American Indian Education, 46*(3), 11–36.

American Psychological Association. (1996, February). Intelligence: Knowns and unknowns. *American Psychologist*. Retrieved September 5, 2011, from http://www.michna.com/intelligence.htm.

Aratani, Y. (2009). *Homeless children and youth: Causes and consequences*. Retrieved July 26, 2011, from http://www.nccp.org/publications/pub_888.html.

Artiles, A. J., Kozleski, E. B., Trent, S. C., Osher, D., & Ortiz, A. (2010). Justifying and explaining disproportionality, 1968–2008: A critique of underlying views of culture. *Exceptional Children, 76*(3), 279–299.

Artiles, A. J., Rueda, R., & Salazar, J. J. (2005). Within-group diversity in minority disproportionate representation: English language learners in urban school districts. *Exceptional Children, 71*(3), 283–300.

Ayers, W., Ladson-Billings, G., Michie, G., & Noguera, P. (2008). *City kids, city schools: More reports from the front row*. New York: New Press.

Banks, J. A., & Banks, C. A. M. (2001). *Multicultural education: Issues and perspectives*. New York: Wiley.

Barrera, M. (2006). Roles of definitional and assessment models in the identification of new or second language learners of English for special education. *Journal of Learning Disabilities, 39*(2), 142–156.

Blanchett, W. J. (2009). A retrospective examination of urban education: From *Brown* to the resegregation of African Americans in special education—it is time to "go for broke." *Urban Education, 44*(4), 370–388.

Blanchett, W. J. (2010). Telling it like it is: The role of race, class, and culture in the perpetuation of learning disability as a privileged category for the white middle class. *Disability Studies Quarterly, 30*(2). Retrieved July 27, 2011, from http://www.dsq-sds.org/article/view/1233/1280.

Blanchett, W. J., Klingner, J. K., & Harry, B. (2009). The intersection of race, culture, language, and disability. *Urban Education, 44*(4), 389–409.

Blanchett, W. J., Mumford, V., & Beachum, F. (2005). Urban school failure and disproportionality in a post-*Brown* era: Benign neglect of the constitutional rights of students of color. *Remedial and Special Education, 26*(2), 70–81.

Bowles, S., & Gintas, H. (1976). *Schooling in capitalist America*. New York: Basic Books.

Bronfenbrenner, U. (1979). *The ecology of human development: Experiments by nature and design*. Cambridge, MA: Harvard University Press.

Brown v. Board of Education, 347 U.S. 483 (1954).

Cartledge, G., & Kourea, L. (2008). Culturally responsive classrooms for culturally diverse students with and at risk for disabilities. *Exceptional Children, 74*(3), 351–371.

Cartledge, G., Singh, A., & Gibson, L. (2008). Practical behavior-management techniques to close the accessibility gap for students who are culturally and linguistically diverse. *Preventing School Failure, 52*(3), 29–38.

Chau, M., Thampi, K., & Wight, V. R. (2010). *Basic facts about low-income children, 2009: Children aged 6 through 11*. Retrieved July 26, 2011, from http://www.nccp.org/publications/pub_973.html.

Chen, W. B., & Gregory, A. (2010). Parental involvement in the prereferral process: Implications for schools. Retrieved July 27, 2011, from http://rse.sagepub.com/content/early/2010/03/11/0741932510362490.

Delgado, C. E. F., & Scott, K. G. (2006). Comparison of referral rates for preschool children at risk for disabilities using information obtained from birth certificate records. *Journal of Special Education, 40*(1), 28–35.

Deschenes, S., Cubàn, L., & Tyack, D. (2001). Mismatch: Historical perspectives on schools and students who don't fit them. *Teachers College Record, 103*, 525–547.

de Valenzuela, J. S., Copeland, S. R., Qi, C. H., & Park, M. (2006). Examining educational equity: Revisiting the disproportionate representation of minority students in special education. *Exceptional Children, 72*(4), 425–441.

Diana v. State Board of Education, No. C-70-37 RFP (N. Cal. 1970).

Dunn, L. M. (1968). Special education for the mildly retarded: Is much of it justifiable? *Exceptional Children, 35*(1), 5–22.

Fall, A. M., & Billingsley, B. S. (2011). Disparities in work conditions among early career special educators in high- and low-poverty districts. *Remedial and Special Education, 32*(1), 64–78.

Gravois, T. A., & Rosenfield, S. A. (2006). Impact of instructional consultation teams on the disproportionate referral and placement of minority students in special education. *Remedial and Special Education, 27*(1), 42–52.

Gregory, A., Skiba, R. J., & Noguera, P. A. (2010). The achievement gap and the discipline gap: Two sides of the same coin? *Educational Researcher, 39*(1), 59–68.

Haager, D., Klingner, J., & Vaughn, S. (2007). *Evidence-based reading practices for response to intervention*. Baltimore: Brookes.

Hanson, M. J. (2004). Families with Anglo-European roots. In E. W. Lynch & M. J. Hanson (Eds.), *Developing cross-cultural competence: A guide for working with children and their families* (3rd ed.). Baltimore: Brookes.

Harry, B. (2008). Collaboration with culturally and linguistically diverse families: Ideal versus reality. *Council for Exceptional Children, 74*(3), 372–388.

Hermes, M. (2007). Moving toward the language: Reflections on teaching in an indigenous-immersion school. *Journal of American Indian Education, 46*(3), 54–71.

Herrstein, R. J., & Murray, C. (1994). *The bell curve: Intelligence and class structure in American life*. New York: Free Press.

Holgate, D. (2009). *Instructional strategies for Native American English language learners (NA-ELLs) in a reading context*. Unpublished doctoral dissertation, Arizona State University. Retrieved July 26, 2011, from http://gradworks.umi.com/33/57/3357266.html/.

Hoover, J. J., Klingner, J., Baca, L. M., & Patton, J. M. (2008). *Methods for teaching culturally and linguistically diverse exceptional leaders*. Upper Saddle River, NJ: Merrill/Pearson.

Hoover, J. J., & Méndez Barletta, L. (2008). Considerations when assessing ELLs for special education. In J. K. Klingner, J. J. Hoover, & L. M. Baca (Eds.), *Why do English language learners struggle with reading? Distinguishing language acquisition from learning disabilities* (pp. 93–108). Thousand Oaks, CA: Corwin.

Individuals with Disabilities Education Act (IDEA), 20 U.S.C. § 1400 (2004).

Jozefowicz-Simbeni, D. M. H., & Israel, N. (2006). Services to homeless students and families: The McKinney-Vento Act and its implications for school social work practice. *Children & Schools, 28*(1), 37–44.

Kaiser, L., Rosenfield, S., & Gravois, T. (2010). Teachers' perception of satisfaction, skill development, and skill application after instructional consultation services. *Journal of Learning Disabilities, 42*(5), 444–457.

Kalyanpur, M., & Harry, B. (1999). *Culture in special education: Building reciprocal family-professional relationships*. Baltimore: Brookes.

Kashi, T. L. (2008). Response to intervention as a suggested generalized approach to improving minority AYP scores. *Rural Special Education Quarterly, 27*(4), 37–44.

Klingner, J. K., deSchonewise, E. A., Onis, C., & Méndez Barletta, L. M. (2008). Misconceptions about the second language acquisition process. In J. K. Klingner, J. J. Hoover, & L. M. Baca (Eds.), *Why do English language learners struggle with reading? Distinguishing language acquisition from learning disabilities* (pp. 17–36). Thousand Oaks, CA: Corwin.

Klingner, J. K., & Harry, B. (2006). The special education referral and decision-making process for English language learners: Child study team meetings and placement conferences. *Teachers College Record, 108*(11), 2247–2281.

Klingner, J. K., Hoover, J. J., & Baca, L. M. (2008). *Why do English language learners struggle with reading? Distinguishing language acquisition from learning disabilities*. Thousand Oaks, CA: Corwin Press.

Klingner, J. K., Méndez Barletta, L., & Hoover, J. (2008). Response to intervention models and English language learners. In J. K. Klingner, J. Hoover, & L. Baca (Eds.), *English language learners who struggle with reading: Language acquisition or learning disabilities?* (pp. 37–56). Thousand Oaks, CA: Corwin.

Klingner, J. K., & Solano-Flores, G. (2007). Cultural responsiveness in response-to-intervention models. In C. C. Laitusis & L. L. Cook (Eds.), *Large-scale assessment and accommodations: What works?* (pp. 229–241). Arlington, VA: Council for Exceptional Children and Educational Testing Service.

Kozleski, E.B., & Smith, A. (2010). The complexities of systems change in creating equity for students with disabilities in urban schools. *Urban Education, 44*(4), 427–251.

Larry P. v. Riles, 343 F. Supp. 1306 (N.D. Cal. 1972), 502 F. 2d 963 (9th Cir. 1974), No. C-71-2270 RFP (N.D. Cal., October 16, 1979), 793 F. 2d 969 (9th Cir. 1984).

Lynch, E. W., & Hanson, M. J. (2004). *Developing cross-cultural competence: A guide for working with children and their families* (3rd ed.). Baltimore: Brookes.

McCray, A. D., Webb-Johnson, G. C., & Neal, L. I. (2003). The disproportionality of African Americans in special education: An enduring threat to equality and opportunity. In C. C. Yeakey & R. D. Henderson (Eds.), *Surmounting all odds: Education, opportunity, and society in the new millennium* (pp. 455–485). Greenwich, CT: Information Age.

McDonough, E. M. (2009). *An examination of differences between instructional consultation teams and traditional student assistance teams in evaluation and identification of minority students for special education.* Unpublished doctoral dissertation, University of North Carolina at Chapel Hill. Retrieved July 26, 2011, from http://gradworks.umi.com/33/66/3366384 .html/.

McMaster, K. L., Kung, S., Han, I., & Cao, M. (2008). Peer-assisted learning strategies: A "tier I" approach to promoting English learners' response to intervention. *Exceptional Children, 74*(2), 194–214.

Mercer, J. R. (1973). *Labeling the mentally retarded.* Los Angeles: University of California Press.

Merriam-Webster's collegiate dictionary (11th ed.). (2003). Springfield, MA: Merriam-Webster.

Mickelson, R. A. (2003). When are racial disparities in education the result of racial discrimination? A social science perspective. *Teachers College Record, 105*, 1052–1086.

Monzo, L. D., & Rueda, R. (2009). Passing for English fluent: Latino immigrant children masking language proficiency. *Anthropology & Education Quarterly, 40*(1), 20–40.

Morrier, M. J., & Gallagher, P. A. (2010). *Racial disparities in preschool special education eligibility for five southern states.* Retrieved July 27, 2011, from http://sed. sagepub.com/content/early/ 2010/08/31/0022466910380465.

National Center for Educational Statistics. (2001). *Characteristics of the 100 largest public elementary and secondary school districts in the United States: 1999–2000.* Retrieved January 18, 2008, from http://nces.ed.gov/ pubs2001/100_largest/discussion.asp.

National Center for Family Homelessness. (2009). *America's youngest outcasts: State report card on child homelessness.* Newton, MA: Author.

National Research Council. (2002). *Minority students in special and gifted education.* Washington, DC: National Academy Press.

Orosco, M. J., & Klingner, J. (2010). One school's implementation of RTI with English language learners: "Referring into RTI." *Journal of Learning Disabilities, 43*(3), 269–288.

Ortiz, A. A., Wilkinson, C. Y., Robertson-Courtney, P., & Kushner, M. I. (2006). Considerations in implementing intervention assistance teams to support English language learners. *Remedial and Special Education, 27*(1), 53–63.

Papalia-Berardi, A., & Hall, T. E. (2007). Teacher assistance team social validity: A perspective from general education teachers. *Education and Treatment of Children, 30*(2), 89–110.

Rinaldi, C., & Samson, J. (2008). English language learners and response to intervention: Referral considerations. *Teaching Exceptional Children, 40*(5), 6–14.

Rodriguez, D. (2009). Meeting the needs of English language learners with disabilities in urban settings. *Urban Education, 44*(4), 452–464.

Safford, P. L., & Safford, E. H. (1998). Visions of the special class. *Remedial and Special Education, 19*, 229–238.

Shifrer, D., Muller, C., & Callahan, R. (2010). Disproportionality and learning disabilities: Parsing apart race, socioeconomic status, and language. *Journal of Learning Disabilities, 44*(3), 246–257.

Skiba, R., & Sprague, J. (2008). Safety without suspensions. *Educational Leadership, 66*(1), 38–43.

Skiba, R. J., Eckes, S. E., & Brown, K. (2009/2010). African American disproportionality in school discipline: The divide between best evidence and legal remedy. *New York Law School Law Review, 54*, 1071–1112.

Skiba, R. J., Simmons, A. B., Ritter, S., Gibb, A. C., Rausch, M. K., Cuadrado, J., & Chung, C. G. (2008). Achieving equity in special education: History, status, and current challenges. *Exceptional Children, 74*(3), 264–288.

Skinner, C., Wight, V. R., Aratani, Y., Cooper, J. L., & Thampi, K. (2010). *English language proficiency, family economic security, and child development.* Retrieved July 26, 2011, from http://www.nccp.org/ publications/pub_948.html.

Skrtic, T. M., & McCall, Z. (2010). Ideology, institutions, and equity: Comments on Christine Sleeter's "why is there learning disabilities?" *Disabilities Quarterly, 30*(2), 1–32.

Span, C. M. (2003). "Knowledge is light, knowledge is power": African American education in antebellum America. In C. C. Yeakey & R. D. Henderson (Eds.), *Surmounting all odds: Education, opportunity, and society in the new millennium* (pp. 3–29). Greenwich, CT: Information Age.

Turnbull, A. P., Turnbull, H. R., Summers, J. A., & Poston, D. (2008). Partnering with families of children with developmental disabilities to enhance family quality of life. In H. P. Parette & G. R. Peterson-Karlan (Eds.), *Research-based practices in developmental disabilities.* Austin, TX: PRO-ED.

Turnbull, A. P., Turnbull, H. R., Erwin, E., Soodak, L., & Shogren, K. (2011). *Families, professionals, and exceptionality: Positive outcomes through partnerships and trust* (6th ed.). Upper Saddle River, NJ: Merrill/ Pearson.

Turnbull, H. R., Shogren, K. A., & Turnbull, A. P. (2011). Evolution of the parent movement. In J. M. Kauffman &

D. P. Hallahan (Eds.), *Handbook of special education* (pp. 639–653). New York: Routledge.

Turnbull, H. R., Stowe, M. J., & Huerta, N. E. (2007). *Free appropriate public education* (7th ed., rev.). Denver: Love.

U.S. Department of Education. (2001). *Survey of the states' limited English proficient students and available educational programs and services.* Washington, DC: Author.

U.S. Department of Education. (2002, July 5). Improving the academic achievement of the disadvantaged: Final rule. *Federal Register.*

U.S. Department of Education. (2008). *IDEA data.* Retrieved February 2, 2008, from https://www.ideadata.org/tables30th/ ar_1-9.xls.

U.S. Department of Education, Office of Special Education Programs. (2005). *IDEA data.* Retrieved July 26, 2011, from http:// www.ideadata.org.

U.S. Department of Education. (2009). *28th annual report to Congress on the implementation of the Individuals with Disabilities Education Act, 2005* (Vol. 1). Washington, DC: Author.

U.S. Department of Education. (2010). *29th annual report to Congress on the implementation of the Individuals with Disabilities Education Act, 2007* (Vol. 1). Washington, DC: Author.

van Garderen, D., & Whittaker, C. (2006). Planning differentiated, multicultural instruction for secondary inclusive classrooms. *Teaching Exceptional Children, 38*(3), 12–20.

Vohs, J. (1993). On belonging: A place to stand, a gift to give. In A. P. Turnbull, J. M. Patterson, S. K. Behr, D. L. Murphy, J. G. Marquis, & M. J. Blue-Banning (Eds.), *Cognitive coping, families, & disability* (pp. 51–66). Baltimore: Brookes.

Wagner, M., Marder, C., Blackorby, J., & Cardoso, D. (2002). *The children we serve: The demographic characteristics of elementary and middle school students with disabilities and their households.* Menlo Park, CA: SRI International.

Wallace, J. M., Goodkind, S., Wallace, C. M., & Bachman, J. G. (2008). Racial, ethnic, and gender differences in school discipline among U.S. high school students: 1991–2005. *Negro Educational Review, 59*(1–2), 47–62.

Wang, M., McCart, A., & Turnbull, A. P. (2007). Implementing positive behavior support with Chinese American families: Enhancing cultural competence. *Journal of Positive Behavior Interventions, 9*(1), 38–51.

Wight, V. R., Chau, M., & Aratani, Y. (2010). *Who are America's poor children? The official story.* Retrieved July 26, 2011, from http://www.nccp.org/publications/ pub_912.html.

Xu, Y., & Drame, E. (2008). Culturally appropriate context: Unlocking the potential of response to intervention for English language learners. *Early Childhood Education Journal, 35*, 305–311.

Yazzie-Mintz, T. (2007). From a place deep inside: Culturally appropriate curriculum as the embodiment of Navajoness in classroom pedagogy. *Journal of American Indian Education, 46*(3), 72–93.

Chapter 4

Alfred, J. L., Slovak, K., & Broussard, C. A. (2010). School social workers and a renewed call to advocacy. *School Social Work Journal, 35*(1), 1–20.

Araujo, B. E. (2009). Best practices in working with linguistically diverse families. *Intervention in School and Clinic, 45*(2), 116–123.

Axlerod, M. I., Zhe, E. J., Haugen, K. A., & Klein, J. A. (2009). Self-management of on-task homework behavior: A promising strategy for adolescents with attention and behavior problems. *School Psychology Review, 38*(3), 325–333.

Barnard, W. M. (2004). Parent involvement in elementary school and educational attainment. *Children & Youth Services Review, 26*(1), 39–62.

Bayat, M. (2007), *Evidence of resilience in families of children with autism.* Journal of Intellectual Disability Research, 51: 702–714.

Beach Center. (1999). Transcripts of focus groups. Unpublished research.

Beach Center. (2000). Transcripts of focus groups. Unpublished research.

Blue-Banning, M. J., Summers, J. A., Frankland, H. C., Nelson, L. L., & Beegle, G. (2004). Dimensions of family and professional partnerships: Constructive guidelines for collaboration. *Exceptional Children, 70*(2), 167–184.

Bryan, T., & Burstein, K. (2004). Improving homework completion and academic performance: Lessons from special education. *Theory into Practice, 43*(3), 213–217.

CADRE: Consortium for Alternative Dispute Resolution in Special Education. (2008). *Part B—Three year annual report summaries for written complaints, mediations and due process.* Eugene, OR: Author. Retrieved January 20, 2007, from http://www.directionservice .org/cadre/statecomprpts.cfm. See also CADRE: *Facilitated IEP meetings; and emerging practice.* Eugene, OR: Author. Retrieved December 29, 2010, from http://www.directionservice.org/ cadre/pdf/Facilitated%20IEP%20for%20 CADRE%English.pdf.

Christenson, S., Palan, R., & Scullin, S. (2009). Family-school partnerships: An essential component of student achievement. *Principal Leadership, 9*(9), 10–12, 14, 16.

Covey, S. R. (1990). *The seven habits of highly effective people: Restoring the character ethic.* New York: Fireside/Simon & Schuster.

Dearing, E., Kreider, H., Simpkins, S., & Weiss, H. B. (2006). Family involvement in school and low-income children's literacy performance: Longitudinal association between and within families. *Journal of Educational Psychology, 98*, 653–664.

D'Haem, J. (2008). Special at school but lonely at home: An alternative friendship group for adolescents with Down syndrome. *Down Syndrome Research and Practice, 12*(2), 107–111.

Epstein, M. H., Polloway, E. A., Foley, R. M., & Patton, J. R. (1993). Homework: A comparison of teachers' and parents' perceptions of the problems experienced by students identified as having behavioral disorders, learning disabilities. *Remedial and Special Education, 14*(5), 40–50.

Eves, L. C., & Ho, H. H. (2008). Young adult outcome of autism spectrum disorders. *Journal of Autism Developmental Disorder, 38*, 739–747.

Falvey, M. A., Forest, M. S., Pearpoint, J., & Rosenberg, R. L. (2002). Building connections. In J. S. Thousand, R. A. Villa & A. I. Nevin (Eds.), *Creativity and collaborative learning* (2nd ed., pp. 29–54). Baltimore: Brookes.

Frederickson, N., & Turner, J. (2003). Utilizing the classroom peer group to address children's social needs: An evaluation of the circle of friends intervention approach. *Journal of Special Education, 36*(4), 234–245.

Geltner, J. A., & Leibforth, T. N. (2008). Advocacy in the IEP process: Strengths-based school counseling in action. *Professional School Counseling, 12*(2), 162–165.

Ginsburg-Block, M., Manz, P. H., & McWayne, C. (2010). Partnering to foster achievement in reading and mathematics. In S. Christenson & A. Reschly (Eds.), *Handbook of school-family partnerships.* New York: Taylor & Francis.

Goddard, R. D., Tschannen-Moran, M., & Hoy, W. K. (2001). A multilevel examination of the distribution and effects of teacher trust in students and parents in urban elementary schools. *Elementary School Journal, 102*(1), 3.

Harniss, M. K., Epstein, M. H., Bursuck, W. D., Nelson, J., & Jayanthi, M. (2001). Resolving homework-related communication problems: Recommendations of parents of children with and without disabilities. *Reading and Writing Quarterly, 17*, 205–225.

Harry, B. (2008). Collaboration with culturally and linguistically diverse families: Ideal vs. reality. *Exceptional Children, 74*(3), 372–388.

Harry, B., Klingner, J., & Hart, J. (2005). African American families under fire: Ethnographic views of family strengths. *Remedial and Special Education, 26*(2), 101–112.

Hastings, R. P., & Taunt, H. M. (2002). Positive perceptions in families of children with developmental disabilities. *American Journal on Mental Retardation, 107*(2), 116–127.

Hoffman, L., Marquis, J. G., Poston, D. J., Summers, J. A., & Turnbull, A. P. (2006). Assessing family outcomes: Psychometric evaluation of the Beach Center Family Quality of Life Scale. *Journal of Marriage and Family, 68*, 1069–1083.

Hoover-Dempsey, K. V., Battiato, A. C., Walker, J. M. T., Reed, R. P., DeJong, J. M., & Jones, K. P. (2001). Parental involvement in homework. *Educational Psychologists, 36*, 195–209.

Houtenville, A. J., & Conway, K. S. (2008). Parental effort, school resources, and student achievement. *Journal of Human Resources, 33*(2), 437–453.

Hoy, W. K. (2002). Faculty trust: A key to student achievement. *Journal of Public School Relations, 23*, 88–103.

Hoy, W. K., & Tarter, C. J. (1997). *The road to open and healthy schools: A handbook for change (elementary and secondary school ed.).* Thousand Oaks, CA: Corwin.

Ivey, A. E., Ivey, M. B., & Zalaquett, C. (2010). Intentional interviewing and counseling: Facilitating client development in a multicultural society. Belmont, CA: Brooks/Cole.

Jayanthi, M., Sawyer, V., Nelson, J. S., Bursuck, W. D., & Epstein, M. H. (1995). Recommendations for homework-communication problems. *Remedial and Special Education, 16*, 212–225.

Jeynes, W. H. (2005a). Effects of parent involvement and family structure on the academic achievement of adolescents. *Marriage and Family Review, 37*(3), 99–116.

Jeynes, W. H. (2005b). A meta-analysis of the relation of parent involvement to urban elementary school student academic achievement. *Urban Education, 40*(3), 237–269.

Jeynes, W. H. (2007). The relationship between parental involvement and urban secondary school student academic achievement: A meta-analysis. *Urban Education, 42*(1), 82–110.

Johnson, J., Duffett, A., Farkas, S., & Wilson, L. (2002). *When it's your own child: A report on special education from the families who use it.* New York: Public Agenda.

Kyzar, K. (2010). *The relationship of perceptions of service and support adequacy to family quality of life for families of children with deafblindness.* Unpublished doctoral dissertation, University of Kansas.

Lee, S. H., Turnbull, A. P., & Zan, F. (2009). Family perspectives: Using a cultural prism to understand families from Asian cultural backgrounds. *Intervention in School and Clinic, 45*(2), 99–108.

Link, Y. (1999). [Untitled article]. *Tapestry, 3*(1), p. 23.

Lo, L. (2008). Chinese families' level of participation and experiences in IEP meetings. *Preventing School Failure, 53*(1), 21–27.

Lohman, B. J., & Matjasko, J. L. (2010). Creating school-family partnership in adolescence: Challenges and opportunities. In S. L. Christenson & A. L. Reschly (Eds.), *Handbook of school-family partnerships* (pp. 312–341). New York: Routledge.

Lynch, A., Theodore, L. A., Bray, M. A., & Kehle, T. J. (2009). A comparison of group-oriented contingencies and randomized reinforcers to improve homework completion and accuracy for students with disabilities. *School Psychology Review, 38*(3), 307–324.

Mantizicopoulos, P. (2003). Flunking kindergarten after Head Start: An inquiry into the contribution of contextual and individual variables. *Journal of Educational Psychology, 95*(2), 268–278.

McBride, B. A., Schoppe-Sullivan, S. J., & Moon-Ho, H. (2005). The mediating role of fathers' school involvement on student achievement. *Journal of Applied Developmental Psychology, 26*(2), 201–216.

Meadan, H., Halle, J. W., & Ebata, A. T. (2010). Families with children who have autism spectrum disorders: Stress and support. *Council for Exceptional Children, 77*(1), 7–36.

Merriam-Webster's collegiate dictionary (11th ed.). (2003). Springfield, MA: Merriam-Webster.

Milsom, A., Goodnough, G., & Akos, P. (2007). School counselor contributions to the individualized education program (IEP). *Preventing School Failure, 52*(1), 19–25.

Mueller, T. G. (2009). IEP facilitation: A promising approach to resolving conflicts between families and schools. *Teaching Exceptional Children, 41*(3), 60–67.

Mueller, T. G., Singer, G. H., & Draper, L. (2008). Reducing parental dissatisfaction with special education in two school districts: implementing prevention and alternative dispute resolution. *Journal of Educational & Psychological Consultation, 18*(3), 191–233.

Munk, D. D., Bursuck, W. D., Epstein, M. H., Jayanthi, M., Nelson, J., & Polloway, E. A. (2001). Homework communication problems: Perspectives of special education and general education parents. *Reading and Writing Quarterly, 17*, 189–203.

National Association for Gifted Children. (2007). *State of the states in gifted education: 2006–2007.* Washington, DC: Author.

Newman, L. (2005). *Family involvement in the educational development of youth with disabilities: A special topic report of findings from the National Longitudinal Transition Study-2 (NLTS-2).* Menlo Park, CA: SRI International.

Nokali, N. E., Bachman, H. J., & Votruba-Drzal, E. (2010). Parent involvement and children's academic and social development in elementary school. *Child Development, 81*(3), 988–1005.

Nye, C., Turner, H., & Schwartz, J. (2006). Approaches to parent involvement for improving the academic performance of elementary school age children. *Campbell Systematic Reviews, 4,* 1–49.

Parish, S. L., Rose, R. A., Grinstein-Weiss, M., Richman, E. L., & Andrews, M. E. (2008). Material hardship in U.S. families raising children with disabilities. *Exceptional Children, 75*(1), 71–92.

Poston, D., Turnbull, A., Park, J., Mannan, H., Marquis, J., & Wang, M. (2003). Family quality of life: A qualitative inquiry. *Mental Retardation, 41*(5), 313–328.

Powers, T. J., Werba, B. E., Watkins, M. W., Angelucci, J. G., & Eiraldi, R. B. (2006). Patterns of parent-reported homework problems among ADHD-referred and non-referred children. *School Psychology Quarterly, 21*(1), 13–33.

Reynolds, A. J., & Shlafer, R. (2010). Parent involvement in early education. In S. Christenson & A. Reschly (Eds.), *Handbook of school-family partnerships* (pp. 158–174). New York: Taylor & Francis.

Salend, S. J., Duhaney, D., Anderson, D. J., & Gottschalk, G. (2004). Using the Internet to improve homework communication and completion. *Teaching Exceptional Children, 36*(3), 34–73.

Santelli, B., Turnbull, A., Marquis, J., & Lerner, E. (2000). Statewide parent-to-parent programs: Partners in early intervention. *Infants and Young Children, 13*(1), 74–88.

Schaffer v. Weast, 126 S. Ct. 528 (2005).

Sheehey, P., Ornelles, C., & Noonan, M. J. (2009). Developing culturally responsive approaches to family participation. *Intervention in School and Clinic, 45*(2), 132–139.

Sheridan, S. M. (2009). Homework interventions for children with attention and learning problems: Where is the "home" in "homework"? *School Psychology Review, 38*(3), 334–337.

Singer, G. (2006). Meta-analysis of comparative studies of depression in mothers of children with and without developmental disabilities. *American Journal on Mental Retardation, 111*, 155–169.

Singer, G. H. S., Marquis, J., Powers, L., Blanchard, L., DiVenere, N., Santelli, B., et al. (1999). A multi-site evaluation of parent to parent programs for parents of children with disabilities. *Journal of Early Intervention, 22*(3), 217–219.

Smiley, A. D., Howland, A. A., & Anderson, J. A. (2008). Cultural brokering as a core practice of a special education parent liaison program in a large urban school district. *Journal of Urban Learning Teaching and Research, 4*, 89–95.

Staples, K. E., & Diliberto, J. A. (2010). Guidelines for successful parent involvement. *Council for Exceptional Children, 42*(6), 58–63.

Starr, E., Foy, J. B., Cramer, K. M., & Singh H. (2006). How are schools doing? Parental perceptions of children with autism spectrum disorders, Down syndrome and learning disabilities: A comparative analysis. *Education and Training in Developmental Disabilities, 41*(4), 315–332.

Stormshak, E., Dishion, T., & Falkenstein, C. (2010). Family-centered, school-based mental health strategies to reduce student behavioral, emotional, and academic risk. In S. Christenson & A. Reschly (Eds.), *Handbook of school-family partnerships.* New York: Taylor & Francis.

Summers, J. A., Behr, S. K., & Turnbull, A. P. (1988). Positive adaptation and coping strengths in families who have hcildren with disabilities. In G. Singer & L. Irvin (Eds.), *Family support services* (pp. 27–40). Baltimore: Brookes.

Summers, J. A., Marquis, J. G., Mannan, H., Turnbull, A. P., Fleming, K., Poston, D. J., et al. (2007). Relationship of perceived adequacy of services, family-professional partnerships, and family quality of life in early childhood service programmes. *International Journal of Disability, Development and Education, 54*(3), 319–338.

Summers, J. A., Poston, D. J., Turnbull, A. P., Marquis, J. G., Hoffman, L., Mannan, H., et al. (2005). Conceptualizing and measuring family quality of life. *Journal of Intellectual Disability Research, 49*, 777–783.

Sweetland, S. R., & Hoy, W. K. (2000). School characteristics and educational outcomes: Toward an organizational model of student achievement in middle schools. *Educational Administration Quarterly, 36*(5), 703–729.

Taub, D. J. (2000). Understanding the concerns of parents of students with disabilities: Challenges and roles for school counselors. *Professional School Counseling, 10*(1), 52–57.

Trainor, A. (2010a). Diverse approaches to parent advocacy during special education home-school interactions. *Remedial and Special Education, 31*(1), 34–47.

Trainor, A. (2010b). Reexamining the promise of parent participation in special education: An analysis of cultural and social capital. *Anthropology & Education Quarterly, 41*(3), 245–263.

Turnbull, A. P., & Morningstar, M. E. (1993). Family-professional partnerships. In M. E. Snell (Ed.), *Instruction of students with severe disabilities* (4th ed., pp. 1–60). New York: Macmillan.

Turnbull, A. P., & Ruef, M. (1996). Family perspectives on problem behavior. *Mental Retardation, 34*, 280–293.

Turnbull, A. P., & Ruef, M. (1997). Family perspectives on inclusive lifestyle issues for individuals with problem behavior. *Exceptional Children, 63*(2), 211–227.

Turnbull, A. P., Summers, J. A., Lee, S. H., & Kyzar, K. (2007). Conceptualization and measurement of family outcomes associated with families of individuals with intellectual disabilities. *Mental Retardation and Developmental Disabilities Research Reviews, 13,* 346–356.

Turnbull, A. P., Turnbull, H. R., Summers, J. A., & Poston, D. (2008). Partnering with families of children with developmental disabilities to enhance family quality of life. In Parette, P. & G. Peterson-Karlan (Eds.), *Research-based practices in developmental disabilities* (pp. 481–500). Austin, TX: PRO-ED.

Turnbull, A., Turnbull, R., Erwin, E. J., Soodak, L. C., & Shogren, K. A. (2011). *Families, professionals, and exceptionality: Positive outcomes through partnerships and trust* (6th ed.). Upper Saddle River, NJ: Merrill/Pearson.

U.S. Census Bureau. (2010). *Current population survey (CPS)-definitions and explanations.* Retrieved from http://www.census.gov/population/www/cps/cpsdef.html.

U.S. Department of Education. (2003). *To assure the free appropriate public education of all children with disabilities: Twenty-fifth annual report to Congress on the implementation of the Individuals with Disabilities Education Act.* Washington, DC: Author.

U.S. Office of Special Education Programs (Ed.). (2005). *Parents' satisfaction with their children's schooling.* Washington, DC: U.S. Office of Special Education.

Wang, M., Mannan, H., Poston, D., Turnbull, A. P., & Summers, J. A. (2004). Parents' perceptions of advocacy activities and their impact on family quality of life. *Research and Practice for Persons with Severe Disabilities, 29*(2), 144–155.

Webster-Stratton, C., & Reid, M. J. (2010). A school-family partnership: Addressing multiple risk factors to improve school readiness and prevent conduct problems in young children. In S. Christenson & A. Reschly (Eds.), *Handbook of school-family partnerships* (pp. 204–227). New York: Taylor & Francis.

Zuna, N. I., Turnbull, A., & Summers, J. A. (2009). Family quality of life: Moving from measurement to application. *Journal of Policy and Practice in Intellectual Disabilities, 6*(1), 25–31.

Zuna, N. I., Summers, J. A., Turnbull, A. P., Hu, X., & Xu, S. (2010). Theorizing about family quality of life. In R. Kober (Ed.), *Enhancing the quality of life for individuals with developmental disabilities: Theory to practice* (pp. 241–278). Dordrecht, the Netherlands: Springer.

Chapter 5

Aaron, P. G., Joshi, R. M., Gooden, R., & Bentum, K. E. (2008). Diagnosis and treatment of reading disabilities based on the component model of reading: An alternative to the discrepancy model of LD. *Journal of Learning Disabilities, 41*(1), 67–84.

Adlof, S., Catts, H., & Lee, J. (2010). Kindergarten predictors of second versus eighth grade reading comprehension impairments. *Journal of Learning Disabilities, 43*(4), 332–345.

Arndt, S., Konrad, M., & Test, D. (2006). Effects of the self-directed IEP on student participation in planning meetings. *Remedial and Special Education, 27*(4), 194–207.

Ausubel, D. (1963). *The psychology of meaningful verbal learning: An introduction to school learning.* New York: Grune & Stratton.

Barnes, M. A., Fuchs, L. S., & Ewing-Cobbs, L. (2010). Math disabilities. In R. L. Peterson & K. O. Yeates (Eds.), *Pediatric neuropsychology* (2nd ed., pp. 297–323). New York: Guilford.

Bender, W. N. (2007). *Differentiating instruction for students with learning disabilities: Best teaching practices for general and special educators.* Thousand Oaks, CA: Corwin.

Bradley, R., Danielson, L., & Hallahan, D. (2002). *Identification of learning disabilities: Research to practice.* Mahwah, NJ: Erlbaum.

Bulgren, J., Deshler, D. D., & Lenz, B. K. (2007). Engaging adolescents with LD in higher order thinking about history concepts using integrated content enhancement routines. *Journal of Learning Disabilities, 49*(2), 121–133.

Bulgren, J., Marquis, J. G., Lenz, B. K., Schumaker, J. B., & Deshler, D. D. (2009). Effectiveness of question exploration to enhance students' written expression of content knowledge and comprehension. *Reading & Writing Quarterly, 25*(4), 271–289.

Carroll, J., Maughan, B., Goodman, R., & Meltzer, H. (2005). Literacy difficulties and psychiatric disorders: Evidence for co-morbidity. *Journal of Child Psychology and Psychiatry, 46,* 524–532.

Choate, K. T. (2009). Wechsler Individual Achievement Test—2nd edition. In J. A. Naglieri & S. Goldstein (Eds.), *Practitioner's guide to assessing intelligence and achievement* (pp. 417–448). Hoboken, NJ: Wiley.

Christ, T. J., Silberglitt, B., Yeo, S., & Cormier, D. (2010). Curriculum-based measurement of oral reading: An evaluation of growth rates and seasonal effects among students served in general and special education. *School Psychology Review, 39*(3), 447–462.

Cook, R. E. (2008). *Adapting early childhood curricula for children with special needs.* Upper Saddle River, NJ: Merrill/Pearson.

Consortium for Evidence-Based Early Intervention Practices. (2010). *A response to the Learning Disabilities Association of America (LDA) white paper on specific learning disabilities (sld) identification.* Unpublished paper.

Coutinho, M. J., & Oswald, D. P. (2005). State variation in gender disproportionality in special education: Findings and recommendations. *Remedial and Special Education, 26*(1), 7–15.

Deshler, D. D., Robinson, S., & Mellard, D. F. (2009). Instructional principles for optimizing outcomes for adolescents with learning disabilities. In G. D. Sideridis & T. A. Citro (Eds.), *Classroom strategies for struggling learners* (pp. 173–189). Weston, MA: Learning Disabilities Association Worldwide.

Deshler, D. D., & Schumaker, J. B. (2006). *High school students with disabilities: Strategies for accessing the curriculum.* New York: Corwin.

Espin, C. A., Shin, J., & Busch, T. W. (2005). Curriculum-based measurement in the content areas: Vocabulary matching as an indicator of progress in social studies learning. *Journal of Learning Disabilities, 38*(4), 353–363.

Estell, D. B., Jones, M. H., Pearl, R., & Van Acker, R. (2009). Best friendships of students with and without learning disabilities across late elementary school. *Exceptional Children, 76*(1), 110–124.

Fagella-Luby, M., & Deshler, D. (2008). Reading comprehension in adolescents with LD: What we know; what we need to learn. *Learning Disabilities Research & Practice, 23*(2), 70–78.

Fletcher, J. M., & Vaughn, S. (2009). Response to intervention: Preventing and remediating academic difficulties. *Child Development Perspectives, 3*(1), 30–37.

Fletcher-Janzen, E., & Reynolds, C. R. (2008). *Neuropsychological perspectives on learning disabilities in the era of RTI: Recommendations for diagnosis and intervention.* Hoboken, NJ: Wiley.

Foegen, A., & Morrison, C. (2010). Putting algebra progress monitoring into practice: Insights from the field. *Intervention in School and Clinic, 46*(2), 95–103.

Frankenberger, W., & Fronzaglio, K. (1991). A review of states' criteria and procedures for identifying children with learning disabilities. *Journal of Learning Disabilities, 24,* 495–500.

Gajria, M., Jitendra, A. K., Sood, S., & Sacks, G. (2007). Improving comprehension of expository text in students with LD: A research synthesis. *Journal of Learning Disabilities, 40*(3), 210–225.

Geary, D. C. (2005). Learning disabilities in arithmetic: Problem-solving differences and cognitive deficits. In H. L. Swanson, K. R. Harris, & S. Graham (Eds.), *Handbook of learning disabilities* (pp. 199–212). New York: Guilford.

Glover, T. A., & Vaughn, S. (2010). *The promise of response to intervention:*

Evaluating current science and practice. New York: Guilford.

Goldstein, S., & Schwebach, A. (2009). Neuropsychological basis of learning disabilities. In C. R. Reynolds & E. Fletcher-Janzen (Eds.), *Handbook of clinical child neuropsychology* (3rd ed., pp. 187–202). New York: Springer.

Gormley, K. A., & McDermott, P. (2011). Traditions of diagnosis: Learning from the past, moving past traditions. In A. McGill-Franzen & R. L. Allington (Eds.), *Handbook of reading disability research* (pp. 162–172). New York: Routledge.

Gregg, N., & Nelson, J. M. (2010). Meta-analysis on the effectiveness of extra time as a test accommodation for transitioning adolescents with learning disabilities: More questions than answers. *Journal of Learning Disabilities.* Prepublished April 7, 2010, DOI:10.1177/002221940355484.

Hale, J. A., & Dunlap, R. F. (2010). *An educational leader's guide to curriculum mapping: Creating and sustaining collaborative cultures.* Thousand Oaks, CA: Corwin.

Hale, J., Alfonso, V., Berninger, V., Bracken, B., Christo, C., Clark, E., Cohen, M., et al. (2008). Critical issues in response-to-intervention, comprehensive evaluation, and specific learning disabilities identification and intervention: An expert white paper consensus. *Learning Disability Quarterly, 33,* 223–236.

Harlacher, J. E., Walker, N. J. N., & Sanford, A. K. (2010). *The "I" in RTI. Teaching Exceptional Children,* 42(6), 30-3.

Horn, E., & Banerjee, R. (2009). Understanding curriculum modifications and embedded learning opportunities in the context of supporting all children's success. *Language, Speech, and Hearing Services,* 40(4), 406–415.

Horn, E., Leiber, J., & Li, S. (2000). Supporting young children's IEP goals in inclusive settings through embedded learning opportunities. *Topics in Early Childhood Special Education, 20,* 206–223.

Individuals with Disabilities Education Act (IDEA), 20 U.S.C. § 1400 (2004).

Johnson, E. S., Humphrey, M., Mellard, D. F., Woods, K., & Swanson, H. L. (2010). Cognitive processing deficits and students with specific learning disabilities: A selective meta-analysis of the literature. *Learning Disability Quarterly, 33,* 3–18.

Kibby, M. (2009). There are multiple contributors to the verbal short-term memory deficit in children with developmental reading disabilities. *Child Neuropsychology,* 15(5), 485–506.

Lagae, L. (2008). Learning disabilities: Definitions, epidemiology, diagnosis, and intervention strategies. *Pediatric Clinics of North America, 55,* 1259–1268.

Lancaster, P. E., Schumaker, J. B., & Deshler, D. D. (2002). The development and validation of an interactive hypermedia program teaching a self-advocacy strategy to students with disabilities. *Learning Disability Quarterly, 25*(4), 277–302.

Lancaster, P., Schumaker, J., Lancaster, S., & Deshler, D. (2009). Effects of a computerized program on the use of the test-taking strategy by secondary students with disabilities. *Learning Disabilities Quarterly, 32*(3), 165–179.

Machek, G. R., & Nelson, J. M. (2010). School psychologists' perceptions regarding the practice of identifying reading disabilities: Cognitive assessment and response to intervention considerations. *Psychology in the Schools, 47*(3), 230–245.

Martin, J. E., Van Dycke, J., Christensen, W. R., Greene, B. A., Gardner, J. E., & Lovett, D. L. (2006). Increasing student participation in IEP meetings: Establishing the self-directed IEP as an evidence-based practice. *Exceptional Children, 72*(3), 299–316.

Martin, J. E., Van Dycke, J. L., Greene, B. A., Gardner, J. E., Christensen, W. R., Woods, L. L., et al. (2006). Direct observation of teacher-directed IEP meetings: Establishing the need for student IEP meeting instruction. *Exceptional Children, 72*(2), 187–200.

Marzocchi, G. M., Oosterlaan, J., Zuddas, A., Cavolina, P., Geurts, J., Redigolo, D., Vio, C., & Sergeant, J. A. (2008). Contrasting deficits on executive functions between ADHD and reading disabled children. *Journal of Child Psychology and Psychiatry, 49*(5), 543–552.

Meltzer, L., & Krishnan, K. (2007). Executive function difficulties and learning disabilities: Understandings and misunderstandings. In L. Meltzer (Ed.), *Executive function in education* (pp. 77–105). New York: Guilford.

Mercer, C. D., & Pullen, P. C. (2005). *Students with learning disabilities.* Upper Saddle River, NJ: Merrill/Pearson.

Montague, M., Penfield, R., Enders, C., & Huang, J. (2010). Curriculum-based measurement of math problem solving: A methodology and rationale for establishing equivalence of scores. *Journal of School Psychology, 48*(1), 39–52.

Morris, D. (2011). Interventions to develop phonological and orthographic systems. In A. McGill-Franzen & R. L. Allington (Eds.), *Handbook of reading disability research* (pp. 279–288). New York: Routledge.

Naglieri, J. A., & Goldstein, S. (2009). *Practitioner's guide to assessing intelligence and achievement.* Hoboken, NJ: Wiley.

Nelson, J. M., & Harwood, H. (2010). Learning disabilities and anxiety: A meta-analysis. *Journal of Learning Disabilities, 20*(10), 1–15.

O'Donnell, L. (2009). The Wechsler Intelligence Scale for Children—4th edition. In J. A. Naglieri & S. Goldstein (Eds.), *Practitioner's guide to assessing intelligence and achievement* (pp. 153–190). Hoboken, NJ: Wiley.

Paratore, J. R., & Dougherty, S. (2011). Home differences and reading difficulty. In A. McGill-Franzen & R. L. Allington (Eds.), *Handbook of reading disability research* (pp. 93–109). New York: Routledge.

Peterson, R. L., & Pennington, B. F. (2010). Reading disability. In R. L. Peterson & K. O. Yeates (Eds.), *Pediatric neuropsychology* (2nd ed., pp. 324–362). New York: Guilford.

Plomin, R., & Kovas, Y. (2005). Generalist genes and learning disabilities. *Psychological Bulletin, 131*(4), 592–617.

Prifitera, A., Weiss, L. G., Saklofske, D. H., & Rolfhus, E. (2005). The WISC-IV in the clinical assessment context. In A. Prifitera, D. H. Saklofske, & L. G. Weiss (Eds.), *WISC-IV: Clinical use and interpretation* (pp. 3–32). Amsterdam: Elsevier Academic.

Scheuermann, A., Harris, M., Faggella-Luby, M. F., Fritschmann, N., Graner, P., & Deshler, D. D. (2009). Closing the performance gap: Learning strategies instruction for adolescents with learning disabilities. In G. D. Sideridis & T. A. Citro (Eds.), *Classroom strategies for struggling learners* (pp. 49–81). Weston, MA: Learning Disabilities Association Worldwide.

Schumaker, J. B., & Deshler, D. D. (2009). Adolescents with learning disabilities as writers: Are we selling them short? *Learning Disabilities: Research and Practice, 24*(2), 81–92.

Searle, M. (2010). *What every school leader needs to know about RTI.* Alexandria, VA: Association for Supervision and Curriculum Development.

Sena, J. D. W., Lowe, P. A., & Lee, S. W. (2007). Significant predictors of test anxiety among students with and without learning disabilities. *Journal of Learning Disabilities, 40*(4), 360–376.

Snowling, M. J., & Hulme, C. (2008). Reading and other specific learning disabilities. In M. Rutter, D. V. M. Bishop, D. S. Pine, S. Scott, J. Stevenson, E. Taylor, & A. Thapar (Eds.), *Rutter's child and adolescent psychiatry* (5th ed., pp. 802–819). Malden, MA: Blackwell.

Stasi, G. M., & Tall, L. G. (2010). Learning disorders in children and adolescents. In J. Donders & S. J. Hunter (Eds.), *Principles and practice of lifespan developmental neuropsychology* (pp. 127–142). New York: Cambridge University Press.

Stecker, P. M., Fuchs, L. S., & Fuchs, D. (2005). Using curriculum-based measurement to improve student achievement: Review of research. *Psychology in the Schools, 42*(8), 795–819.

Strauss, S. L. (2011). Neuroscience and dyslexia. In A. McGill-Franzen & R. L. Allington (Eds.), *Handbook of reading* disability research (pp. 79–90). New York: Routledge.

Swanson, H. L., & Jerman, O. (2006). Math disabilities: A selective meta-analysis of the literature. Review of Educational Research, 76(2), 249–279.

Swanson, H. L., & Jerman, O. (2007). The influence of working memory on reading growth in subgroups of children with reading disabilities. Journal of Experimental Child Psychology, 96(4), 249–283.

Swanson, H. L., & Sáez, L. (2006). Memory difficulties in children and adults with learning disabilities. In H. L. Swanson, K. R. Harris, & S. Graham (Eds.), Handbook of learning disabilities (pp. 182–198). New York: Guilford.

Swanson, H. L., Zheng, X., & Jerman, O. (2009). Working memory, short-term memory, and reading disabilities. Journal of Learning Disabilities, 42(3), 260–287.

Thoma, C. A., & Wehmeyer, M. L. (2005). Self-determination and the transition to postsecondary education. In E. E. Getzel & P. Wehman (Eds.), Going to college: Expanding opportunities for people with disabilities (pp. 49–68). Baltimore: Brookes.

Tomlinson, C. A. (2003). Fulfilling the promise of differentiated classrooms: Strategies and tools for responsive teaching. Alexandria, VA: Association for Supervision and Curriculum Development.

U.S. Department of Education. (2010). 29th annual report to Congress on the Implementation of the Individuals with Disabilities Education Act, 2007 (Vol. 1). Washington, DC: Author.

U.S. Department of Education. (2011). Data accountability center: Individuals with Disabilities Education Act (IDEA) data. Retrieved February 26, 2011, from https://www.ideadata.org.

Vellutino, F. R., Scanlon, D. M., Small, S., & Fanuele, D. P. (2006). Response to intervention as a vehicle for distinguishing between children with and without reading disabilities: Evidence for the role of kindergarten and first-grade interventions. Journal of Learning Disabilities, 39(2), 157–169.

Wagner, R. K., & Torgesen, J. K. (2009). Using the Comprehensive Test of Phonological Processing (CTOPP) to assess reading-related phonological processes. In J. A. Naglieri & S. Goldstein (Eds.), Practitioner's guide to assessing intelligence and achievement (pp. 367–387). Hoboken, NJ: Wiley.

Wehmeyer, M. L., & Field, S. (2007). Self-determination: Instructional and assessment strategies. Thousand Oaks, CA: Corwin.

Wharton-McDonald, R. (2011). Expert classroom instruction for students with reading disabilities: Explicit, intense, targeted . . . and flexible. In A. McGill-Franzen & R. L. Allington (Eds.), Handbook of reading disability research (pp. 265–272). New York: Routledge.

Womack, S. A., Marchant, M., & Borders, D. (2011). Literature-based social skills instruction: A strategy for students with learning disabilities. Unpublished paper.

Woodcock, R. W. (1990). Theoretical foundations of the WJ-R measures of cognitive ability. Journal of Psychoeducational Assessment, (8)3, 231–258.

Woods, L. L., Sylvester, L., & Martin, J. E. (2010). Student-directed transition planning: Increasing student knowledge and self-efficacy in the transition planning process. Career Development for Exceptional Individuals, 33(2), 106–114.

Yeo, S. (2010). Predicting performance on state achievement tests using curriculum-based measurement in reading: A multilevel meta-analysis. Remedial and Special Education, 31(6), 412–422.

Chapter 6

American Speech-Language-Hearing Association (ASHA). (2003). A workload analysis approach for establishing speech-language caseload standards in the schools. Rockville, MD: Author.

American Speech-Language-Hearing Association (ASHA). (2004). Roles and responsibilities of speech-language pathologists with respect to augmentative and alternative communication. Retrieved April 2, 2011, from http://www.asha.org/policy.

American Speech-Language-Hearing Association (ASHA). (2007a). Accents and dialects. Retrieved April 2, 2011, from http://www.asha.org/about/leadership-projects/multicultural/issues/ad.htm.

American Speech-Language-Hearing Association (ASHA). (2007b). Childhood apraxia of speech. Retrieved April 2, 2011, from http://www.asha.org/policy.

American Speech-Language-Hearing Association (ASHA). (2008). Communication facts: Incidence and prevalence of communication disorders and hearing loss in children—2008 edition. Retrieved April 2, 2011, from http://www.asha.org/members/research/reports/children.htm.

American Speech-Language-Hearing Association (ASHA). (2010a). Roles and responsibilities of speech-language pathologists in schools. Retrieved April 2, 2011, from http://www.asha.org/policy.

American Speech-Language-Hearing Association (ASHA). (2010b). Social language use (pragmatics). Retrieved April 2, 2011, from http://www.asha.org/public/speech/development/Pragmatics.htm.

American Speech-Language-Hearing Association (ASHA). (2011a). How does your child hear and talk? Retrieved April 2, 2011, from http://www.asha.org/.public/speech/development/chart.htm.

American Speech-Language-Hearing Association (ASHA). (2011b). Stuttering: Causes and numbers. Retrieved April 2, 2011, from http://www.asha.org/public/speech/disorders/StutteringCauses.htm.

Apel, K., & Swank, L. K. (1999). Second chances: Improving decoding skills in the older student. Language, Speech, and Hearing Services in Schools, 30, 231–242.

Battle, D. (2002). Communication disorders in multicultural populations (3rd ed.). Boston: Butterworth-Heinemann.

Beukelman, D. R., & Mirenda, P. A. (2005). Augmentative and alternative communication: Supporting children and adults with complex communication needs (3rd ed.). Baltimore: Brookes.

Blackstone, S. (2006, September). The effects of modeling aided AAC. Augmentative Communication News, 18(3), 7–11.

Blackstone, S., Hunt-Berg, M., Nygard, J., & Schultz, J. (2004). Social networks: A communication inventory for individuals with complex communication needs and their communication partners. Verona, WI: Attainment.

Bloom, L., & Lahey, M. (1978). Language development and language disorders. New York: Wiley.

Boon, R., Burke, E., Fore, C., & Spencer, V. (2006, Winter). The impact of cognitive organizers and technology-based practices on student success in secondary social studies classrooms. Journal of Special Education Technology, 21(1), 5–16.

Bunce, B. (2008). Early literacy in action: The language-focused curriculum for preschool. Baltimore: Brookes.

Bunce, B., & Watkins, R. (1995). Language intervention in a preschool classroom: Implementing a language-focused curriculum. In M. Rice & K. Wilcox (Eds.), Building a language-focused curriculum for the preschool classroom: Vol. I. A foundation for lifelong communication (pp. 39–71). Baltimore: Brookes.

Caruso A., & Strand, E. (1999). Clinical management of motor speech disorders in children. New York: Thieme.

Catts, H., & Kamhi, A. (1999). Language and reading disabilities. Needham, MA: Allyn & Bacon.

Chomsky, N. (1957). Syntactic structures. The Hague, the Netherlands: Mouton.

Cunningham, P. M., & Allington, R. L. (2007). Classrooms that work: They can all read and write (4th ed.). Boston: Pearson Education.

Downing, J. E. (2005). Teaching communication skills to students with severe disabilities (2nd ed.). Baltimore: Brookes.

Elder, P. S., & Goossens, C. (1994). Engineering training environments for interactive augmentative communication: Strategies for adolescents and adults who are moderately severely developmentally delayed.

Birmingham, AL: Southeast Augmentative Communication Conference Publications.

Foley, B., & Staples, A. (2000, August). *Literature-based language intervention for students who use AAC.* Paper presented at the International Society for Augmentative and Alternative Communication Convention, Washington, DC.

Giangreco, M. (2000). Related services research for students with low-incidence disabilities: Implications for speech-language pathologists in inclusive classrooms. *Language, Speech, and Hearing Services in Schools, 31*(3), 230–239.

Gillam, R., & Gillam, S. (2011). An introduction to the discipline of communication sciences and disorders. In R. Gillam, T. Marquardt, & F. Martin (Eds.), *Communication sciences and disorders: From science to clinical practice* (2nd ed., pp. 3–26). Sudbury, MA: Jones & Bartlett.

Gillon, G. T. (2007). Phonological awareness—Implications for children with expressive phonological impairment. In B. W. Hodson (Ed.), *Evaluating and enhancing children's phonological systems—Research and theory to practice* (pp. 123–141). Greenville, SC: Thinking Publications.

Goossens, C., Crain, S., & Elder, P. (1992). *Engineering the preschool environment for interactive, symbolic communication.* Birmingham, AL: Southeast Augmentative Communication Conference Publications.

Haynes, W., & Pindzola, R. (2012). *Diagnosis and evaluation in speech pathology* (8th ed.). Boston: Pearson Education.

Hoff, E. (2009). *Language development* (4th ed.). Florence, KY: Wadsworth.

Howell, K. W., & Nolet, V. (2000). *Curriculum-based evaluation teaching and decision making* (3rd ed.). Belmont, CA: Wadsworth/Thompson Learning.

Hulit, L. M., Howard, M. R., & Fahey, K. R. (2011). *Born to talk: An introduction to speech and language development* (5th Ed.). Boston: Pearson.

Individuals with Disabilities Education Act (IDEA). 34 C.F.R. 300.8 (2006).

Justice, L. (2010). *Communication sciences and disorders: A contemporary perspective* (2nd ed.). Boston: Allyn & Bacon.

Kuder, J. S. (2008). *Teaching students with language and communication disabilities* (3rd ed.). Boston: Pearson Education.

Kumin, L. (2001). *Classroom language skills for children with Down syndrome: A guide for parents and teachers.* Bethesda, MD: Woodbine House.

Lombardino, L. J., Riccio, C. A., Hynd, G. W., & Pinheiro, S. B. (1997). Linguistic deficits in children with reading disabilities. *American Journal of Speech-Language Pathology, 6,* 71–78.

Losardo, A., & Notari-Syverson, A. (2001). *Alternative approaches to assessing young children.* Baltimore: Brookes.

McCormick, L. (2003). Introduction to language acquisition. In L. McCormick, D. Loeb, & D. Schiefelbusch (Eds.), *Supporting children with communication difficulties in inclusive settings: School-based language intervention* (2nd ed., pp. 1–42). Boston: Allyn & Bacon.

McCormick, L., & Loeb, D. (2003). Characteristics of students with language and communication difficulties. In L. McCormick, D. Loeb, & D. Schiefelbusch (Eds.), *Supporting children with communication difficulties in inclusive settings: School-based language intervention* (2nd ed., pp. 71–112). Boston: Allyn & Bacon.

Musselwhite, C., & Maro, J. (2010a, March). *Active listening.* Retrieved April 2, 2011, from http://www.aacintervention.com/tips/2010%20tips/03March%202010/activelisteningtipmarch2010/Active%20Listening.pdf.

Musselwhite, C., & Maro, J. (2010b, April). *Active listening: Good news, bad news.* Retrieved April 2, 2011, from http://www.aacintervention.com/tips/2010%20tips/04April2010/fwdgoodnewstipapril2010/Good%20News%20-%20Bad%20News.pdf.

Musselwhite, C., & Maro, J. (2010c, May). *Active listening: Link to literacy.* Retrieved April 2, 2011, from http://www.aacintervention.com/tips/2010%20tips/05May2010/activelisteningreadingmaytip/Active%20Listening%20Reading.pdf.

Myles, B., & Simpson, R. (2003). *Asperger syndrome: A guide for educators and parents* (2nd ed.). Austin, TX: PRO-ED.

National Institute of Health. (2011). *Rett syndrome.* Retrieved July 11, 2011, http://www.ncbi.nlm.nih.gov/pubmedhealth/PMH0002503.

Nelson, N. (2010). *Language and literacy disorders infancy through adolescence.* Boston: Allyn & Bacon.

Nelson, N., & Van Meter, A. (2004). *The writing lab approach to language instruction and intervention.* Baltimore: Brookes.

Owens, R. (2012). *Language development: An introduction* (8th ed.). Boston: Allyn & Bacon.

Paradis, J., Genesee, F., & Crago, M. (2011). *Dual language development and disorders: A handbook on bilingualism and second language learning.* Baltimore: Brookes.

Porter, G., & Burkhart, L. (2010). *Pragmatic organization dynamic displays communication books: Designing and implementing PODD communication books.* Victoria, Australia: Cerebral Palsy Education Centre.

Rice, M. L. (1993). "Don't talk to him, he's weird": A social consequences account of language and social interactions. In A. P. Kaiser & D. B. Gray (Eds.), *Enhancing children's communication: Research foundations for intervention* (pp. 139–158). Baltimore: Brookes.

Rice, M., & Wilcox, K. (1995). *Building a language-focused curriculum for the preschool classroom: Vol. I. A foundation for lifelong communication.* Baltimore: Brookes.

Romski, M. A., & Sevcik, R. A. (1988). Augmentative communication system acquisition and use: A model for teaching and assessing progress. *National Student Speech Language Hearing Association Journal, 16,* 61–74.

Romski, M. A., & Sevcik, R. A. (1992). Developing augmented language in children with severe mental retardation. In S. F. Warren & J. Reichle (Eds.), *Communication and language intervention series: Vol. 1. Causes and effects in communication and language intervention* (pp. 113–130). Baltimore: Brookes.

Romski, M. A., & Sevcik, R. A. (1996). *Breaking the speech barrier: Language development through augmented means.* Baltimore: Brookes.

Romski, M. A., & Sevcik, R. A. (2003). Augmented input. In J. Light, D. Beukelman, & J. Reichle (Eds.), *Communicative competence for individuals who use AAC: From research to effective practice* (pp. 147–162). Baltimore: Brookes.

Romski, M. A., Sevcik, R. A., & Forrest, S. (2001). Assistive technology and augmentative communication in inclusive early childhood programs. In M. J. Guralnick (Ed.), *Early childhood inclusion: Focus on change* (pp. 465–479). Baltimore: Brookes.

Roseberry-McKibbin, C., & O'Hanlon, L. (2005). Nonbiased assessment of English language learners: A tutorial. *Communication Disorders Quarterly, 26*(3), 178–185.

Sandall, S., & Schwartz, I. (2002). *Building blocks for teaching preschoolers with special needs.* Baltimore: Brookes.

Sturm, J., & Rankin-Erickson, J. (2002). Effects of hand-drawn and computer-generated concept mapping on the expository writing of middle school students with learning disabilities. *Learning Disabilities Research and Practices, 17*(2), 124–139.

U.S. Department of Education. (2011). *Data accountability center: Individuals with Disabilities Education Act (IDEA) data.* Retrieved February 26, 2011, from https://www.ideadata.org.

Verdolini, K. (2000). Voice disorders. In J. Tomblin, H. Morris, & D. Spriestersbach (Eds.), *Diagnosis in speech-language pathology* (2nd ed., pp. 233–280). San Diego: Singular.

Vygotsky, L. S. (1978). *Thought and language.* Cambridge, MA: Harvard University Press.

Vygotsky, L. S. (1987). *The collected works of L. S. Vygotsky* (Vol. 1). New York: Plenum.

Chapter 7

American Psychiatric Association. (2000). *Diagnostic and statistical manual of mental disorders* (4th ed., revised). Washington, DC: Author.

Appleton, P. (2008). *Children's anxiety: A contextual approach.* New York: Routledge.

Bateson, P., & Martin, P. (1999). *Design for a life: How behaviour develops.* London: Cape.

Benner, G. J., Beaudoin, K., Mooney, P., Uhing, B. M., & Pierce, C. D. (2008). A replication and extension convergent validity study of the BERS-2 Teacher Rating Scale and the Achenbach Teacher's Report Form. *Journal of Child and Family Studies, 17*(3), 427–436.

Billingsley, B. S., Fall, A. M., Williams, T. O., Jr., & Tech, V. (2006). Who is teaching students with emotional and behavioral disorders? A profile and comparison to other special educators. *Behavioral Disorders, 31*(3), 252–264.

Bonanno, R. A., & Hymel, S. (2010). Beyond hurt feelings: Investigating why some victims of bullying are at greater risk for suicidal ideation. *Merrill-Palmer Quarterly, 56*(3), 420–440.

Boos, H. B. M., Aleman, A., Cahn, W., Pol, H. H., & Kahn, R. S. (2007). Brain volumes in relatives of patients with schizophrenia: A meta-analysis. *Archives of General Psychiatry, 64*(3), 297–304.

Borgwardt, S. J., Riecher-Rossler, A., Dazzan, P., Chitnis, X., Aston, J., Drewe, M., et al. (2007). Regional gray matter volume abnormalities in the at risk mental state. *Biological Psychiatry, 61*(10), 1148–1156.

Bowman-Perrott, L. (2009). Classwide peer tutoring: An effective strategy for students with emotional and behavioral disorders. *Intervention in School and Clinic, 44*(5), 259–267.

Bradshaw, C. P., Zmuda, J., Kellam, S. G., & Ialongo, N. S. (2009). Longitudinal impact of two universal preventive interventions in first grade on educational outcomes in high school. *Journal of Educational Psychology, 101*(4), 926–937.

Breedlove, S. M., Watson, N. V., & Rosenzweig, M. R. (2010). *Biological psychology: A introduction to behavioral, cognitive, and clinical neuroscience* (6th ed.). Sunderlund, MA: Sinauer Associates.

Bruns, E. J., Walrath, C. M., & Sheehan, A. K. (2007). Who administers wraparound? An examination of the training, beliefs, and implementation supports for wraparound providers. *Journal of Emotional and Behavioral Disorders, 15*(3), 156–168.

Buckley, J. A., Ryser, G., Reid, R., & Epstein, M. H. (2006). Confirmatory factor analysis of the Behavioral and Emotional Rating Scale—2 (BERS-2) Parent and Youth Rating Scales. *Journal of Child and Family Studies, 15*(1), 27–38.

Bullock, C., & Foegen, A. (2002). Constructive conflict resolution for students with behavioral disorders. *Behavioral Disorders, 27*(3), 289–295.

Burke, J. D., Hipwell, A. E., & Loeber, R. (2010). Dimensions of oppositional defiant disorder as predictors of depression and conduct disorder in preadolescent girls. *Journal of the American Academy of Child and Adolescent Psychiatry, 49*(5), 484–492.

Button, T. M. M., Lau, J. Y. F., Maughan, B., & Eley, T. C. (2008). Parental punitive discipline, negative life events and gene-environment interplay in the development of externalizing behavior. *Psycholology of Medicine, 38*(1), 29–39.

Centers for Disease Control and Prevention. (2010, May 14). *Surveillance for violent deaths—National violent death reporting system, 16 states, 2007.* Retrieved August 3, 2011, from http://www.cdc.gov/mmwr/preview/mmwrhtml/ss5904a1.htm.

Christenson, S. L., Reschly, A. L., Appleton, J. J., Berman, S., Spanjers, D., & Varro, P. (2008). Best practices in fostering student engagement. In A. Thomas & J. Grimes (Eds.), *Best practices in school psychology* (pp. 1099–1120). Washington, DC: National Association of School Psychologists.

Christle, C. A., Jolivette, K., & Nelson, C. M. (2007). School characteristics related to high school dropout rates. *Remedial and Special Education, 28*(6), 325–339.

Connolly, S. D., & Bernstein, G. A. (2007). Practice parameter for the assessment and treatment of children and adolescents with anxiety disorders. *Journal of the American Academy of Child and Adolescent Psychiatry, 46*, 267–283.

Cullinan, D. (2007). *Students with emotional and behavioral disorders: An introduction for teachers and other helping professionals.* Upper Saddle River, NJ: Merrill/Pearson.

Dandreaux, D. M., & Frick, P. J. (2009). Developmental pathways to conduct problems: A further test of the childhood and adolescent-onset distinction. *Journal of Abnormal Child Psychology, 37*, 375–385.

D'Eon, M., Proctor, P., & Reeder, B. (2007). Comparing two cooperative small group formats used with physical therapy and medical students. *Innovations in Education and Teaching International, 44*(1), 31–44.

Dymond, S. K., Renzaglia, A., & Chun, E. (2007). Elements of effective high school service learning programs that include students with and without disabilities. *Remedial and Special Education, 28*(4), 227–243.

Eme, R. F. (2007). Sex differences in child-onset, life-course-persistent conduct disorder: A review of biological influences. *Clinical Psychology Review, 27*, 607–627.

Epstein, M. H. (2004). *Behavioral and Emotional Rating Scale (BERS-2): A strength-based approach to assessment* (2nd ed.). Austin, TX: PRO-ED.

Epstein, M. H., Cullinan, D., Ryser, G., & Pearson, N. (2002). Development of a scale to assess emotional disturbance. *Behavioral Disorders, 28*(1), 5–22.

Farmer, M.Z., Mustillo, S., Burns, B.J., & Holden, E.W. (2008). Use and predictors of out-of-home placements with systems of care. *Journal of Emotional and Behavioral Disorders, 16*(1), 5–14.

Flick, G. L. (2011). *Understanding and managing emotional and behavioral disorders in the classroom.* Upper Saddle River, NJ: Merrill/Pearson.

Foley, R. M. (2001). Academic characteristics of incarcerated youth and correctional educational programs: A literature review. *Journal of Emotional and Behavioral Disorders, 9*(4), 248–259.

Frazier, J. A., McClellan, J., Findling, R. L., Vitiello, B., Anderson, R., Zablotsky, B., Williams, E., et al. (2007). Treatment of early-onset schizophrenia spectrum disorders (TEOSS): Demographic and clinical characteristics. *Journal of the American Academy of Child Adolescent Psychiatry, 46*(8), 979–988.

Gagnon, J. C., & McLaughlin, M. J. (2004). Curriculum, assessment, and accountability in day treatment and residential schools. *Exceptional Children, 70*, 263–283.

Garber, J., & Carter, J. S. (2006). Major depression. In M. Hersen & J. C. Thomas (Eds.), *Comprehensive handbook of personality and psychopathology* (Vol. 3, pp. 165–216). Hoboken, NJ: Wiley.

Goldstein, B. J., Shamseddeen, W., Spirito, A., Emslie, G., Clarke, G., Wagner, K. D., Asarnow, J. R., et al. (2009). Substance use and the treatment of resistant depression in adolescents. *Journal of the American Academy of Child Adolescent Psychiatry, 48*(12), 1182–1192.

Gresham, F. M., Elliott, S. N., Cook, C. R., Vance, M. J., & Kettler, R. (2010). Cross-informant agreement for ratings for social skill and problem behavior ratings: An investigation of the Social Skills Improvement System—Rating Scales. *Psychological Assessment, 22*(1), 157–166.

Heibron, N., & Prinstein, M. J. (2010). Adolescent peer victimization, peer status, suicidal ideation, and nonsuicidal self-injury: Examining concurrent and longitudinal associations. *Merrill-Palmer Quarterly, 56*(3), 388–419.

Huang, L., Stroul, B., Friedman, R., Mrazek, P., Friesen, B., Pires, S., et al. (2005). Transforming mental health care for children and their families. *American Psychologist, 60*(6), 615–627.

Johns, B. H., Crowley, E. P., & Guetzloe, E. (2005). The central role of teaching social skills. *Focus on Exceptional Children, 37*(8), 1–8.

Kamps, D. M., Greenwood, C., Arreaga-Mayer, C., Veerkamp, M. B., Utley, C., Tapia, Y., et al. (2008). The efficacy of classwide peer rutoring in middle schools. *Education and Treatment of Children, 31*(2), 119–152.

King-Sears, M., & Mooney, J. F. (2004). Teaching content in an academically diverse class. In B. K. Lenz, D. D. Deshler, & B. R. Kissam (Eds.), *Teaching content to all: Evidence-based inclusive practices in middle and secondary schools* (pp. 221–257). Boston: Allyn & Bacon.

Klomek, A. B., Sourander, A., Niemela, S., Kumpulainen, K., Piha, J., Tamminen, T., Almqvist, F., et al. (2009). Childhood bullying behaviors as a risk for suicide attempts and completed suicides: A population-based birth cohort study. *Journal of the American Academy of Child Adolescent Psychiatry, 48*(3), 254–261.

Krezmien, M. P., Mulcahy, C. A., & Leone, P. E. (2008). Detained and committed youth: Examining differences in achievement, mental health needs, and special education status. *Education and Treatment of Children, 31*(4), 445–464.

Lane, K. L., Barton-Arwood, S. M., Nelson, J. R., & Wehby, J. (2008). Academic performance of students with emotional and behavioral disorders served in a self-contained setting. *Journal of Behavioral Education, 17*, 43–62.

Lehr, C. A., Johnson, D. R., Bremer, C. D., Cosio, A., & Thompson, M. (2004). *Increasing rates of school completion: Moving from policy and research to practice.* Minneapolis: University of Minnesota, National Center on Secondary Special Education and Transition.

Leone, P. E., Meisel, S. M., & Drakeford, W. (2002). Special education programs for youth with disabilities in juvenile corrections. *Journal of Correctional Education, 53*, 46–50.

Maheady, L., & Gard, J. (2010). Classwide peer tutoring: Practice, theory research, and personal narrative. *Intervention in School and Clinic, 46*(2), 71–78.

McDonell, M. G., & McClellan, J. M. (2007). Early-onset schizophrenia. In E. J. Mash & R. A. Barkley (Eds.), *Assessment of childhood disorders* (4th ed., pp. 526–550). New York: Guilford.

McMahon, R. J., & Frick, P. J. (2007). Conduct and oppositional disorders. In E. J. Mash & R. A. Barkley (Eds.), *Assessment of childhood disorders* (4th ed., pp. 132–183). New York: Guilford.

Meyer, S. E., & Carlson, G. A. (2010). Development, age of onset, and phenomenology in bipolar disorder. In D. J. Miklowitz & D. Cicchetti (Eds.), *Understanding bipolar disorder: A developmental psychopathology perspective* (pp. 35–66). New York: Guilford.

Miller, K. J., Fitzgerald, G. E., Koury, K. A., Mitchem, K. J., & Hollingshead, C. (2007). Self-management, problem-solving, organizational, and planning software for children and teachers. *Intervention in School and Clinic, 43*(1), 12–19.

Miner, J. L., & Clarke-Stewart, K. A. (2008). Trajectories of externalizing behavior from age 2 to age 9: Relations with gender, temperament, ethnicity, parenting, and rater. *Developmental Psychology, 44*(3), 771–786.

Mitchem, K., Kight, J., Fitzgerald, G., & Koury, K. (2007). Electronic performance support systems: An assistive technology for secondary students with mild disabilities. *Journal of Special Education Technology, 22*(2),1–14.

Morris, A. S., Silk, J. S., Steinberg, L., Myers, S. S., & Robinson, L. R. (2007). The role of the family context in the development of emotion regulation. *Social Development, 16*(2), 361–387.

National High School Center. (2007). *Dropout prevention for students with disabilities: A critical issue for state education agencies.* Washington, DC: Author. Retrieved December 13, 2010, from http://www .betterhighschools.org/docs/NHSC_ DropoutPrevention_052507.pdf.

Nelson, J. R., Stage, S., Duppong-Hurley, K., Synhorst, L., & Epstein, M. H. (2007). Risk factors predictive of the problem behavior of children at risk for emotional and behavioral disorders. *Exceptional Children, 73*(3), 367–379.

Posner, M. I., & Rothbart, M. K. (2009). Toward a physical basis of attention and self regulation. *Physics of Life Reviews, 6*(2), 103–120.

Quinn, K. P., & Lee, V. (2007). The wraparound approach for students with emotional and behavioral disorders: Opportunities for school psychologists. *Psychology in the Schools, 44*(1), 101–111.

Quinn, M. M., Rutherford, R. B., Leone, P. E., Osher, D. M., & Poirier, J. M. (2005). Youth with disabilities in juvenile corrections: A national survey. *Exceptional Children, 71*(3), 339–345.

Riccomini, P. J., Witzel, B., & Robbins, K. (2008). Improving the mathematics instruction for students with emotional and behavioral disorders: Two evidence-based instructional approaches. *Beyond Behaviour, 17*(2), 24–30.

Rice, E. H., Merves, E., & Srsic, A. (2008). Perceptions of gender differences in the expression of emotional and behavioral disabilities. *Education and Treatment of Children, 31*(4), 549–565.

Robb, A., & Reber, M. (2007). Behavioral and psychiatric disorders in children with disabilities. In M. L. Batshaw, L. Pellegrino, & N. J. Roizen (Eds.), *Children with disabilities* (6th ed., pp. 297–311). Baltimore: Brookes.

Rose, C. A., Monda-Amaya, L. E., & Espelage, D. L. (2010). Bullying perpetration and victimization in special education: A review of the literature. *Remedial and Special Education, 32*(2), 114–130.

Rudolph, K. D., & Lambert, S. F. (2007). Child and adolescent depression. In E. J. Mash & R. A. Barkley (Eds.), *Assessment of childhood disorders* (4th ed., pp. 213–252). New York: Guilford.

Rudy, H. L., & Levinson, E. M. (2008). Best practices in the multidisciplinary assessment of emotional disturbances: A primer for counselors. *Journal of Counseling and Development, 86*, 494–504.

Saarni, C., Campos, J. J., Camras, L., & Witherington, D. (2006). Emotional development: Action, communication, and understanding. In N. Eisenberg (Ed.), *Handbook of child psychology. Vol. 3: Social, emotional and personality development* (6th ed.). New York: Wiley.

Sacks, G., & Kern, L. (2008). A comparison of quality of life variables for students with emotional and behavioral disorders and students without disabilities. *Journal of Behavioral Education, 17*, 111–127.

SAMHSA. (2011). Major depressive episodes and treatment among adolescents: 2009. *The MSDUH Report.* Retrieved on August 8, 2011, from http://oas.samhsa .gov/2k11/009/AdolescentDepressionhtml .pdf.

Schoenfeld, N. A., & Janney, D. M. (2008). Identification and treatment of anxiety in students with emotional or behavioral disorders: A review of the literature. *Education and Treatment of Children, 31*(4), 583–610.

Severson, H. H., Walker, H. M., Hope-Doolittle, J., Kratochwill, T. R., & Gresham, F. M. (2007). Proactive, early screening to detect behaviorally at-risk students: Issues, approaches, emerging innovations, and professional practices. *Journal of School Psychology, 45*, 193–223.

Sharkey, J. D., You, S., Morrison, G. M., & Griffiths, A. J. (2009). Behavioral and Emotional Rating Scale—2 Parent Report: Exploring a Spanish version with at-risk students. *Behavioral Disorders, 35*(1), 53–65.

Sheese, B. E., Voelker, P., Posner, M. I., & Rothbart, M. K. (2009). Genetic variation influences on the early development of relative emotions and their regulation by attention. *Cognitive Neuropsychiatry, 14*(4/5), 332–355.

Sickmund, M. (2002, March). *Juvenile offenders in residential placement: 1997–1999. OJJDP fact sheet.* Washington, DC: U.S. Department of Justice, Office of Juvenile Justice and Delinquency Prevention.

Situ, M., Li, T., Gao, X., Zhang, X., Fang, H., Zhang, Y., & Huang, Y. (2009). The effect of genetic and environmental factors on the internalizing behavior of children: A twin study. *Zhonghua Yi Xue Yi Chuan Xue Za Zhi (Chinese Journal of Medical Genetics), 26*(6), 639–643.

Southam-Gerow, M. A., & Chorpita, B. F. (2007). Anxiety in children and adolescents. In E. J. Mash & R. A. Barkley (Eds.), *Assessment of childhood disorders* (4th ed., pp. 347–397). New York: Guilford.

Stambaugh, L. F., Mustillo, S. A., Burns, B. J., Stephens, R. L., Baxter, B., Edwards, D., & DeKraai, M. (2007). Outcomes from wraparound and multisystemic therapy in a center for mental health services system-of-care demonstration site. *Journal of Emotional and Behavioral Disorders, 15*(3), 143–155.

Sterzer, P., Stadler, C., Poustka, F., & Kleinschmidt, A. (2007). A structural neural deficit in adolescents with conduct disorder and its association with lack of empathy. *NeuroImage, 37,* 335–342.

Stout, K. E., & Christenson, S. L. (2009). Staying on track for high school graduation: Promoting student engagement. *Prevention Researcher, 16*(3), 17–20.

Stringaris, A., Maughan, B., & Goodman, R. (2010). What's in a disruptive disorder? Temperamental antecedents of oppositional defiant disorder: Findings from the Avon longitudinal study. *Journal of the American Academy of Child and Adolescent Psychiatry, 49*(5), 474–483.

Teeter, P. A., Eckert, L., Nelson, A., Platten, P., Semrud-Clikeman, M., & Kamphaus R. W. (2009). Assessment of behavior and personality in the neuropsychological diagnosis of children. In C. R. Reynolds & E. Fletcher-Janzen (Eds.), *Handbook of clinical child neuropsychology* (3rd ed., pp. 349–382). New York: Springer.

Uhing, B. M., Mooney, P., & Ryser, G. R. (2005). Differences in strength assessment scores for youth with and without ED across the Youth and Parent Rating Scales of the BERS-2. *Journal of Emotional and Behavioral Disorders, 13*(3), 181–187.

U.S. Department of Education. (2009). *Twenty-eighth annual report to Congress on the implementation of the Individuals with Disabilities Education Act, 2006.* Washington, DC: Author.

U.S. Department of Education. (2011). *Data accountability center: Individuals with Disabilities Education Act (IDEA) data.* Retrieved February 26, 2011, from https://www.ideadata.org.

Vannest, K. J., Temple-Harvey, K. K., & Mason, B. A. (2008). Adequate yearly progress for students with emotional and behavioral disorders through research-based practices. *Preventing School Failure, 53*(2), 73–83.

Wagner, M., & Davis, M. (2006). How are we preparing students with emotional disturbances for the transition to young adulthood?: Findings from the National Longitudinal Transition Study—2. *Journal of Emotional and Behavioral Disorders, 14,* 86–98.

Wagner, M., Friend, M., Bursuck, W. D., Kutash, K., Duchnowski, A. J., Sumi, W. C., et al. (2006). Educating students with emotional disturbances: A national perspective on school programs and services. *Journal of Emotional and Behavioral Disorders, 14*(1), 12–30.

Wagner, M., Kutash, K., Duchnowski, A. J., Epstein, M. H., & Sumi, W. C. (2005). The children and youth we serve: A national picture of the characteristics of students with emotional disturbances receiving special education. *Journal of Emotional and Behavioral Disorders, 13*(2), 79–96.

Walker, J. S., & Schutte, K. M. (2004). Practice and process in wraparound teamwork. *Journal of Emotional and Behavioral Disorders, 12,* 182–192.

West, A. E., Henry, D. B., & Pavuluri, M. N. (2007). Maintenance model of integrated psychosocial treatment in pediatric bipolar disorder: A pilot feasibility study. *Journal of the American Academy of Child and Adolescent Psychiatry, 46*(2), 205–212.

White, G. W., Jellinek, M. S., & Murphy, J. M. (2010). The use of rating scales to measure outcomes in child psychiatry and mental health. In L. Baer & M. A. Blais (Eds.), *Handbook of clinical rating scales and assessment in psychiatry and mental health* (pp. 175–194). New York: Humana.

Willcutt, E., & McQueen, M. (2010). Genetic and environmental vulnerability to bipolar spectrum disorders. In D. J. Miklowitz & D. Cicchetti (Eds.), *Understanding bipolar disorder: A developmental psychopathology perspective* (pp. 225–258). New York: Guilford.

Winters, N. C., & Metz, W. P. (2009). The wraparound approach in systems of care. *Psychiatric Clinics of North America, 32*(1), 135–151.

Yeh, M., Forness, S. R., Ho, J., McCabe, K., & Hough, R. L. (2004). Parental etiological explanations and disproportionate racial/ethnic representation in special education services for youths with emotional disturbance. *Behavioral Disorders, 29*(4), 348–358.

Youngstrom, E. (2007). Pediatric bipolar disorder. In E. J. Mash & R. A. Barkley (Eds.), *Assessment of childhood disorders* (4th ed., pp. 253–304). New York: Guilford.

Chapter 8

Adams, Z. W., Derefinko, K. J., Milich, R., & Fillmore, M. T. (2008). Inhibitory functioning across ADHD subtypes: Recent findings, clinical implications, and future directions. *Developmental Disabilities Research Reviews, 14,* 268–275.

Alberto, P. A., & Troutman, A. C. (2008). *Applied behavior analysis for teachers* (8th ed.). Upper Saddle River, NJ: Merrill/Pearson.

American Academy of Child and Adolescent Psychiatry. (2007). *ADHD parents medication guide.* Washington, DC: Author.

American Psychiatric Association (APA). (2000). *Diagnostic and statistical manual of mental disorders* (4th ed., rev.). Washington, DC: Author.

Armenteros, J. L., Lewis, J. E., & Davalos, M. (2007). Risperidone augmentations for attention-deficit/hyperactivity disorder. *Journal of the American Academy of Child and Adolescent Psychiatry, 46,* 558–565.

Barkley, R. A. (2003). Attention-deficit/hyperactivity disorder. In E. J. Mash & R. A. Barkley (Eds.), *Child psychopathology* (2nd ed., pp. 75–143). New York: Guilford.

Barkley, R. A., Fischer, M., Smallish, L., & Fletcher, K. (2006). Young adult outcome of hyperactive children: Adaptive functioning in major life activities. *Journal of the American Academy of Child and Adolescent Psychiatry, 45*(2), 192–202.

Barkley, R. A., Murphy, K. R., & Fischer, M. (2007). *ADHD in adults: Original research and clinical implications.* New York: Guilford.

Blazer, B. (1999). Developing 504 classroom accommodation plans: A collaborative, systematic parent-student-teacher approach. *Teaching Exceptional Children, 32*(2), 28–33.

Brock, S. E., Jimerson, S. R., & Hansen, R. L. (2009). *Developmental psychopathology at school: Identifying, assessing, and treating ADHD at school.* New York: Springer.

Bowen, R., Chavira, D. A., Bailey, K., Stein, M. T., & Stein, M. B. (2008). Nature of anxiety comorbid with attention deficit hyperactivity disorder in children from a pediatric primary care setting. *Psychiatry Research, 157,* 201–208.

Buggey, T. (2007). A picture is worth . . . : Video self-modeling applications at school and home. *Journal of Positive Behavior Interventions, 9,* 151–158.

Bush, G. (2008). Neuroimaging of attention deficit hyperactivity disorder: Can new imaging findings be integrated in clinical practice? *Child Adolescent Psychiatric Clinics of North America, 17,* 385–404.

Bussing, R., Mason, D. M., Bell, L., Porter, P., & Garvan, C. (2010). Adolescent outcomes of childhood attention-deficit/hyperactivity disorder in a diverse community sample. *Journal of the American Academy of Child and Adolescent Psychiatry, 49*(6), 595–605.

Conners, C. K. (1997). *Conners's Rating Scales—Revised technical manual.* North Tonawanda, NY: Multi-Health Systems.

Cortese, S., Lecendreux, M., Mouren, M. C., & Konofal, E. (2006). ADHD and insomnia. *Journal of the American Academy of Child and Adolescent Psychiatry, 45*(4), 384–385.

Da Fonseca, D., Seguier, V., Santos, A., Poinso, F., & Deruelle, C. (2009). Emotion understanding in children with ADHD. *Child Psychiatry Human Development, 40,* 111–121.

Davis-Berman, J. L., & Pestello, F. G. (2010). Medicating for ADD/ADHD: Personal and social issues. *International Journal of Mental Health and Addiction, 8*(3), 482–492.

Demaray, M. K., Elting, J., & Schaefer, K. (2003). Assessment of attention-deficit/hyperactivity disorder (AD/HD): A comparative evaluation of five commonly used, published rating scales. *Psychology in the Schools, 40*(4), 341–361.

Demaray, M. K., Schaefer, K., & Delong, L. K. (2003). Attention-deficit/hyperactivity disorder (ADHD): A national survey of training and current assessment practices in the schools. *Psychology in the Schools, 40*(6), 583–597.

Dopheide, J. A., & Pliszka, S. R. (2009). Attention-deficit–hyperactivity disorder: An update. *Pharmacotherapy, 29*(6), 656–679.

Egger, H. L., Kondo, D., & Angold, A. (2006). The epidemiology and diagnostic issues in preschool attention-deficit/hyperactivity disorder: A review. *Infants and Young Children, 19*(2), 109–122.

Faraone, S. V., Perlis, R. H., Doyle, A. E., Smoller, J., Goralnick, J., Holmgren, M., et al. (2005). Molecular genetics of attention-deficit/hyperactivity disorder. *Biological Psychiatry, 57*, 1313–1323.

Flory, K., Molina, B. S. G., Pelham, W., Gnagy, B., & Smith, B. H. (2006). ADHD and risky behavior. *Journal of Clinical Child and Adolescent Psychology, 53*, 571–577.

Glanzman, M., & Blum, N. J. (2007a). Attention deficits and hyperactivity. In M. L. Batshaw, L. Pellegrino, & N. J. Roizen (Eds.), *Children with disabilities* (6th ed., pp. 345–365). Baltimore: Brookes.

Glanzman, M., & Blum, N. J. (2007b). Genetics, imaging, and neurochemistry in attention-deficit/hyperactivity disorder (ADHD). In P. J. Accardo (Ed.), *Capute and Accardo's neurodevelopmental disabilities in infancy and childhood. Vol. 2: The spectrum of developmental disabilities* (3rd ed.). Baltimore: Brookes.

Harman, P. L., & Barkley, R. (2000). One-on-one with Russell Barkley. *Attention! 6*(4), 12–14.

Holler, R. A., & Zirkel, P. A. (2008). Legally best practices in Section 504 plans. *School Administrator, 65*(8), 38–40.

Hoza, B. (2007). Peer functioning in children with ADHD. *Ambulatory Pediatrics, 7*(1), 101–106.

Hoza, B., Kaiser, N. M., & Hurt, E. (2007). Multimodal treatments for childhood attention-deficit/hyperactivity disorder: Interpreting outcomes in the context of study designs. *Clinical Child and Family Psychology Review, 10*(4), 318–334.

Jitendra, A. K., DuPaul, G. J., Someki, F., & Tresco, K. E. (2008). Enhancing academic achievement for children with attention-deficit hyperactivity disorder: Evidence from school-based intervention research.

Developmental Disabilities Research Reviews, 14, 325–330.

Kern, L., DuPaul, G. J., Volpe, R. J., Sokol, N. G., Lutz, J. G., Arbolino, L. A., et al. (2007). Multisetting assessment-based intervention for young children at risk for attention deficit hyperactivity disorder: Initial effects on academic and behavioral functioning. *School Psychology Review, 36*, 237–255.

Kieling, C., Goncalves, R. R., Tannock, R., & Castellanos, F. X. (2008). Neuroimaging of attention deficit hyperactivity disorder. *Child and Adolescent Psychiatric Clinics of North America, 17*(2), 285–307.

Kiersuk, T. J., Smith, A., & Cardillo, A. (1994). *Goal attainment scaling: Applications and measurement.* Hillsdale, NJ: Erlbaum.

Konrad, M., Fowler, C. H., Walker, A., Test, D. W., & Wood, W. M. (2007). Effects of self-determination interventions on the academic skills of students with learning disabilities. *Learning Disabilities Quarterly, 30*, 89–113.

Larsson, J. O., Larsson, H., & Lichtenstein, P. (2004). Genetic and environmental contributions to stability and change of ADHD symptoms between 8 and 14 years of age: A longitudinal twin study. *Journal of the American Academy of Child Adolescent Psychiatry, 43*, 1267–1275.

Mahone, E. M., & Wodka, E. L. (2008). The neurobiological profile of girls with ADHD. *Developmental Disabilities Research Review, 14*, 276–284.

Makami, A. Y. (2010). The importance of friendship for youth with attention-deficit/hyperactivity disorder. *Clinical Child and Family Psychology Review, 13*(2), 181–198.

Mazzotti, V. L., Wood, C. L., Test, D. W., & Fowler, C. H. (2010). Effects of computer-assisted instruction on students' knowledge of the self-determined learning model of instruction and disruptive behavior. *Journal of Special Education.* DOI 10.1177/0022466910362261.

McQuade, J. A., & Hoza, B. (2008). Peer problems in attention deficit hyperactivity disorder: Current status and future directions. *Developmental Disabilities Research Reviews, 14*, 320–324.

Meltzer, L. (2010). *Promoting executive function in the classroom.* New York: Guilford.

Merriman, D. E., & Codding, R. S. (2008). The effects of coaching on mathematics homework completion and accuracy of high school students with attention-deficit disorder. *Journal of Behavioral Education, 17*(4), 339–355.

Molina, B. S., Hinshaw, S. P., Swanson, J. M., Arnold, L. E., Vitiello, B., Jensen, P. S., Epstein, J. N., et al. (2009). The MTA at 8 years: Prospective follow-up of children treated for combined-type ADHD in a multisite study. *Journal of the American Academy of Child and Adolescent Psychiatry, 48*, 484–500.

Parker, H. C. (1992). ADAPT accommodation plan. *ADD Warehouse.* Retrieved July 7, 2008, from http://www.addwarehouse.com.

Roach, A. T., & Elliott, S. N. (2005). Goal attainment scaling: An efficient and effective approach to monitoring student progress. *Teaching Exceptional Children, 37*(4), 8–17.

Scheirs, J. G. M., & Timmers, E. A. (2009). Differentiating among children with PDD-NOS, ADHD, and those with a combined diagnosis on the basis of WISC-III profiles. *Journal of Autism Developmental Disorders, 39*, 549–556.

Schnoes, C., Reid, R., Wagner, M., & Marder, C. (2006). ADHD among students receiving special education services: A national survey. *Council for Exceptional Children, 72*(4), 483–496.

Smith, B. H., Barkley, R. A., & Shapiro, C. J. (2007). Attention-deficit/hyperactivity disorder. In E. J. Mash & R. A. Barkley (Eds.), *Assessment of childhood disorders* (4th ed., pp. 53–122). New York: Guilford.

Stanford, P., & Reeves, S. (2005). Assessment that drives instruction. *Teaching Exceptional Children, 37*(4), 18–23.

Stevens, J., & Ward-Estes, J. (2006). Attention-deficit/hyperactivity disorder. *Comprehensive Handbook of Personality and Psychopathology, 3*, 316–329.

Upadhyaya, H. P., & Carpenter, M. J. (2008). Is attention deficit hyperactivity disorder (ADHD) symptom severity associated with tobacco use? *American Journal on Addictions, 17*, 195–198.

Vaidya, C. J., & Stollstorff, M. (2008). Cognitive neuroscience of attention deficit hyperactivity disorder: Current status and working hypotheses. *Developmental Disabilities Research Reviews, 14*, 261–267.

Wilens, T. E., Hahesey, A. L., Biederman, J., Bredin, E., Tanguay, S., Kwon, A., et al. (2005). Influence of parental SUD and ADHD on ADD in their offspring: Preliminary results from a pilot-controlled family study. *American Journal of Addictions, 14*, 179–187.

Zirkel, P. A. (2009). Legal perspectives: What does the law say? New Section 405 student eligibility standards. *Teaching Exceptional Children, 41*(4), 68–71.

Chapter 9

American Psychiatric Association (APA). (2000). *Diagnostic and statistical manual of mental disorders* (4th ed., rev.). Washington, DC: Author.

Avchen, R. N., Bhasin, T. K., Braun, K. V., & Yeargin-Allsopp, M. (2007). Public health impact: Metropolitan Atlanta developmental disabilities surveillance program. *International Review of Research in Mental Retardation, 33*, 149–190.

Bambara, L. M., Wilson, B. A., & McKenzie, M. (2007). Transition and quality of life. In S. L. Odom, R. H. Horner, M. E. Snell, & J. Blacher (Eds.), *Handbook of developmental disabilities* (pp. 371–389). New York: Guilford.

Borkowski, J. G., Noria, C. W., Lefever, J. B., Keogh, D. A., Whitman, T. L., Lounds, J. J., et al. (2004). Precursors of mild mental retardation in children with adolescent mothers. *International Review of Research in Mental Retardation, 29*, 197–228.

Borthwick-Duffy, S. A. (2007). Adaptive behavior. In J. W. Jacobson, J. A. Mulick, & J. Rojahn (Eds.), *Handbook of intellectual disabilities* (pp. 279–293). New York: Springer Science/Business Media.

Brady, N. C., & Bashinski, S. M. (2008). Increasing communication in children with concurrent vision and hearing loss. *Research and Practice for Persons with Severe Disabilities, 33*, 59–70.

Brady, N., Warren, S. F., & Sterling, A. (2009). Interventions aimed at improving child language by improving maternal responsivity. In L. Glidden (Ed.), *International review of research in mental retardation* (Vol. 37, pp. 333–357). New York: Elsevier.

Brown, F., Lehr, D., & Snell, M. (2011). Conducting and using student assessment. In M. Snell & F. Brown (Eds.), *Instruction of students with severe disabilities* (7th ed., pp. 73–121). Upper Saddle River, NJ: Merrill/Pearson.

Causton-Theoharis, J. N., Giangreco, M. F., Doyle, M. B., & Vadasy, P. F. (2007). Paraprofessionals: The "sous-chefs" of literacy instruction. *Teaching Exceptional Children, 40*(1), 56–62.

Clark, G. M. (2007). *Assessment for transitions planning* (2nd ed.). Austin, TX: PRO-ED.

Clark, G. M., & Patton, J. R. (2006). *Transition planning inventory: Updated version*. Austin, TX: PRO-ED.

Davies, D. K., Stock, S. E., King, L., Woodard, J., & Wehmeyer, M. (2008). "Moby Dick is my favorite": Evaluating the use of a cognitively accessible portable reading system for audio books by people with intellectual disability. *Intellectual and Developmental Disabilities, 46*(4), 290–298.

Dixon, D. R. (2007). Adaptive behavior scales. In J. L. Matson (Ed.), *International review of research in mental retardation* (Vol. 34, pp. 99–140). San Diego: Elsevier.

Einfeld, S., & Emerson, E. (2008). Intellectual disability. In M. Rutter, D. V. M. Bishop, D. S. Pine, S. Scott, J. Stevenon, E. Taylor, & A. Thapar (Eds.), *Rutter's child and adolescent psychiatry* (5th ed., pp. 820–841). Malden, MA: Blackwell.

Emerson, E. (2010). Deprivation, ethnicity, and the prevalence of intellectual and developmental disabilities. *Journal of Epidemiology Community Health*. DOI:10.1136/jech.2010.111773.

Emerson, E., Graham, H., & Hatton, C. (2006). Household income and health status in children and adolescents in Britain. *European Journal of Public Health, 16*, 354–360.

Ferguson, D. L. (1995). The real challenge of inclusion: Confessions of a "rabid inclusionist." *Phi Delta Kappan, 77*, 281–287.

Fujiura, G. T., & Parish, S. L. (2007). Emerging policy challenges in intellectual disabilities. *Mental Retardation and Developmental Disabilities Research Reviews, 13*(2), 188–194.

Giangreco, M. F., & Broer, S. M. (2007). School-based screening to determine overreliance on paraprofessionals. *Focus on Autism and Other Developmental Disabilities, 22*(3), 149–158.

Grigal, M., & Hart, D. (2010). *Think college! Postsecondary education options for students with intellectual disabilities*. Baltimore: Brookes.

Ismail, S., Buckley, S., Budacki, R., Jabbar, A., & Gallicano, G. I. (2009). Screening, diagnosing and prevention of fetal alcohol syndrome: Is this syndrome treatable? *Developmental Neuroscience, 32*, 91–100.

Jarrold, C., Purser, H. R. M., & Brock, J. (2006). Short-term memory in Down syndrome. In T. P. Alloway & S. E. Gathercole (Eds.), *Working memory and neurodevelopmental conditions* (pp. 239–266). Hove, East Sussex, England: Psychology Press.

Keller, C. L., Bucholz, J., & Brady, M. P. (2007). Yes I can! Empowering paraprofessionals to teach learning strategies. *Teaching Exceptional Children, 39*(3), 18–23.

Kim, R., & Dymond, S. K. (2010). Special education teachers' perceptions of benefits, barriers, and components of community-based vocational instruction. *Intellectual and Developmental Disabilities, 48*(5), 313–329.

Kleinert, H. L., & Kearns, J. F. (2010). *Alternate assessment for students with significant cognitive disabilities: An educator's guide*. Baltimore: Brookes.

Lane, K. L., Fletcher, T., Carter, E., Dejud, C., & Delorenzo, J. (2007). Paraprofessional-led phonological awareness training with youngsters at risk for reading and behavioral concerns. *Remedial and Special Education, 28*(5), 266–276.

Lee, Y., Wehmeyer, M., Palmer, S., Williams-Diehm, K., Davies, D., & Stock, S. (in press). The effect of student-directed transition planning using a computer-based reading support program on the self-determination of students with disabilities. *Journal of Special Education*.

Li, J., Bassett, D. S., & Hutchinson, S. R. (2009). Secondary special educators' transition involvement. *Journal of Intellectual and Developmental Disability, 34*(2), 163–172.

Lytle, R., Lieberman, L., & Aiello, R. (2007). Motivating paraeducators to be actively involved in physical education programs. *Journal of Physical Education, Recreation, and Dance, 78*(4), 26–30.

Martin, J., Jorgensen, C. M., & Klein, J. (1998). The promise of friendship for students with disabilities. In C. M. Jorgensen (Ed.), *Restructuring high schools for all students: Taking inclusion to the next level* (pp. 145–181). Baltimore: Brookes.

McDermott, S., Durkin, M. S., Schupf, N., & Stein, Z. A. (2007). Epidemiology and etiology of mental retardation. In J. Mulick, J. Rojahn, & J. Jacobson (Eds.), *Handbook of intellectual and developmental disabilities* (pp. 3–40). New York: Springer.

Mithaug, D. E., Mithaug, D., Agran, M., Martin, J., & Wehmeyer, M. L. (2007). *Self-instruction pedagogy: How to teach self-determined learning*. Springfield, IL: Thomas.

National Research Council. (2002). *Minority students in special and gifted education*. Washington, DC: National Academy Press.

Newman, L., Wagner, M., Cameto, R., & Knokey, A. M. (2009). *The post–high school outcomes of youth with disabilities up to 4 years after high school: A report from the National Longitudinal Transition Study-2 (NLTS2)*. (NCSER 2009-3017). Menlo Park, CA: SRI International.

Noonan, P. M., Morningstar, M. E., & Erickson, A. G. (2010). Improving interagency collaboration: Effective strategies used by high-performing local districts and communities. *Career Development for Exceptional Individuals, 31*(3), 132–143.

O'Reilly, M. F., O'Reilly, B., Sigafoos, J., Green, V., Lancioni, G., & Machalicek, W. (2007). Educational assessment. *International Review of Research in Mental Retardation, 34*, 141–161.

Palmer, S. B., Wehmeyer, M. L., Gipson, K., & Agran, M. (2004). Promoting access to the general curriculum by teaching self-determination skills. *Exceptional Children, 70*, 427–439.

Percy, M. (2007). Factors that cause or contribute to intellectual and developmental disabilities. In I. Brown & M. Percy (Eds.), *A comprehensive guide to intellectual and developmental disabilities* (pp. 125–148). Baltimore: Brookes.

Quilty, K. M. (2007). Teaching paraprofessionals how to write and implement social stories for students with autism spectrum disorders. *Remedial and Special Education, 28*(3), 182–191.

Rehfeldt, J. D., Clark, G. M., & Lee, S. W. (2010). The effects of using the transition planning inventory and a structured IEP process as a transition planning intervention on IEP meeting outcomes. *Remedial and Special Education*, DOI:10.1177/0741932510366038.

Riggs, C. G., & Mueller, P. H. (2001). Employment and utilization of paraeducators in inclusive settings. *Journal of Special Education, 35*(1), 54–62.

Schalock, R. L., Borthwick-Duffy, S. A., Bradley, V. J., Buntinx, W. H. E., Coulter, D. L., Craig, E. M., et al. (2010). *Intellectual disability, definition, classification, and systems of support* (11th ed.). Washington, DC: American Association on Intellectual and Developmental Disabilities.

Schuchardt, K., Gebhardt, M., & Mäehler, C. (2010). Working memory functions in children with different degrees of intellectual disability. *Journal of Intellectual Disability Research, 54*(4), 346–353.

Shogren, K. A., Bovaird, J. A., Palmer, S. B., & Wehmeyer, M. L. (in press). Examining the development of locus of control orientations in students with intellectual disability, learning disabilities, and no disabilities: A latent growth curve analysis. *Research and Practice for Persons with Severe Disabilities.*

Shogren, K., Palmer, S., Wehmeyer, M. L., Williams-Diehm, K., & Little, T. (2011). Effect of intervention with the Self-Determined Learning Model of Instruction on access and goal attainment. *Remedial and Special Education,* DOI:10.1177/0741932511410072.

Snell, M., & Brown, F. (2011). *Instruction of students with severe disabilities* (7th ed.). Upper Saddle River, NJ: Pearson.

Stevens, S. L. (2006). *An investigation of the content validity, stability, and internal consistency of the Spanish version of the Transition Planning Inventory, Home Form.* Unpublished doctoral dissertation, University of Kansas, Lawrence.

Stinnett, T. A., Fuqua, D. R., & Coombs, W. T. (1999). Construct validity of the AAMR Adaptive Behavior Scale—School: 2. *School Psychology Review, 28*(1), 31–43.

Switzky, H. (2006). *International review of research in mental retardation: Vol. 31. Mental retardation, personality, and motivational systems.* San Diego: Academic Press.

Tassé, M. J., & Havercamp, S. M. (2006). The role of motivation and psychopathology in understanding the IQ-adaptive behavior discrepancy. In L. M. Glidden (Series Ed.) & H. Switzky (Vol. Ed.), *International review of research in mental retardation: Vol. 31. Mental retardation, personality, and motivational systems* (pp. 231–260). San Diego: Academic Press.

Thompson, J. R., Bradley, V., Buntix, W. H. E., Schalock, R. L., Shogren, K. A., Snell, M. E., Wehmeyer, M. L., et al. (2009). Conceptualizing supports and support needs of persons with intellectual disability. *Intellectual and Developmental Disabilities, 47,* 135–146.

Tylenda, B., Beckett, J., & Barrett, R. P. (2007). Assessing mental retardation using standardized intelligence tests. In

J. L. Matson (Ed.), *International review of research in mental retardation* (Vol. 34, pp. 27–97). San Diego, CA: Elsevier.

U.S. Department of Education, Office of Special Education Programs, Data Analysis System (DANS). (2011a). *Children with disabilities receiving special education under Part B of the Individuals with Disabilities Education Act, 2008.* (OMB #1820-0043). Retrieved February 12, 2011, from http://www.ideadata.org/.

U.S. Department of Education, Office of Special Education Programs, Data Analysis System (DANS). (2011b). *Personnel (in full-time equivalency of assignment) employed to provide special education and related services for children with disabilities, 2007.* (OMB #1820-0518). Retrieved February 12, 2011, http://www.ideadata.org/.

Vadasy, P. F., Sanders, E. A., & Peyton, J. A. (2006a). Code-oriented instruction for kindergarten students at risk for reading difficulties: A randomized field trial with paraeducator implementers. *Journal of Educational Psychology, 98,* 508–528.

Vadasy, P. F., Sanders, E. A., & Peyton, J. A. (2006b). Paraeducator-supplemented instruction in structural analysis with text reading practice for second and third graders at risk for reading problems. *Remedial and Special Education, 27*(6), 365–378.

Van der Molen, M. J., Van Luit, J. E. H., Van der Molen, M. W., & Jongmans, M. J. (2010). Everyday memory and working memory in adolescents with mild intellectual disability. *American Association on Intellectual and Developmental Disabilities, 115*(3), 207–217.

Walker, A. R., Uphold, N. M., Richter, S., & Test, D. (2010). Review of the literature on community-based instruction across grade levels. *Education and Training in Autism and Developmental Disabilities, 45*(2), 242–267.

Warren, S. F., Fey, M. E., Finestack, L. H., Brady, N. C., Bredin-Oja, S. L., & Fleming, K. K. (2008). A randomized trial of longitudinal effects of low-intensity responsivity education/prelinguistic mileu teaching. *Journal of Speech, Language, and Hearing Research, 51*(2), 451–470.

Watkins, M. W., Ravert, C. A., & Crosby, E. G. (2002). Normative factor structure of the AAMR Adaptive Behavior Scale—School, Second Edition. *Journal of Psychoeducational Assessment, 20,* 337–345.

Wehmeyer, M., & Agran, M. (2010). Promoting self-determined learning. In J. de la Fuente Arias & M. A. Eissa (Eds.), *International handbook on applying self-regulated learning in different settings* (pp. 205–224). Almeria, Spain: Education and Psychology.

Wehmeyer, M. L., Agran, M., Hughes, C., Martin, J., Mithaug, D. E., & Palmer, S. (2007). *Promoting self-determination

in students with intellectual and developmental disabilities.* New York: Guilford.

Wehmeyer, M. L., & Mithaug, D. (2006). Self-determination, causal agency, and mental retardation. In L. M. Glidden (Series Ed.) & H. Switzky (Vol. Ed.), *International review of research in mental retardation: Vol. 31. Mental retardation, personality, and motivational systems.* (pp. 31–71). San Diego: Academic Press.

Wehmeyer, M. L., Shogren, K., Palmer, S., Williams-Diehm, K., Little, T., & Boulton, A. (in press). Impact of the Self-Determined Learning Model of Instruction on student self-determination: A randomized-trial placebo control group study. *Exceptional Children.*

Yoder, P. J., & Warren, S. F. (2001). Relative treatment effects of two prelinguistic communication interventions on language development in toddlers with developmental delays vary by maternal characteristics. *Journal of Speech, Language, and Hearing Research, 44,* 224–237.

Chapter 10

Bambara, L., Koger, F., Bartholomew, A., & Browder, D. (2011). Building skills for home and community. In M. Snell & F. Brown (Eds.), *Instruction of students with severe disabilities* (7th ed., pp. 529–568). Upper Saddle River, NJ: Merrill/Pearson.

Batshaw, M. L., Shapiro, B., & Farber, M. L. Z. (2007). Developmental delay and intellectual disability. In M. L. Batshaw, L. Pellegrino, & N. J. Roizen (Eds.), *Children with disabilities* (6th ed., pp. 245–261). Baltimore: Brookes.

Baumgart, D., Brown, L., Pumpian, I., Nisbet, J., Ford, A., Sweet, M., et al. (1982). Principle of partial participation and individualized adaptations in educational programs for severely handicapped students. *Journal of the Association for Persons with Severe Disabilities, 7,* 17–27.

Blackstone, S. W., Williams, M. B., & Wilkins, D. P. (2007). Key principles underlying research and practice in AAC. *Augmentative and Alternative Communication, 23*(3), 191–203.

Brown, F., & Snell, M. (2011). Measuring student behavior and learning. In M. Snell & F. Brown (Eds.), *Instruction of students with severe disabilities* (7th ed., pp. 186–223). Upper Saddle River, NJ: Merrill/Pearson.

Brown, F., Snell, M., & Lehr, D. (2011). Meaningful assessment. In M. Snell & F. Brown (Eds.), *Instruction of students with severe disabilities* (7th ed., pp. 67–110). Upper Saddle River, NJ: Merrill/Pearson.

Brown, I., Galambos, D., Poston, D. J., & Turnbull, A. P. (2007). Person-centered and family-centered support. In I. Brown & M. Percy (Eds.), *A comprehensive guide to intellectual and developmental disabilities* (pp. 351–361). Baltimore: Brookes.

Campbell, P. H. (2011). Addressing motor disabilities. In M. E. Snell & F. Brown (Eds.), *Instruction of students with severe disabilities* (7th ed., pp. 291–327). Upper Saddle River, NJ: Merrill/Pearson.

Carter, E. W., Cushing, L. S., & Kennedy, C. H. (2009). *Peer support strategies for improving all students' social lives and learning.* Baltimore: Brookes.

Copeland, S. R., & Keefe, E. B. (2007). *Effective literacy instruction for students with moderate or severe disabilities.* Baltimore: Brookes.

Courtade, G. R., Spooner, F., & Browder, D. M. (2006). Review of studies with students with significant cognitive disabilities which link to science standards. *Research and Practice for Persons with Severe Disabilities, 32*(1), 43–49.

Downing, J. E. (2008). *Including students with severe and multiple disabilities in typical classrooms* (3rd ed.). Baltimore: Brookes.

Downing, J. E. (2011). Teaching communication skills. In M. Snell & F. Brown (Eds.), *Instruction of students with severe disabilities* (7th ed., pp. 461–491). Upper Saddle River, NJ: Merrill/Pearson.

Engleman, M. D., Griffin, H. C., Griffin, L. W., & Maddox, J. I. (1999). A teacher's guide to communicating with students with deaf-blindness. *Teaching Exceptional Children, 31*(5), 64–70.

Falvey, M. A., Forest, M. S., Pearpoint, J., & Rosenberg, R. L. (2002). Building connections. In J. S. Thousand, R. A. Villa, & A. I. Nevin (Eds.), *Creativity and collaborative learning* (2nd ed., pp. 29–54). Baltimore: Brookes.

Ferguson, D. L., & Baumgart, D. (1991). Partial participation revisited. *Journal of the Association for Persons with Severe Disabilities, 16*, 218–227.

Fossett, B., & Mirenda, P. (2007). Augmentative and alternative communication. In S. L. Odom, R. H. Horner, M. Snell, & J. Blacher (Eds.), *Handbook of developmental disabilities* (pp. 330–348). New York: Guilford.

Frey, G. C. (2007). Physical activity and youth with developmental disabilities. In S. L. Odom, R. H. Horner, M. Snell, & J. Blacher (Eds.), *Handbook of developmental disabilities* (pp. 349–365). New York: Guilford.

Gaitatzes, C., Chang, T., & Baumgart, S. (2007). The first weeks of life. In M. L. Batshaw, L. Pellegrino, & N. J. Roizen (Eds.), *Children with disabilities* (6th ed., pp. 47–59). Baltimore: Brookes.

Giangreco, M. F. (2011). Foundational concepts and practices for educating

students with severe disabilities. In M. Snell & F. Brown (Eds.), *Instruction of students with severe disabilities* (7th ed., pp. 1–27). Upper Saddle River, NJ: Merrill/Pearson.

Gropman, A. L., Smith, A. C. M., & Duncan, W. (2010). Neurologic aspects of the Smith-Magenis. In R. D. Nass & Y. Frank (Eds.), *Cognitive and behavioral abnormalities of pediatric diseases* (pp. 231–243). New York: Oxford University Press.

Holburn, S., Gordon, A., & Vietze, P. M. (2007). *Person-centered planning made easy: The picture method.* Baltimore: Brookes.

Hughes, C., & Carter, E. W. (2008). *Peer buddy programs for successful secondary school inclusion.* Baltimore: Brookes.

Jackson, L., Ryndak, D., & Wehmeyer, M. (2010). The dynamic relationship between context, curriculum, and student learning: A case for inclusive education as a research-based practice. *Research and Practice in Severe Disabilities, 34*(1), 175–195.

Jorgensen, C. M., McSheehan, M., & Sonnenmeier, R. M. (2010). *The beyond access model: Promoting membership, participation, and learning for students with disabilities in the general education classroom.* Baltimore: Brookes.

Kleinert, H. L., & Kearns, J. F. (2010). *Alternate assessment for students with significant cognitive disabilities: An educator's guide.* Baltimore: Brookes.

Lee, S. H., Soukup, J. H., Little, T. D., & Wehmeyer, M. L. (2009). Student and teacher variables contributing to access to the general education curriculum for students with intellectual and developmental disabilities. *Journal of Special Education, 43*(1), 29–44.

Lee, S. H., Wehmeyer, M. L., Soukup, J. H., & Palmer, S. B. (2010). Impact of curriculum modifications on access to the general education curriculum for students with disabilities. *Exceptional Children, 76*(2), 213–233.

Lieber, J., Horn, E., Palmer, S., & Fleming, K. (2008). Access to the general education curriculum for preschoolers with disabilities: Children's school success. *Exceptionality, 16*, 18–32.

Light, J., & McNaughton, D. (2009). *Accessible literacy learning: Evidence-based reading instruction for individuals with autism, cerebral palsy, Down syndrome, and other disabilities.* San Diego: Mayer Johnson.

Martin, J., Marshall, L., Maxson, L., & Jerman, M. (1993). *Self-directed IEP: Teacher's manual.* Colorado Springs: University of Colorado, Center for Educational Research.

Mastergeorge, A. M., Au, J., & Hagerman, R. (2010). Fragile X: A family of disorders. In R. D. Nass & Y. Frank (Eds.), *Cognitive and behavioral abnormalities of pediatric*

diseases (pp. 170–187). New York: Oxford University Press.

Mazzocco, M. M. M., & Holden, J. J. A. (2007). Fragile X syndrome. In I. Brown & M. Percy (Eds.), *A comprehensive guide to intellectual and developmental disabilities* (pp. 173–187). Baltimore: Brookes.

McDonnell, J., & Copeland, S. R. (2001). Teaching academic skills. In M. Snell & F. Brown (Eds.), *Instruction of students with severe disabilities* (7th ed., pp. 492–528). Upper Saddle River, NJ: Merrill/Pearson.

McNaughton, D. B., & Beukelman, D. R. (2010). *Transition strategies for adolescents and young adults who use AAC.* Baltimore: Brookes.

Moser, H. W. (2004). Genetic causes of mental retardation. *Annals of the New York Academy of Sciences, 1038*, 44–48.

Mount, B., & O'Brien, C. L. (2002). *Exploring new worlds for students with disabilities in transition from high school to adult life.* New York: Job Path.

Munk, D. D., & Dempsey, T. L. (2010). *Leadership strategies for successful schoolwide inclusion: The STAR approach.* Baltimore: Brookes.

Odom, S. L. (2009). The tie that binds: Evidence-based practice, implementation science, and child outcomes. *Topics in Early Childhood Special Education, 29*, 3–61.

Odom, S. L., Fleming, K., Diamond, K., Lieber, J., Hanson, M., Butera, G., et al. (2010). Examining different forms of implementation in early childhood curriculum research. *Early Childhood Research Quarterly, 25*(3), 314–328.

Parker, A. T., Davidson, R., & Banda, D. R. (2007). Emerging evidence from single-subject research in the field of deaf-blindness. *Journal of Visual Impairment and Blindness, 101*(11), 690–700.

Percy, M. (2007). Factors that cause or contribute to intellectual and developmental disabilities. In I. Brown & M. Percy (Eds.), *A comprehensive guide to intellectual and developmental disabilities* (pp. 125–148). Baltimore: Brookes.

Percy, M., Cheetham, T., Gitta, M., Morrison, B., Machalek, K., Bega, S., et al. (2007). Other syndromes and disorders associated with intellectual and developmental disabilities. In I. Brown & M. Percy (Eds.), *A comprehensive guide to intellectual and developmental disabilities* (pp. 229–267). Baltimore: Brookes.

Potvin, M. C., Prelock, P. A., & Snider, L. (2008). Collaborating to support meaningful participation in recreational activities of children with autism and spectrum disorder. *Topics in Language Disorders, 28*(4), 365–374.

Rowland, C., & Schweigert, P. (2003). Cognitive skills and AAC. In D. R. Beukelman & J. Reichle (Series Eds.), J. C. Light, D. R. Beukelman, & J. Reichle (Vol. Eds.), *Communicative competence for individuals who use AAC: From research to effective practice* (pp. 241–275). Baltimore: Brookes.

Saul, R. A., & Tarleton, J. C. (2010). FMR1-r disorders. *Gene Reviews*. Retrieved August 5, 2011, from http://www.ncbi.nlm.nih.gov/bookshelf/br.fcgi?book=gene&part-fragilex.

Schlosser, R. W. (2003). *The efficacy of augmentative and alternative communication: Toward evidence-based practice*. San Diego: Academic Press.

Schlosser, R. W., Sigafoos, J., Rothschild, N., Burke, M., & Palace, L. M. (2007). Speech and language disorders. In I. Brown & M. Percy (Eds.), *A comprehensive guide to intellectual and developmental disabilities* (pp. 383–401). Baltimore: Brookes.

Silberman, R. K., Bruce, S. M., & Nelson, C. (2004). Children with sensory impairments. In F. P. Orelove, D. Sobsey, & R. K. Silberman (Eds.), *Educating children with multiple disabilities: A collaborative approach* (4th ed., pp. 425–527). Baltimore: Brookes.

Smith, A. C. M., Boyd, K., Elsea, S. H., Finucane, B. M., Haas-Givler, B., Gropman, A., et al. (2010). Smith-Magenis syndrome. *Gene Reviews*. Retrieved August 5, 2011, from http://www.ncbi.nlm.nih.gov/pubmed/20301487.

Snell, M., & Brown, F. (2011). *Instruction of students with severe disabilities* (7th ed.). Upper Saddle River, NJ: Merrill/Pearson.

Snell, M., & Delano, M. E. (2011). Teaching self-care skills. In M. Snell & F. Brown (Eds.), *Instruction of students with severe disabilities* (7th ed., pp. 377–430). Upper Saddle River, NJ: Merrill/Pearson.

Tartaglia, N. R., Hansen, R. L., & Hagerman, R. J. (2007). Advances in genetics. In S. L. Odom, R. H. Horner, M. Snell, & J. Blacher (Eds.), *Handbook of developmental disabilities* (pp. 98–128). New York: Guilford.

Trainor, A. A. (2007). Person-centered planning in two culturally distinct communities: Responding to divergent needs and preferences. *Career Development for Exceptional Individuals, 30*(2), 92–103.

Turnbull, A., Turnbull, H. R., Erwin, E. J., Soodak, L. C., & Shogren, K. A. (2011). *Families, professionals, and exceptionality: Positive outcomes through partnerships and trust* (6th ed.). Upper Saddle River, NJ: Merrill/Pearson.

U.S. Department of Education, Office of Special Education Programs. (2011). Individuals with Disabilities Education Act (IDEA) data. Retrieved January 18, 2008, from https://www.IDEAdata.org/index.html.

Vlaskamp, C., & van der Putten, A. (2009). Focus on interaction: The use of an individualized support program for persons with profound intellectual and multiple disabilities. *Research in Developmental Disabilities, 30*, 873–883.

Wehmeyer, M. L., Agran, M., Hughes, C., Martin, J., Mithaug, D. E., & Palmer, S. (2007). *Promoting self-determination in students with intellectual and developmental disabilities*. New York: Guilford.

Xu, Y., & Filler, J. (2008). Facilitating family involvement and support for inclusive education. *School Community Journal, 18*(2), 53–71.

Zabala, J. (2005). Ready, SETT, go! Getting started with the SETT framework. *Closing the Gap, 23*(6), 1–4.

Zabala, J., Bowser, G., & Korsten, J. (2004/2005). SETT and ReSett: Concepts for AT implementation. *Closing the Gap, 23*(5), 1–4.

Chapter 11

American Psychiatric Association. (2000). *Diagnostic and statistical manual of mental disorders* (4th ed., rev.). Washington, DC: Author.

Anderson, J. S., Druzgal, T. J., Froehlich, A., DuBray, M. B., Lange, N., Alexander, A. L., Abildskov, T., et al. (2010). Decreased interhemispheric functional connectivity in autism. *Cerebral Cortex*. DOI: 10.1093/cercor/bhq190.

Arick, J. R., Young, H. F., Falco, R. A., Loos, L. M., Krug, D. A., Gense, M. H., et al. (2003). Designing an outcome study to monitor the progress of students with autism spectrum disorders. *Focus on Autism and Other Developmental Disabilities, 18*, 75–87.

Autism and Developmental Disabilities Monitoring Network. (2007). Prevalence of autism spectrum disorders [14 sites, United States, 2002]. *MMWR Surveillance Summary* (Vol. 56, pp. 12–28). Atlanta: Centers for Disease Control and Prevention.

Bade-White, P. A., Obrzut, J. E., & Randall, P. P. (2009). Neuropsychological aspects of pervasive developmental and autism spectrum disorders. In C. R. Reynolds & E. Fletcher-Janzen (Eds.), *Handbook of clinical child neuropsychology* (pp. 765–781). New York: Springer.

Baer, D. M., Wolf, M. M., & Risley, T. R. (1968). Some current dimensions of applied behavior analysis. *Journal of Applied Behavior Analysis, 1*, 91–97.

Baron-Cohen, S. (2009). Autism: The empathizing-systemizing (E-S) theory. *Year in Cognitive Neuroscience 2009, 1156*, 68–80.

Baron-Cohen, S., Golan, O., Wheelwright, S., & Hill, J. J. (2004). *Mind reading: The interactive guide to emotions*. London: Jessica Kingsley Limited.

Bellini, S., Peters, J. K., Benner, L., & Hopf, A. (2007). A meta-analysis of school-based social skills interventions for children with autism spectrum disorders. *Remedial and Special Education, 28*(3), 153–162.

Bettleheim, B. (1967). *The empty fortress: Infantile autism and the birth of the self*. London: Collier-Macmillan.

Brosnan, J., & Healy, O. (2011). A review of behavioral interventions for the treatment of aggression in individuals with developmental disabilities. *Research in Developmental Disabilities, 32*(2), 437–446.

Boutot, E. A. (2007). Fitting in: Tips for promoting acceptance and friendships for students with autism spectrum disorders in inclusive classrooms. *Intervention in School and Clinic, 42*(3), 158–161.

Cardon, T. A. (2007). *Initiations and interactions: Early intervention techniques for parents of children with autism spectrum disorders*. Shawnee Mission, KS: Autism Asperger Publishing.

Carr, E. G. (2007). The expanding vision of positive behavior support. *Journal of Positive Behavior Interventions, 9*(1), 3–14.

Carr, E. G., Levin, L., McConnachie, G., Carlson, J. I., Kemp, D. C., & Smith, C. E. (1994). *Communication-based intervention for problem behavior: A user's guide to producing positive change*. Baltimore: Brookes.

Causton-Theoharis, J., Ashby, C., & Cosier, M. (2009). Islands of loneliness: Exploring social interaction through the autobiographies of individuals with autism. *Intellectual and Developmental Disabilities, 47*(2), 84–96.

Cederlund, M., Hagberg, B., & Gillberg, C. (2009). Asperger syndrome in adolescent and young adult males. Interview, self-, and parent assessment of social, emotional, and cognitive problems. *Research in Developmental Disabilities, 31*(2), 287–298.

Chandler, L. K., & Dahlquist, C. M. (2010). *Functional assessment: Strategies to prevent and remediate challenging behaviors in school settings* (3rd ed.). Upper Saddle River, NJ: Pearson.

Cohen, R., Kincaid, D., & Childs, K. E. (2007). Measuring school-wide positive behavior support implementation: Development and validation of the Benchmarks of Quality. *Journal of Positive Behavior Interventions, 9*(4), 203–213.

Colle, L., Baron-Cohen, S., & Hill, J. (2006). Do children with autism have a theory of mind? A non-verbal test of autism vs. specific language impairment. *Journal of Autism and Developmental Disorders, 37*(4), 716–723.

DeBoer, S. R. (2007). *How to do discrete trial training*. Austin, TX: PRO-ED.

Dib, N., & Sturmey, P. (2007). Reducing student stereotypy by improving teachers' implementation of discrete-trial teaching. *Journal of Applied Behavior Analysis, 40*(3), 339–343.

Donnellan, A. M., Hill, D. A., & Leary, M. R. (2010). Rethinking autism: Implications of sensory and movement differences. *Disability Studies Quarterly, 30*(1), 1–26.

Dunlap, G., & Carr, E. G. (2007). Positive behavior support and developmental disabilities: A summary and analysis of research. In S. L. Odom, R. H. Horner,

M. E. Snell, & J. Blacher (Eds.), *Handbook of developmental disabilities* (pp. 469–482). New York: Guilford.

Dunlap, G., Iovannone, R., Kincaid, D., Wilson, K., Christiansen, K., Strain, P., et al. (2010). *Prevent-teach-reinforce: The school-based model of individualized positive behavior support.* Baltimore: Brookes.

Eigsti, I., de Marchena, A. B., Schuh, J. M., & Kelley, E. (2011). Language acquisition in autism spectrum disorders: A developmental review. *Research in Autism Spectrum Disorders, 5,* 681–691.

Fombonne, E. (2005). Epidemiology of autistic disorder and other pervasive developmental disorders. *Journal of Clinical Psychiatry, 66,* 3–8.

Fombonne, E. (2009). Epidemiology of pervasive developmental disorders. *Pediatric Research, 65*(6), 591–598.

Fossett, B., & Mirenda, P. (2007). Augmentative and alternative communication. In S. L. Odom, R. H. Horner, M. E. Snell, & J. Blacher (Eds.), *Handbook of developmental disabilities* (pp. 330–348). New York: Guilford.

Frankel, F., Myatt, R., Sugar, C., Whitham, C., Gorospe, C. M., & Laugeson, E. (2010). A randomized controlled study of Parent-Assisted Children's Friendship Training with children having autism spectrum disorders. *Journal of Autism and Developmental Disorders, 40*(7), 827–842.

Freeman, S., Paparella, T., & Stickles, K. (2009). Autism intervention research: From the reviews to implications for practice. *International Review of Research in Mental Retardation, 38,* 195–238.

Freitag, C. M. (2007). The genetics of autistic disorders and its clinical relevance: A review of the literature. *Molecular Psychiatry, 12,* 2–22.

Furniss, F. (2009). Assessment methods. In J. Matson (Ed.), *Applied behavior analysis for children with autism spectrum disorder* (pp. 33–66). New York: Springer.

Golan, O., & Baron-Cohen, S. (2006). Systemizing empathy: Teaching adults with Asperger syndrome and high functioning autism to recognize complex emotions using interactive multimedia. *Development and Psychopathology, 18*(2), 589–615.

Goldstein, S., Naglieri, J. A., & Ozonoff, S. (2009). *Assessment of autism spectrum disorders.* New York: Guilford.

Gray, C. A. (1998). Social stories and comic strip conversations with students with Asperger syndrome and high-functioning autism. In E. Schopler, G. B. Mesibov, & L. J. Kunce (Eds.), *Asperger syndrome or high-functioning autism?* (pp. 167–198). New York: Plenum.

Horner, R. H., Salentine, S. P., & Albin, R. (2003). *Self-assessment of contextual fit in schools.* Eugene: University of Oregon.

Horner, R. H., Todd, A. W., Lewis-Palmer, T., Irvin, L. K., Sugai, G., & Boland, J. (2006). The School-Wide Evaluation Tool (SET): A research instrument for assessing school-wide positive behavior support. *Journal of Positive Behavior Interventions, 6*(1), 3–12.

Ivey, J. K. (2007). Outcomes for students with autism spectrum disorders: What is important and likely according to teachers? *Education and Training in Developmental Disabilities, 42*(1), 3–13.

Janney, R., & Snell, M. E. (2008). *Behavioral support: Teachers guides to inclusive practices.* Baltimore: Brookes.

Kaland, N., Mortensen, E. L., & Smith, L. (2011). Social communication impairments in children and adolescents with Asperger syndrome: Slow response time and the impact of prompting. *Research in Autism Spectrum Disorders, 5*(3), 1129–1137.

Kasari, C., Locke, J., Gulsrud, A., & Rotheram-Fuller, E. (2010). Social networks and friendships at school: Comparing children with and without ASD. *Journal of Autism and Developmental Disabilities.* DOI 10.1007/s10803-010-1076-x.

Kim, S. H., & Lord, C. (2010). Restricted and repetitive behaviors in toddlers and preschoolers with autism spectrum disorders based on the autism diagnostic observation schedule (ADOS). *Autism Research, 3*(4), 162–173.

Kincaid, D., Childs, K., & George, H. (2005). *School-wide benchmarks of quality.* Tampa: University of South Florida.

Klinger, L. G., O'Kelley, S. E., & Mussey, J. L. (2009). Assessment of intellectual functioning in autism spectrum disorders. In S. Goldstein, J. A. Naglieri, & S. Ozonoff (Eds.), *Assessment of autism spectrum disorders* (pp. 209–250). New York: Guilford.

Klintwall, L., Holm, A., Eriksson, M., Carlsson, L. H., Olsson, M. B., Hedvall, A., Gillberg, C., & Fernell, E. (2010). Sensory abnormalities in autism. *Research in Developmental Disabilities, 32*(2), 795–800.

Kluth, P. (2008). *"You're going to love this kid!": Teaching students with autism in the inclusive classroom.* Baltimore: Brookes.

Koegel, R. L. (2007). Social development in individuals with high functioning autism and Asperger disorder. *Research and Practice for Persons with Severe Disabilities, 32*(2), 140–141.

Krug, D. A., Arick, J. R., & Almond, P. (1993). *Autism screening instrument for educational planning—2.* Austin, TX: PRO-ED.

LaCava, P. G., Golan, O., Baron-Cohen, S., & Myles, B. S. (2007). Using assistive technology to teach emotion recognition to students with Asperger syndrome: A pilot study. *Remedial and Special Education, 28*(3), 174–181.

Landrigan, P. J. (2010). What causes autism? Exploring the environmental contribution. *Current Opinion in Pediatrics, 22*(2), 219–225.

Lee, H. J., & Park, H. R. (2007). An integrated literature review on the adaptive behavior of individuals with Asperger syndrome. *Remedial and Special Education, 28*(3), 132–139.

Lee, S. H., Wehmeyer, M. L., Soukup, J. H., & Palmer, S. B. (2010). Impact of curriculum modifications on access to the general education curriculum for students with disabilities. *Exceptional Children, 76*(2), 213–233.

Llaneza, D. C., DeLuke, S. V., Batista, M., Crawley, J. N., Christodulu, K. V., & Frye, C. A. (2010). Communication, interventions, and scientific advances in autism: A commentary. *Physiology and Behavior, 100*(3), 268–276.

Lord, C. (2010). Autism: From research to practice. *American Psychologist, 65*(8), 815–826.

Love, J. R., Carr, J. E., & LeBlanc, L. A. (2009). Functional assessment of problem behavior in children with autism spectrum disorders: A summary of 32 outpatient cases. *Journal of Autism and Developmental Disorders, 39,* 363–372.

Mandell, D. S., Wiggins, L. D., Carpenter, L. A., Daniels, J., DiGuiseppi, C., Durkin M. S., Giarelli, C., et al. (2009). Racial/ethnic disparities in the identification of children with autism spectrum disorders. *American Journal of Public Health, 99*(3), 493–498.

Matson, J. L., Shoemaker, M. E., Sipes, M., Horovitz, M., Worley, J. A., & Kozlowski, A. M. (2010). Replacement behaviors for identified functions of challenging behaviors. *Research in Developmental Disabilities, 32*(2), 681–684.

May, S., Ard, W., Todd, A. W., Horner, R., Sugai, G., Glasgow, A., et al. (2003). *School-wide information system.* Eugene: University of Oregon.

Mayes, S. D., & Calhoun, S. L. (2010). Impact of IQ, age, SES, gender, and race on autistic symptoms. *Research in Autism Spectrum Disorders, 5*(2), 749–757.

McConnell, S. R. (2002). Interventions to facilitate social interaction for young children with autism: Review of available research and recommendations for educational intervention and future research. *Journal of Autism and Developmental Disorders, 32,* 351–372.

McGee, G. G., Morrier, M. J., & Daly, T. (1999). An incidental teaching approach to early intervention for toddlers with autism. *Journal of the Association for Persons with Severe Handicaps, 24*(3), 133–146.

Naglieri, J. A., & Chambers, K. M. (2009). Psychometric issues and current scales for assessing autism spectrum disorders. In S. Goldstein, J. A. Naglieri, & S. Ozonoff (Eds.), *Assessment of autism spectrum disorders* (pp. 55–90). New York: Guilford.

National Research Council. (2001). *Educating children with autism.* Washington, DC: National Academy Press.

Noens, I., Van Berckelaer-Onnes, I., Verpoorten, R., & Van Duijn, G. (2006). The Comfort: An instrument for the indication of augmentative communication in people with autism and intellectual disability. *Journal of Intellectual Disability Research, 50*(9), 621–632.

Ozonoff, S. (2010). Autism spectrum disorders. In K. O. Yeates, M. D. Ris, H. G. Taylor, & B. F. Pennington (Eds.), *Pediatric neuropsychology: Research, theory, and practice* (pp. 418–446). New York: Guilford.

Richler, J., Huerta, M., Bishop, S. L., & Lord, C. (2010). Developmental trajectories of restricted and repetitive behaviors and interests in children with autism spectrum disorders. *Development and Psychopathology, 22*(1), 55–69.

Risi, S., Lord, C., Gotham, K., Corsello, C., Chrysler, C., Szatmari, P., et al. (2006). Combining information from multiple sources in the diagnosis of autism spectrum disorders. *Journal of the American Academy of Child and Adolescent Psychiatry, 45*(9), 1094–1103.

Rutter, M., Le Couteur, A., & Lord, C. (2003). *Autism Diagnostic Interview—Revised.* Torrance, CA: Western Psychological Services.

Ryan, J. B., Hughes, E. M., Katsiyannis, A., McDaniel, M., & Sprinkle, C. (2011). Research-based educational practices for students with autism spectrum disorders. *Teaching Exceptional Children, 43*(3), 56–64.

Saracino, J., Noseworthy, J., Steiman, M., Reisinger, L., & Fombonne, E. (2010). Diagnostic and assessment issues in autism surveillance and prevalence. *Journal of Developmental and Physical Disabilities, 22*(4), 317–330.

Schroeder, J. H., Desrocher, M., Bebko, J. M., & Cappadocia, M. C. (2010). The neurobiology of autism: Theoretical applications. *Research in Autism Spectrum Disorders, 4*, 555–564.

Schumann, C. M., Bloss, C. S., Barnes, C. C., Wideman, G. M., Carper, R. A., Akshoomoff, N., Pierce, K., et al. (2010). Longitudinal magnetic resonance imaging study of cortical development through early childhood in autism. *Journal of Neuroscience, 30*(12), 4419–4427.

Scott, T. M., Alter, P. J., & McQuillan, K. (2010). Functional behavior assessment in classroom settings: Scaling down to scale up. *Intervention in School and Clinic, 46*(2), 87–94.

Scruggs, T. E., Mastropieri, M., Berkeley, S. L., & Marshak, L. (2010). Mnemonic strategies: Evidence-based practice and practice-based evidence. *Intervention in School and Clinic, 46*(2), 79–86.

Shea, V., & Mesibov, G. B. (2009). Age-related issues in the assessment of autism spectrum disorders. In S. Goldstein, J. A. Naglieri, & S. Ozonoff (Eds.), *Assessment of autism spectrum disorders* (pp. 117–137). New York: Guilford.

Simpson, R., Ganz, J., & Mason, R. (2012). Social skills interventions and programming for learners with autism spectrum disorders. In D. Zager, M. L. Wehmeyer, & R. Simpson (Eds.), *Research-based principles and practices for educating students with autism*. New York: Routledge.

Simpson, R., & Myles, B. (2008). *Educating children and youth with autism: Strategies for effective practice* (2nd ed.). Austin, TX: PRO-ED.

Sodian, B., & Kristen, S. (2010). Theory of mind. In B. Glatzeder, V. Goel, & A. Müller (Eds.), *Towards a theory of thinking* (pp. 189–201). New York: Springer.

Staples, K. L., & Reid, G. (2010). Fundamental movement skills and autism spectrum disorders. *Journal of Autism and Developmental Disorders, 40*(2), 209–217.

Symons, F. J., Byiers, B. J., Raspa, M., Bishop, E., & Bailey, Jr., D. B. (2010). Self-injurious behavior and fragile X syndrome: Findings from the national fragile X survey. *American Association on Intellectual and Developmental Disabilities, 115*(6), 473–481.

Tager-Flusberg, H., Paul, R., & Lord, C. (2005). Language and communication in autism. In F. R. Volkmar, R. Paul, A. Klin, & D. Cohen (Eds.), *Handbook of autism and pervasive developmental disorders* (3rd ed., pp. 335–364). New York: Wiley.

Thompson, T. (2007). *Making sense of autism.* Baltimore: Brookes.

Thompson, T. (2008). *Dr. Thompson's straight talk on autism.* Baltimore: Brookes.

Toro, R., Konyukh, M., Delorme, R., Leblond, C., Chase, P., Fauchereau, F., Coleman, M., et al. (2010). Key role for gene dosage and synaptic homeostasis in autism spectrum disorders. *Trends in Genetics, 26*(8), 363–372.

U.S. Department of Education, Office of Special Education Programs. (2011). *Individuals with Disabilities Education Act (IDEA) data.* Retrieved January 18, 2008, from https://www.IDEAdata.org/index.html.

Wallace, G. L. (2008). Neuropsychological studies of savant skills: Can they inform the neuroscience of giftedness? *Roeper Review, 30*(4), 229–246.

Wehmeyer, M. L., Shogren, K. A., Zager, D., Smith, T. E. C., & Simpson, R. (2010). Research-based principles and practices for educating students with autism spectrum disorders: Self-determination and social interactions. *Education and Training in Autism and Developmental Disabilities, 45*(4), 475–486.

Wiggins, L. D., Robins, D. L., Bakeman, R., & Adamson, L. B. (2009). Brief report: Sensory abnormalities as distinguishing symptoms of autism spectrum disorders in young children. *Journal of Autism and Developmental Disorders, 39,* 1087–1091.

Williams, D. (2010). Theory of own mind in autism: Evidence of a specific deficit in self-awareness? *Autism, 14*(5), 474–494.

Winter-Messiers, M. A., Herr, C. M., Wood, C. E., Brooks, A. P., Gates, M. A. M., Houston, T. L., & Tingstad, K. I. (2007). How far can Brian ride the daylight 4449 express? A strength-based model of Asperger syndrome based on special interest areas. *Focus on Autism and Other Developmental Disabilities, 22*(2), 67–79.

Wolf, J. M., & Paterson, S. J. (2010). Lifespan of PDD/autism spectrum disorders (ASD). In J. Donders & S. J. Hunter (Eds.), *Principles and practice of lifespan developmental neuropsychology* (pp. 239–250). New York: Cambridge University Press.

Chapter 12

Adams, F. V. (2007). *The asthma sourcebook.* New York: McGraw-Hill.

Alati, R., O'Callaghan, M., Najman, J. M., Williams, G. M., Bor, W., & Lawlor, D. A. (2005). Asthma and internalizing behavior problems in adolescence: A longitudinal study. *Psychosomatic Medicine, 67,* 462–470.

Arbour-Nicitopoulos, K. P. (2010). Adolescents' attitudes toward wheelchair users: A provincial survey. *International Journal of Rehabilitation Research, 33*(3), 261–263.

Association for Driver Rehabilitation Specialists. (n.d.). *Driving and cerebral palsy.* Hickory, NC: Author.

Au, K. S., Ashley-Koch, A., & Northrup, H. (2010). Epidemiologic and genetic aspects of spina bifida and other neural tube defects. *Developmental Disabilities Research Reviews, 16,* 6–15.

Bellenir, K. (2006). *Asthma sourcebook* (2nd ed.). Detroit, MI: Omnigraphics.

Benbadis, S. R., & Berkovic, S. F. (2006). Absence seizures. In E. Wyllie (Ed.), *The treatment of epilepsy: Principles and practice* (4th ed., pp. 305–315). Philadelphia: Lippincott, Williams, & Wilkins.

Bennett, T. L., & Ho, M. R. (2009). The neuropsychology of pediatric epilepsy and antiepileptic drugs. In C.R. Reynolds & Fletcher-Janzen, E. (Eds.), *Handbook of clinical child neuropsychology* (3rd ed., pp. 505–528). New York: Springer.

Berg, A. T. (2006). Epidemiologic aspects of epilepsy. In E. Wyllie (Ed.), *The treatment of epilepsy: Principles and practice* (4th ed., pp. 109–116). Philadelphia: Lippincott, Williams, & Wilkins.

Berg, A. T., Langfitt, J. T., Testa, F. M., et al. (2008) Global cognitive function in children with epilepsy: A community-based study. *Epilepsia, 49,* 608.

Bessell, A. G. (2001a). Children surviving cancer: Psychosocial adjustment, quality of life, and school experiences. *Exceptional Children, 67*(3), 345–359.

Bessell, A. G. (2001b, September). Educating children with chronic illness. *Exceptional Parent Magazine, 31*(9), 44.

Best, S. J., Heller, K. W., & Bigge, J. L. (2010). *Teaching individuals with physical or multiple disabilities* (6th ed.). Upper Saddle River, NJ: Merrill/Pearson.

Castro-Giner, F., Künzli, N., Jacquemin, B., Forsberg, B., de Cid, R., Sunyer, J., Jarvis, D., et al. (2009). Traffic-related air pollution, oxidative stress genes, and asthma (ECHRS). *Environmental Health Perspectives, 117*(12), 1919–1924.

Clark, N. A., Demers, P. A., Karr, C. J., Koehoorn, M., Lencar, C., Tamburic, L., & Brauer, M. (2010). Effect of early life exposure to air pollution on development of childhood asthma. *Environmental Health Perspectives, 118*(2), 284–290.

Clayton, D. B., Brock, III, J. W., & Joseph, D. B. (2010). Urologic management of spina bifida. *Developmental Disabilities Research Reviews, 16*, 88–95.

Clayton, S., Chin, T., Blackburn, S., & Echeverria, C. (2010). Different setting, different care: Integrating prevention and clinical care in school-based health centers. *American Journal of Public Health, 100*(9), 1592–1596.

Committee on School Health. (2000). Home, hospital, and other non-school–based instruction for children and adolescents who are medically unable to attend school. *Pediatrics, 106*(5), 1154–1155.

Coster, W. J., & Haltiwanger, J. T. (2004). Social-behavioral skills of elementary students with physical disabilities included in general education classrooms. *Remedial and Special Education, 25*(2), 95–103.

Davies, P. L., Soon, P. L., Young, M., & Clausen-Yamaki, A. (2004). Validity and reliability of the school function assessment in elementary school students with disabilities. *Physical and Occupational Therapy in Pediatrics, 24*(3), 23–43.

DePaepe, P., Garrison-Kane, L., & Doelling, J. (2002). Supporting students with health needs in schools: An overview of selected health conditions. *Focus on Exceptional Children, 35*(1), 1–24.

De Wals, P., Tairou, F., Van Allen, M. I., & Uh, S. H. (2007). Reduction in neural-tube defects after folic acid fortification in Canada. *New England Journal of Medicine, 357*(2), 135–142.

Drum, C. E., Krahn, G. L., & Bersani, H. (2009). *Disability and public health*. Washington, DC: American Association on Intellectual and Developmental Disabilities.

Engelke, M. K., Guttu, M., Warren, M. B., & Swanson, M. (2008). School nurse case management for children with chronic illness: Health, academic, and quality of life outcomes. *Journal of School Nursing, 24*(4), 205–214.

Felix, L., & Hunter, S. J. (2010). Pediatric aspects of epilepsy. In J. Donders (Ed.), *Principles and practices of lifespan developmental neuropsychology* (pp. 359–370). Chicago: University of Chicago Press.

Fisch, B. J., & Olejniczak, P. W. (2006). Generalized tonic-clonic seizures. In E. Wyllie (Ed.), *The treatment of epilepsy:*

Principles and practice (4th ed., pp. 281–304). Philadelphia: Lippincott, Williams, & Wilkins.

Fletcher, J. M., & Dennis, M. (2010). Spina bifida and hydrocephalus. In K.O. Yeates, M. D. Ris, H. G. Taylor, & B. F. Pennington (Eds.), *Pediatric neuropsychology: Research, theory, and practice* (2nd ed., pp. 3–25). New York: Guilford.

Gardiner, R. M. (2000). Impact of our understanding of the genetic aetiology of epilepsy. *Journal of Neurology, 247*, 327–334.

Heller, K. W., Forney, P. E., Alberto, P. A., Best, S. J., & Schwartzman, M. N. (2009). *Understanding physical, health, and multiple disabilities* (2nd ed) Upper Saddle River, NJ: Pearson.

Holmbeck, G. N., DeLucia, C., Essner, B., Kelly, L., Zebracki, K., Friedman, D., & Jandasek, B. (2010). Trajectories of psychosocial adjustment in adolescents with spina bifida: A 6-year, four-wave, longitudinal follow-up. *Journal of Consulting and Clinical Psychology, 78*(4), 511–525.

Hwang, J. L., Davies, P. L., Taylor, M. P., & Gavin, W. J. (2002). Validation of school function assessment with elementary school children. *Occupation, Participation, and Health, 22*(2), 48–58.

Johnson, K. L., Dudgeon, B., Kuehn, C., & Walker, W. (2007). Assistive technology use among adolescents and young adults with spina bifida. *American Journal of Public Health, 97*(8), 330–336.

Kim, H., Kieckhefer, G. M., Greek, A. A., Joesch, J. M., & Baydar, N. (2009). Health care utilization by children with asthma. *Public Health Research, Practice, and Policy, 6*(1), 1–11.

Klima, A., & McLaughlin, T. F. (2007). The effects of a token economy system to improve social and academic behavior with a rural primary aged child with disabiltiies. *International Journal of Special Education, 22*(3), 72–77.

Lindstrom, L., Johnson, P., Doren, B., Zane, C., Post, C., & Harley, E. (2008). Career connections: Building opportunities for young women with disabilities. *Teaching Exceptional Children, 40*(4), 66–71.

Liptak, G. S. (2007). Neural tube defects. In *Children with disabilities* (6th ed., pp. 419–438). Baltimore: Brookes.

Lytle, R., Lavay, B., & Rizzo, T. (2010). What is a highly qualified adaptive physical education teacher? *Journal of Physical Education, Recreation, and Dance, 81*(2), 40–44.

Nelson, K. B., & Chang, T. (2008). Is cerebral palsy preventable? *Current Opinion in Neurology 21*(2), 129–135.

O'Shea, T. M. (2008). Diagnosis, treatment, and prevention of cerebral palsy. *Clinical Obstetrics and Gynecology, 51*(4), 816–828.

Pakula, A. T., Braun, K. V., & Yeargin-Allsopp, M. (2009). Cerebral palsy: Classification and epidemiology. *Physical*

Medicine and Rehabilitation Clinics of North America, 20(3), 425–452.

Pellegrino, L. (2007). Cerebral palsy. In *Children with disabilities* (6th ed., pp. 387–408). Baltimore: Brookes.

Plavnick, J. B., Ferreri, S. J., & Maupin, A. N. (2010). The effects of self-monitoring on the procedural integrity of a behavioral intervention for young children with developmental disabilities. *Journal of Applied Behavior Analysis, 43*(2), 315–320.

Plioplys, S., Dunn, D. W., & Caplan, R. (2007). 10-year research update review: Psychiatric problems in children with epilepsy. *Journal of the American Academy of Child and Adolescent Psychiatry, 46*(11), 1389–1402.

Robb, J. E., & Brunner, R. (2010). Orthopaedic management of cerebral palsy. In M. Benson, J. Fixsen, M. Macnicol, & K. Parsch (Eds.), *Children's orthopaedics and fractures* (3rd ed., pp. 307–325). New York: Springer.

Shorvon, S. D., Andermann, F., & Guerrini, R. (2011). *The causes of epilepsy: Common and uncommon causes in adults and children*. New York: Cambridge University Press.

Soleimnpour, S., Geierstanger, S. P., Kaller, S., McCarter, V., & Brindis, C. D. (2010). The role of school health centers in health care access and client outcomes. *American Journal of Public Health, 100*(9), 1597–1603.

Standen, P. J., Camm, C., Battersby, S., Brown, D. J., & Harrison, M. (2011). An evaluation of the Wii nunchuk as an alternative assistive device for people with intellectual and physical disabilities using switch control software. *Computers in Education, 56*(1), 2–10.

Taras, H., & Brennan, J. J. (2008). Students with chronic diseases: Nature of school physician support. *Journal of School Health, 78*(7), 389–396.

Taras, H., & Potts-Datema, W. (2005). Childhood asthma and student performance at school. *Journal of School Health, 75*(8), 296–312.

Taylor, H. B., Landry, S. H., English, L., & Barnes, M. (2010). Infants and children with spina bifida. In J. Donders & S. J. Hunter (Eds.), *Principles and practice of lifespan developmental neuropsychology* (pp. 169–182). New York: Cambridge University Press.

Thomson, J. D., & Segal, L. S. (2010). Orthopedic management of spina bifida. *Developmental Disabilities Research Reviews, 16*, 96–103.

Tibosch, M. M., Verhaak, C. M., & Merkus, P. J. F. M. (2010). Psychological characteristics associated with the onset and course of asthma in children and adolescents: A systematic review of longitudinal effects. *Patient Education and Counseling, 82*(1), 11–19.

Tsuei, M. P. (2008). A web-based curriculum-based measurement system for class-wide ongoing assessment. *Journal of Computer Assisted Learning, 24*(1), 47–60.

U.S. Department of Education, Office of Special Education Programs. (2011). Individuals with Disabilities Education Act (IDEA) data. Retrieved January 18, 2008, from https://www.IDEAdata.org/index.html.

Vasquez, J. C., Fritz, G. K., Kopel, S. J., Seifer, R., McQuaid, E. L., & Canino, G. (2009). Ethnic differences in somatic symptom reporting in children with asthma and their parents. *Journal of the American Academy of Child Adolescent Psychiatry, 48*(8), 855–863.

Warchausky, S., White, D., & Tubbergen, M. V. (2010). Cerebral palsy across the lifespan. In J. Donders & S. J. Hunter (Eds.), *Principles and practice of lifespan developmental neuropsychology* (pp. 205–220). New York: Cambridge University Press.

Wehmeyer, M. L. (2008). The impact of disability on adolescent identity. In M. Sadowski (Ed.), *Adolescents at school: Perspectives on youth, identity, and education* (2nd ed., pp. 167–184). Cambridge, MA: Harvard Education Press.

Wehmeyer, M. L., Parent, W., Lattimore, J., Obremski, S., Poston, D., & Rousso, H. (2009). Promoting self-determination and self-directed employment planning for young women with disabilities. *Journal of Social Work in Disability and Rehabilitation, 8*(3–4), 117–131.

Weinstein, S. L., & Gaillard, W. D. (2007). Epilepsy. In *Children with disabilities* (6th ed., pp. 439–460). Baltimore: Brookes.

Westerveld, M. (2008). Neuropsychology in pediatric epilepsy. In J. E. Morgan & J. H. Ricker (Eds.), *Textbook of clinical neuropsychology* (pp. 149–157). New York: Taylor & Francis.

Westerveld, M. (2010). Childhood epilepsy. In K. O. Yeates, M. D. Ris, H. G. Taylor, & B. F. Pennington (Eds.), *Pediatric neuropsychology: Research, theory, and practice* (2nd ed., pp. 71–91). New York: Guilford.

Winnick, J. (Ed.). (2010). *Adapted physical education and sport* (5th ed.). Champaign, IL: Human Kinetics.

Yeargin-Allsopp, M., Braun, K. V., Doernberg, N. S., Benedict, R. E., Kirby, R. S., & Durkin, M. S. (2008). Prevalence of cerebral palsy in 8-year-old children in three areas of the United States in 2002: A multisite collaboration. *Pediatrics, 121*(3), 547–554.

Yeates, K. O., Fletcher, J. M., & Dennis M. (2008). Spina bifida and hydrocephalus. In J. E. Morgan & J. H. Ricker (Eds.), *Textbook of clinical neuropsychology* (pp. 128–148). New York: Taylor & Francis.

Chapter 13

Altimier, L. (2008). Shaken baby syndrome. *Journal of Perinatal and Neonatal Nursing, 22*(1), 68–76.

Barr, R. G., Rivara, F. P., Barr, M., Cummings, P., Taylor, J., Lengua, L. J., &

Meredith-Benitz, M. (2009). Effectiveness of educational materials designed to change knowledge and behaviors regarding crying and shaken-baby syndrome in mothers of newborns: A randomized, controlled trial. *Pediatrics, 123*, 972–980.

Case, M. E. (2008). Inflicted traumatic brain injury in infants and young children. *Brain Pathology, 18*, 571–582.

Cheng, M. L., Khairi, S., & Ritter, A. M. (2006). Pediatric head injury. In P. L. Reilly & R. Bullock (Eds.), *Head injury: Pathophysiology and management* (pp. 356–367). London: Hodder Arnold.

De la Paz, S. (2009). Rubrics: Heuristics for developing writing strategies. *Assessment for Effective Intervention, 34*(3), 134–146.

Donders, J. (2008). Subtypes of learning and memory on the California Verbal Learning Test—Second Edition (CVLT-II) in the standardization sample. Journal of Clinical and Experiental Neuropsychology, 30(7), 741–748.

Faul, M., Xu, L., Wald, M. M., & Coronado, V. G. (2010). *Traumatic brain injury in the United States: Emergency department visits, hospitalizations and deaths 2002–2006.* Atlanta: Centers for Disease Control and Prevention, National Center for Injury Prevention and Control.

Fay, T. B., Yeates, K. O., Wade, S. L., Drotar, D., Stancin, T., & Taylor, H. G. (2009). Predicting longitudinal patterns of functional deficits in children with traumatic brain injury. *Neuropsychology, 23*(3), 271–282.

Freeman, S. S., Udomphorn, Y., Armstead, W. M., et al. (2008). Young age as a risk factor for impaired cerebral autoregulation after moderate to severe pediatric traumatic brain injury. *Anesthesiology, 108*, 588–595.

Gillette, Y., & DePompei, R. (2008). Do PDAs enhance the organization and memory skills of students with cognitive disabilities? *Psychology in the Schools, 45*(7), 665–677.

Grados, M. A., Vasa, R. A., Riddle, M. A., Slomine, B. S., Salorio, C., Christensen, J., et al. (2008). New onset obsessive-compulsive symptoms in children and adolescents with severe traumatic brain injury. *Depression and Anxiety, 25*, 398–407.

Hajek, C. A., Yeates, K. W., Taylor, H. G., Bangert, B., Dietrich, A., Nuss, K. E., Rusin, J., & Wright, M. (2010). Relationships among post-concussive symptoms and symptoms of PTSD in children following mild traumatic brain injury. *Brain Injury, 24*(2), 100–109.

Hall, T. (2009). *Explicit instruction: Effective practices reports*. Retrieved November 28, 2010, from http://aim.cast.org/learn/historyarchive/backgroundpapers/explicit_instruction.

Horneman, G., & Emanuelson, I. (2009). Cognitive outcome in children and young adults who sustained severe and moderate traumatic brain injury 10 years earlier. *Brain Injury, 23*(11), 907–914.

Hundert, J. (2007). Training classroom and resource preschool teachers to develop inclusive class interventions for children with disabilities: Generalization to new intervention targets. *Journal of Positive Behavior Interventions, 9*(3), 159–173.

Johnson, A. R., DeMatt, E., & Salorio, C. F. (2009). Predictors of outcome following acquired brain injury in children. *Developmental Disabilities Research Reviews, 15*, 124–132.

Johnson, D., & Johnson, R. (1991). *Cooperation* and *competition: Theory and research*. Edina, MN: Interaction.

Johnson, D., Johnson, R., & Holubec, E. (1998). *Cooperation in the classroom*. Boston: Allyn & Bacon.

Kade, H. D., & Fletcher-Janzen, E. (2009). Brain injury rehabilitation of children and youth: Neurodevelopmental perspectives. In C. R. Reynolds & E. Fletcher-Janzen (Eds.), *Handbook of clinical child neuropsychology* (3rd ed., pp. 459–504). New York: Springer.

Kirkwood, M. W., Yeates, K. O., Taylor, H. G., Randolph, C., McCrea, M., & Anderson, V. A. (2008). Management of pediatric mild traumatic brain injury: A neuropsychological review from injury through recovery. *Clinical Neuropsychologist, 22*, 769–800.

Kraus, J. F., & Chu, L. D. (2005). Epidemiology. In J. M. Silver, T. W. McAllister, & S. C. Yudofsky (Eds.), *Textbook of traumatic brain injury* (pp. 3–26). Washington, DC: American Psychiatric.

Laatsch, L., Harrington, D., Hotz, G., Marcantuono, J., Mozzoni, M. P., Walsh, V., et al. (2007). An evidence-based review of cognitive and behavioral rehabilitation treatment studies in children with acquired brain injury. *Journal of Head Trauma Rehabilitation, 22*(4), 248–256.

Lajiness-O'Neill, R., & Erdodi, L. A. (2011). Traumatic brain injury. In J. M. Kauffman & D. P. Hallahan (Eds.), *Handbook of special education* (pp. 262–276). New York: Routledge.

Lambert, M. A., & Nowacek, J. (2006). 20 ways to help high school students improve their study skills. *Intervention in School and Clinic, 41*(4), 241–243.

Max, J. E. (2005). Children and adolescents. In J. M. Silver, T. W. McAllister, & S. C. Yudofsky (Eds.), *Textbook of traumatic brain injury* (pp. 477–494). Washington, DC: American Psychiatric.

Michaud, L. J., Duhaime, A. C., Wade, S. L., Rabin, J. P., Jones, D. O., & Lazar, M. F. (2007). Traumatic brain injury. In M. L. Batshaw, L. Pellegrino, & N. J. Roizen (Eds.), *Children with disabilities* (pp. 461–476). Baltimore: Brookes.

Scheeler, M. C., Congdon, M., & Stansbery, S. (2010). Providing immediate feedback to co-teachers through bug-in-ear technology: An effective means of peer coaching in inclusion classrooms. *Teacher Education and Special Education, 33*(1), 83–96.

Semrud-Clikeman, M. (2001). *Traumatic brain injury in children and adolescents: Assessment and intervention*. New York: Guilford.

Simpson, D. A. (2006). Clinical examination and grading. In P. L. Reilly & R. Bullock (Eds.), *Head injury: Pathophysiology and management* (pp. 143–163). London: Hodder Arnold.

Slifer, K. J., & Amari, A. (2009). Behavior management for children and adolescents with acquired brain injury. *Developmental Disabilities Research Reviews, 15*, 144–151.

Slomine, B., & Locascio, G. (2009). Cognitive rehabilitation for children with acquired brain injury. *Developmental Disabilities Research Reviews, 15*, 133–143.

Snell, M., & Janney, R. (2005). *Teachers' guides to inclusive practices: Collaborative teaming* (2nd ed.). Baltimore: Brookes.

Thousand, J., Villa, R., & Nevin, A. (2007). *Differentiating instruction: Collaborative planning and teaching for universally designed learning*. Thousand Oaks, CA: Corwin.

U.S. Department of Education. (2011). *Data accountability center: Individuals with Disabilities Education Act (IDEA) data*. Retrieved February 12, 2011, from https://www.ideadata.org.

Vu, J. A., Babikian, T., & Asarnow, R. F. (2011). Academic and language outcomes in children after traumatic brain injury: A meta-analysis. *Exceptional Children, 77*(3), 263–281.

Wehmeyer, M. L., Palmer, S., Agran, M., Hughes, C., Martin, J., & Mithaug, D. (2007). *Promoting self-determination in students with developmental disabilities*. New York: Guilford.

Ylvisaker, M., Todia, B., Glang, A., Urbanczyk, B., Franklin, C., DePompei, R., et al. (2001). Educating students with TBI: Themes and recommendations. *Journal of Head Trauma Rehabilitation, 16*(1), 76.

Chapter 14

Andrews, J. F., & Covell, J. A. (2007). Preparing future teachers and doctoral level leaders in deaf education: Meeting the challenge. *American Annals of the Deaf, 151*(5), 464–475.

Antia, S., Jones, P., Reed, S., & Kreimeyer, K. (2009). Academic status and progress of deaf and hard of hearing students in general education courses. *Journal of Deaf Studies and Deaf Education, 14*, 293–311.

Batshaw, M. L., Pellegrino, L., & Roizen, N. (Eds.). (2007). *Children with disabilities* (6th ed.). Baltimore: Brookes.

Bishop, M. (2010). Happen can't hear: An analysis of code-blends in hearing, native signers of american sign language. *Sign Language Studies, 11*(2), 205–240.

Blackorby, J., & Knokey, A. (2006). *A national profile of students with hearing impairments in elementary and middle school: A special topic report of the special education elementary longitudinal study*. (Special Education Elementary Longitudinal Study [SEELS], U.S. Department of Education, Office of Special Education Programs [OSEP]). Retrieved February 20, 2011, from http://www.seels.net/grindex.html.

Caldwell, D. C. (1973). Use of graded captions with instructional television for deaf learners. *American Annals of the Deaf, 118*(4), 500–507.

Cambria, C., Silvestre, N., & Leal, A. (2009). Comprehension of television messages by deaf students at various stages of education. *American Annals of the Deaf, 153*(5), 425–434.

Cawthon, S. W. (2008). Accommodations use for statewide standardized assessments: Prevalence and recommendations for students who are deaf or hard of hearing. *Journal of Deaf Studies and Deaf Education, 13*(1), 55–76.

Cole, K. M., Cutler, M. M., Thobro, P., & Haas, R. (2009). An exploratory study of psychosocial risk behaviors of adolescents who are deaf or hard of hearing: Comparisons and recommendations. *American Annals of the Deaf, 154*(1), 30–35.

Commission on Education of the Deaf. (1988). *Toward equality: Education of the deaf*. Washington, DC: U.S. Government Printing Office.

Cummins, J. (1988). Second language acquisition within bilingual education programs. In L. Beebe (Ed.), *Issues in second language acquisition* (pp. 145–166). Boston: Heinle & Heinle.

Cummins, J. (1992). Language proficiency, bilingualism, and academic achievement. In P. A. Richard-Amato & M. A. Snow (Eds.), *The multicultural classroom: Readings for content-area teachers* (pp. 16–26). Reading, MA: Addison-Wesley.

Cummins, J. (2003). BICS and CALP: Origins and rationale for the distinction. In C. B. Paulston & G. R. Tucker (Eds.), *Sociolinguistics: The essential readings* (pp. 322–328). London: Blackwell.

Cummins, J. (2009). Pedagogies of choice: Challenging coercive relations of power in classrooms and communities. *International Journal of Bilingual Education and Bilingualism, 12*(3), 261–267.

Easterbrooks, S. R., & Baker, S. (2002). Language learning in children who are deaf and hard of hearing: Multiple pathways. Boston, MA: Allyn & Bacon.

Elliot, S. N., Kratochwill, T. R., & Schulte, A. G. (1998). The assessment accommodation checklist: Who, what, where, when, why, and how? *Teaching Exceptional Children, 3*(2), 10–14.

Gallaudet Research Institute. (1973/1974–2007/2008). *Regional and national summary report of data from the annual survey of deaf and hard of hearing children and youth*. Washington, DC: Gallaudet University.

Gilbert, R. H., Knightly, C. A., & Steinberg, A. G. (2007). Hearing: Sounds and silences. In M. Batshaw, L. Pellegrino, & N. Rozen (Eds.), *Children with disabilities* (pp. 157–184). Baltimore: Brookes.

Halpin, K. S., Smith, K. Y., Widen, J. E., & Chertoff, M. E. (2010). Effects of universal newborn hearing screening on an early intervention program for children with hearing loss, birth to 3 yr of age. *Journal of the American Academy of Audiology, 21*(3), 169–175.

Hanks, J., & Luckner, J. (2003). Job satisfaction: Perceptions of a national sample of teachers of students who are deaf or hard of hearing. *American Annals of the Deaf, 148*(1), 5–17.

Jacobs, P. G. (2010). Psychosocial potential maximization: A framework of proactive psychosocial attributes and tactics used by individuals who are deaf. *Volta Review, 110*(1), 5–29.

Joint Committee on Infant Hearing. (2007). Year 2007 position statement: Principles and guidelines for early hearing detection and intervention programs. *Pediatrics, 120*(4), 898–921.

Karchmer, M., & Mitchell, R. (2003). Demographic and achievement characteristics of deaf and hard-of-hearing students. In M. Marschark & P. Spencer (Eds.), *Oxford handbook of deaf studies, language, and education* (pp. 21–37). New York: Oxford University Press.

Luckner, J. L., & Bowen, S. K. (2010). Teachers' use and perceptions of progress monitoring. *American Annals of the Deaf, 155*(4), 397–406.

Luckner, J. L., & Cooke, C. (2010). A summary of the vocabulary research with students who are deaf or hard of hearing. *American Annals of the Deaf, 155*(1), 38–67.

Marschark, M., Lang, H. G., & Albertini, J. A. (2002). *Educating deaf students: From research to practice*. New York: Oxford University Press.

Marschark, M., Leigh, G., Sapere, P., Burnham, D., Convertino, C., Stinson, M., et al. (2006). Benefits of sign language interpreting and text alternatives for deaf students' classroom learning. *Journal of Deaf Studies and Deaf Education, 11*(4), 421–437.

Marschark, M., Richardson, J. T. E., Sapere, P., & Sarchet, T. (2010). Approaches to teaching in mainstream and separate postsecondary classrooms. *American Annals of the Deaf, 155*(4), 481–487.

Marschark, M., Sapere, P., Convertino, C., Mayer, C., Wauters, L., & Sarchet, T. (2009). Are deaf students' reading challenges really about reading? *American Annals of the Deaf, 154*, 357–370.

Marschark, M., Sapere, P., Convertino, C., & Seewagen, R. (2005). Educational interpreting: Access and outcomes. In M. Marschark, R. Peterson, & E. Winston (Eds.), *Sign language interpreting and* interpreter education (pp. 57–83). New York: Oxford University Press.

Mayer, C., & Leigh, G. (2010). The changing context for sign bilingual education programs: Issues in language and the development of literacy. *International Journal of Bilingual Education and Bilingualism, 13*(2), 175–186.

McDonald, D. M. (2010). Not silent, invisible: Literature's chance encounters with deaf heroes and heroines. *American Annals of the Deaf, 154*(5), 463–470.

Miller, M. S. (2010). Epistemology and people who are deaf: Deaf worldviews, views of the deaf world, or my parents are hearing. *American Annals of the Deaf, 154*(5), 479–485.

Moores, D. F. (2008a). Educational programs for deaf students: Schools and programs in the United States. *American Annals of the Deaf, 153*(2), 122–185.

Moores, D. F. (2008b). Research on bi-bi instruction. *American Annals of the Deaf, 253*(1), 3–4.

Moores, D. F. (2009). Residential schools for the deaf and academic placement past, present, and future. *American Annals of the Deaf, 155*(1), 3–4.

National Institute on Deafness and Other Communication Disorders. (2011). *Cochlear implants. Improving the lives of people who have communication disorders* [Electronic version]. Retrieved February 23, 2011 from http://www.nidcd.nih.gov/health/hearing/coch.asp.

Newman, L., Wagner, M., Cameto, R., Knokey, A. M., & Shaver, D. (2010). *Comparisons across time of the outcomes of youth with disabilities up to 4 years after high school. A report of findings from the national longitudinal transition study-2 (NLTS2)*. Menlo Park, CA: SRI International. Retrieved February 23, 2011, from http://www.nlts2.org/reports/2010_report_2010_09_complete.pdf.

Nicholas, J., & Greers, A. (2006). Effects of early auditory experience on the spoken language of deaf children at 3 years of age. *Ear and Hearing, 27*(3), 286–298.

Nikolaraizi, M., & Makri, M. (2004/2005). Deaf and hearing individuals' beliefs about the capabilities of deaf people. *American Annals of the Deaf, 149*, 404–414.

Nowakowski, M. E., Tasker, S. L., & Schmidt, L. A. (2009). Establishment of joint attention in dyads involving hearing mothers of deaf and hearing children, and its relation to adaptive social behavior. *American Annals of the Deaf, 154*(1), 15–29.

Padden, C., & Humphries, T. (2005). *Inside deaf culture*. Cambridge, MA: Harvard University Press.

Punch, R., Creed, P. A., & Hyde, M. B. (2006). Career barriers perceived by hard-of-hearing adolescents: Implications for practice from a mixed-methods study. *Journal of Deaf Studies and Deaf Education, 11*(2), 225–237.

Robson, G. (2004). *The closed captioning handbook*. Burlington, MA: Focal Press.

Rose, S., McNally, P., Barkmeier, L., Virnig, S., & Long, J. (2008). Silent Reading Fluency Test: Reliability, validity, and sensitivity to growth for students who are deaf and hard of hearing at the elementary, middle school, and high school levels. (Technical Report 9). Minneapolis: University of Minnesota, College of Education and Human Development, Research Institute on Progress Monitoring.

Scheetz, N. A. (2004). Psychosocial aspects of deafness. Boston: Pearson.

Schick, B., Williams, K., & Kupermintz, H. (2006). Look who's being left behind: Educational interpreters and access to education for deaf and hard-of-hearing students. *Journal of Deaf Studies and Deaf Education, 11*(1), 3–20.

Shaver, D., Newman, L., Huang, T., Yu, J., & Knokey, A. (2011). The secondary school experiences and academic performance of students with hearing impairments. *National Longitudinal Transition Study-2 (NLTS2)*(NCSER 2011-3003). Menlo Park, CA: SRI International.

Siegel, L. M. (2000). The educational and communication needs of deaf and hard of hearing children: A statement of principal on fundamental educational choice. *American Annals of the Deaf, 145*(2), 64–77.

Spencer, P. (2004). Individual differences in language performance after cochlear implantation at 1 to 3 years of age: Child, family, and linguistic factors. *Journal of Deaf Studies and Deaf Education, 9*, 395–412.

Stewart, D. A., & Kluwin, T. N. (2001). *Teaching deaf and hard of hearing students: Content, strategies, and curriculum*. Needham Heights, MA: Allyn & Bacon.

Swanwick, R., & Watson, L. (2007). Parents sharing books with young deaf children in spoken English and in BSL: The common and diverse features of different language settings. *Journal of Deaf Studies and Deaf Education, 12*(3), 385–405.

Tevenal, S., & Villanueva, M. (2009). Are you getting the message? The effects of SimCom on the message received by deaf, hard of hearing, and hearing students. *Sign Language Studies, 9*(3), 266–286.

U.S. Department of Education. (1992, October 30). Deaf students education services: Policy guidance. *Federal Register, 57*(211): 49274–49276.

U.S. Department of Education. (2011). *Data accountability center: Individuals with Disabilities Education Act (IDEA) data.* Retrieved February 12, 2011, from https://www.ideadata.org.

Wake, M., Hughes, E., Poulakis, Z., Collins, C., & Rickards, W. (2004). Outcomes of mild-profound hearing impairment at age 7–8 years: A population study. *Ear Hear, 25*, 1–8.

Wauters, L. N., & Knoors, H. (2007). Social integration of deaf children in inclusive settings. *Journal of Deaf Studies and Deaf Education, 13*(1), 21–36.

Wolbers, K. A. (2002). Cultural factors and the achievement of black and Hispanic deaf students. *Multicultural Education, 10*, 43–52.

Chapter 15

Allman, C. B. (2004). *Position paper. Use of extended time*. Louisville, KY: American Printing House for the Blind.

Anthony, T. L. (2000). Performing a functional low vision assessment. In F. M. D'Andrea & C. Farrenkopf (Eds.), *Looking to learn: Promoting literacy for students with low vision* (pp. 32–83). New York: AFB Press.

Anthony, T. L., Bleier, H., Fazzi, D. L., Kish, D., & Pogrund, R. L. (2002). Mobility focus: Developing early skills for orientation and mobility. In R. L. Pogrund & D. L. Fazzi (Eds.), *Early focus: Working with young children who are blind or visually impaired and their families* (2nd ed., pp. 326–404). New York: AFB Press.

Barclay, L. A. (2003). Preparation for assessment. In S. A. Goodman & S. H. Wittenstein (Eds.), *Collaborative assessment: Working with students who are blind or visually impaired, including those with additional disabilities* (pp. 37–70). New York: AFB Press.

Barraga, N. C., & Erin, J. N. (2001). *Visual impairments and learning* (4th ed.). Austin, TX: PRO-ED.

Brasher, B., & Holbrook, M. C. (2006). Early intervention and special education. In M. C. Holbrook (Ed.), *Children with visual impairments: A parent's guide* (2nd ed., pp. 201–237). Bethesda, MD: Woodbine House.

Conroy, P. W. (2005). English language learners with visual impairments: Strategies to enhance learning. *RE:view, 37*(3), 101–108.

Corn, A. L., & Lusk, K. E. (2010). Perspectives on low vision. In A. L. Corn & J. N. Erin (Eds.), *Foundations of low vision: Clinical and functional perspectives* (2nd ed., pp. 3–34). New York: AFB Press.

Corn, A. L., & Sacks, S. Z. (1994). The impact of non-driving on adults with visual impairments. *Journal of Visual Impairment and Blindness, 88*(1), 53–68.

Emerson, R. W., Holbrook, M. C., & D'Andrea, F. M. (2009). Acquisition of literacy skills by young children who are blind: Results from the ABC braille study. *Journal of Visual Impairment and Blindness, 103*(10), 610–624.

Erin, J. N., & Levinson, S. (2007). Assessments: Identifying your child's needs. In S. LaVenture (Ed.), *A parents' guide to special education for children with* visual impairments (pp. 61–89). New York: AFB Press.

Erin, J. N., & Topor, I. (2010). Functional vision assessment of children with low vision, including those with multiple disabilities. In A. L. Corn & J. N. Erin (Eds.), *Foundations of low vision: Clinical and functional perspectives* (2nd ed., pp. 339–399). New York: AFB Press.

Ferrell, K. A. (2000). Growth and development of young children. In M. C. Holbrook & A. J. Koenig (Eds.), *Foundations of education: Vol. 1. History and theory of teaching children and youths with visual impairments* (2nd ed., pp. 111–134). New York: AFB Press.

Ferrell, K. A. (2006). Your child's development. In M. C. Holbrook (Ed.), *Children with visual impairments: A parent's guide* (2nd ed., pp. 73–96). Bethesda, MD: Woodbine House.

Hatlen, P. H. (1996). The core curriculum for blind and visually impaired students, including those with additional disabilities. *RE:view, 28*(1), 25–32.

Hatlen, P. H., & Curry, S. A. (1987). In support of specialized programs for blind and visually impaired children: The impact of vision loss on learning. *Journal of Visual Impairment and Blindness, 81*(1), 7–13.

Huebner, K. M. (2000). Visual impairment. In M. C. Holbrook & A. J. Koenig (Eds.), *Foundations of education: Vol. 1. History and theory of teaching children and youths with visual impairments* (2nd ed., pp. 55–76). New York: AFB Press.

Kirchner, C., & Diament, S. (1999). Estimates of the number of visually impaired students, their teachers, and orientation and mobility specialists. *Journal of Visual Impairment and Blindness, 93*(9), 600–606.

Koenig, A. J., & Farrenkopf, C. (1997). Essential experiences to undergird the early development of literacy. *Journal of Visual Impairment and Blindness, 91*(1), 14–24.

Koenig, A. J., & Holbrook, M. C. (1993). *Learning media assessment of students with visual impairments: A resource guide for teachers.* Austin: Texas School for the Blind and Visually Impaired.

Koenig, A. J., & Holbrook, M. C. (2000). Planning instruction in unique skills. In A. J. Koenig & M. C. Holbrook (Eds.), *Foundations of education: Vol. 2. Instructional strategies for teaching children and youths with visual impairments* (2nd ed., pp. 196–221). New York: AFB Press.

Lee, H., & Ponchillia, S. V. (2010). Low vision rehabilitation training for working-age adults. In A. L. Corn & J. N. Erin (Eds.), *Foundations of low vision: Clinical and functional perspectives* (2nd ed., pp. 760–792). New York: AFB Press.

Lewis, S., & Allman, C. B. (2000). Educational programming. In M. C. Holbrook &

A. J. Koenig (Eds.), *Foundations of education: Vol. 1. History and theory of teaching children and youths with visual impairments* (2nd ed., pp. 218–259). New York: AFB Press.

Lewis, S., & Wolffe, K. E. (2006). Promoting and nurturing self-esteem. In S. Z. Sacks and K. E. Wolffe (Eds.), *Teaching social skills to students with visual impairments: From theory to practice* (pp. 122–162). New York: AFB Press.

Liefert, F. (2003). Introduction to visual impairment. In S. A. Goodman & S. H. Wittenstein (Eds.), *Collaborative assessment: Working with students who are blind or visually impaired, including those with additional disabilities* (pp. 1–22). New York: AFB Press.

Lowenfeld, B. (1973). Psychological considerations. In B. Lowenfeld (Ed.), *The visually handicapped child in school* (pp. 27–60). New York: Day.

Lueck, A. H. (2004). Comprehensive low vision care. In A. H. Lueck (Ed.), *Functional vision: A practitioner's guide to evaluation and intervention* (pp. 3–24). Alexandria, VA: Association for Education and Rehabilitation of the Blind and Visually Impaired.

Lussenhop, K., & Corn, A. L. (2002). Comparative studies of the reading performance of students with low vision. *RE:view, 34*(2), 57–69.

Milian, M. (1997). Teaching braille reading and writing to students who speak English as a second language. In D. P. Wormsley & F. M. D'Andrea (Eds.), *Instructional strategies for braille literacy* (pp. 189–230). New York: AFB Press.

Milian, M. (2000). Multicultural issues. In M. C. Holbrook & A. J. Koenig (Eds.), *Foundations of education: Vol. 1. History and theory of teaching children and youths with visual impairments* (2nd ed., pp. 197–217). New York: AFB Press.

Nelson, K. A., & Dimitrova, E. (1993). Severe visual impairment in the United States and in each state. *Journal of Visual Impairment and Blindness, 87*(3), 80–85.

Pogrund, R. L. (2002). Refocus: Setting the stage for working with young children who are blind or visually impaired. In R. L. Pogrund & D. L. Fazzi (Eds.), *Early focus: Working with young children who are blind or visually impaired and their families* (2nd ed., pp. 1–15). New York: AFB Press.

Pugh, G. S., & Erin, J. (Eds.). (1999). *Blind and visually impaired students: Educational service guidelines.* Watertown, MA: Perkins School for the Blind.

Sacks, S. Z. (2006). Theoretical perspectives on the early years of social development. In S. Z. Sacks & K. E. Wolffe (Eds.), *Teaching social skills to students with visual impairments: From theory to practice* (pp. 51–80). New York: AFB Press.

Scott, E. P., Jan, J. E., & Freeman, R. D. (1995). *Can't your child see? A guide for*

parents of visually impaired children (3rd ed.). Austin, TX: PRO-ED.

Silberman, R. K. (2000). Children and youth with visual impairments and other exceptionalities. In M. C. Holbrook & A. J. Koening (Eds.), *Foundations of education: Vol. 1. History and theory of teaching children and youths with visual impairments* (2nd ed., pp. 173–196). New York: AFB Press.

Simons, B., & Lapolice, D. J. (2000). Working effectively with a low vision clinic. In F. M. D'Andrea & C. Farrenkopf (Eds.), *Looking to learn: Promoting literacy for students with low vision* (pp. 84–116). New York: AFB Press.

Social Security Act, 42 U.S.C. 1382c § 1614 (2011).

Swenson, A. M. (2008). Reflections on teaching reading in braille. *Journal of Visual Impairment and Blindness, 102*(4), 206–209.

U.S. Department of Education. (2011). *IDEA data*. Retrieved April 24, 2011, from https://www.ideadata.org/arc_toc10.asp#partbCC.

Wall, R. S., & Corn, A. L. (2004). Students with visual impairments in Texas: Description and extrapolation of data. *Journal of Visual Impairment and Blindness, 98*, 351–356.

Wolffe, K. E. (2000). Career education. In A. J. Koenig & M. C. Holbrook (Eds.), *Foundations of education: Vol. 2. Instructional strategies for teaching children and youths with visual impairments* (2nd ed., pp. 679–719). New York: AFB Press.

Wolffe, K. E. (2006). Theoretical perspectives on the development of social skills in adolescence. In S. Z. Sacks & K. E. Wolffe (Eds.), *Teaching social skills to students with visual impairments: From theory to practice* (pp. 81–116). New York: AFB Press.

Wolffe, K. E., Sacks, S. Z., & Thomas, K. L. (2000). *Focused on: Importance and need for social skills.* New York: AFB Press.

Young, L. (1997). Adding positive experiences with dogs to the curriculum. *RE:view, 29*(2), 55–61.

Chapter 16

Armstrong, T. (2009). *Multiple intelligences in the classroom* (3rd ed.). Arlington, VA: Association for Supervision and Curriculum Development.

Beghetto, R. A. (2008). Creativity enhancement. In J. A. Plucker & C. M. Callahan (Eds.), *Critical issues and practices in gifted education: What the research says* (pp. 139–154). Waco, TX: Prufrock.

Berlin, J. E. (2009). It's all a matter of perspective: Student perceptions on the impact of being labeled gifted and talented. *Roeper Review, 31*, 217–223.

Betts, G., & Kercher, J. (1999). *Autonomous learner model: Optimizing ability.* Greeley, CO: ALPS.

Betts, G. T., & Carey, R. J. (2010). *Response to intervention and the autonomous learner model: A complete approach to the gifted and talented.* Greeley, CO: ALPS.

Bloom, B. S. (Ed.). (1956). *Handbook I: Cognitive domain.* New York: McKay.

Bloom, B. S. (1985). *Developing talent in young people.* New York: Ballantine.

Borland, J. H. (2008). Identification. In J. A. Plucker & C. M. Callahan (Eds.), *Critical issues and practices in gifted education: What the research says* (pp. 261–280). Waco, TX: Prufrock.

Burke, C. S., Sims, D. E., Lazzara, E. H., & Salas, E. (2007). Trust in leadership: A multi-level review and integration. *Leadership Quarterly, 18*(6), 606–632.

Callahan, C. M., & Dickson, R. K. (2008). Mentoring. In J. A. Plucker & C. M. Callahan (Eds.), *Critical issues and practices in gifted education: What the research says* (pp. 409–422). Waco, TX: Prufrock.

Capper, M. R., Foust, R. C., Callahan, C. M., & Albaugh, S. B. (2009). Grade and gender differences in gifted students' self-concepts. *Journal for the Education of the Gifted, 32*(3), 340–367.

Castellano, J. A., & Frazier, A. D. (2011). *Special populations in gifted education: Understanding our most able students from diverse backgrounds.* Waco, TX: Prufrock.

Chen, J., & McNamee, G. D. (2007). *Bridging assessment for teaching and learning in early childhood classrooms, Pre-K.* Thousand Oaks, CA: Corwin.

Chen, J., Moran, S., & Gardner, H. (2009). *Multiple intelligences around the world.* San Francisco: Jossey-Bass.

Clark, B. (2008). *Growing up gifted: Developing the potential of children at home and school* (7th ed.). Upper Saddle River, NJ: Merrill/Pearson.

Cramond, B., & Kim, K. H. (2008). The role of creativity tools and measures in assessing potential and growth. In J. L. Van Tassel-Baska (Ed.), *Alternative assessments with gifted and talented students* (pp. 203–226). Waco, TX: Prufrock.

Dai, D. Y. (2010). *The nature and nurture of giftedness: A new framework for understanding gifted education.* New York: Teachers College Press.

Davis, G. A., Rimm, S. B., & Siegle, D. (2010). *Education of the gifted and talented* (6th ed.). Upper Saddle River, NJ: Merrill/Prentice Hall.

Douglas, D. (2004). Self-advocacy: Encouraging students to become partners in differentiation. *Roeper Review, 26*(4), 223–228.

Feldman, D. H. (2008). Prodigies. In J. A. Plucker & C. M. Callahan (Eds.), *Critical issues and practices in gifted education: What the research says* (pp. 523–534). Waco, TX: Prufrock.

Feng, A. X., & Van Tassel-Baska, J. L. (2008). Identifying low-income and minority students for gifted programs: Academic and affective impact of performance-based assessment. In J. L. Van Tassel-Baska (Ed.), *Alternative assessments with gifted and talented students* (pp. 129–146). Waco, TX: Prufrock.

Fisher-Doiron, N., & Irvine, S. (2009). Going beyond basics to reach all children. *Principal, 88*(5), 26.

Ford, D. Y. (2008). Intelligence testing and cultural diversity: The need for alternative instruments, policies, and procedures. In J. L. Van Tassel-Baska (Ed.), *Alternative assessments with gifted and talented students* (pp. 107–128). Waco, TX: Prufrock.

Ford, D. Y., Grantham, T. C., & Whiting, G. W. (2008). Culturally and linguistically diverse students in gifted education: Recruitment and retention issues. *Exceptional Children, 74*(3), 289–306.

Galbraith, J., & Delisle, J. (1996). *The gifted kids' survival guide.* Minneapolis: Free Spirit.

Gardner, H. (1983). *Frames of mind: The theory of multiple intelligences.* New York: Basic Books.

Gardner, H. (2006). *Multiple intelligences: New horizons.* New York: Basic Books.

Gardner, H. (2011). *Frames of mind: The theory of multiple intelligences* (3rd ed.). New York: Basic Books.

Gardner, H., & Moran, S. (2006). The science of multiple intelligences theory: A response to Lynn Waterhouse. *Educational Psychologists, 41*(4), 227–232.

Garn, A. C., Matthews, M. S., & Jolly, J. L. (2010). Parental influences on the academic motivation of gifted students: A self-determination theory perspective. *Gifted Child Quarterly, 54*(4), 263–272.

Gates, J. (2010). Children with gifts and talents: Looking beyond traditional labels. *Roeper Review, 32*, 200–206.

Geisler, J. L., Hessler, T., Gardner, R., & Lovelace, T. S. (2009). Differentiated writing interventions for high-achieving urban African American elementary students. *Journal of Advanced Academics, 20*(2), 214–247.

Gifted and Talented Children's Education Act, 20 U.S.C. §3312 (1978).

Greenwood, S. C., & McCabe, P. P. (2008). How learning contracts motivate students. *Middle School Journal, 39*(5), 13–22.

Harter, S. (2006). The self. In W. Damon & N. Eisenberg (Eds.), *Handbook of child psychology: Vol. 3. Social, emotional, and personality development* (6th ed., pp. 505–570). New York: Wiley.

Hertberg-Davis, H. (2009). Myth 7: Differentiation in the regular classroom is equivalent to gifted programs and is sufficient. Classroom teachers have the time, the skill, and the will to differentiate adequately. *Gifted Child Quarterly, 53*(4), 251–253.

Hoh, P. (2008). Cognitive characteristics of the gifted. In J. A. Plucker & C. M. Callahan (Eds.), *Critical issues and practices in gifted education: What the research says* (pp. 57–84). Waco, TX: Prufrock.

Hughes, C. E. (2011). Twice-exceptional children: Twice the challenges, twice the joys. In J. A. Castellano & A. D. Frazier (Eds.), *Special populations in gifted education: Understanding our most able students from diverse backgrounds* (pp. 153–173). Waco, TX: Prufrock.

Kalbfleisch, M. L. (2008). Getting to the heart of the brain: Using cognitive neuroscience to explore the nature of human ability and performance. *Roeper Review, 30*, 162–170.

Kalbfleisch, M. L., & Iguchi, C. M. (2008). Twice-exceptional learners. In J. A. Plucker & C. M. Callahan (Eds.), *Critical issues and practices in gifted education: What the research says* (pp. 707–720). Waco, TX: Prufrock.

Kuo, C. C., Maker, J., Su, F. L., & Hu. C. (2010). Identifying young gifted children and cultivating problem solving abilities and multiple intelligences. *Learning and Individual Differences, 20*, 365–379.

Lee, S. Y., Olszewski-Kubilius, P., Donahue, R., & Weimholt, K. (2008). The civic leadership institute: A service-learning program for academically gifted youth. *Journal of Advanced Academics, 19*(2), 272–308.

Lee, S. Y., Olszewski-Kubilius, P., & Peternel, G. (2010). The efficacy of academic acceleration for gifted minority students. *Gifted Child Quarterly, 54*(3), 189–208.

Maker, C. J. (1993). Creativity, intelligence and problem solving: A definition and design for cross-cultural research and measurement related to giftedness. *Gifted Education International, 9*, 68–77.

Maker, C. J. (2001). DISCOVER: Assessing and developing problem solving. *Gifted Education International, 15*, 232–251.

Martin, L. T., Burns, R. M., & Schonlau, M. (2010). Mental disorders among gifted and nongifted youth: A selected review of the epidemiologic literature. *Gifted Child Quarterly, 54*(1), 31–41.

McCollister, K., & Sayler, M. F. (2010). Lifting the ceiling: Increase rigor with critical thinking skills. *Gifted Child Today, 33*(1), 41–47.

Mrazik, M., & Dombrowski, S. C. (2010). The neurobiological foundations of giftedness. *Roeper Review, 32*, 224–234.

National Association for Gifted Children. (2009). *2008–2009 state of the states in gifted education: National policy and practice data.* Washington, DC: Author.

National Association for Gifted Children. (n.d.). *NAGC position paper on acceleration.* Retrieved March 25, 2011, from http://www.nagc.org/index .aspx?id=383.

National Center for Education Statistics. (2009). *Digest of education statistics.* Washington, DC: U.S. Department of Education.

National Center for Education Statistics. (2010). *Digest of education statistics.* Washington, DC: U.S. Department of Education.

Neumeister, K. L. S., Williams, K. K., & Cross, T. L. (2009). Gifted high school students' perspectives on the development of perfectionism. *Roeper Review, 31,* 198–206.

Newman, S. D. (2008). Neural bases of giftedness. In J. A. Plucker & C. M. Callahan (Eds.), *Critical issues and practices in gifted education: What the research says* (pp. 469–478). Waco, TX: Prufrock.

Newsom, T. (2010). Developing African-American leaders in today's schools: Gifted leadership, the unfamiliar dimension in gifted education. *Black History Bulletin, 73*(1), 18–23.

Pfeiffer, S. I. (2003). Challenges and opportunities for students who are gifted: What the experts say. *Gifted Child Quarterly, 47*(2), 161–169.

Reis, S. M., & Boeve, H. (2009). How academically gifted elementary, urban students respond to challenge in an enriched, differentiated reading program. *Journal for the Education of the Gifted, 33*(2), 203–240.

Renzulli, J. S., & Reed, R. E. S. (2008). Intelligences outside the normal curve: Co-cognitive traits that contribute to giftedness. In J. A. Plucker & C. M. Callahan (Eds.), *Critical issues and practices in gifted education: What the research says* (pp. 303–320). Waco, TX: Prufrock.

Renzulli, J. S., & Reis, S. M. (2010). A technology based application of the schoolwide enrichment model and high end learning theory. In L. Shavinina (Ed.), *International handbook on giftedness* (pp. 1203–1224). New York: Springer.

Rizza, M. G., & Gentry, M. (2001). A legacy of promise: Reflections, suggestions, and directions from contemporary leaders in the field of gifted education. *Teacher Education, 36*(3), 167–184.

Roach, A. A., Wyman, L. T., Brookes, H., Chavez, C., Heath, S. B., & Valdes, G. (1999). Leadership giftedness: Models revisited. *Gifted Child Quarterly, 43*(1), 13–24.

Robinson, W., & Campbell, J. (2010). *Effective teaching in gifted education: Using a whole school approach.* New York: Routledge.

Rogers, K. B. (2007). Matching needs of gifted learners to school possibilities. *Understanding Our Gifted, 19*(2), 15–20.

Sarouphim, K. M. (2002). DISCOVER in high school: Identifying gifted Hispanic and Native American students. *Journal of Secondary Gifted Education, 14*(1), 30–38.

Sarouphim, K. M. (2004). DISCOVER in middle school: Identifying gifted minority students. *Journal of Secondary Gifted Education, 15*(2), 61–69.

Sarouphim, K. M. (2005). DISCOVER across the spectrum of grades: Identifying gifted minority students. *Gifted and Talented International, 20,* 70–77.

Sarouphim, K. M. (2009). The use of a performance assessment for identifying gifted Lebanese students: Is DISCOVER effective? *Journal for the Education of the Gifted, 33*(2), 275–295.

Schader, R. M. (2008). Parenting. In J. A. Plucker & C. M. Callahan (Eds.), *Critical issues and practices in gifted education: What the research says* (pp. 479–492). Waco, TX: Prufrock.

Schroth, S. T., & Helfer, J. A. (2008). Identifying gifted students: Educator beliefs regarding various policies, processes, and procedures. *Journal for the Education of the Gifted, 32*(2), 155–179.

Steenbergen-Hu, S., & Moon, S. M. (2011). The effects of acceleration on high-ability learners: A meta-analysis. *Gifted Child Quarterly, 55*(1), 39–53.

Stephens, K. R., & Karnes, F. (2000). State definitions for the gifted and talented revisited. *Exceptional Children, 66*(2), 219–238.

Tomlinson, C. A. (2008). Differentiated instruction. In J. A. Plucker & C. M. Callahan (Eds.), *Critical issues and practices in gifted education: What the research says* (pp. 167–178). Waco, TX: Prufrock.

Van Tassel-Baska, J. (2005). Gifted programs and services: What are the nonnegotiables? *Theory into Practice, 44*(2), 90–99.

Van Tassel-Baska, J. (2008). *Alternative assessments with gifted and talented students.* Waco, TX: Prufrock.

Van Tassel-Baska, J. (2009). United States policy development in gifted education: A patchwork quilt. In L. V. Shavinina (Ed.), *International handbook on giftedness* (pp. 1295–1311). New York: Springer.

Whiting, G. (2009). Gifted black males: Understanding and decreasing barriers to achievement and identity. *Roeper Review, 31,* 224–233.

Worley, B. B. (2008). Visual and performing arts. In J. A. Plucker & C. M. Callahan (Eds.), *Critical issues and practices in gifted education: What the research says* (pp. 735–748). Waco, TX: Prufrock.

Name Index

Subject Index

Discrimination, 8, 57–58. *See also* Multicultural considerations
Disproportionate representation
 factors associated with, 61–63, 65–71
 multicultural considerations, 58–61
 poverty, 66–68
Distortions, 133
Diversity theories, 56–58. *See also* Multicultural considerations
Dogs, guide, 362
Domains of family life. *See also* Families; Family factors
 emotional well-being, 84–85
 exceptionality-related support, 84–85
 family interaction, 84–85
 parenting, 84–85
 physical/material well-being, 84–85
Down syndrome, 200, 201
Driver's education, 284
DSM-IV-TR. *See Diagnostic and Statistical Manual of Mental Disorders* (DSM-IV-TR)
Duration, 133
Dyskinetic cerebral palsy, 267
Dyslexia, 106

Ear canal, 316
Early childhood instructional strategies
 attention deficit/hyperactivity disorder, 187
 autism, 255–256
 communication disorders, 143
 family-professional partnerships and, 86
 gifted and talented students, 383–384
 hearing loss, 332
 intellectual disability, 207–209
 learning disabilities, 118–120
 multiple disabilities, 230–231
 physical disabilities and other health impairments, 282
 traumatic brain injuries, 303–304
 visual impairments, 364
Early hearing detection and intervention (EHDI) systems, 322, 323
Early identification, 11
Early intervention, hearing loss and, 332
Ears, hearing loss and, 316–317
Echolalia, 243
Ecological inventories, 147–148, 214–215
Economic self-sufficiency, 24
Educability, 12–13
Educational evaluations, hearing loss, 323
Educational factors, intellectual disability, 200–201
Educational placement. *See also* Inclusion
 autism, 259
 communication disorders, 145–146
 emotional or behavioral disorders, 166–168
 hearing loss, 336–338
 Individuals with Disabilities Education Act, 10
 intellectual disability, 212–213
 learning disabilities, 121–122
 multicultural considerations, 60–61
 multiple disabilities, 234–236
 physical disabilities and other health impairments, 284–285
 traumatic brain injuries, 307–308
 visual impairments, 357, 365–366

Education of All Handicapped Students Act (Public Law 94-142). *See* Individuals with Disabilities Education Act (IDEA)
EHDI (early hearing detection and intervention) systems, 322, 323
Electronic memory support aids, 301
Electronic texts, 280, 281
Elementary/middle school instructional strategies
 attention deficit/hyperactivity disorder, 187–188
 autism, 256–257
 communication disorders, 143–144
 emotional or behavioral disorders, 165
 family-professional partnerships, 88
 gifted and talented students, 384–385
 hearing loss, 332–334
 intellectual disability, 209–210
 learning disabilities, 120
 multiple disabilities, 231–232
 physical disabilities and other health impairments, 283
 traumatic brain injuries, 304–305
 visual impairments, 364–365
Elementary Secondary Education Act (ESEA), 19, 22, 30–31, 196
ELLs. *See* English language learners (ELLs)
Embedded learning opportunities, 119–120
Emergency care, asthma, 274
Emotional characteristics
 attention deficit/hyperactivity disorder, 177, 179
 emotional or behavioral disorders, 152–155
 gifted and talented students, 376–377
 hearing loss, 320–321
 learning disabilities, 108
 traumatic brain injuries, 295
Emotional or behavioral disorders. *See also specific disorders*
 assessment, 159–161, 168–169
 case studies, 150–151
 causes of, 157–159
 characteristics, 152–156, 169
 defined, 152
 evaluating students with, 159–161
 IEP design, 161–164
 including students with, 166–168
 individualized education programs, 161–164
 instructional strategies, 165–168
 personal accounts, 162
 social characteristics, 169
Emotional well-being, 84–85
Emotion recognition, 255
Employment
 discrimination and, 21
 individual education programs, 46
 intellectual disability, 211, 212
 least restrictive environment, 17
 special education goals, 24
 supported, 19
 transition planning, 203–204, 334
Empowerment, 84, 90
Encephalitis, 292
English language development, hearing loss and, 317
English language learners (ELLs)
 demographics, 65–66
 disproportionate representation, 65–66
 response to intervention, 76
 visual impairments and, 354, 356
Enrichment, 384–385, 386

Environmental factors
 asthma, 274
 attention deficit/hyperactivity disorder, 179
 autism, 247
 learning disabilities, 109–110
 spina bifida, 270
 visual impairments, 348
Epilepsy, 268, 271–273
Equality of opportunity, 22, 24
Errorless learning, 187–188, 282
ESEA (Elementary Secondary Education Act), 19, 22, 30–31, 196
Ethics and standards for professional practice, 25
Ethnicity. *See* Race/ethnicity
Etiology, 348–349
Eugenics, 56
European Americans
 disproportionate representation, 63
 in gifted and talented programs, 61, 373
 risk ratios, 59–60
 as term, 59
Eustacian tubes, 316
Evaluation. *See also* Assessment; Nondiscriminatory evaluation
 attention deficit/hyperactivity disorder, 180–182
 autism, 247–251
 communication disorders, 136–138
 emotional or behavioral disorders, 159–161
 gifted and talented students, 378–380
 hearing loss, 322–326
 intellectual disability, 202–203
 learning disabilities, 110–115
 multiple disabilities, 223–225
 physical disabilities and other health impairments, 274–276
 traumatic brain injury (TBI), 296–298
 visual impairments, 348–353
Event casts, 142
Event recording, 237
Evidence-based practices, 48–49
Evoked otoacoustic emissions (EOAE) screening, 325
Exceptionality-related support, 84–85
Exclusionary standard, 106
Expanded core curriculum, 352–353, 367–368
Expansions, 142
Experiences, limited by visual impairments, 347
Expressive language disorders, 129
Externalizing behavior, 155–156
Extracurricular inclusion, 17
Eyes, anatomy of, 349

F2F HICs (Family-to-Family Health Information Centers), 94
Facilitated IEP meeting, gifted and talented students, 97
Falls, 296
Families. *See also* Family-professional partnerships
 defined, 82
 demographics of, 82–83
 quality of life, 83–86, 88
 resource information sharing, 92–94
 training, counseling, and home visits, 11
Family factors
 culturally responsive instruction, 77
 disproportionate representation, 63
 emotional or behavioral disorders, 158
 multicultural considerations, 69, 70

Family-professional partnerships. *See also* Families; Partnerships; Partnership Tips
 advocacy, 90, 100–101
 case studies, 80–81
 commitment, 90
 communication, 89–92
 equality, 90
 families, 82–86
 forming, 88–95, 97, 99–100
 homework assistance, 97, 99–100
 participation in the IEP conference, 94–95, 97
 personal accounts, 87
 professional competence, 90
 respect, 90
 trust, 86–87, 90
Family-to-Family Health Information Centers (F2F HICs), 94
Fatigue, 294
FBA (functional behavioral assessment), 249–251
Females. *See* Gender
Field observations, 237
Field of vision, 344
Fingerspelling, 318
First aid, seizures, 272
504 Plans, 182, 183, 184
Fluency, 136–137
Fluency disorders, 134
Focused contrast, 142
Folic acid, 269, 270
Formative analysis, 236
Four-R approach, 63, 64
Fragile X syndrome, 223
Free or reduced-price lunch eligibility, 33
Friendships, 97, 98, 108, 254–255
Full participation, 23–24
Functional behavioral assessment (FBA), 249–251
Functional disorders, 135
Functionally blind, 345
Functional vision assessment (FVA), 349–352

Gender
 emotional or behavioral disorders, 152, 156
 general education students, 6
 gifted and talented students, 376
 intellectual disability, 197
 special education students, 5, 20, 54
General education, increasing time in, 40
General education curriculum
 attention deficit/hyperactivity disorder and, 189–191
 autism, 260
 communication disorders and, 146
 emotional or behavioral disorders and, 168–169
 gifted and talented students, 388
 IDEA and, 17
 intellectual disability, 213–214
 learning disabilities, 123
 multiple disabilities, 236
 physical disabilities and other health impairments, 285–286
 progress in, 30–33
 traumatic brain injuries, 309
 visual impairments, 358–360, 367
Generalization, 199
Generalized anxiety disorder, 153
Generalized seizures, 271, 272
Genetic drift theories, 56
Genetic factors
 asthma, 274